COMPUTER SYSTEMS
ARCHITECTURE

DIGITAL SYSTEM DESIGN SERIES

ARTHUR D. FRIEDMAN, Editor
George Washington University

S. I. AHMAD AND K. T. FUNG
Introduction to Computer Design and Implementation

MICHAEL ANDREWS
Principles of Firmware Engineering in Microprogram Control

J. E. ARSENAULT AND J. A. ROBERTS
Reliability and Maintainability of Electronic Systems

JEAN-LOUP BAER
Computer Systems Architecture

MELVIN A. BREUER
Digital System Design Automation:
Languages, Simulation and Data Base

MELVIN A. BREUER AND ARTHUR D. FRIEDMAN
Diagnosis and Reliable Design of Digital Systems

ARTHUR D. FRIEDMAN
Logical Design of Digital Systems

ARTHUR D. FRIEDMAN AND PREMACHANDRAN R. MENON
Theory and Design of Switching Circuits

COMPUTER SYSTEMS ARCHITECTURE

Jean-Loup Baer

COMPUTER SCIENCE PRESS

Computer Science Press, Inc.
11 Taft Court
Rockville, Maryland 20850

2 3 4 5 6   85 84 83 82 81

Library of Congress Cataloging in Publication Data

Baer, Jean-Loup.
   Computer systems architecture.

   Includes bibliographical references and index.
   1.   Computer architecture.   I.   Title.
QA76.9.A73B33   621.3819'52   79-27039

US ISBN 0-914894-15-3
UK ISBN 0 273 01474 9

621. 381952
B141c

209818

A mes parents.

Preface

The term *Architecture* when applied to *Computer Systems* is relatively recent. Ten years ago, when Foster used it in the title of his book, some University librarians were thoroughly confused. In at least one case, the book was miscatalogued and sent to the School of Architecture specialized library. Even today, there is no entry specific to Computer Architecture in *Computing Reviews,* the Review Journal of the Association for Computing Machinery; papers and books on this topic are indexed under the Computer Systems category. I hope that this omission will soon be remedied since there is now common agreement on the existence of Computer Architecture although there is no consensus on what this field encompasses.

I was guided in my choice of including *Architecture* and *Systems* in the title of this book by the usual definitions of these terms. According to the American College Dictionary, architecture is the "art or science of building, including plan, design, construction and decorative treatment," and system is an "assemblage or combination of parts forming a complex or unitary whole." That modern computers form a system should not require any justification: even the von Neumann machine, the simplified model of a stored program computer, consists of an aggregate of five blocks. The architectural definition requires more elaboration. Because computers are tools to be used by people, I will add "engineering" to the above "art or science" but I will not try to draw the fine line between the Computer Science and Computer Engineering disciplines when it comes to the study of Computer Architecture. I prefer to indicate the features corresponding to "plan, design, construction and decorative treatment" when viewed in the context of sound computer architectures, namely:

- Structure: the static arrangement of the parts (plan);
- Organization: the dynamic interaction of these parts and their management (design);
- Implementation: the design of specific building blocks (construction);
- Performance Evaluation: the behavioral study of the system or of some of its components (decorative treatment!).

Naturally, computers are too young to have the historical richness of architectural masterpieces. But schools of thought exist in which stylistic issues (stack architectures, orthogonal instruction sets, hierarchic and distributed systems etc.), when resolved, give an artistic seal to the final product.

The parallel between the two building processes could be continued. However, our last analogy is to note that while architects work with contractors, electricians, plumbers and the like, computer architects take their decisions after consulting software specialists and chip designers among many others. Nonetheless, even with this help, the range of expertise required from computer architects is very wide and the number of topics covered here is necessarily limited. However, it corresponds broadly to the guidelines set forth by the IEEE Task Force on Computer Architecture with a more systems oriented approach to the subject.

This book is divided into three parts. In the first two, I do not present specific architectures in detail but I draw many examples from current systems such as IBM System/370, CDC 6600, DEC PDP-10 and PDP-11 and also from more powerful or less common machines since it is my belief that advances in the more sophisticated models are echoed in subsequent standard products. In the third part, by contrast, I describe some complete systems.

Part I is an overview of what Bell and Newell have called the Computer Space. Chapter 1 surveys the historical dimension from ENIAC to current microcomputers. Chapter 2 introduces the PMS, ISP, CDL and Petri Net notations which will be used consistently in the remainder of the text. This provides the opportunity of evaluating instruction sets and addressing modes.

Part II is the study of the main (hardware) blocks, their control and their (software/hardware) interactions. Chapter 3 presents algorithms for the four basic arithmetic operations for the fixed and floating-point representations of numbers. The emphasis is on methods used to achieve "engineering" speed-up. Chapter 4 is devoted to central processors and to methods to render them more powerful such as look-ahead, functional unit distribution and automatic detection of parallelism. The concept of a stack computer is also introduced in this chapter. Chapters 5 and 6 deal with the memory hierarchy found in modern computer systems. Chapter 5 is technologically oriented: RAM's and their interleaving, rotational secondary memories and electronic disks are presented. Associative memories are briefly described. Chapter 6 is devoted to the virtual memory concept and to its implementations at the primary-secondary memory and cache-primary memory levels. The tradeoffs between various schemes are examined and evaluated by referring to simulations and actual measurements. Chapter 7 examines microprogramming and its applications to emulation, high-level language interpretation and tuning of architectures. The chapter ends with the presentation of an ideal microprogramming system. Chapter 8 is concerned with input/output: interrupts, channels, I/O devices and an evaluation of asynchronous input/output processing are discussed.

Part III presents specific systems. Because the numerous examples provided in the first two parts give a good representation of a medium-size architecture, I direct my attention mostly to small machines and to supercomputers. Chapter 9 examines the small end of the spectrum with the DEC PDP-11 family, including the VAX 11/780, being the vehicle for minicomputers and the Intel 8080 and Zilog Z8000 being examples of 8-bit and 16-bit microcomputers. The last section of the chapter presents the stack architecture of the Hewlett-Packard HP-3000. Chapter 10 deals with supercomputers. Pipeline processors (Amdahl 470 V/6, CRAY-1, CDC STAR-100, TI ASC), array processors (ILLIAC IV), and multiprocessors (C.mmp, C.m*, PLURIBUS) are discussed. Hardware and software considerations (synchronization, scheduling etc.) are included in the presentation. Finally, Chapter 11 mentions some specialized architectures, gives an overview of several options used to achieve distributed processing and attempts to assess the impact of VLSI on future systems.

This book grew out from notes given to first year Computer Science Graduate Students at the University of Washington. The material has been expanded and is appropriate for a two-quarter, or even a two-semester, sequence at the senior-first year graduate student level. It is suitable for Computer Science, Computer Engineering and Electrical Engineering majors. Although a course on Logical Design is not a formal prerequisite, it is my experience that students with a background in Digital Design can understand some parts of the text more quickly. I assume tacitly that the readers have had some exposure to high-level language programming and I use a Pascal-like notation to express algorithms.

Many colleagues and students have helped me during the preparation of the book. In particular, I would like to thank P. Borgwardt, D. P. Bovet, C. Crowley, C. Ellis, T. Hou, J. Jensen, K. Kim, E. Lazowska, B. Nussbaum, and M. Sievers for their technical and "grammatical" criticisms. I owe a great debt of gratitude to Professor G. Estrin who introduced me to the field of Computer Architecture. Some sections of this text are direct outgrowths of research supported by the National Science Foundation. I might not have written this book if it had not been for the text editing and formatting systems implemented by R. Tomlinson and G. Houston. I am indebted to them and to M. Reidel and H. Sardarov for their typing assistance. The patience and continuing support of my wife Diane Roseman deserves more than the usual amount of credit. Finally, I take full responsibility for any remaining gallicisms.

Jean-Loup Baer

CONTENTS

PART III   Complete Systems: From Micros to Supercomputers

Part I

AN OVERVIEW OF THE COMPUTER SPACE

In the beginning was the secret brain.

Dylan Thomas

Ce que l'on conçoit bien s'énonce clairement,
Et les mots pour le dire arrivent aisément.

Boileau

Very few facts are able to tell their own story, without comments to bring out their meaning.

John Stuart Mill

Chapter 1

HISTORICAL SURVEY OF COMPUTER SYSTEMS ARCHITECTURE

1.1 INTRODUCTION

Defining what is meant by Computer Systems Architecture is not a simple task. First, we must not restrict ourselves to the sole aspect of the hardware. Building black boxes of increasing size and complexity from some primitive entities such as adders, shift registers, or memory chips is certainly part of the process. Interconnecting these boxes through buses, switches, and controllers is also an important contribution to the overall design. But, the harmonious cooperation between the components in the system, the way messages are passed and received, and the blend of hardware and software features which make the system operate must be included. Thus, we shall consider Computer Systems Architecture as the design of the integrated system which provides a useful tool to the programmer. Since the term programmer itself is subject to various interpretations, as in systems programmer, applications programmer, coder, or programmer analyst, we shall study the architecture of computer systems at different levels. In particular, we shall treat:

- the internal workings of the black boxes which are the main components of the system;
- the means of interconnecting these boxes, their parallel activities, and cooperation.

This will imply not only the description of parts of the system and of their interconnections, but also, when necessary, of the supervisory control which might well be a software product.

1

Before proceeding to a short outline, two words of caution are in order. First, since this book is intended as continuing an introductory text on Digital Systems design, it is assumed that the reader has a basic knowledge of digital logic. For example, it is expected that the principles behind the construction of a full adder or a half-adder, the decoding of an instruction, etc., are well understood. We shall seldom be at that level of detail.

Second, this book will often be biased towards the study of large and powerful systems. Although this might not be the trend in the development of computers, we believe that it is in the study of large and powerful machines, even special-purpose ones, that advances in the state of the art are realized. In addition, we shall emphasize the performance aspects in evaluating components and total systems by quoting monitoring studies or by relying on the results of analytical models and simulations.

This philosophy of looking at large computers in order to improve more standard units is neither new nor limited to Computer Architecture. For example, the development of racing cars has had a significant impact on the safety of current automobiles. As early as 1952, shortly after the completion of the IAS machine which since then has become the model of the stored program computer, its inventor, von Neumann, sensed the need for a continued experimentation in building unique systems with "specifications simply calling for the most advanced machine which is possible in the present state of the art." Von Neumann and his associates were able to convince the Atomic Energy Commission, Sperry-Rand, UNIVAC and IBM of the validity of this approach. This resulted in the construction of giant computers such as LARC (UNIVAC) and STRETCH (IBM) which brought forth "major advances in Computer Technology that were rapidly reflected in the product line of these companies." The supercomputers of the seventies might play the same roles and it is perhaps no coincidence that a successful computer using advanced pipeline concepts was built by Texas Instruments, a manufacturer of integrated circuits and small calculators.

This book is divided into three parts. Part I is an overview of what Bell and Newell have called "the computer space." We shall look at the historical development of Computer Systems Architecture, and follow this by a study of the representation of computer systems at various levels. This study of methodologies and notations will allow us to give an overview of the development of systems from structural and behavioral viewpoints. Part II will be centered on the four main components of a von Newmann machine, i.e., the arithmetic-logical unit, memory and the management of a hierarchy of storage components, the control and its orderly implementation via microprogramming, and the connection of input-output devices with the remainder of the system using channels operating in parallel with the main processor. Part III will look at specific systems, such as mini and microcomputers, supercomputers of the array and pipeline families, multiprocessors, and at the impact of new technologies on future systems.

Several important issues are either not treated or barely mentioned. For example, associative processing receives little attention because of its very special-purpose nature and of its high manufacturing cost which makes it noncompetitive at the present time. Geographically distributed computer networks are simply mentioned. Another book would be necessary to treat them at a substantial level. Justice might not have been done to newly emerging architectures such as high-level language direct execution machines. Stack machines do not receive the treatment that their advocates would expect. This is a question of choice for which this author takes full responsibility.

1.2 HISTORICAL SURVEY

Until 1970, it was customary to review the history of electronic computers by providing a classification by generations. We shall adhere to this convention and follow the chronological outline of Rosen's authoritative survey (cf. bibliography at the end of the chapter). For the post 1970 era, we shall point out the trends in computer architecture which indicate a departure from the designs realized in the previous generations. We do not present an encyclopedic overview of the computer genealogical chart. Instead, we shall limit ourselves to what can be considered as the landmarks in the development of computer systems. The prehistoric age of computers, that is the period of mechanical and electromechanical machines, is not covered. The interested reader can consult a fascinating anthology edited by Randell as well as Goldstine's historical account from which the quotes from the previous section were taken. This latter book also provides an interesting view on the birth of the early computers as seen by an active participant.

1.2.1 Generation 0 (Prior to 1950)

The first electronic computers were not the product of commercial enterprises. They were unique realizations, built or contracted by Universities or Government supported research institutions.

ENIAC, completed in 1946 at the Moore School of Engineering (University of Pennsylvania) under the direction of Eckert and Mauchly, can be considered as the first electronic computer. It was made of more than 18000 vacuum tubes and 1500 relays, most of which had to operate simultaneously. ENIAC's primary function was to compute ballistic trajectories. It was able to perform nearly 5000 additions or subtractions per second. Arithmetic operations were done in decimal, serially, with each digit being implemented as a ring of 10 flip-flops. This ring lay-out was certainly inherited from previous electromechanical devices. There was no programming in the sense we give to this word today. The computer was wired in for specific computations and modifications or replacements of programs made new rewirings necessary. Hence, the set-up time was tremendous. Despite these shortcomings, ENIAC was to be used for ten years before being retired.

The idea of having the program stored in memory is generally attributed to von Neumann. While a consultant at the Moore School, he and the originators of the ENIAC designed the first stored program computer named EDVAC. At the same time, Wilkes, who had spent a summer in Philadelphia studying with the investigators of ENIAC, built the EDSAC at Cambridge University (U.K.). EDSAC was the first stored program computer to be operational (1949). Its storage was much more extensive than ENIAC's: it had a primary memory of 1024 words, a mercury delay line acting as a shift register, backed up by a drum of 4600 words. This has to be compared with the 20 registers and 312 words of externally alterable read-only memory of ENIAC. Besides being the first computer to execute stored programs, EDSAC can be considered as the first one to introduce the notion of a memory hierarchy.

The EDVAC project was severely crippled when Eckert and Mauchly left the Moore School to form their own company. Von Neumann, Goldstine and their collaborators at the Institute for Advanced Studies (IAS) in Princeton had already started on a new venture, referred now as the IAS or von Neumann machine. Because the von Neumann machine is still the usual frame of reference for many modern computers, we present its overall structure in some detail.

A von Neumann machine is a system composed of five basic units (cf. Figure 1.1) whose functions can be summarized as follows:

- The *input* transmits data and instructions from the outside world to the memory;
- The *memory* stores instructions and data, intermediate and final results;
- The *arithmetical-logical unit* (*ALU*) performs arithmetic and logical operations;
- The *control* interprets the instructions and causes them to be executed;
- The *output* transmits final results and messages to the outside world.

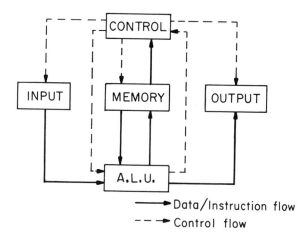

Figure 1.1   A von Neumann machine

For the execution of a non-branching instruction, the following sequence of actions, or *instruction execution cycle*, is undertaken:

1. The control requests and fetches from memory the next instruction to be executed;
2. The control decodes the instruction;
3. Depending on the results of Step 2:

    (a) An operand is fetched from memory, stored in a register of the arithmetic-logical unit and control is given to the latter in order to perform an operation; or

    (b) An operand is stored, from a register of the arithmetic-logical unit, in the memory; or

    (c) A request is made to the input (output) to accept (transmit) a word from (to) the outside world;

4. Upon termination of Step 3, return to Step 1.

In the original IAS machine, whose inner workings are described in the classic proposal by Burks et al., the memory consisted of 4096 (2^{12}) words of 40 bits. The medium used for storage was a cathode ray tube. Mention was made of an automatically managed memory hierarchy. The arithmetic-logical unit was of the single accumulator type and operations were performed in parallel binary mode (this is to be contrasted with ENIAC's serial arithmetic). The internal representation was 2's complement. Floating-point operations were not implemented; maybe the fact that von Neumann and his collaborators were brilliant mathematicians prevented them from realizing the difficulties involved in having the programmers plan their own scaling factors. The control unit was hardwired, with a decoding mechanism allowing for an instruction set of 64 opcodes. The instructions were of the one address type, with the format:

opcode   operand address

with the second operand being implicitly the ALU's accumulator. Since 6 bits had to be reserved for the opcode and 12 bits for the address, two instructions were packed in a single word. Words were also divided into tetrads (4 bits) and hexadecimal notation was advocated for debugging purposes.

Several other machines quite similar to the IAS computer were built subsequently, including ILLIAC at the University of Illinois, JOHNIAC at the RAND Corporation, MANIAC at Los Alamos, WEIZAC at the Weizman Institute in Israel, AVIDAC and ORDVAC at the Argonne National Laboratories.

ENIAC, EDSAC and the IAS-type computers were all geared to perform scientific tasks. The first machine whose goal was real-time computations (aircraft simulator, air-traffic and industrial process control) was Whirlwind I (WWI), started at MIT in 1947 and completed in 1951.

Like all its successors in this line of application, WWI had a short word length (16 bits). With room for 32 opcodes, only 27 instructions were actually implemented leaving a potential addressing space of 2048 words. Using 0.5 μs circuitry, WWI could perform 20,000 operations per second since the limiting factor was the memory cycle. In 1951, memory consisted of over 1200 registers of electrostatic storage tubes. This was soon to be replaced by 2K words of 8 μs cycle time of coincident-current magnetic core memory, a design developed by Forrester at MIT. The advent of core memory has certainly been one of the most important innovations in the history of Computer Systems.

Besides being the first computer with a core memory, the Whirlwind project made a significant contribution to computer science in educating a number of pioneers by making available detailed documentation of the logical design of the main parts of the machine.

Before core, the principal medium used for memory was an electrostatic storage tube, as in the early design of Whirlwind. The first practical version of the electrostatic storage device was due to Williams from Manchester University. But the main architectural advance in the Manchester computer was to be the introduction of index registers. Of importance too was the use of a magnetic drum for secondary memory. The drum was divided into blocks of equal size, or pages. As we shall see later, the automatic management of a paged memory hierarchy was also "initiated" in Manchester a little more than a decade later.

Electrostatic storage was also used in the SWAC (Standard Western Automatic Computer) one of the fastest, and smallest, of the early computers. Its eastern counterpart, the SEAC, used memory delay lines, at least initially. SEAC might have been the first operational stored program computer in the U.S.A. (1950). Its successor, MIDAC, used a three address instruction format (for two operands and a result) with possible indexing on each address. The two index registers were the program counter (for looping) and a base register.

These early computers were operated on an open-shop basis. There was no operating system and only primitive input-output devices. Debugging was generally performed on-line, stepping up instruction by instruction, reading memory contents while the machine was running (this was made relatively easy by the CRT memories), and changing the contents of the registers through console switches. This was facilitated in part by the fact that programming was done in machine language (there existed no high-level language yet) and by the high competence of the mathematician-programmers.

1.2.2 Generation 1 (1950–1958)

The 1950's saw the birth of the computer industry. Rather than following a breadth first review of the genealogical tree, we consider the major companies of the time. Interestingly enough, the current giant, IBM, was not the first one to participate in the commercialization of electronic computers. Its superiority in sales management and public relation activities enabled it to overcome its relatively late start.

When Eckert and Mauchly left the University of Pennsylvania, they formed their own company and started to build BINAC, a small binary computer, intended for the Northrop Corporation. BINAC was not a stored program computer and never worked satisfactorily. Almost at the same time as BINAC was realized, Eckert and Mauchly started on the design of the UNIVAC (UNIVersal Automatic Computer) which was commissioned by the Bureau of the Census for its 1950 calculations. UNIVAC I was delivered in 1951.

One of the major architectural advances of UNIVAC I was its tape system. Magnetic tapes could be read forward and backward with buffering capabilities and error-checking procedures. UNIVAC I was a decimal machine with 12 digits/word. It had a single address instruction format and two instructions were packed in each word. Its memory was still of the mercury delay line type, a factor which made it rapidly obsolete. Its successor, UNIVAC II, had core memory and was upward compatible with UNIVAC I. Late deliveries of this new model (1957) hampered the growth in the computer field of the Remington Rand Corporation which had acquired the Eckert and Mauchly original company.

UNIVAC I was intended, as its name implies, for both scientific and commercial applications. The first paper describing the system listed matrix algebraic computations, statistical problems (census related), premium billings for a life insurance company and logistical problems (this was before the invention of PERT networks) as a sample of the tasks that could be performed by the system. UNIVAC I was certainly the first successful commercial computer.

UNIVAC II was mostly intended for commercial applications. After acquiring Engineering Research Associates in 1950, Remington Rand built the scientifically oriented UNIVAC 1103 and 1103A, the latter delivered in 1956. They were 36 bit machines, using binary arithmetic and 1's complement representation, and a two-address instruction format of the form:

Accumulator = Contents(address 1) op. Contents(address 2).

The UNIVAC 1103 had floating-point hardware and was the first computer provided with a program interrupt capability.

At the time of their delivery the UNIVAC 1103 and the IBM 704 (see below) were the most advanced scientific computers of their generation.

The real entry of IBM in the electronic computer market began with the introduction of the Defense Calculator soon to be called the IBM 701. Prior to that date (1950), IBM's interest in the calculator area had been mostly restricted to office equipment and punch card machines. In the 1930's IBM had manufactured electromechanical devices to complement card punches; in the late 1940's some electronic equipment was added (IBM had an electronic multiplier at that time) to be known as the 600 series or Electronic Calculating Punch. In connection with the Northrop Corporation, a Card Program Calculator (CPC) was designed by coupling a calculating machine with a card punch. The CPC's were not stored program computers and were only semi-automatic in the sense that they needed human intervention to feed their (card) programs. However, they were extremely popular and in high-demand in computing centers, thus setting a base for further IBM deliveries.

IBM, as a company, was not overly interested in the development of early electronic computers. Still, in 1939, Aiken, who was designing an electromechanical machine with relays at Harvard, got some research support from IBM. It has been said that this happened more because of the personal interest of Thomas Watson Sr. in supporting academia, than because of some grandiose vision of the future of the computer industry. Aiken's first machine, the MARK I, was comparatively slow. It took 6 seconds to perform an addition and 12 seconds for a division. It had hardware units performing logarithms, exponentiation, and trigonometrical functions. Its first successor, MARK II, was also electromechanical and it was not until the late 40's that Aiken used electronics in MARK III. The last of the series, MARK IV, was completed in 1952.

By 1950, the need for high speed computing became evident. IBM then announced the 701 which was delivered, early, in 1953. This was the first realization in the IBM 700/7000 series of scientific computers whose elements came to be regarded as the models for the first and second generation of scientific computers.

The IBM 701, of which more than a dozen were delivered, was a typical von Neumann machine. We shall describe in more detail one of its successors, the 7094. At this point, it is sufficient to say that the 701 used 2K words of unreliable electrostatic storage with a memory word of 36 bits. Two instructions were packed in a single word; I/O transmissions were under program control. The next product in the line, the 704 (1956) had 4K words of core memory, 3 index registers and hardwired floating-point operations. Although some relay computers, such as one developed at the Bell Laboratories and MARK II, had floating-point hardware, this was a first for an electronic computer. Because of the larger number of opcodes, the extension of the address field and the necessary encoding of the index registers, the instruction format could not fit in a half-word. The new full word instruction was kept until the end of the series. It was also in the 704 that indirect addressing first appeared.

The 701 and 704 still processed I/O requests as in the original IAS model, i.e., all transfers had to be routed through the ALU's accumulator. The shared access of main memory by the central processor and peripheral equipment was made possible by the introduction of data channels in the IBM 709. This new concept, in conjunction with interrupt capabilities, can be seen as the first major architectural departure from the von Neumann model. It is still present in most modern computers. The 709, operational by 1958, was to be a short lived model due to the advent of transistorized logic.

On the business-oriented side, IBM's 701 counterpart was the 702, a character-oriented machine with a primary memory of 10,000 characters using, as the 701, electrostatic technology. Although it was delivered (early again) in 1955, the unreliable memory, the relative lack of speed of the ALU and the unbuffered I/O tape system made it difficult for the 702 to compete with UNIVAC I. Less than a year after delivery of the 702, its successor, the 705, was ready. Core memory, buffered tape I/O systems with special hardware controllers and a faster model (model III) brought the 705's performance up to that of UNIVAC II. Timely deliveries and good service support from the manufacturer tilted the scales towards IBM.

UNIVAC and IBM were not the only companies interested in the computer market. Raytheon and Honeywell, at first separately and then in a common venture, collaborated on the design of the Datamatic 1000, a large data processing computer with core memory and 48 bit (12 digit) words. Delivered two years after the 705, it was never successful. RCA which had been involved in manufacturing the Selectron, the storage medium for the IAS machine, switched to the development of core memories when the Williams tubes superseded the Selectrons. RCA went on to build the BIZMAC's, business-oriented machines with variable word-lengths. An interesting feature of the BIZMAC was the possible interconnection of the central computer with electronic sorters directly linked to printers or card punches. The interconnection was realized through a relay-based switch. As in the Datamatic case, the BIZMAC hit the market too late and was almost obsolete when delivered. Burroughs was also involved early in the computer field but with minimal impact at that time.

We mentioned earlier that some early computers, e.g. EDSAC, had a magnetic drum as secondary memory. In fact, by 1950, some systems had been built with drums as their main memory. The advantages of low price per bit and large capacity rendered drums attractive despite their 5-25 ms. average access times. Drum computers, as they were to be known, were not intended for large and fast systems. But they provided a good alternative to those users who had limited requirements. The realization of cyclic primary memories such as drums had started with the development of the mercury delay lines. A typical example was the Pilot ACE based on a preliminary design of Turing and modified for practical purposes by Huskey. It was a precursor of the English Electric Deuce, the Bendix G-15 and the Packard-Bell 250. By the early 50's, several other manufacturers, for example NCR and ElectroData Corporation later absorbed by Burroughs, had drum computers on the market. In 1954, IBM announced the 650 which had a faster but somewhat smaller (2000 words of 10 digits) drum than most of its competitors. Initially the input/output was only through card devices but later models had printers and tapes. Floating-point hardware, index registers, a core memory buffer for tapes and disks and a larger drum (4000 words) were extensions which made the 650 a rival difficult to beat.

It was during this period that the first software efforts in the area of assemblers and loaders, high-level languages and compilers, and operating systems were fostered.

To alleviate the burden of programming in machine language, frequently used functions, for example floating-point emulators, were available in EDSAC as system routines. Absolute loaders appeared with the IBM 701. Assembly languages were widely used with first generation machines. User groups, such as SHARE for IBM customers, even tried early standardizations such as SAP for the 704.

With the advent of drum machines came assemblers optimized with respect to the fetching of the next instruction (e.g. SOAP for the IBM 650). Macroassemblers were available on the IBM 702 and successors.

Under the influence of Grace Hopper, the UNIVAC group was very active in the development of high-level languages. Mathmatic, a precursor of ALGOL, and Flowmatic, an ancestor of COBOL, were designed in the early 50's. At IBM, Speedcode, an interpreter, and PACT (through SHARE), were available on the 701. During the period 1954–1957, Backus and his coworkers developed FORTRAN for which a compiler was available, albeit not bug-free, by the time the 709 was delivered. The influence and wide usage of FORTRAN and of its compilers are well known.

Supervisors or operating systems were necessary as soon as I/O devices faster than card equipment became more common. The Whirlwind investigators had already sensed the need for a "comprehensive system." Batch processing, the grouping of a collection of jobs separated by control cards, were the rule when tape-to-tape systems prevailed. In this mode of operation, the input was transferred from card to tape, and the output from tape to printer, on a satellite computer. The job control language, that is cards indicating the nature of the following decks, was still rather simple. Input/Output manipulations were standardized and this was at the same time eased and made mandatory by the use of high-level languages. Complex (for the time) operating systems were designed, for example SOS (a SHARE enterprise).

With the development of batch processing, the user was isolated from the machine. Debugging was off-line, and it was the beginning of eternal complaints about turn-around times! But the convenience for many applications of programming in high-level languages and the freedom from worrying about I/O transactions overcame, in most cases, the lack of man-machine interactions.

1.2.3   Generation 2 (1958–1964)

The passage from the first to the second generation was essentially due to a technological change. Ten years had to pass from the discovery of the transistor by Bardeen and Brattain in 1948 to its application in digital computer circuitry. By 1958 the engineering problems had been solved and vacuum tubes were then abandoned. Transistors presented cost advantages, were smaller and dissipated much less heat. Therefore orders of magnitude more components could be used in the construction of computers.

IBM again was not the first company to deliver a fully transistorized machine. NCR, and more successfully RCA, were the front runners with some small transistor machines. In addition, the RCA 501 (operational in 1959) was offered with a COBOL compiler which, in spite of being excruciatingly slow (on an already slow machine) and a cumbersome software package for the 501's memory size, gave RCA a welcome boost to re-establish itself in the computer field after rather shaky beginnings.

But if IBM was not the leader in the application of the new technology, it was not far behind. The first IBM transistorized computer, the 7070 delivered in 1960, was business-oriented and was intended to replace the 650 and 705. But since it was incompatible with the latter, most customers were unhappy and it was soon to be replaced with the 7080 which was compatible with its predecessors. This issue of compatibility would again arise when third generation computers were to appear. The 7080 was a decimal, character-oriented machine of rather large capacity. To satisfy smaller customers, two extremely popular machines were delivered in 1961: the 1620 (6 bits/character) and the 1401 (7 bits/character). It is reported that IBM sold approximately two thousand 1620's and twenty thousand 1401's. Like the 702 and 705, the 1401 was a variable word length decimal machine; instructions and data were stored as characters and the delimiter was the setting of a special bit in the first character (hence the 7 bit/character) since data was "read" from left to right.

Other companies like CDC, Burroughs, Honeywell, General Electric, and the already mentioned NCR and RCA also cashed in on the small machine market. Honeywell was particularly successful, first with the H-800, fast and inexpensive, and then with the 200 series which was upward compatible with the IBM 1401 and replaced it in some installations when IBM switched to System/360.

On the scientific side, IBM's successor to the 709 was to be initially a one-of-a-kind machine, the 709TX, specially commissioned by the Department of Defense. IBM was not willing to stop the production of the 709 less than a year after its initial delivery. However, pressures from competitors obliged IBM to give up on the production of the 709 and to begin that of what was to be the 7090. On-time deliveries (1959) offset the inconveniences of incompletely debugged machines, and further improvements in reliability made the 7090 the successful computer of its generation. Hundreds of them were sold, at several million dollars per unit. The 7094 was an enhancement of the 7090, and the 7040/7044 series was a cheaper, smaller and slower version.

Since the 7000 series has become a model for the second generation of computers, we elaborate somewhat on its structure. A typical 7094 configuration is shown in Figure 1.2. Table 1.1 depicts the hardware evolution in the series. Comparing Figure 1.2 with Figure 1.1, we see that the main architectural change is in the presence of data channels allowing asynchronous concurrency between I/O and compute operations. Minor modifications are apparent in the integration of the arithmetic-logical and control units into a single central processing unit (CPU) which has control over the initiations of channel programs, and in the wide variety of external devices. Within the CPU itself, we see a proliferation of opcodes (cf. Table 1.1)

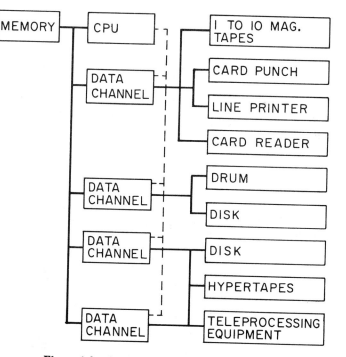

Figure 1.2 A typical IBM 7094 configuration

Table 1.1 The IBM 700/7000 Series

Model number	First delivery	CPU technology	Memory technology	Cycle time (μs)	Memory size (K)	Number of opcodes	Number of index registers	Hardwired floating-point	I/O overlap (channels)	Instruction fetch overlap	Speed ratio (approximate)
701	1952	vacuum tubes	Williams tubes	30	2–4	24	0	no	no	no	1
704	1955	vacuum tubes	core	12	4–32	80	3	yes	no	no	2.5
709	1958	vacuum tubes	core	12	32	140	3	yes	yes	no	4
7090	1960	transistor	core	2.18	32	169	3	yes	yes	no	25
7094 I	1962	transistor	core	2	32	185	7	yes (double precision)	yes	yes	30
7094 II	1964	transistor	core	1.4	32	185	7	yes (double precision)	yes	yes	50

from 24 to 185, an increase in the number of index registers, and for more powerful machines, hardwired double-precision (72 bits) floating-point and instruction look-ahead. In terms of raw speed the largest gap is due to the technological change from vacuum tubes to transistors (709 to 7090), along with a sharp decrease in memory cycle time. In the latest model, the 7094 II, the conjunction of a fast memory cycle and of the overlap of many functions results in a very powerful machine.

Yet, the operation of the CPU was very much in the style of that of the ALU and control unit of the IAS computer. Instructions kept their one address format, with an implicit accumulator and the addition of address modification through indexing and/or indirect addressing. The basic instruction execution cycle presented earlier remained valid, if I/O operations were discarded and interrupt checking inserted at the beginning of the cycle. This cycle required between one (for a transfer) and 19 memory cycles (for a double-precision floating-point divide) to execute.

Further enhancements in the 7090/7094 structure allowed the presence of two banks of 32K words of memory which could be selected under program control. The first time-sharing system implemented at MIT took advantage of this feature. The coupling of a 7090/7094 with a 7040/7044 (the latter monitoring I/O operations) was a very popular configuration in large scientific centers.

UNIVAC's transistorized scientific computer, the 1107, successor of the 1103, was operational three years after the launching of the IBM 7090. It was too late to be a major competitor. The real importance of the 1107 is that it provided a good test bed for the 1108 which was to become a successful third generation computer. On the business data processing side, UNIVAC III continued the line which had started with BINAC but this particular model was too expensive for its limited performance and never became very popular.

Several companies which were making some profit in the small to medium size computer field tried at that time to break into the medium to large size market. Two of them were particularly successful: CDC and Burroughs.

CDC was formed in 1957 by some UNIVAC dissidents. Their first machine was the 1604, a scientific 48 bit-word computer, slower but less expensive than the IBM 7090. It was followed by the 3600, an improved and faster version, which had a multiport- multibus CPU-I/O channels-Memory connection, a design to be carried on in several subsequent systems. In 1964 CDC delivered its first 6600, a machine whose architecture presented several important innovations, such as multiple functional units, and which was the most powerful computer of its time. Since then, the CDC 6600 and its descendants have kept CDC in a leading role related to the development of supercomputers. We shall come back later to the CDC 6600 since it presents characteristics which also qualify it as being a member of the third generation.

The departure from strict von Neumann architectures was not limited to CDC products. In 1963, Burroughs delivered the B-5000, a rather slow machine, with the B-5500 (1964) improving on the speed. The B-5000 can be considered as the first machine designed to efficiently process a high-level language, in this case ALGOL-60. The stack organization, the descriptor (pointer) based addressing and the segmented approach to the virtual memory concept are three features (some will say advances) which would stay with the Burroughs line. A few machines have been built following these principles: the English Electric KDF-9, a series of ICL computers, and some minicomputers (cf. the Hewlett-Packard 3000 described in Chapter 9). The concept of high-level language machines has been developed throughout the years and is becoming increasingly popular and more cost-effective with the advent of microprogramming and writable control stores. It is also important to note that while Burroughs was introducing segmentation, the first virtual memory system using paging was realized at Manchester University on an ATLAS computer (1962).

In the late fifties and early sixties, two companies, Digital Equipment Corporation (DEC) and Scientific Data Systems (SDS), were started. They were to influence the systems of the next generation, DEC by introducing minicomputers (the DEC PDP-1 in 1960), SDS by providing sophisticated hardware interrupt systems which would be used in time-sharing systems. DEC's PDP-5 (1963) was a precursor of the very popular PDP-8, and SDS's 910-920 (1962) were the early products of the 900-9000 series.

During this period, there was no lack of activity in the giant computer area. Multiprocessors and multifunctional unit CPU's were introduced to provide more computing power. In 1958, the National Bureau of Standards sponsored the PILOT project. PILOT was a multiprocessor, each CPU being assigned a specific task: arithmetic, bookkeeping and I/O respectively. This philosophy of distributed computing under the supervision of a master control was later advocated for the design of computer utilities. In the Ramo-Wooldridge RW-400 (a "polymorphic" computer) multiple CPU's and memories were interconnected as functionally independent modules. This was for reliability as well as for speed-up purposes, making the RW-400 a prototype of current computer networks and proposed reconfigurable computers. In the Bull Gamma-60, concurrency of operations in the separate functional units was under control of the assembly language programmer through some pseudo-operations. This tight-coupling of functional units under the supervision of either hardware or software will be encountered again.

The two leaders in the scientific computing field, IBM and UNIVAC, were also involved in the development of supercomputers. Started a year apart, UNIVAC's LARC completed in 1960, and IBM's STRETCH (or 7030) delivered in 1961, were designed according to different philosophies. With LARC, UNIVAC's intention was to freeze the technology at a given point and balance the system accordingly without taking into account potential component improvements, while IBM's goal for STRETCH, as indicated by the name, was to use the most advanced techniques and the latest components as they evolved. It is somewhat ironical that neither LARC (only 2 models built) nor STRETCH (7 machines delivered) were commercially successful.

LARC had two processors: a CPU which utilized a binary-coded decimal floating-point representation and extensive overlap in the instruction cycle (making it a forerunner of pipeline processors) in connection with interleaved memory, and an I/O processor with its own memory for its stored program. Unhappily, compute-bound and I/O bound tasks were both providing bottlenecks for the two processors instead of increasing the throughput. This inadequacy in the management of multiprogrammed processes prevented LARC from being widely accepted.

The design specifications for STRETCH called for a factor of improvement of 100 over the IBM 704. In fact, it never realized much more than a 50:1 ratio, which did not make it cost-effective when the 7094 appeared (cf. Table 1.1). The main new feature in STRETCH was a look-ahead unit allowing fetching and partial interpretation, and/or execution, of several instructions following the one pointed to by the program counter. Very elaborate schemes, too complex to be totally successful, were needed to recover the program state when interrupts or program branching occurred. This experience proved profitable for subsequent machines. Besides this look-ahead feature supported by an interleaved memory, STRETCH had a very extensive instruction set and data types, many out of the ordinary such as Boolean vectors and variable length integers. Finally, protection for multiprogrammed tasks was partially embedded in the hardware by the use of two bound registers.

Neither LARC nor STRETCH could be considered as "true" multiprocessors in the sense that they had only one CPU. Burroughs was the first company to introduce (1962) a multiprocessor with identical CPU's. This machine, the D-825, could have up to 4 processors connected to 16 memory modules via a cross-bar switch. The D-825 was intended for military applications; its cross-bar scheme was to be kept by Burroughs for its dual processor B-5000 and would reappear in the design of more recent multi-processors.

As mentioned earlier, FORTRAN had appeared just prior to the beginning of Generation 2. Its success, and the recognized need for high-level languages, turned the late fifties and early sixties into an era of prime development for computer languages. On the scientific side, an international committee of mathematicians and computer scientists developed ALGOL (1958) which was revised in 1960 (hence the name ALGOL-60) and finalized in 1962. The formal definition of its syntax using what is now known as the Backus-Naur Form (BNF) was to become a model for future language descriptions. But the lack of standard I/O procedures prevented the wide acceptance of ALGOL-60 by American manufacturers (Burroughs excepted). On the other hand, researchers and educators used, and continue to use, ALGOL and its dialects as effective means of communication. On the business side, COBOL, originated in 1959 with a first official version in 1960, was also a committee-designed language under the auspices of the Department of Defense. DOD's main interest in the venture was to have available a language which would be truly compatible for a large variety of machines (CO standing for common). Although this goal was not quite completely reached, DOD's strong influence as the largest computer user imposed COBOL as a standard. To this day, FORTRAN and COBOL, with numerous small changes, are still considered to be (maybe for the worse rather than for the better) the standard high-level programming languages of the non-academic community.

In 1963, another commitee, this one consisting of IBM users, launched a new programming language which was to become PL/I. It was supposed to bring together the best points of FORTRAN and COBOL with a smattering of ALGOL constructs. The result was a cumbersome language with many attractive features but slow in compilation and execution. Although the language has a vocal set of advocates, it does not enjoy the popularity of its predecessors.

This period saw a proliferation of new procedural languages. Among those which are still in use and quite popular, APL is the most interesting since it is particularly well suited to interactive computing.

A new field in Computer Science, namely Artificial Intelligence, emerged with the second generation of computers. The expanded memory sizes and increased speeds of operation allowed the execution of programs which could not have been dreamed of before. List processing languages such as IPL, COMIT (for the translation of natural languages) and LISP were developed. LISP is still very widely used and is a standard for artificial intelligence languages.

As we said before, a major architectural change during this period was the introduction of channels and their asynchronous parallel operation with, and under the control of, the CPU. Because of the permitted concurrency between CPU and I/O operations, management of I/O routines and assignment of files to the external devices could not be left to the discretion of the users. The operating system had to be in charge of all I/O related activities and the concept of a resident I/O supervisor became the rule. The users were required to rely on it and schemes to protect it from malicious or inadvertent destruction were needed. This led to hardware enhancements such as relocation registers and memory locks, and provided the basis for the multiprogramming and time-sharing systems of the next generation. Other improvements to the operating systems of that time included the development of a large number of utility routines (dumps, time-out routines, etc. ..) and more elaborate linking loaders allowing users to choose from libraries of high-level language processors and assembly packages.

1.2.4   Generation 3 (1964–197?)

The passage from the first to the second generation was unequivocally a matter of technological advance. No such claim can be made for the transition to the third generation. Three factors can be identified which certainly played important roles for the new appellation: the advent of integrated circuits, the generalization of multiprogrammed operating systems, and the new IBM series of computers, System/360, which was a complete and incompatible departure from the 7000 series.

1.2.4.1   *Medium-scale Machines*

By 1964, IBM had a firm grip on the computer market. The announcement of a new series of computers, named System/360, came as no surprise since it had been in the design stage since 1961. From the users' viewpoint however, the unpleasant fact was the incompatibility, except by emulation, of the 360's with their 7000's ancestors. On the other hand the six 360 models announced, namely models 30, 40, 50, 60, 62 and 70, were all upward compatible and had the same instruction set implemented by microprograms in the lower models.

Figure 1.3 shows the general organization of System/360. As can be seen

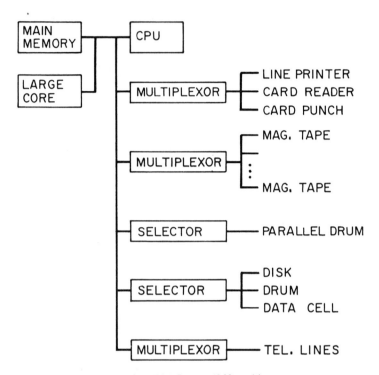

Figure 1.3   IBM System/360 architecture

by comparing Figures 1.2 and 1.3, there is no major conceptual change in the overall architecture between the 360 and the 7090. Minor changes, not included in the figure, are that the main memory of the 360 is faster and can be expanded up to 1 million words in some models, and there is a greater diversification in the type of data channels and peripheral equipment. The large core storage of Figure 1.3 is a memory running approximately one order of magnitude slower than main core with correspondingly lesser cost.

The principal difference between System/360 and the 7000 series lies in the CPU. Instead of a 36-bit word, we have a 32-bit or 4-byte (one byte is 8 bits) word with a machine which can be considered at the same time word and byte (or character) oriented. The single accumulator and 7 index registers of the 7094 have been replaced by 16 general registers and 4 double-length floating-point registers. An extensive instruction set, almost 150 opcodes, provides for word, byte, integer, decimal and floating-point operations. The instructions, of different lengths, can be for register to register, register to memory, memory to register, or memory to memory operations. Interrupt capabilities are enhanced with a limited built-in priority system modifiable by the programmer, memory protection is implemented through memory locks, and a program status double-word contains the pertinent information on the state of the running program. These last three features are meant to ease the design of multiprogrammed operating systems.

We shall return frequently to some specific features of System/360 in the course of this book since the series is representative of current computers.

IBM did not limit the 360 line to the above six models. Models 60, 62 and 70 soon disappeared to be replaced by models 65 and 75. In 1967, IBM introduced the model 67, the first IBM computer for the general public using the virtual memory concept, and the model 44 designed for scientific and real-time applications. In the large computer arena, a sequence of models dubbed 9X culminated in the 360/91 of which only a few, about 20, were delivered. Raw speed was attained by using some of the techniques pioneered in STRETCH and pipelined multifunctional units. This brief incursion into the supercomputer field was rapidly abandoned for two reasons: fear of an antitrust suit which was to come about nonetheless a few years later, and the forthcoming arrival of the model 85 built around the cache memory concept and performing as well as the 91 with a simpler architecture. Soon, the model 195 was to capture the best features of the 91 and of the 85. On the other end of the scale, the model 20 was introduced to satisfy former users of the 1400 series.

In 1970, IBM announced System/370 which presented no advance compared to the 360 except for a different circuit technology. There are several compatible models: 115, 125, 135, 145, 155 and 165 with cache, 158, 168 and 3033 with paging systems. New models appear periodically.

A number of IBM competitors have built systems which resemble System/360. RCA with the Spectra line (1965) presented computers which were compatible with the 360 and whose ranges of performance lay between consecutive models of the IBM series. In particular, RCA tried to corner the time-sharing market with an early virtual memory based operating system. The financial aspects of the enterprise were so dismal that RCA quit the computer manufacturing business (too soon according to some financial analysts) and sold out to UNIVAC. This acquisition broadened the base of the latter company which was very successful with its scientific computers, the 1108 and the 1110, successors of the 1107. An interesting aspect of the incompatibility between the 7000 series and System/360 is that it boosted UNIVAC's 1108 which could rely on previously developed software to which a number of 7094 users converted.

Before introducing the Sigma series, SDS had enjoyed a fair success with the 900's and 9000's. They were 24-bit word machines, with a highly sophisticated interrupt system, which were geared towards time-sharing and mostly real-time process control applications. With the same objectives in mind, but also hoping to make a dent in IBM's share of the market, SDS, which became a part of Xerox in 1969, launched the Sigma series. The higher models were 32-bit word machines with byte addressing capabilities as in the 360. They kept the interrupt philosophy of the 900's. The Sigma 7 and 9 were available with paging options while the 5 was not. Later the 16-bit word Sigma 2 and 3 appeared. Again, they were intended mostly for process control. Microprogrammed versions of the Sigmas have also been available. But the Xerox machines never achieved a total success, their relative failures often caused by inadequate or late software deliveries. In 1976, Xerox decided to leave the mainframe manufacturing part of the computer business and sold out its maintenance operations to Honeywell.

As we mentioned earlier, Honeywell had been very wise in marketing its H-200 which was compatible with IBM's 1401, and hence it capitalized on the 360's incompatibility. During this period of time Honeywell was (a distant) second to IBM in the business-oriented data processing field with a selection ranging from a small 100 unit to the rather powerful 8000's. The demise of the General Electric computer division and its transfer to Honeywell in the early seventies added to the latter's line the scientific GE-600's which included the GE-645, the hardware backbone for the MULTICS system. We shall return to MULTICS, a joint venture between GE, and then Honeywell, MIT and the Bell Telephone Laboratories, when we discuss virtual memory systems. The MULTICS project is still at the forefront of research, both in software and hardware, for the protection and privacy of users in a time-sharing environment. Along with the acquisition of GE, Honeywell inherited a French company, Machines Bull, the manufacturer of the Gamma-60. With the recent addition of the Xerox Sigmas and with the announcement of a new series of minicomputers, Honeywell is very well equipped but still far from IBM's share of the market.

Of all IBM competitors, Burroughs has consistently been striving to present alternate architectures. In the late sixties it introduced the B6700, an improved version of the stack-oriented B5500 with a better organization for multiprogrammed operating systems. Recently (1972), the B1700 has been the first (mini) computer to allow, at least from the programmer's viewpoint, a bit-addressable memory. At the same time, the B1700 can be considered as the first machine in industrial production which directly interprets a variety of high-level languages.

1.2.4.2 *Mini and Supercomputers*

With IBM shying away from smaller models, the minicomputer explosion proved profitable to DEC which had a brilliant start with the first mass produced minicomputer, the PDP-8 (over 12,000 units sold since 1965), and which can still be considered as the leading manufacturer of minicomputers with its PDP-11 line (over 10,000 units sold between 1972 and 1975). The minicomputer explosion, or as some call it revolution, was due to a combination of hardware and software technological advances, and of economical factors which allowed the dedicated use of small processors for a large variety of applications. For example, the PDP-8 had the same structure as its antecedent the PDP-5 (older by 3 years), but its performance was 3 times as good for half the price. The PDP-11 is even faster, presents more options, has a longer word length (16 bits instead of 12), and still is in the same price range.

Two typical minicomputer configurations are shown in Figures 1.4.a and 1.4.b. The major point to notice, while comparing their architectures to that of a medium size computer (cf. Figure 1.3), is the absence of sophisticated data channels. Direct Memory Access (DMA) interfaces do exist in a simplified manner and, as a consequence, there is a relative paucity of I/O devices for a given installation, although the variety of devices which can be attached to the system is in no way limited. Furthermore, transfer rates will be slow. The following factors, not shown in the figure, used to be instrumental in the classification of a computer in the mini category: small word sizes (less than or equal to 16 bits), a limited memory addressing range (64K bytes is an often cited figure corresponding to an address field of 16 bits), restricted arithmetic capabilities (in general hardwired or even microprogrammed floating-point operations are not available, and integer multiply and divide are optional), and a much more limited set of language processors, utility routines, and software packages available to the users. But, as we shall see in Chapter 9, some of these limitations have been overcome, and even 32 bit "minicomputers" have been introduced on the market (e.g., the DEC VAX 11/780).

A 1974 survey (Datamation July 1974) listed 23 manufacturers of minicomputers for 44 models with Data General, General Automation, Hewlett-Packard, Honeywell, Interdata, Microdata, and Varian being the best known companies competing with DEC.

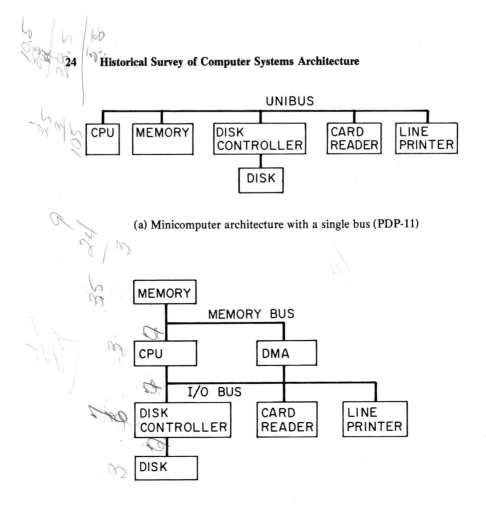

(a) Minicomputer architecture with a single bus (PDP-11)

(b) Minicomputer architecture with DMA

Figure 1.4 Minicomputer organizations

DEC did not limit itself to minicomputers. The PDP-10, first delivered in 1967 and which since then has been the recipient of several upgradings, is a versatile machine (paged virtual memory system, cache buffer, extensive priority interrupt scheme) with a highly sophisticated software support and a large library of language processors. Geared towards efficient interactive programming, it has been propelled in a leadership position for this mode of computing. The DEC System-20 is the PDP-10's successor with a similar architecture. In 1978, DEC started the delivery of a new "supermini computer," the VAX 11/780, which has a 32-bit word length, virtual memory, a cache, but no data channels (although naturally there are DMA paths).

The other end of the spectrum, i.e., the large computer scene, has been dominated by CDC. The CDC 6600, introduced in 1964, presented some major innovations for a system which was not, and has not become, a prototype. In particular, the design of a CPU with a set of dedicated arithmetic functional units controlled by a hardware scheme allowing the execution of independent instructions out of sequence was the first of this magnitude which was ever implemented. The central processor speed-up was further enhanced by an instruction stack by-passing in some instances the fetching of instructions from core, hence reducing contention for that resource, and the systematic interleaving of memory banks. Overall parallelism was attained by 10 Peripheral Processor Units (PPU), each with its own private memory, sharing arithmetic circuitry and access to main memory on a time-multiplexed basis. The PPU's communicated with the channels and held parts of the Operating System. Multiprogramming and protection were facilitated by a pair of registers delimiting the contiguous area of core allotted to each user. The CDC 6600 is, to our knowledge, the last computer of significant size which did not include interrupts in its architecture.

Building on the immediate acceptance of the 6600 by the community of scientific users of large systems, CDC continued the line with the 6400 (1966), slightly less powerful with its integrated arithmetic unit, and with the 6500 (1968), a dual processor 6400. In 1969, the 7600 appeared on the market. While still being upward compatible with the 6600, the main differences are a set of pipelined functional units, a four fold speed-up in the basic processor cycle, and a slightly different organization for the PPU-CPU interactions. To this date, the 7600 can be considered as the supercomputer with the largest number of units sold. Currently, CDC manufactures the CYBER series which is identical to the 6000's, except for a few additional instructions for character handling and new circuit technology. The staying power of the 6000 series which is still widely used, some 13 years after the delivery of the first model, and which still serves as a point of reference to evaluate powerful processors is quite remarkable.

CDC also continued its 3000 series, and by joining forces with NCR has some openings on the peripheral market. Its last supercomputer, the STAR-100, will be discussed later.

Specific applications (weather prediction, nuclear energy problems) require a tremendous amount of raw computing power which will be provided by supercomputers. Some supercomputers of the third generation were based on the architectures of less powerful models. For example, the IBM 360/91 was not much different from other System/360's. The CDC 7600 borrows much from the 6000 series. Currently, the architects of these models, G. Amdahl for IBM and S. Cray for CDC respectively, have formed their own companies to produce supercomputers which are in direct line with their prior efforts. The Amdahl 470 V/6 is compatible with System/370 (it can run under the same operating systems). The differences are in a more advanced semiconductor technology, allowing the labelling of the machine as being of the 4th generation, a basic cycle time (32 ns.) two to three times as fast as the higher models of System/370, a larger associative map for virtual address translation, and, last but not the least, significantly much tighter packaging which results in a decrease in wiring connections and a higher expected reliability. The CRAY-1 which follows the 7600 is a 64-bit machine with 12 pipelined functional units, a minor cycle (12.5 ns) twice as fast as its predecessor's, a very large set of programmable high-speed registers, and an instruction set containing both scalar and vector instructions.

Because the applications like those cited above often require the processing of ordered data such as vectors or matrices, a great speed advantage can be achieved by performing arithmetic operations in parallel. This is the basic idea behind the array processors such as ILLIAC IV where 64 processors operate synchronously under the supervision of a single control unit, and of the pipeline processors such as CDC's STAR-100 and Texas Instrument's Advanced Scientific Computer where the arithmetic units are segmented and able to process several instructions, in different stages, at the same time. We shall return to these special architectures in Chapter 10.

1.2.4.3 *Operating Systems Developments*

We noted that the coming of more complicated operating systems was one of the reasons for the passage from the second to the third generation. In contrast, the state of the art in programming languages advanced only minimally. FORTRAN and COBOL are still the most widely used high-level languages. BASIC, simple minded as its name implies, was designed in the early sixties to provide easy access to the machine in a time-sharing environment for casual users. It has nicely fulfilled its charter. PL/I has some followers but they are found almost uniquely among clever programmers on IBM equipment, or the versions available are only subsets of the original language (although at least one non-IBM large operating system, namely MULTICS, has been written in PL/I). ALGOL-60 has continued to be very popular among computer scientists for algorithm communication, and ALGOL-60 lingua is proliferating in Computer Science textbooks. A number of languages were derived from ALGOL. The three most important to date are: ALGOL-68 with a very rigorous definition of its semantics, SIMULA 67 with its class concept which allows a more flexible dynamic memory allocation than ALGOL's block structure, and Pascal, widely used in the teaching community, with its explicit type checking leading to better error detection at compile time. System implementation languages, midway between assemblers and high-level languages, extensible languages and languages for Artificial Intelligence applications approaching natural languages have been designed and implemented. None of them have yet received the wide acceptance of the major languages of the second generation.

If the programming languages have not evolved much, the art, or science, of programming has been closely scrutinized. Without involving ourselves in a discussion of Structured Programming, we shall simply note that the design of modular programs and the attempts at proving their correctness are healthy trends which are to be emphasized in the future. These methodologies are of particular importance for the realization of large and complex systems such as those encountered today.

By now, all medium to large computer systems operate under a multiprogramming scheme. Jobs can be entered from different sources: CRT displays or teletypes can be used in an interactive mode if the system provides for an on-line file system; remote job entry stations can add jobs to the batch queue; jobs (or processes) can spawn their own processes for subsequent or concurrent execution. Since multiprogramming implies a sharing of resources, of which the main store is the most important, advances in operating systems include enhancements in the automatic management of hierarchies of memory (virtual memory system), scheduling and allocating of other resources such as channels, devices or even CPU's in a multiprocessing environment, synchronization of concurrent processes, and protection between processes. As a matter of course, these improvements have influenced the architectures of the third generation. For example, several forms of address mapping have been implemented, some of them helped by the presence of small associative memories. Access to rotating secondary devices can be optimized with some advance position sensing of the arms and/or read-write heads. Special-purpose processors can be included in the overall system, e.g., front-end processors for line polling in an installation with a large number of interactive terminals. As a general rule, we can state that users have demanded more of the system, be it for man-machine interaction facilities or for better turn-around, and these requests have been translated into new features in the operating systems, sometimes in a contradictory fashion. Finally some of these features have been or are in the process of being translated into microcoded primitives.

After having been promised LSI (Large Scale Integration) for many years and after having to be contented with MSI (M for medium) until the beginning of the 1970's, after having seen a consolidation in software design but no new revolutionary advances, and after having observed that the new IBM series, System/370, presents no architectural features which can be considered as real novelties, can we say (in the mid or even later 70's) that we are still in the third generation? It might be more appropriate to label the current era as "late" third unless the advent of computer networks and the proliferation of mini and microcomputers, leading possibly to distributed function architectures, mark the birth of a fourth generation. We do not intend to answer this question in this chapter, and limit ourselves to introducing two major areas that we have not touched upon and which are greatly influencing the ways in which computers are used and are built. The first one is the utilization of computer networks which has now become economically viable and which will certainly become more prevalent in the future. The second is the advent of microprocessors and their impact on future systems.

In the last decade, we have seen the beginnings of the sharing and accessing of information between computer systems, or networking. These computers are in general geographically remote, as for example in the world-wide ARPANET, but can also be scaled down to be rather close to each other like in the Irvine Distributed Computer System or the Xerox PARC Ethernet. The distinction that is made between networks and multiprocessors is that in the former case computers in the network do not share main memory. Communication is through messages and appropriate protocols. We shall not discuss geographically remote computer networks since an entire volume should be devoted to them. However we shall keep in mind their prime importance. We shall briefly introduce local networks in Chapter 11.

Microprocessors, or computers on a chip, have been commercially available since 1971. The first microprocessor, the Intel 4004, had a 4-bit arithmetic-logical unit. Since then 8-bit (e.g., Intel 8080) and 16-bit (e.g., National PACE, Intel 8086, Zilog Z8000, and Motorola 68000) microprocessors have been manufactured. They have generated an exceptional market, that of hand-held calculators of various complexity and price range. Many other applications using single microprocessors have since been devised (cf. Chapter 9). With the flexibility brought by microprogramming, microprocessors have been able to replace minicomputers in cases where speed was not at a premium, much in the same way as earlier minicomputers had taken the place of medium-sized computers. With the projected continuing decrease of microprocessors' cost, it is safe to predict that they are going to contribute more and more to the complete system's architecture. Distributed function systems, where general and/or special function units handle concurrent tasks and are "loosely" connected, have started to appear. The organizational challenges are in the control, allocation, synchronization and cooperation of these independent units. Networks of microcomputers might replace medium and even large computers when means to communicate efficiently are developed.

It appears then that the future in Computer Architecture will see more departures from the original von Neumann model. This has been somewhat transparent in this short historical review and will become more apparent when we study the individual units comprising current computers. The advances due to technological breakthroughs will have even more impact as will be seen when looking at the relationships between these units. The constant changes in speed, cost and flexibility of the various components will be reflected in the design and implementation of computer systems.

1.3 BIBLIOGRAPHICAL NOTES AND REFERENCES

[Stone 75], [Hayes 78], and [Kuck 78] are current texts providing a good overview of Computer Architecture. [Bell and Newell 71] contains reprints of the most important papers which appeared prior to 1970. In supplement to [Randell 73] and [Goldstine 72], [Wilkes 72] and [Tropp 74], among many others, can be consulted for their personal impressions on the early days of computing. [Rosen 69] is the most complete survey on the history of Computer Architecture although its account of the third generation is necessarily incomplete. [Rosin 69], [Denning 71] and [Rosen 72] cover the developments in Programming Languages and Operating Systems up to approximately the same time. A recent conference traces the history of Programming Languages [ACM 78]. It is hoped that it will be followed by meetings of the same type providing historical insights on other facets of Computer Science. The parution of an *Annals of the History of Computing* Quarterly is also a step in this direction.

More specific bibliographies will be given at the end of each chapter.

References

1. ACM SIGPLAN History of Programming Languages Conference, *SIGPLAN Notices, 8,* Aug. 1978.

2. Bell, C. G. and A. Newell, *Computer Structures: Readings and Examples,* McGraw Hill, New York, N.Y., 1971.

3. Burks, A. W., Goldstine, H. H. and J. von Neumann, "Preliminary Discussion of the Logical Design of an Electronic Computing Instrument," *U.S. Army Ordnance Department Report,* 1946 (Also reprinted in 2).

4. Denning, P. J., "Third Generation Computer Systems," *Computing Surveys, 3,* (Dec. 1971), 175-216.

5. Goldstine, H. H., *The Computer from Pascal to von Neumann,* Princeton University Press, 1972.

6. Hayes, J. P., *Computer Architecture and Organization*, McGraw Hill, New York, N.Y., 1978.

7. Kuck, D., *The Structure of Computer and Computations*, vol. 1, Wiley, New York, N.Y., 1978.

8. Randell, B. ed., *The Origins of Digital Computers*, Springer-Verlag, Berlin, 1973.

9. Rosen, S., "Electronic Computers: A Historical Survey," *Computing Surveys, 1*, (Mar. 1969), 7-36.

10. Rosen, S., "Programming Systems and Languages," *Comm. ACM, 15*, (Jul. 1972), 591-600.

11. Rosin, R. F., "Supervisory and Monitor Systems," *Computing Surveys, 1*, (Mar. 1969), 37-54.

12. Stone, H. S. ed., *Introduction to Computer Architecture*, SRA, Chicago, Ill., 1975.

13. Tropp, H., "The Effervescent Years: A Retrospective," *IEEE Spectrum, 11*, (Feb. 1974), 70-81.

14. Wilkes, M. V., "Historical Perspectives—Computer Architecture," *Proc. AFIPS 1972 Fall Joint Comp. Conf., 41*, AFIPS Press, Montvale, N.J., 1972, 971-976.

Chapter 2

DESCRIPTION OF COMPUTER SYSTEMS

In this chapter our goal is to present descriptive tools and notations which can help in the design, analysis and synthesis of computer systems at various levels of detail. In Section 1, we delineate these levels emphasizing those of primary importance to the computer architect. Section 2 looks at the global structure of the system introducing the PMS notation, a semi-graphical means of communication which has become quite widely used. The third section is devoted to the description of processors. We choose to present ISP as one of the programming-language oriented mechanisms available at this level. This section also reviews instruction sets and types of addressing. In Section 4, we focus on the register transfer level which is of importance in the design of control units. Finally, the last section presents some techniques used to model the dynamic flow of information throughout the system.

2.1 LEVELS IN THE REPRESENTATION OF COMPUTER SYSTEMS

There are several levels at which we would like to describe computer systems, namely, from top to bottom.

Level 1 Global System Structure

The overall system structure is laid out. That is, the principal components such as processors, channels, main memory modules, input/output devices and so on, as well as their interconnections, are identified. Ideally, we would include their static characteristics, e.g., the number of memory banks, and the dynamic attributes, for example, the possibility of concurrency between a processor and associated channels.

Level 2   The Processor Description

At this level the goal is to represent the architecture of each individual component and of the logical interfaces as seen, for example, from the Operating System's viewpoint. This is most important when the component is programmable. Hence the emphasis is on processors, their instruction set, the internal data representation and the description of the instruction execution cycle, in a manner such that the actions transparent to a programmer will not be shown.

Level 3   The Register Transfer Level

The objective here is to get an understanding of the internal workings of a given component, or part of it, by describing actions such as the transfer of information between (not necessarily programmer addressable) registers. The description of a functional unit or of an input/output interface belongs to that level.

Levels 4 and 5   Logical Design and Circuit Design Levels

The descriptions at these levels used to be in terms, respectively, of gates and flip-flops, and of transistors, resistors and the like. Today, these two levels are integrated, at least from the architect's viewpoint, within the design of chips. Since these chips can either be memory elements or can perform complex functions (cf. the microprocessors of Chapter 9), the distinction between level 3 and subsequent levels is less clear than it used to be.

In this book, we concentrate on topics falling within the scopes of the first three levels. Chip design will not be considered, but the cost-performance influences brought upon by the availability of the new technologies will not be discarded. For the first three levels, means of communicating architectural concepts in a unified manner would be very useful. Unfortunately, there are no standard notations and the goal of this chapter is to introduce those that we consider the most appropriate and to indicate how and when they can be used. The emphasis will be on the top two levels, since they are closest to our interest, while it is recognized that it is the third one which has received the most attention, probably because it is easier to describe actual hardware and to simulate it within that frame of reference.

Descriptions of computer systems can be further divided into graphical and language-oriented notations. For level 1, graphical representations are to be highly recommended since they give a good appraisal of a global view of the system. For this purpose we shall use informal block diagrams and PMS, a notation which blends a pictorial approach with some written footnotes. At level 2, a programming language representation seems more suitable. ISP appears to be at the present time the best language. There exist a number of Computer Hardware Description Languages, CHDL's, which can be used for level 3. The most well-known are AHPL, a derivative of APL, and CDL. Both languages have their advantages and disadvantages. We shall (not very frequently) use the more readable CDL.

The descriptive vehicles listed above are meant to show mostly the static features of the system. In addition, we might be interested in the dynamics of the system, i.e., the representation of the information flow. Again, graphical representations are most convenient in this case and we shall rely on Petri Nets and their extensions for this purpose. They will be useful at all three levels by attaching various degrees of interpretation to them.

It is to be noted that we have not mentioned analytical models which describe the behavior or predict the performance of the system. A general study of these methodologies falls outside the scope of this book. We shall use specific models when necessary in the course of particular studies (e.g., in the analysis of interleaved memories).

2.2 GLOBAL SYSTEM STRUCTURE

2.2.1 Block Diagrams and PMS

In the previous chapter, we have given some schematic views of the organizations of a von Neumann machine, of second and third generation computers, and of minicomputers. We have used block diagram representations where each component of the system was identified by a "black box". Physical interconnections were shown as lines joining boxes but, except for the von Neumann model, we have not attempted to pictorially describe the potentially different control and data paths.

Since we wanted to give an overall view of the type of systems that we were mentioning, there was no reason to dwell on details such as the number of channels which could be attached to an IBM 7094, or the maximum memory size that one could address in a System/360. In fact, in the latter case, this could be dependent on the model under description, and even more on the details of a given installation. However, some common features are apparent in Figures 1.1 to 1.4. There are boxes for processors (central and channels), memories (primary and secondary), and input/output devices. Lines connecting them represent the transfer paths, i.e., the switches and links between processors and memories. The Processor, Memory, Switch combination stands out as the backbone of the whole system and consequently should be at the base of any substantial descriptive notation. PMS, a notation due to Bell and Newell, is an answer to this requirement.

Before looking at PMS and its use in the description of specific computer configurations, we must mention the fact that block diagrams, at various degrees of sophistication, are still the most widely used means of displaying a system's architecture. With the aid of graphics packages and plotting devices, these block diagrams can be machine processed and therefore easily modified and edited. Figure 2.1 shows an example of what can be obtained. The layout of the figure, the amount of text included in each box or accompanying a connecting line, and the blowing up or zooming on parts of the pic-

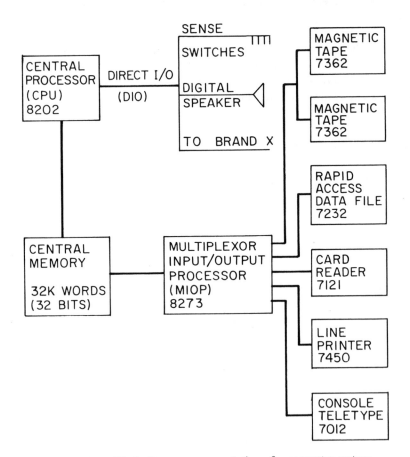

Figure 2.1 Block diagram representation of a computer system

ture are conveniently left to the discretion of the programmer. The man-machine interaction can be achieved via an intelligent CRT terminal (e.g., the Tektronix 4014 in the figure), or minicomputer with graphics capability (e.g., the depicted IMLAC PDS-1D), linked to a medium sized computer supporting a language with graphics extensions. After engineering the layout, and editing it through several iterations on the display, it can be printed on a hardcopy terminal with plotting capabilities (e.g., the Gencom in the figure) or encoded and written on a tape to be processed (offline) by a plotter.

The flexibility of the above package hides its lack of formality. PMS is an

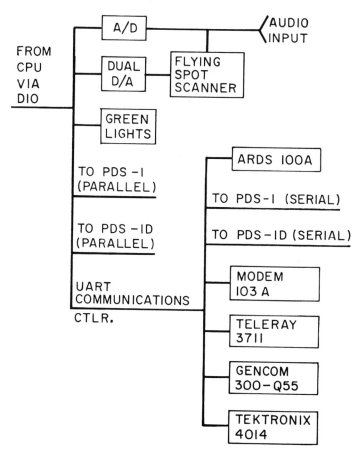

Figure 2.1 Continued

attempt at laying down systematically the rules to describe the system, i.e., identify the main components and their attributes in an orderly fashion. The notation blends a graphical approach, similar to the block diagram, with the ability to describe numerous attributes in a compact fashion. To introduce PMS we proceed mostly by examples. The reader interested in the complete notation should consult the original reference.

There are seven primitive components in the notation.

Memory M   This component stores information over time without modifying its contents or format. The information is stored in terms of individually addressable units, hence the need for an addressing system. This component can be further divided into subcomponents, or modules.

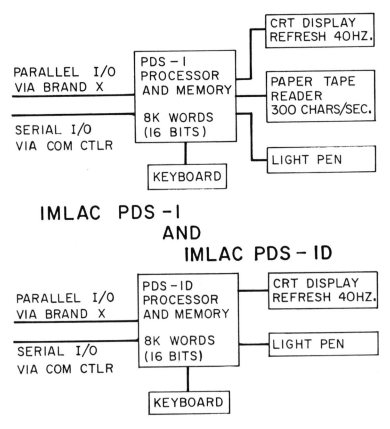

Figure 2.1   Continued

Link L   As its name implies this component connects other components. It transfers information without altering it.

Switch S   A switch builds links, or transfer paths of control and data. A switch has a set of links associated with it that it can enable or disable.

Control K   This component evokes the other PMS components. With the exception of the processor *P*, which has an implied control within itself, *K* is the only active component of the system.

Data-Operations D   It is in this component that units of information are altered (as in an arithmetic-logical unit).

Transducer T   The communications to the outside world are represented by transducers. They transform the representation of data without altering its meaning.

Processor P   This is the component able to interpret a stored program, that is a sequence of instructions. It is not a purely primitive component as the above six, since generally it consists of a combination of local storage *M*, of a control unit *K*, and of data-operation units *D* interconnected by links *L* and switches *S*. However, as we shall see, it is rare that we will want to subdivide *P*'s.

The seven primitives of PMS are sufficient to yield as much descriptive power as the most uninterpreted block diagrams. For example, the von Neumann model of Figure 1.1 becomes the PMS description of Figure 2.2.a. By lumping together the *K* and the *D* to form a *P*, and by merging the two *T*'s into a single one, we obtain the description of Figure 2.2.b. The next step, not necessary here but which will be mandatory in more detailed examples, is to denote the major function of each component. *P* in this case stands for central processor, abbreviated Pc. *M*, the primary memory is denoted Mp. Attached to the *T* are external devices *X*'s, and the total picture

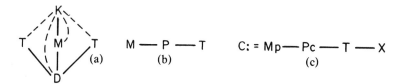

Figure 2.2   PMS description of a von Neumann machine

yields the definition (operator $:=$) of a stored program computer C (Figure 2.2.c).

A more complex description, but still a schematic one, is found in Figure 2.3 which is the direct correspondent to the block diagram of Figure 1.3 modeling the System/360. Abbreviations of the form Pio and Ms are self-explanatory. Another functional attribute has been added to some of the components, e.g., disk for Ms or multiplexor for Pio. More generally, to each primitive Z of a PMS description we can attach a list of attributes and their values with the notation:

$$Z(a_1:v_1, a_2:v_2, \ldots, a_n:v_n),$$

where a_i is the ith attribute and v_i its value. For example, Pio('Multiplexor) is an abbreviation for P(function:input/output; name:multiplexor). When the shortened forms of the attributes have evident meanings, their functional characteristics can be omitted.

PMS provides a systematic way of displaying the main features of each component. A comprehensive list of what can be associated with each of the components can be found in the formal definition of the notation, but it is certainly not exhaustive. In order to illustrate the power of the method, we give two examples: a PMS description of a particular model in the System/370 series, namely the Model 155, and the PMS description of the

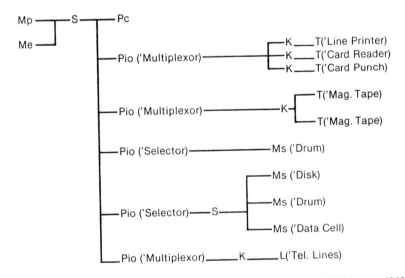

Figure 2.3   PMS description of the general architecture of an IBM System/360

Sigma 5 installation as depicted in Figure 2.1. The first one is still generic in spirit while the second is very specific.

For a central processor Pc with an integrated central processor unit, we do not need to delineate the data-operations components (the D's). The data paths in the arithmetic-logical unit need to be mentioned only if their width is not the same as that of the data transfer portion of the bus from Mp to Pc (from the logical rather than physical point of view). For instance, this is the case in the System/370 description since the data paths vary from model to model, but unnecessary in the Sigma 5's. The type of control used, such as the possibility of microprogrammed operations, is another important parameter. The instruction set, data types, details of the microprogramming operation, and the internal interrupt configurations are examples of functions which should not be described in detail at the PMS level, but rather at levels 2 and 3. However, if there are some salient features, such as an extensive interrupt system for the Sigma 5, a comment can be inserted to that effect. The cycle time of the Pc, the number of instructions/word or of words/instruction, and the internal storage capacity (labelled Mps) that has to be saved when the current process has to relinquish the use of the Pc are features which most often will be included in the description.

As a matter of convenience, this list of attributes will be inserted as footnotes in the figures in order not to overcrowd the pictorial part of the description. Referring to Figures 2.4 and 2.5, the notation $a \sim b$ means the interval from a up to b, $\sim a$ means an interval around a of undetermined scope, $a|b|c$ means one of a or b or c, and #a:b, where a and b are both integers, means $(b - a + 1)$ identical units.

Modern computer systems have a hierarchy of memories. Primary memory Mp and secondary memory Ms have already appeared in our diagrams. In Figure 2.4, we see a third memory, Mcache, which serves as a buffer between Mp and Pc, and we have already noted that Mp could be extended via an Me (cf. Figure 2.3). Mp, Mcache, and Me are random access memories built around the same principles but with different technologies, sizes, speeds, and costs. Hence, they will share the same attributes. On the other hand the most common Ms, until now, have been rotating devices whose characteristics are very different from the Mp's, and therefore they will have different attributes. If and when the so-called electronic disks (charge-coupled devices and bubble logic memories) become cost-effective as Ms's, we will have to introduce new attributes. We shall return to the memory hierarchy problem in Chapters 5 and 6. In this chapter, we restrict ourselves to the description of systems built around the technology available in the late 70's.

We start by examining what characterizes Mp's. The first keyword is technology. Until 1970 all third generation computers used core memories. With

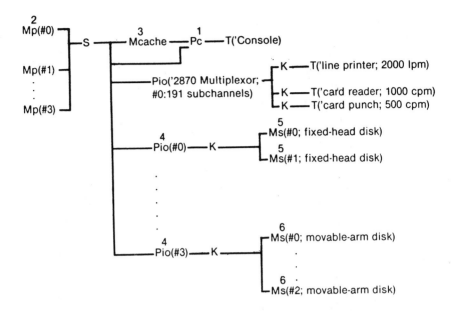

1. Pc ('Model 155; cycle-time : 115ns.; microprogrammed 72 bit hoz.; 8b/byte; data-path: 4 bytes; (2 | 4 | 6) bytes/instr.; Mps ~ 88 bytes)
2. Mp (core; 256 KBytes; t.cycle: 2.1 μs; 16 bytes/transfer)
3. Mcache (monolithic; 8KBytes; t.cycle: 230ns.; 4 bytes/transfer)
4. Pio ('2880 Block Multiplexor; transfer rate: 3MB/sec)
5. Ms ('2305 fixed-head disk; capacity: 5MBytes; t.access: 5ms.; transfer rate: 1.5 MB/sec)
6. Ms ('3330 movable-arm disk: (2|4|6|8) drives; capacity : 100MB/drive; t.seek : 10–55 ms.; t.access ~ 8.4ms.; transfer rate : 806 KB/sec)

Figure 2.4 PMS generic description of the IBM System/370 Model 155

advances in semiconductor technologies and LSI, this is not the case any-more; for example, in the original series System/370 computers, the lower models had monolithic technology memories while the larger models used core. Of course, in the latter case, Mcache's provide a faster memory com-plex as seen from the Pc's viewpoint. Technology has influenced the second attribute, that is the speed factor. When core was used, the cycle time (sum of read and write) was sufficient to characterize the memory's performance. In the case of semiconductors, both access and cycle times may have to be given. The final important attribute is size. As we shall see shortly, it is one of the main parameters in defining the power of the overall system.

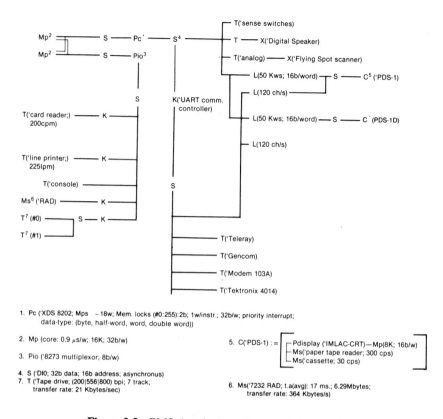

1. Pc ('XDS 8202; Mps ~18w; Mem. locks (#0:255):2b; 1w/instr.; 32b/w; priority interrupt;
   data-type: (byte, half-word, word, double word))

2. Mp (core: 0.9 μs/w; 16K; 32b/w)

3. Pio ('8273 multiplexor; 8b/w)

4. S ('DI0; 32b data; 16b address; asynchronus)

7. T ('Tape drive; (200|556|800) bpi; 7 track;
   transfer rate: 21 Kbytes/sec)

5. C('PDS-1) : = ⎡ Pdisplay ('IMLAC-CRT)—Mp(8K; 16b/w)
                ⎢ Ms('paper tape reader; 300 cps)
                ⎣ Ms('cassette; 30 cps)

6. Ms('7232 RAD; t.a(avg): 17 ms.; 6.29Mbytes;
   transfer rate: 364 Kbytes/s)

Figure 2.5   PMS description of a specific installation

The PMS notation allows the representation of modules in Mp. In Figures 2.4 and 2.5 we can see the Mp increments that can be added to the system, the potential interleaving and the bandwidth of transmission on the memory bus.

Currently, in order to support multiprogrammed operating systems, all medium to large computer systems have a secondary memory in the form of a rotating device, either drum, fixed-head disk or movable-arm disk. In all cases, the parameters of importance are the capacity, or size, of the device and the timing factors associated with it, namely, the average access time (half of the rotation time although this can be less in the case of a paging drum), the transfer rate and the seek time when the device is a disk with a movable arm.

As seen in the figures, the Mp-Ms transition goes through a Pio, or channel, and a controller, or K, for the Ms device. The labelling of a channel as a P rather than a K is a matter of choice. We prefer the former, since as we shall see in Part 2, we can consider channels as special-purpose stored program processors. A Pio description is simpler than that of a Pc. We will distinguish selectors from block multiplexors and (byte) multiplexors (their internal descriptions belong, like that of a Pc, to levels 2 and 3). The only attributes of interest might be the number of subchannels in a multiplexor along with the transfer rates that they allow. As for K's, the mere mention of their presence is sufficient. Nonetheless, they should not be forgotten for some information can be gained by displaying them. For example, a common K shared by several T's or Ms's indicates that these devices cannot be on the path of transmission simultaneously. This is illustrated in both figures. From the second figure, we see that the two magnetic tape drives in the Sigma 5 installation cannot be operated at the same time. As for T devices, D operators and X peripherals, when they occur, the main parameters will almost always be a matter of common sense.

We remark that the address translation mechanism between Mcache and Mp, or for that matter any virtual memory mapping between Mp and Ms, is difficult to represent in PMS. It can be argued that it should be done at levels 2 and 3 of the description since the hardware used is not visible in the global structure. At any rate, we feel that it is worth mentioning whether the system is a paging or segmented one. The size of the associative memory used, if any, can be embedded as an attribute of Pc. In the case of a cache, the name Mcache is sufficient to gather that such a buffer is being used.

The third primitive which gave PMS its name is rarely shown with attributes. The switch S describes the connections between components and is necessarily a part of the graphic description. It seldom must be expanded, although exceptions occur, as for instance with the direct input-output feature of the Sigma 5 (cf. Figure 2.5). The main attribute of a switch is the concurrency that it allows between its terminals. This is of primary importance in multiprocessor structures where an objective is to maximize parallel transfers of information. This will be examined in more detail in Part III. Like D's within Pc's, S's within other components will not be detailed in the figures. However, they are subsumed by some attributes and/or components. For example, in Figure 2.4, the path from Mp to an Ms ('movable-arm disk) seems to pass through only a single S. In fact, the total selection consists of a switch (decoder) to select the Mp on the memory bus, a switch (e.g., in the operating system) to select the disk and drive, another one to choose the appropriate cylinder and one to position the arm on the right track, and finally a last switch for delineating the sector which corresponds to the block of information to be accessed. In a global structure, we are certainly not interested in all these subswitches. But when we study rotating devices and the advantages brought forth by independent seeks and rotational position sensing, we might need to go down to this lower level.

The last primitive is the link L. In Figure 2.4 we do not show any. In Figure 2.5 the two pairs of L's which are present are connecting two C's: the Sigma 5 at one end and either of the PDS-1 or PDS-1D at the other. Again, like previous primitives, links might appear at lower levels in the descriptions. A register to register transfer needs a link; a memory bus, or an I/O bus, is a link; this is true also of an interface between a Pio and a K; more generally, an S is a terminal for a link, although, as we have just shown, not all links have S's as terminals. As before, these details are not germane to the global structure of the system. On the other hand, all links where the speed of transmission is of interest should be shown. Thus, the main attributes will be the information rate of transmission and the concurrency which indicates whether the link is only one-way (simplex), two-way but allowing information transfer only in one direction at a given time (half-duplex), or two-way without restriction (full-duplex).

2.2.2 Uses of PMS

The strength of PMS is that it provides a standard terminology. It can be used to describe an installation without having recourse to local and/or manufacturer jargon. It is certainly preferable to know that a DIO is an S, or that a Rapid Access Data File is nothing else than an Ms ('fixed-head disk) than to have to check in manuals. In the same vein, PMS can be one of several appropriate means of communicating requests for bids. The intended buyer could set up a request as a generic PMS description, somewhat in the fashion of Figure 2.4, and the prospective vendor would respond with a specific description similar in spirit to the one of Figure 2.5. Of course, more attributes would be required (not forgetting one of the most important, namely the cost) along with descriptions at lower levels when need be. For us, PMS will serve as a way to avoid the introduction of too many synonyms and will provide some unification against a potential deluge of acronyms. Naturally, we shall not always abide by PMS, and we might prefer terms like channel to Pio, or functional unit to D, when the context recommends it. But, adhering as much as possible to PMS should enhance the pedagogical value of this book.

Given a PMS description, what can be learned about the main features of the system under study? First, an appraisal of its global power can be obtained by looking at two factors: the cycle-time, or speed, of the Pc and the size of the Mp. Assuming a single Pc, the inverse of the cycle time provides an upper bound on the number of MIPS (millions of instructions per second) executable by the processor. The real MIPS factor depends on the instruction mix, the bandwidth that the Mp-Pc switch can support and, in multiprocessor structures, on the number of Pc's (this is still quite an approximation; more exact measures will become apparent in Parts II and III). The Mp size is also primordial since, among other effects, it directs the number of programs which can be present simultaneously in Mp (the multiprogramming load) and hence has a monitoring effect on the compute versus I/O bound mix that the overall system can support. Less important, but still of considerable value, is the capacity(s) of the Ms device(s) and its transfer rate. But for a quick assessment with only a qualitative value, we can surmise that the Pc(cycle-time) and Mp(size) are sufficient.

A second type of information readily available from a PMS description is the intended use of the system in a general functional sense. Installations which are oriented towards scientific computations will have a tendency to be powerful, according to the criteria of the above paragraph, and will have an Mp with large word length or a large data path width in the Pc in order to compute data with sufficient precision using hardwired instructions. Business-oriented and information retrieval systems will have a Pc with bytes (or characters) as units of addressing in the instruction set, and the overall system will have more input/output capabilities than in the previous environment. Process control and smaller installations will generally be built around minicomputers of small word length, low capacity Mp, and a few often highly specialized Ms and T's. General-purpose computing facilities can be further distinguished if they cater mostly to batch oriented customers or to time-sharing users. In the former type of computing, many T's will be used for remote job entry terminals, while in the latter, L's and Pio('Communication Controller) or Pio('Front-end) will be in the picture. Also, very large systems, either multiprocessors or local networks, will be distinguishable through their PMS descriptions. Much about the concurrency of operation, potential contention for resources, and means of information transfer can be learned by studying the S and L configurations.

PMS is not restricted to descriptions at level 1. It has been used quite extensively at levels 2 and 3. We shall follow the same principle when PMS's use will provide a clarification in the exposition (see e.g., the PMS descriptions in Chapter 4 for powerful Pc's, Chapter 8 for I/O subsystems and in Part III, Chapters 9 through 11).

2.3 THE PROCESSOR DESCRIPTION

2.3.1 ISP

Within PMS we have identified the system's main architectural components. Some of these, that is P's and K's, control its general behavior. At the next level in the hierarchy of descriptions, we need a notation that will allow the specification of the nature and sequence of operations allowable in these controlling components. Because this control is generally implemented through a stored program, our focus will be on the internal operation of the Pc and on its interactions with other primitives such as Mp and Pio's. Thus, our goal is to replace the often ill-written and barely comprehensible basic operations and programming reference manuals by some easily readable notation general enough to be machine independent. Additional qualities such as simplicity, extensibility and flexibility will be welcome.

What we need then is a descriptive vehicle which facilitates the formalization of a hierarchy of storage devices from the flip-flop to Mp, including registers and memory cells and possibly pages and memory modules, of the contents of these memory cells, i.e., instruction formats and data types, of the outcomes of the execution of the Pc's repertoire, and finally of the interpretation of the instruction execution cycle. These requirements point to a programming language approach. Namely, the storage devices are akin to simple and aggregate data structures. Data types and instruction formats correspond to the declaration of variable types. The description of the instruction set is analogous to that of the syntax and semantics of the allowable statements, and the interpretation of the instruction cycle can be seen as a directive of how the flow of control is realized.

Two languages stand out among those which have been used for this purpose. The first one is APL in which algorithms can be communicated in a compact and precise fashion, and the second is ISP (Instruction Set Processor) specially designed for our topic of discussion. Although APL has been nicely extended into AHPL (A Hardware Programming Language) and hence can also be used at level 3, our choice will be ISP for two main reasons: like APL it can be used at level 3, and it is much more readable (some foes of APL have referred to that language as being "write only"). Both APL and ISP allow for some description of the parallelism inherent in the operation of modern computers, but not to the degree necessary. Let us elaborate on this important point.

Very often more than one storage device will be affected by the execution of an instruction. A typical example is the setting of flip-flops, known as condition codes, as the result of some arithmetic operation. These condition codes are tested for subsequent branching. The descriptive language must be able to show that the result of the arithmetic operation not only modifies the contents of some accumulator or register but also that the condition codes are set at the same time. ISP can express this type of concurrency quite nicely. But ISP is not as convenient for representing another type of parallelism present in medium to large systems, namely the *overlap* of parts of the instruction cycle over different consecutive instructions. This is based on the fact that an internal operation in the Pc will require more than one access to Mp, and that the cycle time of Mp is slower than that of Pc. Consider, for example, the instruction cycle for an operation of the form:

$$\text{Register} \leftarrow \text{Register operator Mp}[z]$$

as shown in Figure 2.6 (recall the description of the instruction cycle in the von Neumann machine in Chapter 1). The next instruction address calculation (step 6), in this case an increment in the location counter, can be performed in parallel with any of steps 1 to 5. ISP will be able to describe this to a certain extent, that is, it will show it as being done concurrently with one of those steps. However, the overlap of instruction i with some of its successors, as represented in an ideal situation in Figure 2.7, allowing the concurrent execution of some of the steps 1 to 5 applied to different operands, cannot be described by an ISP program (we shall return several times to this overlap problem also named *look-ahead* processing or *pipelining*). Therefore, in our Pc descriptions we shall keep in mind this weakness in ISP's power. Although the end results of each action will be correct, their time occurrences might not be exact. Furthermore, if several instructions can occur in parallel as in a multifunctional unit Pc, then ISP becomes inadequate. This is one motivation behind the introduction of graph models later in this chapter.

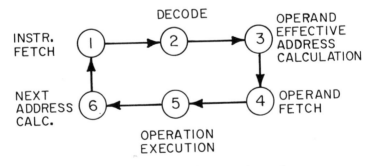

Figure 2.6   Instruction execution cycle

INSTR.

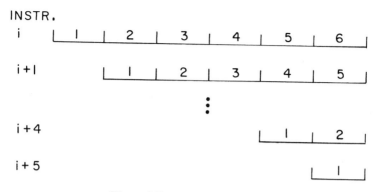

Figure 2.7 Ideal overlapping

As in the preceding section, our discussion of ISP is based on examples. The formal notation is due to Bell and Newell; these authors have worked out numerous instances of processor descriptions written in ISP. We shall frequently refer to Figure 2.8 which is a partial ISP description of the Pc of a Xerox Sigma 5.

As we said earlier, an ISP description, or program, contains information relevant to the Pc and Mp states as seen from the programmer's viewpoint. We start with the "declaration" of the Pc state. The Sigma 5 is a general register machine with 16 registers, 7 of which can be used as index registers, and with register 0 often playing a special role. In ISP notation, this is indicated by:

$R[0:15]\langle 0:31\rangle$	16 registers of 32 bits
$R0 := R[0]$	Alias for register 0
$XR[1:7] := R[1:7]$	Index registers

The status of the running program is encoded in a PSD (program status double word) which is declared as:

$PSD\langle 0:63\rangle$	Program Status Doubleword

The first 4 bits of the PSD are the condition codes mentioned earlier. The breaking up of the PSD is indicated by a redefinition of its components, as:

$CC\langle 1:4\rangle := PSD\langle 0:3\rangle$	Condition codes

or similarly for the instruction address, or location counter:

$IA := PSD\langle 15:31\rangle$	Location counter

Since IA will always be accessed in its entirety, we need not to break it up like

Pc State

R[0:15]⟨0:31⟩	General registers
R0 := R[0]	Register 0
XR[1:7]: = R[1:7]	Index registers
PSD⟨0:63⟩	Program status doubleword
CC⟨1:4⟩ := PSD⟨0:3⟩	Condition codes
FMC⟨0:2⟩ := PSD⟨5:7⟩	Floating point mode control
FS := FMC⟨0⟩	Floating significance
FZ := FMC⟨1⟩	Floating zero
FN := FMC⟨2⟩	Floating normalize
MS := PSD⟨8⟩	Master-mode-slave-mode
DM := PSD⟨10⟩	Decimal mask
AM := PSD⟨11⟩	Arithmetic mask
IA := PSD⟨15:31⟩	Instruction address
WK⟨0:1⟩ := PSD⟨34:35⟩	Write-key
IIS⟨0:2⟩ := PSD⟨37:39⟩	Interrupt inhibits
CI := IIS⟨0⟩	
IJ := IIS⟨1⟩	
EI := IIS⟨2⟩	
RSP := PSD⟨56:59⟩	Register block pointer

MWP[0:255]⟨0:1⟩   Memory write-protect registers
IR⟨0:33⟩ := Instruction □00   Instruction register

PC Panel

SS⟨1:4⟩	Sense-switches
Address Stop	Panel switch
⋮	⋮
Data	Panel switch
Compute	Panel switch

Mp State

Mp[0:3] [0:1FFF₁₆]⟨0:31⟩   4 Modules of Mp

Instruction formats

i⟨0:31⟩	Instruction
ib := i⟨0⟩	Indirect bit
op⟨0:6⟩ := i⟨1:7⟩	Operation code
gr⟨0:3⟩ := i⟨8:11⟩	General register field
ir⟨0:2⟩ := i⟨12:14⟩	Index register field
address⟨0:16⟩ := i⟨15:31⟩	Operand address
value⟨10:19⟩ := i⟨12:31⟩	Immediate value
hop⟨0:3⟩ := op⟨0:3⟩	Half opcode

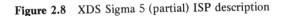

Figure 2.8   XDS Sigma 5 (partial) ISP description

Data Types

byte := 8 bits
half-word := 2 bytes
word := 4 bytes
double-word := 2 words
integer/int := data type (2's complement; carrier (1|2|4) bytes)
log /ff := data-type (referent: binary; component : 1 word)
floating-point/fp := data-type (referent: number;
                component-list: sign, exponent,
                mantissa; sign := 1b;
                exponent := 7b; mantissa :=
                24b fraction; referent-ex-
                pressions:$(-1 \uparrow \text{sign}) \times$
                $(16 \uparrow (\text{exponent} -64)) \times$ mantissa;
                carrier: 1 word; format: (sign:
                word⟨0⟩, exponent:word⟨1:7⟩,
                mantissa:word⟨8:31⟩))

floating-point-double
  precision/dfp := data-type (component-list:
            fp □ continued mantissa; continued-
            mantissa := 32b; carrier:2 words)

Functions (hexadecimal notation is used for the opcodes)

ba := $(70 \leq op \leq 75)$	Byte addressing
ha := $(50 \leq op \leq 58)$	Halfword addressing
wa := $((04 \leq op \leq 07)\|(26 \leq op \leq 4F)\|$	Word addressing
$(64 \leq op \leq 65))$	
dwa := $(08 \leq op \leq 1F)$	Double word addressing
X0 := (ir = 0)	Index = 0 test
CC0 := ((R[gr] = 0) → (CC⟨3:4⟩ ← 00);	Result is 0
(R[gr] < 0) → (CC⟨3:4⟩ ← 01);	Negative
(R[gr] > 0) → (CC⟨3:4⟩ ← 10)	Positive
CC1 := (CC⟨2⟩ ← R[gr]⟨16⟩)	

      ⋮

CC25 := ...

Effective address calculation

EA := (ba → Z⟨15:33⟩; ha → Z⟨15:32⟩;	Effective address length
wa → Z⟨15:31⟩; dwa → Z⟨15:30⟩)	
Z⟨15:33⟩ := (⌐ ib → Z';	Indirect addressing
ib → (address⟨0:16⟩ ← Mp[address]⟨15:31⟩;	
next Z'))	
Z'⟨15:33⟩ := (X0 → address □00;	Indexing
⌐ X0 → address □00 + (ba → R[ir];	with register
ha → R[ir]□0; wa → R[ir]□00;	shifting
dwa → R[ir]□000)	

Figure 2.8 Continued

Instruction Interpretation

```
] interrupt → (IR ← Mp[IA]□00; IA ← IA + 1;
                 next instruction execution)
interrupt → not at this level
```

Memory Access Data Types

EB⟨0:6⟩ ← Mp[EA]   Effective byte

⋮

ED⟨0:63⟩ ← Mp[EA]   Effective double word

Instruction Set

```
Instruction execution : = (
  /* Immediate instruction */
      LI ( : = op = 22) → (R[gr] ← value; CC0);          Load Immediate

          ⋮

  /* Load and Store Operation */
      LB ( : = op = 72) → (R[gr]⟨0:23⟩ ← 0;             Load byte
                           R[gr]⟨26:31⟩ ← EB; CC2)

          ⋮

      LW ( : = op = 32) → (R[gr] ← EW;CC0)               Load word

          ⋮

  /* Arithmetic operation */

          ⋮
```

Figure 2.8   Continued

the CC's. The decomposition can be carried on several levels down, as for instance in the inhibit interrupt codes in Figure 2.8.

Concatenation is expressed by the operator '□'. For example, the instruction register is 34 bits long, two more than a memory word, and this is shown as:

IR⟨0:33⟩ := instruction □ 00

The declaration of the Pc state is followed by that of the control panel, i.e., sense switches and display lights used by the operator. Details are not significant here.

The Mp state description can be straightforward; we simply have to declare the Mp size available. If we want to be more specific, that is, be consistent with a PMS description, then we can show module configurations (cf. Figures 2.5 and 2.8). If instead of a 32K word Sigma 5 we had a 64K word

Sigma 7 with paging hardware and page size of 512 words, then we could write:

Mp[0:7][0:15][0:511]⟨0:31⟩   128 pages of 512 words

(Note the free mixing of decimal and hexadecimal notation for this attribute in Figure 2.8).

The description of instruction formats (there might be more than one for a given machine and in fact there are two for the Sigma 5 as shown in the figure) does not present any special difficulty and follows the same pattern as the description of the Pc state. However, it can become extremely cumbersome for machines with a large variety of opcodes like the PDP-11 (cf. Chapter 9). In the case of data types, several observations are in order. First, we use the same metalinguistic operator as in PMS to show alternatives and the operator '/' for abbreviations purpose, e.g.:

integer/int := 2's complement (1|2|4) bytes

This shows details of implementation important to a programmer such as the numbering system used in the internal representation of integers and the possible lengths, or ranges. This is more apparent in the floating-point cases which are illustrated in detail in Figure 2.8.

We now turn our attention to the treatment of the 6 steps of Figure 2.6. We start by declaring "functions" that will be called upon later on. We partition the instruction set according to its opcodes (only the relevant subset of these partitions is shown) and mode of addressing into *ba* (byte), *ha* (half-word), *wa* (word), and *dwa* (doubleword) addressing. The Boolean function XO is true if there is no indexing. The condition code settings are also elaborated (Figure 2.8 is not complete by any means but one should recall that we are summarizing a reference manual 200 pages long). By examining the function CCO, we can see the syntax of ISP statements which is of the form:

condition → action 1; action 2; . . .; action *n*

where all actions can be performed in parallel. If we wish to indicate a constrained sequencing, we use the operator "next". This is shown in the effective address calculation where after a successful test for indirection, the indirect addressing is performed and only then can indexing be initiated (post-indexing). This is then expressed as:

ib → address⟨0:16⟩ ← Mp[address]⟨15:31⟩; next Z′

The explanation of how addressing is achieved in the Sigma 5 takes several pages in the reference manual because bytes or halfwords are logically addressable while from the Pc-Mp viewpoint all addresses refer to words. In ISP, only a few lines are needed. First, the effective address length is computed according to the type of operation. Then, indirect addressing is tested, and if needed is performed. This is followed by an indexing operation with a shift in the index register prior to the address modification. The assignments of *EA, Z* and *Z'* in the ISP description speak for themselves better than we can do without a lengthy discourse.

The interpretation of the instruction execution cycle comes next. We have lumped into the same (parallel) actions steps 1 and 6 of Figure 2.6. At this level of description we do not elaborate on the interrupt structure. The only information available from the ISP description is that interrupt conditions are tested prior to the fetching of a new instruction.

The description of the instruction set would of course take more space. The decoding portion (cf. step 2 in Figure 2.6) is embedded in the condition, or predicate, determining the actions to follow. The descriptions of individual operations are simple, concise and precise. The usual repetitions of programming manuals cannot be avoided but are shortened by the use of functions (cf. condition codes setting and the use of CCO).

The operation of channels, i.e., Pio's, and controllers, that is *K*'s, can also be described with ISP. A good example can be found in Bell and Newell's book where the descriptions of a channel, Pio('7909), attached to an IBM 7094, and of the Pc('7094) instructions to the Pio('7909) are given. The unusual amount of comments in the Pio portion indicates that ISP is not well suited to this level of description. Similarly, the almost total absence of these comments and the rather poor readability of a *K*('disk) description (which can be seen in the same chapter of the cited book) seem to show that ISP might not be the answer to all hardware descriptions and that the Computer Hardware Description Languages presented in the next section are needed.

2.3.2   Type of Instructions

A quick survey of the ISP's of second and third generation computers shows no major advances in the logical structures of the processors and few differences in the capabilities of the instruction sets. However, two trends are apparent: a move from the unique double-length accumulator to a set of general registers, and a more complex relocation scheme for segments of program and data. Both of these minor changes have their impact on the instruction sets. Because of the presence of more than one accumulator, single address instructions will be replaced by the 1-address + general register scheme explained below. The advent of multiprogrammed operating systems is responsible for the dynamic relocation requirements and associated means of protection of users' and systems' programs. Less important effects such as more extensive data types will increase the number of instructions found in general-purpose Pc's. Finally, because read-only memories are quite cheap, extensive microprogramming allows the introduction of machine language instructions that perform high-level language functions.

Looking at the instruction formats of Pc's provides a way of classifying processors. The primary factor is the number of Mp addresses which are encoded in the instruction. This will of course depend on the number of accumulators present in the Pc state. We can have:

- 0-address instructions.

    These are typical of stack computers that we shall introduce in Chapter 4. But many third generation computers, e.g., the IBM System/360 and 370, the PDP-11 and the CDC 6000 series, have instructions which refer only to registers. In the case of stack computers, the accumulators are implicit and hence the instructions are simply opcodes, while in the RR (register-register) format of the 370 the instructions are of the form:

    R[gr1] ← R[gr1] operator R[gr2]

    and are special forms of the 1-address + general register case. Similarly, one could say that the CDC 6600 instructions are 3-address instructions.

- 1-address instructions.

    These are basically the instructions modelled after those of the von Neumann machine. In most instructions an accumulator is implied as an operand and result. The use of an index register in the effective address calculation of the other operand should not lead us to misconstrue the fact that a single address is going to be generated. The IBM 7094 and most computers of the second generation had instructions following this format. Nowadays, some stack computers like the HP-3000 use this format with the implied accumulator, if any, being the top of the stack.

- 1-address + general register instructions.

    The Sigma 5 ISP descriptions show how these instructions are encoded. The term "general register" might be misleading on some occasions. For example, in the Sigma 5, we saw that some but not all of these registers could be used as index registers. In the IBM System/370, we have 16 general registers and 4 additional floating-point accumulators. In the CDC 6000 series, the 24 general registers are partitioned into 3 groups, of different length and function, i.e., either accumulators, address registers, or index registers.

- 2-address + general register (optional) instructions.
  Two operands can be accessed from Mp. In third generation computers a typical instruction using this format would be of the form:

  MOVE, Count   A, B

  where "Count" bytes starting at address A are transferred to the Mp area starting at address B. But, we also have "true" 2 address instructions, for example in the PDP-11.

- 3-address instructions.
  Although it could be envisioned, and in fact had been implemented in some early computers, this scheme had been completely abandoned for some time. With the facilities provided by microprogramming, this type of instructions has reappeared as for example in the DEC VAX 11/780 (cf. Chapters 7 and 9).

In the preceding discussion, we have not included the problem of determining the location of the next instruction. This was not an oversight since the general rule is that this next instruction is the one sequentially following the current instruction in Mp except in case of jumps. Therefore, there is no need to encode it in the instruction. This was not true in the early days of computing where Mp was implemented as a drum. In the IBM 650, which had such a rotating device for Mp, a field in the instruction was allowed to explicitly indicate the location of the next instruction. Therefore depending on the time of execution of the instruction and the latency of the drum, an optimizing assembler could place the next instruction in the appropriate location so that the access time to move it to the instruction register would be minimized.

Although we just said that 3-address instructions are scarce, this statement could be construed as being in contradiction with the 3-register format found in the CDC 6000. But, as noted earlier, this 3-register instruction has no Mp operand reference and can fall under the 0-address heading. Therefore, the above classification is not always exact; for example, in a stack computer some operations (those for loading and storing) will necessitate an Mp address. Very often a Pc instruction set will have instruction formats falling in several of the above categories. Nonetheless, it is fair to say that the trend in third generation machines was towards the 1-address + general register configuration with register-register operations as well. This is true of the Pc's for the IBM System/360 and 370, the CDC 6000 series, the DEC PDP-10 and

System-20 etc. This will often imply that instructions can be of different lengths for a given Pc. In the IBM System/370, there are 5 instruction formats. The RR format, already mentioned, which is half a word long; the RX format similar to the RR but replacing a register by an Mp address, the RS format involving 2 registers and an Mp address (for special types of branching and multiple loading or storing of registers) and the SI format with an immediate value field and an Mp field (in contrast with the Sigma 5 where the immediate value replaces the Mp address) which are a word long, and a 6-byte SS format for instructions like the MOVE presented before. In the CDC 6000 series, instructions can be 15 bits long (a quarter of a word) when involving only registers, 30 bits long when an Mp address is needed, and even 60 bits long in the Cyber 70's for character manipulation. At the other end of the "power" spectrum, a minicomputer like the PDP-11 has 13 instruction formats of length 1, 2, or 3 (16-bit) words. The current trend seems to be in a proliferation of instruction formats and/or addressing modes.

The general registers serve many purposes: they can be accumulators, index registers, base registers (see below), stack pointers, subroutine linkage registers and recipients of temporary variables. Because of this generality it is unnecessary to have specific instructions applied uniquely, for example, to index registers and, as a side benefit, the instruction length can be reduced (recall the RR format for a System/370). Certainly foremost in the minds of the computer designers who use a general register scheme is the hope of reducing the number of references to Mp with shorter instructions and, most of all, with the registers used for temporary storage since access to their contents is usually much faster than retrieval of the contents of an Mp cell (although difficult to believe this is not true in some systems!). This concept was pushed to its extreme in the CDC 6000 and 7000 series where all arithmetic operations have to be of the register-register form.

Several recent studies show that going from a single accumulator and 3 index register machines such as the IBM 7090 to a machine with 16 general and 4 floating-point registers such as the System/370 does not yield a decrease in Mp addressing as significant as one would intuitively expect. Table 2.1 gives typical percentages obtained when tracing the executions of four different programs on a Sigma 5. The programs were respectively a FORTRAN IV compute bound scientific program, an I/O bound FORTRAN IV run, a simulation mixing FORTRAN and assembly language, and a compilation of XPL, a dialect or more precisely a subset of PL/I, written in XPL. We can observe the following. The flexibility of byte, halfword, word, and doubleword addressing is barely cost-effective, especially for halfword addressing, and might not be taken advantage of as much as possible by the

Table 2.1   Instruction mixes (percentages)

Traces Instructions	FORTRAN Scientific 0.54×10^6 inst.	FORTRAN I/O 0.55×10^6 inst.	FORTRAN & Ass. Lang. Simulation 0.65×10^6 inst.	XPL Compiler 1.3×10^6 inst.
Type of addressing				
ba	<1	8.5	6.4	13.2
ha	0	≪1	.5	7.
wa	84.5	66.5	77.2	55.7
dwa	1.5	1.4	2.	1.8
immediate	13.2	23.3	14.	22.3
Type of instructions*				
load/store	37.8	27.4	37.7	46.4
branch	19.9	39.4	37.8	24.3
Integer arith.	6.9	33.8	16.4	24.3
F. p. arith.	27.4	<1	2.5	0
logical/shift	7.9	5.5	2.5	7.8
Misc.	<1	6.1	5.	<1
Number of operand/in- struction ($\times 100$)				
from Mp	58.6	34.5	40.6	46.4
from register	7.5	2.4	7.5	7.
Indirect addressing	3.6	4.7	2.7	2.1

*The total may exceed 100 since some instructions belong to several categories.

programmers and compiler writers. The load and store instructions, hereafter called M-type for Mp and Move, comprise between 27% and 46% of the total number of instructions executed, the arithmetic and logical operations, A-type, between 26% and 42% and the flow of control instructions, P-type for Procedural, between 20% and 40%. Finally, a memory operand fetch is generated approximately at every other instruction.

These figures are typical of third generation computers and also of minicomputers such as the DEC PDP-11 (cf. Chapter 9 Table 9.4). They stem from the fact that programs written in high-level languages are composed mainly of assignment statements, IF statements and procedure calls or branches. The summary of three studies of programs written in an experimental system programming language (SAL), XPL, and FORTRAN shown in Table 2.2 confirm this fact. (These statistics are static, i.e., generated at compile time in contrast with those of Table 2.1 which were dynamic, that is

Table 2.2   Percentages of types of executable statements
in three high-level languages (static measures)

Statement type	SAL	XPL	FORTRAN
Assignment	47	55	61
Procedure calls	25	17	5
Tests	17	17	10
Loops	6	5	9
Returns	4	4	4
Go To's	0	1	9

measured during execution.) Furthermore, most expressions on the right-hand side of an assignment statement have none or one operator (between 70% and 80% for both static and dynamic measures). In the case of System/370 it has been observed that the average instruction length is almost one word, implying either a paucity of RR formats or a large amount of SS instructions, and that M-type instructions comprise between 36% and 50% of the total (this higher percentage compared to the Sigma's can be explained by the differences in addressing methods), the A-type between 10% and 20% and the P-type between 28% and 48%. Since traces of programs also exist for a second generation machine like the IBM 7090, yielding percentages of 49% for M-type, 25% for A-type, and 20% for P-type, we can try and compare these figures. In Table 2.3 are the ratios of M/A and P/A for the IBM 7090 trace (which is the well-known Gibson mix reportedly biased towards scientific computations, hence against SS instructions), a System/360 composite trace, the averages of columns 1 and 3 of Table 2.1 for the Sigma 5, a more "scientific" trace for the System/360, and a general technical mix for the DEC PDP-10. This latter machine has a rich instruction set (in particular for branches), 16 general registers (no special floating-point accumulators;

Table 2.3   Instruction type ratios

	M/A (Scientific)	P/A
IBM 7090	1.95	.8
System/360	2.9	2.5
Sigma 5	1.10	.85
System/360		
(floating-point only)	1.4	1.65
PDP-10	1.5	1.1

the word size is 36 bits sufficient for single precision arithmetic), and no base registers. It appears at first glance that instead of an increment in percentage of "useful" instructions, i.e., A-type, with respect to the other 2 types when using a general register machine, we have regressed and are doing more bookkeeping. This is even more blatant in the 360 case than in the Sigma's or PDP-10's. But several factors should be taken in consideration before reaching such a conclusion.

- The ratio M/A should instead by computed in terms of Mp addressing; For the IBM 7090 it becomes $(M+A)/A$, i.e., 2.95, since all A-type refer to an Mp operand. For the other three Pc's we can keep the same ratios by estimating that most M-type have an Mp operand while most A-type are of the RR format.

- In System/360 the address field is only 12 bits long; Since only 4K bytes can be directly addressed in an RX instruction, some registers are used as base registers, hence requiring frequent loads and stores, mostly in large programs and in the absence of an optimizing compiler.

- The System/360 does not have indirect addressing; Indirect addressing has a tendency to increase the Mp ratio for the single accumulator machine, mostly for P-type if computed in a manner similar to that of the M-type, since many branches are taken "indirect".

- Many registers are reserved by the compiler; For example in the Sigma 5 FORTRAN IV compiler, only 4 registers are left for accumulator duties once the index, I/O, linkage and function results registers have been reserved. If double precision floating-point is used, then we only have 2 accumulators!

Therefore, although there does not seem to be any advantage in the general register scheme in terms of their use as accumulators, their flexibility is nonetheless fundamental for the realization of complex multiprogrammed operating systems, the possibility of shared segments of code and data, and the efficient handling of large address spaces. However, providing an excess of registers is not an advantage either because the whole set of registers has to be saved during context switching (in a multiprogramming environment) since they are part of the Pc state. In the case of the PDP-10 it has been shown that for all programs measured, 90% of the time 10 or fewer registers would suffice. Similarly, 10 registers are sufficient for 90% of these same programs, 98% of the time (see the CRAY-1 presentation in Chapter 10 for another view of register use in a powerful machine).

2.3.3   Addressing and Instruction Formats

The problem of being able to address a large Mp, either real or virtual, is apparent in the ISP description. Leaving aside for the moment the virtual memory concept, we can see several methods of effective address calculation.

With each mode of addressing we must associate a code indicating how the effective address is to be calculated. In some cases, it is embedded in the opcode itself (cf. Figure 2.8); in others a special field is reserved for that purpose, as for example the indirect bit in the Sigma 5. In Figure 2.9, we show a sample of formats with various associated schemes for addressing on which we now elaborate. Naturally the register-register format does not require any Mp addressing.

- Immediate addressing

    Although it does not really belong in a discussion of Mp addressing, we include the immediate mode for reasons of completeness. Several alternatives exist, all of them using a constant included in the instruction itself. Generally it will be through opcode specification that this type of addressing will be encoded. In the case of the Sigma 5, the immediate value is loaded or used as an operand for arithmetic and logical operations in conjunction with the contents of a general register (cf. the LI description in Figure 2.8). On the other hand in System/370, the immediate operand is only 1-byte long and used mostly for logical operations in the SI format. In the CDC 6000 series only immediate loading of registers is permitted while, in contrast, the PDP-11 allows a large number of immediate operations even with two "constant" operands (although the PDP-11 immediate addressing mode is in fact a disguised indexing mode with the index register being the program counter).

- Direct addressing

    The address field of the instruction contains the Mp address. This scheme is the simplest and generally the default case, hence requiring no special encoding. But the address generation might not be sufficient for two main reasons. First, the field reserved for that purpose may be too small to allow the addressing of the complete range of Mp, and, second, we might want to increment or decrement the effective address in a uniform fashion, as for example while accessing elements of an array. This latter facility comes with the use of index registers.

- Index addressing

    The effective address is going to be the sum of the direct address and of the contents of one of a set of previously designated registers. As noted before, the current trend is to have any of the general registers usable as

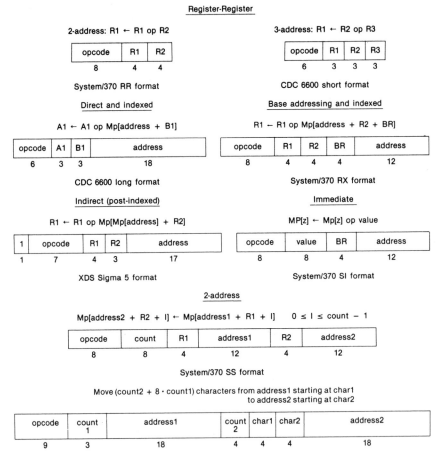

Figure 2.9 Sample of instruction formats

an index register (cf. System/370), but in other machines like the CDC 6000 only specific registers can be used for that purpose. Generality will be more expensive in terms of instruction space. For example, it costs 4 bits in System/370 (1 out of 15 registers with 0 indicating no indexing) while only 3 bits are needed in the Sigma 5 or the CDC 6000. All current major computers have index register capabilities.

Note that the Mp range which can be addressed is the maximum value that the contents of a register can assume when considered as a positive integer, i.e., $(2^n - 1)$ if the length is n bits (in fact it is more precisely $(2^n - 1 + 2^{|address|} - 1)$ where $|address|$ is the length of the direct address field). So, it would appear that the use of index registers is sufficient to solve our problem of limited addressing. But if index registers are thus employed, we lose their help for our primary purpose in introducing them: the easy incremental modification of the effective address. Hence the need for one of the two next schemes.

- Base addressing

    With another register field, called base, such that the contents of this new register can be added to the (indexed) effective address, we meet our two original requirements. An interesting point in that scheme is that a segment of program or data can be placed anywhere in Mp as long as its starting address is known and can be loaded in the appropriate base register. System/370 makes extensive use of this property which allows non-contiguity in the program segments. The direct address is now called a displacement within the segment. This relocation can also be coupled with an independent protection mechanism for each segment. For example, code segments could be "read only" while data segments could be "shared" (read/write). The base registers can also be embedded in the hardware and be transparent to the programmer. A pair of such registers is used in the CDC 6000 series so that when a program, which has to be stored along with its data in a contiguous partition of Mp, is loaded its starting address is stored in the first base register called RA (relocation address). The program itself is compiled or assembled with respect to origin 0. When the effective address EA has been computed it is checked against the contents of the second register, named FL for field length, which corresponds to the highest address with respect to origin 0 which can be referenced. If EA > FL, then an error condition will occur and the program will be aborted; otherwise the absolute address is computed as RA + EA. If there are two sets of such relocation registers, then each program can have two segments. Some sharing of code, i.e., of one of the segments can be done. This is the implementation chosen for the PDP-10 and the UNIVAC 1108.

Looking at Figure 2.9, we see that the base addressing as performed in System/370 is costly in the instruction format layout (4 bits), as well as in the allocation of registers for that function. The displacement is necessarily small when compared to the complete addressable Mp range.

- Indirect addressing

    Instead of using a register in order to be able to address the full Mp range, we can use a memory location to contain the effective address. The problem is to decide which locations can play this role. A solution which presents itself immediately is to use the cell whose address is the (possibly indexed) direct address to contain the effective address. This is generally called indirect addressing and is recognizable in the instruction format with a single bit. If we use indexing prior to indirect addressing any memory location can contain the effective address. If we wish to index after the indirection (post-indexing like in the Sigma 5) then only $(2^{|address|} - 1)$ cells can contain indirect addresses. This number is more than sufficient. Indirect addressing can be performed on several levels. For example if the leftmost bit is used in the instruction format to indicate indirect addressing, we can continue to perform indirection as long as the previous indirect address has the leftmost bit on. In most cases indirect addressing is limited to a single level (Sigma 5, PDP-11, IBM 7090) because with each indirection we require an Mp fetch, that is, a time consuming operation.

This time cost is the drawback of indirect addressing. When we compare base and indirect addressing, we see that the latter provides more generality since any Mp location can be used, we waste less important Pc resources, that is a Mp location versus a general register, and less space in the instruction format. Indirect addressing is not as convenient for segmentation and protection purposes.

- Two operand addressing

    Either of the above schemes, or a combination thereof, could theoretically be used for each operand. System/370 uses base addressing (non-indexed) and the CYBER 70 direct addressing. The latter type, exemplified in Figure 2.9, shows an interesting point, that is the difficulty in upgrading an architecture.

The CYBER 70 has the same instruction set as the CDC 6000 series, with the short format (15 bit) and the long format (30 bit) instructions, and in addition four 60 bit operations for character handling. In order to keep a compatible way of obtaining the direct addresses, they are put in the positions that they would have occupied in two consecutive 30 bit instructions. The number of characters handled and the position of the starting characters in the first words of the source and destination addresses also have to be specified. Since a word can contain 10 characters, the character fields are 4 bits each leaving 7 bits for the count. The constraints on the layout are:

$$
\begin{array}{ccccc}
\text{opcode} & & \text{address 1} & & \text{address 2} \\
\longleftrightarrow & \longleftrightarrow & \longleftrightarrow & \longleftrightarrow & \longleftrightarrow \\
9 & 3 & 18 & 12 & 18
\end{array}
$$

This obliges one of the fields to be split into two and leads to the awkward format of Figure 2.9.

There are other addressing mechanisms. Stack addressing and the use of descriptors will be explained in Chapters 4 and 6. Minicomputers such as the PDP-11 often have a very comprehensive addressing mechanism combining most of the above schemes. A more thorough treatment can be found in Chapter 9. With the advent of microprogrammed Pc's and the lower cost of read-only memories, new machines have richer instruction sets (see, e.g., the DEC VAX 11/780 Chapter 7 Section 3.3. and Chapter 9 Section 3.7). Some very powerful computers can have part of their instruction set tailored to their main purposes. Typical examples are the pipeline or vector processors which can treat streams of operands and have instructions designed to that effect (cf. Chapter 10).

Before closing this Pc description, it is reasonable to ask why we did not use ISP in connection with Figure 2.9. We feel that for examples of isolated functions a sample figure and associated comments bring out the main points more clearly. The reader is encouraged to work out Exercise 5 for his own judgment.

2.4   THE REGISTER TRANSFER LEVEL

2.4.1   Computer Hardware Design Languages

At this level we want to describe the behavior of a PMS primitive or of interconnections between modules. These register transfer actions are of direct concern to the computer designer, but not necessarily to the logic designer.

As a matter of fact, the notation could be useful not only to describe but also to help carry out the design and checking of intended structural and behavioral decisions. This could be performed for example through simulation. Therefore, we again see that programming languages are convenient tools since the main actions will be (register) assignments controlled by a set of predicates (Boolean expressions on gates and/or timing factors).

Many attempts have been taken at defining CHDL's, that is Computer Hardware Design (or Description) Languages. ISP is certainly a member of this category. It can be further classified as a procedural language with asynchronous control. It is then better suited for describing modules at a level where clocks and timing factors are not of the utmost importance (and this is closer to the philosophy of this book which is concerned more with architectural properties than with the complete design of elements of a computer system). On the other hand CDL (Computer Design Language), introduced by Y. Chu, is geared towards synchronous systems and allows for both procedural and mainly non-procedural control actions. The distinction between these two modes will become clear below where we briefly introduce the language. This is in order to give the flavor of a CHDL rather than to provide a design tool. In fact, CDL is more noted for its pedagogical properties than for its use in industrial environments. When we use CDL in this book, comments and program structure will be sufficient for a clear understanding.

It is important to note that any programming language could be used instead of a CHDL since the main purpose is to describe (hardware) algorithms. We can justify CHDL's only because they bring more clarity and impose less complexity in the data and control structures geared to the specific application. In particular, issues such as parallelism (as discussed in the previous section), timing signals, and synchronization in the use of resources can be handled more economically in a special-purpose environment. On the other hand, some concepts such as recursion can be avoided if not relevant or at least less important than in general algorithmic developments.

2.4.2   CDL

Like all programming languages, CDL consists of sequences of declarative and executable statements. The former are further divided into storage and control structures. As previously, we proceed mostly by examples. Figure 2.10 represents the linkage between a Pc and an Mp with the only registers and buses shown being those involved in the instruction fetch. The CDL program describing this sequence of steps is found in Figure 2.11.

In general, storage structures will be registers. The register statements declare these registers, giving them names and lengths. For example:

Register,	MAR(0–16),	$Memory Address Register
	MDR(0–31),	$Memory Data Register

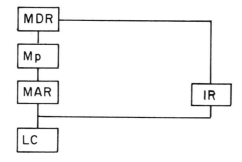

Figure 2.10   Registers and buses for basic instruction fetch

Register,   MAR (0–16) $ Memory Address Register
                 MDR (0–31) $ Memory Data Register
                 LC (0–16) $ Location Counter
                 IR (0–31) $ Instruction Register
                 INTRP $ Interrupt flip-flop
Subregister,   IR (IND) = IR(0), IR(AD) = IR(15-31)
Memory,   M(MAR) = M(0-131072, 0-31)
Comment,   normal sequencing

/STARTOFFETCH/   IF(INTRP ≠ 0) THEN GO TO INTERSEQ;
                     MAR ← LC;
                     MDR ← M(MAR), LC ← countup LC;
                     IR ← MDR;
                     execution cycle;
                     GOTO STARTOFFETCH;
/INTERSEQ/   Interrupt sequence
                              ⋮
                     GOTO STARTOFFETCH;

Figure 2.11   A CDL program (partial)

declare the registers associated with Mp. The '$' delimits the beginning of comments.

Subregisters, i.e., parts of registers, are declared in a fashion similar to ISP's mode of operation:

Register,   IR(0-31), $Instruction Register
Subregister,   IR(IND)=IR(0), IR(OP)=IR(1-7),
                 IR(GR)=IR(8-11), IR(IX)=IR(12-14),
                 IR(AD)=IR(15-31),

and concatenation, or cascade of registers, are formed using the (ill-chosen) operator '–':

Register,	A(0–35),MQ(0–35),
Subregister,	MQ(M)=MQ(1-35),
Casregister,	AMQ=A-MQ(M),

(the reader will have recognized the declaration of a double-length accumulator as in the IBM 7090).

Identical registers can also form aggregate structures, that is an array of registers as in:

Array-register,   GR(0–15,0–31), $16 General registers
                                          $of 32 bits

Mp can be declared in a similar fashion. However, the memory address register used to access Mp has to be declared beforehand. For example, the Mp in Figure 2.11 has 128K words of 32 bits (notice that some of the flexibility of multisubscripts found in ISP has disappeared).

Other storage structures commonly used will be switches and lights, i.e., those elements belonging to the Pc control panel state. Logic networks, e.g., combinational circuits similar to those found in the design of a full adder, can also be declared through so-called terminal statements. In the same vein, a decoder declaration has the form:

Register,	BCD(0–3),	
Decoder,	BIN(0–9)=BCD,	$BIN(i) is true if
		$BCD(0–3)=i

(Notice that the decoder has only 10 output lines out of the 16 possible values of BCD).

The declaration of control structures is not always necessary. For example, none of them shows up in Figure 2.11. Two types of control structures can be used: registers and clocks. A clock statement declares a clock giving it its name and its number of phases, as e.g.:

Clock,   P(1–3), $Three-phase clock

The execution statements, or micro-instructions, are based on register transfers. The right side of the assignment statement can be an expression involving several registers. The basic operators are the usual logical and shift instructions, increment and decrement by 1, and add and subtract. Conditional micro-instructions are also permitted by use of the (possibly nested) IF... THEN... ELSE construct. Functions, or (non-basic) operators as they are called in CDL, can also be declared making CDL an easily extensible language.

The sequencing of the micro-instructions can be performed in one of two ways, which can be mixed in any program. The basic entity is the execution statement which is preceded by a label enclosed in slashes '/'. Under "normal sequencing", the rules of flow of control are those of conventional procedural programming languages (cf. Figure 2.11, and note the use of ',' to indicate parallelism and of ';' to show sequentiality). But this flow of control can also be regulated by predicates (Boolean expressions) instead of labels and control statements. To illustrate this point, we again consider the example of Figure 2.11 but we now assume the following:

- We have a command signal which indicates that we are in a FETCH cycle. For example, FETCH could have been declared as a register control structure, or, more likely, in a decoder statement;
- We have declared a 3-phase clock;
- The fetch sequence consists of:
  - Transfer of LC to MAR (Phase 1);
  - Memory read cycle and increment of LC (Phase 2);
  - Transfer of MDR into IR (Phase 3).

In CDL this could be expressed as shown in Figure 2.12.

This mode of sequencing can also be expressed with the use of the contents of a control register as an operand in a (control) Boolean expression. Chu's book has a number of such examples.

Register,	⋮	$ see Figure 2.11
	F(0 − 3),	$ Control
	⋮	
Decoder,	K(0 − 9) = F,	
Terminal,	⋮	
	FETCH = K(9),	$ Fetch Command
	⋮	
Clock,	P(1 − 3),	$ 3-phase
	⋮	
/FETCH ∗ P(1)/	MAR ← LC,	$ ∗ is logical AND
/FETCH ∗ P(2)/	MDR ← M(MAR), LC ← countupLC,	
/FETCH ∗ P(3)/	IR ← MDR,	$ Notice "," instead of ";"
	END	$ End of Sequence

Figure 2.12 A CDL program with clocked statements (partial)

2.5 MODELING THE DYNAMICS OF THE SYSTEM

2.5.1 Dynamic Information Flow

The two notations that we have introduced in previous sections have to be considered as static in the sense that they describe either an overall structure or depict the rules dictating the execution of instructions or of hardware algorithms. The way information flows through PMS primitives is of course indicated by buses and within a particular module by programming language control statements. However, the dynamic sequences of events needed to perform particular actions are not represented in as clear a fashion as one would like.

This is not a difficulty inherent in Computer Architecture. Very few algorithmic processes are amenable to a notation which reflects the sequences of possible executions. Some examples can be drawn from formal language theory: regular expressions are the most evident. In Software Engineering practice, flowcharts indicate how execution proceeds much in the same manner as the source language. There is no gain in formalism (in fact there might be some precision lost) but the pictorial representation helps in the understanding process. However flowcharts are restricted to the modeling of the flow of control while the representation of data structures—and data flow—is generally non-existent. In Systems Architecture several factors increase the complexity of the representation, particularly when we do not want to restrict ourselves to descriptions but want also to include means for analysis and evaluation, i.e., provide a design tool.

We wish to represent the flow of control, the structures (hardware and software "data structures") in which information is stored and massaged, the creation and deletion of processes, and the allocation and occupancy of resources during the processes' lifetimes. Currently, there is no model which is completely satisfactory.

This is an area of intense investigation with various modeling apparatus. We shall limit ourselves to Petri Nets and their extensions which have already received a wide following. Petri Nets and derivatives are used for the representation of concurrent activities. They allow for the modeling of control flow (in a richer and more formal way than flowcharts do) and when supplemented by some data representation they can be of interest to Systems Architects. They also are convenient for the analysis of properties such as deadlock. They can be, and have been, used as models at all three levels discussed in the previous sections as well as for software systems.

2.5.2   Petri Nets and Derivatives

Although Petri Nets have been used as rigorous models for parallel processes, as Turing machines have been for sequential algorithms, our presentation will be informal (see the bibliography for references on Petri Nets).

A Petri Net consists of a set of *places* $P = (p_1, p_2, \ldots, p_n)$ corresponding to conditions which may hold in the system, a set of *transitions* $T = (t_1, t_2, \ldots, t_m)$ representing events which may occur, and a set of directed arcs connecting places to transitions and transitions to places.

A place may contain *tokens* which signify the holding of the corresponding condition. Graphically, places are denoted by circles; transitions, by bars; and tokens, by dots inside a place. A net has associated with it an initial *marking*, or state, which is the number of tokens initially assigned to each place in the net. A transition may *fire* when all its input places (places linked to the transition by an arc directed from the place to the transition) are full (contain a token). After firing, a token is removed from every input place and a token is added to every output place (places linked to the transition by an arc directed from the transition to the place). The firing of a transition corresponds to the occurrence of the event. Petri Nets may be generalized to allow a weight to be associated with each arc indicating the number of tokens transferred along the arc during transition firing and, in the case of an input place and arc, the number of tokens required to enable a transition. The default weight is one. The state of the system, or marking, is modeled by the number of tokens on each place. Hence transition firing represents a state modification.

Figure 2.13 illustrates some of these concepts. Figure 2.13.a shows a Petri Net and its initial marking. Figure 2.13.b is the same net after firing of transition t_1. Note that we had a choice of firing either t_1 or t_2. This is known as (forward) conflict. Figure 2.13.c is the same net after firing of transition t_3. If the initial transition to fire had been t_2, no other transition could have fired and the net would have been dead. In contrast, a net is said to be live for some marking if it is possible to fire any transition by some sequence of transition firings (also called execution sequence). We can see that two transitions can fire simultaneously, for example t_1 and t_5 with the marking of Figure 2.13.c. This exemplifies a major advantage of Petri Nets over conventional flowcharts, namely, the possibility of representing asynchronous computational structures. Furthermore, since place p_3 will never hold more than one token (the reader should verify this point) transitions t_3 and t_4 are mutually exclusive. This type of modeling power is extremely convenient for the representation of semaphores and critical sections which will be discussed

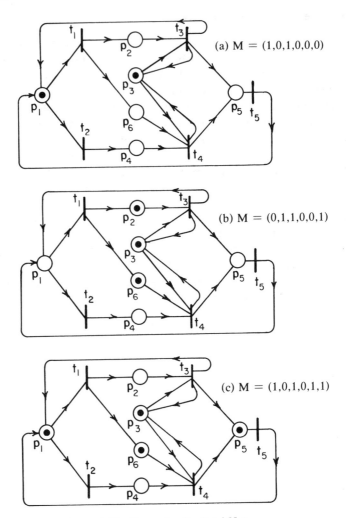

Figure 2.13   Example of a Petri Net

in Chapter 10. Finally, some places can receive more than one token. If the net is designed in such a way that no place can receive more than one token, the net is said to be safe. If the maximum number of tokens that can be received by any place is not finite, the net is said to be unbounded.

An extension which enhances the descriptive power of the Petri Net model, as described above, is disjunctive logic (in contrast to the conjunctive logic of transition firing). A decision or branch is modeled in Petri Nets by a single place (e.g., the firing of t_1 or t_2 in Figure 2.13). The conflict between the competing transitions is arbitrarily resolved. The disadvantage of this approach is a slight discrepancy in the descriptive model since such a conflict usually represents a data dependent decision. That is, it should be shown in the net as an event or transition firing. Disjunctive logic allows the decision making event to be modeled as a transition. It will be denoted by a '+' at the input or output of the transition.

At first glance, it would appear that such a trivial change should not modify the representative power of the Petri Nets. But this modification is sufficient to transform the extended Petri Net to as powerful a theoretical model as a Turing Machine. From the descriptive viewpoint it allows for the testing of an empty place, a feature which cannot be accomplished by non-extended Petri Nets. A further discussion of this topic is outside the scope of this book (cf. the bibliography for references).

To give a flavor of the use of Petri Nets and associated data flow or data structures, we proceed again by example. Figure 2.14 is a representation of the control flow in the execution of an instruction in a single accumulator arithmetic-logical unit. We have intentionally named the transitions by the events they represent in order to facilitate the interpretation. We have to associate a data storage structure with this Petri Net. Several alternatives are

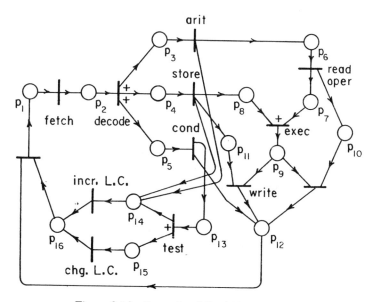

Figure 2.14 Example of Petri Net modeling

possible: for example a labelled block diagram, or ISP or CDL declaration statements. If the former is chosen, a slight expansion to Figure 2.10 should suffice to obtain a block diagram, or data graph, with registers such as the location counter LC, the instruction register IR, the memory address register MAR and memory data register MDR, the accumulator A and an opcode decoder playing the role of a decider. Data operators are placed on directed links connecting these registers and, when activated, will perform the required transfers.

It remains to formalize the interactions between control and data graphs. For example, Patil and Dennis have chosen a protocol where the firing of a transition is decomposed into the following parts:

- Enable the control transition (i.e., check if the firing conditions are met);
- Remove the tokens from the input places and send a ready signal to the associated data operator in the data graph; (this is shown by the labelling in the data graph.)
- Wait for an acknowledge signal from the data operator;
- Put tokens on the transition's output places.

Returning to Figure 2.14 we see that three types of operations are considered: arithmetic, store and conditional. The initial marking will activate the *fetch* transition which brings the operation in the instruction register in order to be decoded. The transfer from a Mp location to the instruction register IR is part of the data flow and is not shown here. The ready signal from the transition *fetch* would activate the transfer through a data link from LC to MAR and a read cycle for Mp would be generated, followed by a transfer from MDR to IR, upon which an acknowledge signal would be sent back to the *fetch* transition. This refinement could be modeled explicitly, but, in contrast to CDL's possibility of representing clocks, all operations in Petri Nets are performed in an asynchronous fashion. The advantage of the latter approach is that the correctness of the system, e.g., the proper termination of algorithms, is independent of the time taken by individual operations and can be checked by implementation independent methods. After the fetch operation is completed, the *decode* transition will be activated and a decider in the data flow graph will indicate, with the acknowledge signal, which of the places p_3, p_4, or p_5 will become full. This is indicated by the disjunctive logic extension. The *arit, store* and *cond* transitions have no links with the data graph and show only flow of control. The remainder of the net is self-explanatory. Notice that when either the *store* or the *arit* transition is fired, the transition *incr.L.C.* (increment location counter) can be activated in parallel with some other transition such as *exec*. Unlabelled transitions are present to indicate the flow of control and have no connections with the data graph.

The need for modeling asynchronous structures as an aid to designing distributed function architectures and networks is arising with the increasing number of these types of systems. Petri Nets and equivalent graph models of computations can be used to describe the control functions. Some more complete systems embedding structural (control and data flow) and behavioral (prediction of performance) features are under investigation, but it is too soon to pass judgment on the approaches being taken.

2.6 BIBLIOGRAPHICAL NOTES, REFERENCES AND EXERCISES

PMS and ISP have been introduced in [Bell and Newell 71]. Brief summaries of these notations can be found in a special issue of *Computer* devoted to CHDL's. AHPL and CDL are also presented there, but [Hill and Peterson 73] and [Chu 72] have to be consulted respectively for thorough treatments. PMS and ISP have also been used for analysis of systems [Knudsen 72, Barbacci 76]. A monument to the descriptive power of APL is the complete specification of IBM System/360 written in that language [Falkoff, Iverson, and Sussenguth 64]. A good comparison between CHDL's at the register transfer level can be found in [Barbacci 75]. Technical symposia on CHDL's, their design, uses and applications are organized on a regular basis.

There is an extensive literature on Petri Nets and other graph models of computations. [Peterson 77]'s survey can lead to other references. [Hack 74] gives formal definitions of Petri Nets as well as a discussion of their theoretical power. The example in Section 6 was adapted from [Patil and Dennis 72]. Among many uses of Petri Nets or equivalent graph models, the LOGOS project for hardware and software system specifications has been the most advanced [Rose 72].

The statistics for instruction mixes of Section 3 were taken from [Flynn 74], [Jensen 76] for the Sigma traces, [Lunde 75 and 77] for the PDP-10 statistics, [Alexander and Wortman 75] for XPL, and Table 2.2 is derived from [Tanenbaum 78].

References

1. Alexander, A. and D. Wortman, "Static and Dynamic Characteristics of XPL programs," *Computer, 8,* (Nov. 1975), 41–46.

2. Barbacci, M. R., "A Comparison of Register Transfer Languages for Describing Computers and Digital Systems," *IEEE Trans. on Comp., C-24,* (Feb. 1975), 137–150.

3. Barbacci, M. R., *"The Symbolic Manipulation of Computer Descriptions: ISPL Compiler and Simulator,"* Tech. Report, Carnegie-Mellon University, 1976.

4. Bell, C. G. and A. Newell, *Computer Structures: Readings and Examples,* McGraw Hill, New York, N.Y., 1971.

5. Chu, Y., *Computer Organization and Microprogramming.* Prentice-Hall, Englewood Cliffs, N.J., 1972.

6. *Computer* Special Issue on Hardware Description Languages, Dec. 1974.

7. Falkoff, A. D., Iverson, K. E. and E. H. Sussenguth, "Formal Description of System/360," *IBM System J., 3,* 1964, 198-262.

8. Flynn, M. J., "Trends and Problems in Computer Organizations," *Proc. IFIP Congress 1974,* North-Holland, Amsterdam, 1974, 3-10.

9. Hack, M., "The Recursive Equivalence of the Reachability Problem and the Liveness Problem for Petri Nets and Vector Addition Systems," *15th IEEE SWAT Symposium,* 1974, 156-164.

10. Hill, F. J. and G. R. Peterson, *Digital Systems: Hardware Organization and Design,* John Wiley and Sons, New York, N.Y., 1973.

11. *International Symposium* on Computer Hardware Description Languages and Their Applications, 1975.

12. Jensen, J. E., *Dynamic Task Scheduling in a Shared Resource Multiprocessor,* Ph.D. Dissertation, University of Washington, 1976.

13. Knudsen, M. J., *PMSL, An Interactive Language for System-Level Description and Analysis of Computer Structures,* Ph.D. Dissertation, Carnegie-Mellon University, 1973.

14. Lunde, A., "More Data on the O/W Ratios", *Comp. Architecture News, 4,* (Mar. 1975), 9-13.

15. Lunde, A., "Empirical Evaluations of Some Features of Instruction Set Processor Architectures", *Comm. ACM, 20,* (Mar. 1977), 143-153.

16. Patil, S. S. and J. B. Dennis, "The Description and Realization of Digital Systems," *Compcon Digest,* 1972, 223-227.

17. Peterson, J. L., "Petri Nets", *Computing Surveys, 9,* (Sep. 1977), 223-252.

18. Rose, C. W., "LOGOS and the Software Engineer", *Proc. AFIPS 1972 Fall Joint Comp. Conf.,* 41, AFIPS Press, Montvale, N.J., 1972, 311-323.

19. Tanenbaum, A., "Implication of Structured Programming for Computer Architecture", *Comm. ACM, 21,* (Mar. 1978), 237-246.

Exercises

1. Give a PMS description of your computer installation. The level of detail should be comparable to that of Figure 2.5.

2. Give a partial ISP description of the main computer of Exercise 1. The level of detail should be comparable to that of Figure 2.8.

3.   Indicate the features of the processor described in Exercise 2 which cannot be accurately represented by ISP. Can you suggest enhancements to ISP to remedy the situation?

4.   Assume that your local computing resources consist of 3 installations located in different buildings. You intend to connect them in a local network and have prepared a Technical Report to that effect. Show how to lay out the first pages of this report as a PMS description of the network with little detail. What are the main components and their attributes that you would select to indicate?

5.   Give an ISP description of the instruction formats for the CDC 6600—CYBER 70 (cf. Figure 2.9).

6.   Give an ISP equivalent to the CDL program of Figure 2.11.

7.   Verify that the Petri Net of Figure 2.13 is neither live nor safe.

8.   Verify that the extended Petri Net of Figure 2.14 is live and safe.

9.   Show how one can test the absence of a token on a place by using conjunctive and disjunctive logic in an extended Petri Net.

Part II

THE BUILDING BLOCKS AND THEIR INTERACTIONS

We look before and after
And pine for what is not

Shelley

It isn't really
Anywhere!
It's somewhere else
Instead!

Alan Alexander Milne

Chapter 3

ARITHMETIC ALGORITHMS

The second part of this book, starting with this chapter, examines the main components of a computing system, first in a stand-alone fashion and then in connection with other components.

The heart of a computing system resides in the module(s) where information is massaged and transformed. In our PMS descriptions this focal point was simply called a Pc. The goal of the ISP notation was to elucidate the Pc's behavior from the programmer's viewpoint. But, as we saw earlier (recall Figure 2.2), Pc is an abbreviation for a number of submodules. In particular, data operators, D's, either as separate entities or in a unique arithmetic-logical unit (ALU), are those components where the numerical algorithms are performed. In this chapter, we consider the implementation of these algorithms, in a hardware sense, with no concern yet about how to interconnect and/or integrate the various operations (this will be done in the next chapter).

Before dealing with data transformations, we must discuss the internal representation of this data. We shall start by rapidly reviewing some numbering systems for the representation of integers and then look at the implementation of the four basic arithmetic operations (addition, subtraction, multiplication, and division). The next step will be to introduce floating-point formats and look at the four basic operations anew with real numbers in floating-point form. Some aspects of the ALU which deal with character, or alphanumeric, information will be covered to conclude this chapter.

Our approach is far from encyclopedic. We shall mostly be concerned with efficient implementations and not with a history of digital system design. We shall also restrict ourselves to algorithms which are cost-effective and implementable for word lengths of current interest, and therefore will not be concerned with algorithms which are more powerful theoretically but only when the number of bits is sufficiently large. Similarly, we shall simply mention numbering systems which can be extremely advantageous in some special situations but which lose most of their appeal in general applications. The bibliography at the end of the chapter will provide pointers to references the interested reader should consult.

3.1 NUMBER SYSTEMS

3.1.1 Positional Number Systems

The great majority of digital computers use positional number systems to represent numerical information. In this mode of representation, a number is encoded as a vector of digits where each digit is weighted according to its position. Associated with the number system is a *base* (or radix) b such that the range of each digit is from 0 to $b - 1$. Therefore, a number x in base b is represented as follows:

$$x = (x_n, x_{n-1}, \ldots, x_i, \ldots, x_1, x_0, x_{-1}, \ldots, x_{-m})$$

with its value (we consider only positive numbers for the time being) denoted $|x|$:

$$|x| = \sum_{i=-m}^{n} x_i b^i$$

Integers are such that only terms with non-negative powers of the base are taken in the summation; only negative ones are required for fractions.

The main positional system in use by humans is the decimal system ($b = 10$). The ordinary representation is in the form of strings of digits with a decimal point separating the integer and fraction parts. Although decimal machines have been built, all modern computers use the binary system ($b = 2$). The disadvantage of having to convert from the externally used decimal to the internal binary is more than compensated for by the gains in storage efficiency and the ease in implementing the basic operations. In contrast to the paper representation, the fractional point is simply implied within the computer's internal encoding.

Storage structures, that is registers and memory cells, are of finite length and therefore the range of representable numbers is itself limited. For a positional number system in base b with n positions (where b and n are integers), we can consider b^n to be the precision or "number of numbers" which can be accommodated. For each position there is a requirement of b symbols, so that we can define:

$$E = nb$$

as a measure of storage efficiency. We want to minimize E under the constraint of a given precision:

$$N = b^n$$

i.e., we want to choose b such that:

$$E = nb = b \ln N / \ln b$$

is minimal (where ln is the natural logarithm).

Differentiating with respect to b yields:

$$\frac{dE}{db} = \frac{\ln N(\ln b - 1)}{(\ln b)^2}$$

which is null for $\ln b = 1$, or $b = e$ (the naperian base of value $2.73..$). It can be easily verified that we have a minimum for this choice.

Evidently a radix must be an integer. From the storage efficiency viewpoint, base 3 is slightly superior to base 2 since $3/\ln 3$ is smaller than $2/\ln 2$. But because bistable electronic devices are certainly more common than tristable ones, a radix 2 is far more appealing. From a practical standpoint it is the only logical choice for a digital system.

As pointed out before, the human mind is accustomed to the decimal notation. Reading and writing lengthy strings of 0's and 1's, the two binary digits or bits used in the binary system, is not only extremely unpleasant and cumbersome but it is also an error prone process. To facilitate communication between the binary internal representation and some notation more akin to our way of thinking, octal ($b = 8$) and hexadecimal ($b = 16$) have often been employed. The associated compacting factors of three for octal and four for hexadecimal (in terms of representation as compared with binary) are an enormous asset, especially for system programmers with respect to memory dumps. Since these number systems have bases which are powers of 2, the conversions between binary and octal or hexadecimal are trivial. The choice between octal and hexadecimal is dictated by the word length, that is on being a multiple of 3 or 4, and, in case it is both, on ancillary issues such as the number of bits used for encoding characters.

The more general problem of converting a number written in source base b_s to a number in destination base b_d can be handled in several ways.

The common methods use either division or multiplication. We have to distinguish between integer and fraction conversion.

a) Conversion of integers

Let $(x_n, x_{n-1}, \ldots, x_i, \ldots, x_0)$ be an integer in base b_s and $(X_m, X_{m-1}, \ldots, X_j, \ldots, X_0)$ its conversion in radix b_d.

i) Multiplication method (using b_d arithmetic).

We perform the summation:

$$|X| = \sum_{i=0}^{n} x_i b_s^i$$

in radix b_d arithmetic.

Example 3.1 Let $x = 7632$ in octal or $x = (7632)_8$ (we use conventional rather than vector-like representations). Converting to decimal yields:

$$|X| = (((7 \cdot 8 + 6) \cdot 8 + 3) \cdot 8 + 2) \text{ (using Horner's rule)}$$

or $X = 3994$ in decimal. □

ii) Division method (using b_s arithmetic)

We have $X_0 = |x| \bmod b_d$ where the division is performed in radix b_s. Continuing in the same fashion for successive digits, from the least to the most significant, we have:

$$x = Q_0 b_d + X_0,$$

$$Q_0 = Q_1 b_d + X_1, \quad \text{etc.}$$

The procedure terminates with the X_i' such that $Q_i = 0$.

($\lfloor x \rfloor$ is the floor of x, i.e., the largest integer smaller than or equal to x. We shall also use $\lceil x \rceil$ as the ceiling or smallest integer greater than or equal to x).

Example 3.2 Converting $x = (7632)_8$ to decimal.

We have $X_0 = 7632 \bmod 12$, where the division is performed in octal, and the remainder is an octal number. The reader can verify that:

$$X_0 = 7632 \bmod 12 = (4)_8 = 4 \text{ and } \lfloor 7632/12 \rfloor = 617$$

$$X_1 = 617 \bmod 12 = (11)_8 = 9 \text{ and } \lfloor 617/12 \rfloor = 47$$

$$X_2 = 47 \bmod 12 = (11)_8 = 9 \text{ and } \lfloor 47/12 \rfloor = 3$$

$$X_3 = 3 \bmod 12 = (3)_8 = 3$$

and $X = 3994$. $\qquad\qquad\qquad\qquad\qquad\qquad\qquad\qquad$ □

b) Conversion of fractions

We have now $x = (x_{-1}, x_{-2}, \ldots, x_{-n})$ and we want to find the conversion $X = (X_{-1}, X_{-2}, \ldots, X_{-m})$. The first important observation to make here is that a fraction represented with a finite number of digits in base b_s does not necessarily have a terminating representation in base b_d. However, we can get the first m digits of the conversion by again using either multiplication or division.

i) Multiplication method (using b_s arithmetic)

We multiply by b_d obtaining:

$$X_{-1} = \lfloor |x| b_d \rfloor$$

The fractional part of $|x| b_d$, say $^-X_{-1}$ is then used to compute:

$$X_{-2} = \lfloor ^-X_{-1} b_d \rfloor \text{ and } ^-X_{-2}$$

and so on with:

$$X_{-i} = \lfloor ^-X_{-(i-1)} b_d \rfloor \text{ and } ^-X_{-i} \text{ being}$$

$$^-X_{-i} = X_{-(i-1)} b_d - X_{-i}.$$

Example 3.3 Let $x = (.7632)_8$ to be converted to decimal with four fractional digits.

$$.7632 \cdot 12 = (11.6004)_8 \text{ yielding } X_{-1} = 9$$

$$.6004 \cdot 12 = (7.405)_8 \text{ yielding } X_{-2} = 7$$

$$.405 \cdot 12 = (5.062)_8 \text{ yielding } X_{-3} = 5$$

$$.062 \cdot 12 = (0.764)_8 \text{ yielding } X_{-4} = 0$$

hence $X = .9750\ldots$. $\qquad\qquad\qquad\qquad\qquad\qquad\qquad\qquad$ □

ii) Division method (using b_d arithmetic).

We simply divide $|x|$ by b_s using b_d arithmetic.

Example 3.4 As before let us convert $x = (.7632)_8$ to decimal. This can be written:

$$(((2/8 + 3)/8 + 6)/8 + 7)8 = .9750 \ldots . \qquad \square$$

Thus, to convert a number from one base to another we have the choice of two methods for integers and two methods for fractions, that is 4 possible algorithms. Most often we will wish to convert from binary (or octal or hexadecimal) to decimal and vice-versa. For hand calculations we are more comfortable with decimal arithmetic and will tend to favor methods a(i) and b(ii) when converting from binary to decimal, and methods a(ii) and b(i) when converting from decimal to binary. When the process is automated by program, or microprogram, divisions should be avoided and binary arithmetic is preferable. Since we cannot always use binary multiplication, table look-ups can be inserted as well as tricks such as the simulation of decimal arithmetic by binary processes. For example, multiplying a binary number by 10 can be performed by shifting left 3 places (multiplication by 8) and adding the original number twice (cf. Exercises 1 and 2).

3.1.2 Integer Representation

If only positive integers were to be represented, an n-bit word would allow a range of 0 to $2^n - 1$. With the need to represent both positive and negative numbers the 2^n possibilities have to be encoded such that there will be equal (or almost equal) intervals for both signs, an easy way of distinguishing between positive and negative entities, i.e., an easy sign test, a simple detection of 0, and efficient ways of performing the four basic operations. This latter constraint can be reduced to the handling of addition and subtraction as we shall see later in this chapter. Three positional numbering systems have been used to this effect: sign and magnitude, one's complement, and two's complement. All three permit an easy sign test by checking a single bit. The other criteria lead to important differences.

Sign and magnitude

In this representation, a designated bit, in general the leftmost one, indicates the sign of the integer (0 for $+$, 1 for $-$). The interval of representation is therefore $[-(2^{n-1} - 1), 2^{n-1} - 1]$. One of the inconveniences is the dual representation of 0, namely $+0$, or true zero, and -0 (notice that the conventional human system is decimal sign and magnitude and that we are not overly bothered by this dual representation of 0). The real trouble with sign and magnitude comes during the addition of numbers of opposite signs because we have to compare their magnitudes in order to know the sign of the result. This will not be required in the other two systems.

Sign and magnitude was quite common in computers up to the third generation. For example, it was the system used in the IBM 7000 series. Today it is still frequent in the representation of mantissas in floating-point formats (cf. Section 4 in this chapter).

One's complement

One's (or 1's) complement is the binary case of the more general diminished radix complement system (DRC). Non-negative integers in the interval $[0, 2^{n-1} - 1]$ are represented as in a binary positional system. To represent negative integers in the interval $[-(2^{n-1} - 1), 0]$, we first represent their absolute values as above and then complement bit by bit, i.e., replace 0's by 1's and 1's by 0's. More generally, for a positional system in base b, we replace each digit x_i by $(b - 1) - x_i$. For the decimal system, we have a 9's complement representation and in hexadecimal a F's complement (where A, B, ..., F are the hexadecimal symbols for 10, 11, ..., 15).

As in sign and magnitude, sign recognition is trivial since the leftmost bit is 0 for positive integers and 1 for negative ones. Unhappily we still have a dual representation of 0, since an n-bit word full of 0's is complemented in a word full of 1's. But, as will be seen in Section 2, addition and subtraction are simple to implement by comparison with sign and magnitude. Complementation requires only a bit by bit process.

Two's complement

Two's (or 2's) complement is the binary case for the radix complement system (RC). Non-negative numbers in the range $[0, 2^{n-1} - 1]$ are represented as in the DRC system. A negative integer x of absolute value $|x|$ is represented as if it were a positive integer of value $2^n - |x|$, where of course n is the number of bits in the word. For all practical purposes, each bit is complemented as in the 1's complement representation and a 1 is added in the least significant position (this requires an addition which can involve all n bits). In a positional number system of base b, the complement of a positive integer x is found in the same manner, that is by complementing in the DRC fashion and adding 1 in the least significant digit. The pseudo-positive number resulting in the operation is $b^n - |x|$ since:

$$\sum_{i=0}^{n-1} (b - 1 - x_i)b^i + 1 = (b - 1)(1 + b + \cdots + b^{n-1}) - |x| + 1$$

$$= b^n - |x|$$

The sign test is as in the two other number systems. There is a unique representation of 0 since a string of 0's complements itself. (The reader who wishes to verify this assertion might be bothered by the carry-out from the sign bit which has all the appearances of an overflow. This carry can be discarded as will be shown in some detail in the next section.) The interval of representation is $[-2^{n-1}, 2^{n-1} - 1]$ with -2^{n-1} represented by a 1 followed by $n - 1$ 0's (note that it is also self-complementing but this is not a problem since 2^{n-1} is not in the allowed range of representation). Addition and subtraction will be slightly simpler than in 1's complement but, as is readily observed, complementation is somewhat more difficult.

The following example illustrates the encoding of integers in these three systems.

Example 3.5 Assume that we have a 4-bit word ($n = 4$). Then the numbers $+6$ and -6 have the following representations in the three systems just discussed:

	$+6$	-6
sign and magnitude	0110	1110
one's complement	0110	1001
two's complement	0110	1010

□

The greater ease in addition and subtraction is amplified when multiplication and division are considered. This is one of the reasons, coupled with the unique representation of 0, why 2's complement seems to be currently preferred. Of the major computers in service today, only the CDC 6000 and Univac 1100 series use 1's complement. But Seymour Cray, designer of the CDC 6600, seems to have changed his mind: his latest machine, the superpowerful CRAY-1, uses 2's complement.

3.1.3   Other Number Systems

Single base positional number systems are not the only ones of interest, whether they are intended for human use, digital computer internal representation, or mathematicians. For example, we use a mixed radix (positional) system to keep track of time. Several non-positional systems are commonly used, in conjunction with binary. Table 3.1 illustrates three of them.

The *Binary-Coded Decimal* (*BCD*) system is such that it encodes a string of n decimal digits into a string of n 4-bit entities which are the binary translations of the individual digits. The storage efficiency is only 10/16th of the binary scheme. The ease in conversion from decimal to BCD has made this system attractive for the implementation of decimal instructions using a decimal data referent. If signed numbers are to be considered then an extra bit is necessary. Since the length of computer words has never been of the form $4n + 1$, an extra 3 bits will be wasted. Arithmetic operations are performed by combining binary rules for the operations on single digits and decimal rules for carries.

A variation on BCD is the *excess-3 code*. Here, each decimal digit, again a 4-bit entity, is its BCD encoding to which has been added 3. For example, 8 is 1000 in BCD and 1011 in excess-3. An advantage of the excess-3 code is that a 1's complement of the whole word yields a 9's complement in excess-3. For example, 0100 is the complement of 8 and is the excess-3 code for 1. A second, and maybe more interesting, property of

Table 3.1   Some non-positional number systems

	BCD	Excess-3	Gray code
0	0000	0011	0000
1	0001	0100	0001
2	0010	0101	0011
3	0011	0110	0010
4	0100	0111	0110
5	0101	1000	0111
6	0110	1001	0101
7	0111	1010	0100
8	1000	1011	1100
9	1001	1100	1101

this system is that binary carries out of the individual digits correspond to decimal carries. This is so since adding two digits in excess-3 code will yield an excess of 6. Hence, if the result were greater than 9 (or 1111) a decimal carry should be generated. The binary addition will provide the same effect. The reader can verify that the addition rules for the excess-3 code are such that, if there is no carry out of the leftmost position when adding two excess-3 digits in binary, then one should subtract 3, while if a carry is generated 3 has to be added (cf. Exercise 3).

Another series of codes which have been useful are the *Gray codes*. Table 3.1 shows one of them called *reflected binary*. In this non-positional system, the codes of two consecutive integers differ by only a single bit. This property is advantageous when one wants to digitize a continuous and slowly varying process, as for example in some analog, or mechanical, to digital translations.

The *residue number system* has attracted much theoretical attention. The basic idea is to represent an integer x of value $|x|$ as a vector of digits:

$$x = (x_n, x_{n-1}, \ldots, x_1),$$

where each x_i is computed as

$$x_i = |x| \bmod m_i$$

with m_n, m_{n-1}, $\ldots$, m_1 being positive integers containing no common factors.

Example 3.6 In the residue system with $m_2 = 5$ and $m_1 = 3$ the decimal integer 13 has the representation $(3, 1)$, since $13 \bmod 5 = 3$ and $13 \bmod 3 = 1$. ▢

The conversion from a positional to a residue system presents no difficulty. But the opposite conversion is not simple. That a unique solution exists is a consequence of the *Chinese Remainder Theorem* that we state without proof (cf. Exercise 4).

Theorem Let m_1, m_2, $\ldots$, m_n be positive integers relatively prime in pairs, i.e., m_i and m_j have no common factors for all i and j such that $i \neq j$, and let $m = m_1 \cdot m_2 \cdots m_n$. Then for integers a, x_1, x_2, $\ldots$, x_n there exists a unique number $|x|$ such that:

$$a \leq |x| < a + m \text{ and } x_i = |x| \bmod m_i \quad 1 \leq i \leq n.$$

If we let $a = 0$ and let each x_i be less than m_i we have a representation of nonnegative integers in the interval $[0, m - 1]$. By letting $a = -m/2$, we have a representation for both positive and negative integers.

The residue number system is such that addition, subtraction and multiplication can be performed on a digit by digit basis without any need for carry, that is:

$$(x_n, x_{n-1}, \ldots, x_1) *(y_n, y_{n-1}, \ldots, y_1) =$$

$$((x_n *y_n) \bmod m_n, (x_{n-1} *y_{n-1}) \bmod m_{n-1}, \ldots, (x_1 *y_1) \bmod m_1)$$

where $*$ is either $+$, $-$, or $\times$.

Besides the conversion problem, the other disadvantages of the residue number system are in the difficulties in sign testing, in comparing the magnitudes of two numbers, and in performing division. The absence of carry propagation for the three other operations is particularly well suited for processing in parallel of all digits in a synchronous fashion. However, to our knowledge, the disadvantages listed above have always prevented an industrial implementation.

3.2 ADDITION AND SUBTRACTION

3.2.1 Addition in Positional Number Systems

Given a positional number system in base b, the addition of two n-digit positive numbers, the addend x and the augend y:

$$x = (x_{n-1}, \ldots, x_1, x_0), \qquad y = (y_{n-1}, \ldots, y_1, y_0),$$

results in a sum $s = (s_n, s_{n-1}, \ldots, s_1, s_0)$ where s_n can only take one of the two values 0 or 1 independently of b. When s_n is 1, it will often be considered as an *overflow*. The addition algorithm can be expressed (in a Pascal-like notation) as:

1. $c_0 \leftarrow 0$ (c_0 is the initial carry-in);
2. **For** $i: = 0$ **step** 1 **until** $n - 1$ **do**
   begin
   $\qquad s_i \leftarrow (x_i + y_i + c_i) \bmod b$;
   $\qquad c_{i+1} \leftarrow \lfloor (x_i + y_i + c_i)/b \rfloor$
   end;
3. $s_n \leftarrow c_n$;

Since $x_i + y_i \leq 2(b - 1)$ and the initial $c_0 = 0$, the maximum value for any c_i will be $\lfloor (2(b - 1)+1)/b \rfloor = 1$.

In this algorithm each digit is examined once. Hence, the process is of complexity $O(n)$ (we say that a function $g(n)$ is of complexity order $f(n)$, written $O(f(n))$, if there exists a constant k such that $g(n) \leq kf(n)$ for all but some finite (possibly empty) set of values of n ($n \geq 0$). Thus, saying that the addition algorithm is $O(n)$ is synonymous to saying that it runs in a number of steps proportional to n). Since all digits have to be examined, no theoretical improvement can be expected. But, naturally, implementation considerations are important for hardware realizations.

We can easily design a similar algorithm for subtracting a subtrahend y from x with generation of borrows instead of carries at each digit subtraction. Hardware considerations and the complement number systems already introduced render unnecessary the distinction between addition and subtraction, as we shall see in the next section.

For the binary case, we can translate step 2 of the algorithm in terms of true (1) and false (0) boolean values as:

$$s_i \leftarrow (x_i \oplus y_i) \oplus c_i \ (\oplus \text{ is the exclusive-or operator});\qquad(1)$$
$$c_{i+1} \leftarrow x_i \cdot y_i + (x_i + y_i) \cdot c_i \ (\cdot \text{ and } + \text{ are the logical AND and OR}).$$

Many direct realizations of system (1) are possible. The choice will depend on the availability of the type of gates: OR, AND, NOT, NAND, NOR, EOR etc. . . . . In general, the implementation of a 1-bit full adder will be performed by connecting two half-adders as shown in Figure 3.1.a. A half-adder with inputs A and B realizes the two outputs:

$$S \leftarrow A \oplus B$$
$$C \leftarrow A \cdot B.$$

The system (1) is then constructed as shown in Figure 3.2 since we can write c_{i+1} as:

$$c_{i+1} \leftarrow x_i \cdot y_i + (x_i \oplus y_i) \cdot c_i\qquad(1')$$

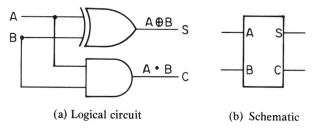

(a) Logical circuit   (b) Schematic

Figure 3.1 Half-adder

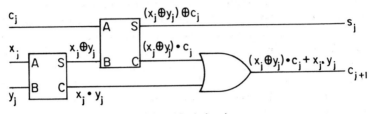

(a) Logical circuit

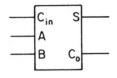

(b) Schematic

Figure 3.2   Full adder

Full adders are available from all Integrated Circuit manufacturers. As we shall see, a full adder is too small a building block for most ALU's since progress in medium to large scale integration has permitted designers to conceive of more powerful constructs on a single chip.

A single full adder and a 1-bit storage device, or flip-flop, to retain the potential carry are sufficient for a hardware implementation of the addition algorithm. If we assume that the inputs and outputs are in shift registers, or that selection circuits exist to obtain the n digits serially, then the addition may proceed exactly as in the algorithm. Serial adders are not used in the design of central processors or ALU's because they are too slow and too cumbersome or restrictive. However they are conceivably useful in serial devices like magnetic bubble logic or CCD memories.

3.2.2   Addition and Subtraction of Signed Integers

Before turning our attention to the design of parallel adders, we state the rules for addition and subtraction for the binary systems discussed previously. Let x be the augend, y the addend or subtrahend, and s the result. All three numbers are contained in n-bit registers, the nth bit being the sign bit, that is:

$$x = (x_n, \ldots, x_2, x_1), \qquad y = (y_n, \ldots, y_2, y_1), \qquad s = (s_n, \ldots, s_2, s_1)$$

Sign and magnitude

If the numbers are of the same sign $(x_n = y_n)$, the sum is also of the same sign. We add the $(n - 1)$-bit magnitudes according to system (1) and set s_n to x_n. If c_n is 1 we have a magnitude which cannot be encoded with $(n - 1)$ bits; this is called an *overflow*.

If x and y are of different signs $(x_n \neq y_n)$ we have to find which of the two magnitudes is largest. If it is x, then we subtract y from x and set s_n to x_n. Otherwise we do the opposite. In order to avoid this magnitude check we can use the following modification.

Let us always subtract y from x when the two numbers are of different signs. The result s and borrow b are given by:

$$s_i \leftarrow x_i \oplus y_i \oplus b_i \qquad 1 \leq i \leq n - 1, b_1 = 0$$

$$b_{i+1} \leftarrow \bar{x}_i \cdot y_i + (\bar{x}_i + y_i) \cdot b_i. \tag{2}$$

If $x_n = 0$, $y_n = 1$, $(x \geq 0, y < 0)$, and $b_n = 0$, i.e., there is no generated borrow in the last position, then $|x| > |y|$ and the result is correct. We can set s_n to 0. If $b_n = 1$, that is $|x| < |y|$, then the result, negative, is the 2's complement of the true magnitude (cf. Exercise 5). In this second case we set s_n to 1 and take the 2's complement of the magnitude.

If $x < 0$ and $y \geq 0$ and $|x| > |y|$ the correct result is generated by the subtraction. If the contrary is true, then we have to repeat the steps of the above paragraph modified for this particular case. It should be remarked that a "negative" 0 can be generated when $x < 0$ and $y = -x$.

In summary we can write the algorithm:

1. **If** subtraction **then** set $y_n \leftarrow \bar{y}_n$;
2. **If** $x_n = y_n$ **then**
   begin add magnitudes according to system (1);
           If $c_n = 1$ **then** overflow **else** $s_n \leftarrow x_n$
   end;
3. **If** $x_n \neq y_n$ **then**
   begin subtract magnitude of y from that of x
           according to system (2);
           If $b_n = 0$ **then** $s_n \leftarrow x_n$
           else $s_n \leftarrow y_n$ and 2's complement $(s_{n-1}, \ldots, s_1)$;
   end;

One's complement

The addition process consists of first performing the operations laid out in system (1) with $1 \le i \le n$ (that is the sign bits are also added). Then, if a carry-out is generated, i.e., if c_{n+1} is 1, it is added to the result. In practical realizations this end-around carry, the line out of the last adder, will be connected to the initial carry c_1. To justify this procedure we have to consider the following three cases. (Subtraction is handled like addition by simply taking the one's complement of the subtrahend and adding. If both true and false values are available from the contents of a register this requires no extra time delay.)

1. Both operands positive: **then** $c_{n+1} = 0$;
       if $s_n = 1$ **then** overflow;
2. Operands of different signs: **if** $c_{n+1} = 0$ **then** end
       else add 1 (end-around carry);
3. Both operands negative: **then** $c_{n+1} = 1$ and 1 is added
       (or c_1 is set to 1 initially); **if** $s_n = 0$ **then** overflow.

The overflow conditions in cases 1 and 3 are evident. Of course no overflow can occur in case 2. To show the correctness of the procedure, recall that a negative number x has for 1's complement representation the n-bit "positive number" $2^n - 1 - |x|$ where $|x|$ is the absolute value of x. Also, any result which looks like a magnitude greater than $2^n - 1$ will generate a carry-out of the leftmost position of the word. In other words, c_{n+1} will be 1.

Analyzing case by case we have:

- Case 1. $x \ge 0$, $y \ge 0$. The result is $|x| + |y|$ which represents the positive number $x + y$.
- Case 2. $x > 0$, $y \le 0$ or $x < 0$, $y \ge 0$. These two subcases are treated similarly and we proceed only with the first one. We still have to distinguish (for analysis sake only and not in the algorithm) between the subcases $|x| > |y|$ and $|x| < |y|$.

(i) $|x| > |y|$. Then the desired result is $|x| - |y|$.

The sum yields $|x| + 2^n - 1 - |y|$. Since $|x| > |y|$, a carry-out will be generated and a 1 added. That is we subtract 2^n (the carry-out) and add 1 (end-around carry) resulting in:

$$|x| + 2^n - 1 - |y| - 2^n + 1 = |x| - |y|,$$

the desired result.

(ii) $|x| < |y|$. Then the desired representation is $2^n - 1 + (|x| - |y|)$.

Proceeding as above yields:

$$2^n - 1 + |x| - |y|$$

with no carry-out. This is the desired result.

Note that in (i), $x_n = 0$, $y_n = 1$, and $c_{n+1} = 1$ implies that $c_n = 1$ and hence $s_n = 0$ (cf. system (1)). In the same manner, we see that s_n will be set to 1 in case (ii). Another important point to note is that when $x = -y$, and x and y are added, then the negative 0 will be obtained.

- Case 3. $x < 0$, $y < 0$. Now the desired result is $2^n - 1 - (|x| + |y|)$. The sum yields:

$$2^n - 1 - |x| + 2^n - 1 - |y|.$$

A carry-out is generated. Suppressing it and adding 1 yields:

$$2^n - 1 - (|x| + |y|)$$

the desired representation.

Returning to cases 1 and 3, we see that we have an overflow if the signs are the same and either:

$$s_n = 1 \text{ and } c_{n+1} = 0 \text{ (case 1), or}$$

$$s_n = 0 \text{ and } c_{n+1} = 1 \text{ (case 3).}$$

But in case 1 for s_n to be 1, c_n has to be 1 and conversely for s_n to be 0 in case 3, c_n has to be 0. Hence we have:

$$\text{overflow} \leftarrow c_n \oplus c_{n+1}.$$

As mentioned in the discussion of case 3, the null value generated through addition will be a "negative" 0. In order to avoid this we can use a subtractor instead of an adder. That is, if the operation called for is an addition we complement one of the operands and subtract it from the other, while if the operation is a subtraction we go on without complementing. As a matter of fact, we can now use a system similar to system (2) instead of system (1) and obtain the "true" 0 (cf. Exercise 6).

Two's complement

This analysis proceeds in the same way as in the 1's complement case. The difference is that when x is negative its representation is the "pseudo-positive number" $2^n - |x|$. Again we can distinguish 3 cases.

- Case 1. Both operands positive. As in 1's complement.
- Case 2. Operands of different signs.
  If $x > 0$, $y \leq 0$, $|x| > |y|$ the sum is $|x| + 2^n - |y|$. The carry out is discarded (subtraction of 2^n) and the result is correct. If $|x| < |y|$ the sum is a negative number, there will be no carry out and the representation is correct. It is easily verified that discarding the carry-out yields correct results for the case where $x \leq 0$, $y > 0$.
- Case 3. Both operands negative. Then the sum is $2^n - |x| + 2^n - |y|$. Again discarding the carry-out yields $2^n - (|x| + |y|)$, the desired representation.

Overflow detection is as in the 1's complement system. The main difference that can be observed in the arithmetic rules for the 1's and 2's complement is in the treatment of the carry-out which is simply discarded in the latter system and ended-around in the former. We should also remark that subtraction is no more complex in 2's complement than in 1's complement since the subtrahend can be 1's complemented and a carry-in c_1 of 1 instead of 0 be input to the rightmost addition block.

The addition-subtraction algorithm of the sign and magnitude system can be further modified in such a way that a 2's complement adder is sufficient. When the operands are of the same sign (for an addition, or of opposite signs for a subtraction), there is no change to the previous algorithm. When the operands are of different signs (we assume $x > 0$, $y < 0$ and an addition), we take the 2's complement of the magnitude of y and add it to the magnitude of x. If a carry-out is generated ($c_n = 1$) then $|x|$ was greater than $|y|$ and the result is correct. It remains to set s_n to 0. On the other hand if no carry-out was generated, then the 2's complement of the result is the true magnitude. We also have to set s_n to 1. Analysis of the remaining possibilities follows the same patterns as those of the previous paragraphs.

In our discussion of hardware implementations of adders, we shall restrict ourselves to the 2's complement system. There is no inherent difficulty in modifying the designs so that they can be applied to the other two systems.

3.2.3 Parallel Adders

Ripple adder

Instead of having all bits of the operands pass sequentially through a single full-adder, we can present the n bits of the 2 operands in parallel to n full-adders. These full-adders are connected in such a way that the carry-out from full-adder i, c_{i+1}, is the carry-in for full-adder $i + 1$, for $1 \le i \le n - 1$. There is an input line from the outside to the carry-in c_1 and an output connection giving c_{n+1}. A schematic description of an adder of this type is shown in Figure 3.3 for a 4-bit adder. Figure 3.4 is a functional diagram for the same adder as can be found in a catalog of integrated circuits.

Because a carry can be propagated from c_1 to the last sum and carry outputs, that is ripple through the n full-adders (hence the name ripple adder), the worst case timing is n full-adder levels. If we were to design a synchronous ALU, this is the time that we would have to choose for the completion of an addition. If the adder is self-timing or asynchronous, and if a signal can be delivered when all outputs are stable, then we will not have to wait that long. It has been shown (experimentally) that on the average the longest carry transition sequence passes through $\log (5n/4)$ adders (where log is the logarithm in base 2; unless otherwise specified we shall keep this notation). This $O (\log n)$ figure for the asynchronous adder compared to the $O(n)$ of the synchronous ripple adder seems to indicate a strong advantage for the asynchronous approach. However, there are disadvantages in having to sense the completion, which increases hard-

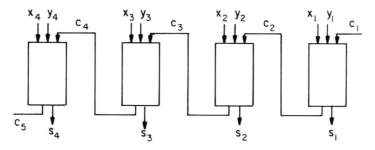

Figure 3.3 Ripple adder (schema)

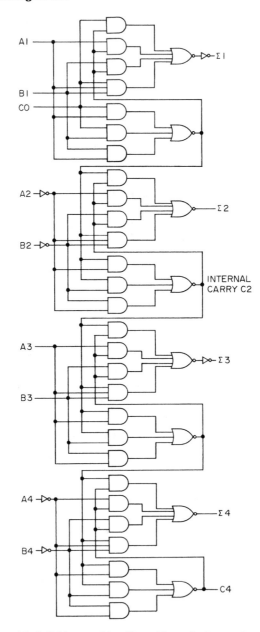

Figure 3.4   Four-bit full binary adder (from Texas Instruments catalog SN74LS83 functional block diagram)

ware requirements and decreases speed, and in ensuring that stabilization has been reached. For these reasons, asynchronous logic at this level has seldom been used.

Carry look-ahead adders

If we examine how a carry ripples from full-adder i to full-adder $i + 1$, i.e., if we examine equation (1'), we see that the transmission can be decomposed into:

carry generation:	$g_{i+1} \leftarrow x_i \cdot y_i$;
carry propagation:	$p_{i+1} \leftarrow x_i \oplus y_i$;
and	$c_{i+1} \leftarrow g_{i+1} + p_{i+1} \cdot c_i$.

Starting with an initial carry-in c_1, or $g_1 = c_1$, we have the recurrence:

$$c_{i+1} \leftarrow g_{i+1} + \sum_{j=1}^{i} \left(\prod_{k=j+1}^{i+1} p_k \right) \cdot g_j \tag{3}$$

(Σ and Π are the logical OR and AND operators).
For example, for a 4-bit adder we would have:

$c_2 \leftarrow g_2 + (p_2 \cdot c_1)$

$c_3 \leftarrow g_3 + (p_3 \cdot g_2 + p_3 \cdot p_2 \cdot c_1)$

$c_4 \leftarrow g_4 + (p_4 \cdot g_3 + p_4 \cdot p_3 \cdot g_2 + p_4 \cdot p_3 \cdot p_2 \cdot c_1)$

$c_5 \leftarrow g_5 + (p_5 \cdot g_4 + p_5 \cdot p_4 \cdot g_3 + p_5 \cdot p_4 \cdot p_3 \cdot g_2 + p_5 \cdot p_4 \cdot p_3 \cdot p_2 \cdot c_1)$

Each of the c_i's is now a two-level expression in x_j, y_j, and c_1, $1 \le j \le i$. The terms in parentheses are the propagate terms. The logical lay-out of a typical 4-bit adder of this type, called carry look-ahead (CLA) because a carry can be generated or predicted before its corresponding sum bit has been obtained, is shown in Figure 3.5. There is approximately the same number of gates as in the ripple adder of Figure 3.4 but the worst case timing is now 4 (gate) levels instead of 8. According to the manufacturer, the speed increase is 3-fold.

The fan-in fan-out restrictions in circuitry prevent a direct extension of system (3) to adders for large word lengths. In the same manner as full-adders are cascaded into a ripple adder, CLA's can be connected with the

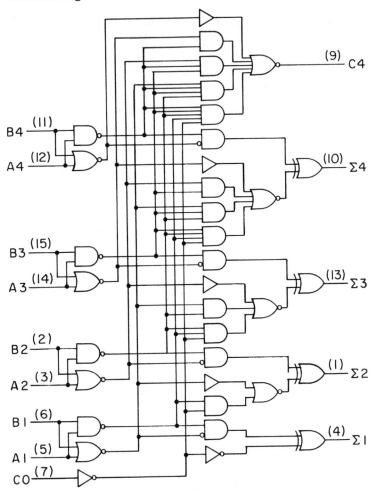

Figure 3.5   Four-bit carry look-ahead adder (from Texas Instruments catalog SN74LS283 functional block diagram)

carry-out from one being the carry-in of the next. Figure 3.6 is a schematic description of such an arrangement. A carry look-ahead box is the equivalent of a 4-bit CLA with the carry-out generated as in (3).

This concept can be extended to several levels. We can group the n bits into A groups of b bits, and generate a G term, and a P term for each group. For example, for group a (bits $(a - 1)b + 1$ to ab), we have:

$$P_a \leftarrow \prod_{i=(a-1)b+2}^{ab+1} p_i, \qquad G_a \leftarrow \sum_{j=(a-1)b+1}^{ab} \left(\prod_{i=j+1}^{ab+1} p_i \right)\cdot g_j + g_{ab+1} \qquad (4)$$

The carry-out of group a, denoted by C_a is then:

$$C_a \leftarrow G_a + \sum_{j=1}^{a-1} \left(\prod_{i=j+1}^{a} P_i \right)\cdot G_j, \qquad (5)$$

and therefore the carry at position k $(k = ab + 1 + m,\ 0 \le m \le b - 1)$ is:

$$c_k \leftarrow g_k + \sum_{j=ab+2}^{k-1} \left(\prod_{i=j+1}^{k} p_i \right)\cdot g_j + \prod_{i=ab+2}^{k} p_i \cdot C_a. \qquad (6)$$

In most medium to large Pc's, the ALU contains CLA's grouped as above. For example the CDC 6600 (word length 60 bits) has groups of 3 bits, with the groups combined in 4's to make 5 sections which are finally combined together. In the IBM 360/91 (floating-point adder,

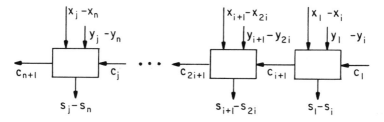

Figure 3.6   One-level Carry-Look-Ahead adder

mantissa of 56 bits), there are sections of 2 groups of 4 bits, while in the integer adder of System 370/158 there are 2 sections of 4 groups of 4 bits. For a 100 bit adder, a 15-fold speed up over a ripple adder can be obtained with an increase of 40 percent in switching elements.

Carry-save adders

If instead of having to add only two operands, we need to add m of them, $m > 2$, as for example in multiplication, we can speed-up this cumulative operation by letting the carry propagation happen only during the last addition. We again use n full-adders but, instead of connecting them as in the ripple adder, we leave them unconnected and take as input three of the m operands, say x, y, and z. The two outputs generated:

$$ss_i \leftarrow x_i \oplus y_i \oplus z_i,$$

$$cs_{i+1} \leftarrow x_i \cdot y_i + (x_i \oplus y_i) \cdot z_i, \tag{7}$$

along with another of the original inputs can be considered as inputs to another (or the same) block performing the operations of system (7). This process is repeated until only two operands, or partial sums, are left. The last addition requires a ripple adder (or any adder implementing system (1)).

We shall see in the next section how several stages of carry-save adders can be efficiently connected for the implementation of fast multiplication.

3.3 MULTIPLICATION AND DIVISION

3.3.1 The Multiplication Scheme

Given two n-digit positive integers, the multiplicand x and the multiplier y, represented in a positional number system of radix b, say:

$$x = (x_{n-1}, \ldots, x_0), \text{ and } y = (y_{n-1}, \ldots, y_0)$$

their product p is a $2n$-digit positive number:

$$p = (p_{2n-1}, \ldots, p_0)$$

which can be obtained by the following algorithm.

1. Set $p_j \leftarrow 0$, $0 \le j < 2n$;
2. **For** $i: = 0$ **step** 1 **until** $n - 1$ **do**
3. **If** $y_i \ne 0$ **then begin** $k \leftarrow 0$;

          For $j: = 0$ **step** 1 **until** $n - 1$ **do**

            begin $t \leftarrow x_j \cdot y_i + p_{i+j} + k$; ($*$ In base b $*$)

               $p_{i+j} \leftarrow t \bmod b$; $k \leftarrow \lfloor t/b \rfloor$

            end; ($*$ of For j $*$)

            $p_{i+n} \leftarrow k$

      end;

This is the usual right to left paper and pencil method with the accumulation of digits being done as soon as possible instead of letting all partial products be developed and added at the end. Because of the nested loops on i and j, it is easy to see that we have an $O(n^2)$ process. While the $O(n)$ addition scheme cannot be improved upon for the reasons we have already mentioned, this is not the case for multiplication. Numerous investigations have taken place on how "fast" we can multiply. From the theoretical computer scientist's viewpoint, the measure of interest is the number of digit multiplications without concern for overhead and operations such as addition and shifting.

The basic idea used in the speed-up is to split multiplicand and multiplier in halves as follows (we assume x and y to be $2n$-digit entities and their product has $4n$ digits; furthermore we assume, without loss of generality, that $b = 2$):

$$x = X_1 \cdot 2^n + X_0$$

$$y = Y_1 \cdot 2^n + Y_0$$

with $X_1 = (x_{2n-1}, \ldots, x_n)$ and $X_0 = (x_{n-1}, \ldots, x_0)$, and Y_1 and Y_0 being treated similarly. The product p is now:

$$p \leftarrow (2^{2n} + 2^n)X_1 \cdot Y_1 + 2^n(X_1 - X_0) \cdot (Y_0 - Y_1) + (2^n + 1)X_0 \cdot Y_0 \quad (8)$$

In order to obtain p by equation (8) we have replaced one $2n$-bit multiplication by 3 n-bit multiplications, or in terms of timing:

$$T(2n) \leq 3T(n) + cn \quad (9)$$

for some constant c related to addition and shifting times ($T(m)$ is the time to perform the multiplication of 2 m-bit numbers).

The solution to recurrence equation (9) can be found by classical techniques and it can be shown that: *209818*

$$T(n) \leq 3cn^{\log 3}$$

That is the multiplication process has been reduced from $O(n^2)$ to $O(n^{1.59})$.

Instead of splitting multiplier and multiplicand into two parts, one can be more sophisticated and improve still more. Using techniques borrowed from algorithms for the Fast Fourier Transform, a procedure of order $O(n \log n \log \log n)$ is known. What is not known, however, is if there exists a faster method, and even if there exists a limit to how fast one can go (that is how close to $O(n)$ one can be).

From the computer architect's viewpoint, the above technique presents little practical interest since the overhead is prohibitive (the pay-off starts only for large n) and the controlling circuits too complicated. The hardware schemes which follow represent a different philosophy. Our goal in introducing the theorists' research is to demonstrate that there exist a set of common problems in which practical and theoretical computer science have vested interest. Although the angles of approach might appear as widely different, they are certainly less so than one or two decades ago.

3.3.2   Multiplication of Binary Integers

Basic scheme for signed integers

Let $x = (x_n, \ldots, x_1)$, $y = (y_n, \ldots, y_1)$, and $p = (p_{2n}, \ldots, p_1)$ be the multiplicand, multiplier and product. Using a ripple, or a carry look-ahead, adder with a shift register the multiplication scheme given in the preceding section can be slightly modified and implemented as follows for a positive multiplicand x and a positive multiplier y yielding the positive product p.

1. **Set** $p_j \leftarrow 0, 1 \le j \le 2n$;
2. **For** $i: = 1$ **step** 1 **until** n **do**
3.   **If** $y_i \ne 0$ **then begin** $c_i \leftarrow 0$;
$$\qquad \textbf{For } k: = 0 \textbf{ step } 1 \textbf{ until } n - 1 \textbf{ do}$$
$$\qquad \textbf{begin } c_{i+k+1} \leftarrow p_{i+k} \cdot x_{k+1}$$
$$\qquad\qquad\qquad + (p_{i+k} \oplus x_{k+1}) \cdot c_{i+k};$$
$$\qquad\qquad p_{i+k} \leftarrow p_{i+k} \oplus x_{k+1} \oplus c_{i+k}$$
$$\textbf{end};$$
$$\qquad p_{i+n+1} \leftarrow c_{i+n+1}$$
end;

This algorithm can be directly implemented for the sign and magnitude representation. The $(n - 1)$ bit magnitudes are multiplied as above, p_{2n-1} is set to 0, and the product's sign, p_{2n} is:

$$p_{2n} \leftarrow x_n \oplus y_n.$$

For the 1's and 2's complement systems we have to be more careful. If x and y are both positive, there is no difficulty. However, if one (or both of them) is negative, and if we blindly follow the above algorithm, we shall obtain an erroneous result. Very often, we will first convert to sign and magnitude, and therefore avoid the problems, at the cost of two (or three) conversions. It might be more interesting to always stay in the same representational system. We consider here only the 2's complement case and encourage the reader to work out the same analysis for the 1's complement.

We assume first that x is negative and y is positive. The desired result, a negative number, should be in the 2's complement representation of $x \cdot y$, i.e., $2^{2n} - |x \cdot y|$. The algorithm, as currently described, would yield:

$$(2^n - x) \cdot y = 2^n \cdot y - |x \cdot y|$$

The corrective action in this case is to perform a sign extension of the multiplicand, that is to have a negative x be represented as $2^{2n} - |x|$ instead of $2^n - |x|$. The product now becomes:

$$2^{2n} \cdot y - |x \cdot y|$$

Since all carry-outs will be discarded, we obtain the correct representation.

An apparent criticism to this solution is that it looks like we require a $2n$-bit adder since x has doubled in length. However, an n-bit adder and a $2n$-bit shifter are sufficient. The example of Figure 3.7 on 4-bit numbers demonstrates the technique. The multiplicand x is in an n-bit register, the multiplier and the product share a $2n$-bit shift register. The multiplier is at the least significant digit end, and the product, initially 0, at the most significant end. When the least significant bit is 0, the shift register is shifted right once with the sign of the multiplicand being injected as the leftmost bit. When it is 1, the multiplicand is added to the n most significant bits, the register is shifted right once and its n most significant bits are replaced with the $(n + 1)$ bits resulting from the addition (n bits) to which is concatenated, to the left, the sign of the multiplicand. (If x is negative, the reader can verify that a carry-out is generated after the first such process and it corresponds to the most significant bit of the accumulated product while if x is positive a 0 will be put in that position.) This procedure is repeated for the n bits of the multiplier, resulting in the desired 2's complement representation.

When the multiplicand is positive and the multiplier is negative, we could extend y in the same manner. But this is going to double the number of iterations (although the skipping to be described shortly would prevent it). A better short cut is to generate $x \cdot (2^n - y)$ and then perform the

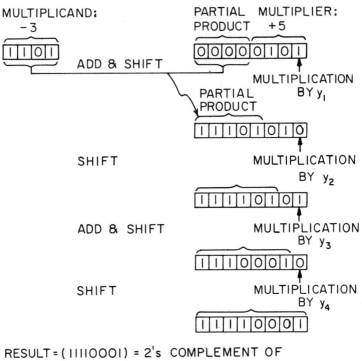

RESULT = (IIIIOOOI) = 2's COMPLEMENT OF
(OOOOIIII) = -15

Figure 3.7   Multiplication in 2's complement: multiplicand negative, multiplier positive

additional subtraction $2^n \cdot x$. This subtraction is in fact the addition $2^{2n} - 2^n \cdot x$ and the result is $2^{2n} - |x \cdot y|$. Figure 3.8 shows an example on 4-bit integers.

When both x and y are negative, we "expand" x as in Figure 3.7 and perform the subtraction as in Figure 3.8. The resulting operation takes the form:

$$(2^{2n} - x) \cdot (2^n - y) - (2^{2n} - 2^n \cdot x) = 2^{3n} - 2^{2n} \cdot y + x \cdot y - 2^{2n}$$

with everything greater than 2^{2n} being discarded. Hence we have $x \cdot y$, a positive number, as a result. (See Exercise 10.)

In the remainder of this section, we consider only positive numbers. The extra conversions into sign and magnitude, or the methods just out-

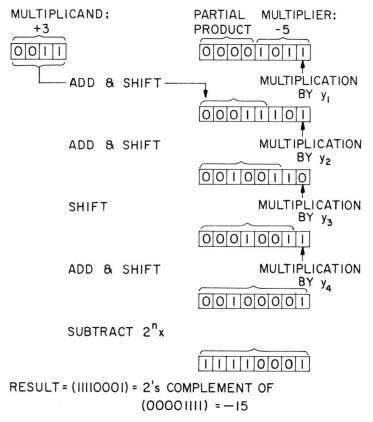

Figure 3.8 Multiplication in 2's complement: multiplicand positive, multiplier negative

lined, are generally used in conjunction with other forms of speed-up, to be covered now, to treat negative numbers. The speed-up methods that are presented are viewed as an engineering approach and should not be confused with the aforementioned theoretical investigations.

Recoding the multiplier

When the current multiplier bit is 0, no addition is performed in the actual implementation of the multiplication scheme and the partial product is simply shifted right one position. This is governed by the jump in step 3 of the algorithm. This can be generalized to shifts of variable lengths if strings of 0's can be detected. This latter process is often referenced to as skipping over 0's. If the adder is also an efficient subtractor, as for example in the 2's complement representation, we can also skip over strings of 1's. To justify this operation, consider a substring of 1's in the multiplier of the form (* is either 0 or 1):

$$* * * *011110* *   \text{(multiplier bits)}$$

$$\uparrow \quad \uparrow\uparrow$$
$$j \quad i(i - 1)   \text{(bit position)}$$

The multiplication process between bits y_j and y_i in the original algorithm computes:

$$x \cdot (2^i + 2^{i+1} + \cdots + 2^{j-1}) = x \cdot (2^j - 2^i).$$

Thus the $(j - i)$ additions can be replaced by one addition and one subtraction. A flag is needed to control whether addition, subtraction, or skipping is to be done. We rephrase the algorithm as (with global vector operations replacing system (1) or its equivalent for subtraction):

1. **Set** $p_j \leftarrow 0, 1 \le j \le 2n$; flag $\leftarrow 0$;
2. **For** i: $= 1$ **step** 1 **until** n **do**
         If $(y_i = 1$ **and** flag $= 0)$ **or** $(y_i = 0$ **and** flag $= 1)$ **then**
3.   **If** $y_i = 0$ **then begin** $p \leftarrow p + x$; flag $\leftarrow 0$ **end**
                  else begin $p \leftarrow p - x$; flag $\leftarrow 1$ **end**;

An interesting remark to be made here is that when the multiplier is negative and the 2's complement representation is used, this recoding scheme will automatically subtract the mandatory $2^n \cdot x$ that we have just discussed. This stems from the fact that the sign bit is 1 and the virtual sign extension is like a string of 1's.

In the worst case there is no skipping over 0's when the straightforward algorithm is implemented. With a multiplier of the form $0101\ldots0101$ and the skipping over 0's and 1's, we still have n operations to perform. This is why quite often the decoder will check if there is a single 1 surrounded by 0's so that a single addition instead of an addition and a subtraction is generated. If skipping over 0's is allowed for any length, it has been shown that on the average the shift length is 2. If both strings of 0's and 1's can be skipped, then the average shift length increases to 3. But the circuitry needed to implement variable shifts of any length might be too cumbersome. With an upper bound on the shift length of 4, the above figures are closely approximated for a common range of n. It is also worthwhile to notice that very often we shall have long strings of 0's or 1's at the most significant part of the multiplier when it is a small constant. Similarly, normalized floating-point numbers will have a tendency to have mantissas with long strings of 0's or 1's at their least significant end (cf. Section 4 in this chapter).

An alternative to skipping over strings of 0's and 1's is to recode c bits of the multiplier at a time and to have $2^c - 1$ multiples of the multiplicand available before the start of the multiplication. For example, with $c = 2$, then x, $2x$, and $3x$ should be ready. If bits y_i and y_{i+1} of the multiplier are 00, a right shift of length 2 is performed. If the bits are 01, then x is added before the shift. If the bits are 10, it will be an addition of $2x$ and if they are 11, it will be $3x$. In step 2 of the original algorithm, i is incremented by 2.

This recoding scheme can be combined with the skipping over 0's and 1's. Table 3.2 indicates how this can be done for 2 bits at a time with the generation of only $2x$ and $4x$, i.e., with only left shifts of the multiplicand. To understand Table 3.2 one must pay attention to the fact that bits y_i and y_{i+1} are those recoded while bit y_{i+2} is used to indicate the possible termination of a string. Furthermore two extra 0 bits are implicit at the least significant end and an extra 0 bit at the leftmost end is assumed. For example, the 6-bit multiplier (011001) = 25 is recoded as:

$$0 \; 01 \; 10 \; 01 \; 00$$

extra bit   extra bits
$$-4 \cdot 2^{-2} x$$
$$2 \cdot 2^0 \cdot x$$
$$-2 \cdot 2^2 \cdot x$$
$$2 \cdot 2^4 \cdot x$$

that is $(32 - 8 + 2 - 1) \cdot x = 25x$.

If instead of the recoding of Table 3.2 we wish to use the flag technique described earlier, then x and $2x$ are sufficient for a 2-bit recoding (cf. Exercise 11).

These techniques have been used, some in conjunction with the carry-save adder trees to be described next, in multipliers such as the integer multipliers of the IBM System 370/158 and 168 (skipping over 4 0's or 4 1's), the floating-point multipliers of the same models (decoding 4 bits at a time with a generation of $2x$, $3x$, and $6x$, a left shift to obtain $4x$ and $12x$, and a combination of at most 3 of those to obtain anything between x and $15x$), the IBM System 360/91 floating-point multiplier which follows

Table 3.2 Multiplier 2-bit recoding with skipping

Multiplier			Added product	Explanation
y_{i+2}	y_{i+1}	y_i		
0	0	0	0	No string
0	0	1	+2	End of string of 1's
0	1	0	+2	Single 1
0	1	1	+4	End of string
1	0	0	−4	Beginning of string
1	0	1	−2	+2 for end and −4 for beginning
1	1	0	−2	Beginning of string
1	1	1	0	String of 1's

the decoding of Table 3.2, the CDC 6600 multiplier which treats 2 bits of the multiplier at a time after having generated x, $2x$, and $3x$, and the multipliers of the ILLIAC IV which decode 8 bits at a time.

Using carry-save adders

Given 3 operands, the carry-save adder (CSA) generates two outputs as per system (7). If n operands have to be added, as for a multiplication, we can take advantage of the CSA speed by using the following algorithm.

1. Set ss_j and cs_j to 0, $1 \le j \le 2n$;
2. For $i: = 1$ **step** 1 **until** n **do**
      If $y_i \ne 0$ **then**
         For $k: = 0$ **step** 1 **until** $(n - 1)$ **do**
3.   **begin** $ss'_{i+k} \leftarrow ss_{i+k} \oplus cs_{i+k} \oplus x_i$;
               $cs'_{i+k+1} \leftarrow ss_{i+k} \cdot cs_{i+k} + (ss_{i+k} \oplus cs_{i+k}) \cdot x_i$;
               $ss_{i+k} \leftarrow ss'_{i+k}$;
               $cs_{i+k+1} \leftarrow cs'_{i+k+1}$
      end;
4. Add ss and cs in a conventional $2n$-bit parallel adder according to system (1).

Since CSA's are much less complex than parallel adders, we can use more than one without an undue increase in the cost of the multiplier. In Figure 3.9, we show how 3 CSA's can be used. A clock phases the operations of

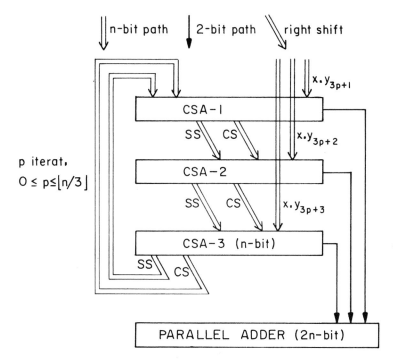

Figure 3.9 Multiplier with Carry-Save adders

each CSA such that the whole operation, minus the last ripple addition, would take n CSA levels. Thus it does not appear that we have gained anything by going from 1 to 3 CSA's. However if overlapping operations are permitted, for example multiplier recoding done in parallel with the partial product accumulation, there is a definite improvement in duplicating the hardware. Moreover, if we increase the number of CSA's, then parts of the multiplication process per se are performed concurrently. In Figure 3.10, we show how the inclusion of one more CSA permits some parallel additions (we have given only a schematic description of the CSA's organization and have left out the parallel adder). The number of iterations has now decreased from $n/3$ to $n/4$ for a total time of $3n/4$ CSA levels. More generally, if we had $(n - 2)$ CSA's we can build a tree of depth 0 (log n), i.e., generate the sum up to the ripple addition in 0 (log n) CSA levels. This order of magnitude is obtained by the following construction. We group the n operands in triples as inputs to a top level of CSA's. We obtain (approximately) $2n/3$ outputs which can again be fed in triples to a second level of CSA's. We continue this construction until only 2 out-

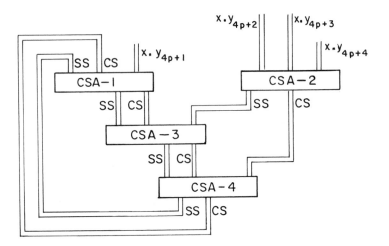

Figure 3.10   Multiplier with 4 CSA's

puts are left. Evidently we have a logarithmic depth, since we decrease the number of inputs by one third at each level. That $(n - 2)$ CSA's are needed is easily proven by induction on the number of operands (cf. also Exercise 12). Such a configuration is called an adder, or Wallace, tree. A 14 CSA's Wallace tree to add 16 operands is shown in Figure 3.11. It is not the unique way to obtain the minimal depth and methods of grouping the CSA's for a given purpose will be discussed in Chapter 4.

In general, we will not wish to invest in $(n - 2)$ CSA's. Only a limited number of them will be connected as in Figure 3.10 and an iterative process will be implemented. Recoding of the multiplier can be used concurrently, with shifts of 2 (or more) instead of single shifts. For example, the floating-point multiplier in the CDC 6600 uses 3 CSA's with a 2-bit recoding of the multiplier for each half of the multiplier (see below for splitting the multiplication process). In the IBM System 360/91 there is a carry-save adder tree of 6 CSA's also with a 2-bit multiplier recoding. We shall return to these designs in the next chapter. In the ILLIAC IV processing elements, each ALU has a 4-layer CSA tree, with an 8-bit recoding of the multiplier. The CDC STAR-100 uses a full Wallace tree for its 32-bit multiplier, while 64-bit multiplies are handled in 4 32-bit multiplications (and not 3 as the theoreticians would recommend).

The log-sum process

If instead of having one hardware multiplier for 2 n-bit operands, we had

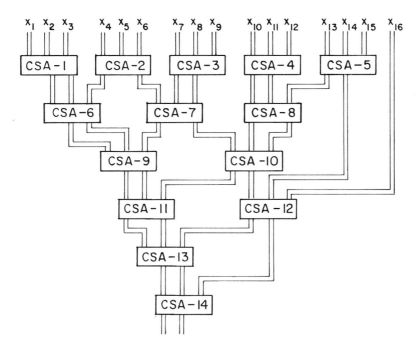

Figure 3.11   Wallace tree

two multipliers each of which can handle an n-bit multiplicand and an $n/2$-bit multiplier, we could perform in parallel the multiplications of the multiplicand by the upper-half of the original multiplier and by its lower half. If the multiplication time for a full multiplication is:

$$T_1 = n (A + S),$$

where A is the add time and S the shift time, then with two multipliers it becomes:

$$T_2 = n/2 \cdot (A + S) + A,$$

the extra addition being done on the overlapping parts of the two resulting products. We can generalize the process to m multipliers and attain a speed of:

$$T_m = \lceil n/m \rceil \cdot (A + S) + \lceil \log m \rceil \cdot A$$

At the limit we have 0 (log n) additions of n-bit operands. This log-sum process of summing n operands is never fully used but, as we shall see, can exist for some applications in array processors. For our present discussion, it is sufficient to point out that duplication of multipliers is rare and limited to a very small m. A striking example is the CDC 6600 multiplier with $m = 2$.

3.3.3   Division

Division of positive integers

The multiplication process has for inputs an n-digit multiplicand and an m-digit multiplier and produces as output an $(n + m)$-digit product. Division has for inputs an $(n + m)$-digit dividend x and an n-digit divisor y to produce two outputs, an $(m + 1)$-digit quotient q and an n-digit remainder r such that:

$$x = y \cdot q + r, \qquad 0 \le r < y$$

In the ordinary paper and pencil method, assuming a base b positional number system, the integer division requires some guess work. The first digit of q, say q_m, is given a value; the product $y \cdot q_m$ is computed and subtracted from x. If the subtraction yields a negative result, q_m was too large and a new value (a smaller one) has to be tried. If the result was positive but larger than (or equal to) y, then q_m was too small and a larger value is necessary. The right digit q_m is such that:

$$0 \le x - y \cdot q_m < y$$

Once q_m has been generated, the process continues for q_{m-1} replacing x by $x - y \cdot q_m$ and so on until q_0 is obtained. The last partial dividend is the remainder r.

The above process is called a restoring division since we restore the dividend when we have made a wrong guess. When $b = 2$, i.e., when we are in the binary system, there are only two possible guesses: 0 or 1. This means that the algorithm (still a restoring one) with x and y being n-digit, or:

$$x = (x_{n-1}, \ldots, x_0), \qquad y = (y_{n-1}, \ldots, y_0),$$

$$q = (q_n, \ldots, q_0), \qquad r = (r_{n-1}, \ldots, r_0)$$

can be expressed as:

1. Expand x into $x' = (x_{2n-2}, \ldots, x_n, x_{n-1}, \ldots, x_0)$
   by letting all $x_i, n \leq i \leq 2n - 2$, be 0, (we perform a sign extension).
2. For $i: = 1$ **step** 1 **until** n **do**
   Set $z \leftarrow x' - 2^{n-i} \cdot y$ (as in system (1) for example)
   If $z \geq 0$ **then** $q_{n+1-i} \leftarrow 1$ and $x' \leftarrow z$
          else $q_{n+1-i} \leftarrow 0$ and do not modify x'
3. $r \leftarrow x'$.

Figure 3.12 shows how the algorithm can be implemented with a subtractor and a $2n$-bit shift register in a manner similar to the multiplication
of Figure 3.7. The "else" part of step 2 is deceptively simple. If the subtraction yields a negative result, we have to perform an addition to restore
x'. This can be avoided by the use of a non-restoring technique. Although

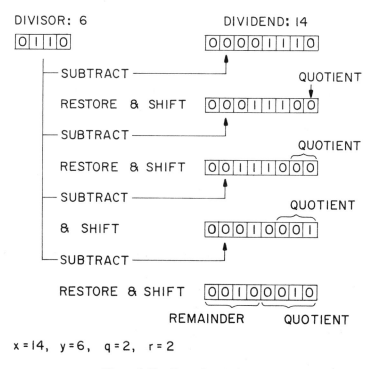

Figure 3.12 Restoring division

this last scheme is not limited to the binary system, we restrict ourselves to it since it happens to be the most prevalent case (and also for the sake of clarity in explanation).

As stated earlier the only two guesses for a binary system are 0 or 1. Returning to step 2, when z is negative (when we guessed wrong), we have:

$$x' - 2^{n-i} \cdot y < 0$$

After this subtraction, and assuming that $i \neq n$, we add $2^{n-1} \cdot y$ and subtract $2^{n-i-1} \cdot y$, i.e., we perform:

$$z_1 \leftarrow x' - 2^{n-i} \cdot y + 2^{n-i} \cdot y - 2^{n-i-1} \cdot y, \text{ or}$$

$$z_1 \leftarrow x' - 2^{n-i-1} \cdot y$$

If instead we do not restore z and add $2^{n-i-1} \cdot y$ when z is negative, we obtain:

$$z_2 \leftarrow x' - 2^{n-i} \cdot y + 2^{n-i-1} \cdot y, \text{ or}$$

$$z_2 \leftarrow x' - 2^{n-i-1} \cdot y = z_1$$

The only difficulty in this method is when the last quotient bit yields a negative remainder. This happens if we had for some j:

$$r' \leftarrow x' - 2^{j+1} \cdot y + (2^j + 2^{j-1} + \cdots + 2^0) \cdot y < 0$$

The correct remainder should have been the partial remainder generated at the same time as the jth quotient bit, that is:

$$r \leftarrow r' + y$$

Thus the non-restoring algorithm for binary positive integers becomes:

1. Expand x into x' as in the restoring algorithm; sign $\leftarrow 1$
2. **For** $i := 1$ **step** 1 **until** n **do**
       Set $z \leftarrow x' - \text{sign} \cdot 2^{n-i} \cdot y$;
       If $z \geq 0$ **then** $q_{n+1-i} \leftarrow 1$ and sign $\leftarrow 1$
             else $q_{n+1-i} \leftarrow 0$ and sign $\leftarrow -1$;
       $x' \leftarrow z$;
3. **If** $q_0 = 1$ **then** $r \leftarrow x'$
             else $r \leftarrow x' + y$;

Figure 3.13 shows two examples of non-restoring division with the alternative of step 3.

Non-restoring division in 2's complement

Although many divide units, or ALU's, first convert 1 or 2's complement numbers in sign and magnitude form before attempting a division, and then apply variations of the above algorithm, some of them directly use the original representation system. (Note that in the sign and magnitude algorithm we will need to add and subtract, that is convert back and forth in pseudo-complement form.) In the following we restrict ourselves to the 2's complement notation.

Given x and y, we want q and r to be such that:

$$x = y \cdot q + r, \text{ with } r \text{ and } x \text{ of the same sign and } 0 \leq |r| < |y|$$

The first modification to the algorithm for positive integers is a slightly different sign extension. If x and y are $(n + 1)$-bit quantities, with x_n and y_n encoding their respective signs, q_n the first bit of the desired $(n + 1)$-bit quotient will be:

$$q_n \leftarrow x_n \oplus y_n.$$

The sign extension should also allow for the generation of n additional quotient bits, that is we require a sign extension of x of n bits. Now, if the (partial) dividend z (initially the extended x) and y are of the same sign, then we subtract y (we add its 2's complement). On the contrary, if z and y are of opposite signs, then we will add y. In both cases it will tend to decrease the absolute value of z. When applied to the first quotient digit, this yields:

$$z \leftarrow x - (1 - 2q_n) \cdot 2^{n-1} \cdot y,$$

where the x on the right hand side of the expression stands for an extended x. If the resulting partial dividend z and y are of the same sign, then q_{n-1} should be set to 1. For example, assuming x, y and z to be positive, q_n would be 0 and we can reason as in the case of the positive integer division. If the three quantities are negative, q_n is again 0 and we try to decrease x in absolute value. If our result is again negative we did not overshoot (our guess was right) and the first bit of the positive quotient should be 1. If now x is positive, y is negative, i.e., q_n is 1, and the resulting z is negative, as y, our "guess" was wrong because $2^{n-1} \cdot y$ is larger in absolute

Divisor: 3 = (0011)   Dividend: 10 = (1010)

Expand Dividend	0001010	
Subtract divisor	− 0011	

Result (negative)	− 0001110	Quotient bit: $q_3 = 0$
Add divisor	+ 0011	

Result (negative)	− 0000010	Quotient bit: $q_2 = 0$
Add divisor	+ 0011	

Result (positive)	+ 0000100	Quotient bit: $q_1 = 1$
Subtract (divisor)	− 0011	

Result (positive)	+ 0001	Quotient bit: $q_0 = 1$

Remainder (0001) = 1 Quotient (0011) = 3

i.e.   10 = 3.3 + 1

Divisor: 4 = (0100)   Dividend: 10 = (1010)

Expand Dividend	+ 0001010	
Subtract divisor	− 0100	

Result (negative)	− 0010110	Quotient bit: $q_3 = 0$
Add divisor	+ 0100	

Result (negative)	− 0000110	Quotient bit: $q_2 = 0$
Add divisor	+ 0100	

Result (Positive)	+ 0000010	Quotient bit: $q_1 = 1$
Subtract divisor	− 0100	

Result (negative)	− 00010	Quotient bit: $q_0 = 0$
	+ 0100	Add divisor

+ 0010	Remainder (0010) = 2 Quotient (0010) = 2

10 = 4.2 + 2

Figure 3.13   Nonrestoring division

value than x. We should enter a 0 in the quotient bit (wrong guess) but since the latter is in 2's complement representation we enter the complement, that is a 1. The same type of reasoning applies for the 8 possible cases.

We can repeat the above process up to the last quotient bit q_0. At this point we have to resolve two small problems. The first one is that we wish to have the remainder r and the original dividend x be of the same sign, and the second is related to the 2's complement representation which will be off by 1 if the quotient is negative since, in essence, we have generated the 1's complement.

Therefore, if the last partial dividend generated, call it z^0, and x are of the same sign, we can set r to z^0 and q_0 to 1. This is evident if y is also of the same sign. On the other hand, if y were of the opposite sign, then r is correct, q_0 is correct and therefore a 0 should be entered in that position per our previous discussion. The transformation from 1's to 2's complement would add a 1 in the last quotient position, hence q_0 should be set to 1.

If x and z^0 are of different signs we have two cases:

- If x and y are of the same sign (and hence z^0 is of a different sign), then we should set q_0 to 0 and restore r as $z^0 + y$. If x and y are positive this is the scheme that we have already seen for positive integers. If x and y are negative the quotient is positive and 0 is the bit generated for a wrong guess.
- If x and y are of different signs and z^0 is of the sign of y, then we should again correct r to be $z^0 - y$. q_0 is set to 1 (wrong guess for a negative quotient) and q is incremented by 1 for the 1's to 2's complement representation.

The algorithm is then as follows. Let

$$x = (x_n, \ldots, x_0), y = (y_n, \ldots, y_0), q = (q_n, \ldots, q_0) \text{ and } r = (r_n, \ldots, r_0).$$

x's extension which at the same time holds the partial dividend will be a $2n$-bit vector z. As previously we use vector operations in lieu of system (1).

1. Perform a sign extension of x into $z = (z_{2n-1}, \ldots, z_{n+1}, z_n, \ldots, z_0)$;
2. $q_n \leftarrow x_n \oplus y_n$; sign $\leftarrow q_n$;
3. For $i: = 1$ **step** 1 **until** $n - 1$ **do**
   begin
   $\qquad z \leftarrow z - (1 - 2 \cdot \text{sign}) \cdot 2^{n-i} \cdot y$; (where the subtraction is the 2's complement addition)

4. **If** $z = 0$ **then** $q_{n-i} \leftarrow 1$; $q_j \leftarrow 0$ $(0 \leq j < n - i)$; $r \leftarrow 0$ and end;
    else if $z_{2n-i} = y_n$ **then** $q_{n-i} \leftarrow 1$ and sign $\leftarrow 0$
    else $q_{n-i} \leftarrow 0$ and sign $\leftarrow 1$
    end;
6. $z \leftarrow z - (1 - 2 \cdot \text{sign}) \cdot y$;
7. **Set** r, q_0 and q according to Table 3.3 (the $n - 1$ high order bits of z are dropped in the assignment of z to r).

Figure 3.14 shows the application of the algorithm on 2 examples.

Faster division schemes

Division can be speeded up much in the same ways as multiplication. Multiples of the divisor can be subtracted, strings of 0's and 1's can be generated in the quotient, but the complexity of the methods as well as the relatively low frequency of divide operations are deterrents to the implementation of these difficult algorithms. We shall see in the next section how fast multipliers can be used for the division of normalized fractions in a convergence process.

3.4 FLOATING-POINT OPERATIONS

In our presentation of numbering systems and in the subsequent treatment of arithmetic operations, we dealt mainly with signed integers. The same

Table 3.3 Last step in non-restoring 2's complement division

Line #	x_n	y_n	z_n	Action
0	0	0	0	$q_0 \leftarrow 1; r \leftarrow z$
1	0	0	1	$q_0 \leftarrow 0; r \leftarrow z + y$
2	0	1	0	$q_0 \leftarrow 1; r \leftarrow z$
3	0	1	1	$q_0 \leftarrow 1; q \leftarrow q + 1; r \leftarrow z - y$
4	1	0	0	$q_0 \leftarrow 1; q \leftarrow q + 1; r \leftarrow z - y$
5	1	0	1	$q_0 \leftarrow 1; r \leftarrow z$
6	1	1	0	$q_0 \leftarrow 0; r \leftarrow z + y$
7	1	1	1	$q_0 \leftarrow 1; r \leftarrow z$

Divisor y = 3 (0011)   Dividend x = -5 (1011)

Step 1	Expand x	111011	

| Step 2 | $q_3 \leftarrow 1$ | | |

Step 3	Add $2^2 \cdot y$	001100	$2^2 y$
		111011	

Steps 4,5 $q_2 \leftarrow 1$, sign $\leftarrow 0$ 000111

Step 3   Subtract $2^1 y$ 111010 $-2y$

Steps 4,5 $q_1 \leftarrow 1$, sign $\leftarrow 0$ 000001

Step 6   Subtract y   111101 $-y$

Step 7   Line 5   111110

$$q_0 \leftarrow 1$$

$$\rightarrow q = (1111) = -1; r = (1110) = -2 \text{ and } -5 = 3 \cdot (-1) + (-2)$$

Divisor y = -2 (1110)   Dividend x = $+5$ (0101)

Step 1   Expand x   000101

Step 2 $q_3 \leftarrow 1$

Step 3   Add $2^2 y$ 000101
                                                    1110 $2^2 y$

Steps 4,5 $q_2 \leftarrow 1$, sign $\leftarrow 0$ 111101

Step 3   Subtract $2^1 y$ 00010 $-2y$

Steps 4,5 $q_1 \leftarrow 0$, sign $\leftarrow 1$ 000001

Step 6   Add y   111110   y

                                                    111111

Step 7   Line 3 Subtract y   000010

                                                    000001

$$q_0 \leftarrow 1 \qquad q \leftarrow (1101) + (0001) = (1110)$$

$$\rightarrow q = (1110) = -2; r = (0001) = +1 \text{ and } \qquad 5 = (-2) \cdot (-2) + 1$$

Figure 3.14 Nonrestoring division in 2's complement notation

algorithms could be applied to real numbers with a provision for scaling, that is for keeping track of the implied binary fractional point. This would have to be done in a prior analysis of the program and with the insertion of adequate shifts. Although the earliest computers were operated under these conditions, it was soon recognized that this was too much of a burden to impose on programmers as well as too error prone a process.

This scaling is also avoided in the technical literature and in non-automated computations. Scientists cannot easily grasp the meaning of, and would hate to have to perform operations such as:

$$12,300,000,000 \times 0.0000000678.$$

Instead they use what is often called the scientific notation and write:

$$123.10^8 \times 6.78 \cdot 10^{-8}.$$

Similarly, real numbers can be represented by a computer word (or concatenation of words) in the format:

$$m \cdot r^e$$

called *floating-point* in contrast with the integer or fixed (binary) point form. In this format, m is the *mantissa*, e the *exponent* (or characteristic), and r the *radix*. In addition to the fact that the scaling problem has disappeared, we shall have an expanded range of values that can be represented over the one available in the fixed-point notation.

We start this section by showing some alternatives for floating-point formats. We continue by discussing the changes imposed in the four arithmetic operations.

3.4.1 Floating-point Formats

Several factors have to be weighted in the choices for m, e, and r in a floating-point format. In particular, the range of values to be accommodated and the precision that we wish to attain are the two most important factors. Since both the exponent and the mantissa will share one (or more) word, giving more room to one is cutting short the other. More precisely, increasing the range, i.e., having a wider choice of exponents, will decrease the length of the mantissa, and therefore diminish the precision. The decrease of the exponent length will have the opposite effect. The third parameter, that is the choice of the exponent's radix, also has an influence on both range and precision. Choosing a small radix, like $r = 2$, will provide a smaller range while a larger radix will result in the loss of more significant bits when alignment of mantissas will be necessary.

However, there are some decisions which can be taken without too much hesitation. The mantissa will be either an integer or a pure fraction; then, the implied binary point will be either at the right or at the left of the field occupied by the mantissa. Furthermore, this quantity will have to be represented in one of the three numbering systems already discussed. The exponent will be a signed integer, with several choices for its representation. Finally, the radix will be chosen according to the word length for reasons of precision and range as explained above, but will always be a power of 2.

Most floating-point formats consist of 3 fields, and occasionally 4, namely: mantissa sign, exponent, and mantissa, with the exponent sign being the (rarely explicit) fourth field. If it is not present, since both positive and negative integers have to be encoded, an "excess" notation is generally used for the exponent. If the exponent field is a bits long, all exponents e are biased by 2^{a-1}, that is they are represented by $e + 2^{a-1}$. Conversions of real numbers to and from integers, be they realized by software or hardware, will have to take this into account. Some examples to follow shortly will explain the procedure more easily than a long discourse.

Before proceeding further, we examine Figure 3.15 which shows the formats used in five different machines and which cover most of the practical options (cf. also Exercises 15 and 16). The Burroughs B5500 format uses sign and magnitude for both the exponent and the mantissa which is considered as an integer. This is one of the few computers of the post-60 era which has a 4-field format. The word length of 48 bits combined with a small exponent width calls for a rather large r. The choice of radix 8 leads to a largest real number representable of the order of 10^{72} (cf. Exercise 14). In the CDC-Cyber series, the mantissa is again an integer but this time the representation is in 1's complement. The exponent is in excess-1024 notation since we have 11 bits in the exponent field. With the large word length of 60 bits, a radix 2 gives good precision and a more than adequate range for a scientific machine (largest number representable 10^{322}). Since the 1's complement notation is used for the mantissa, a negative real number is represented as the 1's complement (of the 60 bit word) of its absolute value. This presents a slight difficulty due to the two possible representations of 0 in that system. Thus both $(2000)_8$ and $(1777)_8$ can be considered as 0 exponents. The latter is kept for the so-called indefinite operands and negative exponents are biased by $(1777)_8$ while non-negative ones are biased by $(2000)_8$. In Systems/360 and /370 and in the Sigma 5 the mantissa is a fraction, the exponent is in excess-64 notation and,

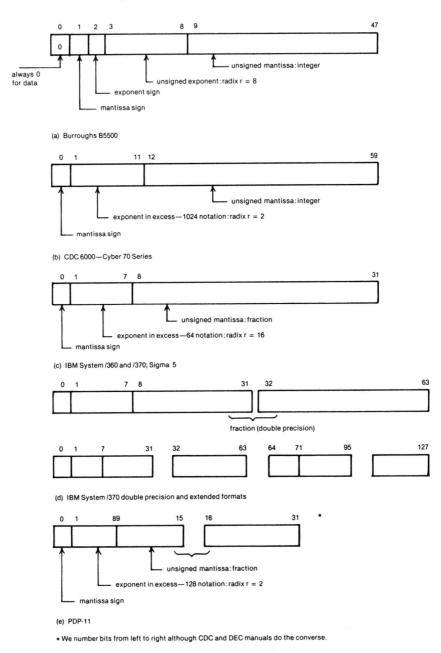

(a) Burroughs B5500

(b) CDC 6000—Cyber 70 Series

(c) IBM System /360 and /370; Sigma 5

(d) IBM System /370 double precision and extended formats

(e) PDP-11

* We number bits from left to right although CDC and DEC manuals do the converse.

Figure 3.15   Floating-point formats

because of the short word length, the radix is 16. While the mantissa of the IBM machines is in sign and magnitude representation, that of the Sigma is in 2's complement. The largest number representable is approximately 10^{76}, but the precision is quite often not sufficient since alignment will be performed by groups of 4 bits. In this case, a fraction extension is implemented with an extra word. Finally the minicomputer PDP-11 (word length 16 bits) requires two words for single precision and 4 for double precision. The mantissa is a fraction, the exponent is in excess-128 notation, and the radix is 2 yielding a largest representable number of 10^{38}.

Since precision is important, we will attempt to always have as many significant bits as possible in the mantissa. This is accomplished by *normalizing* the real number, that is by having its most significant digit, in base r, at the leftmost position in the mantissa, decreasing the exponent accordingly. Thus a normalized positive number in the CDC format will have a 1 in bit 12 (and it will be 0 for a normalized negative number). For the IBM System/370, the leftmost hexadecimal digit must be different from 0, i.e., at least one of the bits 8 through 11 must be 1. The requirement is similar for a positive number in the Sigma 5 while for a negative number in this latter machine the converse must be true: at least one of these same bits must be 0. By convention, operands and results are normalized in the PDP-11 representation. Hence, the mantissa's leftmost bit is always a 1 and does not have to be stored. Of course the hardware is cognizant of this fact and performs the necessary maskings.

Instruction sets will in general allow for normalized and unnormalized operations in single and double precision. Most compilers generate only normalized operations and library routines, or macros, are used for real to integer and integer to real conversions. Zero, which can be represented by a mantissa of 0 and any exponent, will be converted to a "true" zero (a word full of 0-bits) upon recognition of the null value in an assignment or as the result of an arithmetic operation. Special provisions are often made for the handling of positive and negative "infinite" values which correspond to overflow and underflow situations.

To end this presentation of floating-point formats, we sketch algorithms for the conversions to and from these formats to either decimal notation or fixed-point notation.

(i) Conversion from floating to fixed point (assuming an excess notation for the exponent and an integer representation for the mantissa).

1. Check mantissa sign; if minus and the mantissa is not in sign and magnitude representation perform the complementation;
2. Extract the exponent and subtract the excess yielding e;

3. Multiply the mantissa by r^e (if an integer is desired, shift the mantissa left or right depending on the sign of e by $e \log r$ places), and assign the sign as determined in step 1.

(This algorithm can be generalized without difficulty to other formats as shown in the examples to follow.)

Example 3.7a Let $(6056\ 2777\ 7777\ 7777\ 7777)_8$ be a floating-point number in CDC format. Its decimal equivalent can be found by following the above algorithm.

Step 1. Negative sign. Taking the 1's complement yields:

$1721\ 5000\ 0000\ 0000\ 0000$;

Step 2. Extract the exponent $(1721)_8$ and subtract the excess $(1777)_8$; this yields:

$(-56)_8 = -46$;

Step 3. The mantissa is 5.2^{45} and therefore the real number is:

$-5.2^{45} \cdot 2^{-46} = -2.5$.

(A right shift of 46 places in the uncomplemented mantissa would have yielded $0000...0010$, the integer 2 which is the absolute value of the integer conversion of the real number.)   □

Example 3.7b Let $(5BCA\ 0000)_{16}$ be a floating-point number in the IBM System/370 notation. (Note that in both examples the numbers are normalized.)

Step 1. Sign positive;
Step 2. Extract the exponent $(5B)_{16}$ and subtract the excess $(40)_{16}$ yielding:

$(1B)_{16} = 27$;

Step 3. The mantissa $(CA\ 0000)_{16} = 12/16 + 10/256 = .789...$, hence the real number is $.789 \cdot 16^{27}$.

If instead the floating point number had been $(41CA\ 0000)_{16}$, a right shift of 6 hexadecimal digits to take the hexadecimal point to the right of the word, followed by a left shift of 1 hexadecimal digit for the (41-40) exponent, i.e., a right shift of 20 places, would have yielded the integer equivalent $(0000\ 000C)_{16} = 12 = \lfloor .789 \cdot 16 \rfloor$.   □

(ii) Conversion from fixed to floating-point (under the same assumptions as above).

1. Check the sign; if negative convert the absolute value;
2. Transform the fixed-point value into an integer in radix r multiplied by the appropriate value of r^e;
3. Add e to the excess for the exponent field;
4. Normalize if necessary (or wanted);
5. If negative convert in the notation used.

Example 3.8a   Convert -2.5 into normalized CDC format.

Step 1. Remember negative sign and convert 2.5;
Step 2. $(2.5)_{10} = (10.1)_2 = (101)_2 \cdot 2^{-1}$;
Step 3. $(1777)_8 - 1 = (1776)_8$ so that the unnormalized representation is:

(1776 0000 0000 0000 0005);

Step 4. To normalize we shift the mantissa 45 positions left so that bit 12 becomes 1. At the same time, we decrease the exponent by $(45)_{10}$ or $(55)_8$. The exponent field becomes:

$(1776) - (55) = (1721)_8$,

and the normalized representation of 2.5 is:

1721 5000 0000 0000 0000;

Step 5. Now, we take the 1's complement for the final representation:

6056 2777 7777 7777 7777.   □

Example 3.8b   Convert $+1$ in normalized IBM System/370 format.

Step 1. Sign positive;
Step 2. $(1)_{10} = (1)_{16} = (.1)_{16} \cdot 16^1$;
Step 3. Add 1 to $(40)_{16}$ yielding $(41)_{16}$ and the representation:

4110 0000;

Step 4. The number is already normalized;
Step 5. The number is already in the correct sign representation.   □

3.4.2 Floating-point Arithmetic

Addition and subtraction

Given $x = m_1 \cdot r^{e_1}$ and $y = m_2 \cdot r^{e_2}$, their sum z (evidently the same analysis will hold for the difference) is:

$$z = (m_1 + m_2 \cdot r^{-(e_1 - e_2)}) \cdot r^{e_1}, \text{ assuming } e_1 \geq e_2.$$

The addition therefore proceeds in three steps (four if normalization is included):

1. Detect the operand with the largest exponent;
2. Shift the mantissa of the operand with the smallest exponent by $(e_1 - e_2) \log r$ places;
3. Add the (shifted) mantissas;
4. Normalize.

We examine these steps in more detail.

The easiest way to compare two operands is to perform the subtraction of one from the other and to check the sign of the result. Since the absolute value of $e_1 - e_2$ is the shift count needed in step 2, we can merge the two actions into one. If the exponents are represented in excess notation, that is if in fact their representation is $2^{a-1} + e_1$ and $2^{a-1} + e_2$, we can perform the subtraction by adding the 1's complement of the second to the first following the 1's complement rules for addition (cf. Exercise 18). If an end-around carry is generated during the exponent's subtraction, then e_1 was greater than e_2 and m_2 can be gated to the shifting unit of the adder. The completion of the subtraction will yield the shift count. If on the other hand e_2 was larger than or equal to e_1, then there will be no end-around carry, m_1 can be gated to the shifter and the shift count will be the 1's complement of the result of the subtraction.

Example 3.9   IBM System/370 format.

Add (4Axx $xxxx$) and (4Cyy $yyyy$). $e_1 = 10$, $e_2 = 12$, $e_1 - e_2 = -2$, so m_1 should be gated to the shifter and the shift count is 2 hex digits, or 8 bits. Following the procedure in the above paragraph entails the complementing of 4C into 33 (note that we are complementing only the 7 bits of the exponent's field) and its addition to 4A, resulting in:

$$
\begin{array}{r}
100\ 1010\ (4A) \\
+011\ 0011\ (33) \\
\hline
111\ 1101\ (3D)
\end{array}
$$

Since there is no end-around carry, m_1 should be gated to the shifter and the shift count is the 1's complement of 3D, or 02 hex digits.   □

The second part of step 2, the shifting, presents no difficulty. We shall see in the next section how shifting can be done in synchronous as well as asynchronous fashion.

Step 3, that is the addition of the two mantissas, has been covered in detail in Section 2. We can apply any of the techniques used in the addition of integers. A slight modification is necessary for the handling of overflow. When we add two n-bit integers of the same sign, we can obtain an $(n + 1)$-bit result. In fixed-point notation, this is an overflow situation, while in floating-point it is not since we can correct it by increasing the exponent by 1 and by shifting the resulting mantissa by log r. This "virtual" overflow is handled automatically in the hardware of hardwired floating-point units.

Example 3.10   IBM System/370 format.

Add (4A83 F263) and (4AA3 627A).
Steps 1 and 2. No shifting since exponents are the same;
Step 3. 83 F263
$\underline{+A3\ 627A}$
127 54DD

The virtual overflow results in a one hex, or 4 bits, right shift and an increase in the exponent yielding:

4B12 754D.

(Note that a rounded result would have been 4B12 754E.)   □

Step 4, the post-normalization is again a straightforward shifting. When leading 0's are detected in the mantissa, they are removed by groups of log r, the mantissa is shifted left accordingly, and the exponent decreased by 1.

In general, floating-point adders will also have extension capabilities for the mantissa (e.g., the CDC 6600 uses a $97 + 1$ (for virtual overflow) adder). Provisions are made for detecting real overflow, i.e., overflow or underflow on the exponent, as well as for zeroing the exponent in case of a null resulting mantissa.

Multiplication

Given $x = m_1 \cdot r^{e_1}$ and $y = m_2 \cdot r^{e_2}$, their product p is:

$$p = m_1 \cdot m_2 \cdot r^{e_1 + e_2}$$

If x and y are normalized their product will either be normalized or the mantissa will be off by a single (base r) digit. All floating-point units take this into account and the post-normalization is always embedded into the hardware. The algorithm (for normalized inputs) is then:

1. Add the two exponents performing the necessary adjustments to obtain the correct excess notation;
2. Multiply the mantissas;
3. Post-normalize the resulting mantissa if it is not normalized.

Consider first step 2. If each mantissa occupies n bits, the resulting product will be $2n$ bits long and only the high order half will be kept for single precision results. Discarding the lower half means that the exponent is not $(e_1 + e_2)$ but $(e_1 + e_2) + n/\log r$ when the mantissas are integers. Thus step 1 consists of adding the exponents, subtracting the excess weight since it is counted once in each of the two exponent representations, and possibly adding $n/\log r$ to take the lower half discard into consideration. Step 3 has already been elaborated upon.

Example 3.11   CDC 6600 format.

Multiply (2101 4600 0000 0000 0000) and (2020 4000 0000 0000 0000).

Step 1. Add $(2101 + 2020 - 2000 + 60)_8$, where $60_8 = 48$ (the discard of the 48 rightmost bits). This yields 2201;

Step 2. Multiply the mantissas. The 96 bit result is:

   2300 0000 0000 $\cdots$ 0000;

Step 3. The result is unnormalized. Post-normalization implies a left shift of a single place and a decrement of the exponent by 1 giving the result:

   2200 4600 0000 0000 0000.   □

We have previously presented fast methods of implementing the multiplication of integers. In the floating-point case, the exponent calculation can be done in parallel. Some examples will be described in Chapter 4.

Division

Given a dividend $x = m_1 \cdot r^{e_1}$ and a divisor $y = m_2 \cdot r^{e_2}$, the quotient q is:

$$q = m_1/m_2 \cdot r^{e_1 - e_2}$$

The division process then consists of three steps much in the same fashion as multiplication, that is:

1. Subtract the exponents performing the necessary adjustments;
2. Divide the mantissas keeping only the quotient;
3. Post-normalize if necessary and/or wanted.

If e_1 and e_2 are represented in excess notation, then the resulting exponent is represented by the difference of the exponents (or of their encodings) to which one adds the "excess". If the original operands are normalized, the resulting quotient is also normalized but again we have here the possibility of a "virtual" overflow. If m_1 is considered as a $2n$-bit integer and m_2 as an n-bit one, then the resulting quotient is an $(n + 1)$-bit entity and the leftmost bit can very well be significant. As in the multiplication case, the hardware will take care of it automatically, increasing the exponent by 1 and shifting the mantissa by $\log r$ bits to the right.

Example 3.12 IBM System/370 format.

Divide (4296 0000) by (4420 0000).

Step 1. $42 - 44 + 40 = 38$;
Step 2. $(96\ 0000)/(20\ 0000) = (12C\ 0000)$.

We have a virtual overflow which is corrected as mentioned above to yield:

(3912 0000) □

In fact, the division of mantissas starts by normalizing (in binary) at least the divisor and in general both operands, injecting the correct number of 0's at the right end of the quotient (or equivalently decreasing the number of iterations in the subtraction loops). If instead of performing a restoring or non-restoring scheme, we want to use the floating-point multiplier, the quest for a quotient can be replaced by that of a reciprocal (the CRAY-1 computer does not have a machine instruction for division but only one for a reciprocal). This is called the convergence method for reasons which will be obvious in the next paragraph.

We assume, without loss of generality, that we wish to find $q = x/y$, where x and y are n-bit normalized binary fractions. This problem can be replaced by that of finding the (real) number r such that $y \cdot r = 1$, and hence $q = x \cdot r$. This process can be implemented iteratively by choosing successive factors r_i such that $y \cdot r_1 \cdot r_2 \cdots r_n$ converges to 1. The critical point is therefore the choice of the r_i's. Under the above assumptions, this is facilitated by the fact that y, a normalized binary fraction, is of the form:

$$y = 1 - z, \qquad 0 \le z \le 1/2$$

Hence r_1 can be chosen as $1 + z$, yielding:

$$y \cdot r_1 = (1 - z) \cdot (1 + z) = 1 - z^2, \text{ with now } 0 \le z^2 \le 1/4,$$

that is, $y \cdot r_1$ of the form:

$$0.11xxxx \cdots$$

Now choosing r_2 to be $(1 + z^2)$ will yield $y \cdot r_1 \cdot r_2$ of the form:

$$0.1111xx \cdots$$

For example, for a 56 bit mantissa as in the IBM System/360 model 91 which uses this method, we need 6 r_i's (although as we shall see in the next chapter this can be speeded up). The use of binary arithmetic provides another benefit, namely the ease in getting the r_i's. We observe that if the partial product $y \cdot r_1 \cdot r_2 \cdots r_{k-1}$ is of the form $(1 - z_k)$, the next factor r_k can be taken as:

$$2 - (1 - z_k)$$

i.e., the 2's complement of the partial product. We shall see in Chapter 4 how this method can be implemented with the use of a fast floating-point multiplier.

3.5 OTHER FUNCTIONS OF THE ALU

Until now, we have only discussed the arithmetic chores of the ALU. As its name implies, it has also to provide capabilities for logical functions. The combinatorial circuits necessary to realize any of the 16 Boolean functions of two variables are extremely simple when compared to the more sophisticated algorithms of this chapter. Microcomputers and ALUs on a chip are generally able to perform addition, subtraction and these 16 Boolean functions in parallel on 4 (or 8 and now 16) bits at a time.

Standard instruction sets present a wide variety of load and store operations. The ALU has to generate addresses to pass to the Memory Address Register (cf. Chapter 5) and henceforth will need an adder for indexing purposes. Either the ALU's integer adder, or a shorter and less complex one, can be utilized.

Comparisons and conditional branches will also require an adder. In general, comparisons of two items will be handled by subtracting one from the other and testing the sign of the result. This will be done by setting either internal flip-flops, or some accessible to the programmer (recall the condition codes of the Sigma 5 in Chapter 2). Testing of the flip-flops will direct the flow of control.

Decimal arithmetic, sometimes not available in the hardware, can be implemented separately, for example with a serial adder, or be treated in the general-purpose ALU's adder controlled through microprogram (cf. Chapter 7). Character-oriented instructions can likewise have a special unit devised for them or use the common resources. There will be no design complexities, most of the work being done by the firmware or the software.

All instructions sets include a variety of shift instructions. The basic arithmetic operations also require shifting capabilities. Very often the adder will be connected to a shift register and associated counter. Capabilities for logical shifts with sign extensions and for circular shifts (rotates) are common. In some powerful machines where several events can occur at the same time, there is a need for synchronous shifting, that is an operation for which timing is independent of the number of bits being shifted. This is not the case for ordinary shift registers where the shifting time is dependent on the count and is of the form:

$$t = s + a \cdot n$$

where s is some set-up time and a is the subsequent delay for a single bit shift.

A synchronous shift can be implemented as follows. The shift count c can be written (with $c_i = 0$ or 1) as:

$$c = \sum_{i=0}^{a} c_i \cdot 2^i, \text{ where } 2^{a+1} - 1 \text{ is the maximum shift count.}$$

Then the shift unit can be constructed with a columns of temporary registers as shown in Figure 3.16. If $c_i = 0$, then bits from column i pass directly to their corresponding ones in column $i + 1$. On the other hand if $c_i = 1$, then bit j of column i will be transferred to bit $j + 2^i$ in column

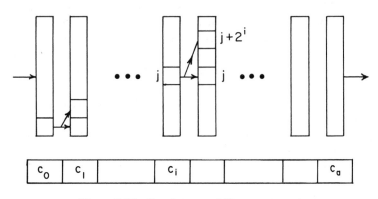

Figure 3.16   Synchronous shift arrangement

$i + 1$ (we assumed a straightforward left shift; for a right shift, the count can be considered as negative, i.e., $c_i = -1$, and bit j would be passed to bit $j - 2^i$; in the cases of circular shifts, these numbers are to be taken modulo n, the word length; sign extensions present no difficulty).

Since we have to pass through the a columns, independently of c, the timing is always the same, i.e.:

$$t = s + a'$$

where s is again a set-up time and a' is a constant linked to the time for a bit to traverse from one column to the next. Very often, floating-point units which use a radix different from 2 will have a base r as well as a base 2 shifter.

Finally, embedded in any ALU are encoders and decoders, counters, flip-flops, time-pulse generators etc. . . . . Their design is outside the scope of this book and can be found in any good text on logical and circuit design. Our next task is to see how building blocks, such as adders, can be connected to form units capable of executing instructions.

3.6   BIBLIOGRAPHICAL NOTES, REFERENCES AND EXERCISES

Knuth's historical account of number systems and his algorithmic discussion of the 4 basic operations are as brilliant as can be expected [Knuth 69]. He also discusses the residue number system following the ideas first expressed in [Svoboda and

Valach 55] and later independently in [Garner 59]. [Blaauw 76] is a thorough treatment of the hardware implementation of the four basic operations in fixed point format. There is some emphasis on evaluating the various schemes available and some of our figures have been taken from this book. [MacSorley 61] is a very comprehensive survey on high speed binary arithmetic. The log $5n/4$ figure for carry propagation can be found in [Reitweisner 60]. The carry look-ahead principle can be traced back to [Weinberger and Smith 56], while the carry-save adder technique is much more ancient since Babbage already knew of it. The $O\ (n^{1.59})$ multiplication technique first appeared in [Karatsuba and Ofman 62] and the $O\ (n \log n \log \log n)$ method is due to [Schonage and Strassen 71]. The recoding of Table 3.2 is from [Anderson et al. 67] and the Wallace tree construction was first published in [Wallace 64]. Fast and complex division algorithms can be found in [Robertson 58], and the convergence method is clearly explained in [Anderson et al. 67]. The synchronous shift of Section 3.5 has been used in the CDC 6600 and is "rediscovered" periodically [Thornton 70].

For more advanced study of Computer Arithmetic the reader can consult [Kuck 78] and [Hwang 79].

References

1. Anderson, S., Earle, J., Goldschmitt, R., and D. Powers, "The IBM System/360 Model 91: Floating-point Execution Unit," *IBM Journal of Research and Development, 11,* (Jan. 1967), 34–53.

2. Blaauw, G., *Digital Systems Implementation,* Prentice-Hall, Englewood Cliffs, N.J., 1976.

3. Garner, H., "The Residue Number System," *IRE Trans. Elec. Comp., EC-8,* (Mar. 1959), 140–147.

4. Hwang, K., *Computer Arithmetic. Principles, Architecture and Design,* Wiley, New York, N.Y., 1979.

5. Karatsuba, A., and Y. Ofman, "Multiplication of Multidigit Numbers on Automata," *Dokl. Akad. Nauk. SSSR, 145,* (1962), 293–294, (in Russian).

6. Knuth, D., *The Art of Computer Programming vol. 2. Semi-numerical Algorithms,* Addison-Wesley, Reading, Mass., 1969.

7. Kuck, D., *The Structure of Computers and Computations,* vol. 1, Wiley, New York, N.Y., 1978.

8. MacSorley, O., "High Speed Arithmetic in Binary Computers," *Proc. of the IRE, 49,* (Jan. 1961), 67–91.

9. Reitwiesner, G., "The Determination of Carry Propagation Length for Binary Addition," *IRE Trans. Elec. Comp., EC-9,* (Mar. 1960), 35–38.

10. Robertson, J., "A New Class of Digital Division Methods," *IRE Trans. Elec. Comp., EC-7,* (Sept. 1958), 218-222.

11. Schonage, A., and Strassen, V., "Schnelle Multiplikation grosser Zahlen," *Computing,* 7, (1971), 281-292.

12. Svoboda, A., and M. Valach, "Rational Numerical Systems of Residual Classes," in *Stroje na Zpracovani Informaci,* 3, (1955), 247-295.

13. Thornton, J., *Design of a Computer. The Control Data 6600,* Scott, Foresman and Co., Glenview, Ill., 1970.

14. Wallace, C., "A Suggestion for a Fast Multiplier," *IEEE Trans. Elec. Comp., EC-13,* (Feb. 1964), 14-17.

15. Weinberger, A. and J. Smith, "A One Microsecond Adder Using One Megacycle Circuitry," *IRE Trans. Elec. Comp., EC-5,* (Jun. 1956), 65-73.

Exercises

1. Give an algorithm to convert integers from decimal to binary using only binary shifts and additions. Give a CDL description of the algorithm assuming that the decimal number is encoded in BCD in a source register S and that the resulting binary integer is to be found in a destination register R. Temporary registers can be used to hold masks or constants.

2. Give an algorithm to convert integers in the range $[0, 2^{31} - 1]$ from binary to decimal using binary arithmetic and no division. A limited amount of table look-up is allowed (e.g., a table with 10 entries). The output should be in BCD form.

3. Give an algorithm for the addition of two numbers in excess-3 code representation in a style similar to the one in Section 2.1.

4. Prove the Chinese remainder theorem.

5. Prove that if $|y| > |x|$, $y < 0$ and $x \geq 0$, and $|y|$ is subtracted from $|x|$ according to system (2), then $(s_{n-1}, \ldots, s_1)$ is the 2's complement representation of $|x| - |y|$. Apply the same reasoning to the case $x < 0$ and $y \geq 0$.

6. Obtain system (2) directly from a truth table and prove that it is correct for a sign and magnitude implementation. Show that the system

$$s_i \leftarrow (x_i \oplus y_i) \oplus \bar{b}_i \qquad 1 \leq i \leq n,\ b_1 = 0$$

$$b_{i+1} \leftarrow \bar{x}_i \cdot \bar{y}_i + (\bar{x}_i + \bar{y}_i) \cdot b_i \qquad\qquad (10)$$

yields a correct subtraction type of adder for a 1's complement representation. "Add" $+4$ and -4 represented in 1's complement in a 4-bit word using systems (1) and (10). Discuss your results.

7. Given 6-bit registers, convert the decimal numbers 6, 9, 23, −9, −30, into sign and magnitude, 1's and 2's complement. Then perform the operations:

$$6 + 9, 9 + 23, 6 - 9, 6 - 23, 23 - 6, -30 - 23, -9 - 23,$$

in these three systems and justify your answers.

8. Give a block diagram of a 3-level carry look-ahead adder with 2 sections of 4 groups of 4 bits. What is the worst case speed-up when compared with a ripple adder (assume 2's complement).

9. Give a multiplication scheme similar to the pencil and paper algorithm of Section 3.1 but which proceeds with a left to right scan of the multiplier. What are the disadvantages of such a method (an advantage is that the most significant bits are obtained first, an interesting situation for floating-point multiplications).

10. In the spirit of Figure 3.7 and 3.8 perform the multiplication of −4 by −3 in 2's complement. Repeat the examples of Figure 3.7 and 3.8 for the 1's complement system after having set forth the rules for multiplying in that system.

11. Provide a table similar to Table 3.2 and an algorithm akin to the skipping over 0's and 1's multiplication method for a 2-bit multiplier recoding with only the multiplicand and its double being available.

12. Show that a good approximation of the depth of a Wallace tree is:

$$\frac{\lceil \log (n - 3) \rceil}{0.6} \le a \le \frac{\lceil \log (n - 3) \rceil}{0.6} + 1, \ 5 \le n \le 200$$

13. Find examples similar to those of Figure 3.14 for the 6 remaining cases of Table 3.3.

14. Compute the ranges of real numbers representable in each of the formats of Figure 3.15.

15. Modify the real to integer and the integer to real conversion algorithms for the case where the mantissa is a fraction.

16. A computer has a word length of 24 bits with the sign of the mantissa in the leftmost bit in a floating-point format where 5 bits are reserved for the encoding of the exponent. The exponent radix is 4, excess notation is used, the binary point is assumed at the left of the mantissa and numbers are represented in 2's complement.

    (a) State in some convenient decimal notation the largest representable number.

    (b) Is the number $(26260000)_8$ normalized?

(c) Convert $(51520000)_8$, a floating-point number in the above format, in decimal notation.

(d) Convert the decimal real number 1.75 in normalized format.

17. Transcribe the formats of Figure 3.15 in ISP notation.

18. Prove that a 1's complement subtraction of numbers in excess-notation yields a 1's complement representation of their difference.

Chapter 4

POWERFUL CENTRAL PROCESSORS

In our presentation of the ISP notation, we showed what had to be included in the description of the central processor (Pc) state from the programmer's view-point. In Chapter 3, we presented some algorithms for performing arithmetic on data or, in PMS terms, we described the behavior of some of the D-units of the ALU. Now our goal is to specify how these D-units can be integrated with some control K and some internal storage M to form the central processor Pc as shown in Figure 2.2.a.

Our emphasis will not be on the implementation of the control. The current trend is to microprogram Pc's, in micro and minicomputers as well as in larger machines (e.g., the whole IBM System/370 line is microprogrammed) and even in supercomputers (like the CDC STAR-100). This will be seen in Chapter 7. For the time being, we shall imply a decoding of the control flow and show its logical implications; but we shall not elaborate on its implementation except in specific instances when describing an existing machine if some parts of the control present outstanding features.

We start this chapter with the basic hardware requirements for the building of a small Pc. Looking at the instruction execution cycle will point out the places where performance improvements can be achieved: namely, instruction overlaps, look-ahead features and multifunctional units. We shall continue with a general view of the parallel execution of instructions and associated look-ahead principles. The CDC 6600 central processor design will provide us with an interesting case study for many of these performance enhancements. Pipelining within functional units, a generalization of instruction overlap, will be introduced with the IBM System/360 Model 91 as a vehicle for presentation. We shall conclude this chapter with some remarks on the design of stack processors.

135

4.1 BASIC REQUIREMENTS FOR A Pc

The Pc as seen from the programmer's viewpoint consists of the following:

- A set of registers which define the state of the system;
- A set of registers which contain operands for and temporary results of computations;
- An arithmetic-logical unit (ALU) which executes instructions according to their opcodes and associated operands as implied in the description of the instruction set.

From the designer's point of view, three main blocks are also present, namely:

- An *instruction unit* (I-unit) whose role is to fetch and decode instructions, to generate the operands' effective addresses and to fetch and/or store these operands. After appropriate decoding of the instruction and fetching of the operands, orders are passed to an execution unit which will perform the operations;
- An *execution unit* (D-unit) which can either be integrated around a single "block" of hardware (or a chip), or which is composed of several functional units. Its role is to execute the orders sent by the I-unit;
- *Storage registers,* some accessible to the programmer, and some internal to the Pc (either in the I- or the D-unit).

Of course these three building blocks are connected via data and control paths in a way transparent to the programmer who sees only the end results of the computations as described by ISP. But the designer is responsible for the location of the registers encoding the program state, for the amount of concurrency allowed in the D-unit and in the transfers in and out of the register block etc., that is, decisions which influence the speed of the computations but not their correctness.

Starting with the instruction unit, we look at the minimal hardware which is required for a Pc with an integrated D-unit able to perform integer (parallel) addition and subtraction, as well as shifts, logical operations and comparison (a typical minicomputer basic instruction set). In these needs, we do not include entities such as clocks, multiplexers etc., and we stay mostly at the level of detail that could be described in ISP with some incursions into the CDL domain.

Figure 4.1.a shows the basic blocks in an I-unit. They are:

- An instruction register (*IR*) holding the current instruction. Its opcode part can be gated to a decoder (*DC*), a part of the control unit, which

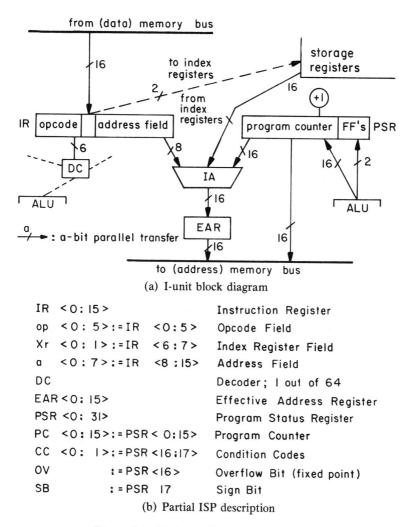

(a) I-unit block diagram

IR	<0:15>	Instruction Register
op	<0:5>:=IR <0:5>	Opcode Field
Xr	<0:1>:=IR <6:7>	Index Register Field
a	<0:7>:=IR <8:15>	Address Field
DC		Decoder; 1 out of 64
EAR	<0:15>	Effective Address Register
PSR	<0:31>	Program Status Register
PC	<0:15>:=PSR<0:15>	Program Counter
CC	<0:1>:=PSR<16:17>	Condition Codes
OV	:=PSR<16>	Overflow Bit (fixed point)
SB	:=PSR 17	Sign Bit

(b) Partial ISP description

Figure 4.1   Basic requirements of an I-unit

will either exercise control lines in the ALU (or D-unit) or activate the transfer to the first instruction of a microprogram for that opcode, depending on the control structure.

- An effective address register (*EAR*) holding the address of the operands to be fetched or stored. This *EAR* is connected to the output of an adder which can take as input the address field of the instruction register on the one hand, and either the program counter or an index register selected by the index register field in the *IR* on the other hand. The adder itself can be part of the D-unit or be a dedicated "address" adder (*IA*) in the I-unit as shown in the figure.

- A program status register (*PSR*) which contains the program counter (*PC*) and often some flip-flops (bits) indicating the results of conditions such as the sign of a result, a possible overflow etc., (recall the condition codes in Chapter 2). If instructions are restricted to occupying a full word, then some means of incrementing the program counter by 1 must be provided. If the instruction length is variable this will be reflected in a slightly more sophisticated increment procedure as well as in the packaging into parcels of instructions from a buffer to the *IR* (this is the case when several instructions can be embedded in a single word). In order to implement conditional jumps, both the *EAR* and the *PC* should be accessible to the ALU (perhaps in a unidirectional sense).

Figure 4.1.b gives a partial ISP description of a 16-bit word I-unit (cf. also Exercise 1).

We now turn our attention to the D-unit (cf. Figure 4.2). Its nucleus is an ALU (*DA*) which can perform the operations mentioned earlier. Its operands are·contained in a double length accumulator (*AQ* and *MQ*) with shifting

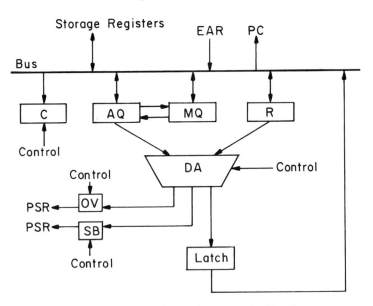

Figure 4.2   Basic requirements of a D-unit

capabilities and another single length register R. Some flip-flops which could be part of the I-unit's PSR are set by logical conditions such as overflow or sign detection. A counter (C) holds shift counts and is also used in the multiplication and division algorithms (these two operations can be implemented as hardwired logic or can be simulated in software, or more generally microprogrammed).

It is somewhat difficult to distinguish between the registers which are part of the D-unit and those which are storage registers. For example, if we were to consider a Pc with a set of general registers like those of the IBM System/370, then the AQ-MQ and R registers of Figure 4.2, as well as the counter C, could be embedded in the ALU (DA). The instruction's first task would be to gate the appropriate general registers to these (now internal) registers. We shall see examples of this scheme which is currently most prevalent. In particular, in microprocessors the ALU is on a chip along with a set (often called file and even sometimes misnamed stack) of registers and part of the control logic. But previous single accumulator machines, like the IBM 7090, had designs which more resemble that shown in Figure 4.2 with the AQ and MQ directly accessible by program, and the DA being an adder.

Assuming a modern design implying a set of registers accessible by the programmer, let us call it SR, we must show the data paths between the I-unit, the D-unit, SR, and the primary memory Mp (we leave aside for the moment I/O interconnections).

Access to and from Mp is required for the IR (receive data), EAR (send address), the storage registers SR (send and receive data), and PC (send address). Therefore, we need a Pc-Mp *bus*, often called the memory switch, whose characteristics will be described in the next chapter. Communication between SR, PC, and EAR (or IR) and the ALU (or DA) is also needed for loading and storing operands exercising the adder (SR), for immediate values and/or shift counts (PC and EAR), and for returning jump addresses (PC). In contrast to the memory switch, this D-bus is not represented in a PMS description. But when concurrency in the Pc becomes a major objective in the design (be it at the microprogram or at the multifunctional unit level) its design and control become extremely important and it can be subdivided into several data and control paths. This will become quite apparent in our study of the CDC 6600 and in Chapter 7.

4.2 SPEEDING UP THE INSTRUCTION CYCLE

We now examine the instruction cycle (recall Figure 2.6) and look at the resources in the I-unit and in the D-unit which are busy during each of the five elementary steps. For each of these steps we note which resources have to be free at the beginning and which ones can be released at the completion. This will allow us to determine those resources which are critical and which may have to be duplicated, if we want to realize as much concurrency as possible. Table 4.1 summarizes this allocation procedure using the terminology of the previous section.

Step 1, the instruction fetch, stores the next instruction in *IR*. The address of the instruction is found in *PC* which can be modified at the termination of the step, and the memory switch (Mp switch) is used for the transfer. Step 2, decoding and program counter incrementing (we assume nonbranching instructions, a restriction that will be taken care of soon), requires free use of the decoder *DC* and of *PC*. The former can be released after having performed its task, while on the other hand *PC* has to be kept untouched until step 1 is to be called on again. The effective address calculation, step 3, requires the use of *IR*, some register from *SR* (which is not of interest here), the I-unit adder *IA*, and the effective address register *EAR*. At the end of this step, *IR* and *IA* can be released since all the information encoded in the instruction has been extracted (*IR*), and we have at most one addition in *IA* per instruction. The next step, operand fetch, requires the use of Mp switch and of *EAR* whose contents set in the previous step have not been modified. At the end of step 4, both Mp switch and *EAR* can be released. The last step takes place uniquely in the D-unit and requires also that D-bus be free.

If we were to assume that all five steps take the same amount of time, or in other words that the ideal overlap of Figure 2.7 can be realized, all resources which are used for a duration of more than one step and which have to be left untouched are to be either duplicated or modified so that no information is lost. In particular this is true of *PC* since instructions will be fetched at every step (we shall have five instructions at various stages of processing). *PC* has to be incremented in step 1 (and this presents no difficulty) and some buffer is needed to store incoming instructions while *IR* still holds the one in the decoding stage and for which an effective address calculation is performed

Table 4.1   Resource allocation in an instruction cycle

Step #	Function	Resources needed	Resources released
1	Instruction fetch	IR, Mp switch	PC, Mp switch
2	Decode and increment program counter	IR, DC, PC	DC
3	Effective address calculation	IA, EAR, IR	IA, IR
4	Operand fetch	EAR, Mp switch	EAR, Mp switch
5	Execution	D-Bus, D-unit	D-Bus, D-unit

(steps 2 and 3). If *IR* is loaded at the end of step 1 and released only at the end of step 3, and if a new instruction is fetched at every step, it is not difficult to foresee the disaster! We shall have an almost continuous overflow situation in the buffer since it fills up twice as fast as it is being emptied. Other areas of conflict in this too perfect a scheme are found in the use of the same resource in two different steps like the Mp switch in steps 1 and 4.

Even if we could modify our instruction cycle so that concurrency of fetches could be done and appropriate buffers for instructions and operands set up, we would still be far from a realistic design because of the assumptions of equal times for each step. We would have to assume a worst case for each stage and pay penalties: for example, an add instruction would take as long as a floating-point divide if they both were hardwired, or every instruction would be treated as referencing an operand whose address is indexed. Therefore we have to be a little more cautious in our approach.

With Table 4.1 we can divide the steps into three groups following the resource requirements: instruction fetch (step 1 and part of 2), I-unit tasks (remainder of step 2, steps 3 and 4), and D-unit tasks (step 5). If the Mp switch is constrained to be accessed sequentially and hence cannot be time-shared by the instruction fetch (I-fetch) and the I-unit, then either the I-unit and the D-unit can overlap or the I-fetch and the D-unit can work in parallel. A possible arrangement is the one shown in Figure 4.3. This resource vs. time graph is called a *Gantt chart*.

Now if Mp is organized in such a way that it is as easy to fetch a double word as it is to fetch a single one, then with the addition of a buffer to hold the extra word we can realize the overlap of Figure 4.4. Here we have the first inkling of look-ahead, that is some work is done before it is actually needed. It might very well turn out that this prefetching will be useless if the preceding instruction is a successful branch. Although branching instructions occur

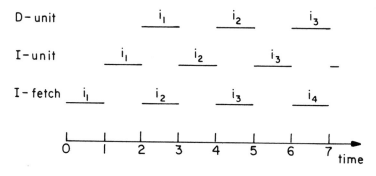

Figure 4.3 Simple overlap

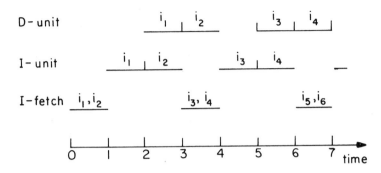

Figure 4.4   Overlap with double instruction fetch

approximately every 3 instructions (cf. Table 2.1), the execution of a successful branch as the first of two instructions loaded simultaneously is much less
frequent. And, as we see below, we can further enhance the process to take
care of the branches, at least partially.

Returning to Figures 4.3 and 4.4, if t is the (worst-case) time to execute the
tasks in either I-fetch, I-unit, or D-unit, and assuming that these worst-cases
are the same in each stage of the instruction cycle, then we have:

t_0 = time to execute n instructions without overlap = $3nt$
t_1 = time to execute n instructions with simple overlap = $(1 + 2n)t$
t_2 = time to execute n instructions with prefetching = $(1 + \lceil 3n/2 \rceil)t$

that is respective improvements of 50 and 100 percent.

These figures are slightly misleading since in the no-overlap case (t_0) we do
not need a worst-case timing, and also the worst cases in each stage might be
different (there should be a t_f, t_i and t_d defined for each stage; cf. Exercise 2).
However, the improvement factors quoted above give a good feel of the advantages derived through overlap and look-ahead.

The timing of Figure 4.4 requires that Mp be divided into two banks which
can be accessed independently (this was the case in the IBM 7094 whose instruction cycle could be abstracted as in Figure 4.4). This is referred to as
memory interleaving (cf. Chapter 5). With more extensive memory interleaving, instruction and operand fetches can be done concurrently. The ideal
situation is depicted in the Gantt chart of Figure 4.5 with:

t_3 = time to execute n instructions with ideal overlap = $(2 + n)t$.

The reader will certainly have noticed that a double instruction fetch is no

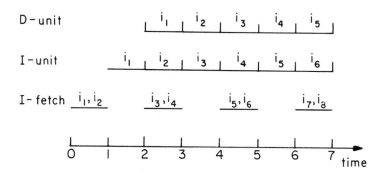

Figure 4.5   Ideal overlap with double instruction fetch

longer necessary under these ideal conditions. Figure 4.6 is therefore the optimal situation (recall Figure 2.7). The advantage of prefetching is that it minimizes the possibility of contention for memory modules since instruction and operand fetches will overlap half as often. The diagram of Figure 4.5 is a realistic representation of the IBM System/360 model 75 instruction cycle.

Having achieved what appears to be as close to an optimal overlap as possible, what other actions can be done in order to further speed-up the instruction cycle? Three areas where improvements can be readily realized present themselves immediately:

- Speed-up the instruction fetch;
- Speed-up I-unit processing;
- Speed-up D-unit processing.

But these speed-ups have to be done concurrently since it would be worthless to have two extremely fast stages if the third one is going to act as a bottleneck.

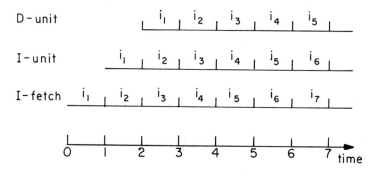

Figure 4.6   Ideal overlap

Until recently the weak point in the chain was the Mp cycle. With the advent of interleaved memories, of caches and of semi-conductor memories without a destructive read-out, instruction and operand fetches can be done much faster. These advances in the Mp switch structure, in technology and in hierarchies of memory will be discussed later. Their influence on Pc design will be that more than one instruction can be prefetched efficiently and that some operands can be present while the D-unit is busy processing a previous instruction. Hence, buffers for instructions as well as for operands and operand addresses will be necessary. For example, the IBM System/370 model 155 allows prefetching of 3 words (an average of 3 instructions) but disallows operand preloading. On the other hand, the look-ahead features of the model 165 are more elaborate.

The overlap features in the Pc of the model 165 are shown in some detail in Figure 4.7 (the Mp switch and the D-units are oversimplified). An instruction buffer *IB* can hold two double words, or 16 bytes, that is 4 instructions on the average. This corresponds to a prefetching of one 'unit' since the Mp switch bandwidth is 8 bytes. The *IB* is connected to the unique instruction register *IR* which prepares instructions to be executed by the D-units. Up to

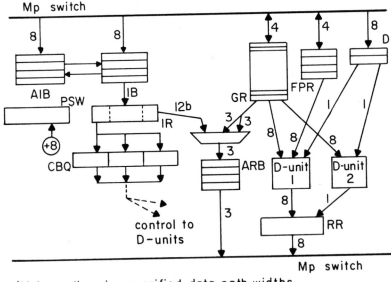

(Unless otherwise specified data path widths are in bytes; the notation I2b indicates a data path of width 12 bits)

Figure 4.7   IBM System/370 Model 165 overlap features

3 instructions can be decoded in advance and they are stored in a circular buffer queue (*CBQ*). The decoding can be delayed by conditions such as the unavailability of required resources or such as the address adder *IA* being busy computing the effective address of an operand needed for a previous instruction. These conditions will be couched in more general terms in the next section and more complex case studies will be treated later.

Associated with *IB* is an auxiliary instruction buffer *AIB* of the same capacity. *AIB* plays an active role only when an instruction which can bring a break in the sequential control flow is encountered (e.g., a branch or an EXECUTE instruction which in effect interprets another instruction). In that case, one stream of instructions, the most likely according to predictions based on opcodes, general register use and other factors, is loaded into *IB*, while the other one is concurrently filling *AIB*. If the prediction of success turns out to be incorrect, *IB* and *AIB* are swapped (this swapping is unnecessary for branch instructions and a one-way traffic from the *AIB* to *IB* appears to be sufficient).

The address adder *IA* is a three-input adder since System/370 uses base addressing. Its output is connected to an effective address register buffer *ARB* which can hold four 3-byte addresses. Data operands can also be prefetched in *DB* (two 8-byte registers).

In addition to the double buffering scheme of the IBM System/370 model 165, the instruction fetch phase can be further optimized, to its extreme, by avoiding it as much as possible. This is feasible when we have a look-behind as well as a look-ahead facility. The instruction buffer, as we have considered it up to now, is a first-in-first-out (FIFO) queue. As an instruction becomes decoded it disappears from the buffer. Keeping the same structure in mind, i.e., a FIFO queue, let us add the provision for a decoded, and even executed, instruction to be kept in the buffer until the *m* instructions following it in its sequential stream have been decoded. The new buffer structure looks like the one shown in Figure 4.8.a. The current instruction is in *IB*(PC), the look-ahead part is between *IB*(PC-1) and *IB*(first), and the look-behind portion between *IB*(PC+1) and *IB*(last). If the instruction at *IB*(PC) is not a branch, execution proceeds as in the look-ahead features previously described. A new unit, say a word, is fetched through the Mp switch, all locations in the buffer are moved up one position, and *IB*(last) disappears. However, if we have a branch and if this branch is successful and its target is between *IB*(PC) and *IB*(last), then we do not have to perform an I-fetch since the next instruction is already there (cf. Figure 4.8.b). This type of operation is appropriately called *loop-mode* since it corresponds to a branch backwards in the flow of control. Very often it will be executed more than once and the look-ahead feature can be disconnected since all instructions in the loop are

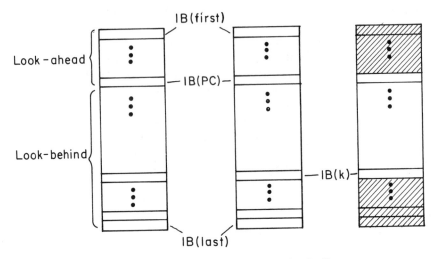

Figure 4.8   Look-behind instruction buffer

in the buffer (Figure 4.8.c). The Mp switch can now service operand fetches and stores exclusively and the I-fetch cycle is simply reduced to a (hardware) pointer modification in the look-behind portion of the buffer. When the branch becomes unsuccessful, or in other words the loop is terminated, normal operations again take place. Implementations of such schemes will be discussed shortly with examples drawn from the CDC 6600 and the IBM System/360 model 91. The CDC 7600, the IBM System/360 model 195, ILLIAC IV and the CRAY-1 have similar features.

The time consuming step in the I-unit phase is the operand fetch. As before the best way to minimize this operation is to avoid it. This means that register-register instructions should be used as much as possible. This is the principle followed by the CDC series. General register machines, like the IBM System/370, are not always successful in this respect as was reported in Chapter 2. Vector processors use the interleave features to their maximum efficiency. Speeding up the memory hierarchy with the introduction of fast buffers, or caches, so that its cycle time matches that of the D-units is also a factor but, as we shall see, the randomness of data access, as compared to the sequentiality of instructions, leaves more room for inefficiency.

In order to accelerate the D-unit processing—and certainly we cannot avoid the data computations—one can first utilize efficient algorithms as discussed in the previous chapter. In general, this will imply that several D-units, each one tailored to a set of functions, will be present as was the case in the IBM System/370 model 165 shown in Figure 4.7. It has two D-units, one centered around a 64-bit adder for fixed and floating-point arithmetic, and the other built around a byte serial adder for character processing and decimal operations. This gain can be further enhanced if we allow several D-units to operate in parallel (this is not the case in the model 165). If we permit overlaps in D-unit executions, then we need some hardware control mechanism which can check on the permissible order of operations. These controls can become quite complex and their requirements will be discussed in the next section. In the same vein, if concurrency is allowed in the execution then programs should be modified so that they take advantage of this mode of operation. This implies detection of parallelism and scheduling, topics that will also be covered briefly in the next section.

4.3 LOOK-AHEAD AND PARALLELISM

4.3.1 Models of Look-ahead Processors

In the previous section we saw how the overlap of instruction fetch, decoding and operand fetch, and finally execution per se, could speed up the instruction execution cycle. The most simplifying assumption we made was to postulate that the three steps took the same amount of time. If we relax this assumption, then we might obtain a Gantt chart similar to that of Figure 4.9.a which is one of many possible situations. The salient facts in this particular example are:

- Each of the 3 stages can be delayed (and not necessarily by a stage in the previous instruction). For example, the D-unit execution in instruction $i + 3$ is delayed because the D-unit step in instruction $i + 2$ is not completed;
- I-fetches cannot overlap; when I-unit steps overlap, this corresponds only to operand fetches performed concurrently. This is to say that in our model there is a unique decoder. In the following, we shall consider loading and fetching of operands as part of the D-unit tasks. Therefore, the revised timing chart is the one of Figure 4.9.b.
- An instruction can terminate after one of its successors (in the sequential stream) is already finished. In our example, instruction $i + 1$ is completed before instruction i.

The challenge in the design of a look-ahead processor which allows these out-of-order terminations is to control the execution of instructions so that the results obtained are the same as those which would have resulted from strict sequential execution. Furthermore, we would like to obtain a minimal

Instr.

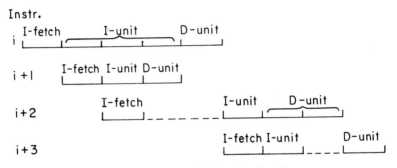

(a) Look-ahead with fetch in I-unit

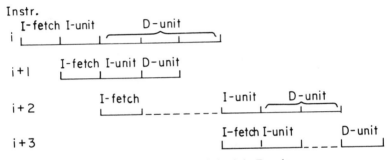

(b) Look-ahead with fetch in D-unit

Figure 4.9 Look-ahead and parallelism schematic timing

completion time. As can be expected this optimality criterion is in direct opposition with the hope of retaining a rather simple control. The complexity of the implementation will grow with the desire to be as close to optimal as possible.

We start with a rather simple model. The processor consists of m functional units, $D_1, D_2, \ldots, D_m$ and n general registers (accumulators) R_1m R_2, $\ldots, R_n$. Each of the D_i is restricted to a specific set of operations; for example, D_i is a floating-point adder or a multiplier. Instructions will be of the form:

$R_i \leftarrow D_h(R_j, R_k)$ (Arithmetic-logical)

If $P(R_i)$ **then goto** L (Predicate or branch on condition)
    else next (sequential) instruction

Note that functional units operate only on registers. Load operations are of the form:

$$R_i \leftarrow D_{\text{load}}$$

and stores can be viewed as:

$$\emptyset \leftarrow D_{\text{store}}(R_i)$$

(This model can be modified to fit a one address + general register scheme).

The instructions are fetched, in a look-ahead fashion, in an instruction buffer. The I-fetch takes a single unit of time which we shall refer to as *minor cycle*. In other words, we assume that there is no degradation because of memory contention. This corresponds rather faithfully to a loop-mode execution, the period of time when the look-ahead processor is most efficient. Similarly, if the decoding part of the I-unit step allows the instruction to proceed, we shall assume that a minor cycle will be sufficient to schedule the operation to a specific D_i.

When the decoding prevents this scheduling (or in our new terminology when the instruction cannot be *issued*) for reasons which will be soon apparent, subsequent instructions cannot be issued either. Therefore, the unique decoder-scheduler services instructions on a first-in-first-out basis.

What are the conditions which prevent an instruction from being issued? The first one, which is resource oriented, is the unavailability of a functional unit to perform the task.

Example 4.1   Assuming a single adder, with an addition time of 4 units and a single multiplier with a multiply time of 10 units, the sequence:

$$S_1: \quad R_1 \leftarrow R_2 + R_3$$
$$S_2: \quad R_4 \leftarrow R_2 * R_5$$
$$S_3: \quad R_6 \leftarrow R_3 + R_6$$

executes according to the timing chart shown in Figure 4.10.

In addition to the delay due to the D-unit conflict between the first and the third instructions, this figure also shows that under our assumptions of perfect look-ahead and unique decoding the I-fetch and I-unit steps can be lumped into a single I-unit step. This unique step will be delayed when the conditions for "issue" are not met.   □

The second factor which can prevent an instruction from being issued is procedural. It happens when two instructions are dependent on each other, that is when the order in which they are completed will have an impact on the values being computed. If S_i and S_j are two instructions, let I_i and I_j be their

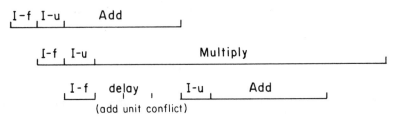

Figure 4.10   Functional unit conflict

respective domains (I stands for input), and O_i and O_j be their ranges (O is for output). If there is no deviation from the sequential flow of control between S_i and S_j, i.e., the two instructions are in the same sequential "block", then these two instructions can be processed in parallel if and only if:

- They do not store values in the same variable (register);
- The result of one is not an input operand for the other.

Translating these requirements in terms of domains and ranges yields:

$$O_i \cap O_j = \emptyset$$
$$O_i \cap I_j = \emptyset \quad \text{, for all } (i, j), i \neq j, \qquad (1)$$
$$O_j \cap I_i = \emptyset,$$

where $\emptyset$ is the empty set.

In the instruction sequence of Example 4.1:

$$O_1 = \{R_1\}, \ I_1 = \{R_2, R_3\}$$
$$O_2 = \{R_4\}, \ I_2 = \{R_2, R_5\}$$
$$O_3 = \{R_6\}, \ I_3 = \{R_3, R_6\}$$

so that we have:

$$O_1 \cap O_2 = \emptyset \quad\quad O_1 \cap O_3 = \emptyset \quad\quad O_2 \cap O_3 = \emptyset$$
$$O_1 \cap I_2 = \emptyset \quad\quad O_1 \cap I_3 = \emptyset \quad\quad O_2 \cap I_3 = \emptyset$$
$$O_2 \cap I_1 = \emptyset \quad\quad O_3 \cap I_1 = \emptyset \quad\quad O_3 \cap I_2 = \emptyset$$

and all three operations can be processed in parallel (or are independent) from the procedural viewpoint.

Example 4.2   Consider the sequence:

$$S_1: R_1 \leftarrow R_2 + R_3$$
$$S_2: R_1 \leftarrow R_4 * R_5$$

We have:

$$O_1 = \{R_1\} \text{ and } O_2 = \{R_1\}, \text{ hence } O_1 \cap O_2 \neq \emptyset$$

S_1 must be completed before S_2 can proceed. $\qquad \square$

Example 4.3 Consider the sequence:

$$S_1: R_1 \leftarrow R_2 + R_3$$
$$S_2: R_4 \leftarrow R_1 * R_5$$

Now $O_1 = \{R_1\}$, $I_2 = \{R_1, R_5\}$ and hence $O_1 \cap I_2 \neq \emptyset$. Again S_2 has to wait for completion of S_1. $\qquad \square$

In designing our simple processor, we need to keep track of the availability of the D-units and of the use of the registers. The first task is easy: we associate a "busy" bit with each unit. When b_h, the bit associated with D_h, is 0, an instruction can be issued to D_h. At this point b_h is set to 1 and this prevents any further issuing to D_h. At completion of the operation in D_h, b_h is reset to 0.

Looking at Examples 4.2 and 4.3, it appears at first glance that a single bit would be sufficient for testing register availability. The bit r_k associated with R_k would be set to 1 when R_k is in the range of an issued instruction. It would disallow the further issuing of any instruction having R_k either in its range or in its domain. When R_k receives its value, at the completion of the instruction for which it is an output variable, r_k can be reset to 0. This scheme fails, however, when we consider the case where R_k is in the domain of an instruction S_i ($R_k \in I_i$) and in the range of S_j ($R_k \in O_j$) which follows S_i. The third condition of system (1) is not fulfilled and S_j cannot proceed since there is a risk of having its result stored in R_k before having used R_k as an operand of S_i. Setting a bit r_k when R_k is either in the domain or in the range of S_i would resolve that conflict, but it would also disallow the concurrent execution of two instructions which have common elements in their domain. Since several instructions can have non-disjoint domains, and since they all have to be completed before a common element can be part of the range of a subsequent instruction, we need counters to monitor the register utilizations.

Let C_k be the counter associated with R_k. Initially C_k is set to 0. When R_k is in the range of some instruction S_i, its counter is set to 1. If it is in its domain, C_k is decremented by 1 (if it is both in the range and domain, it is set to 1 since no other instruction can use it). At completion of an instruction, all elements of its range have their counters reset to 0 and all elements in its domain have their counters incremented by 1 (with the same exception as above where the counter will be reset to 0). Now, an instruction:

$$S_m: \quad R_i \leftarrow D_h(R_j, R_k)$$

can proceed when:

$b_h = 0$ (unit free)
$C_i = 0$ (result register R_i is neither a result nor an operand for a previous instruction)
$C_j \leq 0$ (the operands R_j and R_k are not results of previous incom-
$C_k \leq 0$ pleted instructions)

After issuing the instruction to D_h, we set (as an indivisible operation):

$$b_h \leftarrow 1 \ (D_h \text{ busy})$$
$$C_i \leftarrow 1 \ (\text{result register})$$
$$C_j \leftarrow C_j - 1$$
$$C_k \leftarrow C_k - 1$$

and at the completion of the operation:

$$b_h \leftarrow 0$$
$$C_i \leftarrow 0$$
$$C_j \leftarrow C_j + 1$$
$$C_k \leftarrow C_k + 1$$

If two operations are completed at the same time, we assume a fixed priority, based for example on unit numbers, for resetting counters and registers.

Example 4.4   Let us assume an integrated I-fetch-I-unit time of 1 cycle, an add time of 2 cycles, and a multiply time of 4 cycles. There is a single D_{add} and a single D_{multiply}. Consider the sequence:

$$S_1: \quad R_1 \leftarrow R_2 + R_3$$
$$S_2: \quad R_2 \leftarrow R_4 * R_5$$
$$S_3: \quad R_3 \leftarrow R_3 + R_4$$
$$S_4: \quad R_6 \leftarrow R_6 * R_6$$
$$S_5: \quad R_1 \leftarrow R_1 + R_5$$
$$S_6: \quad R_2 \leftarrow R_3 + R_4$$

The acyclic directed graph of Figure 4.11.a shows the procedural precedence relationships. There is an arc between S_i and S_j if $i < j$ and at least one of the three conditions in system (1) is not realized. Figure 4.11.b shows only

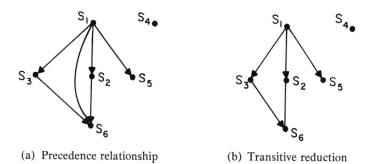

(a) Precedence relationship   (b) Transitive reduction

Figure 4.11   Procedural precedence relationships

the essential precedence relations; that is, if S_i has to be completed before S_j and S_k, and in turn S_j must complete before S_k, then the arc (S_i, S_k) is redundant. The graph in Figure 4.11.b is the transitive reduction of the one in Figure 4.11.a (the arc (S_1, S_6) has disappeared).

The timing sequence is shown in Figure 4.12. S_2 is delayed because $C_2 = -1$. S_4 is delayed because b_{multiply} is 1 and, similarly, S_6 is delayed because b_{add} is 1. The completion time is 15 units.   □

This last example shows that a small number of functional units and the procedural dependencies both contribute to the slow-down of operations. The first delaying action can be remedied by having several D-units which can execute the same operations. If such hardware investments seem to be too costly, we can use *virtual D-units* as follows. Instead of not issuing an instruction to a busy D-unit the request is put in a FIFO queue attached to the unit. When the latter becomes free, it selects the first instruction (if any) in

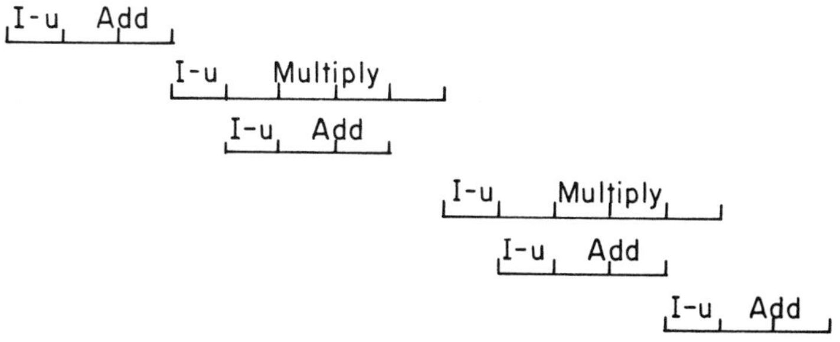

```
I-u   Add
  I-u      Multiply
    I-u   Add
            I-u      Multiply
              I-u   Add
                      I-u   Add
```

Figure 4.12   Simple look-ahead example timing

its queue. The advantage is that now only procedural dependencies prevent the issuing of instructions. Figure 4.13 shows the execution of the sequence of Example 4.4 under these new assumptions. The completion time has been reduced to 12 units (cf. Exercise 4); one should notice an instance of result register conflict delaying the issue of S_6.

Of course, replicating D-units, either in a real sense or with the aid of FIFO queues, is necessarily limited. A bound on the number of instructions which can be issued must be selected. It should be related to the frequency of occurrence of specific instructions, their execution time and the capacity of the look-ahead buffer. When the queue of a specific D-unit is filled, issuing of an instruction to that D-unit should be forbidden until completion of the current instruction. In essence, we replace the busy bit introduced earlier by a counter initialized to the maximum length of the queue (or the maximum number of units). With each instruction issued to a particular unit, the counter is decremented by 1, and it is incremented by 1 when the instruction is finished. The busy bit test is replaced by a test for zero on the counter.

When in the previous sections we discussed the requirements of the Pc, we saw that the D-units could either directly access the storage registers or that they could have their own internal operand buffers. If this latter situation were incorporated in our model, as justified by examination of actual implementations, then the condition $I_i \cap O_j = \emptyset$ is not required in order to allow concurrency between instruction S_i and its successor S_j. At S_i issue time, the contents of the registers in its domain are transferred into the internal buffers of the D-unit which is to perform the operation. We might pay some small time penalty for this transfer but parallelism is enhanced. Furthermore, the control is simplified since there is no need for a counter/register anymore and we can return to the original single bit scheme.

In the same way, results can be buffered in the D-unit awaiting the completion of previous operations. Thus, the condition $O_i \cap O_j = \emptyset$ can also be

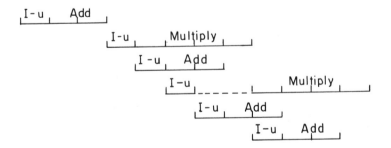

Figure 4.13   Look-ahead with virtual D-units

removed. Of course a second bit per register is needed for control purposes, so that at most one delayed store occurs for a given register.

Conflicts of the form $I_j \cap O_i \neq \emptyset$ must remain since they have logical implications on the correctness of the results.

Figure 4.14 shows the Gantt chart of the sequence of Example 4.4 assuming domain buffering and no virtual D-unit. The completion time is 13 units. Note that the first multiplication is not delayed anymore.

Assuming virtual (or duplication of) units and register buffering, can we still improve our look-ahead processor? The following example shows that while some procedural conflicts cannot be avoided, they need not stop the subsequent issuing of instructions.

Example 4.5 (a) Consider the sequence:

S_1: $R_1 \leftarrow R_2 + R_3$
S_2: $R_4 \leftarrow R_1 * R_5$
S_3: $R_6 \leftarrow R_3 + R_6$

Since there is a procedural conflict between S_1 and S_2, the latter would not be issued if we followed the rules that we have set forth until now. However, if it is *conditionally issued* by reserving the multiply unit for it and indicating which registers it needs and which ones it is going to change, then we could thereafter issue and execute S_3.

(b) Consider the sequence:

S_1: $R_3 \leftarrow R_1 / R_2$
S_2: $R_4 \leftarrow R_1 * R_3$
S_3: $R_1 \leftarrow R_2 + R_5$

It is not difficult to see that if S_2 is conditionally issued as in the previous

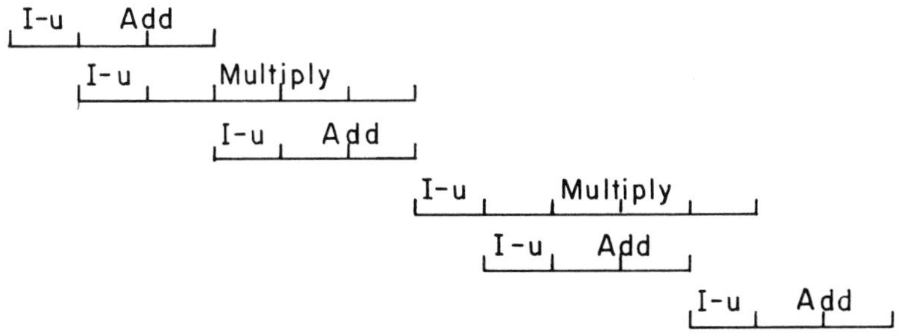

Figure 4.14 Look-ahead with D-unit buffering

sequence, then S_3 can proceed and will be completed before the start of S_2 (we assume that division takes 6 units of time). Hence, we have to prevent the storing of the result of the addition in R_1 until the starting time of the multiplication.   □

This example shows that if we want to implement "forwarding", we need a controlling device which indicates when values associated with registers are available, as well as when results can be stored into registers. In order to do so, we can associate with each D-unit input buffer a bit indicating whether a value is in the buffer or whether it is waiting for the completion of an operation in some other D-unit. In that case, instead of a value being stored in the buffer, we put in it a tag which identifies the D-unit which will send the value. When the bits of both operands are set to "values" the operation can proceed. When an instruction in a D-unit is completed, the control searches all tags in the other D-units which are waiting for that particular completion. Transfer from the output register to buffers is then authorized and this might allow the start of some conditionally issued operations. To take care of the conflict described in Example 4.5.b, the control makes sure that all conditionally issued instructions having the current result register in their domain have their corresponding bits set to "values". Otherwise, the storing action is to be delayed.

It is evident that this searching takes time, unless it can be done in an associative fashion (cf. Chapter 5) or unless there are a limited number of units (i.e., if the length of the queues is restricted). Two specific implementations mixing to various degrees the virtual unit, buffering, and conditional issue concepts will be examined in the next sections.

4.3.2   Automatic Detection of Parallelism (intra-statement)

The previous examples always had sequences of machine language instructions. Nothing was said about how these sequences were reached. The issuing of instructions was dictated by the original ordering and the rules of system (1). These rules are general enough so that they apply to any two statements or group of statements. We shall discuss their usefulness later in the context of multiprocessor systems.

However, within a look-ahead processor with multi-functional units as described previously the level at which parallelism is important is between instructions. Therefore from the programmer or compiler viewpoint, concurrency has to be indicated, or detected, within statements mostly in arithmetic expressions. To ask a programmer to order code in such a way that the processor will achieve a high order of parallelism is not a viable alternative. Thus, it will be the compiler's role to automatically detect which instructions can be performed in parallel and to order them so that the completion time of the sequence is minimized.

Several methods have been proposed for automatically detecting parallelism within statements. These methods can be generalized to blocks of statements with a single entry, the first statement, and a single exit, the last statement, and no branching or looping. The most important criteria by which the various algorithms differ are:

- *The type of machine for which they are intended to generate code.*
  For example, if a multiprocessor stack computer (cf. Section 4.6) is to execute the code the algorithm presented below should not be followed.
- *The arithmetic rules which can be used.*
  If the reordering of operands and the use of the commutativity law for some operators is not permitted, then the resulting sequence might show less potential for parallelism than if it were possible to take advantage of the reordering and commutativity. In what follows, we shall use commutativity and associativity, but not distributivity.
- *The amount of parallelism obtained.*
  This can be measured by the height of the tree representing the computation of the arithmetic expression. (The height of a tree is defined as the maximum level of its nodes, with the root having level 1 and any other node having the level of its father plus 1; the tree of Figure 4.15.a has height 5.) Under the conditions stated in the previous paragraph, the algorithm to be described yields a minimal number of levels. However, if blocks of statements are treated as an entity, the algorithm might not be optimal.
- *The type of code generated.*
  This is again an issue which is dependent on the target processor. We shall use the format:

$$R_i \leftarrow D_h(R_j, R_k)$$

  with no restriction on the number of registers. This is consistent with the models of look-ahead processors studied previously.
- *The number of passes over the input string.*
  For a given arithmetic expression the optimal tree (without distributivity) of height k can be obtained in k passes.

The algorithm is best explained through an example. Consider the arithmetic expression:

$$A + B + C + D * E * F + G + H;$$

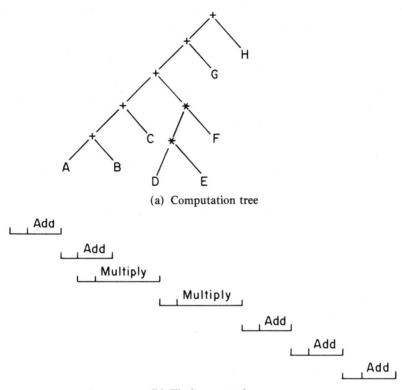

(a) Computation tree

(b) Timing example

Figure 4.15   Computation of A+B+C+D*E*F+G+H without automatic
detection of parallelism

where we assume that A, B, ... H, are already in registers. The code that a
compiler would usually generate is:

$$S_1: \quad T_1 \leftarrow A + B$$
$$S_2: \quad T_1 \leftarrow T_1 + C$$
$$S_3: \quad T_2 \leftarrow D * E$$
$$S_4: \quad T_2 \leftarrow T_2 * F$$
$$S_5: \quad T_1 \leftarrow T_1 + T_2$$
$$S_6: \quad T_1 \leftarrow T_1 + G$$
$$S_7: \quad T_1 \leftarrow T_1 + H$$

(A reader unfamiliar with the compilation of arithmetic expressions should study the part of Section 6 relative to the reverse Polish notation before proceeding here).

The generated code corresponds to the inorder traversal of the tree of Figure 4.15.a. (The inorder traversal of a binary tree is defined, recursively, as traverse in inorder the left subtree, visit the root, traverse in inorder the right subtree.) Figure 4.15.b shows the Gantt chart obtained using a look-ahead processor with a single adder, a single multiplier, no virtual unit, and no forwarding (buffering has no effect in this particular instance). The completion time is 23 units (cf. Exercise 6).

A first, and trivial, observation is that the order of execution of S_2 and S_3 can be exchanged. A forwarding scheme would in effect perform this transformation. Under the same assumptions as above, a gain of 3 time units would result. However, there is additional potential parallelism; for example, C and G can be added while D and E are multiplied.

We now present an algorithm which yields a tree with minimal height. The algorithm uses multiple passes, one per level. All instructions generated during a pass can be executed in parallel as far as procedural conditions are concerned. The result of an operation, that is the left-hand side of a generated instruction, replaces in the output string the operands and operator which constitute its right-hand side. At the end of a pass, the output string becomes the input string for the subsequent pass. Scanning of the input string proceeds from left to right without back-up. The relative precedence of operators is the usual, namely:

> precedence 0: $'('$, $')'$, $';'$
> precedence 1: $'+'$, $'-'$
> precedence 2: $'*'$, $'/'$
> precedence 3: $'**'$ (exponentiation)

Although the algorithm that we describe can be easily extended to expressions with parentheses as well as to unary and non-commutative operators, we restrict ourselves to the case of operators $'+'$ and $'*'$ for clarity. The result of a call to the SCAN procedure is a triplet (left operator (LO), operand (ITEM), right operator (RO)). SCAN will assign to LO the preceding value of RO (initialized to $'+'$), and ITEM and RO will receive the next two lexical entities which, in this simplified case, are necessarily an operand and an operator. A double entry stack is used to store operands (STACK(1,I)) and operators (STACK(2,I)) whenever they cannot be part of a temporary result. The stack is initially empty.

The generation of instructions will depend on the relative precedences of LO, RO, and the operator at the top of the stack. The algorithm for a given pass is:

While forever **do**
  begin call SCAN;
    if LO = ';' **then begin while** STACK **not** empty **do**
                          begin Insert STACK(2,TOP) and
                                    STACK(1,TOP) in the output string;
                                    Pop the stack
                      end;
                      exit for this pass
            end;
    if (precedence (RO) > precedence (LO)) **or** (STACK is empty)
      then Push ITEM and RO on top of the STACK
      else [precedence(RO) ≤ precedence (LO)]
        if (STACK **not** empty) **and** (precedence(STACK(2, TOP) =
        precedence(LO))
        then begin Generate (T_i ← (STACK(1, TOP),
                      STACK(2, TOP), ITEM);
                  Insert T_i and RO in output string;
                  Pop the stack
        end
        else Insert ITEM and RO in the output string
  end.

Table 4.2 is the application of the algorithm to the example expression. Figure 4.16.a is the resulting tree, of height 4, and Figure 4.16.b is the Gantt chart of the execution of the sequence of code generated:

S_1: $T_1 ← A + B$
S_2: $T_2 ← D * E$
S_3: $T_3 ← C + G$
S_4: $T_4 ← T_2 * F$
S_5: $T_5 ← T_1 + T_3$
S_6: $T_6 ← T_5 + T_4$
S_7: $T_7 ← T_6 + H$

(Note that it does not correspond to any intuitive traversal of the tree, except for deepest level first, an ordering which cannot be easily obtained.)

The completion time is 17 units with the same modeling assumptions as above. It is optimal under these conditions.

4.3.3   Deterministic Scheduling (a first look)

We stated earlier that the compiler's role was to detect parallelism and to schedule operations in such a way that execution time would be minimized.

Table 4.2 Illustration of the algorithm for automatic detection of parallelism

Pass 1:   Input $A + B + C + D * E * F + G + H$;

LO	ITEM	RO	STACK $(1,-)$	$(2,-)$	CODE GEN.	OUTPUT
+	A	+	A	+	$-$	$-$
+	B	+	$-$	$-$	$T_1 \leftarrow A + B$	T_1 +
+	C	+	C	+	$-$	$-$
+	D	*	D	*	$-$	$-$
			C	+		
*	E	*	C	+	$T_2 \leftarrow D * E$	T_2 *
*	F	+	C	+	$-$	F +
+	G	+	$-$	$-$	$T_3 \leftarrow C + G$	T_3 +
+	H	;	$-$	$-$	$-$	H ;

Pass 2:   *Input* $T_1 + T_2 * F + T_3 + H$;

LO	ITEM	RO	STACK $(1,-)$	$(2,-)$	CODE GEN.	OUTPUT
+	T_1	+	T_1	+	$-$	$-$
+	T_2	*	T_2	*	$-$	$-$
			T_1	+		
*	F	+	T_1	+	$T_4 \leftarrow T_2 * F$	T_4 +
+	T_3	+	$-$	$-$	$T_5 \leftarrow T_1 + T_3$	T_5 +
+	H	;	$-$	$-$	$-$	H ;

Pass 3:   Input $T_4 + T_5 + H$;

LO	ITEM	RO	STACK $(1,-)$	$(2,-)$	CODE GEN.	OUTPUT
+	T_4	+	T_4	+	$-$	$-$
+	T_5	+	$-$	$-$	$T_6 \leftarrow T_5 + T_4$	T_6 +
+	H	;	$-$	$-$	$-$	H ;

Pass 4:   Input $T_6 + H$;

LO	ITEM	RO	STACK $(1,-)$	$(2,-)$	CODE GEN.	OUTPUT
+	T_6	+	T_6	+	$-$	$-$
+	H	;	$-$	$-$	$T_7 \leftarrow T_6 + H$	T_7

Since the number of instructions is finite, this second goal can always be obtained but possibly only through enumerative methods. Our interest is mainly in algorithms which run in time proportional to some power of the number of operations, i.e., in polynomial time algorithms of order $O(n^a)$ where n is the number of instructions to schedule and a is a constant.

Given a directed graph representation of a computation to be performed, for example the graph of Figure 4.11 or the trees of Figures 4.15 and 16, the amount of time needed for each operation, and characteristics of the system such as the number of D-units and the degree of overlap, the (so-called)

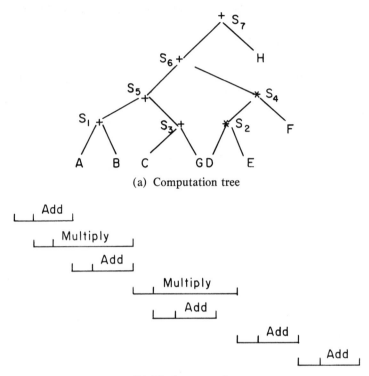

(a) Computation tree

(b) Timing example

Figure 4.16   Computation of A+B+C+D*E*F+G+H with automatic
detection of parallelism

deterministic scheduling algorithms yield sequences of instructions such as
those shown in previous examples. The goal in these algorithms is to arrive at
optimal orderings, where optimality is a criterion which might depend on
several factors.

Deterministic scheduling algorithms which yield optimal schedules in
polynomial time have been found only for a few restricted cases (for a more
complete discussion, see Chapter 10). Even if we restrict ourselves to tree
tasks by imposing our optimization to be done on a statement per statement
basis which is consistent with our previous detection of parallelism, we are
still severely limited. Hence, we may have to rely on heuristics which have
been thoroughly tested and which are known, either through theoretical
analysis or by simulation, to be close to optimality.

We start with a simplified model of a parallel processor and of the tasks to be run on it. The procedural precedence relations of the tasks form a tree. We assume that all tasks take the same amount of time to be executed on the identical D-units and that there are a sufficient number of these available so that no instruction will be delayed by the lack of an available D-unit. We further assume there is no I-fetch-I-unit time delay, and finally that the function to be optimized is the time to complete all tasks (i.e., the time at which the root of the tree will have been executed).

A priority list is set up with the tasks ranked in decreasing level order. For example, labelling the nodes of the tree of Figure 4.16 with the statement numbers generated by the algorithm described through Table 4.2, we obtain the priority list (this is one of several which could have been obtained):

$$L = (S_1, S_2, S_3, S_5, S_4, S_6, S_7).$$

At time 0, we scan the list from left to right and schedule all operations which are allowed to be executed (in our example S_1, S_2, and S_3). It should be noted that besides these operations at the highest level, there could be some at lower levels which are also ready to be processed. At the subsequent time unit, we can schedule those operations all of whose procedural predecessors have terminated. In our example, this would be S_5 and S_4. We continue in this manner until the root has been reached. The completion time is equal to the number of levels in the tree and is clearly optimal.

In the above algorithm, we have not really made use of the priority list. When we restrict the number of processors, this list will play a crucial role in the process. In the unconstrained algorithm, an upper bound on the number of processors needed to obtain an optimal schedule is equal to the number of nodes whose two immediate successors are variables (or initially in registers). If we assume that we have fewer processors than this bound, then the following algorithm, a slight modification of the above, still yields an optimal schedule.

Let n be the number of processors. Set up the list L as previously specified. At time 0 scan the list, from left to right, and schedule the first n (if there are fewer than n candidates, schedule them all) operations which have no predecessors. For example, with $n = 2$ for the same tree as before, we would schedule S_1 and S_2. We repeat this step at subsequent time units, always starting from the left of L and skipping over already scheduled instructions and over instructions which still have predecessors that have not yet been terminated. Continuing our example, the execution would proceed as follows:

Time 0: S_1 and S_2
Time 1: S_3 and S_4

Time 2: S_5
Time 3: S_6
Time 4: S_7

The required time is 5 time units which is an optimal schedule for this tree using 2 processors.

It has been proven than an optimal schedule will be obtained if we set up the priority list in level order and if we follow the previous algorithm for the assignment of tasks to processors. This procedure, known as *Hu's algorithm* or "cutting the longest queue," corresponds to a critical path length schedule. Extending this concept to directed acyclic graph structures and to trees with unequal task times is a natural idea. This does not result in optimal schedules, as we shall now demonstrate.

Leaving aside the acyclic graph representation (to be treated in Chapter 10), we consider a tree structure with unequal (integer) task times, a limited number of processors and the same goal of minimizing the total completion time. We are somewhat closer to the look-ahead processor models seen before, but we are still making some rather strong simplifications such as neglecting the I-fetch-I-unit times and the specificity of the D-units.

We extend Hu's algorithm by computing the levels as follows. The root is assigned level t_0 where t_0 is the time required to execute the task represented by the root. If t_i is the time to execute the ith task and its successor is task j at level k, then the level assigned to i is given by level$(i) = k + t_i$.

The priority list is again built in decreasing level order. For our example of Figure 4.16.a, this would yield:

$$L = (S_2, S_1, S_3, S_4, S_5, S_6, S_7)$$

assuming an add time of 1 unit and a multiply time of 2 units. The scheduling algorithm is the same as before with the additional constraint that some processors might be busy at the start of a new time unit. With the same tree, we have:

Time 0: S_2 and S_1
Time 1: S_3 (and one processor is still busy finishing S_2)
Time 2: S_4 and S_5
Time 3: nothing
Time 4: S_6
Time 5: S_7

This schedule requires 6 time units which in this particular instance can be shown to be optimal.

However, now consider the tree of Figure 4.17.a. A priority list based on levels is:

$$L = (S_1, S_2, S_5, S_3, S_4, S_7, S_6, S_8)$$

which yields the schedule of Figure 4.17.b and a completion time of 7 units. However, the schedule of Figure 4.17.c results in 6 units, which is optimal for this tree. It can be shown that for the assumptions of this example, Hu's extended algorithm is always within one time unit of optimal (cf. Exercise 9).

If we attempt to make our scheduling model be closer to the designs of look-ahead processors, it becomes extremely difficult to obtain significant analytical results. For example, assigning specific instruction sets to the D-units implies a new model for which only general bounds can be obtained. If we reinstate the delay due to I-fetch-I-unit operations, then the only result of significance is that it is better to start with those instructions which occupy most the D-units (cf. Exercise 10).

The allocation of specific D-units is a problem comparable to that of

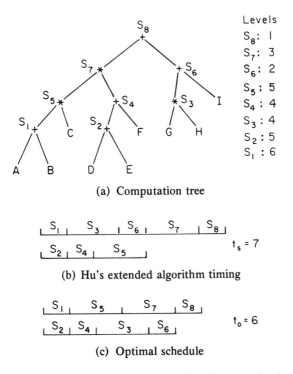

(a) Computation tree

(b) Hu's extended algorithm timing

(c) Optimal schedule

Figure 4.17 Hu's extended algorithm is not optimal

allocating registers in order to minimize the number of fetch and stores (with of course a limited number of registers). In our example sequences, we have avoided this register assignment. This problem is one of the class of "hard" problems for which it is strongly conjectured that there exists no polynomial time solution. A number of good heuristics have been devised and can be found in books treating compiler construction.

4.4 THE CDC 6600 CENTRAL PROCESSOR

4.4.1 General Description

As we mentioned in Chapter 1, the CDC 6600, introduced in 1964, was a major step forward in the design of powerful computers. There are four features in the 6600 which at that time were advances in the state of the art, namely:

- Separation of the computational function into specialized units which can operate concurrently under the supervision of a hardware control unit;
- Interleaving of primary memory modules;
- Introduction of I/O peripheral processors with their own instruction set and internal memory (and shared circuitry) to process the I/O function;
- Addition of facilities for multiprogramming such as relocation registers.

In this section we concentrate on the first of these four features.

Figure 4.18.a is a very simplifed PMS description of the complete CDC 6600 system. In Figure 4.18.b we have enlarged the Pc part in order to show the multiplicity of D-units and associated control (Figure 4.18.c is a more conventional representation of the processor). As can be seen, the Pc consists of:

- Ten D-units: a shifter, a Boolean logic network, two increment units which perform, among other tasks, the load and store operations to and from memory and registers, a branch unit which may operate in conjunction with an increment unit, a floating-point adder, an integer adder, two floating-point multipliers, and a floating-point divider.
- Twenty-four registers, partitioned into three sets:
  8 X registers (X0-X7), 60 bits/register, which are used as accumulators;
  8 A registers (A0-A7), 18 bits/register, which are used as address registers;
  8 B registers (B0-B7), 18 bits/register, which are used as index registers.
  The interconnection between these registers and central memory Mp will be explained shortly.

Mp³(#0:31) — S ──┬── Pc¹

└── K('Extended core coupler) ──── Ms('Extended core)

└── K('Read and write pyramids;)

Mp⁴(#0:9)─ S ───── Pp²(#0:9) ──── Stm──── Kio(#1:12)

1. cf. Figure IV.18.b
2. Pp('Peripheral Processor; 12b/w)
3. Mp(core; 1 μs/w; 4096 w; 60b/w)
4. Mp(core; 1 μs/w; 4096 w; 12b/w)

(a) General PMS description

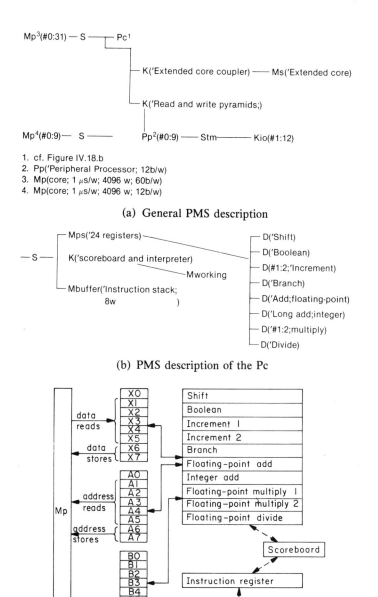

(b) PMS description of the Pc

(c) Conventional description of the CDC 6600 central processor

Figure 4.18   The CDC 6600

- A look-ahead buffer, or instruction stack, of 8 words. Since instructions are either 15 or 30 bits, the buffer contains from 16 to 32 of them.
- A hardware control scheme which decides when to issue an instruction, to which D-unit it is intended (interpreter) as well as when to forward and/or buffer contents of registers (scoreboard). This control requires some temporary storage (flip-flops) which have been designated as Mworking in the figure.

With the exception of the branch and increment units, all other D-units only address the registers and hence respond to short instruction formats. These are similar to the instructions used in the look-ahead processor models (recall Figure 2.9 for the CDC instruction formats). The load and store operations are quite original and unique to the CDC architecture. In order to load the contents of memory location L (we ignore the relocation problem which has been alluded to in Chapter 2) into accumulator X_i, we have to set the corresponding address register A_i to the effective address L. This will automatically initiate the transfer. The effective address L can be:

- A direct address (a constant in the address field of the long instruction);
- The sum of a direct address and the contents of either an address register A_i, or of an index register B_i, or of an accumulator X_i;
- The sum of the contents of an index register B_j and the contents of either an address register A_i, an index register B_i, or an accumulator X_i;
- The difference between the contents of an address register A_j and the contents of either an address register A_i or an index register B_i.

The first two cases require a long instruction format since a direct address is requested. In the other two cases, a short instruction format is sufficient. An important restriction on the data paths between Pc registers and Mp (and at the same time a potential increase in concurrency) is that only registers X1 through X5 can be loaded while only the contents of X6 and X7 can be stored into memory. A0 and X0 have no direct link with memory and can be used as temporary scratchpad registers. The B registers do not have access to Mp and B0 always contains the value 0. This provides easy encoding for "no-indexing" conditions as well as rapid access to a commonly used value. Figure 4.19 shows a partial ISP description which illustrates these features.

4.4.2   Design of the D-units and of the Instruction Buffer

The general block diagram of a D-unit is shown in Figure 4.20. Besides the circuitry performing the hardware algorithm, we notice that internal buffering of the input and output operands is provided. A decoder is also present to

Pc state

.

.

.

X[0:7]⟨59:0⟩   Accumulators

A[0:7]⟨17:0⟩   Address registers

B[0:7]⟨17:0⟩   Index and arithmetic registers
                                           (no connection with Mp)

B[0] := 0

Instruction format (abbreviated)

   i⟨0:29⟩   some instructions are only 15 bits
  fm⟨0:5⟩ := i⟨0:5⟩   opcode
 fmi⟨0:8⟩ := i⟨0:8⟩   extended opcode
  ir⟨0:2⟩ := i⟨6:8⟩   register 1
  jr⟨0:2⟩ := i⟨9:11⟩   register 2
  kr⟨0:2⟩ := i⟨12:14⟩   register 3
   k⟨0:17⟩ := i⟨12:29⟩   address size constant

Instruction execution

.

.

.

instruction-exec := (···

    "SA$_i$ A$_j$ + K"(fm ± 50) → (A[ir] ← A[jr] + K; next F-S;

    .

    .

    .

    F-S := (0 < ir < 6) → (X[ir] ← Mp[A[ir]]);

       (6 ≤ ir) → (Mp[A[ir]] ← X[ir]))

Figure 4.19 Partial ISP description for Load-Store operations of the CDC 6600

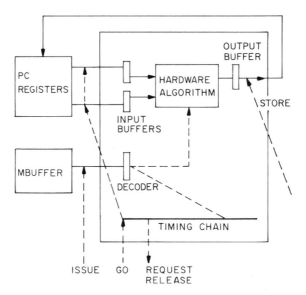

Figure 4.20   General block diagram of a CDC 6600 D-unit

further specify which of the subfunctions allowed in the D-unit is to be performed. The timing chain sends messages to and receives orders from the control, including the following:

- The "issue" order from the scoreboard will initiate the transfer of part of the opcode into the D-unit decoder;
- The "read" order, triggered by a "go" from the scoreboard, will be sent when both input operands are ready to be transferred (i.e., have their correct values) into the internal registers;
- The "request release" is a message from the D-unit to the scoreboard asking if the result can be stored in a Pc register. The message has to be sent before the completion of the operation so that there will be no delay in storing in the absence of conflict;
- The "store" order from the scoreboard acknowledges the "request release" message and allows the transfer of the result in the appropriate Pc register.

From the perspective of the D-units, the unit of time is a minor cycle (100 ns.), one tenth of the memory cycle of Mp which is a major cycle. This one to ten ratio is related to the sharing of circuitry by the 10 Pp's (Peripheral processors) during a major cycle.

The above timing scheme is well illustrated by the design of the simplest of the functional units, namely the Boolean logic unit.

Boolean Unit

The Boolean unit performs the logical AND, OR, or Exclusive-Or of two operands (possibly complemented using the 1's complement system) contained in accumulators X_i and X_j and transfers the result into X_k. Direct transfer from one (complemented) register to another is also performed in the Boolean unit.

All operations take 300 ns., or 3 minor cycles, from the time the inputs are sampled and found available in the Pc registers until the result is stored in the X_k Pc register.

A typical timing sequence is as follows. We assume that an "issue" order has already been delivered by the scoreboard and that the opcode has been (or is in the process of being) transmitted to the Boolean logic unit. At time 0, a "go Boolean" order is given by the scoreboard which has checked that the Pc registers X_i and X_j, used as input operands, are ready to be read. The Boolean logic unit then issues a "read" and the contents of X_i and X_j are transferred into the internal registers. One minor cycle after the "go Boolean" signal the operands, or their complements as directed by the decoder, are in the black box labelled hardware algorithm in Figure 4.20 which, in this instance, is a combinatorial network. At most 125 ns. later, the result of the operation, as selected by the decoder signals, is in the internal output buffer. A "request release" signal was sent to the scoreboard 75 ns. after the "go Boolean", that is even before the operands were in the internal buffers, in order to let the control have time to respond through a "store" order if X_k, the Pc result register, was free. The whole operation from "issue" to a result in X_k takes 300 ns. when there is no conflict. However, an extra minor cycle is required before being able to "issue" another instruction to the Boolean logic unit.

Another advantage in the design of these special-purpose D-units is that the "black boxes" labelled hardware algorithms can be tailored to specific algorithms. Thus, some of the more advanced techniques described in Chapter 3 will be used. We briefly review a few implementation details.

Integer Adder

The integer adder performs 1's complement addition and subtraction of 60 bit integers. A "borrow" look-ahead adder is used with the logic equations described in Exercise 6 of Chapter 3. Conceptually, we have a 3-level CLA. The input operands consist of 20 groups of 3 bits (A modules) and the final

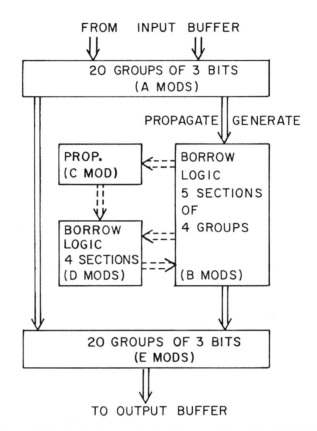

Figure 4.21   Path diagram in the integer adder of the CDC 6600

sums consist of 20 groups of 3 bits (E modules). Some of the outputs of the A modules are directed towards the E modules, while others corresponding to borrow generate and borrow propagate bits are passed to the borrow logic which consists of five sections (B modules) (inputs to a section come from 4 groups). The borrow logic is terminated by the use of a single C module or 4 extra sections (D modules). The longest path has 16 logic levels (inversions) while the shortest has 5 levels. Of course, design is geared for the critical path. An add (or subtract) takes 3 minor cycles.

Shifter

The shift unit design follows the outline for a synchronous shifter given in Section 6 of Chapter 3. It performs shifts in 3 minor cycles. In addition, the shift unit implements the normalize instruction as well as the pack and un-pack operations which are used in the transformations to and from fixed-point and floating-point representations.

Since the CDC 6600 is essentially intended for performing high-speed arithmetic, and since it was thought that floating-point numbers would be used most often, it does not include an integer multiplier or an integer divider. As a matter of fact, a programming "trick" discovered long after the machine was in operation allows integer multiplies with operands of less than 48 bits (cf. floating-point multiplier description below). In the CYBER systems, means of multiplying integers of 60 bits are provided without having to pass through the pack and unpack instructions. For divide operations however, these transformations are still mandatory. This is easily justified by the low frequency of occurrence of such instructions.

Floating-point Adder

In Chapter 3, we have seen the format used in the CDC 6600 as well as the basic addition algorithm for the floating-point representation system. This D-unit can perform single and double precision addition and subtraction. Because of the 1's complement representation, there is room for an extra exponent value which is used for "indefinite" operands. These can result from combining null values (e.g., in division) or so-called infinite values obtained from overflow and underflow conditions. The rules for combining these are described in CDC reference manuals.

When adding (or subtracting) two floating-point numbers, x and y, found in the internal registers of the D-unit, the first step is to detect the larger exponent. A subtract network of 12 bits, similar to the one described in the integer adder but with a shortest critical path, is used for this purpose. The technique described in Chapter 3 to detect the larger of x and y through the end-around carry must be modified slightly since in the case where the two exponents are of different signs their bias differs by 1. It can be easily shown (cf. Exercise 11) that:

$$(x \geq y) \leftarrow \text{(end-around-borrow)} \oplus \text{(exponent-sign-alike)}$$

While the subtraction is completed, the mantissa corresponding to the small exponent is entered in a synchronous shifter similar to the shift unit pre-viously presented but somewhat simpler since only right shifts are necessary. At the completion of the subtraction the shift count is known. A maximum of 96 is allowed. It corresponds to the least significant addition in double preci-sion. Hence a 7 column shifter is required.

The mantissa adder is a 98-bit (two extra bits, one for the sign and one for the virtual overflow) version of the integer adder. Virtual overflow is corrected during transmission to the output internal buffer.

From the above discussion, it is obvious that single and double precision operations take the same amount of time, 4 minor cycles in this instance. It is interesting to compare this figure with the 3 minor cycles of either the integer add or of the shift. Out of the 3 cycles, one is spent in transferring into the internal buffers, and 75 ns. are required between the completion of the hardware algorithm and the transmission of the result from the black box to the internal output buffer. Thus, the ratio of execution between the integer and floating-point adds is not 4/3 (the minor cycles ratio) but rather 225/125, i.e., 1.8. Furthermore, if normalized results are wanted, a normalize instruction (another 4 cycles) must be executed.

Floating-point Multiplier

The CDC 6600 multiplier takes advantage of three of the speed-up methods mentioned in Chapter 3, namely:

- Carry-save adders (CSA) are used;
- Two parallel trees of CSA's each handle one half of the multiplier bits;
- The multiplier is recoded two bits at a time.

This last scheme, the recoding, uses the multiplicand X_k, as well as $2X_k$ and $3X_k$. Thus, the first action performed in the D-unit is to shift X_k left one position and to add it to itself. Once this is done, the two halves of the multiplier are handled in parallel in two 3-layer CSA networks. Each network handles 24 bits of the multiplier. Since each layer encodes two bits of the multiplier, 4 iterations through each network are required. The pseudo-sum and pseudo-carry vectors are passed from one layer to the next with a right shift of two places. At the end of each iteration, a holding register will contain the partial product (in pseudo form) of the multiplicand with 6 bits of the multiplier. It is shifted right 6 places, and during the next iteration the true sum of the rightmost 6 bits can be performed (cf. Figure 4.22). After 4 iterations, each of the two networks has generated 72 (24 + 48) pairs of bits of pseudo-sums and pseudo-carries, of which 24 have been completely added. The rightmost 48 bits of the network corresponding to the upper half of the multiplier are in the same position as the leftmost 48 bits generated by the lower half. In a schematic way, this can be viewed as:

```
upper XXXX XXXX XXXX XXXX YYYY YYYY
lower                XXXX XXXX XXXX XXXX YYYY YYYY
```

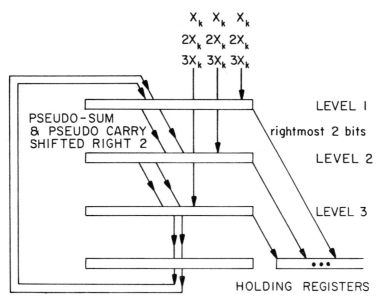

Figure 4.22 Carry-save adder network for half of the multiplier

where X's are pairs of (octal) pseudo-sums and pseudo-carries and Y's are (octal) digits for which the true sums have already been performed. As can be seen it remains to do a 72-bit addition on 3 or 4 operands. This can be performed by the lower CSA network which must be slightly expanded (since in the multiplication it required only 48 bits). At the same time, a carry propagation network is activated for the last addition.

The exponent calculation is done in parallel. It requires two additions, one for the exponents and one to add 48 (corresponding to the new mantissa). In case of a virtual overflow, it is necessary to subtract one. Normalized operands yield a normalized result. The overall operation takes 10 minor cycles.

Integers of up to 48 bits can also be multiplied using this D-unit by specifying a double precision multiply since the 48 bits generated in the lower half are those that must be kept.

Floating-point Divider

The basic method used is restoring division (the pencil and paper process) and simultaneous generation of two bits of the quotient by parallel subtraction of multiples of the divisor and choosing the smallest remainder. The exponent calculation is done in parallel as in the multiplier. This algorithm requires 25 (1 + 48/2) restoring subtractions, each one requiring one minor cycle. The overall operation takes 29 minor cycles.

An interesting instruction performed in the divide unit, although completely independent of the division, is the "population count". It is implemented within the divide D-unit, and its opcode appropriately selected, because of the low frequency of occurrence of the divide operation. "Population count" counts the number of bits set to 1 in an X register. A logsum tree of adders is used, the leaves of the tree receiving their inputs from circuits adding the number of bits set to 1 in consecutive sequences of 4 bits. The overall process takes 8 minor cycles.

The remaining D-units are used for moving data between Mp and Pc registers and for breaking the flow of control.

Increment Units

These units are used to perform the load and store operations from and to Mp, as well as the loading of B registers from other registers and the loading of X registers (lower 18 bits) directly from the contents of A and B registers. In order to compute the effective address L, or to add and subtract contents of A and B registers, an 18 bit adder is shared by the two units.

When an SA_i instruction is issued, the effective address L is sent directly to the A_i register and to Mp through the central storage "stunt box" (cf. Chapter 5). If no memory conflict occurs, the result is available in X_i (for a load) or X_i is available as a result register (for a store) after 8 minor cycles.

The increment units are also used in conjunction with the branch unit to accomplish tests between two B registers, as well as to compute the effective branch address.

Branch Unit and Instruction Stack

This D-unit is somewhat different from the others because:

- It is not self-sufficient and it operates in conjunction with either the increment units or the integer adder for the testing of the 60 bit accumulators;
- It causes the cessation of instruction issuing to any D-unit.

Once the effective branch address T has been computed, and the success of the branching decision has been assessed, the new instruction will be fetched from either Mp or Mbuffer (the instruction stack in CDC terminology). The choice depends on the distance between the source address IA (the address of the instruction being currently executed) and the target address T as well as on the validity of the instruction already in Mbuffer. To that effect, a depth value D and a pointer P are maintained. D measures how many words in Mbuffer are valid with D between 0 and 7. When a branch out of the stack is performed, D is reset to 0. After that, it is incremented by 1 for any incoming word put in the buffer up to a maximum of 7. P points to the word holding the instruction currently executed (i.e., P points to the position of IA in the buffer). After the computation of T, the absolute value of $T - P$ (the distance between source and target addresses) is tested. If this distance is greater than 7, the branch is out of the stack and the word at address T is brought from Mp. If the distance is less than 7, further testing is necessary to see if T is within the range of validity. For example, if P points to the first word of the stack and D is the current depth, then if:

$$-D < T - P < 0$$

the next instruction is valid in Mbuffer (hence the look-behind adjective often associated with Mbuffer). In this case, we can operate in loop-mode and save on Mp fetches for instructions. Because of jumps within loops already being executed in loop-mode, the test for validity might be more complex (cf. Exercise 12).

When the branch is towards a location already in Mbuffer, it can be executed in 8 minor cycles in conjunction with an increment unit, 9 minor cycles in conjunction with the integer adder, and 14 minor cycles if T is of the form (constant + contents of a B register). When a word from Mp is referenced, 6 extra minor cycles are required.

The RJ (return jump) instruction used for subroutine calls and returns is also implemented through the Branch unit. It requires 14 minor cycles and D is always reset to 0 after this instruction. Its ISP description is as follows:

"RJ k" (opcode= 010) $\rightarrow$ ($M[k]\langle 59{:}30\rangle \leftarrow 04_8 \,\square\, 00_8 \,\square\, IA + 1;$
next ($IA \leftarrow k + 1; p \leftarrow 3$))

where $0400(IA + 1)$ is an unconditional jump to location $IA + 1$. The value of p set to 3 indicates that the leftmost instruction in the word at address IA is the next one to be executed.

As seen in the above description, the traffic between Pc and the internal registers of D-units is heavy and time consuming (one minor cycle per transfer). Consequently, some concurrency in this part of the execution process would be desirable. Figure 4.23 shows how this is accomplished with 4 sets of data buses. One of them (set 4) is dedicated to communication with Mp while the others are equipartitioned, transfer traffic wise, between the D-units. Since the 4 sets can be used at the same time, up to 7 registers can be trans-

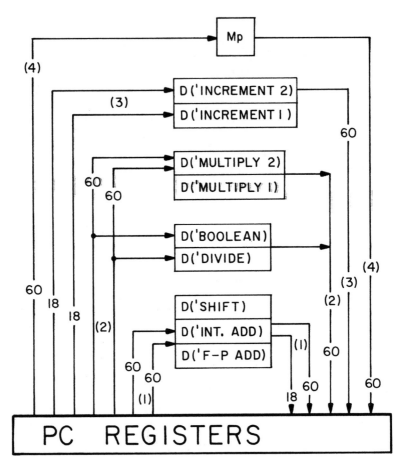

Figure 4.23   Data buses between D-units and the registers of the Pc

ferred simultaneously. The data buses are also arranged in such a way that a result can be entered into a selected register and read out on another bus for input to another D-unit in one minor cycle. This explains why results are available to other D-units a minor cycle before the current one becomes free again.

4.4.3   Controlling the D-units: the Scoreboard

In order for an instruction to be executed on a given D-unit, it must have fulfilled a series of requirements upon which we now elaborate (cf. the Petri Net of Figure 4.24 for a schematic representation of the process):

- It has been brought into Mbuffer, has been interpreted, and is ready to be issued (place 1);
- To be ready, the D-unit to which it is to be sent must be free (place 2) and the Pc register which has to receive the result must not have been reserved for a similar purpose in a previous, and as yet incompleted, instruction (place 3).

Once the instruction is issued (transition *issue*), several conditions are true, namely:

- The next instruction is ready to be fetched and interpreted (place 4);
- The D-unit is reserved and is waiting for a "go read" signal which will happen when the input operands are ready to be transferred (place 5).

When the input operands are ready (places 7 and 8), i.e., are not waiting to receive results from previous incompleted instructions, the reading takes place (transition *read*). This frees the two registers for possible storing (places 9 and 10) and the hardware black box internal to the D-unit can be activated (place 11). This activation takes place (transition *exec*) and

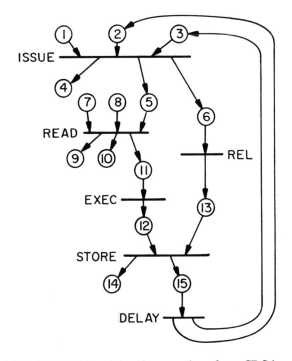

Figure 4.24   Petri Net describing the execution of one CDC instruction

simultaneously (or perhaps even before) a "request for release" message is sent to the scoreboard (transition *rel*). When the hardware algorithm is finished (place 12), and upon availability of the result register (place 13), the store signal (transition *store*) will initiate the transfer of the result to the appropriate Pc register which will then contain the computed value (place 14). However, an extra minor cycle is required before the D-unit can be reused and before the same Pc result register can be used in the same capacity (place 15 and transition *delay*).

Before delineating the hardware requirements of the control mechanism, we look at the interpretation of the instruction with rather liberal abstraction of the complex low level details.

We assume that the next instruction word has been fetched from Mp and has entered Mbuffer. At this point, the first 30 bits of the word are sent through a series of internal registers to an "instruction register" U. For a short instruction only the leftmost 15 bits are kept. At the same time, an instruction fetch is initiated, the pointer P is moved down one position (or equivalently the instruction word is moved up one position), and a parcel pointer p points to the next instruction in the current word if any; this latter case corresponds to the $p \leftarrow 3$ instruction in the ISP formulation of the RJ instruction. The transfer to the U register takes one minor cycle for short and 2 minor cycles for long instructions. It is from the U register that the instruction will be issued to a D-unit (in the absence of conflict).

When the next instruction word is fetched from Mp it takes 8 minor cycles before it enters Mbuffer. Since it takes one minor cycle per parcel to process a word of instructions (in the best case), up to 4 minor cycles per word of instructions can be saved by working in loop-mode. This is in addition to the decrease in Mp contention.

The CDC control unit, or scoreboard, allows buffering, since the D-units have internal registers, and forwarding, but there is no provision for virtual units. Therefore, the hardware requirements are:

- A bit per D-unit denoted as BUSY(D_i) for the ith D-unit, which indicates whether D_i is busy (BUSY(D_i) = 1) or free (BUSY(D_i) = 0);
- An entry per register holding the name of the D-unit, if any, which is going to use the register to store its result. Every unit, as well as each set of data buses, is given a number for that purpose. The set of 24 entries, one for each of the X, B, and A registers, will be called the *XBA* set.

A test for issue is performed as follows. The opcode of the instruction designates the D-unit, say D_a, as well as the type of the result register. The number of the latter, say X_k, is also in the instruction lay-out. If BUSY(D_a) is false and $XBA(X_k)$ is empty then the instruction can be issued.

In addition to BUSY(D_a), several other signals are associated with each D-unit. If D_a has inputs from X_i and X_j and a result to be stored in X_k, these signals are as follows:

- Three register entries F_i, F_j, and F_k which contain encodings for the names of X_i, X_j, and X_k;
- Two entries Q_i and Q_j indicating which D-units (if any) compute values which should be stored in X_i and X_j before using the latter as operands;
- Two read flags (flip-flops) R_i and R_j indicating when X_i and X_j can be transferred into the internal registers of D_a.

When the instruction is issued, BUSY(D_a) is set and the code for D_a is entered in $XBA(X_k)$. Then F_i, F_j, and F_k are assigned their codes, in general through a direct transfer from the instruction register U. Q_i and Q_j are set by copying the $XBA(X_i)$ and $XBA(X_j)$ entries. If Q_i (respectively Q_j) is empty, the read flag R_i (R_j) is set. When both R_i and R_j are set, a "go read" signal can be generated. Otherwise, assuming that Q_i contains the encoding for D_b, we must wait for completion of the latter. When D_b receives permission to store in X_i, after positive answer to a request release message, it clears the $XBA(X_i)$ entry and at the same time (through a hardwired emulation of an associative search) all Q_m entries in other D-units which have the same contents. In our case, this will set R_i. Since several units can be ready to read at the same time because they were held up by the same conflicts, a hardware priority scheme is implemented to resolve the contention for the data buses.

Finally, upon a request release message, the scoreboard must check whether there is any other D_h which has an F_m holding the X_k tag (X_k is the result register of D_a) and for which R_n, the read flag of the other operand, is not yet set. Because conflicts in result registers are forbidden, one can see that R_m, corresponding to X_k, will always be set. If the situation just described occurs, then another attempt will be made at every consecutive minor cycle until R_n and R_m are both set (cf. Exercise 17). Then, the old value of X_k can be read into D_h's internal buffer and, at the subsequent minor cycle, the result from D_a can be stored in X_k.

As an example Table 4.3 shows how

$$C1.(Y(K) - Y1) + C2.(Y(K) - Y2)^2$$

would be computed, with no attempt at code optimization, although result register conflicts have been intentionally avoided. It is assumed that instructions are read from Mp and that there is no conflict between operand and instruction fetches. Table 4.4 shows the differences in timing when we operate in loop-mode. Of course, more optimization is possible (cf. Exercise 13).

Table 4.3   Computation of C1·(Y(K) − Y1) + C2·(Y(K) − Y2)^2

Word				ISSUE	START	RESULT	UNIT TFREE	FETCH
1		SA1	C1 (fetch C1)	1	1	4	5	9
		SA2	K (fetch K)	3	3	6	7	11
2	(1,2)	SB1	X2 (B1−X2)	9	11	14	15	
	(2)	SA3	B1+Y (fetch Y(K))	10	14	17	18	22
3	(1)	SA4	Y1 (fetch Y1)	17	17	20	21	25
	(2)	FX5	X3-X4 (Y(K)−Y1)	19	25	29	30	
	(2)	NX6	B0,X5	20	29	33	34	
4	(1,2)	FX7	X6*X1 (C1*(Y(K)−Y1))	25	33	43	44	
		SA1	C2 (fetch C2)	26	26	29	30	34
5	(1)	SA4	Y2 (fetch Y2)	33	33	36	37	41
	(2)	FX0	X3-X4 (Y(K)−Y2)	35	41	45	46	
	(2)	NX5	B0,X0	36	45	49	50	
6	(1,2)	FX3	X5*X5 ((Y(K)−Y2)**2)	41	49	59	60	
	(2,3)	FX4	X3*X1 (C2*(Y(K)−Y2)**2)	44	59	69	70	
	(2,3)	FX2	X7+X4 (unnormalized expression)	46	69	73	74	
	(2,3)	NX6	B0,X2	50	73	77	78	

(1) Delay in issue due to Mp fetch
(2) Delay in start due to inavailability of read operands
(3) Conflict in D-units

Tables 4.3 and 4.4 can be read as follows. The ISSUE column indicates whether the test:

$$BUSY(D_i) \text{ is false and } XBA(X_k) \text{ is empty}$$

is true. The START column corresponds to a "go read" and shows when the operation can start within the D-unit. The RESULT column gives the time of

Table 4.4 Computation of $C1 \cdot (Y(K) - Y1) + C2 \cdot (Y(K) - Y2)^2$ in loop-mode

Word				ISSUE	START	RESULT	UNIT FREE	FETCH
1		SA1	C1	1	1	4	5	9
		SA2	K	3	3	6	7	11
2		SB1	X2	5	11	14	15	
	(2,3)	SA3	B1+Y	7	14	17	18	22
3	(3)	SA4	Y1	15	15	18	19	23
	(2)	FX5	X3−X4	17	23	27	28	
	(2)	NX6	B0,X5	18	27	31	32	
4	(2)	FX7	X6*X1	20	31	41	42	
		SA1	C2	21	21	24	25	29
5		SA4	Y2	23	23	26	27	31
	(2,3)	FX0	X3−X4	28	31	35	36	
	(2,3)	NX5	B0,X0	32	35	39	40	
6	(2)	FX3	X5*X5	34	39	49	50	
	(2,3)	FX4	X3*X1	42	49	59	60	
	(2)	FX2	X7+X4	43	59	63	64	
	(2)	NX6	B0,X2	44	63	67	68	

(2) Delay in start due to inavailability of read operands
(3) Conflict in D-units

completion of the operation, i.e., the time of availability of the result as input to another unit. The computing times (RESULT − START) are those given in the descriptions of the individual units. The column FREE indicates when the D-unit which has just completed its task is again free, that is when the BUSY(D_i) bit will be reset. Finally, the FETCH column shows the times when operands fetched from Mp will be in their respective registers.

Instructions are grouped into words of 60 bits. The K_i's are direct addresses of 18 bits and therefore all instructions referencing them will be long

(30 bits) instructions. In non-loop mode, words of instructions have to be transferred to Mbuffer. It takes at least 8 minor cycles after issuing the first instruction of word i before the first instruction of word $(i + 1)$ can be issued. In loop-mode, the only constraint is that the first instruction of word $(i + 1)$ has to wait 2 minor cycles after the issuing of the last instruction of word i. In the tables, this can be seen for example in the issue times of the first instruction of word 2 (SB1 X2). Within a word, it takes one cycle to issue a short and 2 cycles to issue a long instruction.

Both tables also show how conflicts in D-units can delay issuing of instructions. For example, in Table 4.4 the first instruction of word 3 cannot be issued at time 9 because both increment units are still busy. It will have to wait until one of them becomes free. This happens at time 15.

In addition to the possibility of delays in issuing, Tables 4.3 and 4.4 show examples of delays due to the unavailabilities of operands. For example, the same instruction as above (SB1 X2), although issued at time 9 in Table 4.3 and at time 5 in Table 4.4, cannot start in either case until time 11 because X2 loaded by the preceding instruction will not be available until then. Similarly, in Table 4.3, the first instruction of word 4 is issued at time 25 but only starts at time 33 when both operands are ready (the delay is due to storing into X6 in the preceding instruction).

If we trace the execution of this 4th word of instruction in Table 4.3 we have:

(i) FX7 X6*X1 (short instruction)

Can be issued at time 25, 8 time units after the issuing of the first instruction of word 3. There is no D-unit conflict since both multiply units are free and no result register conflict since X7 has not been used. The instruction cannot start until time 33 as explained above. Once started, the multiplication takes 10 minor cycles. Therefore, the result is available at time 43 and the unit is free at time 44.

(ii) SA1 C2 (long instruction)

Can be issued at time 26, one minor cycle after the preceding short instruction since there is no conflict in either D-unit or result register. Can start immediately (time 26). Will take 3 minor cycles to complete. The result in A1 will be available at time 29, the increment unit will be free at time 30, and the contents of the memory location Mp [C2] will reach X1 at time $26 + 8 = 34$.

The relevance of such an organization with a more restricted instruction format is worth studying (cf. Exercise 14). The next section sheds some light on a different approach.

4.5   THE IBM SYSTEM 360/91 AND 360/195 CENTRAL PROCESSORS

4.5.1   General Description

The Model 91 was intended to be the most powerful representative of IBM System/360. However, it was abandoned rather rapidly reportedly for a combination of political and technical reasons. Concerning ourselves only with the latter, a possible explanation for the early withdrawal of the Model 91 lies in the introduction of the Model 85 which, in spite of a less sophisticated Pc, was able to outperform the Model 91 with the use of a cache memory (cf. Chapter 6). The technological advances of the 91 and of the 85 were consolidated in the Model 195. A few minor features were added in the System/370 version. Because the Model 91 is better documented in the open literature we shall concentrate on its design.

The basic philosophy of the Model 91 is to operate to the greatest possible extent in an overlap, or pipeline, mode. The inherent speed limitations in gate propagation times and the worst case design necessary at each step in the overlap limit the number of stages. The designers of the Model 91 had a goal of obtaining a "result" every 60 ns. This is the time necessary to perform the shortest of the steps in the instruction execution cycle, namely the decoding (in fact there is more to that step than simply a determination of the opcode). Since the Mp cycle time is an order of magnitude larger than this 60 ns. minor cycle, extensive buffering techniques and look-ahead processing are necessary to approach such an ideal execution rate. Furthermore the execution part of the cycle, the one which involves the D-units, must be optimized in order to match the other parts of the cycle. To that end, multiple functional units, tailored to the algorithms to be implemented, will be used.

Figure 4.25 shows the general organization of the Pc. An instruction unit (Kins·unit) receives instructions from a look-ahead buffer (Mbuffer and Mab), decodes them, and when necessary issues orders to a fixed point or to a floating-point unit. Each of these has internal buffers for orders (Mfi and Mxi) and for operands (Mfo and Mxo) as well as data paths to and from the 16 general registers (fixed unit) and the 4 floating-point registers (floating-point unit). The fixed point unit has a single Dfx which can execute an instruction in one minor cycle while the floating-point unit is composed of an adder-subtracter Das and of a multiplier-divider Dmd. Details on the implementation of Das, Dmd, and on their control are forthcoming. Finally, buffers for data and addresses for storage back to Mp (Msc, Msa, Msd) are also provided.

The look-ahead buffer operates under the same general principles as those

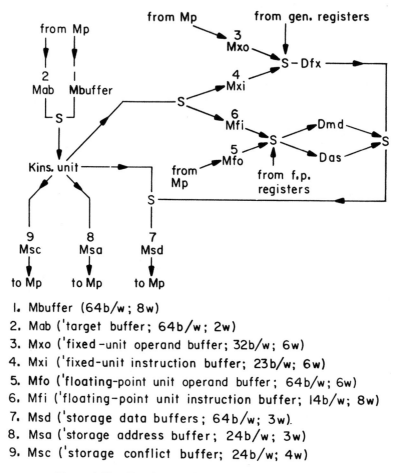

I. Mbuffer (64b/w ; 8w)
2. Mab ('target buffer; 64b/w; 2w)
3. Mxo ('fixed-unit operand buffer; 32b/w; 6w)
4. Mxi ('fixed-unit instruction buffer; 23b/w; 6w)
5. Mfo ('floating-point unit operand buffer; 64b/w; 6w)
6. Mfi ('floating-point unit instruction buffer; 14b/w; 8w)
7. Msd ('storage data buffers; 64b/w; 3w).
8. Msa ('storage address buffer; 24b/w; 3w)
9. Msc ('storage conflict buffer; 24b/w; 4w)

Figure 4.25   IBM System/360 Model 91 Pc description

described for the System/370 Model 165 (cf. Section 2 in this Chapter). Processing in loop mode is also possible and the implementation is similar to that of the CDC 6600. Instruction issuing first implies the checking of the instruction length. This is slightly more complex than in the CDC system because the unit of information for transfer to and from Mp is the double word and instructions (2, 4 or 6 bytes) can cross over (double) word boundaries. After the whole instruction has been loaded in the instruction register, and if further processing requires the fixed (or floating) point unit, the Kins. unit checks whether Mfi (or Mxi) is full. If this is not the case, then instruction dependency is tested. In addition to result register conflicts for the 16 general registers (but not for the 4 floating-point registers as will be seen later) resolved through a simple counter scheme, this also includes locking of the condition code settings.

The counter scheme is shown in Figure 4.26. Associated with each general register R_j is a counter C_j. If an instruction alters R_j without using it as a source operand (R_j is a result register), the counter is incremented at decode time and decremented after execution of the instruction. Instructions which only alter R_j can be decoded and issued, but the last part of their execution has to wait until the previous instruction also altering R_j is over (cf. instructions i and $i + 1$ in the figure). Those instructions which use R_j as a source have to wait until C_j is null before they can be sent to the fixed-point unit (cf. instruction $i + 3$). Evidently, all subsequent instructions become blocked even if they do not reference R_j at all (cf. instruction $i + 4$).

Regarding the locking of condition codes, recall that in the System/360 architecture transfer of control is implemented via a test on condition codes (CC's). (In System/360, not all instructions alter the CC's.) Since instruc-

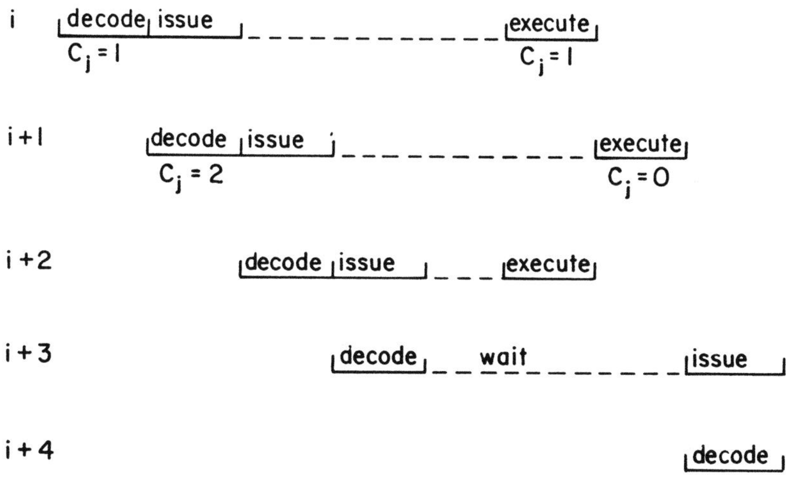

Instructions i and (i+1) alter R_j (of associated counter C_j)

Instruction i+3 uses R_j

Instructions i+2 and i+4 do not reference R_j

Figure 4.26 Counter scheme for register conflict

tions can be executed out of sequence before the branch instruction is reached, the last (sequential) instruction affecting the CC's must be tagged. Simultaneously, removing of tags of previously decoded instructions which have not yet completed is accomplished. It is only when no more tags are present that the CC's can be tested. Figure 4.27 illustrates the process with the final CC settings defined by the execution of instruction $(i + 2)$ even if the execution of instruction i terminates later.

Because of the out-of-sequence possibilities, interrupts as we are used to seeing them would imply a substantial amount of recovery. Therefore, an "imprecise" interrupt philosophy is adopted, namely, it interrupts the fetching of instructions and allows termination of all instructions which were in the processing stage, including those which may have been waiting in some buffer.

The instruction formats used in System/360, the base addressing concept appearing in most of the operand fetches (cf. also Exercise 14), and the floating-point formats have already been discussed. With these differences in mind, an ISP description of System/360 would have a strong resemblance to the one given for the Sigma 5 in Chapter 2.

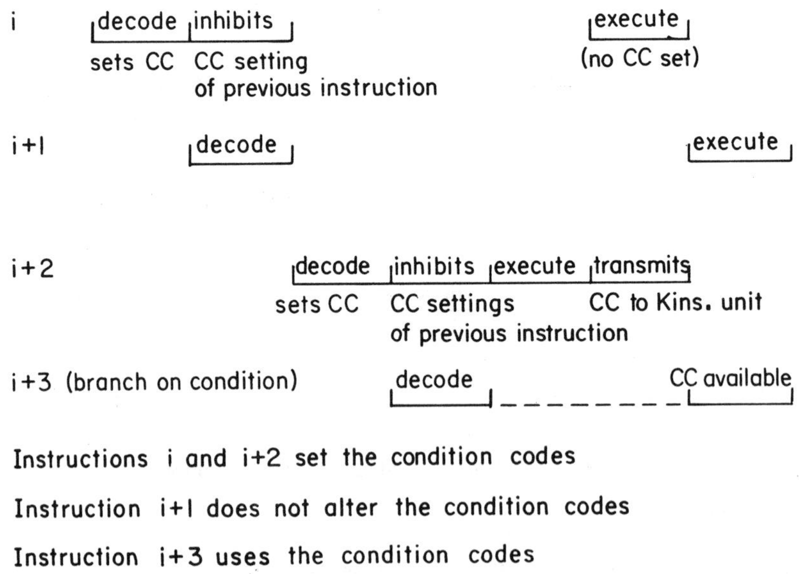

i   decode inhibits   execute
     sets CC CC setting   (no CC set)
              of previous instruction

i+1   decode   execute

i+2   decode inhibits execute transmits
                             sets CC CC settings   CC to Kins. unit
                                      of previous instruction

i+3 (branch on condition)   decode   CC available

Instructions i and i+2 set the condition codes

Instruction i+1 does not alter the condition codes

Instruction i+3 uses the condition codes

Figure 4.27   Tagging schemes for condition code settings

4.5.2 Design of the Pipelined Floating-point Units

In order to achieve the processing rate of one result/minor cycle of 60 ns., the floating-point units are tailored to their respective algorithms, namely addition and subtraction for Das and multiplication and division for Dmd. The presence of operand and order buffers facilitates the implementation of virtual D-units. Their control will be explained later. However, even with this duplication of D-units, it was not feasible in the mid-sixties to conceive of an adder or of a multiplier performing their operations on 56 bit mantissas in 60 ns. Quoting directly from [Anderson, S. F. et al. 67] "The add unit requires 2 cycles for execution and is limited to one new input per cycle .... Further study of pipelining techniques would indicate that a 3 cycle multiply and a 12 cycle divide are possible." These figures will be discussed after our presentation of the designs.

As indicated in the above quotation, a new input can be gated into the adder at every minor cycle although one add by itself requires two cycles. This is made possible by an overlap feature within the adder. A similar technique is used within Dmd although overlap of consecutive operations is not allowed.

In the description of these D-units, we shall use the term pipeline instead of overlap since it is the accepted one (in general overlap is used for concurrency within steps of the instruction execution cycle while pipeline is reserved for concurrency within D-units).

Floating-point Adder

The algorithm used in the implementation of Das is the one presented in Section 4.2 of Chapter 3. The first two steps are performed in one cycle, the addition of the fractions in a second cycle, and normalization in a third cycle. A schematic description is shown in Figure 4.28 with indications on where latches for temporary storage of data are needed.

The exponent subtraction and the determination of the smallest operand follow the description given previously. The exponent subtractor is a 7-bit CLA. The preshifter is limited to 2 columns: the first one is for right shifts of 0, 1, 2, or 3 hexadecimal digits and the second for either 0, 4, 8, or 12 digits. This implies a maximum right shift of 15 digits, which is sufficient since the mantissas are 14 digits long. The post shifter used in the normalization stage has a similar design, the only difference being that left shifts are now implemented instead of right shifts. The fraction adder is a two-level CLA; the first level consists of 14 groups where each group receives its inputs from 4 bits of the operands; the outputs of these groups are paired as inputs to 7 sections. With this decomposition an input every cycle appears to be reasonable.

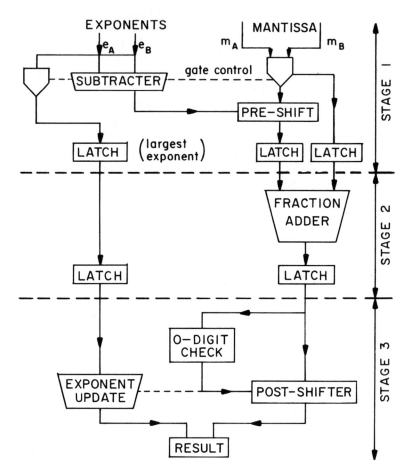

Figure 4.28 Pipelined floating-point adder

Floating-point Multiplier and Divider

The same hardware is shared by the multiplier and the divider. Pipelining is used but only internally, not as in the adder for overlap of different instructions.

The multiplication is speeded up by a recoding of the multiplier and by the use of a carry-save adder (CSA) network. Unlike the CDC 6600, only powers of two of the multiplicand are needed, i.e., only appropriate shifts will have to be implemented, and the recoding of the multiplier two bits at a time follows the one given in Table 3.2.

In the actual realization, six groups of 2 bits are recoded simultaneously and the resulting six multiples of the multiplicand added to the partial product. Since the multiplier is 56 bits long, 5 iterations in the CSA network are required. In addition to the six multiples of the multiplicand, the sum and carry generated at the previous iteration must be added. Hence six CSA's (i.e., 8-2) will have to be present. Several possibilities for the topology of the network can be envisioned (cf. Figure 4.29). The circuit of Figure 4.29.a has

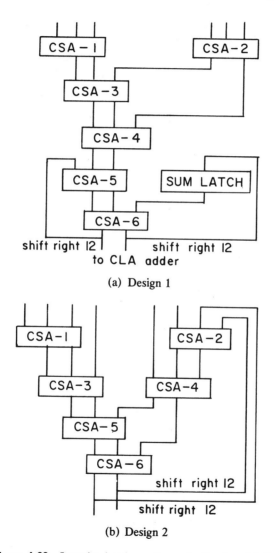

(a) Design 1

(b) Design 2

Figure 4.29 Iterative hardware for a pipelined multiplier

the advantage that it better matches the time required for new inputs to arrive at CSA-5 with the time required for the sum of the previous iteration to be stabilized in a latch input to CSA-6. The design of Figure 4.29.b requires slightly less hardware but time-wise is not as optimized. Therefore, the design of Figure 4.29.a was selected.

The internal pipelining consists of 4 stages (cf. Figure 4.30). In stage 1, 12

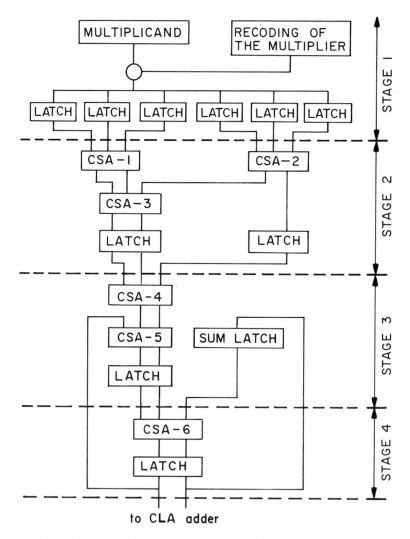

Figure 4.30   Pipelined multiplier for the IBM System/360 Model 91

bits of the multiplier are recoded and the 6 inputs are prepared. Stages 2 and 3 consist of two levels each in the CSA network. Stage 4 is the last level.

The overall mantissa multiplication is a stream of 5 operations in the pipeline since 12 bits are recoded at a time in stage 1 and the multiplier is 56 bits long. Assuming a perfect overlap, and since we have 4 stages, we shall have a minimum execution time of $(4 - 1) + 5 = 8$ time or clock units. A clock unit, the time to execute one stage in the pipeline, is quoted at 20 ns.; this amounts to a total time of almost 3 cycles of 60 ns. each (cf. Exercise 15). A last carry-propagate addition with a CLA adder similar to the one used in Das must still be performed. Hence the claim of a multiplication of 3 cycles appears quite difficult to achieve; a figure of 4 cycles seems more reasonable (this is the figure used in some other papers relative to the Model 91).

It is interesting to note that when prenormalization is necessary it is done while the operands are in the buffers prior to multiplication, and more importantly prior to division.

The exponent is generated in parallel with the iterative hardware computing the mantissa. Two exponents are computed: one is the sum of the original exponents, and the other takes care of a potential virtual underflow. Naturally, the correct one is selected.

The sharing of the hardware between the multiplier and the divider is motivated by the use of the convergence method for the division algorithm (recall Chapter 3 Section 4.2). Nonetheless, there still remain a number of difficulties in taking advantage of the iterative hardware. Among the most important, we can cite:

- The multipliers are of variable length: the first one determined by table look-up is 7 bits, the second is 14 and lengths are doubled until the fifth iteration;
- The result of a multiplication is the multiplicand for the next iteration so that a unique result is needed and hence the CLA has to be included in the loop;
- Two results have to be generated during each iteration: the product of the multiplier and the denominator which yields the next multiplier, and the accumulated product of the numerator by the successive multipliers which converges towards the quotient.

Some of these problems are not as serious as they appear at first glance. For example, the consecutive multipliers all have a leading string of 1's (except for the first one which is short), so that only the last multiplication has an actual multiplier longer than 12 bits and must go through two iterations in the CSA network. Since in this last multiplication we need not generate a next multiplier but only the resulting quotient, a single repetition through the CSA network will be done during the entire process. In a similar vein, a speed-up can be obtained by pipelining part of the CSA-tree and the CLA addition. The overall configuration is shown in Figure 4.31 and a Gantt chart for the timing in Figure 4.32. The latter indicates that a minimum of 16 clock units is necessary. These clock units correspond to two levels in the CSA and an addition in the CLA. It thus appears that the claim of 12 cycles is somewhat unwarranted since it would imply that a clock unit is of the order of 40 ns. This seems incompatible with the figures given previously for the adder and the iterative hardware of the multiplier.

Even if we were to double the original estimates, the division in the Model

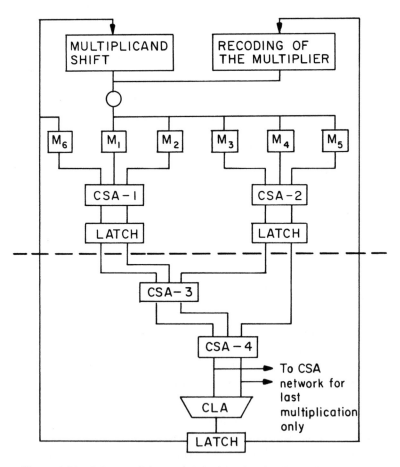

Figure 4.31   Schema of the use of the iteration hardware for a divider using the convergence method

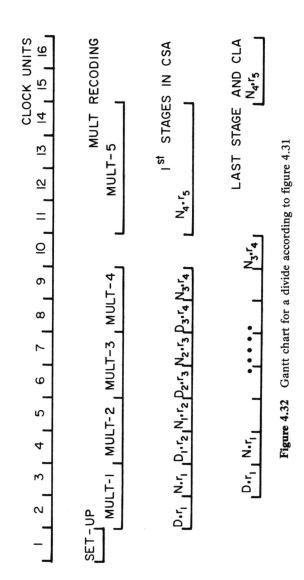

Figure 4.32 Gantt chart for a divide according to figure 4.31

91 would take only half of the time of that of the CDC 6600 with no special hardware. The convergence algorithm is therefore a rapid method. The computation of the exponent is treated as in multiplication, and since it is performed in parallel, it does not slow down the operation.

4.5.3   Hardware Control of the Virtual D-units

In addition to the instruction and operand buffers, the floating-point unit uses the concept of virtual D-units (called *reservation stations* in the IBM terminology). The two stage pipelined adder has 3 virtual D-units and the multiplier-divider has two. Both Das and Dmd receive orders of the form:

$$R_i \leftarrow R_i \text{ op. } R_j$$

where the R_j can be the contents of some memory location. In that case, a transfer to an internal buffer will take place so that from the perspective of the D-unit every operation looks like a register-register instruction. R_i will be the sink and R_j the source. The data paths interconnecting registers and (virtual) D-units are simpler than those found in the CDC 6600: a single common data bus, Scom, is time-shared by all.

As explained in Section 3 of this chapter, a tagging scheme is needed for the reservation stations. Similarly, a tag will be used with the 4 floating-point registers and with the 3 store data buffers which are the only registers that can receive results. The unit is represented in Figure 4.33. It shows the 3 virtual adders and the 2 virtual multiplier-dividers and their source and sink registers. Notice that an instruction such as loading a floating-point register in Mfp will consist of a transfer from Mp to Mfo and then to Mfp through Scom. Neither Das nor Dmd is involved in that process.

Since the 4 floating-point registers are the only ones which can be both sink and source in an instruction, the resources which affect them must be identified. They are the 6 operand buffers, the 3 adders (from now on we consider the virtual D-units as if they were real) and the 2 multipliers. Tags will therefore be 4 bits wide to identify these 11 entities. Although a 12th tag could be used to identify a "no tagging" without extra cost, the usual busy bit has been retained.

Associated with each source and sink buffer within the D-units is a tag which will store the tag of the source or sink if the value of the register is not yet available (that is, if the busy bit was on at the time the operation was scheduled).

We now elaborate on the implementation of the virtual D-unit concept as found in the Model 91. When the next instruction found in Mfi is decoded,

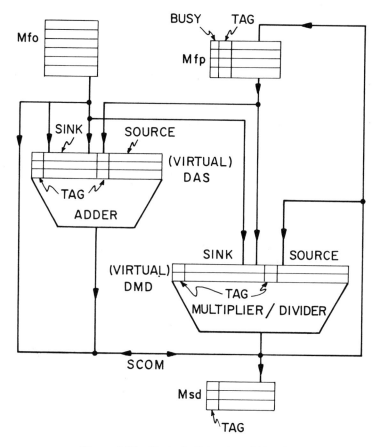

Figure 4.33   Control of the virtual D-units

its execution proceeds according to the Petri Net of Figure 4.34. We assume that only one operand is in Mfp (i.e., the source is in Mfo). We shall also talk in terms of Das but both of these assumptions do not restrict the generality of the net. In order to proceed, we must first have an available unit (place 1). If the busy bit of R_i (the floating-point register) is off (place 2), the transition t_1 can fire. Its actions include:

- Transfer (when Scom is free) the contents of R_i into the appropriate sink or source station in Das; similarly, transfer the contents of the other operand;
- Set BUSY(R_i) on;

- Set Tag(R_i) to the code of the Das which will execute the instruction (place 3).

Some time after the real adder has started the execution of the addition (place 4), it will perform a request for the use of Scom (transition t_2). The scheduling of Scom is implemented through a hardware priority scheme. When Scom becomes free (place 5), the adder's result will be sent back to the sink whose bit will be turned back to off (place 6). Das will again become available. But the broadcasting of the tag associated with the sink to all D-units must also take place (transition t_3).

To see why this is mandatory, assume that in the interval of time following the firing of t_1 and preceding that of t_3, another usage of a D-unit, say Das, involving R_i was scheduled. If a free Das was found, then the instruction should be prepared in the reservation station (transition t_4) although BUSY(R_i) is on (place 7). The events occurring when t_4 fires are:

- Set the tag in the new Das to the tag associated with R_i;
- Update the tag of R_i to point to the new Das (place 8).

Now, when a broadcast such as the one done by the firing of transition t_3 occurs, every D-unit tests if the broadcast tag is the same as the one encountered in their sink or source tag station. If the match is successful, the result of the adder is directly input to the reservation station and tag(R_i) is set to indicate a value. When both sink and source have received their contents, the operation can proceed.

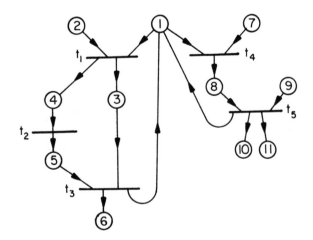

Figure 4.34　Petri Net of the hardware controller for the virtual D-unit scheme

For example, let us assume that we want to compute the sequence:

R1 ← R1 + R2
R1 ← R1 + R2

and that initially all resources are free.

Since there is a free Das, say Das1, and since both BUSY(R1) and BUSY(R2) are false, we can schedule the first addition. This involves:

- the transfer of the contents of R1 and R2 in the sink and source registers of Das1;
- the setting of the tags of these source and sink registers to "values";
- the setting of BUSY(R1) to true and of Tag(R1) to the code given to Das1 (we shall denote this by Tag(R1) = "Das1");
- the setting of BUSY(Das1) to true.

These actions correspond to the firing of transition t_1 in the Petri Net of Figure 4.34. Since the real adder is free, transition t_2 can fire immediately after t_1. But during the execution of the first addition, we want to prepare the second operation (i.e., meet the conditions for transition t_4 to fire). Since a second virtual Das, say Das2, is free, we can transfer the value of R2 in the source register. But the value of R1 is not ready yet. Therefore, we will set the tag of the sink register of Das2 to the current tag of R1 ("Das1"), keep BUSY(R1) to be true, and reset Tag(R1) to "Das2" to indicate that this is the unit which will store its final value in R1. Now, when the real adder terminates its first computation, it will broadcast the "Das1" tag (transition t_3). This will be recognized by the sink register of "Das2" which will receive the output value of the adder. Since Tag(R1) = "Das2", the value of R1 will not be modified. Upon receiving its value, the sink register of Das2 will turn its tag into "value" and the real adder can proceed with the second addition. When this second operation is completed a "Das2" tag will be broadcasted, recognized by R1, and the output value will be stored in the register R1 (transition t_5).

As in the CDC case, this hardware scheme does not supersede the detection of parallelism and a sophisticated scheduling. But even without this added software much can be gained through this concept of the virtual D-unit.

4.6 STACK PROCESSORS (A FIRST LOOK)

Among the various types of addressing discussed in Chapter 2, the 0-address format, or stack addressing, stands out as completely different from other forms. A *stack* is a linear list for which all insertions and deletions are performed at one end called the *top* (of the stack). Generally, accesses are restricted to the top of the stack but not necessarily to the single topmost element. The insertion operation is also called PUSH and the deletion operation is called POP. It is assumed that the reader knows the mechanics for handling stacks in sequential and linked allocations.

In this section, we see how stack addressing can be used efficiently for the evaluation of arithmetic expressions; we do not elaborate on other aspects of stack computers such as the ease they provide for executing block-structured languages. Besides the Burroughs B5000-B6700 series which can be considered as the paradigm of the stack computer, hardware stacks are present in the ICL 2900, a recent British entry in the computer market, and in a number of minicomputers such as the Hewlett-Packard HP 3000 (cf. Chapter 9).

4.6.1   Polish Notation for Arithmetic Expressions

Arithmetic expressions can easily be translated into suffix or "reverse Polish notation" (from its originator Lukaciewicz). This concept can be extended in such a way that a compiler can be built to transform the executable part of a high-level language source program into an intermediate string which follows the rules of the suffix notation: when a n-ary operator is to be executed its n operands are immediately preceding it.

As an example, let us consider the expression:

$$A + B + C * (D + E + F * G) .$$

It is well understood in the context of programming languages that a fully parenthesized version of this expression is:

$$((A + B) + (C * ((D + E) + (F * G))))$$

that is, a multiplication operator takes precedence over an addition. The usual precedence operations between operators have already been given in Section 3 and we repeat them here:

Precedence 0: $'('$, $')'$, $';'$
Precedence 1: $'+'$, $'-'$
Precedence 2: $'*'$, $'/'$
Precedence 3: $'**'$ (considered as a unique operator for exponentiation).

The transformation of the input string representing the arithmetic expression into an output string, image of the same expression written in reverse polish notation, can be obtained by applying the following algorithm. We use a stack, named STACK, to temporarily store operators which cannot yet be placed in the output string. By definition an operator ⊢ of precedence 0 is the initial token in the stack. SCAN(ITEM) is a procedure which returns the next lexical entity in the input string and OUTPUT(X) places X in the output string. The algorithm is then:

1. PUSH(' ⊢ '); [Initialize]
2. **While forever do**
   begin SCAN(ITEM); [Get next lexical entity]
3. **If** ITEM is an operand **then** OUTPUT(ITEM) [ITEM is an operand]
4. **else case** ITEM **of**   [ITEM is an operator]
4.1 '(' : PUSH(ITEM);
4.2 precedence(ITEM) > precedence(TOP(STACK)): PUSH(ITEM);
     [Because of precedence]
4.3 ')' : **begin while** TOP(STACK) ≠ '(' **do**
                begin OUTPUT(TOP(STACK)); POP **end**;
                POP
           end;
4.4 ';' : **begin while** TOP(STACK) ≠ ' ⊢ ' **do**
                begin OUTPUT(TOP(STACK)); POP **end**;
                POP; quit
           end;
4.5 precedence(ITEM) ≤ precedence(TOP(STACK)): [Generate
     elements of the output string]
     begin
        while precedence(ITEM) ≤ precedence(TOP(STACK)) **do**
        begin OUTPUT(TOP(STACK));POP **end**;
        PUSH(ITEM)
     end;
5. **end** [of forever]

(Errors in the syntax of the input string can easily be detected; this type of analysis is outside the scope of this book and belongs to the theory of compiler construction.)

The application of this algorithm to the example string is shown in Table 4.5. It results in the reverse polish string:

$A\ B\ +\ C\ D\ E\ +\ F\ G\ *\ +\ *\ +$

Table 4.5   Illustration of the algorithm to generate a reverse Polish notation

Input : $A + B + C * (D + E + F * G);$

Step	Item	Stack	Output added at each step
1		⊢	
3	A	⊢	A
4.2	$+$	⊢ $+$	
3	B	⊢ $+$	B
4.5	$+$	⊢ $+$	$+$
3	C	⊢ $+$	C
4.2	$*$	⊢ $+ *$	
4.1	$($	⊢ $+ * ($	
3	D	⊢ $+ * ($	D
4.2	$+$	⊢ $+ * (+$	
3	E	⊢ $+ * (+$	E
4.5	$+$	⊢ $+ * (+$	$+$
3	F	⊢ $+ * (+$	F
4.2	$*$	⊢ $+ * (+ *$	
3	G	⊢ $+ * (+ *$	G
4.3	$)$	⊢ $+ *$	$* +$
4.4	$;$		$* +$

Output : $AB + CDE + FG * + * +$

The evaluation of an expression written in reverse polish notation is straightforward and faithfully follows the definition of the notation. The string is scanned from left to right until an operator is encountered. The n-ary operator op is immediately preceded by its n operands and the result:

$$op (o_1, o_2, \ldots, o_n)$$

can be generated. It is given some name, say T_i, and T_i replaces the $n + 1$ symbols $o_1, \ldots, o_n$, op in the input string. The left to right scan is repeated, starting from T_i.

Returning to our example string, the code generated for a one-address machine would then be:

```
LOAD A
ADD B
STORE T1   (New string T1 C D E + F G * + * +)
LOAD D
ADD E
```

STORE T2   (New string T1 C T2 F G * + * +)
LOAD F
MUL G
ADD T2   (Taking advantage of the commutativity of the + and *
MUL C   operators)
ADD T1

Similarly, for a one address + general register machine, we would have:

L,R1 A
A,R1 B
L,R2 D
A,R2 E
L,R3 F
M,R3 G
A,R2 R3
M,R2 C
A,R1 R2

Let us assume now that a (hardware) stack is available. A push operation will insert an operand at the top of the stack; an n-ary arithmetic operator will find its n operands in the n topmost locations in the stack, will pop them, perform its operation and will push the result back. Then, the same expression as before will be evaluated as (cf. Table 4.6 for the contents of the stack):

PUSH A
PUSH B
ADD
PUSH C
PUSH D
PUSH E
ADD
PUSH F
PUSH G
MUL
ADD
MUL
ADD

The first major difference that can be seen by inspecting the code generated in these three evaluations is that in the stack processor case a single left to right scan is performed, i.e., the stack mechanism takes care of the

Table 4.6 Contents of the stack during the evaluation of AB + CDE * + * +

PUSH A	PUSH B	ADD	PUSH C	PUSH D	PUSH E	ADD	PUSH F	PUSH G	MUL	ADD	MUL	ADD
A	B	A+B	C	D	E	D+E	F	G	F*G	D+E+F*G	C*(D+E+F*G)	Final
	A		A+B	C	D	C	D+E	F	D+E	C	A+B	expression
				A+B	C	A+B	C	D+E	C	A+B		
					A+B		A+B	C	A+B			
								A+B				

management of temporaries. An astute compiler could of course optimize the code for the register machines so that fewer temporaries, or registers, would be needed (in fact no temporary at all for this particular expression). But a general observation is that fewer operand fetches will be necessary in the stack processor. Furthermore, instructions will be shorter since all of the procedural types (A-type in Chapter 2) simply require an opcode. The ratio of these A-type instructions to M-type might at first glance appear to be higher for the stack type of organization since all temporaries (fetches and stores) are avoided. But if the number of hardware registers used to implement the stack is smaller than the number of operands, or temporary results, residing in the stack at a given time, then the stack will overflow in Mp and this becomes equivalent to a STORE followed later by a LOAD. Also, since one address + general register machines have instruction formats which combine an operand fetch and an arithmetic or Boolean operation, it becomes difficult to compare the relative efficiency of the two organizations for the evaluation of arithmetic expressions (we emphasize once more that stack computers have other features which enable them to be more attuned to the execution of block-structured languages). A measure of efficiency could be to minimize the product:

$$\text{number of instructions} \cdot (\text{memory cycle/instruction})$$

(cf. Exercise 16). For example, we could say that in System/370 an RR instruction is 1/2 memory cycle (a half-word fetch) while an RX would be 2 memory cycles (1 for the instruction fetch and 1 for the operand fetch). In the case of a stack machine, assuming that a PUSH or POP is encoded in 1/2 word, then a PUSH or POP operation would take 3/2 cycles and an arithmetic operation would take 1/4 assuming that it is encoded in a byte. Of course these latter figures do not take into account the potential overflow of the stack in Mp.

4.6.2   Realization of Stack Processors

The hardware implementation of a stack mechanism requires as a minimum the capabilities to push an item on the stack and to detect an overflow if the stack is already full, and to pop the top of the stack into some location, or register, and detect underflow when the stack is empty. A stack of n entries of bit width w can be realized as follows.

We consider $(w + 1)$ shift registers, labelled 0 through $w - 1$ with the $(w + 1)$st named POINTER. These registers are n bits long (cf. Figure 4.35). An entry in the stack has its leftmost bit (say bit 0) in register 0, bit 1 in regis-

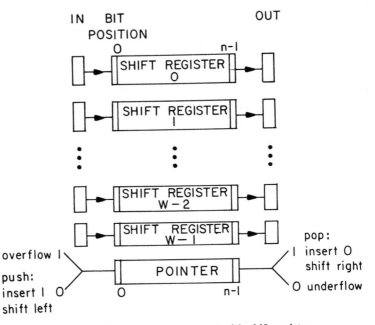

Figure 4.35   Stack implemented with shift registers

ter 1, and so on with the rightmost bit in register $w - 1$. Of course, all bits corresponding to the same entry are in corresponding positions in all w registers. Shift register POINTER indicates the number, and relative positions, of the entries in the stack. Since the only valid operations are POP and PUSH, the string of bits set to 1 in POINTER (where a 1 indicates the presence of an entry) will always be contiguous.

In order to push the contents of IN on the top of the stack, we test if bit 0 of POINTER is 0 (when the stack is empty POINTER is set to all 0's). If this is the case, we gate IN into the leftmost positions of the w registers, insert a 1 in position 0 of POINTER, and perform a circular left shift of one position of all $w + 1$ registers. Implicitly then, the top of the stack will be at the rightmost position. If bit 0 of POINTER had been a 1 when we had tried the push operation we would have had an overflow. We shall soon see how to handle this situation. To pop the stack into some register OUT (e.g., a memory location or an arithmetic register of the ALU) we initiate a symmetric procedure. We test if bit $n - 1$ of POINTER is a 1. If this is true, we transfer the rightmost bits of the w registers into the corresponding positions in OUT, set bit position $n - 1$ of POINTER to 0 and perform a circular right shift of 1 position for all $w + 1$ registers. If bit $n - 1$ of POINTER had been a 0, it would indicate an underflow.

Underflow is a logical situation which should be cleared by some exception program; it could be handled as a trap (or internal interrupt; cf. Chapter 8). Overflow on the other hand can either be considered as a limitation on the power of the stack mechanism for a given implementation, or there should be a way to allow this overflow to be handled. Examples where overflow might occur are when the stack is used to store return addresses of procedure calls or resumption points of interrupt routines. The stack depth limits the nesting of procedures or the generality of the interrupt priority scheme. Hence, since the (hardware) stack depth might be quite limited, we might want to have it "overflow" in Mp (note that since Mp is itself not infinite, we still have an overflow problem; but we might want to keep this feature as a check against infinite loops!).

The PUSH and POP routines have to be modified to handle the Mp extension. An additional register S will point to the word in Mp which holds the entry $n + 1$ in the stack with entry $n + 2$ being in the previous sequential memory cell. A pair of limit registers S_L and S_H indicate respectively whether the extension is empty (contents of S = contents of S_L), or whether we have an overflow on the Mp extension (contents of S = contents of S_H before the PUSH operation). The two procedures can be modified as follows.

PUSH(IN)

1. **If** POINTER(0) = 0, **then** proceed as before;
2. [Hardware stack overflow].
   If $S = S_H$ **then** overflow (abort the task);
   $S \leftarrow S + 1$; Circular left shift the $w + 1$ registers;
   POP (into Mp(S)) using the previously defined POP operation;
   PUSH(IN) as previously defined.

POP

1. **If** POINTER($n - 1$) = 0 **then** underflow (and trap);
2. [POP the hardware stack]
   Proceed as defined previously;
   If $S = S_L$ **then** end;
3. [Insert from Mp]
   PUSH(Mp(S)) but without the last shifting operation; $S \leftarrow S - 1$;

These procedures are illustrated in Figure 4.36 which shows some snapshots of the stack manipulations of Table 4.6. We have assumed a stack of 2 entries, i.e., $n = 1$.

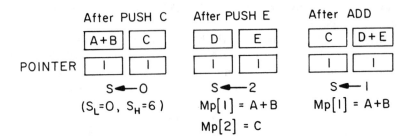

Figure 4.36 Snapshots of a stack with Mp extension

It should be noted that in our implementation model the execution of an arithmetic expression proceeds as follows:

- Transfer the contents of positions $(n - 1)$ and $(n - 2)$ of the stack into internal registers of the ALU;
- After performing the arithmetic operation transfer the result back into position $(n - 2)$;
- Rotate all $w + 1$ registers right one position;
- If $S \neq S_L$ then perform step 3 of the POP routine.

This is quite inefficient if a PUSH immediately follows the arithmetic operation since we would transfer one entry of the stack back and forth from Mp. To avoid this overhead, we can modify once more the PUSH and POP routines. For the first one, we allow the insertion to be done at the rightmost position, as:

PUSH(IN)

0.5. [Is there space at the rightmost end?]
   If POINTER$(n - 1) = 0$ **then** transfer IN in position $(n - 1)$
   of the w registers and set POINTER$(n - 1)$ to 1;
   Else steps 1 and 2 as before.

For the POP routine, as well as for the execution of an arithmetic operation, we must transfer the first non-null entry. If we limit ourselves to the possibility of having a single void entry at the top of the stack, then the POP routine becomes:

POP

1. **If** POINTER$(n - 1) = 0$ **and** POINTER$(n - 2) = 0$ **and** $S = S_L$ **then** underflow

2. **If** POINTER($n - 1$) $= 0$ **do**

    2.1. Shift the ($w + 1$) registers right one position and set POINTER(0) to 0.

    2.2. **If** $S \neq S_L$ **then** perform previous step 3.

3. Perform steps 2 and 3 as defined previously.

The modifications to the protocol of the execution of an arithmetic expression and generalizations of the above procedures are left to the reader (cf. Exercise 17).

The Burroughs B6700 stack mechanism is quite similar in principle to the one just discussed. Machine instructions are of variable length; 8 bits (corresponding to a single opcode) is the most common. Data and "control" words are 51 bits long as shown in Figure 4.37; the first 3 bits are used as tags identifying the various word types.

Each current process has a stack extension attached to it. This portion of Mp contains local variables, temporary storage (the stack extension of the previous paragraphs), and references (descriptors) to procedures and arrays. The register stack consists of two double length registers A and B. Because of this limited depth, registers A and B are implemented as regular registers instead of as a vector of 102 (2.51) shift registers of 2 bits. Two extra flip-flops, F_A and F_B, serve as POINTER and indicate whether A and B are empty. The PUSH and POP procedures and the protocol for the execution of an arithmetic expression are similar to the last set of those presented above.

Loading of local variables (not temporaries) is simply done by putting their displacement from S_L in the A register and the LOAD (PUSH) instruction loads the contents of that memory location into the A register. Naturally, ancillary stack operations might also be performed. STORE is executed according to the same principle. Descriptors are used when subscripted variables are involved (cf. Chapter 6). Finally, the hardware implementation of the block structure and procedure calls is aided by the use of registers keeping track of the static block structure and of the dynamic calls in a manner very similar to the chaining process devised in Randell and Russell's classical implementation of an ALGOL-60 compiler. This last feature is absent from the B-5500 and from the HP-3000.

This latter machine (cf. Chapter 9 Section 5) has a stack of 4 registers. Measurements have shown that an operand reference to memory (LOAD or STORE) occurs every 3 instructions on the average (compare with Table 2.1) and that the stack extension adds another 4% to the Pc-Mp traffic. Simulations have shown that with 2 registers in the stack this percentage would double and that no real advantage would be gained by having more than 4 registers.

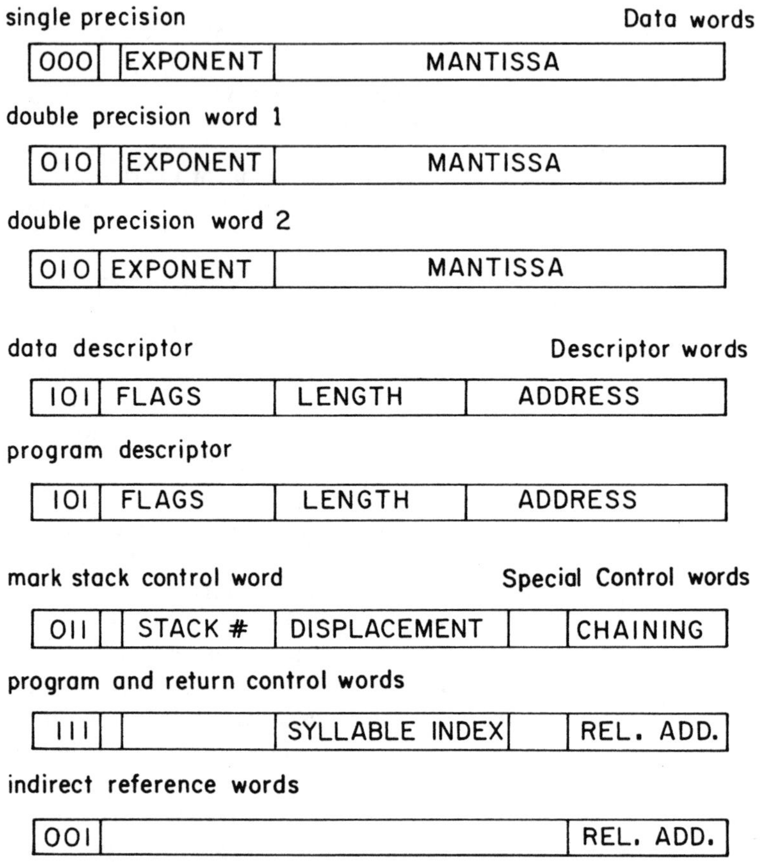

single precision   Data words

| 000 | EXPONENT | MANTISSA |

double precision word 1

| 010 | EXPONENT | MANTISSA |

double precision word 2

| 010 | EXPONENT | MANTISSA |

data descriptor   Descriptor words

| 101 | FLAGS | LENGTH | ADDRESS |

program descriptor

| 101 | FLAGS | LENGTH | ADDRESS |

mark stack control word   Special Control words

| 011 | STACK # | DISPLACEMENT | CHAINING |

program and return control words

| 111 | | SYLLABLE INDEX | REL. ADD. |

indirect reference words

| 001 | | REL. ADD. |

Figure 4.37 Formats of data and control words in the Burroughs B6700
(incomplete)

4.7 BIBLIOGRAPHICAL NOTES, REFERENCES AND EXERCISES

Among many references which look at the basic Pc requirements, we can cite [Abd-Alla and Meltzer 76]. [Katzan 71] contains a lot of information about the various IBM System/370 models. For more details IBM manuals can be consulted. An excellent discussion of overlap and pipelining can be found in [Chen 75]. More of the material also covered by Chen will be found in Chapter 10. [Keller 75] is a good introduction to the problems of look-ahead processing. Many of the ideas of Section 3 are due to [Tomasulo 67] and [Thornton 70]. The conditions for inter-statement parallelism were first defined in [Bernstein 66]. The intra-statement parallelism detection algorithm of Section 3.2 comes from [Baer and Bovet 68]. Its optimality is proven in [Beatty 72].

The application of the law of distributivity is treated in [Kuck, Muraoka, and Chen 72]. Tree traversals are thoroughly examined in [Knuth 68].

Hu's algorithm first appeared in [Hu 61]. An analysis of Hu's extended algorithm, or critical path length scheduling, can be found in [Kaufman 74] while the treatment of more general bounds is examined in [Graham 72]. The register assignment problem is treated in detail in [Aho and Ullman 73].

Section 4 on the CDC 6600 is based on [Thornton 70]. The Petri Net of Figure 4.24 is abstracted from [Shapiro and Saint 70]. Program optimization with respect to the detection of intra-statement parallelism and register allocation for the 6600 is described in [Allard, Wolk, and Zemlin 64].

A whole issue of the IBM Journal of Research and Development was devoted to the IBM System/360 Model 91. We have already cited the three main references in this and the previous chapters.

The use of stacks in the design of Pc's is described in [McKeeman 75]. Specifics on the Burroughs B6700 stack mechanism can be found in [Hauck and Dent 72]. [Organick 73] is an excellent tutorial on the B6700 organization and on the general use of stacks in addition to the one for the Pc. [Randell and Russell 64] is a classic reference for the compilation of block-structured languages using the Polish notation concept. [Blake 77] gives some interesting statistics on the use of the HP-3000.

References

1. Abd-Alla, A. and A. Meltzer, *Principles of Digital Computer Design,* Vol. 1, Prentice-Hall, Englewood Cliffs, N.J., 1976.

2. Aho, A. V. and J. D. Ullman, *The Theory of Parsing, Translation, and Compiling,* Vol. II, Prentice-Hall, Englewood Cliffs, N.J., 1973.

3. Allard, R. W., Wolk, K. A. and R. A. Zemlin, "Some Effects of the 6600 Computer on Language Structure", *Comm. ACM, 7,* (Feb. 1964), 112-119.

4. Anderson, D. W., Sparacio, F. J. and R. M. Tomasulo, "The IBM System/360 Model 91: Machine Philosophy and Instruction Handling", *IBM Journal of Research and Development, 11,* (Jan. 1967), 8-24.

5. Anderson, S. F., Earle, J. G., Goldschmitt, R. E. and D. M. Powers, "Floating-point Execution Unit", *IBM Journal of Research and Development, 11,* (Jan. 1967), 25-33.

6. Baer, J.-L. and D. P. Bovet, "Compilation of Arithmetic Expressions for Parallel Computations", *Proc. IFIP Congress 1968,* North-Holland, Amsterdam, 1968, 340-346.

7. Beatty, J., "An Axiomatic Approach to Code Optimization for Expressions", *Journal ACM, 19,* (Oct. 1972), 613-640.

8. Bernstein, A. J., "Analysis of Programs for Parallel Processing". *IEEE Trans. Elec. Comp., E-15,* (Oct. 1966), 746-757.

9. Blake, R. P., "Exploring a Stack Architecture", *Computer, 10,* (May 1977), 30–39.

10. Chen, T. C., "Overlap and Pipeline Processing", in *Introduction to Computer Architecture,* H. Stone ed., SRA, Chicago, Ill., 1975, 375–431.

11. Graham, R., "Bounds on Multiprocessing Anomalies and Packing Algorithms", *Proc. AFIPS 1972 Spring Joint Computer Conf., 40,* AFIPS Press, Montvale, N.J., 1972, 205–217.

12. Hauck, E. A. and B. A. Dent, "Burroughs B6500/B7500 Stack Mechanism", *Proc. AFIPS 1968 Spring Joint Computer Conf., 32,* AFIPS Press, Montvale, N.J., 1968, 245–251.

13. Hu, T. C., "Parallel Sequencing and Assembly Line Problems", *Operations Research, 9,* (Nov. 1961), 841–848.

14. Katzan, H., *Computer Organization and the System/370,* Van Norstrand Reinhold, New-York, N.Y., 1971.

15. Kaufman, M., "An Almost-optimal Algorithm for the Assembly-line Scheduling Problem", *IEEE Trans. Comp., C-23,* (Nov. 1974), 1169–1174.

16. Keller, R., "Look-ahead Processors", *Computing Surveys, 7,* (Dec. 1975), 177–196.

17. Knuth, D., *The Art of Computer Programming, Vol. 1,* Addison-Wesley, Reading, Mass., 1968.

18. Kuck, D. J., Muraoka, Y., and S. C. Chen, "On the Number of Operations Simultaneously Executable in FORTRAN-like Programs and Their Resulting Speed", *IEEE Trans. Comp., C-21,* (Dec. 1972), 1293–1309.

19. McKeeman, W. M., "Stack Processors", in *Introduction to Computer Architecture,* H. Stone ed., SRA, Chicago, Ill., 1975, 281–317.

20. Organick, E. I., *Computer System Organization. The B5700/B6700 Series,* Academic Press, New-York, N.Y., 1973.

21. Randell, B. and L. Russell, *Algol 60 Implementation,* Academic Press, London, 1964.

22. Shapiro, R. M. and J. Saint, "A New Approach to Optimization of Sequencing Decisions", *Annual Review Automatic Programming, 6,* part 5, 1970.

23. Thornton, J. E., *Design of a Computer Systems, the Control Data 6600,* Scott, Foresman and Co., Glenview, Ill., 1970.

24. Tomasulo, R. M., "An Efficient Algorithm for Exploiting Multiple Arithmetic Units", *IBM Journal of Research and Development, 11,* (Jan. 1967), 25–33.

Exercises

1. Complete the ISP description of Figure 4.1.

2. Assuming the following values for I-fetch (t_f), I-unit execution (t_i), and D-unit execution (t_d), compute the times necessary to execute 100 instructions in the cases:

   (a) no overlap;
   (b) simple overlap (recall Figure 4.3);
   (c) ideal overlap (recall Figure 4.6);

   Now if preloading of one instruction modifies t_f so that it becomes $t_f' = 4t_f/3$, compute the times to execute 100 instructions for:

   (d) overlap with double instruction fetch (recall Figure 4.4);
   (e) ideal overlap with double instruction fetch (recall Figure 4.5);

   Conclude by comparing the results in the two cases:
   (i) $t_f = 2, t_i = 2, t_d = 1$;   (ii) $t_f = 5, t_i = 2, t_d = 5$.

3. Give formulas for the execution times of n instructions for the 5 overlap cases of Exercise 2 for all possible orderings of t_f, t_f', t_i, and t_d.

4. What is the minimal completion time of the sequence in Example 4 under the assumption of no buffering and no virtual D-unit, but with as many real multipliers and adders as necessary. How many multipliers and adders are needed? Could you improve the execution time by scheduling the statements in a different order while still keeping the procedural constraints.

5. Repeat Exercise 4 assuming only one multiplier and one adder but allowing virtual units and buffering.

6. Compute the completion times of the sequences corresponding to the trees of Figures 4.15 and 4.16 assuming a single adder and a single multiplier, 3 virtual units per real unit, buffering and forwarding.

7. What is the maximal depth of the stack in the algorithm for automatic detection of parallelism assuming only $'+'$ and $'*'$ operators? What happens when parenthesis are introduced?

8. Give algorithmic descriptions for Hu's algorithm and its extension when tasks are of unequal (integer) times.

9. Show that for $n = 2$ processors if tasks are of time 1 or 2, and if the procedural precedence relationships form a tree, then Hu's extended algorithm is within one time unit of optimality. More generally, show that if t_0 is the optimal completion time, t_s the completion time under Hu's extended algorithm, and t_h the completion time under Hu's extended algorithm when tasks of time k are replaced by a chain of k tasks of unit time, then:

$$t_0 \le t_s \le t_h + k - \lfloor k/n \rfloor$$

10. Assume a Pc with a single D-unit and a I-unit-I-fetch time of t_m. Let $t_1, t_2, \ldots,$ t_r be execution times of instructions which could be processed in parallel (i.e., in any order). Show that if:

$$t_1 \ge \cdots \ge t_d \ge t_e = t_f = \cdots = t_j \ge t_m \ge t_n \ge \cdots \ge t_r,$$

and if t_{inc} and t_{dec} are the respective completion times when the instructions are processed in order 1, 2, $\ldots$, d, e, $\ldots$, j, n, $\ldots$ r and in the reverse order then:

$$t_{\text{inc}} - t_{\text{dec}} = t_m - t_1$$

Assuming now that there are as many D-units as instructions, show that:

$$t_r - t_m \le t_{\text{inc}} - t_{\text{dec}} \le t_r - t_1$$

11. Consider the CDC 6600 floating-point format. Prove that if x and y are two floating-point numbers, then when subtracting the exponent of y from that of x in a 1's complement adder:

$$(x \ge y) \leftarrow \text{(end-around carry)} \oplus \text{(exponent sign alike)}$$

12. Give a general test on branching within a look-behind buffer given T the effective branch address, IA the branch instruction address, P the location of the branch instruction in the buffer, and D the depth of valid instructions in the buffer.

13. Optimize the code of Table 4.3 assuming that the computation is performed only once. Consider now the loop

    for K:= 1 **step** 1 **until** 50 **do**
        Z(K) := C1 * (Y(K) − Y1) + C2 * (Y(K) − Y2) ** 2;

    Give a timing table similar to Table 4.3 for the first iteration of the loop, and similar to Table 4.4 for subsequent iterations. Optimize. What is the trade-off between conflicts in result registers and extra fetches and loads?

14. We assume now that we have a 360/6600 Pc, i.e., a machine whose instruction set is similar to that of System/360's and which has 10 D-units as in the CDC 6600. Arithmetic-logical operations are of the form:

$$R_i \leftarrow R_i \text{ op. } R_j$$

and instructions of the form:

$$R_i \leftarrow R_i \text{ op. } Mp[a]$$

are forbidden. Instructions which reference Mp are load, store, and branch instructions. The machine has 8 floating-point registers and 8 index or address registers. Register to register transfers are handled by the Boolean unit. A word is 32 bits long with either short (16 bits) or long (32 bits) instructions.

(a) Using ISP describe possible instruction formats for short and long instructions.

(b) Summarize the timing rules for instruction fetch which differ from those of the CDC 6600; assume an Mbuffer of 16 words.

(c) Repeat Exercise 13 for this new architecture. Is Mbuffer long enough? What is the minimum size of Mbuffer allowing a loop-mode operation for this particular expression?

(d) Compare the use of 3 register instructions (as in CDC 6600) versus 2 register instructions (as in this 360/6600) with respect to multi-functional units Pc's.

15. Show that 8 clock times are sufficient for the iterative hardware of Figure 4.29.a when mantissas of 56 bits are multiplied. How many clock time units would be necessary if the design of Figure 4.29.b was adopted assuming that the CSA network is again decomposed into 3 stages?

16. Consider the expression:

$$A + B * (C - D * E)/(F + G)$$

Transform it into reverse Polish notation. Generate code for a stack, a one address, and a one address + general register machine. Now assuming the availability of the following instruction formats:

- Stack machine: short instruction 8 bits for an opcode, long instruction 24 bits for an opcode and an Mp address.
- One address machine: 24 bits for an opcode and an Mp address.
- One address + general register: short instruction 16 bits for an opcode and 2 registers, long instruction 32 bits for an opcode, one register, and an Mp address.

Compare the lengths of the programs for the above expression. You can assume that the machines have word lengths of 32 bits with instructions allowed to cross over word boundaries. How many memory cycles will be needed if we have 16 registers and the stack is 6 words deep? What happens if the stack is only 2 deep? Can you derive any general conclusion from this exercise?

17. Give the Gantt Chart for the computation of:
   R2 ← R3 / R5   (/ takes 20 units)
   R1 ← R2 + R4   (+ takes 4 units)
   R4 ← R6 * R6   (* takes 10 units)
in a CDC 6600-like environment.

Chapter 5

THE MEMORY HIERARCHY

In Chapter 1, we related how technological developments generated the introduction of faster, larger and less expensive memory devices. Very early, computer systems were not limited to a single memory level but the components were embedded in a hierarchy with each increasing level in the hierarchy consisting of modules of larger capacity, slower access time and cheaper cost/bit. As shown in our study of fast central processors, (main) memory access time has often been the reason for bottlenecks in execution. Instruction (look-ahead stacks) and data buffers were designed to reduce this slowing effect. Today, large scale integration (LSI) allows the manufacturing of fast semiconductor Random Access Memories (RAM's) which can be conveniently used for the lower levels of the hierarchy. However, optimization of the access to primary memory is still desirable.

As we shall soon see, there exists a gap in the access times between the various levels of the hierarchy. Emergent technologies such as Charge Coupled Devices (CCD's) and Magnetic Bubble Memories might be the bridge needed between current Mp and Ms, the latter implemented at the present time through rotational devices. However, because of the requirements for large amounts of on-line storage, disks will still be competitive. And the need for off-line and archival stores makes removable disk packs and magnetic tapes unavoidable.

From the above discussion it is clear that the study of "memory" in Computer Systems Architecture should provide a discussion of the various components of the hierarchy as well as of the management of the transfer of information between the different levels. This latter aspect will be the subject of Chapter 6.

We start this chapter by introducing the physical devices which form the components of a memory hierarchy. Their main attributes, in the PMS sense, will be listed and discussed. The next section is devoted to primary memory, Mp, and its organization. In Section 3 we study *interleaving*, a means to optimize access to Mp. In Section 4, we shall present some of the current devices used for secondary memories, i.e., drums and disks, and will briefly show the potential of the so-called electronic disks. The chapter ends with a brief look at associative memory.

To be consistent with the philosophy previously expressed, very little will be said about technological aspects of the various components. Their physical properties will be abstracted as much as possible but in such a way that an understanding of the operational constraints will be maintained.

5.1 COMPONENTS OF THE MEMORY HIERARCHY

The design of a memory hierarchy is guided by the desire to:

- try to match the Pc speed with the rate of information transfer from the lowest element of the hierarchy;
- attain adequate performance at a reasonable cost.

The speed criterion can be rephrased as: to attain a relation between the frequencies of access of the units of information with their placement in the hierarchy. Of course the latter will vary in time. Cost can be decomposed into two factors: a structural factor which limits the size of the faster, and hence more expensive, components; and a dynamic factor imposed by the management of transfers between levels which are time-consuming and which require the use of other resources besides the memory (e.g., channels, operating system, etc. . . .). It is interesting to remark that the dynamic component of the cost can take forms which depend on the type of installation and the functions to be optimized (e.g., throughout vs. response-time).

From a structural viewpoint a memory hierarchy consists of L levels. At each level i, the memory, M_i, has components characterized by *size*, or *capacity*, S_i, (average) *access time*, T_i, and *cost/bit*, C_i. A level might contain several modules, $M_i{}^j$, not necessarily identical but closely related in function and attributes S_i, T_i, and C_i (e.g., two disks of different capacity with average access time of the same magnitude).

Connections between modules at level i and levels $i - j$, ($j = 1, \ldots, i, i \neq 0$) and $i + j$ ($j = 1, \ldots, L - i, i \neq L$) are characterized by their *transfer rates*, or *bandwidth*, B_k, with k being the highest level of the two connected modules, and by the physical amount of information transferred, R_k. Multilevel connections can exist, as for example between cache and Ms.

A contemporary computer system could have a memory hierarchy of up to 6 levels with interconnections as shown in Figure 5.1. Table 5.1 indicates

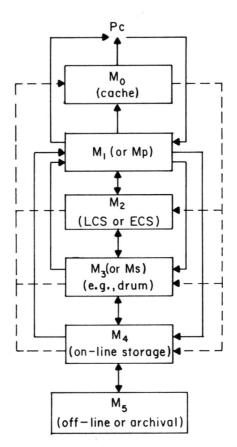

Figure 5.1   Levels and interconnections in a memory hierarchy

typical values for the attributes S_i, T_i, C_i, B_k, and R_k. Naturally, many systems will have only part of the range shown in Figure 5.1 and the values given in Table 5.1 are only indicative of the current state of the art.

Level 1 consists of Mp which until 1970 was always core. Since then MOS (metal oxide semiconductor) technology has gradually become prevalent and it is expected that core memory will virtually disappear by 1985. Currently, Mp size can be as large as a few million bytes ($1M = 10^6$). The access time is slightly less than a microsecond for the random access to a word (hence the name Random Access Memory or RAM). This access time depends on the size of the chips from which the RAM's are built. A bigger chip implies a longer access time at a decreased cost. The cost/bit is a few tenths of a cent

Table 5.1 Parameters of the components of a memory hierarchy

Component	Technology	Typical sizes S_i	Average access time T_i	Cost/bit (cents) C_i	Transfer unit R_k	Transfer rate B_k
cache	semi-conductor (bipolar)	4–16K bytes	.1 μs	3	1 word	40M bytes/sec
Mp	semi-conductor (MOS)	8K–1M words	0.5–1 μs	.5	1–16 words	4M bytes/sec
	core	8K–1M words	0.5–1 μs	.7	1–16 words	4M bytes/sec
LCS	core	64K–1M words	5–10 μs	.3	1–16 words	500K bytes/sec
ECS	core	64K–1M words	6–10 μs	.3	8 words	500K bytes/sec
fixed-head disk	magnetic	5M bytes	5–15 ms	.05	1K–4K bytes	1M bytes/sec
drum	magnetic	5M bytes	5–15 ms	.01	1K–4K bytes	1M bytes/sec
movable-arm disk (one drive)	magnetic	10–800M bytes	25–60 ms	.005	4K bytes	1M bytes/sec
tape (2400 feet reel)	magnetic	50M bytes	seconds	.00001	80–10K bytes	300K bytes/sec

Index i for level.
Index $k = \max(i, j)$ for a transfer from level i to/from level j.

(cf. Figure 5.2), a price which will decrease by a factor of 10 within a decade (for semiconductor memories). Transfers (R_k) to and from the central processor registers are also on a single word basis for each module, although from the Pc-Mp switch viewpoint it might appear that R_k is related to the interleaving capabilities (cf. Section 3; also multiword operands occur in some systems. For example in the IBM System/370, the "STM" instruction stores 2 to 16 general registers into 2 to 16 consecutive memory locations).

Systems with high performance requirements often use a high-speed buffer, or *cache memory* (M_0 in the figure), between Mp and Pc. The access time is approximately 0.1 μs, i.e., an order of magnitude faster than that of Mp, and consequently semiconductors are mandatory (either MOS or bipolar technology). Typical sizes are a few kilobytes (1K $= 10^3$). Access to Pc is on a word basis and transfers to and from Mp are by blocks of 1 to 16 words. In Figure 5.1, a one-way transfer between M_1 and M_0 is indicated. This is not always the case as will be discussed in Chapter 6. Similarly, there exist systems which allow direct transfers from M_2 or M_3 to M_0.

The Large Core Storage (LCS) and Extended Core Storage (ECS) level is, as the name implies, a direct extension of Mp. Typical access times are a few microseconds but the price per bit is not significantly less than that of Mp. LCS works on a word basis while access to ECS consists of a small seek time followed by a block transfer time. R_k is generally a few words (a superword or sword of 8 words in the CDC 6000 series). This level is generally connected to M_1 and M_3.

At the next level we have shown a *drum* or *fixed-head disk*. These rotational devices are the components most often used currently as Ms in a virtual memory environment or for small-to-medium systems. Their average access time, the sum of rotational latency and transfer time, is of a few milliseconds for blocks, or sectors, of 1K to 4K bytes. Their capacity is

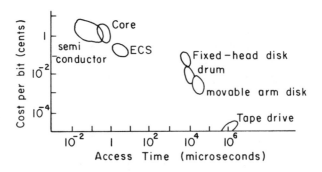

Figure 5.2   Current memory technology (circa 1978)

several Mbytes for a price of a few hundredths of a cent per bit. It is usually connected to Mp, M_2 if present and M_4 when it exists.

Level 4 corresponds to permanent file storage. It will generally support one or more *movable-arm disks*. Smaller installations could have a fixed-head disk and magnetic tape drives instead, while in large systems mass storage subsystems based on "virtual" disks and automatic retrieval of magnetic cartridges might be present. The movable-arm disk access time is longer than for the fixed-head because of the *seek time* needed to move the arm to the right cylinder (cf. Section 4). The seek time is on the average of the same order as the rotational latency. Transfer times and transfer units are approximately the same as for fixed-head disks but the capacity is 4 to 5 times larger.

At the last level are off-line and archival storage with removable disk packs on movable-head disks and magnetic tapes. The latter are cheaper and slower, and have to be sequentially accessed for efficient use. They can store on the order of 50 Mbytes but this often depends on the configuration of the records on the tape (cf. Chapter 8). The transfer rate is one order of magnitude slower than for disks and the access time depends on the position of the last record accessed. Record lengths, i.e., R_k, can vary widely from a few bytes to several thousand bytes. At this level, devices such as floppy-disks, cassettes, etc. ... should also be included. We consider them more like input/output devices than elements of the memory hierarchy. This may be proven incorrect in the context of small and even medium installations.

A cursory examination of Figure 5.2 reveals the existence of an access-time gap between core and semi-conductor memories on the one hand, and rotating devices on the other. Naturally, computer manufacturers have invested and are still in the process of investing substantial research resources to try to find devices which would bridge this gap. The so-called "electronic disks" which have not yet been mass produced may provide the anticipated solution. The three most commonly proposed technologies are:

- Charge-Coupled Devices (CCD's)
- Magnetic Bubbles
- Electron Beam

Their place in the memory hierarchy in terms of cost and access time as of 1982 are shown in Figure 5.3; other attributes are shown in Table 5.2. For comparison purposes, we have also included MOS RAM's in the latter table with the same projections. As can be seen, the memory gap could be filled by many of these technologies. The choice will depend on a number of engineering details allowing mass production which are not yet sufficiently resolved to warrant firm forecasts. It is for this reason that some of the devices which do

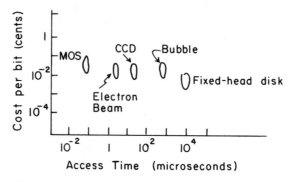

Figure 5.3   Projected memory technology (circa 1982)

Table 5.2   Projected attributes of the electronic disks (circa 1982)

Technology	Typical sizes	Average access time	Cost/bit (cents)
CCD	1–5 M words	25 μs	.02
Bubbles	1–5 M words	750 μs	.02
Electron beam	1 M word	4 μs	.02
MOS	2 M words	.1 μs	.05

not appear to be competitive have been included in the table. We shall return to these aspects later in this chapter.

The numbers given in Tables 5.1 and 5.2 must be taken as estimates. Caution is required when forecasting in rapidly changing technologies. For example, it has been reported that MOS RAM's are becoming faster than bipolar RAM's. Considering the cost factor, the demise of the bipolar technology could be predicted. However, improvement of bipolar memories may also be forthcoming.

It has been almost implicit in our presentation that there exist two natural boundaries in the memory hierarchy. The first one is at the man-machine interface, that is, at the on-line-off-line storage border. In PMS terms, the devices are more like transducers T_i than memories M_i. The second occurs between those components directly accessed by the Pc and those whose information has to be transferred to Mp before being available to Pc. While the first boundary requires human intervention, e.g., mounting a tape or typing a message on a teletype, the second will be either transparent as in a virtual memory environment, or at least will be programmable and will not impede the normal flow of operations. In this chapter and the next we consider only the elements, and their management, which interact in this latter boundary.

5.2. PRIMARY MEMORY

5.2.1 Random-Access Memories

The memories at the lowest level of the hierarchy, that is, M_1 or M_p and the cache M_0, belong to the class of *random-access memories* (RAM's). RAM's can be characterized as consisting of a number of identical i-units (in general words), each accessible through a unique hardwired address, and each of same access duration independent of the location of the i-unit and of previous accesses. Storage, or writing, and retrieval, or reading, in RAM's require:

- A storage medium organized in such a way that i-units (in the following, we refer to i-units as words) can be read and written as entities;
- An address register (MAR) to hold the address of the word being accessed;
- A data register (MDR), or buffer, to hold the information being read or written;
- Sensors to read;
- Transducers (drivers) to write.

Schematically, a RAM is as shown in Figure 5.4.

The storage medium is an array of bits, with the bits subsequently grouped into words. Since the atomic unit of information is the bit, the physical storage medium must be such that one can:

- Sense one of two stable states which will respectively model 0 and 1. This sensing will be used for reading;
- Switch from one state to another as often as needed for writing purposes.

This sensing and switching will be performed through the application of an external energy source. The requirement for stability implies that the states should be separated by some high energy barrier and that the energy stored be some discrete quantity. This has led to the selection of media such as magnetic ferrite cores, where the magnetic moment is the measured quantity, and transistor cells where the circulated current is used to identify the states.

Regardless of the storage medium, we can see that reading implies the

to and from Pc, Pio etc...

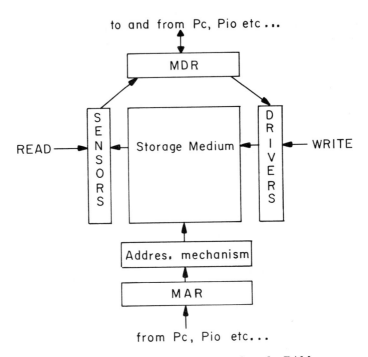

Figure 5.4   Schematic representation of a RAM

selection of a word and the sensing of each bit of the word, and that writing implies the selection of a word and a further discrimination over which bits to switch from one state to another, i.e., a bit selection. Hence, any storage cell will have to be able to receive inputs from a word selector, a bit selector, and a sensor. However, the latter two terminals can be shared since they are used in the mutually exclusive operations of reading and writing.

Before proceeding with actual implementations of the storage array, we briefly discuss the addressing mechanism. The address of the word to be read or written into is found in the MAR. Assuming that the RAM has a capacity $S = 2^n$ b-bit words, the MAR is n bits wide. A straightforward decoding will require $O(S)$ gates to obtain an one-out-of-S output. This technique will be called *linear selection*. However, if the technology allows either sensing or switching states, or both, by the application of fractions of the energy source such that the applied sum is sufficient to carry over the energy barrier, then the decoding can be made simpler by splitting the address into two halves. Now, only $O(\sqrt{S})$ gates are necessary, $\sqrt{S}$ for the upper half of the address and $\sqrt{S}$ for the lower half. The word selected will be at the intersection of these two one-out-of-$\sqrt{S}$ decoders and hence, the name *coincident selection*.

5.2.2 Magnetic Ferrite Core Memories

This section is included for historical interest. The hurried reader may omit it and move directly to the more modern technologies of Section 5.2.3.

Physical Properties

Magnetic ferrite cores, or cores in short, have been the dominant medium for RAM's until the mid-seventies. The basic storage cell is a toroid core threaded by a number of conductive wires. The physical properties of the core are shown in the idealized BH curve of Figure 5.5. The value of the flux density B distinguishes the two stable states. The energy source, here a magnetizing force, is proportional to the sum of the current passing through the wires threading the core. The writing and reading of a single bit can be performed as follows.

To write a 1 in a bit, a sufficiently large positive current is applied such that the corresponding magnetic field H will be greater that the threshold value H_c. If the bit was already in "state 1", i.e., point C on the curve, nothing would happen. It it were in "state 0", i.e., point F, it would follow the curve from point F to G and then A since $H > H_c$. After passing A, it would reach C and remain in the stable "state 1". The current i need not be

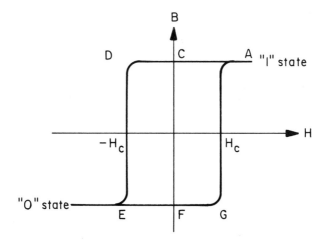

Figure 5.5 Idealized hysteresis curve

applied on a single wire but the sum of the currents applied should be greater than or equal to i.

To read the value of a bit the only physical property which can be used is a change of state. For example, currents of sum smaller than $-i$ in some of the wires are sent and sensed on an additional one if there was a change in the flux. If indeed there was one, it can be amplified, and transformed into the setting of the corresponding bit (flip-flop) of the MDR. For example, if the core was in "state 1", i.e., point C, a current $-i$ will make it switch to "state 0", i.e., point F, and the recorded change will set the appropriate flip-flop to 1. On the other hand, if it was already in "state 0", nothing would happen.

The writing and reading procedures just presented have two defects. First, reading is destructive. Although its previous contents are correctly recorded in the MDR, the entire word will be set to 0. Second, we have shown how to write a 1 but not how to write selectively a 1 or a 0. Thus, the procedures have to be modified and consist of two passes.

Procedure READ

1. Sense all bits in the given word and amplify results in the MDR (this clears the word);
2. Write back the contents of the MDR.

Procedure WRITE

1. Sense all bits in the given word without storing it in the MDR (this clears the word);
2. Write back the contents of the MDR.

The reader will have noticed that we have not yet taken care of the selective writing. This can be done either by some logic at the MDR level, or with the use of an inhibit wire to be discussed shortly. At this time, we want to emphasize the fact that a read cycle can be decomposed into two parts: an access time and a regeneration time. At the end of access time, typically half of the cycle time, the information is available in the MDR, and therefore to the Pc, but the RAM is not yet ready to accept a new command until the completion of its regeneration. This will be important when we look at memory interleaving.

Memory Organization

Depending on the number of wires threading individual cores, we have different memory organizations. With the coincident current mode, we have what has been called 3D memories; linear selection corresponds to the 2D memories, and in between, with aspects of both methods, is the 2-1/2D organization.

3D Organization

From a geometrical viewpoint, 3D core memories of $w = 2^n$ b-bit words consist of b planes of w cores. That is, the bits in position i of the w words are in the same plane. Thus, there will be one sense wire and one inhibit wire per plane connected to the relevant bit in the MDR. In addition, each core will be threaded by 2 wires, the X and Y-wires, which will drive part of the current needed for switching or sensing states. The X-wire will correspond to the decoding of the lower half of the address (in the MAR) and the Y-wire to the upper half. Figure 5.6 shows an array of 16 words of b bits. The read and write procedures to follow show that we could have merged the inhibit and sense windings since they are always used at different times and could be shared.

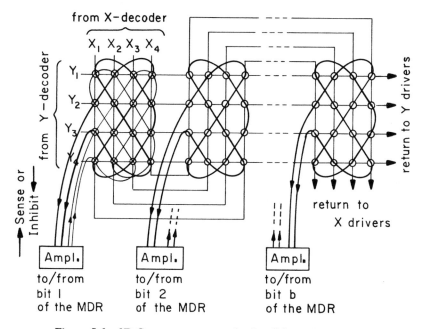

Figure 5.6   3D Core memory organization (16 words of b bits)

Procedure READ

1. Send-$i/2$ over the X-wire and Y-wire corresponding to the decoding of the respective halves of the address; amplify the sense signals and send them to the MDR;
2. Regenerate by sending $i/2$ on the same X-wire and Y-wire and $-i/2$ over the inhibit wire for those bits which are 0 in the MDR.

For example, to read the word at address 1110, the $X_2(10)$ and $Y_3(11)$ wires will be activated (we assume a 16 word memory); after amplification the word at address 14 (1110) will be cleared out and it will be re-written in step 2.

Procedure WRITE

1. Clear the word by sending $-i/2$ over the X-wire and Y-wire as above but do not amplify the sense signals, i.e., do not alter the MDR;
2. As in step 2 of procedure READ.

This organization requires:

- $w \cdot b$ cores to store the information;
- 1 X-decoder with $n/2$ inputs and $2^{n/2} = \sqrt{w}$ outputs;
- 1 Y-decoder with $n/2$ inputs and $2^{n/2}$ outputs;
- $2 \cdot 2^{n/2} = 2\sqrt{w}$ drives for the X and Y wires;
- b sense inhibit wires.

A memory with a 3D organization can be found in the CDC 6000 series.

2D Organization

Conceptually the 2D scheme appears simpler than the 3D's because of the linear selection of words. Geometrically, the 2D memory appears as b lines of width w (cf. Figure 5.7). The cores only have to be threaded by 2 wires, one to select the word and one per bit. The latter bit line can be used for sensing and switching. For such a layout the read and write procedures become:

Procedure READ

1. Send $-i$ over the selector word wire. Amplify the signals sensed on the bit lines and send those signals to the associated bits in the MDR.
2. Regenerate by sending i over the word line and $-i/2$ over the bit lines of those bits set to 0 in the MDR.

Procedure WRITE

1. As 1 above but without altering the MDR;
2. As 2 above.

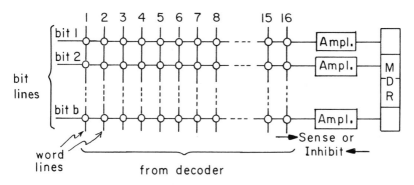

Figure 5.7 2D Core memory organization (16 words of b bits)

This organization requires:

- $w \cdot b$ cores to store the information;
- one decoder with n input and $2^n = w$ outputs;
- w drives;
- b sense-inhibit lines.

At first glance, it seems that we pay dearly for the apparent simplicity of the layout, namely w drives instead of $2\sqrt{w}$ and the same complexity ratio for the decoding. But the 2D memory has the advantage of needing one less wire per core. Since the speed of switching and sensing is related to the size of the core, faster memories can be attained with the 2D organization.

2-1/2D Organizations

It would be advantageous to take the best of two worlds, that is a small number of threads and a minimal number of drives. This leads to 2-1/2D organizations.

The first 2-1/2D organization (derived from the 3D) has the main advantage that there is no need for an inhibit wiring. Thus the connections to the MDR and the regeneration cycle are simpler. Figure 5.8 shows how this is done. As in the 3D case there is still a coincident current selection but each bit plane has its own set of X-drivers. Reading proceeds essentially as in the 3D case with the difference that all b X_i-wires are conducting an $-i/2$ current. To write, after clearing of the word as before, $i/2$ is sent on the Y_j-wire and $i/2$ on only those X_i-wires which have their corresponding bits set to 1 in the MDR.

A memory organization of this type was used for the IBM System/360. As can be seen, $(b-1)\sqrt{w}$ more drives are needed than in the 3D case and the

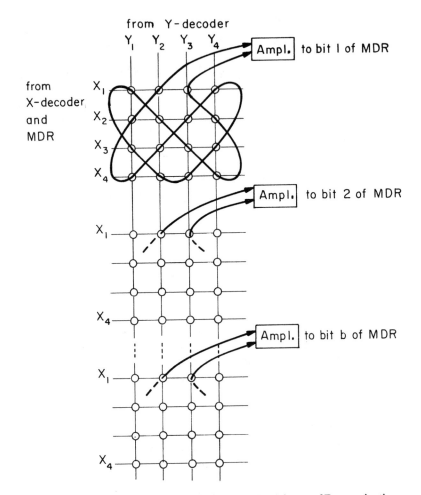

Figure 5.8   2½D memory organization derived from a 3D organization
(16 words of b bits)

results of the X-decoder to *b* bit planes must be fan-out. This additional logic
is compensated by the suppression of the inhibit function.

In the second layout (derived from the 2D) the number of word lines is
reduced and the bit lines are replicated (cf. Figure 5.9). The advantage is
that there are shorter bit (sense) lines which have shorter delays and require
less powerful amplifiers. The price paid is some added switching logic at the
MDR interface in order to select the appropriate bit line when sensing or

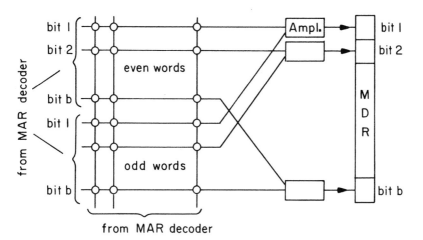

Figure 5.9   2½D memory organization derived from a 2D organization

regenerating. If g words are grouped on the same word line, then an extra 1-out-of-g decoder is needed (notice that the MAR decoding still requires the equivalent of a 1-out-of-w decoder).

This latter 2-1/2D and the 2D organizations are not as common for core memories as they are for RAM's with transistor cells.

5.2.3 Electronic RAM's

Physical Properties

The basic cell in a "static" electronic RAM will be a flip-flop. In its simplest form it can consist of two transistors cross-connected in the usual fashion (cf. Figure 5.10.a). The two stable states of this classical configuration are differentiated by whether transistor T_1 or T_2 is on. For example if T_1 is on, i.e., a current flows through T_1 to ground, then the potential at point V_1 is null. In that case the base of T_2 is grounded and T_2 is held off. This implies that $V_B = V_C$ and the base of T_1 is also at that potential keeping T_1 on. Therefore we have a stable state. A similar argument would hold for the other stable state corresponding to T_2 on and T_1 off.

In the following we shall not continue at this level of detail and consider the idealized cell of Figure 5.10.b. Connected to the flip-flop are two bit/sense lines, one for each stable state, and a word line connecting all bits of a given word. Such an idealized cell will, in general, consist of more than two transistors (up to as many as 6 in some MOS realizations). Normally the

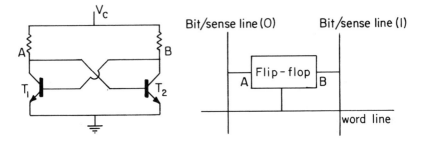

Figure 5.10   Basic cell in an electronic RAM

word line is held at a potential close to 0. A coincidence of pulses on the word line and one of the bit/sense lines results in a stable state. For example, assume that we want to write a 0 corresponding to the state $V_A = 0$ (T_1 on). If both the word line and the bit/sense line(0) are receiving pulses such that the bit/sense line(0) is brought to ground when V_A is already 0, then nothing will happen. On the other hand if $V_A = V_C$, then T_2 would have been on. But now $V_A = 0$ and T_2 is turned off. Reasoning as before we can see how the stable state will be reached.

In order to read, a small pulse is applied on the word line without changing the bit/sense lines. If $V_A = 0$, this will cause a small current to flow through T_1 and a small decrease in the current in the bit/sense line (0). This can be sensed, amplified, and transmitted to the appropriate bit of the MDR. Naturally, a similar signal would be sent on the other line if V_B had been 0.

The previous discussions point out a very important difference between the reading and writing processes for core and electronic RAM's, namely that in the latter case sensing is not destructive. Consequently, bit lines and sense lines can be shared and inhibit lines are unnecessary. Furthermore, in the cycle time, which is the sum of the access and regeneration times, the second component will be smaller than the first one instead of being of about the same value as in core memories. It cannot be completely avoided since the states are disturbed and a stabilization period is required. The need for sense lines only also indicates that 2D and 2-1/2D organizations derived from 2D will be more likely. However, 3D electronic RAM's have been manufactured with reading and writing triggered by coincident pulses on the X and Y lines. The savings in decoding are counterbalanced by the need for more devices per memory bit cell hence yielding lower densities. This consideration leads us to discuss the organization of semiconductor RAM's.

Organization

The mass fabrication of chips containing of the order of 1K to 64K bits imposes constraints on the semiconductor RAM's which are quite different from those for core. When core memories are manufactured, the cost per bit decreases with the storage capacity. In the semiconductor case, cost reductions are obtained by increasing the packaging density. This is limited by factors such as the number of pin connections available, the area taken on the board, and the logic (decoding) which can be put on the chip. Some of these problems can be alleviated with technological innovations. For example, the power dissipation can be reduced, and hence the chip density increased, by using "dynamic" MOS cells which are refreshed periodically. But even in current and predicted states of the art, i.e., with chips of 64K bits or more, there is a need for linking these chips together in order to achieve an adequate memory capacity.

The manner in which chips are linked depends on several parameters. The most important ones are:

- n the number of words;
- b the number of bits/word;
- S_c the capacity (in bits) of a chip;
- The amount of decoding logic available on a chip;
- The availability of coincident word lines.

Even with knowledge of these parameters we shall have several options. For example, let $n = 1024$ (1K), $b = 16$, $S_c = 256$. We assume that the amount of decoding logic is not restricted and that coincident word lines are not permitted. We give two organizations (cf. Figure 5.11) which can be considered at the opposite ends of the spectrum. The reader is encouraged to find middle-of-the-road solutions which will often be more appealing than either of the two presented below (cf. Exercise 4).

Regardless of the organization, we need 64 chips ($1024 \cdot 16/256 = 64$). In a first layout, we can assume that each chip carries the bit in position i for 256 words. Thus we divide our chips into 4 groups, and on each chip we have 256 word lines and a unique (double) bit/sense line. The external decoding is a 1-out-of-4 for groups and the decoding on the chip is 1-out-of-256. This latter figure might make the task somewhat formidable for a 256 bit chip! Notice that this organization is as close to 2D as can fit within our constraints (cf. Figure 5.11.a).

At the other extreme, a second possibility is to consider that each chip is storing 16 words (cf. Figure 5.11.b). The external decoding selects 1-out-of-64 for chips, the internal decoding is 1-out-of-16 for word lines, and each

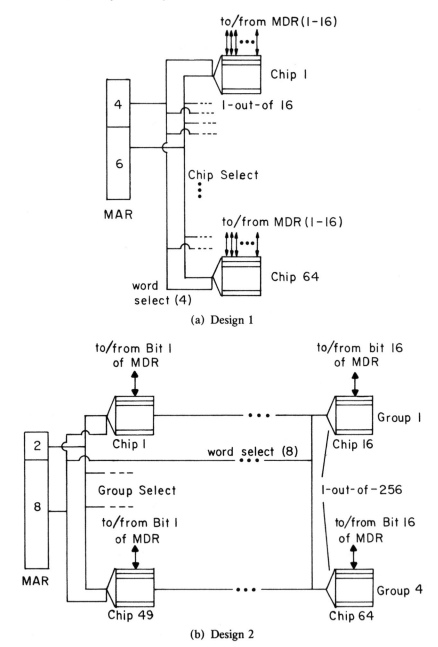

(a) Design 1

(b) Design 2

Figure 5.11 Chip organization in a RAM

chip carries 16 bit/sense lines. This is the most "vertical" approach. It allows an easy expension for n but none is possible for b. This is not too critical since in general b will be fixed at design stage. As indicated earlier, other organizations might be more flexible.

5.2.4 Error—Correcting Codes

From the preceding sections it is readily apparent that the cost-performance characteristics of electronic RAM's surpass those of ferrite cores. One feature which could be in doubt is the reliability of "dynamic" electronic RAM's. However, the low cost of introducing extraneous bits for error detection and correction makes the mean time between failures of semiconductor memories ten times larger according to some manufacturers. In this section we present some error (detecting and) correcting codes (ECC).

ECC's can be classified according to the number of erroneous bits which can be detected (1 bit errors, 2 bit errors, multiple bit errors) and corrected. The simplest ECC is a 1-error detected or *parity checking* code. Given a memory word, we append an extra bit so that the sum of the '1' bits is always even (*even parity*) or always odd (*odd parity*). Thus, if the original n-bit word were:

$$(x_1, x_2, \ldots, x_n),$$

we append the parity bit c_0 such that:

$c_0 = x_1 \oplus x_2 \oplus \cdots \oplus x_n$ (for odd parity, i.e., $c_0 = 1$ if the word contains an odd number of '1' bits).

Now, upon transmission of this word, we check whether:

$$c_0 \oplus x_1 \oplus x_2 \oplus \cdots \oplus x_n = 0.$$

If not, this means that one of the bits $c_0, x_1, x_2, \ldots, x_n$ which was 0 became 1, or conversely one which was 1 became 0 (assuming only a single bit is in error). The scheme is extremely simple, inexpensive (one bit and an n-input EOR circuitry), but rather weak since it can only *detect* single bit errors and cannot indicate their location.

Since memory bits have become much less expensive, the use of more complex and powerful error correcting and detecting schemes is justified. For example, several models of the IBM System/370, the CRAY-1 and many powerful computers, and the DEC VAX 11/780 have 8 bit ECC's appended to 64-bit words to detect and correct single bit errors, detect double bit errors, and detect 70% of multiple (larger than 2 bit) errors. These schemes are based on Hamming codes which we now present.

For a code of n-bit words, the minimum number of bits which must be changed to convert one valid word to another is called the *minimum distance* of the code. For example, a word of n bits which can assume any of the 2^{n-1} values of $n - 1$ bits and a parity bit forms an n-bit code of minimum distance 2. In general, a distance k code will detect up to $(k - 1)$ errors.

Consider now the case when we want to detect and *correct* one error. Detection implies a minimum distance of 2. If we create a code with minimum distance 3 (by adding more ECC bits) a single error will result in a pattern which will be at distance 1 from one valid pattern and at distance 2 or more from all others. Hence, it will be possible to detect and correct a single bit error. It we were interested only in error detection, this same minimum distance of 3 would allow us to detect single and double bit errors. It we want to be able to detect double bit errors and detect and correct single bit errors, then we have to increase the minimum distance to 4.

Let us see how a single bit error in an n-bit word can be corrected. We must append m correcting bits $c_0, c_1, \ldots, c_{m-1}$ to the n-bit word such that we can uniquely determine which of the $(n + m)$ bits is in error as well as the error-free condition. Thus the 2^m error-correcting patterns must be such that:

$2^m > n + m + 1$, or for all practical purposes, (i.e., with $m < n - 1$ and $n \geq 5$)

$2^m > 2n$

and $m = \lceil \log_2 n \rceil + 1$

For example, let us design a single error correcting scheme for an 8-bit word. ($m = 4$). Let c_0, c_1, c_2, c_3 be the ECC bits. We can consider these c_i bits to be in position 2^i in the $(n + m)$ bit word, i.e., our $(8 + 4)$ bit word would have the configuration:

$$(y_1, y_2, \ldots, y_{10}, y_{11}, y_{12}) = (c_0, c_1, x_1, c_2, x_2, x_3, x_4, c_3, x_5, x_6, x_7, x_8)$$

Every index j can be written as a power of 2 (recall the synchronous shifter of Chapter 3 Section 5). A bit c_i will be the parity check for all y_j such that j includes 2^i in its representation. That is:

c_0 is the parity check for bits $y_1, y_3, y_5, y_7, y_9, y_{11}$
c_1 is the parity check for bits $y_2, y_3, y_6, y_7, y_{10}, y_{11}$
c_2 is the parity check for bits $y_4, y_5, y_6, y_7, y_{12}$
c_3 is the parity check for bits $y_8, y_9, y_{10}, y_{11}, y_{12}$

and conversely:

y_1 will be checked by c_0 $(1 = 2^0)$,
y_2 will be checked by c_1 $(2 = 2^1)$,
y_3 will be checked by c_0 and c_1 $(3 = 2^0 + 2^1)$,

$$\vdots$$

y_{12} will be checked by c_2 and c_3 $(12 = 2^2 + 2^3)$

Now, upon transmitting the word, we can compute:

$$c'_0 = y'_1 \oplus y'_3 \oplus \cdots \oplus y'_{11} \quad \text{and} \quad e_0 = c_0 \oplus c'_0$$

$$\vdots$$

$$c'_3 = y'_8 \oplus y'_9 \oplus \cdots \oplus y'_{12} \quad \text{and} \quad e_3 = c_3 \oplus c'_3$$

Assume a single error on a given y_j. Then, all e_i such that c_i checks y_j will be one's. Performing the sum

$$j = \sum_0^3 e_i 2^i$$

will indicate the erroneous bit. In the above example, let us assume y_9 to be in error. It is checked by c_0 and c_3. Hence e_0 and e_3 will be 1, and

$$j = 2^0 + 2^3 = 9$$

gives the index of the erroneous bit.

If we wish to detect double errors as well as correct single errors, then the minimum distance must be increased by 1 by adding a parity check bit for the whole word, with:

$$c_m = y_1 \oplus y_2 \cdots \oplus y_{n+m}$$

Assume a single error. The parity over the whole word will be incorrect and the above scheme will detect the faulty bit. If the faulty bit is c_m itself, then j will be 0. If a double error occurs, c_m will be correct but some of the c_i bits will be incorrect. No correction can take place. Some multiple errors (but not all) can be detected.

In terms of implementation, the c_i check bits are generated at Mp write time (in fact they will be appended at one end of the word and not scattered among "useful" bits). At a subsequent Mp read, a check bit generator circuit regenerates the c_i check bits which are then compared to those previously stored. Error correction (or detection) can then take place. For example in System/370 the corrected word is sent to Pc and Mp.

5.2.5 Read-Only Memories

Although they are never used as a primary memory component, we include here *read-only memories* (ROM's) because they are a special case of a random-accessed memory. As the name implies, they are used for permanent storage, i.e., they cannot be altered. We shall see how they can be used when we study microprogramming (cf. Chapter 7). They have also been utilized in the design of arithmetic functions, Boolean circuits, character generators in display devices, code translators as e.g., from ASCII to EBCDIC, etc.

Like a RAM, a ROM is randomly accessed; it needs an MAR and the results of a read operation will be stored in an MDR. Since no writing has to be performed it can be constructed with various technologies, the most common being diodes, bipolar and MOS transistors. The information to be stored is entered once, generally by the manufacturer, and can be mass produced in the same manner as ordinary integrated circuits. Some programmable ROM's (PROM) are also available; their initial writing requires a more complex process which cannot be efficiently reproduced on a large scale basis.

Programmable logic arrays (PLA's) have been developed as a variation of ROM's. Basically, a PLA is an array of AND and OR gates on a single integrated circuit chip. This logic array can realize a set of combinational functions expressed in a sum of products form. The input consists of the n input variables and their complements, i.e., $2n$ input lines. From these inputs, a number of product terms can be generated via the AND gates. These terms are then ORed to form the final outputs. At the present time, PLA's can be constructed with as many as a few hundred AND terms. The main differences between PLA's and ROM's, from the conceptual viewpoint, are that in the PLA case some of the input addresses can be ignored and that different addresses can provide the same output. Thus, a better storage efficiency can be attained.

PLA's are as fast as ROM's but, in the late 70's, are still an order of magnitude more expensive. It is not yet clear whether they will supplant completely ROM's in the near future.

5.3   INTERLEAVED MEMORIES

From our discussion of core memories, we could conclude that the cost/bit would decrease with expanding capacity. This is because a linear increase in the logic of the MAR and MDR corresponds to exponential growth in size. But several factors argue against using an enormous monolithic Mp. First, as size increases speed decreases mainly because of longer delays. Also, the cost reduction might not be as straightforward to compute as would be implied by the simplistic reasoning just given: for example, with a larger capacity more powerful amplifiers and drivers are required. Second, an installation is usually fitted to the processing needs and financial assets of the moment. Modular increases can be allowed if the logic of the Mp permits it; partitioning Mp into several modules will facilitate the upgrading. Third, if Mp consists of several self-contained modules, then each of them can be working independently. This has two important implications, namely Mp can be shared by several processors, Pc's or Pio's, and overlapping of memory operations can be realized. The sharing of Mp by several processors will be studied in detail in Chapter 8, where we treat cycle stealing, i.e., the contention between Pc and Pio's for a memory cycle, and Chapter 10, where we examine the memory interference problem between several Pc's competing for memory cycles.

The case for partitioning core memories into several components need not be repeated for semi-conductor RAM's. There, the technology readily lends itself to modularization.

In this section, we restrict ourselves to the study of interleaving, to be defined shortly, and of its influence on the Mp-Pc interface when the central processor is the unique generator of memory requests. Our figures of merit will be the instruction execution rate and the average number of busy memory modules.

5.3.1 Analysis of Interleaving

We say that a memory is n-way interleaved if it is composed of n modules numbered $0, 1, \ldots, n - 1$, and if words at address i are in module number $i \bmod n$. Thus, consecutive instructions, or rather words of instructions, will be placed in consecutive modules, thus facilitating prefetching or look-ahead. Similarly, some data structures can also be mapped according to this scheme. For example, the elements of a vector, the elements of a column of a matrix stored in row major order, and the contents of a stack or queue stored sequentially will also be placed on separate (mod n) modules. If the n memory modules can be operated independently, and time-share the memory bus, then the rate of transfer between Mp and Pc could be at best n times as large as with a single component. Naturally, dependencies in programs, that is branches, randomness in accessing data, and the succession of instruction and data references will dramatically reduce this factor of n. The analyses to follow are attempts at estimating the gains which can be attained by memory interleaving.

Before proceeding with the analyses, we note that the implementation of interleaving is straightforward. Given a memory address it must be directed to the correct module. If n is a power of two, e.g., 2^k, the switching is done by decoding the k lower bits of the address. Each module is given a tag from 0 to $2^k - 1$ and accepts the address whose lower bits match its tag. If the word at that address and also its $(n - 1)$ neighbors are desired, then all modules are activated to retrieve the word corresponding to the address with the k lowest bits truncated. If n is not a power of two, then Mp is divided into banks where each bank consists of 2^k modules. Bank recognition can be done by examining the high-order bits of the address. The fact that all n memory modules cannot be addressed at once in this case is not damaging since, in general, only m modules, $m < n$, need be accessed in order to match processor and memory cycles.

In order to evaluate the gains which can be attained by memory interleaving, we again examine the instruction execution cycle as depicted in Figure 2.6, considering only instructions of the form:

$$R_i \leftarrow R_i \text{ op Mp [EA]},$$

which are typical of general-register machines. As before, we can easily modify the models to better suit given architectures. To reflect the memory technology we divide the memory cycle t_c into an access time t_a and a stabilization, or regeneration, time t_s, with t_a and t_s being of the same order of magnitude. Because the decode and effective address calculation steps are far less time-consuming than a memory access, we group them into a single time step t_d. We omit the incrementation of the location counter from our timing diagrams since it can be performed concurrently with the instruction fetch. Figures 5.12.a and 5.12.b show Gantt charts for the instruction cycle time t_i when interleaving is not implemented. The two cases correspond respectively to D-unit execution times, either smaller than t_s, i.e., t_{e_1}, or larger or equal than, t_s, i.e., t_{e_2}. In the first case, we have:

$$t_{i_1} = 2t_c$$

and in the second

$$t_{i_2} = 2t_c + (t_{e_2} - t_s).$$

If f_1 and f_2 are the relative frequencies of operations of the first and second types respectively, and if we denote by t_i, t_{e_1}, and t_{e_2} expected values rather than values of instances of random variables, we have:

$$t_i = 2t_c + f_2(t_{e_i} - t_s). \tag{1}$$

We refer again to the Gantt charts, but this time under the assumption that we have interleaving and that instruction and operand fetches are directed towards different memory modules (cf. Figure 5.13 shown only for the t_{e_1} case).
Then:

$$t_{i_1} = 2t_a + t_d + t_{e_1},$$
$$t_{i_2} = 2t_a + t_d + t_{e_2},$$

that is:

$$t_i = 2t_a + t_d + t_e,$$

where t_e is the average D-unit execution time.

To be more precise, we have to take into accout the possibility of a conflict between the instruction and operand fetches. If each of the n modules is equally likely to be accessed, then we have two potential delays. The first one is for the operand fetch; it is of length $(t_s - t_d)$ and has probability $1/n$. The second is for the next instruction fetch; it is of length $(t_s - t_{e_1})$, also has

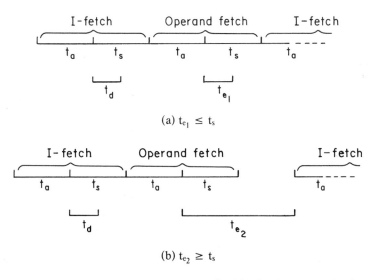

(a) $t_{e_1} \le t_s$

(b) $t_{e_2} \ge t_s$

Figure 5.12 Instruction execution cycle (revisited) without interleaving

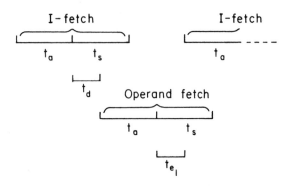

Figure 5.13   Instruction execution cycle with interleaving and no conflict

probability $1/n$, but occurs only for instructions of the first type. After these observations, we can modify our expected timings as:

$$t_{i_1} = 2t_a + t_d + t_{e_1} + (1/n)(t_s - t_d) + (1/n)(t_s - t_{e_2}),$$
$$t_{i_2} = 2t_a + t_d + t_{e_2} + (1/n)(t_s - t_d),$$

and finally,

$$t_i = 2t_a + t_d + t_e + (1/n)(t_s - t_d) + f_1(t_s - t_{e_1})/n. \qquad (2)$$

With n large, t_d small and a fast processor, i.e., t_e small, we see that t_i is close to $2t_a$. Comparing this with the result of equation (1) shows that a two-fold speed up can be gained if $t_a = t_s = t_c/2$. This is not unexpected and can be easily deduced from Figures 5.12 and 5.13.

But if the Pc is powerful and Mp is large, we shall introduce prefetching buffers and/or multiple execution units in order to try and match instruction execution and memory cycles. Let us examine interleaving under these new conditions.

Consider first the prefetching of n instructions since we have n-way interleaving. After they are prefetched, they are decoded, and the n operands in turn are fetched. The execution of the instructions is overlapped with the next fetch cycle. For the time being, we assume no precedence dependencies; the only limitation in the program's execution flow is through conflicts in memory accesses in case of operands and branches in case of instructions (for slightly different models, see Exercises 6-8). Let us start with an investigation of the latter situation.

When the program is loaded into Mp, the instructions are sequentially allocated to the n modules. But at execution time branches occur which disrupt this ordering. If λ is the frequency of execution of instructions which correspond to a successful transfer of control, then the probability of executing k sequentially ordered instructions is $(1 - \lambda)^k$. Let $P(k)$ be the probability of having $(k - 1)$ sequential instructions and of the k-th being a successful branch. Then:

$$P(k) = (1 - \lambda)^{k-1} \cdot \lambda.$$

Now, the expected number of instructions to be executed without transfer of control in a prefetch of n instructions is:

$$\text{IF} = \sum_{k=1}^{n-1} k \cdot (1 - \lambda)^{k-1} \cdot \lambda + n \cdot (1 - \lambda)^{n-1}$$

$$\text{IF} = \frac{1 - (1 - \lambda)^n}{\lambda} \tag{3}$$

IF can represent the number of memory modules doing useful work; $\text{IF} \cdot b$, b being the word length, is the average bandwidth of Mp. Similarly, we can say that an instruction access time is:

$$t_a \frac{\lambda}{1 - (1 - \lambda)^n},$$

i.e., it is equally distributed over IF modules.

The problem is more complex, or the model farther from reality, when we look at operand fetches. The simplest way to account for interleaving is to assume an equal probability of access to each module for any fetch. The expected number of fetches without module conflict is the (expected) length of a sequence of integers drawn with repetition from the set $\{1, 2, \ldots, n\}$ until such a repetition occurs. The probability of k integers being different and the $(k + 1)st$ being one of the first k, that is, the probability $Q(k)$ of a sequence of length k is:

$$Q(k) = \frac{n}{n} \cdot \frac{n-1}{n} \cdot \frac{n-2}{n} \cdots \frac{(n-k+1)}{n} \cdot \frac{k}{n} = \frac{(n-1)!k}{(n-k)!n^k}$$

and the average number of operand fetches is

$$\text{OF} = \sum_{k=1}^{n} \frac{(n-1)! \cdot k^2}{(n-k)! \cdot n^k} \tag{4}$$

It can be shown, and this is not a trivial problem, that:

$$OF = \sqrt{\frac{\pi n}{2}} - \frac{1}{3} + \frac{1}{12}\sqrt{\frac{\pi}{2n}} + O(n^{-1}), \tag{5}$$

$$OF = O(\sqrt{n}).$$

This result is pessimistic since it assumes complete randomness in the data fetches. There exist data structures for which this is not true and for which sequentiality is at least partially realized. To model this effect, we consider the sequence of n data addresses $r_1 r_2 \cdots r_n$ having the following Markovian probabilities:

- $P(r_1) = 1/n$, i.e., random access to the first reference;
- $P(r_{i+1}) = \alpha$ if $r_{i+1} = (r_i + 1) \bmod n$, i.e., we favor module $(j + 1)$ with probability α when the last reference was to module j (with $j = r_i \bmod n$);
- $P(r_{i+1}) = \beta$ if $r_{i+1} \neq (r_i + 1) \bmod n$, with $\beta = (1 - \alpha)/(n - 1)$, i.e., when the favored module is not accessed, we randomly access one of the others.

We can compute OF as before. Let $Q(w \geq k)$ be the probability that the k first accesses are to different modules. We can consider these k requests as a first request to module 0 (it can be any module), j requests of the α type, and $(k - j - 1)$ requests of the β type. Let $C_n(j, k)$ be the number of these sequences of length k with j α-requests. Then the mean value of the cumulative distribution of Q is;

$$OF = \sum_{k=1}^{n} \sum_{j=0}^{k-1} \alpha^j \beta^{k-j-1} C_n(j, k), \tag{6}$$

which can be shown to have the closed form

$$OF = \sum_{k=1}^{n} \sum_{j=0}^{k-1} \alpha^j \beta^{k-j-1} \sum_{h=1}^{k-1-j} (-1)^h \binom{j+h}{h}\binom{k-1}{j+h}(n-j-h-1)_{k-j-1} \tag{7}$$

where $(n - j - 1)(n - j - 2) \cdots (n - k + 1)$ is denoted $(n - j - 1)_{k-j-1}$.

At this point the reader who is not well versed in combinatorics might feel slightly lost. The important point of equation (7) is that OF grows exponentially with α. In order to gain an understanding of how a given value for OF might be derived, suppose that we have $n = 8$ and a sequence of data requests 4 1 2 3 6 7 2 $\cdots$ denoted as $r_1 r_2 r_3 r_4 r_5 r_6 r_7$. The first six memory access are to different modules and we have:

$P(r_1) = 1/n = 1/8$,
$P(r_2) = P(r_5) = \beta$,
$P(r_3) = P(r_4) = P(r_6) = \alpha$,

and consequently the sequence has a probability $(1/n) \alpha^3 \beta^2$.

In general, the processor cycle will be only $m (m < n)$ times faster then t_a. For example in the CDC 6600 and IBM System 360/91 we saw that the memory cycle time t_c, that is $2 \cdot t_a$, was about 10 times slower than the minor cycle regulating the central processor. Therefore, we might wish to request only m words instead of n. Equation (3) and (6) can be rewritten as:

$$IF_m = \sum_{k=1}^{m} k \cdot P(k) + m \cdot \sum_{k=m+1}^{n} P(k),$$

$$IF_m = \frac{1 - (1 - \lambda)^m}{\lambda}, \tag{8}$$

$$OF_m = \sum_{k=1}^{m} k \cdot Q(w \geq k) + m \cdot \sum_{k=m+1}^{n} Q(w \geq k) \tag{9}$$

with the understanding that we know how to compute $Q(k)$.

A pause is needed here to evaluate how realistic these models are. For example, we know that formula (5) yields a pessimistic result from the interleaving viewpoint, but is optimistic in the sense that we neglected data dependencies. If $n = 16$, OF $\simeq 4$ according to this formula and is independent of program behavior.

The $\alpha - \beta$ model has two parameters: α and λ (maybe it should be called the $\alpha - \lambda$ model!). Table 2.1 gives us an upper bound for λ since we have there a record of the frequency of branches both successful and unsuccessful. Hence a λ between 0.1 and 0.25 is quite reasonable. According to equation (8) we have:

With $\lambda = 0.25$, $IF_m \simeq 3.75$ for $m \geq 12$, and
with $\lambda = 0.125$, $IF_8 \simeq 5$ and $IF_{16} \simeq 7$.

Since we can consider n as a ratio of t_a/t_e, for a fixed t_a there is no point in overoptimizing t_e. With regard to the prefetching of instructions, it appears that (according to this model) an 8-way interleaving is adequate.

While λ, and hence IF_m, are independent of n this is no longer true of α. Since OF_m grows exponentially with α, it should be interesting to see what average bandwidth can be obtained under various hypotheses about the values assumed by α. Figure 5.14 shows plots of OF_m vs. m for different α with t_a being fixed. The plot $\alpha = 1/n$ corresponds to random selection of the data, as in short programs with no arrays nor sequentially allocated lists. Increasing values of α correspond to programs with more and more structured data. Examinations of programs written for the IBM System/360 have shown that α is between 0.12 and 0.25 for a 32-way interleaving.

In the $\alpha - \beta$ model, as in any model, we have omitted some considerations which might be of importance. Foremost among them is data dependency. This will be dealt with soon. In addition we assumed single word instructions, single word data, and, for the computation of OF_m, we have neglected precedural dependencies, that is, we computed OF_m rather than OF_{IF}. Also, we have assumed that all modules will be addressed synchronously as per the addressing scheme described previously. This is less realistic for data requests.

Simulation on traces for IBM System/360 programs have shown that the model is optimistic. Only half of the predicted data interleaving was realized. Although the sample of traces (only two) is too small to warrant definite conclusions, it points out that there is a tendency to frequently refer to the same module.

How then, can a system which permits some conflicts be designed? Taking one clue from the extended buffering of the IBM System/360 Model 91, we can have a buffer B storing requests. The system would look like the one in

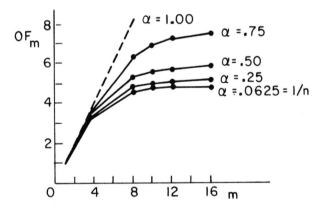

Figure 5.14   Average number of active memory modules during data requests in the α-β model

Figure 5.15. Prefetching of instructions will prevent conflicts in the fetch cycle. The buffer of size L contains data requests which were addressed to busy modules. Let

$$b_1 b_2 \cdots b_j, \quad j \leq L,$$

be the contents of the buffer, and assume that m fetches per processor cycle are requested; m_i will be instruction requests generated as previously and m_0 will be operand requests. These m_0 are taken first from $b_1 b_2 \cdots b_j$, and then from the data requested by the m_i instructions. If a conflict arises between an m_0 and an m_i, or between two m_0 requests, the second occurrence is stored in B. We proceed in this fashion until either the m_0 requests have been processed, or B is full. Simulations have shown that such a scheme doubles OF. However, instruction execution can occur even more out of sequence than before. Thus, there is an increasing need for a virtual D-unit implementation in the central processor.

From the above analyses, in spite of some weaknesses in the models, we can surmise definite gains due to interleaving. Before closing this section, we describe an implementation of an interleaving scheme.

5.3.2 The CDC 6600 Stunt Box

The scheduling of address requests to the 32-way interleaved memory of the CDC 6600 is accomplished by a device called the Stunt Box. Conceptually (cf. Figure 5.16) it consists of a priority network receiving requests from

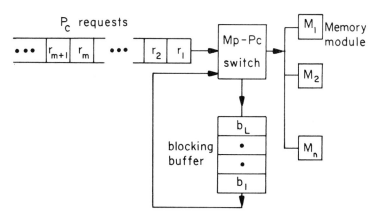

Figure 5.15   Interleaving with a blocking buffer

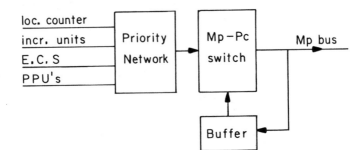

(a) Block diagram of the Stunt box

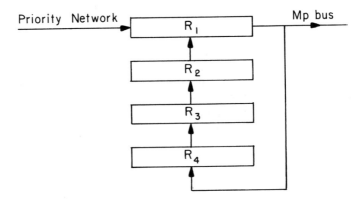

(b) Register queue

Figure 5.16   Memory interleaving in the CDC 6600

several sources, an Mp − Pc switch delivering addresses to the address bus and receiving messages upon the success or failure of the request, and a buffer storing rejected requests.

The priority network ranks addresses coming from the two increment units (operand fetches), the program counter (instruction fetches), the Extended Core Storage coupler, and the ten peripheral processor units (Pio's) in this order. It is highly unusual to give priority to the central processor over I/O processors but, in this instance, it can be explained by the facts that the Pio's have their own memory and that the machine is expected to run mostly compute-bound jobs.

The switch and the buffer are in essence lumped into a single entity called the hopper. It is mainly composed of four registers connected as a circular queue. We must provide some detailed timing information to explain its functioning (cf. Figure 5.16).

Recall that in this architecture a major cycle time of 1000 ns. corresponds to the memory cycle t_c. The processor cycle time, or minor cycle, is 100 ns. or $t_c/10$. The machine operates in a synchronous way and, from the processor's viewpoint, events occur at minor cycle intervals. At every minor cycle, an address is sent to the Mp bus along with tags indicating the type of order and source or destination. We do not dwell on the details of the tag generator which is a major component of the stunt box but which has no conceptual feature of interest. The address and tags request is entered into R_1 before being sent on the bus. Twenty-five nanoseconds later, denoted as time t_{25}, it will be sent on the bus and at t_{75} will be transferred to R_4. It will percolate up the circular queue reaching R_3 at t_{150} and R_2 at t_{225}. Before t_{300}, the module requested will either have acknowledged its acceptance of the request or sent back a message notifying that it is busy. In the former case at t_{300} a new request, if any is waiting, is taken from the output queue of the priority network and the process starts anew. In the latter case the contents of R_2 are transmitted to R_1 and the same request is sent again. We leave it to the reader to verify that in the worst case less than 3 major cycles will have elapsed before the servicing of a given request (cf. Exercise 9).

As can be seen, the $\alpha - \beta$ modified model has some features of the stunt box. Modifying the stunt box such that instruction prefetching could be allowed, as in the IBM 360/91, would make the α-β model even more realistic.

5.4 SECONDARY MEMORY DEVICES

As shown in Figure 5.1, the components of the memory hierarchy above the level of Mp have no direct connection with the Pc. (Some of the following discussion might be erroneous when applied to core extension devices which will be considered later in this section.) The information must be transmitted through either M_1 or M_0. The amount of information transferred, R_k, will always be a multiple of R_1. Several factors account for the magnitude of R_k. The first is the technology of the device. Among the others, the main one is the time overhead required to access a given i-unit on the secondary devices. While primary memory components were of the random access type, this is no longer true of secondary memory devices. Now, the time for an element of the "block" R_k stored on a device at level k to be accessible by Pc, through a reference to M_1, is:

$$t_k = t_a + t_t,$$

where t_a is the access time and t_t the transfer time. A transfer in the other direction, i.e., from M_1 to M_k, has the same form.

In general, t_a will be device dependent and independent of the size of R_k, while t_t will depend on both the device and the magnitude of R_k. Once the block R_k has been accessed, t_t is simply proportional to the size of R_k. Optimization will therefore be directed towards reducing t_a.

In this section we consider three types of secondary memory devices:

- Rotational devices, that is drums and disks, where any R_k can be directly accessed, hence the term direct access storage device (DASD) often given to them;
- Core extensions to main memory, i.e., Large Core Storage (LCS) and Extended Core Storage (ECS);
- Electronic disks, i.e., Magnetic Bubble, Charge-Coupled Devices, and Electron Beam memories.

Our emphasis will be on DASD's. However most of the scheduling strategies and their analyses will be deferred until Chapter 8 where we consider I/O devices. Here we simply describe the performance of these devices, so that we can categorize them in the PMS framework as Ms devices rather than T's. This will be of great importance when we consider the management of the memory hierarchy. Core extensions and electronic disks will be treated more briefly because the impact of the former on Systems Architecture has been rather limited and that of the latter is still unknown.

5.4.1   Direct Access Storage Devices

Magnetic Recording

Like core memories, direct access storage devices, drums and disks, and some sequential access devices, e.g., magnetic tapes, use properties of magnetism in order to store information. But the process is not achieved by a current passing through wires threading static cores. The basic principle involved is that of moving a magnet past a conducting coil and thus inducing a voltage in the coil. The sense of that voltage will depend on the relative direction of the magnet's motion with respect to its poles.

To realize this recording, a surface of magnetic material is moved under a fixed coil named the *head*. To write, pulses are sent to the head and magnetic patterns will be recorded on the surface below, with different patterns for positive and negative currents. To read, the same surface passes under the head, or under a similar one, generating a current of the same polarity as the one already recorded.

The four main recording techniques are: return to zero (RZ), non-return to zero (NRZ), non-return to zero inverted (NRZI) and phase recording (PR). An example of each is shown in Figure 5.17.

In the RZ mode, each "1" bit generates a positive pulse and each "0" bit a negative one. In the non-return to zero methods, changes in the signals will be recorded only when there is a change in the original string. In the NRZ method, there is no change when two consecutive bits are identical. In the NRZI, the polarity changes for each 1 recorded and stays the same for a 0. Finally in the PR (or Ferranti or Manchester or phase encoding or phase modulation) scheme, a 1 is represented by a positive signal followed by a negative one and a 0 by a negative followed by a positive. The important point in this latter method is that the flux change is in the middle of the recording interval.

The advantage of RZ is that it is self-synchronizing. However, it requires twice the flux change compared to the NRZ methods and therefore the packing density is smaller. NRZI is self-clocking if several bits are recorded in parallel and an odd parity bit is used. Since there is always a "1" bit, if the parallel tracks at each bit are ORed then a change will necessarily be re-

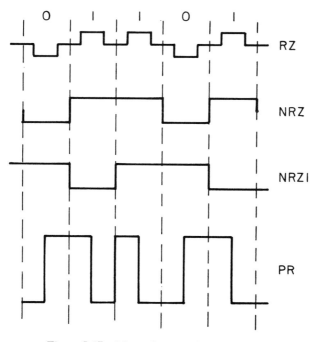

Figure 5.17 Magnetic recording techniques

corded and again we have a self-timing scheme. This will be used principally for magnetic tapes at medium density. PR is mostly used for high density because there is no D-C component.

The reader interested in details on magnetic recording techniques should consult a computer design reference. Our interest is more in the organization and performance of the DASD's.

Drums

As mentioned in our historical survey, drum memories were present in early systems even sometimes as primary memories. Today, they are generally used as paging and/or swapping devices in systems which have storage devices of larger capacity as back-ups.

A drum is basically a rotating cylinder coated with a thin layer of magnetic material. Conceptually, the drum is divided into strips, or *tracks*, passing under read/write heads (cf. Figure 5.18). The tracks consist of consecutive slots, or cells, each able to record a bit. A separate track serves as a timing device. Naturally the cylinder rotates at constant speed and the timing track will have permanent signals determining time units for the drum.

Small drums have 15 to 25 tracks at approximately 1K bit/track. Therefore their capacity is 25K bits, that is between 2.5 and 5K bytes. Large drums have from 500 to 1000 tracks, each storing 10^5 bits, yielding a capacity of 10M bytes. They rotate from 100 to 3600 rpm, and some drums have been designed to go faster by one order of magnitude. A typical drum such as the IBM 2303 has the following characteristics:

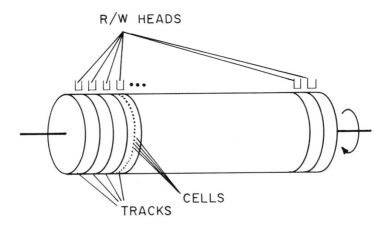

Figure 5.18   Magnetic drum memory

- 800 tracks at 39,000 bits/track yielding a capacity of 32M bits or 4M bytes;
- Rotational speed 3500 rpm;
- Diameter 10.7 inch, length 12 inches, i.e., 67 tracks/inch.

Accessing of a drum for reading and writing can be in one of two modes: parallel or serial. In the first case, n tracks are read (or written) in parallel and n amplifiers are needed. In the second (as e.g., in the IBM 2303), only one head at a time is selected. Words are stored serially and tracks are divided into sectors. Addressing consists of a track number and a sector number. Sectors, in general, are multiples of the word length.

The time to transfer information from the drum to Mp, or vice- versa, consists of an accessing time and a transfer time, yielding:

$$T = t_a + t_t.$$

On the average t_a will be half of a rotation of the drum, assuming a first-in-first-out queue of requests (other scheduling techniques will be considered in Chapter 8). Therefore,

$$t_a = \frac{1}{2 \cdot \text{rotational speed}}.$$

For the IBM 2303, we have $t_a = [60/(2 \cdot 3500)] \cdot 1000 = 8.6$ ms, a typical figure for drums of that size. To assess the value of t_t, we assume serial operation. If there are s equal size sectors/track, then the transfer time of one sector is $t_t = 2t_a/s$. For example, if we look again at the same device, $s = 39,000/32 = 1218$ and $t_t = (2 \cdot 8.6)/1218 \simeq 15 \cdot 10^{-3}$ ms. Thus, it takes approximately 15 μs to transfer a word but the overhead is three orders of magnitude larger. Consequently, we shall have to transfer blocks of words, or records, in this case at least 256 words to be efficient ($t_t \simeq 4$ ms or $t_a/2$). To get an idea of what record size is reasonable, we can compute the data transfer rate per second. In the IBM 2303 it will be 2.3M bits/second (cf. Exercise 9).

Because it is often used in systems with virtual memory, we introduce here the paging drum concept. Physically a paging drum is similar to an ordinary drum but it is always addressed in sectors of equal size corresponding to the page size of the virtual memory (cf. next chapter). Its control is such that it can implement a scheduling policy which takes advantage of this equality in sector sizes. From the controller's viewpoint the requests to the paging drum can be sorted into s buckets corresponding to the s starting addresses of the sectors (cf. Figure 5.19). The operation of the paging drum is then as follows. Each incoming request is placed in its corresponding bucket on a FIFO basis. When the drum's head is under the address corresponding to bucket i, it fulfills the first request (if any) in that bucket.

It is interesting to see how much we gain with such a scheme. We define the efficiency e of the scheduling technique as:

$$e = \frac{t_t}{t_a + t_t}.$$

The efficiency e is always less than or equal to 1 and its difference from 1 is a measure of the overhead incurred in the access time. For the ordinary FIFO scheduling scheme, we have:

$$e_F = \frac{1}{(s/2) + 1} = \frac{2}{s + 2}.$$

Determining e_p for the paging drum is more complex. Under the assumption that the number of requests r is constant, i.e., as soon as a request is serviced another one enters the queue, it can be shown that the expected number of requests serviced during one rotation is:

$$E[k] = \frac{2rs}{2r + s - 1} \quad \text{(Note that if } r = 1 \text{ and } s = 1, \text{ that is with a single buffer, then } E[k] = 1).$$

and therefore:

$$e_p = \frac{2r}{2r + s - 1}.$$

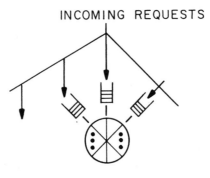

INCOMING REQUESTS

Figure 5.19   Paging drum organization

It is easily verified that $e_p > e_F$ for $r > 0$.

Disks

Disks are used to provide a larger capacity at the secondary memory level. In mini to medium computer installations, a single disk is often sufficient to hold the systems programs and most of the users' files if removable disk packs are available. In larger installations, several disks are present. In all cases some archival storage, such as magnetic tapes, is necessary for back-up purposes.

Like drums, disks are direct access storage devices. Their appearance is that of a stack of long-playing records rotating around a common axis. Each disk is coated with a magnetic material and rotates under (and over for the other side) a read/write head supported by an arm. The arm is part of a comb assembly such that each arm supports two heads, or two sets of heads, one for each side of the disk. If the arm is fixed and holds several heads we have what is called a fixed-head disk (cf. Figure 5.20.a) while if the arm can move we have a movable-arm disk (cf. Figure 5.20.b). The functioning of the former is similar to that of drums while timing for the latter will have to include a potential arm movement, or *seek time*.

Information on the disk is recorded on tracks as on a serial drum. In the movable arm case, all heads move together and are aligned under the same tracks on the different disks. These aligned tracks form a *cylinder*.

An example of a fixed-head disk is the IBM 2305 Model 2. It consists of six disks. Four sets of heads are positioned at 90 degree angles around the surfaces, each consisting of 64 addressable tracks plus 8 spares, that is a total of 768 addressable tracks. Each access mechanism contains 18 heads, hence covering a fourth of the tracks. Each track can store almost 15K bytes giving a total capacity of over 11M bytes. The rotation time is 10 ms and the transfer rate 1.56M bytes/second. In the Model 1 the average access time is divided by two by storing odd bytes of a record on one surface and even bytes on the other, with two sets of heads being paired off at 180 degrees. For the same reason as for drums, tracks are divided into sectors.

In the case of the movable-arm disk, the time to pass information between Mp and Ms is of the form:

$$T = t_s + t_r + t_t,$$

where t_r, the rotation time, is similar to the access time t_a of drums, t_t is the transfer time as before, and t_s is the seek time, or time required to reach the right cylinder. This time is not a linear function of the number of cylinders as

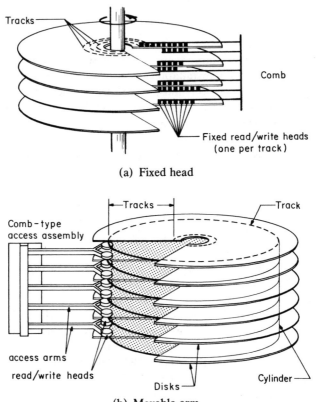

(a) Fixed head

(b) Movable-arm

Figure 5.20   Magnetic disk memories

exemplified by Figure 5.21 for the IBM 2314 (see also Exercise 10) and by the following equation for a DEC RK-11:

$$t_s = (6 + 2n) \qquad 0 < n \leq 8, t_s \text{ in ms},$$
$$= 16 + 3n/4 \qquad 9 \leq n \leq 24,$$
$$= 26 + n/3 \qquad 25 \leq n \leq 200.$$

Table 5.3 shows some of the important performance characteristics for three common disks.

In some disks, the time to pass information can be divided into two phases: the seek time and the "transfer" time. This is of interest when several disk drives share a channel, or Pio, since the channel can be released after

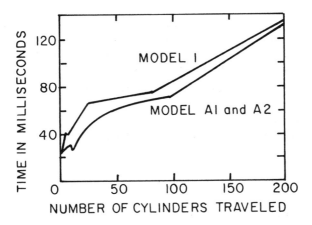

Figure 5.21 Seek time vs. number of cylinders traversed in the IBM 2314 disk

Table 5.3 Movable-arm disk characteristics.

	DEC RK-11	IBM 2314	IBM 3330
Tracks/disk	200	200	404
Track capacity	48K bits	59K bits	104K bits
Disk capacity	20M bits	233M bits	800M bits
#Disk/pack	1	11	11
#Recording surfaces	2	20	19
Average rotation time	40ms	12.5ms	8.4ms
Seek time: Minimum	10ms	25ms	10ms
Average	50ms	60ms	30ms
Maximum	85ms	130ms	55ms

the seek command has been given. This rotational position sensing method requires that tracks be divided into sectors of equal size (recall the paging drum!). We shall see later how it can facilitate scheduling (Chapter 8 Section 3).

5.4.2   Core Extensions to Main Memory

Core extensions to Mp have been rarely used with the exception of the Extended Core Storage (ECS) devices in the CDC 6000 series. This is because the cost per bit is too high for Large Core Storage (LCS) or ECS to successfully compete against either electronic RAM's or drums (cf. Figures 5.2). The comparison is even worse with respect to electronic disks.

As their names imply, LCS and ECS are core memories. LCS works exactly as a core RAM. Typical access times are one order of magnitude larger than Mp's for an equal maximum capacity, and half the cost per bit. We have the same characteristics for ECS with the exception that a small "seek" time is needed. For example, in the CDC 6000 series, information is transferred in groups of 8 words called superwords or swords, with a time penalty to be paid for the first sword. But since ECS can be interleaved the transfer rate can match Mp's cycle.

An advantage of LCS over ECS, and over direct access storage devices, is that its contents can be transferred directly on a word by word basis to the Pc registers. Hence LCS can contain code which will be executed from LCS without having to pass through Mp. This property has been used in several System/360 installations. In the CDC systems, the main uses of ECS are for the storage of frequently accessed portions of the operating system which do not have to permanently reside in Mp and for transmission of files between processors linked by this device.

5.4.3   Electronic Disks

As mentioned previously, for a long time computer manufacturers have tried to fill the gap between RAM's and DASD's. The technologies which have been investigated to date share some common characteristics such as the absence of mechanical apparatus to access information and the use of serial addressing techniques.

As for DASD's, the read/write operations in an electronic disk require two phases: accessing the right bits first and then acting. Therefore we shall have the equivalent of an access time t_a and of a transfer time t_t. As we shall see, t_a is too large for electronic disks to compete with RAM's for the implementation of primary memories.

We present now an overview of 3 types of electronic disks which have been advocated. As usual, we refer the reader to specialized publications for details on the physical features and principles behind each technology.

Magnetic Bubble Memory

This device is based on remanent magnetization as for ferrite core RAM's and magnetic drums and disks. The fabrication techniques are reminiscent of those used for integrated circuits, that is we shall have chips of bubbles.

Conceptually, the memory appears as a shift register of circulating bubbles. Each bubble, a magnetic cylindrical domain, has a diameter of a few microns. Creation, annihilation, sensing and replication of bubbles are handled in a somewhat unified fashion. Because these functions are expensive and take some room on the chip, there is usually only a single occurrence of them on a given chip.

Since there is a shift register and one access point, the average access time t_a for a bit will be $N/2$ for a register of capacity N. To reduce t_a the chip is organized in several minor loops connected to a major loop (cf. Figure 5.22). It is on this major loop that reading (sensing) and writing (generating) is done. The transfer of bubbles from the minor loop to the major loop may be a transfer and replicate, or a transfer and annihilate (on the minor loop). In the latter case reading implies a rewriting. In general, for ease of detection, only every other bubble is used in the major loop. Let K be the number of minor loops of length N. The major loop contains $2K$ positions, with only K "useful" ones. Let s be the shifting rate, and t_i be the time it takes for the bubble in the first position in the major loop to reach the read sensor. Bits will be accessed, either individually, or in blocks of K bits (i.e., the bits are interleaved among the minor loops). The average access time for a bit is:

$$\text{av. access time} = \text{av. minor loop access} + \text{av. major loop shift}$$
$$= N/2 \cdot s + K/2 \cdot 2s + t_i$$

where the $2s$ indicates the restricted availability of positions in the major loop. Similarly, the average read time for a block will be:

$$\text{av. read time} = N/2 \cdot s + K \cdot 2s + t_i$$

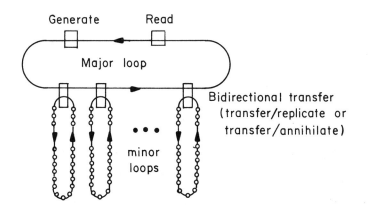

Figure 5.22 Major/minor loop arrangement of a Magnetic Bubble Memory

and the average cycle time, which includes a regeneration of the block at the next round-trip of the minor loop:

$$\text{av. cycle time} = 3N/2 \cdot s, \text{ assuming } N > 2K.$$

Typical figures for N and K are in the hundreds. For example, a 100K bit chip could consist of 144 minor loops of 641 bits (a Texas Instrument product in 1977). The shifting rate is currently of 10 μs/bit with hopes to reduce it by one order of magnitude. But, even in the latter case, this would result in a transfer rate of 1M bit/second, that is, 10 times slower than current drums and disks. Of course, the access time would be of the order of 5 ms if the shifting rate is 10 μs/bit and 500 μs for a shifting rate of 1 μs/bit. There, we would see some advantage over DASD's.

However, the performance appears limited and the future of magnetic bubble memories might reside more in storage for intelligent terminals than in secondary memory devices. Their projected low cost, their small size and weight, and the small amount of required power will soon make them competitive for the replacement of cassette tapes.

Charge-Coupled Devices (CCD)

In CCD shift registers the information is represented as a quantity of charge in a potential well in an MOS structure. The generation and propagation of these charges are achieved by applying multiphase clock pulses to clock lines which serve as electrodes in the MOS structure. Because of some transfer inefficiency, the CCD's must be refreshed but at a frequency much lower than the shifting rate. Shift rates two, and possibly three, orders of magnitude faster than those of bubble memories can be achieved. However, CCD's are volatile. They require low power, the sensing apparatus is small and can be put on the MOS structure easily, and the packaging is as simple as those of RAM's.

The basic operations needed for read and write are charge injection, charge detection, charge regeneration and, of course, charge movement in the shift register. Three main types of CCD organization have been proposed (cf. Figure 5.23). In the *serpentine*, or synchronous, organization all shift registers are simultaneously clocked and are connected in tandem. The internal shift rate is equal to the input/output data rate. The serpentine layout provides the opportunity of building long blocks (a few hundred bits) with a high shifting rate. In the *serial-parallel-serial* scheme (SPS), a horizontally shifting register is filled at input time. Once full, it is transferred into N parallel vertically circulating registers which, in turn, will be connected to a

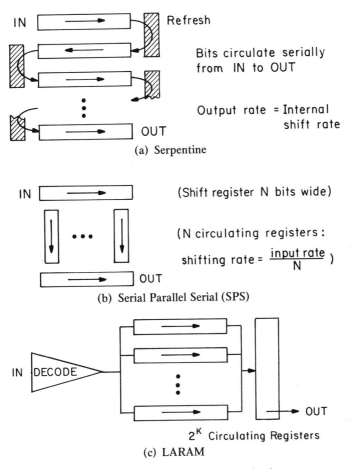

(a) Serpentine

(b) Serial Parallel Serial (SPS)

(c) LARAM

Figure 5.23   CCD Shift register organizations

horizontal output register. Thus the vertical registers have to run at $1/N$ times the frequency of the horizontal ones. From input to output, a bit passes through $N + M$ steps if each vertical register has M positions, and the delay from input to output is $N \cdot M$ times the horizontal shift rate. Advantages include high packing densities and low power dissipation. However, access is slower than in the serpentine case. The last organization called *line-addressable RAM*, or LARAM, is quite close to an MOS RAM structure. It includes a decoder which selects a "line" register, i.e., one of several CCD registers. These line registers form the inputs to a mutiplexer which feeds the

CCD output register. This organization allows fast access to blocks but is limited, as are RAM chips, by the number of pin connections of the decoder.

It appears that CCD's will have access times of 10-100 μs with transfer rates of the order of several Mbits/second. They might very well soon take position in the memory hierarchy between Mp RAM's and disks, or in lieu of the latter.

Electron-Beam Addressed Memories (EBAM)

In this technology, storage is on an MOS target addressed by an electron beam. Storage is recorded by the presence or absence of a charge on the target, and addressing is performed by appropriately deflecting the beam. Random addressing of a bit is thus possible, and block addressing is done with a TV-like scan. Read and write are dependent on particular implementations. In all cases reading consists of the sensing of the changes brought by the addressing of a charge by the electron beam. Writing occurs by monitoring the potentiality of an electrode during the addressing of a particular area of the target.

Reading is partially destructive and refreshing is necessary, but at a very low frequency (e.g., every minute). It appears that EBAM's will be faster than CCD's, maybe more expensive, and will be of limited capacity. They could replace LCS or ECS in the hierarchy, but might be too small for drum or disk substitutes.

5.5 ASSOCIATIVE MEMORY

In all the memory devices that we have considered, reading and writing is done via the mechanism of a memory address. *Associative memories* (AM's) have the capability of addressing items by content rather than by location. Thus, instead of answering queries of the form, "What is the contents of location LOC?", an AM responds to questions of the form, "Is there a location containing item XYZ?". In order to do this efficiently, all locations must be searched in parallel. Consequently, each bit of the AM requires logic in addition to the simple two stable states of addressable memories. The cost is therefore much greater, and has been too prohibitive for the implementation of large scale AM's. Recently, some parallel processor architectures have been realized using the associative concept. We delay their presentations until Chapter 11 and restrict ourselves here to AM's.

An associative memory, or content-addressable memory, has the general organization of Figure 5.24. Logically, the storage array is word-organized.

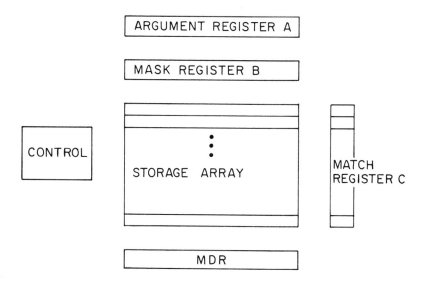

Figure 5.24 Associative memory organization

An *argument register* A holds the pattern to be matched with a *mask register* B indicating which bits of the argument must be found equal, or unequal, depending on the setting of the control. A *match register* C indicates which words in the array have the corresponding contents. The MDR contains the result of the query, i.e., the contents of the first, in some sense, cell matching the masked argument. Control permits matches on bit equality or inequality and directs the selection of a number of commands.

For an AM of w b-bit words, the A, B and MDR registers have b bits and the C register has w bits. In addition to the usual reading and writing, the AM must be able to efficiently perform the compare operation. In a word-organized AM, all words are compared in parallel to the contents of the A register, or parts thereof as indicated by the B register. Obviously, this imposes a large amount of circuitry per bit. In a bit-organized AM, each column of the storage array, i.e., each bit line if the array were a 2D configuration, is compared to a single bit of the argument. Of course, this is slower but also much cheaper. (Notice that in this case another w-bit register is needed.)

Since a unique answer is expected, there is a single MDR. However, several words of the AM may match the argument, or maybe none of them will. It is therefore necessary to sense if there is at least one match and to be able to select one such match (in general the first in some given ordering) out of many. These operations are performed on the match register.

Typical operations that an AM can perform are:

Equal	Unequal
Less than	Greater than
Less than or equal to	Greater than or equal to
Maximum value	Minimum value
Between limits	Not between limits
Next higher	Next lower

For example to perform a "greater than" search on non-negative integers, we have the following algorithm.

0. Initialize C register to all 0's;
1. Scan A from left to right until the first "0" bit is found; call that bit the target bit;
2. Complement the target bit;
3. Mask all bits at the right of the target bit;
4. Perform match on equality, ORing matches in C;
5. Restore target bit to 0;
6. Find next "0" bit at the right of the target bit; if none then end else choose this bit as the new target bit and go to step 2.

As can be seen all steps except step 4 must be performed either in the Pc or by the control of the AM. The advantage is that the loop is executed a maximum of b times while in a conventional memory w iterations are needed.

With LSI techniques AM's could become more cost effective. However, the high pin/circuit ratio and the high power dissipation are still major road blocks. Successful associative processing can be done only if the AM can be distributed among several processors. As we see in the next chapter some small AM's can be used to enhance the power of a conventional system.

5.6   BIBLIOGRAPHICAL NOTES, REFERENCES AND EXERCISES

The technological data regarding device performances as in Tables 5.1 and 5.2 can be found in numerous articles and forecasts as e.g., [Martin and Frankel 75] and [Turn 74]. Discussions of RAM's and of magnetic recording are a standard feature in textbooks such as [Matick 75]. A thorough discussion of error correcting codes appears in [Peterson and Weldon 72]. Interleaving has been modeled and analyzed by several investigators. Equations (1) and (2) in Section 3, as well as the basis for Exercises 5 and 6, can be found in [Strecker 70]. The model leading to equation (4) is due to [Hellerman 67] and the closed form of equation (5) has been obtained by [Knuth and Rao 75]. The α-β model, its equations, and Figure 5.14 are from [Burnett and Coffman 70, 73, 75] while equation (7) was obtained directly by [Chang, Kuck and Lawrie 77]. Simulation results on traces of IBM System/360 program are reported in [Terman 75] and [Baskett and Smith 76]. As usual [Thornton 70] is the source for consideration on the CDC 6600.

The paging drum analysis can be found in [Denning 72] and [Burge and Konheim 71]. Details on the IBM disks can be found in IBM manuals or in [Katzan 71]. Figure 5.21 is from [IBM 69]. Uses of LCS are reviewed in [Williams 72]. Some data on electronic disks is presented in [Feth 76]. More details on bubble memories can be found in [Bobeck, Bonyhard and Gensic 75], on CCD devices in [Amelio 75] and [Panigrahi 76], and on EBAM in [Kelly 75] and [Hughes et al. 75].

The concept of associative memories is very old. A survey and a bibliography of over 100 references can be found in [Parhami 73].

References

1. Amelio, G. F., "Charge-Coupled Devices for Memory Applications," *Proc. AFIPS 1975 Nat. Comp. Conf.*, *44*, AFIPS Press, Montvale, N.J., 1975, 515-522.

2. Baskett, F. and A. J. Smith, "Interference in Multiprocessor Computer Systems with Interleaved memories," *Comm. ACM*, *19*, (Jun. 1976), 327-334.

3. Bobek, A. H., Bonyhard, P. I. and J. E. Gensic, "Magnetic Bubbles—An Emerging New Memory Technology," *Proc. IEEE*, *63*, (Aug. 1975), 1176-1195.

4. Burge, W. H. and A. C. Konheim, "An Accessing Model," *JACM*, *18*, (Jul. 1971), 400-404.

5. Burnett, G., and E. Coffman, Jr., "A Study of Interleaved Memory Systems," *Proc. AFIPS 1970 Spring Joint Comp. Conf.*, *36*, AFIPS Press, Montvale, N.J., 1970, 467-474.

6. Burnett, G., and E. G. Coffman, Jr., "A Combinatorial Problem Related to Interleaved Memory Systems," *JACM*, *20*, (Jan. 1973), 39-45.

7. Burnett, G., and E. G. Coffman, Jr., "Analysis of Interleaved Memory Systems Using Blockage Buffers," *Comm. ACM*, *18*, (Feb. 1975), 91-95.

8. Chang, D., Kuck, D., and D. Lawrie, "On the Effective Bandwidth of Parallel Memories," *IEEE Trans. on Comp.*, *C-26*, (May 1977), 480-489.

9. Denning, P. J., "A Note on Paging Drum Efficiency," *Computing Surveys*, *4*, (Mar. 1972), 1-3.

10. Feth, G. G., "Memories: Smaller, Faster and Cheaper," *IEEE Spectrum*, (Jun. 1976), 37-43.

11. Hellerman, H. *Digital Computer System Principles*, McGraw Hill, New-York, N.Y., 1967.

12. Hughes, W. C., Lemmond, C. A., Parks, H. G., Ellis, G. W., Possin, G. E., and R. H. Wilson, "A Semiconductor Nonvolatile Electron Beam Accessed Mass Memory," *Proc. IEEE, 63,* (Aug. 1975), 1230-1240.

13. IBM System/360 Component Descriptions—2314 Direct Access Storage Facility and 2844 Auxiliary Storage Control, Form A26-3599-2, 1969.

14. Katzan, H., *Computer Organization and the System/370*, Van Nostrand Reinhold, New-York, N.Y., 1971.

15. Kelly, J., "The Development of an Experimental Electron-Beam Addressed Memory Module," *Computer*, *8*, (Feb. 1975), 32-43.

16. Knuth, D. and F. Rao, "Activity in an Interleaved Memory," *IEEE Trans. on Comp.*, *C-24*, (Sep. 1975), 943-944.

17. Martin, R., and H. Frankel "Electronic Disks in the 1980's," *Computer, 8,* (Feb. 1975), 24-31.

18. Matick, R., "Memory and Storage," in *Introduction to Computer Architecture*, H. Stone ed., SRA, Chicago, Ill., 1975, 175-248.

19. Panigrahi, G., "Charged-Coupled Memories for Computer Systems," *Computer*, *9*, (Apr. 1976), 33-41.

20. Parhami, B., "Associative Memories and Processors: An Overview and Selected Bibliography," *Proc. IEEE, 61,* (Jun. 1973), 722-730.

21. Peterson, W. W. and E. J. Weldon, *Error-Correcting Codes*, MIT Press, Cambridge, Mass., 1972.

22. Strecker, W., *An Analysis of the Instruction Execution Rate in Certain Computer Structures*, Ph.D. Dissertation, Carnegie-Mellon University, 1970.

23. Terman, F., "A Study of Interleaved Memory Systems by Trace Driven Simulation," *Proc. Symposium on the Simulation of Comp. Systems*, 1976, 3-9.

24. Thornton, J. E., *Design of a Computer—The Control Data 6600,* Scott, Foresman and Co., Glenview, Ill., 1970.

25. Turn, R., *Computers in the 1980's*, Columbia University Press, New-York, N.Y., 1974.

26. Williams, J., "Large-Core Storage in Perspective," *Computer Design*, (Jan. 1972), 45-50.

Exercises

1. Give read and write procedures for cores threaded with 2 and 3 wires in a 2 1/2 D organization.

2. Show that if groups consist of only 2 words in a 2 1/2 D core organization derived from a 2D memory, then these words can share a single sense line. Give the procedures for reading and writing.

3. Assuming an equal cost for word and bit lines, what is the optimal group size for a 2 1/2 D organization derived from the 2 D? Is this a fair assumption?

4. Find a 2 1/2 D organization different than those given in the text for a 1K RAM with 16 bit/word and 256 bit chips. Describe possible 3D organizations.

5. The 2-out-of-5 code for decimal digits is as follows.

	Weights
Digits	7 4 2 1 0
0	1 1 0 0 0
1	0 0 0 1 1
2	0 0 1 0 0
3	0 0 1 1 0
4	0 1 0 0 1
5	0 1 0 1 0
6	0 1 1 0 0
7	1 0 0 0 1
8	1 0 0 1 0
9	1 0 1 0 0

What is its minimal distance? Design a single error correcting and detecting code based upon this 2-out-of-5 code.

6. Perform the analysis as in Equations (1) and (2) of Section 3 assuming an instruction buffer of n instructions. The access time to the buffer t_b is much smaller than t_a. Consider the 2 cases:

$$t_e + t_b + t_d < t_s$$

$$t_e + t_b + t_d \geq t_s$$

The time to load the buffer is t_c. Take into account the possibility of branches.

7. Perform the analysis as in Equations (1) and (2) of section 3 assuming a prefetch of instruction $(i + 1)$ during the execution time t_e of instruction i. Assume that there is no branching, i.e., no conflict between two consecutive instructions. Repeat this analysis assuming that only every other instruction references an Mp operand (this is consistent with Table 2.1).

8. Discuss the $\alpha - \beta$ model. How can it be modified to be more realistic? Describe

an overall design for a simulation of this model, assuming that program traces are available.

9. What is the worst delay for a memory access in the CDC Stunt Box?

10. Given the rotational speed r in rpms and the capacity t of a track of a drum or fixed-head disk, define:

    - the average access time t_a;
    - the transfer time/word assuming serial operation;
    - the data transfer rate in bits/second.

    Which of these performance characteristics are changed when the DASD is a movable-arm disk? Is further data from the manufacturer required?

11. Given a disk with N cylinders, what is the average number of cylinders moved per seek assuming that requests are independent of the current position of the arm?

12. Modify the algorithm for "greater than" in an AM to be "greater than or equal".

Chapter 6

MANAGEMENT OF THE MEMORY HIERARCHY

In this chapter we consider the hardware/software interactions necessary to efficiently manage transfers of information between the various levels of the memory hierarchy. We concentrate on the first two interfaces, i.e., Mp − Ms ($M_1 − M_2$) where Ms is a rotating device, and $M_0 − M_1$ where M_0 is the cache. We start by considering the available static and dynamic options emphasizing the virtual memory concept. The next section is devoted to paging systems and their characteristics. Section 3 treats segmented systems. Section 4 gives two examples of virtual memory systems. Finally, in Section 5, we discuss cache memories.

6.1 STATIC AND DYNAMIC MEMORY MANAGEMENT SCHEMES

6.1.1 Virtual Memory and Overlays

For any installation programmers will frequently develop software that will not fit in main memory. And, if there is enough Mp available, system programmers will increase the multiprogramming load, that is, the number of tasks simultaneously resident in Mp. This lack of storage capacity is even more evident for cache memories (naturally back-up files and archival data cannot remain accessible on-line for very long if efficient throughput is desired).

Management of the memory hierarchy takes various forms, ranging from a completely dynamic hardware scheme to a static software method with the possibility of human intervention. The amount of overhead spent in the management of the memory hierarchy at the interface between levels i and $(i + 1)$ should be no greater than the amount of time used in transferring in-

269

formation between the two levels, that is approximately of the order of the access time of M_{i+1}, or smaller. This performance rule imposes a dynamic hardware scheme for the $M_0 - M_1$ interface and permits a slow method at the $M_2 - M_3$ level. In fact, at that point, operator interactions might be needed, and therefore a completely automatic procedure is out of the question. At the $M_1 - M_2$ level there exist several possibilities with the choice often dictated by the machine architecture. In the following we assume that the main memory allocated to a given task is too small to contain the storage requirements of that task, either because of the size of the program and associated data, or because of the constraints imposed by the multiprogramming load.

At the Mp − Ms level we can choose between an automatic (dynamic) management method, the virtual memory scheme, and a programmer-based method, a manual (static)· one, using software directives to overlay parts of the allocated Mp during execution. We shall not dwell on this second aspect since it imposes no special architectural requirement. Multiprogramming protection in that case is provided by relocation registers (recall Chapter 2). Overlaying is still often encountered in medium to small computers and was the rule until the early sixties in larger machines. In the 1970's, all manufacturers of medium to large computers have some products running under virtual memory operating systems.

6.1.2 The Virtual Memory Concept

Most of our terminology will be borrowed from Denning's authoritative survey. The discussion to follow assumes the Mp − Ms interface unless otherwise specified.

The main advantage of a virtual memory scheme is to give the programmer the illusion that his addressing space is not limited by the portion of Mp allotted to his program, but only by the range of the effective address calculation. As we noted in Chapter 2, this last sentence should not be construed to say that in a virtual memory system we can address only 2^n words, if n is the length of the address field in an instruction. The segmenting scheme of the Burroughs B5500 and the addressing mechanism of System/370 are examples to the contrary. The important fact is that the actual size of Mp, or of the allocation given to a particular task, can in theory be much smaller than the total size occupied by the program and associated data. In addition to this advantage, virtual memory allows multiprogramming without the requirement of contiguous partitions for each user, permits better main memory utilization, facilitates protection, and increases user's convenience since virtual memory is transparent to the user. Virtual memory can also be implemented with a virtual space smaller than the real space, as for example in the DEC PDP-10 and PDP-11.

Naturally, there are disadvantages to the virtual memory concept. They are mostly related to the potential inefficiency of some operations such as the address translation necessitated at each memory reference and the overhead incurred in the operating system to handle exceptions. This will be discussed later, once the virtual memory scheme has been properly defined.

The set of addresses that a task can reference will be called the (virtual) address space V. The set of physical locations in Mp allotted to the task will be the memory space M, of cardinality $|M|$, which is also called *primary memory allocation* (PMA). When at execution time reference to some address is made in the object code, this will be a reference to a virtual address. Therefore, there must be a scheme to map the address space into the memory space. Such a function f, called an address map, is defined by:

$$f: \quad V \to M \text{ such that if } x \in V$$
$$f(x) = \begin{cases} y \text{ if } x \text{ is in } M \text{ at location } y \\ \text{undefined otherwise.} \end{cases}$$

Figure 6.1 is an example of an address map.

In the case where $f(x)$ is undefined, we have an exception, or *missing-item fault*. The item that we want to reference has to be brought into Mp. Three rules govern this transfer of information: the *replacement rule*, which indicates which item is to be displaced from Mp and written back on Ms; the *loading rule*, which decides at which time the missing-item should be brought into Mp; and the *placement rule*, which dictates where the missing-item is to be placed in Mp.

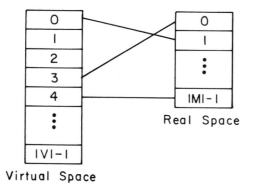

Figure 6.1   Example of an address map

The type of allowable missing-item defines the type of virtual memory system. This missing-item could be as small as a word, as in caches. But then, in order to be completely general, the mapping device should be as large as the smallest of the two physical memories. At the Mp — Ms interface, we shall require this generality and therefore blocking, i.e., the grouping of several words into a single missing-item, will be imposed. Depending on the size of these blocks, we can distinguish between:

- Segmentation, where the blocks are of unequal length (cf. Burroughs B5500, Burroughs B6700);
- Paging, where the blocks are of equal length (cf. Ferranti ATLAS, the first computer with virtual memory, RCA Spectra 70, Xerox Sigma 7, DEC PDP-10, etc., ...);
- Segmentation with paging, where blocks (segments) are multiples of pages (cf. MULTICS, IBM 360/67, 370/158 and 168, Amdahl 470V/6).

In this context, a memory reference can be considered as consisting of a block (segment or page) number and of a displacement within that block. The mapping device must translate the starting (virtual) address of a block into its real address, if it is in Mp, or must generate a fault, if it is absent. Two implementations are possible, namely direct and associative mapping.

The *direct mapping* device consists of n entries corresponding to the $|V|/p$ possible virtual pages, where p is the page size in a paging system, or to n segments in a segmented one. Limiting our example to a paging system, entry i in the table contains the starting address of the real page, or *frame*, into which virtual page i is mapped, or a pattern indicating that page i is not present in Mp. In the case of pages of size $p = 2^k$ (the only practical choice) an effective virtual address of n bits can be decomposed into a page number, the $(n - k)$ leftmost bits, and a line number or displacement, the k rightmost bits. The mapping device translates the $(n - k)$ leftmost bits into a frame number, generally of same length $(n - k)$ bits, to which the line number is concatenated. Figure 6.2 summarizes the process.

Direct mapping can be implemented in hardware by a set of $|V|/p$ fast registers. For example, the Xerox Sigma 7 has 256 registers of 9 bits corresponding to a virtual memory of 2^{17} words (128K) and a page size $p = 512$. This mapping is also feasible without the fast registers by keeping the map in Mp at the cost of one reference (in the table) per memory reference, i.e., with a slow-down penalty of two-to-one solely for the address translation. In the case of segmented systems, the segment number has to be used as an index for the table.

When an *associative map* is used, it contains those pairs (x, y) for which $f(x) = y$. The search is by content: search x to find y. Figure 6.3 shows such a device for a paging system. If "page" and "frame" are replaced by seg-

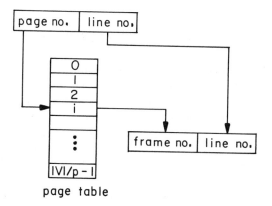

page table

Figure 6.2 Direct mapping

ment, the operation is still valid. In the case of a paging system, we need $|M|/p$ entries in the table. As we saw in the preceding chapter, the cost of associative memories is such that it prohibits a fully associative map.

In general, we shall have a combination of direct and associative mappings for reasons of cost and efficiency: some have already been pointed out, and some will soon become apparent.

6.2 PAGING SYSTEMS

In this section we study in some detail the organization of the most prevalent type of virtual memory systems, paging systems. Most of what follows also

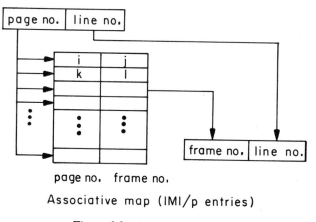

page no.   frame no.

Associative map (IMI/p entries)

Figure 6.3 Associative mapping

applies to segmented systems, with segments consisting of a number of pages. We shall often cite examples drawn from Systems/360 and /370 and from MULTICS, implemented originally on a GE-645, which are of this latter type.

In the last fifteen years, an enormous amount of literature has been published concerning the modeling and monitoring of paging systems (cf. Section 6 which refers to extensive bibliographies and surveys). Our bias here is towards pragmatic results which have influenced the design of the architecture of paging systems, where architecture is used in its broadest sense to include parts of the operating systems. This is not to say that theoretical studies should be neglected. On the contrary some of them, as we shall see, have had profound impact.

The *principle of locality* is central to the successful operation of paging systems. This principle states that, during execution, a process is going to favor a subset of V, that is only a subset of its pages need to be mapped onto frames to allow seldom interrupted execution intervals. This locality of reference can be decomposed into two components, namely:

- *Temporal locality*, which is the tendency for a program to reference in the near future those pages referenced in the recent past. Loops, constants, and temporary variables or working stacks are constructs which lead to this concept;
- *Spatial locality*, which is the tendency for a program to reference neighbor pages, i.e., if page i is referenced at time t, pages $i - k$ to $i + k$ will probably be referenced in the near future. Sequential portions of code and traversals of arrays give credence to this notion.

Naturally, temporal and spatial locality coexist during a program's execution.

Before proceeding with a specific discussion of paging systems, we need a few more definitions. A program is represented as a set of addresses $a_{i,j}$. These addresses are partitioned into pages of equal size p. Thus, we can also speak of a program as the set P of pages

$$P = \{p_1, p_2, \ldots, p_N\} \text{ where } P \subseteq V$$

Each address is of the form $a_{i,j} = p_i d_j$ where $p_i \in P$ and $0 \le d_j < p$ is the line number or displacement. We will often use i instead of p_i when referring to page p_i.

From the (virtual) memory viewpoint the execution of a program is a string of memory references:

$$r_1, r_2, \ldots, r_i, \ldots, r_n,$$

where n is the total number of references, and $r_i = p_j$, $1 \leq i \leq n$, $1 \leq j \leq N$. When $r_i = p_j$ and p_j is not in Mp, we have a *page fault*. We will abide by the usual rule for the study of paging systems, i.e., we consider the memory reference as the unit of (virtual) time.

6.2.1 Address Translation Mechanism and Page Size

As stated in the previous section the address translation mechanism can use either direct or associative mapping, both of which present advantages and difficulties.

Direct mapping implies as many hardware translation registers as there are possible pages in a virtual space (a maximal N or N_{max}). This number is sufficiently small in medium size machines which typically function in a uniprogramming environment with swapping in and out of tasks. The paged Xerox Sigmas have a translation mechanism of this type. However in the case of large systems, such as IBM System/370 or MULTICS, N_{max} becomes too big for a direct scheme. Direct mapping is fast since the penalty of the address translation is only a reference to a specific mapping register. With current technology, this can be of the order of one-tenth of the Mp memory cycle.

The associative mapping overhead is of the same order of magnitude. The constraint here is not the size of N_{max} but that of M_{max}, the maximum number of frames. Since recent estimates show that associative memories cost between two and three orders of magnitude more than RAM's, the map would cost as much as Mp for page sizes of a few hundred words, if it were completely associative.

Therefore, we shall use a combination of the two types of mapping. A small associative memory will contain the frame-page pair most likely to be referenced (this will be explained soon) and a page table, in Mp, will contain the remaining map. A register (PP for page table pointer) points to the start of the current process ' page table. Figure 6.4 shows how the address translation is performed. If a match is found in the associative mapping, the direct search is cancelled. If both the associative and the direct searches fail, then a page fault occurs and a new task is brought in. The contents of PP are changed so that they point to the page table of the new task. The modifications to the associative memory will be discussed later but it should be noted that it might be desirable to modify the AM not only at task switching time, but also during the execution of the task if the Mp frame allocation (PMA) is larger than the size of the AM. This mini-replacement rule will be discussed along with the page replacement algorithm. Typical numbers of entries in the AM are 8 for the IBM System/360 Model 67, 16 for MULTICS on the GE-645 (now Honeywell 6180), and 128 for the IBM System/370 Model 168

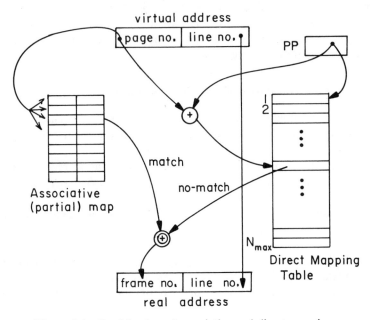

Figure 6.4 Combination of associative and direct mappings

and DEC VAX 11/780 where the AM is replaced by a translation look-aside buffer addressed through a hashing technique. In the Amdahl 470V/6 this buffer size is doubled. For the Model 168, the cost of a match is one cycle (80 ns) while a no-match and translation through the page table takes from 8 to 26 cycles. However, the Model 168 is a segmented machine and therefore an additional level of page table referencing is needed (cf. Section 3). Direct and associative mapping can be combined in other ways. This will become clear when we treat cache memories (cf. Section 5).

Sharing of code and data in a paging environment is not simple if it is to be done entirely dynamically, i.e., without indication at load time of which pages are sharable. Consider first the case of a pure (or reentrant) procedure, e.g., a compiler, to be shared by two users. Each task will have its own map. Since the pure procedure is referenced by other procedures and itself, it must occupy the same relative positions in the virtual spaces of the tasks sharing it. This is shown in Figure 6.5.a where P is shared by tasks A and B. When task B is initiated after task A has been running, its map should be brought up to date by indicating which pages belonging to P are in Mp, and where. The virtual space placement requirement of the shared code is not stringent if the pure procedures are part of an often used package such as a compiler. On the

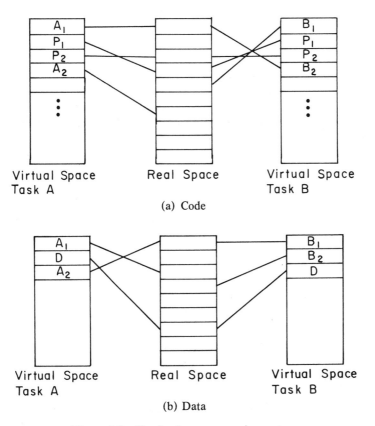

(a) Code

(b) Data

Figure 6.5 Sharing in a pure paging system

other hand, this binding process required from the loader is quite cumbersome if the routines are seldom used.

Data can also be shared if it is not used, directly or indirectly, for referencing purposes. Then there is no restriction on its placement (cf. Figure 6.5.b). But the difficulty resides in the recognition of which of the pages in Mp are shared when we perform task switching. As we shall see, segmented systems provide better handles for sharing of both code and data (cf. Exercise 4).

Now that we know how to perform an address translation, our next task is to choose a page size. In segmented systems, the sizes of the blocks can be unequal and therefore they can be logically tied to program structures such as procedures or data arrays (cf. Section 3). In a paging system, the page size p is arbitrary and in general will be a compromise, the constraints imposed being the efficiency of the secondary memory device, the space taken by the page tables, and the average sizes of the logical program entities just mentioned. Notice that as p increases, the amount of wasted space in the last page in the virtual space will also increase. This is called *internal fragmentation*, in contrast to *external fragmentation* which appears only in segmented systems and which will be defined later.

Of the three factors mentioned, the efficiency of Ms operation is the most influential. As we saw in the preceding chapter, the latency of a (paging) drum is such that blocks of at least 256 words (1K bytes) must be transferred. A moving arm disk will require a block size at least four times as big and even then might not be practical unless clusters of consecutive (small) pages can be transferred on a single request (as in the VAX 11/780 VMS system).

As p gets smaller, the percent of information accessible via associative mapping decreases for a fixed size AM. At the same time, the direct mapping tables grow, along with the dictionaries indicating the placement of the pages on Ms. This *table fragmentation* is therefore another argument against too small a page size.

On the other hand, extensive measurements on programs have shown that logical blocks are much smaller than 1000 words. Most procedures occupy less than 100 words. Thus segments, and hence page sizes, should be small. One could even envision different page sizes for code and data. The MULTICS system was planned this way ($p = 64$ for code and 1024 for data) but the scheme had to be abandoned because of difficulties in hardware implementation.

Since page transport is so costly, most paging systems use a p in the range 128-1024 words (p will always be a power of 2). It is interesting to speculate on the influence that electronic disks will have on this parameter. Table 6.1 lists the page sizes of some virtual memory systems.

During a run, not all pages of a given program will be transferred into Mp.

Table 6.1   Common page sizes

Computer	Page size (in words)
IBM 360/67	1024 (32 bit)
IBM 370/168	512 or 1024 (32 bit)
MULTICS	1024 (36 bit)
RCA Spectra 70/46	1024 (32 bit)
Xerox Sigma 7	512 (32 bit)
DEC PDP-10, 20	512 (36 bit)
CDC STAR-100	4K (bytes)
DEC VAC 11/780	128 (32 bit)

For example, during the compilation of some source programs not all error procedures will be called. The number of words $M(p)$ brought into Mp has been experimentally shown to be of the form:

$$M(p) = a + b \log_2 p, \quad \text{for} \quad 64 \le p \le 2048$$

Figure 6.6 shows the resulting $M(p)$ vs. p for a program of $0.25 \cdot 10^6$ references written in FORTRAN IV.

The *superfluity* of a program is defined as follows. Let S_i be the number of references to page p_i during the interval $[r_k, r_1]$ where $r_k = p_i$ is the reference bringing p_i in Mp (i.e., a page fault to p_i) and r_1 is a page fault resulting in the replacement of p_i (or $r_1 = r_n$ if p_i remains until the end of the program). Let f be the number of page faults. Then the superfluity S is defined as:

$$S = ((\sum_{i=1}^{N} S_i)/f) \cdot p \quad \text{(recall than N is the total number of virtual pages)}$$

Surprisingly, no correlation between S and either page size or replacement algorithms has been found.

6.2.2   Replacement Algorithms and Memory Management

The management of the primary memory allocated (PMA) to a task takes various forms depending on design choices. The foremost criteria are whether tasks are to be partitioned into fixed or variable areas (assuming a multiprogramming environment), and whether replacement algorithms are to be local, i.e., involving only the PMA of the faulting task, or global, that is taking into account the history of all resident tasks. Before discussing the merits of each particular implementation, we present a number of algorithms which define the page(s) to be replaced when the operating system dictates

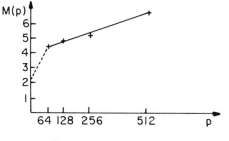

Figure 6.6   M(p) vs. p

that such an action is required. For each of these rules we indicate the hardware needed, if any, in addition to the mapping device. As we shall see, each replacement algorithm is an attempt at modeling program behavior, that is attempting to predict the future locality of a program on its recent past history (except for the unrealizable optimal algorithms).

Let $C_t = \{p_1, p_2, \ldots, p_n\}$ be the set of resident pages (or the set of resident pages for a given task; the distinction will be clear in the context of local and/or global rules) at (reference) time t. If $r_t = p_j$ is such that $p_j \notin C_{t-1}$ then we must load p_j in Mp. Under fixed partitioning, C_t has constant cardinality and hence some $p_i \in C_{t-1}$ has to be replaced to make room for p_j once C_t has been filled to capacity. In a variable PMA policy the cardinality of C_t can increase, i.e., a page fault might result in C_t becoming $C_{t-1} \cup \{p_j\}$. However, if for a given task we do not want to have $|C|$ become as large as $M(p)$, we shall have to reduce C_t at chosen instants. Although this is not a replacement in the strict sense of the word, we shall include those rules in our "replacement algorithms".

The algorithms that we present have not always been implemented in their purest forms (in fact some of them are not realizable in real-time). We shall discuss later some of the concessions which must be made for practicality.

Random Replacement (Local or global, fixed or variable partitioning)

A p_i is randomly chosen from C_t when a replacement is needed. This policy is contrary to the principle of locality and hence is not recommended. However, it has been shown to be of interest in instances where locality is not apparent, for example in some information management systems where transactions imply a sequential search through a data base. For this rule no extra hardware is needed and bookkeeping in the operating system is minimal.

First-in-First-out (*FIFO*) *Replacement* (Local and fixed partitioning; can be extended to global and variable partitioning)

The pages in C_t are ordered according to their loading sequence. When $|C_t|$ reaches the PMA, the first page loaded becomes the first one to be replaced. Subsequent pages are removed in the same fashion.

Example 6.1 Consider a program with 8 virtual pages $\{a, b, \ldots, h\}$ and the reference string

$$a\ b\ a\ d\ g\ a\ f\ d\ g\ a\ f\ c\ b\ g$$

Assume a PMA of 4 pages.

After 5 references (and 4 page faults) $C_5 = \{a, b, d, g\}$. At time 7, we have a page fault for f and hence we must replace a member of C_6 ($C_6 = C_5$). The first page loaded in, a, is replaced resulting in $C_7 = \{b, d, g, f\}$ (where C_t is an ordered set). It is easy to see that subsequent page faults will occur at times 10, 12, 13 and 14 resulting in a total of 9 page faults (including the initial loading) and $C_{14} = \{a, c, b, g\}$. $\quad\square$

As above, there is no need for extra hardware. The operating system must keep a queue of loaded pages. The overhead at page fault, that is the insertions and deletions in the queue, is minimal compared to the time it takes to retrieve pages from secondary memory.

FIFO and some variations making it global and variable have been and are used in many operating systems.

"Clock" or First-in-Not-Used-First-Out (FINUFO) Replacement (Local and fixed partitioning can be extended to global and variable partitioning)

One problem with FIFO is that a frequently referenced page can be replaced too often. The clock algorithm is an attempt to alleviate this disconcerting feature. To do this, we keep a FIFO queue as before, but with two additions. First, we associate with each entry in the queue a "use" bit which will be turned on when the page corresponding to that entry in the queue is referenced after its initial loading. Second, we make the queue circular with a pointer, say P, pointing to the next page to be replaced. At page fault time, we examine the use bit of the page pointed to by P. If it is off, we have found the page to be replaced; we do so, insert the loaded page in its place, and advance P one position (modulo $|C_t|$ of course). If it is on, we turn the use bit off and advance the pointer one position. We continue in this fashion until P points to a page whose "use" bit is off.

Example 6.2 Assume the same operating conditions as in Example 6.1. At time 6, the circular queue looks like:

$a\ b\ d\ g$
v use bit (v means on)
P

The use bit of a was set on at time 3. At time 7, the reference to f causes a page fault; b is replaced since a's bit was on, a's bit is turned off, and the circular queue is:

$a\ f\ d\ g$
   P

After the next 4 references, all members of C have been re-referenced, and the circular queue is:

a f d g
v v v v
   P

The next reference, to c, causes a page fault and d will be replaced. This example shows that "clock" simply reverts to FIFO for a high locality of references.

The reader may verify that in this example we have 8 page faults with the circular queue at time 14 being:

g f c b
P   □

To implement this algorithm, we need a "hardware" bit for each frame. This bit is set at each memory reference to the frame. This can be done during the mapping process if the bit is included in the mapping tables. Thus, there will be no time overhead and little extra hardware. The operating system function is still simple.

This algorithm has been used in MULTICS, for both Mp and the associative memory management, and in the University of Michigan MultiProgramming Supervisor (MTS) and in the original version of CP-67, two operating systems for the IBM System/360 Model 67. It has also been known as the *Look-Aside-Memory* (LAM) replacement algorithm.

Least-Recently-Used (LRU) Replacement (Local and fixed partitioning; can be extended to global and variable partitioning)

Clock was an improvement over FIFO but had no reordering of pages according to the number or recentness of references. This latter constraint can be implemented if instead of using a queue and reference bit, we use a "stack" which is reordered at each reference. Let p_i be in position d $(d > 1)$ of the stack at reference $(t - 1)$, and $r_t = p_i$. Then p_i is moved into position 1, at the top of the stack and all entries in positions 1 to $(d - 1)$ at time $t - 1$ are moved down one position. At page fault time, the page at the bottom of the stack (note this is not really a stack since the middle of it can be accessed) is chosen for replacement. It is the one which has not been referenced for the longest time; hence, the term Least Recently Used (LRU).

Example 6.3   Assume the same operating conditions as in Example 6.1. At time 6, the stack is (left to right is top to bottom):

a g d b

The next reference causes a page fault; *b* is replaced and the stack becomes:

f a g d

Continuing in this fashion, using LRU, we shall have 8 page faults and a final stack:

g b c f   □

A pure LRU algorithm is somewhat impractical since the order in the stack might change at every memory reference. Each move in the stack implies a memory access and the overhead is unbearable unless the stack is stored in a very fast memory buffer. In this case, the stack shifting can be done in parallel with the memory reference. To our knowledge, only one true LRU implementation exists at the Mp − Ms level, that of the CDC STAR-100. There, the associative memory covers the 16 most recently referenced pages, i.e., the 16 top positions in the stack, and repositioning the remainder of the page table in Mp is speeded up by the vector (pipeline) hardware. The longer search and shift times are not significant when compared to other parameters of the system.

The LRU used in the CDC STAR-100 is local with each process having its own stack. Other systems using LRU approximations (cf. Section 4) often take a global approach. In that case, it would appear that LRU not only becomes global but also variable since pages are stolen from other tasks. However, there exist local variable LRU algorithms which will be presented later.

Optimal Replacement in a Fixed Partition (Local and fixed partitioning)

All algorithms presented up to now relied only on past information. With knowledge of the future, an optimal algorithm could be devised where optimality is defined as the minimum number of page faults. The MIN, or optimal, algorithm, due to Belady, generates the minimum number of page faults as follows. Assume C_t has reached its PMA and $r_t = p_j$ is not in C_{t-1}. Let r_{t_i} ($t_i > t$) be the next reference to p_i belonging to C_{t-1} (if p_i is not referenced again let $t_i = n + 1$). Then, remove from C_{t-1} the page p_i with largest t_i, i.e., remove the page which is not going to be referenced for the longest time. Naturally MIN is not realizable in real time. Its interest is to provide a yardstick for other replacement algorithms.

Example 6.4   Assume the same operating conditions as in Example 6.1 At time 7, we have a page fault for *f*. We have $t_a = 10$, $t_b = 13$, $t_d = 8$ and $t_g =$

9. Thus, b is replaced and $C_7 = \{a, d, f, g\}$. At time 12, we have a page fault for c; $t_a = t_d = t_f = 15$ and $t_g = 14$. We can remove any of a, d, or f. The next reference is a page fault, and again we remove one of the two not selected at the previous step. For this particular reference string we have 7 page faults.   □

After having presented the most common fixed-local rules, it is worthwhile to try and to compare their performance. No analytical result is known besides the optimality of MIN, but very strong experimental evidence shows that on the average the number of page faults, for algorithm A denoted f_A, can be ranked as:

$$f_{RAND} > f_{FIFO} > f_{CLOCK} > f_{LRU} > f_{MIN}$$

Figure 6.7 shows the behavior of the last 4 algorithms on the program already mentioned for Figure 6.6 for a fixed page size ($p = 256$). All four curves, f vs. PMA, have the same shape idealized in Figure 6.8.a. This so-called *parachor curve* is typical. In order to run efficiently, we would like to be at the right of the knee of the curve (with a small page fault-rate) while at the same time keeping a small PMA (being as far left as possible). These two constraints indicate that a normal mode of operation would be at the knee of the curve. In fact, at that position we try to minimize the *space-time product*, an accepted criterion for the cost of running a program in a paging environment, that we define here as:

$$SP = M(n + f\rho),$$

where n is the number of references

   M is the (fixed) PMA

   f is the number of page faults

   ρ is the (average) time to transfer a page from Ms to Mp.

The LRU and MIN algorithms have an additional advantage over FIFO and "clock," namely, the stack property. A replacement algorithm A has the stack property if for all t, $t = 1, 2, \ldots, n$, and for a PMA x:

$$f_t^x \geq f_t^{x+1} \geq f_t^{x+2} \geq \cdots \geq f_t^M = f_t^{M+1},$$

where f_t^x is the number of page faults, up to reference t, for a PMA x. In other words when the PMA of a program running in a paging system with a "stack" replacement algorithm is increased, it is assured that the program will generate fewer (or at worst as many) page faults. We leave as an exercise

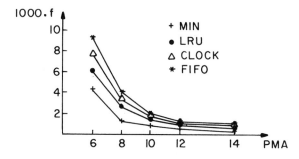

Figure 6.7   Comparison of local replacement algorithms with fixed PMA's

the proof that MIN and LRU are stack algorithms while FIFO and "clock" are not (cf. Exercises 8 and 9). Because of this stack property which allows the simulation of programs, via reference traces, for all PMA at one time, the LRU algorithm has had a profound impact on the study of the behavior of programs in a paging environment. It has become the standard for fixed PMA algorithms. On the other hand, algorithms like FIFO are said to present anomalies. Figure 6.9.a and b show the influence of the page size on the fault rate for a given PMA. For the same program as in previous figures, we can see that in one case 16 pages of 128 words yield a minimum number of

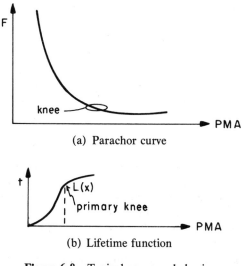

(a) Parachor curve

(b) Lifetime function

Figure 6.8   Typical program behavior

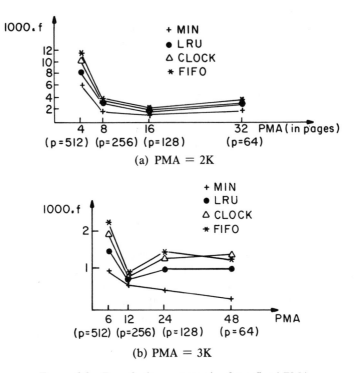

Figure 6.9   Page-faults vs. page size for a fixed PMA

page faults for all 4 algorithms, while in the other case (larger PMA) either 12 pages of 256 words or 48 pages of 64 words are better (notice also that in the figure there is a point where $f_{FIFO} < f_{CLOCK}$). It is possible to construct reference strings for which halving the page size (in a fixed PMA) will more than double the number of page faults in a variety of replacement algorithms such as LRU or FIFO. This is one more argument against too small a page size.

Until now, we have not paid much attention to the cost of pushing, or writing back, the replaced pages on Ms. If these pages have not been modified, then nothing should be done. This is the case for pages of pure (re-entrant) code. Very often, a "modified" bit will be included in the page tables and set on only when a store to a location in that page is generated. Some replacement algorithms will try to first replace those pages which are not modified (or "clean" by opposition to "dirty" pages which have been modified). For example, we could implement a revised FIFO algorithm by:

1. Replace the first "clean" page if one exists in the first m entries in the queue (where m is a parameter of the system);
2. If step 1 fails, replace the first page in the queue.

A similar variation could be done on shared pages by having a step stating "do not replace a shared page" (such a scheme exists in the TSS operating system for the IBM System/360 Model 67 and the VMS system for the VAX 11/780).

With the inclusion of pushes we can redefine the space time product as:

$$SP = M(n + f\rho) + \alpha\rho P$$

where $0 \le \alpha < 1$ is a parameter and P is the number of pushes.

We look now at some variable PMA rules.

Working-Set Replacement (Local or global; variable partitioning)

The moving-window or working set replacement algorithm has had the same type of impact on variable policies as LRU has had for fixed PMA rules. Let T be a window size, i.e., an interval of (virtual) time expressed in number of references. The working set at time t for a window T is the set of pages which have been referenced in the interval $(t - T + 1, t)$, that is:

$$WS(t, T) = \{ p_i \mid r_u = p_i, t - T + 1 \le u \le t \}$$

A page is replaced (deleted from Mp) at time t if it does not belong to $WS(t, T)$. Notice that a page is not necessarily replaced at page fault time. The definition of the space time product now becomes:

$$SP = \overline{M}n + \sum_{i=1}^{f} M_i\rho \tag{3}$$

where $\overline{M}$ is the average working set size and M_i the WS size at the ith page fault.

Example 6.5 Assume the same string as in Example 6.1 and a window of 4 references. At times 4 and 5, the working set is $\{a, b, d, g\}$. At time 6, b is "replaced", or, discarded, since it has not been referenced in the last 4 units. A representation of the execution of the string is:

WS														
					g		g	g	g	g	g	c	b	g
				d	d	g	f	f	f	f	f	g	c	b
		b	b	b	b	d	d	d	d	d	d	f	f	c
	a	a	a	a	a	a	a	a	a	a	a	a	a	f
time	1	2	3	4	5	6	7	8	9	10	11	12	13	14
Page fault	*	*		*	*		*					*	*	*
WS size	1	2	2	3	4	3	4	4	4	4	4	4	4	4

There are 8 page faults and a steady state mean working set size (after $t = 4$) of a little less than 4.   □

An experimental hardware implementation of the *WS* concept exists on the MANIAC II computer at the Los Alamos Scientific Laboratory (the MANIAC II has since been retired). Its components are a working set register, 64 page-frame registers corresponding to the 64 1K frames of Mp, and a *T*-register. The *T*-register is associated with a clock used to decrement an 8-bit counter which, when reaching 0, is reinitialized to the value contained in the *T*-register. Each of the page frame registers has the format:

bit 0: clean or dirty bit
bit 1: alarm bit
bit 2–5: clock-counter
bit 6–15: page number (index in a page table).

The working set register has its rightmost 64 bits corresponding at time *t* to the encoding of *WS*(*t*, *T*) (the other part of the *WS* register is of no concern here). That is, if bit *i* is on in the working set register, then page *i* is part of the working set.

Every time the counter associated with the *T* register-clock becomes null, the clock-counters in the page frame registers are incremented by one. This is done selectively only for those page frame registers which have their corresponding bit set in the *WS* register. When the clock-counter of a given page overflows, i.e., when the frame has not been referenced for the equivalent of a window time, the alarm bit of that frame is set. However, the page is not discarded and the program is not interrupted at this point (in contrast to a pure *WS* strategy). When a page is referenced, the counter is reset to 0, and if the alarm bit were on, it is also set off. Obviously, the *WS* register and the page table are part of the processor state.

At page fault time, a page is pulled from secondary memory. If there is no room for it, then a page with its alarm bit on is replaced. If no such page exists, then one of the previous replacement algorithms can be used to select a page to be replaced. We shall see later an approximation to the working set in a production-type setting without the additional hardware present in the MANIAC II.

As seen in equation (3), there are two parameters of importance for evaluating the performance of a *WS* policy: the page fault rate, as in previous rules, and the mean working set size. They both depend on the values given to the window T. For an increasing window we shall have a smaller fault rate and a larger *WS* size. Plotting the page fault rate vs. the average *WS* size for a given window, we obtain curves similar in shape to the parachor curve of Figure 6.8.a. The next logical question is then to compare a *WS* policy with a fixed replacement algorithm. Experimental evidence indicates that curves of the form shown in Figure 6.10 are to be expected, that is, *WS* more closely models the behavior of programs (there have been cases where *WS* behaves better than MIN).

The main reason for the superiority of *WS* is that it does not have to guess the right PMA. In a fixed PMA rule, if the PMA is too small for one locality and too large for another, the number of page faults will be large in the first locality and there will be some wasted Mp frames in the second. On the other hand, *WS* will adapt its size to changes of localities.

This adaptation of course is not smooth. In Figure 6.11 we show how the *WS* size will change during the transition from one locality to another. During the transition, the set of resident pages will first be the union of the sets belonging to either locality and then pages belonging to the first locality will slowly disappear. There have been attempts at removing this overshoot as well as proposals for *WS* strategies with variable windows. To our knowledge, none of them have been implemented in production systems.

While the (fixed) size of the PMA is difficult to estimate for the previous rules, the width of the window is also hard to evaluate. Several proposals have been made, almost all related to ρ the time to transfer a page from Ms to Mp. However, it appears that if the space-time product is used as a measure of efficiency, then the working-set policy attains a minimum for a large range of T. This is not true for a fixed allocation where the range of optimum

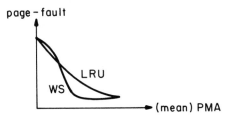

Figure 6.10 Typical parachor curves for LRU and WS policies

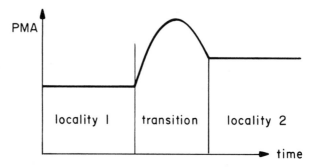

Figure 6.11   Adaptation of WS to changes in locality

PMA is small. In general, the space time product in a *WS* policy is comparatively smaller than the one for LRU, assuming that the PMA of the latter is
approximately the same as the mean working set size.

Page-Fault-Frequency Replacement (Local or global; variable partitioning)

The *page-fault-frequency* (PFF) *rule* is also an attempt at having the primary
memory allocation follow variations in localities. The page fault frequency
defined as the reciprocal of T', the interpage fault time, is monitored (T' expressed in the same unit as the window T of the *WS* algorithm). At page fault
time, if the PFF is greater than some predefined value P no replacement occurs and the PMA is increased by one by loading the faulting page. On the
other hand, if the PFF is less than P then all pages not referenced since the
last page fault are discarded.

The main difference between PFF and *WS* is that in the former actions
take place only at page fault times; in essence, T represents a lower limit on a
(variable) window size. No hardware implementation of PFF exists to date
although there are indications that a minicomputer manufacturer is interested in applying the concept. It should be significantly simpler than a *WS*
implementation (cf. Exercise 12). Comparing PFF and *WS* does not yield
great differences. Overshoots such as the one depicted in Figure 6.10 can be
more pronounced in the PFF algorithm. For example, taking the cumulative
results of 8 programs traced by Graham shows that:

- A minimum space time product was achieved by:
  MIN in 5 cases
  WS in 3 cases

- In the 5 cases where MIN was optimal:

PFF was second best in 2 cases
LRU was second best in 3 cases

- Accumulating the minimal space time products for the 8 programs, we have:

MIN	12.84
LRU	16.82
WS	15.63
PFF	15.28

But PFF can present anomalies in its behavior. For example, an increase in the window size resulting necessarily in an increase in the mean memory allocation can yield a larger number of page faults. *WS* is free of such peculiarities.

Optimal Variable Replacement (Local or global; variable partitioning)

As MIN is optimal for a fixed PMA, a VMIN for a variable environment can be designed. However, we have to choose a criterion for optimality. This was easy for MIN since the only performance parameter of importance was the page fault rate. For VMIN, we would like to use the space-time product. To this date, no optimal algorithm using the space time product has been designed. The difficulty is that the cost of a page fault increases with the resident PMA at page fault time (cf. Equation (3)). If we relax this assumption, we can define an optimal algorithm which minimizes a cost C:

$$C = fR + \overline{M} n U \tag{4}$$

where U is the cost of a reference to a page in Mp and R is the cost of a page fault (i.e., all page faults have the same cost independently of the PMA at exception time).

We obtain a minimal C for a given R/U as follows. A page p_i is removed at time t if it was not referenced between r_t and $r_{t+R/U}$, since the cost of keeping it in Mp during R/U references would be greater than bringing it back from Ms. Thus, we have a working set algorithm with a "forward" window of size R/U. We can plot the page fault rate vs. the average working set size for a given R/U as embodied in:

$$C = f'R/U + \overline{M} \tag{5}$$

where f' is the page fault rate. Taking the concave envelope of the lines generated for various R/U's we get a "parachor" curve. It can be proven that no other variable space algorithm can perform better than the points on this curve under the assumption leading to equation (4). Obviously, VMIN is not realizable in real-time and can only serve as a benchmark.

Since in general the variable algorithms are better than those based on fixed PMA's, we could ask why we should bother with the latter. Several arguments can be put forth. The first is a historical one. The working-set concept, and its derivatives, came to existence in the late sixties, a few years after several virtual memory schemes had been in operation with fixed replacement algorithms. The second, is that extensions to fixed rules, such as global FIFO and global LRU to be described shortly, have their roots in the fixed PMA rules. Other arguments such as the beliefs that locality sizes can be predicted in advance and that fixed partitions are easier to handle from the operating system viewpoint may appear more specious. Therefore, an examination of (primary) memory management policies is in order.

Mp Management

We can distinguish four classes of memory management.

- Equipartition;
- Variable partitions, without correlating the variation to program localities;
- Variable partitions by extending fixed local rules to global rules;
- Variable partitions based on a working-set concept.

We can certainly simplify the functions of the operating system by giving to each program an equal amount of PMA. The multiprogramming load is constant and allocation/deallocation of programs is a trivial matter. Unhappily, this policy can quickly lead to an excess of paging activity which brings the progress of each task at a standstill, since everyone is waiting on the over-committed paging channel. There is no way to adjust the sizes of the PMA's, even if the locality sizes of the resident programs were such that they would fit in main memory. It has been shown that the variance in locality sizes is large enough to warrant a little more complexity in the operating system to implement variable partitioning. Although theoretical models and experimental results argue forcefully against fixed partitioning, it is still present in a number of "modern" operating systems.

A measure of performance which can also be used to judge the efficiency of a virtual memory scheme is the *life-time function*. This function $L(x)$, defined as the mean (virtual) time between page faults for a memory policy with space constraint x, is simply the inverse of $f(x)$ the page-fault function. Its shape is indicated in Figure 6.8.b although there is some evidence that secondary knees might appear. $L(x)$ has been used advantageously in models and experiments in situations where the page-fault function was not adequate. In particular, we can observe in $L(X)$ a convex region from the origin to its knee, assumed unique, and then a concave region. By studying this life time function it has been shown that, depending on its convexity, among fixed partitioning policies, either:

- fixed partitions of unequal size yield better performance than equipartition, and, furthermore, equipartition can be the worst possible; or,
- if $L(x)$ is insufficiently convex, then equipartition can be optimal.

However, the knowledge that unequal partitions may be better does not help in choosing the sizes of the partitions. When varying partitions are implemented, some tasks will be favored over others. If we want to keep a constant multiprogramming level this can be accomplished simply by giving (page residence) priorities to tasks in a round-robin fashion. For example, a task will not relinquish any of its resident pages for the next k page faults, even if it is the culprit, thus possibly increasing its PMA (where k is a parameter of the system). Replaced pages come from the other tasks under some global rule. This biasing is unrelated to the current locality of the favored task but nevertheless it can be shown to be beneficial. Experiments have demonstrated that a biased round-robin policy, with a global FIFO replacement for the other tasks, gives a better result than local FIFO for fixed and (approximately) equal partitions. This conclusion can be generalized by arguments linked to the convexity of the life-time function.

A policy following the changes in program behavior should still be better. We can readily conceive of expanding the fixed local replacement algorithms, described previously, into global rules by considering the histories of all resident tasks rather than that of each of them individually. Thus, global FIFO, FINUFO and LRU, or at least some approximations thereof, exist in systems such as MULTICS and several versions of CP-67 and VS (virtual storage) System/370's. Experiments run on a CDC-STAR 100 have given results showing the superiority of global LRU over fixed (equipartition) LRU, with page fault ratio improvements as large as 3 to 1. When global LRU is used on the same program replicated twice, it behaves better than fixed LRU on each program to which would be given half of the actual main memory. This can be explained by one program temporarily stealing pages from the other, thus progressing more rapidly, and the processes being interleaved with changes in locality. But memory management under a global policy is subject to *"thrashing,"* or overcommittment of primary memory allocation. If the multiprogramming level is too high, pages will be taken from the least recently used program's resident set. But these pages will soon have to be recalled since this program is the next to be executed. Even if the load is well controlled, a task can lose some of its pages belonging to the current and next localities during locality transitions. Thus, both locality and load controls are required.

These controls are what the working set policies (approximations to and variants of the working set and PFF-like replacements) tend to achieve. The estimates of the working set sizes depend only on the individual programs and hence we can embed a provision in the policy that prevents the stealing of a page from the working set of a resident program. In order to do so, we use a supplementary task from which pages can be taken away. It would be the only one which would run with a PMA less than its working-set size. When (if ever) all its pages have been discarded, this is considered as the deallocation of the task and its role as a page source is given to another resident task. Tasks are allocated only if their working-set will fit in main memory.

Typical examples of memory management will be discussed in Section 4. We close this study of the replacement rules by mentioning a few facts about the handling of the associative page tables.

When the associative map contains only a few entries, like 8 to 16, the replacement of missing entries in the table follows quite closely the type of replacement used for pages and frames. For example, "clock" is used in MULTICS and a variant of it called "sweep" in System/360 Model 67. "Sweep" differs from "clock" in that if all entries have been referenced, the one in the first position will be replaced. When the "associative" map is a buffer of about a hundred entries, a hashing mechanism is used (cf. IBM System/370 and Amdahl 470/V6). In both cases the replacement can take place during the mapping and referencing process. To stress the importance of the associative map, recall that in the IBM System/370 Model 168 if the page entry is in the "associative" map, called Translation Lookaside Buffer (TLB), only 1 Pc cycle is necessary for the mapping, while if it is not there from 8 to 26 cycles can be spent in the table look-up (assuming no page fault).

6.2.3   Demand Paging and Prepaging

Up to now, we have always implied that pages were loaded in Mp only when they were accessed at page fault time. This loading rule is called *demand paging* and it is the only one implemented in production type virtual memory systems, except for the VAX/VMS system as described later. However, we could ask the following question, namely: can we predict future exceptions and preload a page, and, if this is possible, for which type of Mp-Ms interface is it beneficial? We must then differentiate between page faults, that is interruptions in the program, and page pulls, that is the number of pages transferred. Our attempt is to trade some improvement in the life-time function by having longer intervals between program interruptions with more page transfers since our predictions are not completely accurate. Again using the space-time product as a measure of cost, we can write (assuming fixed partitions):

$$SP = M(n + f_1\rho_1 + f_2\rho_2 + \cdots + f_k\rho_k) \tag{5}$$

with f_i being the number of page faults with i page transfers and ρ_i the cost to transfer these i pages. For example, ρ_1 will be equal to ρ as defined for equation (1). If we have an LCS type device for Ms, then ρ_1 will be the access time of a word in LCS multiplied by the page size in LCS and there would be no advantage, cost-wise, in doing even perfect predictions. But if the paging secondary memory is a FIFO drum, we can assume that the accessing time will be shared among the i transfers. For example, if $i = 2$ we can assume the average transfer time to be:

$$T_2 = t_a' + t_t$$

where t_a' will be the time to reach the second page, or 2/3 of the rotation, and t_t the time to transfer a page (the first one will already have been transferred since it will be found after a third of the revolution). Thus:

$$\frac{T_2}{T_1} = \frac{2/3\ t_r + t_t}{1/2\ t_r + t_t}\ .$$

Assuming 6 pages/track we would have:

$$\frac{T_2}{T_1} = \frac{2/3 + 1/6}{1/2 + 1/6} = \frac{5}{4}\ ,$$

and hence we could set ρ_2 to 1.25ρ.

Although bringing several pages at once might be cheaper, care must be exercised since other factors in the space time product can be influenced. First, if we have a fixed partition, M is constant and hence i pages have to be replaced if i are brought in. If we have a working-set like policy, then $\overline{M}$, the average PMA, is bigger. These constraints have limited most experimentations to attempt only a single page preloading. The prediction algorithm which appears to be most successful, when no information about the task is given, is as follows. With each (virtual) page p_i we associate another page called its predictee PRED(i). Initially PRED(i) is p_{i+1}. Let LAST (initially 0) be the page number of the last page for which a page fault occurred. When $r_t = p_i$ is an exception, we load p_i on demand, and if preloading has not occurred on the previous page fault, or if preloading occurred and the page preloaded was not referenced (incorrect prediction), we set PRED[LAST] to p_i. If PRED[i] is not already in Mp, we also preload that page. By updating PRED[LAST] we try to dynamically follow the program's behavior.

Experimental results have shown that such a policy is worth pursuing for small page sizes, that is when the number of page frames allocated is rather large. Since it appears that there is a trend towards smaller pages, we can envision the implementation of some preloading mechanism in future operating systems.

For example some prepaging is present in the operating system VAX/VMS for the DEC VAX 11/780 which is a paging machine with a small (128 word) page size. This prepaging can be done in one of two ways. First, a user can specify an "explicit" cluster of pages to be fetched together whenever a page fault to one of its members has occurred. Second, the system can impose a "default" cluster. When a page fault to a page not in an "explicit" cluster is recorded, the "default" cluster is brought in its entirety from Ms. Since it appears that only the size of the "default" cluster, and not its membership, is mentioned and since the operating system imposes a fixed primary memory allocation we can surmise that erroneous guesses in the "default" size are going to be paid dearly (initial measurements have confirmed this fact).

Specific prepaging algorithms have been investigated for programs manipulating mostly large arrays (matrix problems, large data bases). They are successful in that environment, but again their use has to be monitored with care.

6.3   SEGMENTED SYSTEMS

6.3.1   Segmentation (Stack Processors Revisited)

The division of tasks into parts of equal sizes is not a natural one. Programmatic entities such as procedures (or subroutines), local data associated to procedures, blocks, and arrays appear to be better units. The process of splitting a task into such units is called *segmentation*. The virtual memory concepts described previously for paging systems can be applied with a few modifications to segmented systems.

Segmented systems have addresses of the form (s_i, d_j) where s_i is a segment number and d_j a displacement within that segment. Associated with each task is a segment table, or map, giving the translation between the segment number and a real address which is the base address of the first word of the segment. The table also contains information on the length of the segment and extra bits or locks for protection purposes (e.g., read-only segment). As in paging systems, a register contains the address of the segment table for the current process. (From the operating system's viewpoint, a segment table is just another segment.)

Let us consider what happens during the address translation process (cf. Figure 6.12 in which we could have included some associative mapping to make it more like Figure 6.4). The (virtual) address is of the form (s_i, d_j), where s_i added to the contents of the segment table register (STP) points to the corresponding entry in the segment table. A flag indicates whether the segment is in Mp. If so, a check is performed to determine if d_j is greater than l_i the length of the segment. If it were, an error routine would be called and the program aborted. If it is not, then the protection locks are checked. Assuming that the operation is valid, d_j then is added (not concatenated) to the real address found in the table entry to yield the effective (real) address. Thus, if the segment is in Mp, this computation presents little difference from the one for a paging system. There is a better protection facility, which is linked to the program structure, but a slightly more complex mechanism since an addition is required to form the final address.

Now consider the case where the segment is not in Mp. The first task is to check if there is room for the segments, i.e., if there exists in Mp a free area

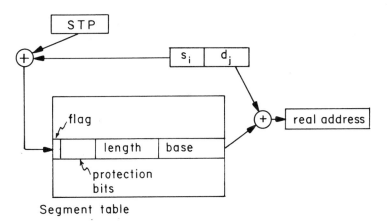

Segment table

Figure 6.12   Address translation in a segmented system

of length l_i. To do this, the structure of information in Mp must be closely examined. This information is generally in the form of two linked lists, one for the reserved segments, those currently in use by the loaded task, and one free list, or list of available space (LAVS). The latter is often implemented as a singly linked list of segments sorted in ascending order of their base address. Each free segment also carries its size. A snapshot of Mp at a given instant will have the checkerboard appearance of Figure 6.13 where only the structure of LAVS is shown in detail. FIRST is a pointer to the first free segment. The first word of each segment contains its size and a pointer to the next segment (fields SIZE and LINK).

Given a missing segment of size L, the following algorithm, named FIRST-FIT, reserves an Mp area for it, if possible.

FIRST-FIT Algorithm

1. Set $Q \leftarrow$ FIRST (we assume at least one block (or segment) in LAVS. This restriction can be easily eliminated);
2. If $SIZE(Q) > L$, then assign to s_i a segment of size L at address $Q + SIZE(Q) - L$; Set $SIZE(Q)$ to $SIZE(Q) - L$ and return successfully;
3. If $SIZE(Q) = L$ then assign to s_i the segment pointed to by Q; Delete the segment from the list (this involves simple pointer manipulations on which we do not elaborate); return successfully;
4. If $SIZE(Q) < L$, then if $LINK(Q) \neq$ NIL (where $Q =$ NIL indicates the end of the list) set $Q \leftarrow LINK(Q)$ and return to step 2, otherwise return unsuccessfully.

In general, step 2 will be of the form "If $SIZE(Q) > L + C$" where C is some constant of the system (for example 11 in the Burrough B5500). This is to prevent small blocks of size less than C from accumulating, since such small blocks are never requested. Naturally step 3 has to be changed to:

$$\text{"If } L \leq SIZE(Q) \leq L + C\text{".}$$

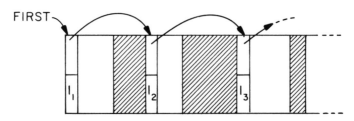

Figure 6.13   Checkerboarded memory (dashed blocks are reserved)

There are many variations of this algorithm which are beyond the scope of this book and which can be found in texts on data structures. We mention this particular method because it is good for our requirements (the variations in segment sizes and their life-times), and because it is the one used in the Burroughs B5000-B6000 series, the paradigm for segmented system as described here. In these machines, the searching process is assisted by the hardware with a special instruction called LINKED LIST LOOK UP.

If the reservation algorithm returns successfully, the Mp area is allocated to the segment, adequate entries are stored in the segment table, the reserved list is modified, and the task can be resumed. If the reservation fails, we have the choice between compaction and replacement.

Compaction consists of moving free blocks into one continuous area of memory and reserved blocks into another. After this process, the LAVS has only one block; hopefully, it has a large enough size to fulfill the request.

The problems with compaction are that, (1) it is time consuming, and (2) since reserved blocks are moved, segment table entries must be modified. This implies that reserved segments carry their segment table address, or that there exists a master list of all segments (this will be also useful for sharing purposes as will be seen later). In the latter case, the master list, itself a segment which is not movable, is updated. Copies of the relevant updates are sent to each segment table. In the B6700 this is facilitated by a special hardware instruction performing the equivalent of an associative search.

Replacement is equivalent to a page replacement algorithm. The only difference is that a large enough block must be replaced. The reserved area being a (doubly) linked list, insertion and deletion are easy to perform. Once a block has been selected for replacement, changes must be made in the segment tables owning it as in the compaction procedure. However, only a single block will be replaced and this requires much less overhead.

The choice then is a question of assessing the cost of a secondary-primary access versus the compaction time. In the Burroughs machine, replacement was the solution which was chosen. One reason is that there is no segment table for a given task. Rather a "stack" vector points to a stack number for each task. In that stack are constants and simple variables, as well as descriptors for other segments such as procedures, blocks and arrays. An address can be viewed as having the form $a \cdot b \cdot c \cdot d$, where a is a stack number, b a location within that stack, c (possibly omitted) a descriptor, i.e., a pointer to another segment, and d a displacement within that segment. Of course, d could also be a descriptor which would then have an "e" following it and so on. To speed-up the process, base registers are used to point directly to some lower levels in the segment hierarchy. A disadvantage is the number of memory cycles needed for an address translation, that is the number of indirect references. Since the descriptor itself carries information on its status, there is no table look-up and no limitation in the number of possible segments other than the length of a descriptor; in other words, it is unlimited for all practical purposes.

Within a paging system, there is no checkerboarding of Mp and hence no main memory unused, except for some vacant space at the end of the last page. This internal fragmentation has to be contrasted to the external fragmentation incurred in a segmented system. There, the LAVS often contains small free blocks which are not claimed because of their limited size. Direct comparisons are difficult. For example using the modification of the FIRST-FIT algorithm (that is with the use of a constant C), there is some internal fragmentation in the segmented system and, by deliberate choice, a diminished external fragmentation. Quoting Denning "fragmentation is not as serious in practice as it could be, but then again it cannot be ignored".

Another problem which appears in segmented systems as described thus far is that some segments might be unduly large, e.g., a few thousand words. Two possibilities can be used to circumvent the problem: the first one is to limit the size of segments (e.g., 1024 words is the maximum for the Burroughs B5500), and the second is to split large segments into pages.

The first solution is not appealing since it is really in contradiction with the philosophy of the method. For example, if the segment size is limited to 1000 words, a vector of 2000 elements should be restructured as a two-dimensional array of 2 $\times$ 1000 (at the cost of one more descriptor reference per access). The second solution can lead to a generalization of segmentation which we now consider.

6.3.2 Segmentation and Paging

Segmentation and paging can be combined in two ways. When the paging philosophy is the dominating factor, we have what has been called *linear segmentation*. On the other hand, when the segmentation viewpoint is carried over we have a *segmented name space*. In both cases, segments are now divided into pages. A (virtual) address is of the form (s_i, p_j, d_l) where s_i is a segment number, p_j a page number within the segment, and d_l a displacement within the page. A segment consists of one or more pages. The address translation mechanism is summarized in Figure 6.14. A register (STP) points to the current segment page table. Let us assume that s_l has already been referenced and has a corresponding entry in the table. Then, associated with this entry is a pointer to a page table. Entry j in the page table indicates whether there exists a corresponding frame or whether there is a page fault. In the former case, the real address is finally computed by concatenating the

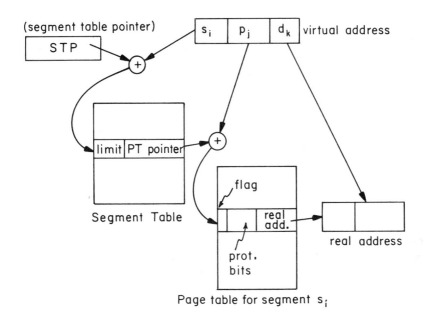

Figure 6.14   Segmented (and paged) address translation

displacement to the entry in the page table. Page faulting will be handled as in paging systems. The case of a missing s_i entry in the segment table is more lengthy to examine. We shall return to this problem of "making the segment known".

From Figure 6.14 we see that the protection for out of range addresses is now in the segment tables (the limit field) while protection bits are in the page tables. This latter choice is mandatory for linear segmentation but not for segmented name implementations, where protection bits could, and should, appear in the segment table. This distinction will become clear. But the most important observation is that an address translation is done through two indirect references instead of one as in pure paged or pure segmented systems. Thus the penalty can be extremely severe unless some associative mapping and/or fast buffers are used for the mapping. This is why current segmented virtual memory systems such as those implemented in the IBM System/370 Model 168 or the Amdahl 470 V/6 have large translation look-aside buffers (TLB).

These last two systems employ a linear segmentation scheme. This is simply an extension of paging and there is no program-related meaning to the notion of segment. In the IBM System/370 Model 168, there are 256 possible segments each having either 32 pages of 2K or 16 pages of 4K bytes. Figure 6.15 shows the two virtual address formats for this mechanism which allows segments of 64K bytes (some operating systems allow segments of 1024K bytes). The advantage of linear segmentation over paging is that it reduces the number of page entries for a given program. But it is worthwhile only if the TLB is large enough to avoid most segment and page table references. We shall return to this system in more detail in the next section.

By contrast, the segmented name space can be conceived as a set of linear name spaces. Each logical entity (task) is itself a segment (hence our previous comments on the position of protection bits). In MULTICS, there exists the possibility of 2^{18} segments of 2^8 pages of 2^{10} words. It is in this type of system that the "segment made known" procedure can be complex.

A complete discussion of how this is handled is outside the scope of this book and special publications on MULTICS or a text on operating systems should be consulted (cf. Section 6). We offer only a brief explanation of the effective address computations and a simplistic overview of the dynamic linking.

One possibility would be to have a linking-loader examine which segments are in a given process, where a process is a set of associated tasks. It would then fill the segment table of that process with the entries corresponding to these segments. This static binding is the one used in the Burroughs B6700. However, in MULTICS all linking is dynamic and segments are referenced symbolically. This accrues generality, protection, sharing, and ease in system programming (MULTICS is written in PL/1). Of course, a new dimension of complexity is added. To help dynamic linking, the following hardware is provided:

- a descriptor base register (DBR) (or STP in Figure 6.14). It will be the only register whose contents are a real address;
- a procedure base register (PBR) which points to the entry in the segment table corresponding to the current executing procedure;
- an instruction counter (IC) which contains the displacement (in the following we shall call displacement the 18 bit corresponding to (page + displacement field)) within the current procedure;
- 8 address base registers;
- 2 working registers;
- 4 pairs of pointer registers pointing to segments different from the one containing the current executing procedure.

We have two types of instructions (cf. Figure 6.16), one corresponding to internal references within the current procedure, say CP, and one to external

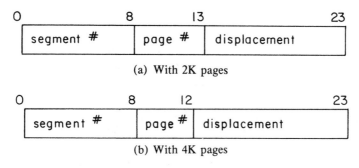

(a) With 2K pages

(b) With 4K pages

Figure 6.15   (Virtual) Address formats in the IBM System 370/ Model 168

references. They are distinguished by the value of bit 29 in the instruction, and hence the names of type 0 for internal and type 1 for external reference.

The formation of the next effective instruction address is immediate if it is within CP. The contents of IC are added to the address pointed to by the entry pointed to by PBR (note that one indirect reference has been avoided). In case of (internal) branching, the standard modifications are made.

Since sharing is at the core of the MULTICS system, procedures will generally be reentrant and therefore data will be in different segments. Associated with each procedure segment is a local, or stack, data segment and a linkage segment needed for the linkage between procedures and non-local data. Non-local data, as well as arguments for and locations of called procedures, will be obtained indirectly through the linkage segment. With some simplification, we can state that the 4 pairs of pointer registers point re-

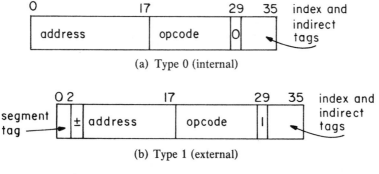

(a) Type 0 (internal)

(b) Type 1 (external)

Figure 6.16   Instruction formats in MULTICS

spectively to the stack, linkage, argument and base (or general data) segments.

Let us see how a direct address reference is handled. This is the general mode for local data. In the Type 1 instruction format, 15 bits are devoted to an operand address. A six bit tag indicates whether index addressing is to be done. If so, one of 8 registers is chosen. The segment tag (3 bits) points to one of the 8 registers forming the 4 pairs. This register holds an "external" address, i.e., a pointer to an entry in the segment table. But if one of its control bits is on, as is always the case in the current system, it must be considered in association with another (hence the pairing) which contains an "internal" address and which acts as a second index register. The generalized (indexed direct) address calculation is summarized in Figure 6.17. It must be followed by the mapping of Figure 6.14 (although there is a possibility of speed-up to shunt the DBR reference).

Indirect addressing is very important in MULTICS since it allows a program to travel from segment to segment. Unlike most machines with indirect addressing, there is no limitation in the number of levels of indirection. Indirect addressing is determined by the tag bits in the right hand side of the instruction formats and exists in both type 0 and type 1 instructions. Upon indirect addressing, a double word is fetched from the direct address computed as before. The rightmost six bits of the first word, tag 1, indicate whether indirect addressing is to be continued (format *its* or indirect transfer

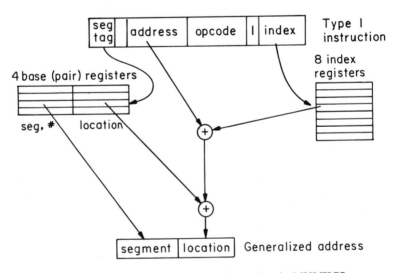

Figure 6.17   Generalized address formation in MULTICS

through segment), or has reached its last level (format *itb* or indirect transfer through base). In the first case, (cf. Figure 6.18) the indirect double word of address:

field 1 $\square$ field 2 + contents (index tag)   ($\square$ is the concatenate operator)

is fetched, and the contents of tag 1 is retested. In the second case, the word at the address computed as above is the final address.

This indirect addressing process is used for dynamic linking. A reference to an external (symbolic) segment, say s_j, will be compiled as an indirect reference to a (double) word in the linkage segment of the compiled procedure. We have assumed that all segments had entries in the segment table. The first time through however, the linkage section will indicate the absence of a link to s_j. A call to the supervisor will take place. The directory is searched for the symbolic segment name. If the segment has already been referenced by another procedure in the same process, its local name in the segment table is returned and the linkage segment appropriately updated. If it has not yet been referenced by the current process, then a new entry is made in the local segment table and again the linkage segment is updated as before. Although the segment is not known by the process, it might be "known" by another, and some (or all) of its pages might be in Mp. The two instances of the same segment have different local names but they share the same page table. We have just described how sharing is done in that case (cf. Figure 6.19). After this first call to the unlinked segment s_j, all subsequent references from CP to s_j will encounter a known segment and proceed as explained in the previous paragraph.

This dynamic binding presents numerous advantages for protection between tasks. Most of the steps needed for the generalized address calculation are handled by special hardware registers. Sharing is simple and static linking is avoided.

As an aside, we stated earlier that sharing in a paging system was difficult. The same is true for a linear segmented space. The sharing is also not very convenient for a name segmented space with static binding. One possibility

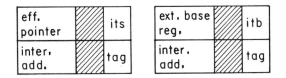

Figure 6.18 Doubleword entries for indirection in MULTICS

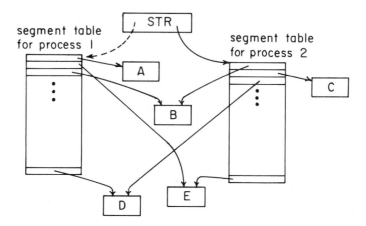

Figure 6.19   Sharing in a segmented name space (A, B, ..., are page tables)

would be to have a segment table for shared segments. But this might require one more level of indirection. In the Burroughs B6700, which does not have segment tables, sharing of library routines is made possible by giving them a large virtual name (there are many routines which have some preassigned names).

At this point we shall compare the behavior of programs running under a paging or a segmented system.

6.3.3 Segmentation vs. Paging. Program Behavior

After having discussed the various implementations of virtual memory systems, we shall examine and try to see the advantages and disadvantages as well as the overall limitations of each scheme.

Let us first consider the hardware requirements. The mapping devices, associative memory or TLB, and parts of the page and/or segment tables can be realized by small inexpensive TLB's. If those "associative" memories are sufficiently large then the overhead of address translation will be negligible. However, the Mp requirements for the page and segment tables can be quite large and inject a third form of fragmentation, or unused space. This table fragmentation is due to the fact that page table space has to be reserved for the worst case, i.e., for all pages of the given task or segment even if they are not all going to be referenced. No conclusive data exists for this third form of fragmentation which can nonetheless be considered of little importance. An alternative is to page the page tables with the unlikely risk of having two page faults for a single memory reference.

Another inherent problem of virtual memory that we have not discussed yet is the handling of I/O. Most of the time, channels (cf. Chapter 8) do not have access to the hardware map and are given real addresses for commands and data. Hence, the supervisor must translate virtual addresses into real ones and be aware of potential non-contiguity when transferring data from buffer to user's PMA, and vice-versa. Furthermore, those frames involved in the transfer should not be disrupted until the completion of the I/O process and should not be available for replacement. Therefore, the supervisor has to trace all memory references in the channel program to insure correct operating conditions. The time overhead can be quite significant.

In terms of mapping, paging systems, or segmented systems with paging, are certainly simpler to implement. Furthermore, the placement rule is avoided, hence limiting the overhead at page fault time. Naturally, the division of tasks into pages is quite arbitrary and a lot of effort has been and is still under way to tailor program behavior to paging environments. This need not be done in segmented systems wherein the division into segments is the logical one.

Interesting statistics have been gathered by Batson and his co-workers on segment sizes for ALGOL 60 programs running on a Burroughs B5500. We summarize some of their results here, but the reader is warned that generalizations should be avoided because of the nature of the language (block-structure) and of the machine. However, some tentative conclusions can be drawn and applied to a more customary environment.

The statistics are for three types of segments: code, local data, and array data. Two types of measurements were made: static measures involving all segments loaded in Mp each considered once, and dynamic measures where the sizes were weighted by the number of times a segment was entered and exited during the course of the computation. In general, static measures had higher means and variances than dynamic ones, thus giving credence to the belief that small segments are more important. But the most important conclusion is that for all 3 types the segment sizes were small, with means of the order of 100 words (approximately 400 instructions, cf. Chapter 4, Section 6) in the static and 40 words in the dynamic cases for code, and with sizes of less than 30 words for 90% of the local data segments, and of less than 125 words for 90% of the arrays. The mean for data segments is much larger because of the presence of a few large blocks.

These statistics have at least two interesting implications for the design of virtual memory systems. The first is that in a segmented system we shall have many small blocks. Therefore the placement rule might be lengthy since long lists will have to be traversed; compaction time could be horrendous and thus is to be avoided. Second, the placement of segments into pages does not have to be an arbitrary process. Since segments are small, a few of them can be clustered in the same page. Improving program behavior can be done by a judicious choice of program restructuring.

The loading and linking process used in non-virtual systems consists of setting a "go-file" which contains a relocatable binary form of the task. In general, the loader processes subroutines and associated data in the order given by the programmer and then follows up with routines taken from the library. For production programs, recompilation is not done for the whole task but only for those routines to be modified. The loader's layout might quickly become a rather random arrangement which does not reflect the connectivity of various elements of the program. Splitting it into pages might produce unwanted results, such as separating code from its associated local data, or code loops crossing page boundaries. In order to avoid these disastrous effects, program restructuring can be done by the following three proposed approaches:

- a priori, by the compiler and/or the loader on information gathered by the compiler;
- dynamically, during the program's execution;
- a posteriori, after the program's execution and in preparation for the next execution.

Difficulties in handling the map have prevented the implementation of the second solution. The first one has been proposed mainly to restructure code in small pages and could be of interest for cache memories (cf. Section 5), although recent work has shown its feasibility for larger page sizes. The last one can be implemented in two ways. The first method consists of tracing the program, gathering statistics on the connectivity between various segments, and then applying a clustering program to assemble in the same set of pages those segments which are highly bonded. Spectacular results have been obtained in reducing page faults but the overhead price is quite high. The second method consists of monitoring inter-segment instructions which yield page faults. A clustering algorithm is then applied according to this information. The process must be repeated at least twice, so that perturbations caused by restructuring will not counterbalance a structure which may have been correct initially.

Program restructuring is not the only answer to improving program behavior. Since most page faults are produced by data references, the program data structures must be carefully laid out. Although the virtual memory scheme is transparent to the programmer, knowledge of the virtual memory environment and of parameters such as the page size are of paramount importance to the efficient programmer.

6.4 REPLACEMENT ALGORITHMS—TWO IMPLEMENTATIONS

In Section 2 we discussed a number of replacement algorithms. We now outline how the two most popular ones, global LRU and pure working set, are approached in production systems. There is no special hardware involved, that is neither shifting stack-like associative memory for LRU, nor MANIAC II-like registers for the working set strategy.

6.4.1 LRU Implementation in OS/VS

Global LRU is approximated in the operating systems for the IBM System/ 370 Model 168. A series of operating systems has been designed for this machine but our subject of discussion, the handling of page replacements, has remained essentially the same.

The addressing structure using linear segmentation has been described before. OS/VS1 has pages of 2K bytes while OS/VS2 can have 2K or 4K bytes (cf. Figure 6.15). A translation look-aside buffer (TLB) of 128 entries serves the role of an associative memory. A virtual address is "hashed" in order to get its corresponding entry in the TLB. Up to six "virtual spaces" (tasks) can have entries concurrently in the TLB. When a new task is initiated and given its turn to execute, the entries in the TLB corresponding to the first (in a FIFO sense) of the other six are invalidated. The hardware involved for this bookkeeping is simply a set of six registers containing the origin (virtual) address of each task. A control register contains the identification of the currently executing task (ID) and each TLB entry has a field containing that ID. An ID of 0 indicates an invalid entry.

In addition to the ID, the virtual and the corresponding real addresses, an entry in the TLB has a field for storage protection, for a reference bit turned on by a reference to an address in the frame, and for a change bit turned on by a store to an address in the frame.

The frames are divided into four sets: available, page I/O, fixed, and active. Each set has one or more FIFO queues.

The available frames form a queue. At initialization time, all frames are available except those reserved for the nucleus of the operating system. As tasks are initiated, or as page faults occur, frames will be taken from the available queue. There is also a mechanism (to be described) to insert frames into the available queue when a page is replaced. The number of available frames is always kept above a given threshold H, a parameter set at system generation time which must be such that it is neither too small (in order to avoid thrashing) nor too large (so that unoccupied Mp is not wasted and thus preventing tasks from being initiated).

The page I/O frames form two queues. The input queue contains the addresses of the frames that are to be filled. These frames are taken from the available queue. The output queue contains the addresses of the frames whose contents have to be written back to Ms. Once this "push" is finished, the frame address can be inserted into the available queue.

The fixed frames contain those critical parts of the operating system which cannot be paged, for example the routine which handles page faults! There is a provision for allowing users to be able to "fix" some of their pages.

The active queues contain those pages used by initiated programs, i.e., those forming the current multiprogramming load. The queues are ranked according to an activity criterion with the high activity queue containing the most recently referenced frames. The ranking of a frame in a queue is done at intervals depending on program interruptions and quantum terminations. At these times, frames which have been referenced since the last ranking are moved to the high activity queue with their reference bit turned off. This is easily done by looking at the reference bit which is present not only in the TLB but also in the page tables. The frames which are not referenced during that interval are moved down from queue activity n to queue activity $(n - 1)$. When a page is supposed to leave the lowest activity queue, it either joins the available queue if the change bit is off (we have a "clean" page), or the output queue (we have a "dirty" page). The process is summarized in Figure 6.20.

The passage from a low activity queue to a non-active queue might happen when a page fault occurs. Assume first that the request is for a single page, that is there is no program initiation nor recall from a program which had been deallocated and is now to be reallocated. The page I/O output queue and the available queue are first scanned. If the missing page is found there, it is given back to the faulting task. If it is not there, or if there is a need for more than one page as in the cases just mentioned, then the system has to act with caution in order to avoid thrashing. Let A be the number of pages requested and C the number of pages in the available queue. If $R = C - (A + H)$ is positive, A pages are taken from the available queue and there is no transfer from the lowest activity queue. If R is not positive, then the lowest activity queue is interrogated. Frames which have not been referenced join the available and output queues as explained above until R is reached. If it is not possible to grant the request of A frames then a task must be deactivated.

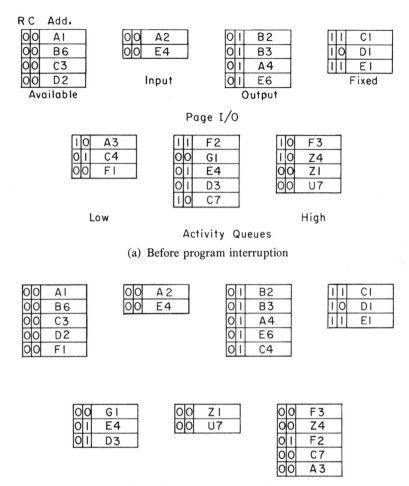

Page I/O

(a) Before program interruption

(b) After program interruption

Figure 6.20   System queues in OS/VS

The selection is done according to priorities fixed at system generation time. Similarly potential reactivation is checked periodically. It depends on the number of pages needed versus the size of C.

As can be seen, the high activity queue represents the top of the LRU stack. The stack instead of being changed at every memory reference is modified only at rather lengthy intervals. No special hardware is needed, and the approximation is sufficient so long as the multiprogramming level is well monitored (i.e., so long as H is well chosen).

6.4.2 Working-Set Implementation in VMOS

A working-set management strategy is approximated in the Virtual Memory Operating System (VMOS) for the Spectra (UNIVAC) Series 70 systems. The hardware of these machines resembles closely that of the IBM System/360 Model 67. From the paging mechanism viewpoint, it is not very different from the Model 168. Pages are 4K bytes and segments are used only to differentiate tasks. Page table and AM entries have reference and change bits.

In VMOS, tasks can be either active or inactive. If active, they are either using the Pc, ready to use it, waiting for a page I/O, or waiting for a peripheral I/O. Only active tasks can compete for Mp. Inactive tasks can become active only if the addition of their working-sets, or estimates (with the estimation procedure to be presented below), is such that:

$$\sum_{j=1}^{i} WS_j \leq |Mp| < \sum_{j=1}^{i+1} WS_j$$

where WS_j, $1 \leq j \leq i + 1$ are the estimates of the resident, or resident-to-be, tasks and $|Mp|$ is the primary memory allocated to the multiprogrammed tasks. This deliberate overcommitment is justified by two facts: the estimates are pessimistic and tend to yield maximum memory sizes, and a minimum of 8 pages is given to every task. Since this system is a highly interactive one, a significant proportion of tasks will be waiting for peripheral (terminal) I/O and can be deactivated harmlessly. Thus, even if this overcommitment is indeed real, thrashing will be avoided by task deallocation.

The reference bit is used in order to approximate the working-set policy. The following (somewhat simplified) scanning routine is activated:

- at page fault time for the faulting task;
- at least every 4000 task instructions (as monitored by the Pc clock);
- for all tasks on peripheral I/O wait, only when the Pc is to become idle.

These last two cases are for Pc bound and I/O bound tasks which are non faulting.

The scanning routine checks the reference bit. If it has been turned on, it is turned off and the corresponding frame is given a "count" of the cumulative Pc time since the bit has been checked on. If it is off, the off-time, that is the cumulative Pc time since it has been checked off, is checked and the following actions take place:

- If off-time > MAX (some system parameter), the frame joins the output queue or the available queue depending on the change bit;
- If MIN < off-time < MAX (MIN is another system parameter) the page is not freed but joins an LRU queue. In essence this queue contains the next pages to be released when needed;
- If off-time < MIN the page remains in its task's working-set and its off-time is updated. Therefore, a page is protected for at least MIN time.

Estimation of the working-set is simple. The initial size is 8 pages. After each page fault, the previous estimate is increased by one and after pages are sent to the available and output queues, the estimate is decreased by the number of pages sent. However, the estimate is always kept at at least 8 pages.

At page fault time one out of three alternatives might occur:

- If the page is still in Mp, it is given back to the faulting task's working-set;
- If the current task's working set is less than its estimate, then the following are tried in order until one succeeds:
  a) Take a frame from the available queue. Initiate a read from Ms for the missing page.
  b) Take a frame from the output queue. Initiate a write for Ms and, at completion, a read from Ms.
  c) Take the front page of the LRU queue of the task. Initiate a read or a write-read as needed. (Note that pages can leave the LRU queue if they have been rereferenced since their insertion.)
  d) Deactivate the task. Include the members of its working set in the available or output queues.
- If the working-set of the current task has reached its estimate, then the actions are as above but in the order:
  (c) —
  (a) and increase estimate by one
  (b) and increase estimate by one
  (d) —

The rationale behind these decisions is that a task which has not reached its estimate should try and reach it and should not lose pages since then the Mp is overcommited and there is a high risk of thrashing.

A task which has reached its estimate is supposedly in a steady-state (locality-wise). Hence, if it has extraneous frames, they should be released or this private pool should be used first if needed.

A number of details have been omitted. For example, writing of the output queue does not have to be initiated solely at page fault time. It is also worth noting that task deallocation is not a scheduling function but is enforced by the paging algorithm.

6.5 CACHE MEMORIES

6.5.1 Cache Systems and Paging Systems

The virtual memory concept is not limited to the Mp-Ms interface. With the advent of fast inexpensive RAM memories, instruction and operand fetch times can be matched with Pc execution times by providing buffers of nontrivial size at a reasonable cost. As we saw in Chapter 4, instruction look-ahead is mandatory for powerful processors; cache memories will provide this look-ahead capability as well as a fast scratchpad area for operands.

The term "cache" was coined by Conti; the first realization appeared in the IBM System/360 Model 85. Since then, caches have been present in the product lines of most medium to large computers and even in large minicomputers such as the PDP 11/70 and 11/60 and the Data General ECLIPSE.

Conceptually, there is only a small difference between a cache system and a paging system. The implementations, however, are far apart because of speed constraints. In a paging system, the ratio of access times between Mp and Ms is approximately 4 orders of magnitude. In the cache-Mp case, it will be only one, since caches are random access memories of access time of less than 100 ns. (e.g., 50 ns.) for an Mp access time of .5 to 1 μs. A missing-item fault is very costly in a paging system, and hence the page fault rate should be of the order of 10^{-4}. In a cache, it can be a few percent without unduly slowing down the system.

Because of these timing facts, it is evident that a missing item fault in a cache has to be handled by the hardware. The operating system must not be involved since a call to it would take longer than the reference to the addressed word in the missing item. Also, the missing item size must be matched to the speed of the secondary memory, Mp. Therefore missing-items, hereafter called *blocks*, will be a few words long. Because of the blocks' sizes, a completely general mapping is out of the question since the map would be as large as the cache itself. The different implementations that we describe next will be variations on specific mapping themes that will tend to be as general as possible.

While blocks will be loaded on demand, writing each "dirty" block will be done in one of two manners, the choice often being dictated by the map implementation: either we will wait until the block has to be replaced, or every word to which a store is made will be written back in the cache and in Mp simultaneously. The former policy will be called a "write back" policy and the latter will be referred to as a "write through" policy. The replacement algorithms will be less elaborate than in paging systems since they are implemented only in hardware. We now present several potential cache organizations.

6.5.2 Cache Organization

Cache organizations differ primarily in the way blocks in Mp are mapped into blocks in the cache. Secondary effects are cache size, block size which in general corresponds to the amount of information transferred from Mp to the cache on a missing-item fault, the write back policy, and the replacement algorithm. We start by describing the original cache system implemented in the IBM System/360 Model 85, called sector organization.

Sector Organization

The cache and Mp are divided into sectors, or pages (cf. Figure 6.21). A sector in Mp can map into any sector in the cache. However, sectors are not the items which will be transferred. This is due to the following two reasons:

- If the sector size is large enough, like a few hundred words, then the transfer would be too time consuming leaving the Pc idle for several microseconds;
- If the sector size is too small, then the mapping device is too large.

Therefore, we keep sectors large enough so that the mapping device is small and we divide sectors into blocks of a few words. The block size is related to the memory interleaving so that all words of the block can be transferred in one Mp cycle time from Mp to the cache. Naturally, we need some marking device to identify those blocks in the cache which belong to the currently mapped sector. A "valid" bit is used for this purpose (cf. Figure 6.21.b). Thus, the replacement algorithm will work sector by sector and within a sector blocks have fixed positions. A tag is also associated with each sector, indicating the Mp sector to which it corresponds.

The Pc retrieves the contents of a given word in the following manner. The address is divided into three components (s_i, b_j, d_k) as in a linear segmented system. The high-order bits s_i correspond to the sector. The first action is then an (associative) search of the tags in the cache to see whether one corresponds to s_i.

If there is a match, then b_j is an index for the block in that sector. The validity bit corresponding to b_j is checked: if it is valid, d_k is the index of the addressed word in the block.

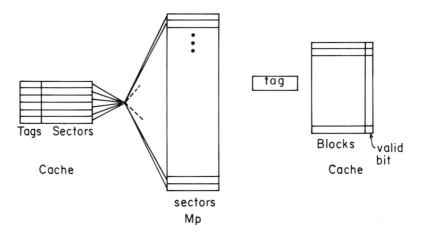

Figure 6.21   Cache with sector organization

If there is a match on s_i and the valid bit of b_j is off, this indicates the correct sector but a wrong block. The correct block is fetched from Mp and stored in its preassigned place in the cache's corresponding sector. The current components of that block are overwritten and the valid bit is turned on.

If s_i does not match this indicates a sector fault. A sector has to be replaced to make room for s_i. After the replacement algorithm chooses such an s_a, the tag is modified to reflect the presence of s_i and b_j is read into its assigned location. All valid bits in the sector are turned off except that of b_j which is turned on.

A write through policy is almost mandatory here since otherwise it may be necessary to write back a complete sector at replacement time. It is not possible to write back on a block per block basis since an invalid block could be part of a sector replaced long ago and whose address has therefore been discarded.

In the IBM System/360 Model 85, the cache contains 16 sectors of 1K bytes (for a total capacity of 4K words). Each sector is divided into 16 blocks of 64 bytes. When a block is brought in the cache on a block fault, the accessed word is fetched first and sent in parallel to the Pc and to the cache (in fact a double word is sent). The rest of the 64 bytes follows since the memory is 4-way interleaved. A write through policy is used. The replacement algorithm is true LRU. The hardware to do this is not extensive since there are only 16 sectors.

Direct Mapping Organization

This organization does not have sectors. Blocks are of size geared to optimal transfer as in the previous scheme. Since sectors are absent each block carries its own tag. In order to reduce the size of the map, each block has a preassigned location in the cache. For a cache of N blocks, blocks k, $k + N$, $k + 2N$, etc. ..., of Mp will be mapped into block k of the cache. The b_j bits of the (s_i, b_j, d_k) address therefore designate the cache block, and the tag has to match the high-order s_i bits in order to have the correct block. Notice that in such an organization there is no associative searching to be done, no valid bit, and no need for a replacement algorithm. An entry in the cache can be viewed as a pair "tag-block" (cf. Exercise 19).

In terms of additional hardware and control, this is a very simple organization. However, efficiency problems might occur due to poor placement of programs and/or data. For example, in a loop for the addition of two vectors, both vectors and the program could be placed in blocks of addresses corresponding to multiples of N thus sharing the same cache block. Conflicts would occur at every memory reference. This is the main drawback of this organization (nonetheless implemented on the PDP 11/60 with blocks of 1 word).

Set Associative Organization

This type of implementation maintains the simplicity of the direct mapping scheme almost in its entirety. However, some flexibility is added by allowing Mp blocks to be in a set of contiguous cache blocks (cf. Figure 6.22). For example, if we have N blocks in the cache, we can divide these N blocks into $N/2$ sets. Now, Mp blocks 0, $N/2$, N, $3N/2$ etc ... map into set 0, Mp blocks k, $N/2 + k$, etc ... into set k. The "middle order" bits designate a set and the "high-order" bits are to be matched against one of the tags of the blocks in the set. Therefore there is a limited searching (maximum number of comparisons equals the number of blocks in a set) and a local replacement algorithm within a set.

Figure 6.23 shows the layout of the cache in the IBM System/370 Model 165. The buffer is 8K bytes (or 16K); the blocks are 32 bytes. As in the Model 85, there is a 4-way interleaving of memories and the 8 bytes addressed first are brought in parallel in the cache and in Pc. The buffer contains 256 blocks grouped in 64 sets (columns) of 4 blocks each. Similarly, Mp is laid out into "columns" (modulo 32 bytes, modulo 64 columns, i.e., modulo 2048 bytes). Each block of Mp can occupy any of the 4 blocks in the corresponding set of the cache. When reference is made to a block, field d_j of the address yields the column and field s_i the block. Field s_i is compared with the 4 possible ad-

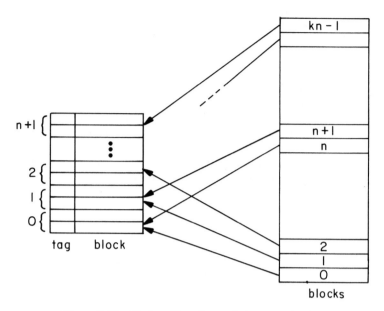

Figure 6.22   Cache with set associative organization

dresses (in the address array) of present blocks. These 4 addresses are shifted locally under a LRU scheme for possible replacement.

The PDP 11/70 also has two blocks per set; the block size is only two words and a "random" replacement algorithm is used (cf. Chapter 9 Section 3.5).

In the Amdahl 470 V/6, cache optimization is pushed further. The buffer is divided into two halves of 8K bytes each. Each half contains 256 32-byte (8 word) blocks. In addition to the tag, each block has bits identifying the words which have been changed while the block was in use. Write back of these words is done at block replacement time. The replacement algorithm is LRU between each corresponding block of the two halves. A single bit per block in one of the two halves is thus sufficient. The cache can be loaded either from Mp or from a channel.

To retrieve a word, the blocks corresponding to the "middle-order" address bits in the two halves of the cache are read simultaneously. The tags are then compared to the "high order" bits and the word in the matching block, if any, is delivered to the Pc. If there is no match, the block replacement is similar to that of the model 165 described previously.

There is no difficulty in implementing a write back policy in the cases of direct mapping and set associative organizations. At block replacement time,

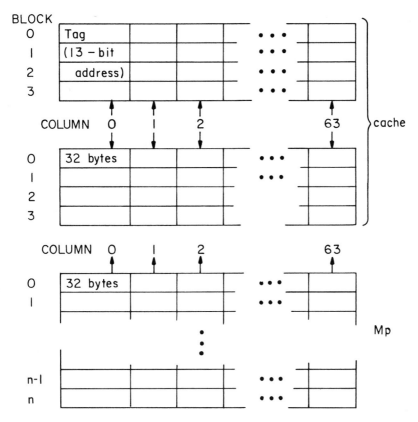

Figure 6.23 Cache organization for the IBM System/370 Model 165

the placement in the cache indicates the b_j bits and the tags associated with each block in the cache carry the s_i bits.

Yet, there exists an additional difficulty. In most systems which have a cache, I/O operations can proceed in parallel with computations performed by the Pc. Let us look at the implications that this has on the cache's design. We first consider the case of a transfer from Mp to Ms (or any I/O device). To make the example more concrete, we assume that a frame at address L_0, and of size p, is to be written back on Ms. If a write through policy is implemented then the information in Mp is correct and the transfer can proceed without having to worry about the cache. If write back is used, there might be some blocks in the cache images of blocks in Mp, at addresses between L_0 and $L_0 + p$, that contain some information which has been modified in the cache and not in Mp. Before the transfer, these blocks must be written back. However, many such blocks could exist, thus slowing down unduly the process currently in possession of the Pc. To take care of this problem, we may want to have all transfers to and from Mp pass through the cache. Then, the information present in the cache will always be correct. The drawback of this method, implemented in the Amdahl 470 V/6, is that the cache access is more complex since there are more sources for request (therefore, a priority mechanism has to be built in the access mechanism), and also there are more opportunities for block conflicts. However, this solution solves the problems of transfers to and from Mp.

With the write through policy, there is no difficulty in the transfer from Mp to Ms. But, consider the transfer of a page from Ms to that same frame at address L_0 in Mp. There might still be some blocks in the cache images of the information contained in the frame which is being replaced. Therefore, the cache has to "listen" to what is happening on the I/O bus and mark as invalid those blocks at addresses between L_0 and $L_0 + p$ (this is the solution chosen in the IBM 370/168 and in the VAX 11/780), or replace those blocks with the information being transferred.

6.5.3   Evaluation of a Cache System

As in a paging system, a number of parameters influence the performance of a cache, namely: cache size, block size and addressing structure. The impact of the replacement algorithm is minimal and the write back policy has not been shown to be a main factor.

The common metric used to measure the efficiency of a cache system is the *hit ratio h* which is a percentage defined as

$$h = \frac{\text{number of memory references to the cache}}{\text{total number of memory references}} \cdot 100$$

$(1 - h$ is the *miss ratio* comparable to a page fault rate). If t_b is the cache access time and t_c the Mp cycle time then an average access time can be computed as

$$t_a = t_b + (1 - h)t_c \qquad \text{(we assume that we always try to access the cache first before generating an Mp reference.)}$$

This is a rather idealistic way to measure the cache's effectiveness. We have implied that cache fetches dominate the instruction cycle. This is not actually true since a cache fetch could be as low as 50 ns. We have also dismissed factors such as memory interference, e.g., during write backs and block faults, and more generally parameters such as the number of memory references per instruction and the locality of code and data. However, t_a is a sufficiently accurate evaluation for most purposes.

For a given cache size, there exists an "optimal" block size. Figure 6.24.a showing the miss ratio vs. block size for a fixed buffer capacity can be compared with Figure 6.9 for a paging system. Other measurements corroborate the fact that block sizes of 64 or 128 bytes are best. But the block size is not a dominant factor since the curves are quite flat. Total cache size is important; as could be expected the miss ratio decreases with an increase in buffer capacity. The curves obtained are quite comparable to parachor curves for fixed local PMA policies in a paging system. Figure 6.24.b indicates the influence of cache size along with that of set size for a set associative policy (set size one is direct mapping while infinite set size is for a fully associative or paging system). As long as the set size is greater than one, the number of blocks per set is not that important.

A difference between paging and cache systems is that at program switching time the contents of the cache could become completely invalid. Simulation experiments have shown that clearing the cache periodically, even at short intervals, does not radically degrade the cache's effectiveness.

From these typical figures and other experiments, we can conclude that caches of size 8 to 16K with block sizes of 64 to 128 bytes and with a set associative mapping scheme will yield hit ratios of over 95%.

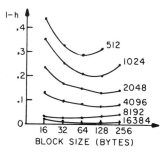

(a) Miss ratio vs. block size for a given cache capacity

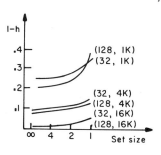

(b) Miss ratio vs. set size for a given (block size, cache capacity)

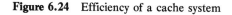

Figure 6.24   Efficiency of a cache system

6.6   BIBLIOGRAPHICAL NOTES, REFERENCES AND EXERCISES

Denning's survey is still the basic reference for a discussion of virtual memory systems [Denning 70]. Numerous theoretical results on paging systems are discussed at length in [Coffman and Denning 73]. Superfluity was first defined in another survey [Kuck and Lawrie 70]. [Belady 66] is a classic study of replacement algorithms for fixed primary allocation. Some implementation issues are well covered in [Alexander 69]. The logarithmic behavior of $M(p)$ was also mentioned in Belady's paper. Figures relative to program behavior in a fixed PMA are taken from [Baer and Sager 72]. The stack algorithms were first defined in [Mattson, Gecsei, Slutz and Traiger 70].

Denning's first presentation of the working set can be found in [Denning 68]. The MANIAC II implementation is described in [Morris 72]. Proposals for modifications to Denning's working set policy can be found for example in [Smith 76]. The page-fault-frequency algorithm was devised by Chu and Opderbeck (see e.g., [Chu and Opderbeck 76]). Graham's thesis [Graham 76] includes some useful comparisons between MIN, LRU, WS and PFF. The VMIN algorithm is due to [Prieve and Fabry 75]. Anomalies in variable PMA policies are discussed in [Franklin, Graham and Gupta 78].

Memory management and the pros and cons of the various partitioning techniques are reviewed in [Denning and Graham 75]. This article also includes an extensive bibliography on the subject. Experimental results on the biased FIFO policy can be found in [Belady and Kuehner 69], and on the global vs. local LRU in [Oliver 74]. Prepaging is discussed in [Baer and Sager 76] and in [Trivedi 76].

Segmented systems are the trademarks of the Burrough B5000-B6000 series. Organick's book [Organick 73] is a good description of these systems but the virtual memory aspect is not emphasized. [Doran 76] provides a comparison between the B6700 and MULTICS approaches. For the latter another book by Organick is available [Organick 72]. More tutorials on the sharing aspect can be found in Operating Systems books such as [Shaw 74] and [Watson 70] and for a detailed development [Daley and Dennis 68] should be consulted. The dynamic memory allocation problem is discussed at length in [Knuth 68]. [Randell and Kuehner 68] presents the various alternatives for virtual memory implementations.

[Batson and Bundage 77] is the reference for statistics gathered on segmented systems. It also refers to previous papers in the same area. [Ferrari 76] gives a nice summary of the efforts involved and of the results which can be obtained through restructuring. Some techniques that programmers could use to improve program performance are presented in [Morrison 73]. The multi-pass loader technique has been developed by [Babonneau, et al. 77]. A priori restructuring has been thoroughly investigated in [Snyder 78].

The OS/VS1 operating system paging algorithm is described in [Wheeler 73] and VMOS in [Fogel 74]. The cache implementation in the IBM System/360 Model 85 was first described in [Conti, Gibson and Pitkowsky 68 and Liptay 68] and [Conti 69] reviews alternate cache organizations. This is also the purpose of [Bell, Casasent and Bell 74] although this latter paper is more directed towards smaller machines.

[Kaplan and Winder 73] describe cache effectiveness in detail. Figure 6.24 is based on their paper. [Strecker 76] reports on simulation experiments which led to the design of the cache for the PDP 11/70. [Smith 78] discusses prepaging in a cache and also gives some interesting details on the cache organizations of the IBM System/370 Model 168 and of the Amdahl 470 V/6.

References

1. Alexander, M. T., *Time-Sharing Supervisor Programs,* The University of Michigan, May 1969.

2. Babonneau, J. Y., Achard, M. S., Morisset, G., and M. B. Mounajjed, "Automatic and General Solution to the Adaptation of Programs in a Paging Environment", *Proc. 6th Symp. on Oper. Systems Principles,* (1977), 109-116.

3. Baer, J.-L. and G. R. Sager, "Measurement and Improvement of Program Behavior Under Paging Systems", in *Statistical Computer Performance Evaluation,* W. Freiberger, ed., Academic Press, New York, N.Y., 1972, 241-264.

4. Baer, J.-L. and G. R. Sager, "Dynamic Improvement of Locality in Virtual Memory Systems", *IEEE Trans. on Soft-Eng., SE1,* (Mar. 1976), 54-62.

5. Batson, A. P. and R. G. Bundage, "Segment Sizes and Lifetimes in ALGOL 60 Programs", *Comm. ACM, 20,* (Jan. 1977), 36-44.

6. Belady, L. A., "A Study of Replacement Algorithms for a Virtual Storage Computer", *IBM Systems Journal, 5,* (1966), 78-101.

7. Belady, L. A. and C. J. Kuehner, "Dynamic Space Sharing in Computer Systems", *Comm. ACM, 12,* (May 1969), 282-288.

8. Bell, J., Casasent, D., and C. G. Bell, "An Investigation of Alternative Cache Organizations", *IEEE Trans. on Comp., C-23,* (Apr. 1974), 346-351.

9. Chu, W. W. and H. Opderbeck, "Program Behavior and the Page-Fault-Frequency Replacement Algorithm", *Computer, 9,* (Nov. 1976), 29-38.

10. Coffman, E. G. and P. J. Denning, *Operating Systems Theory,* Prentice Hall, Englewood Cliffs, N.J., 1973.

11. Conti, C. J., Gibson, D. H., and S. H. Pitkowsky, "Structural Aspects of the System 360/85; General Organization", *IBM Systems Journal, 7,* (1968), 2-14.

12. Conti, C. J., "Concepts for Buffer Storage", *Computer Group News, 2,* (Mar. 1969), 9-13.

13. Daley, R. C. and J. B. Dennis, "Virtual Memory Processes and Sharing in Multics", *Comm. ACM, 11,* (May 1968), 306-311.

14. Denning, P. J., "The Working Set Model for Program Behavior", *Comm. ACM, 11,* (May 1968), 323-333.

15. Denning, P. J., "Virtual Memory", *Computing Surveys, 2,* (Sep. 1970), 153-189.

16. Denning, P. J. and G. S. Graham, "Multiprogrammed Memory Management", *Proc. IEEE, 63,* (Jun. 1975), 924-939.

17. Doran, R. W., "Virtual Memory", *Computer, 9,* (Oct. 1976), 27-37.

18. Ferrari, D., "The Improvement of Program Behavior", *Computer, 9,* (Nov. 1976), 39-47.

19. Fogel, M., "The VMOS Paging Algorithm", *Operating Systems Review, 8,* (1974), 8-16.

20. Kranklin, M. A., Graham, G. S. and R. K. Gupta, "Anomalies with Variable Partitions Paging Algorithms", *Comm. ACM, 21,* (Mar. 1978), 232-236.

21. Graham, G. S., *A Study of Program and Memory Policy Behavior,* Ph.D. Dissertation, Purdue University, 1976.

22. Kaplan, K. R. and R. V. Winder, "Cache-Based Computer Systems", *Computer, 6,* (Mar. 1973), 30-36.

23. Knuth, D., *The Art of Computer Programming, Vol. 1, Fundamental Algorithms,* Addison-Wesley, Reading, Mass, 1968.

24. Kuck, D. T. and D. H. Lawrie, "The Use and Performance of Memory Hierarchies", in *Software Engineering,* J. Tou, ed., Vol. 1, Academic Press, New York, N.Y., 1970, 46-71.

25. Liptay, J. S., "Structural Aspects of System 360/85; The Cache", *IBM Systems Journal, 7,* (1968), 15-21.

26. Mattson, R. L., Gecsei, J., Slutz, D. R. and I. L. Traiger, "Evaluation Techniques for Storage Hierarchies", *IBM Systems Journal, 9,* (1970), 78-117.

27. Morris, J. B., "Demand Paging through Utilization of W. S. on the MANIAC II", *Comm. ACM, 15,* (Oct. 1972), 867-872.

28. Morrison, J. E., "User Program Performance in Virtual Storage Systems", *IBM Systems Journal, 12,* (1973), 216-237.

29. Oliver, N. A., "Experimental Data on Page Replacement Algorithms", *Proc. AFIPS 1974 Nat. Comp. Conf., 43,* AFIPS Press, Montvale, N.J., (1974), 179-184.

30. Organick, E. I., *The Multics System: An Examination of its Structure,* MIT Press, Cambridge, Mass., 1972.

31. Organick, E. I., *Computer System Organization. The B5700/B6700 Series,* Academic Press, New York, N.Y., 1973.

32. Prieve, B. G. and R. S. Fabry, "VMIN—An Optimal Variable-Space Page Replacement Algorithm", *Comm. ACM, 19,* (May 1976), 295-297.

33. Randell, B. and Kuehner, C. J., "Dynamic Storage Allocation Systems", *Comm. ACM, 11*, (May 1968), 297-304.

34. Shaw, A. C., *The Logical Design of Operating Systems,* Prentice-Hall, Englewood Cliffs, N.J., 1974.

35. Smith, A. J., "A Modified Working-Set Paging Algorithm", *IEEE Trans. on Comp., C-29*, (Sep. 1976), 907-914.

36. Smith, A. J., "Sequential Program Prefetching in Memory Hierarchies", *Computer, 11*, (Dec. 1978), 7-21.

37. Snyder, R., "On a priori Program Restructuring for Virtual Memory Systems", *Proc. 2nd Int. Coll. on Oper. Syst.,* IRIA, (Oct. 1978).

38. Strecker, W., "Cache Memories for PDP-11 Family Computers", *Proc. 3rd Symp. on Comp. Arch.,* (1976), 155-157.

39. Trivedi, K. S., "Prepaging and Applications to Array Algorithms", *IEEE Trans. on Comp., C-25*, (Sep. 1976), 915-921.

40. Watson, R., *Time Sharing System Design Principles,* McGraw-Hill, New York, N.Y., 1970.

41. Wheeler, T. F., "O.S./VS1 Concepts and Philosophies", *IBM Systems Journal, 13*, (1974), 213-229.

Exercises

1. Recall the ISP description of the Sigma 5 (Figure 2.8). Modify the effective address calculation if the machine is a Sigma 7 with 256 pages of 512 words. Include the direct map in the declarations of the Mp state.

2. Give a Petri Net (or extended Petri Net) description of the address translation mechanism as in Figure 6.4.

3. Which of the following two drums would you choose:
   Drum A   Drum B
   256 tracks, 2K words/track   64 tracks, 8K words/track
   8 ms rotation time   16 ms rotation time

   a) for a swapping device (i.e., paging in a uniprogramming environment);
   b) for a multiprogrammed paged system with a light load;
   c) for a multiprogrammed paged system with a heavy load.

4. Explain how the use of base registers ease the stringent requirements imposed in the text for sharing in a paging environment?

5. Computer XYZ has a (virtual) address space of 2^{18} words, i.e., generates 18 bit addresses. However, it can be delivered with an Mp range of 128K to 1M words.

A virtual memory system is envisioned. How would you implement the address translation mechanism?

6. Find an example string where
$$F_{\text{FIFO}} > F_{\text{CLOCK}} > F_{\text{LRU}} > F_{\text{MIN}}$$

7. Find example strings where
a) $F_{\text{FIFO}} < F_{\text{CLOCK}}$
b) $F_{\text{FIFO}} < F_{\text{LRU}}$

8. Prove that LRU and MIN are stack algorithms.

9. Show that FIFO and "clock" are not stack algorithms (Hint: Find a counter-example).

10. Modify the space time product formulation of equation (3) in section 2.3 to include the cost incurred by pushing pages.

11. Show that by increasing the window size in a working set algorithm, the page fault rate is decreased and the average working-set size is increased. What can be said about the space-time product?

12. Design a hardware implementation for the PFF algorithm.

13. A true LRU replacement algorithm implies that the set of pages in primary memory be reordered at every reference. Thus, an associative memory with shifting capabilities is necessary. Since such associative memories are rather expensive, only approximations to LRU have been (and are) implemented. Assume that as a systems designer you had to step in after some initial design of the hardware. You are asked to produce a multiprogramming paging system with each user requesting a fixed number of frames, either through a job control statement or by default, and with no sharing among users. You have at your disposal a shifting associative memory of 8 entries corresponding to the possibility of mapping directly the addresses of 8 frames. The address field of your instruction is 18 bits. Your paging device is a drum with a sector size of 256 words. It could be a paging drum if you so desire.

The minimum main memory for which your system has to work is 64K, 8K of which will be taken by the resident system. You want to have the possibility of multiprogramming at least 5 users whose virtual space is assumed to be between 10K and 100K.

(a) Explain your choice of the page size. Give the replacement algorithm you would like to see implemented, which should be some approximation to LRU. Show the structure of the associative map and of page tables in memory.

(b) Explain what happens when a page fault occurs. What actions are taken besides the choice of the page to be replaced?

(c) Assume now that, with the same hardware, you do not restrict the user to a fixed primary memory allotment. Do you foresee any changes in the replacement algorithm? If no, justify your answer. If yes, what changes in the replacement algorithm should seem profitable?

(d) The Operating Systems designer wants you to use some form of predictive loading. Do you need extra hardware? Is your replacement algorithm more difficult?

14. Discuss the following global replacement policy known as AC/RT (due to Belady and Tsao). To a process P_i, we associate two variables AC_i and RT_i which are updated at each page fault of P_i. AC_i counts the fraction of P_i's resident set referenced since the last page fault. RT_i counts the fraction of the last K (K a parameter of the system) page faults of P_i which recalled the most recently replaced page.

(a) What is the significance of AC_i and RT_i? Should they be high or low for a program to avoid too many page faults? (The replacement algorithm is as follows: if RT_i is low, choose a page from P_i, otherwise replace a page from P_j chosen as the process with smaller AC_j.)

(b) What is the danger of such a policy? How would you implement a load control policy?

(c) Design the hardware for such a memory management policy.

15. What is the average number of blocks traversed in a FIRST-FIT reservation policy? Give an algorithm similar to FIRST-FIT but such that instead of always starting at the beginning of the list, one starts from where one left off. What are the changes in the list structure? What is the average number of blocks traversed?

16. Should restructuring work better for small or for large pages? What about prepaging? Justify your answers.

17. Design your own restructuring algorithm. On what would your clustering be based (do not give a clustering algorithm)?

18. In a segmented system with paging, most page tables reside in Mp? What about segment tables?

19. Explain why cache memories are often called associative memories. Is the term accurate? Is it representative of the address translation mechanism? Would you call the TLB used in the IBM System/370 Model 168 a "cache"?

20. System X has a paged virtual memory mechanism. It also has a set associative cache. Describe the order in which the virtual-real address translation and the cache search are performed.

21. Given a machine with a 24 bit effective byte address, how would you delineate fields in this 24 bit address for sector, tags, blocks (of 8 words), sets and words (assuming 4 bytes/word) if a cache were to be included?

(a) with a sector organization (sectors of 128 blocks);
(b) with a direct mapping scheme (256 blocks);
(c) with a set associative scheme (128 sets of 2 blocks).

Chapter 7

THE CONTROL UNIT AND MICROPROGRAMMING

In introducing the PMS notation we said little about control units and controllers (primitive K). In general, they were either absent from PMS descriptions or shown without attributes. However, a control unit was one of the four basic components of the von Neumann machine. It quickly disappeared from structural descriptions by being included within the Pc. In our presentation of powerful processors we expanded on how operations had to be controlled without showing explicitly the means to do so. This chapter's goal is to indicate how control units for processors can be designed. We shall always have a Pc in mind, although the same concepts and techniques could be applied to more special-purpose processors. Our emphasis will be on microprogramming which has now become the standard and most flexible way to implement controlling functions.

Section 1 describes the necessary components of a control unit by reviewing what has to be controlled, namely the resources which have to be altered, the sources and sinks of transfers and the data paths, and the timing sequences of required controlling signals. Section 2 is devoted to microprogramming: its implementation via read-only memories, the variations between vertical and horizontal techniques, and the presentation of some example architectures. The third section looks more closely at three typical microprogramming applications: emulation, high-level language direct execution, and tuning of architectures. Finally, in Section 4, we describe the components of a microprogramming system.

7.1 COMPONENTS OF A CONTROL UNIT

7.1.1 Data Paths and Internal Registers

If we add to the previously defined basic storage registers and active components (ALU) of a Pc (cf. Chapter 4 Section 1) the Mp machinery needed to fetch instructions and operands, we can schematically revise Figure 4.1 and Figure 4.2 in the more general, yet less complex, representation of Figure 7.1. In the center of the figure is a "black box" labelled "control" which directs the operations of the other units according to the sequence of steps appearing in the instruction execution cycle.

We reexamine the 6 basic steps of the instruction execution cycle. We have already examined the resources' occupancy in order to maximize overlap. Without trying to achieve an extreme optimization, we found that a division between an I-unit (fetching and decoding instructions, generating effective operand addresses and monitoring their access) and a D-unit (executing instructions) was logical, if Mp references could be avoided to a large extent. This led to the introduction of buffers for instructions (look-ahead) and data. Similarly, from the viewpoint of the control unit, there is a fetch and an execution phase. However, the fetch phase will be almost entirely restricted to the instruction fetch and decode. Instructions which require additional Mp accesses will do so during the execute phase, or even during a third phase if indirect addressing is allowed.

Before delving into the alternatives which can be considered in order to implement the "control", we should be more precise about the types of actions to be controlled. We shall place ourselves at the register transfer level (level 3 in Chapter 2). The internal workings of each D-unit, e.g., the sequence of actions necessary to perform an integer addition in a carry-look-ahead adder, will not be considered. In other words a local control within a D-unit is assumed. Similarly, a "read" or "write" command to Mp is a sufficient indication to perform the required action. Naturally, the MAR (and MDR if need be) must have their correct contents before the order is given. But on the other hand, if the ALU consists of an integer adder, shifter and a counter, then control sequences will have to be given for operations such as (integer) multiply or floating-point add.

Thus our view is that of a centralized global control with local (decentralized) independently controlled units. For example, looking at the machine of Figure 7.1, the types of data movements controlled by the black box include the following:

- Fetch an instruction, with the sequence:
  MAR ← LC
  LC   ← LC + 1
  Read
  IR   ← MDR
- Effective address calculation:
  EAR ← AP + R[IR]   *
- Fetch an operand and add it to a register:

MAR ← EAR
Read
R[gr] ← R[gr] + MDR   *

etc . . . .

The two "actions" marked with an * are more complex than they appear since they require selective gating from some register to (or from) an adder. We have already implied a number of buses or direct connections: for example, between any (index) register to the EA-unit, any register to the D-unit, and the MDR to the D-unit. We have shown neither the relative timings of these actions, when they start, nor how to select which one to invoke.

Thus a first requirement is to indicate what are the data paths between registers and between registers and D-units. Direct connection paths gating each bit position in a (source) register to corresponding positions in other (sink) registers are relatively expensive. There is a need for decoding logic, or multiplexing, triggered by the control at both the source and sink ends. This

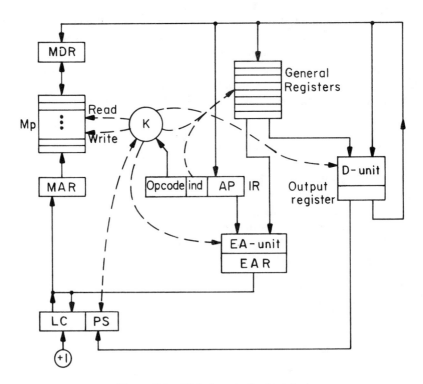

Figure 7.1 Global centralized control

type of connection would be used, in our example, between the general registers and the internal registers of the D-unit and EA-unit. Buses, on the other hand, require less circuitry but are to be time-shared. The connections between the Mp registers (MAR and MDR) and other elements will be performed in that manner. This corresponds to the Mp − Pc switch of the PMS notation, or memory bus. Concurrency of transfers is lost but this is not critical.

This division between direct paths and (memory) bus should not be seen as a mandatory design consideration. As we shall see, there might be a variety of buses internal to the Pc.

7.1.2   Alternative Designs for the Control Unit

Our interest is centered around the design of the K unit in the Pc and not in the local D-unit control. As said above, this K unit will initiate register-register transfers on the data paths and invoke the actions of the D-units. These transfers occur at specific locations called *control points*. When a control point is activated, there is a state transition within the control which thus can be considered as the realization of a finite state machine, since the number of possible states is necessarily bounded. These state transitions can occur in one of the following two ways:

* Synchronous, with all state transitions taking one or more clock cycles. (We can distinguish between "synchronous fixed" where all transitions take the same number of cycles, and "synchronous variable" where some operations take multiple (fixed) cycles without effecting a state transition.)
* Asynchronous, with state transitions being activated when all "inputs" are ready. At termination some conditions indicating stabilization are set (cf. a safe Petri Net firing).

Of these two modes, synchronous (variable) is most frequently used within the Pc with some parts of the system being asynchronous (typical examples are found in the Mp-Pc switch protocols).

The implementation can take two forms: hardwired (random) logic and microprogramming which is now almost exclusively used. We present a short overview of the former, mostly for historical reasons.

Our machine controlled in a variable synchronous scheme is a stripped down version of Figure 7.1 shown in Figure 7.2. It is a single accumulator Pc without index registers. A clock gives basic quanta of time. The fetch step takes 4 quanta and the execute phase is zero, one or more multiples of 4 quanta (cf. Figure 7.3). A fetch flip-flop is set to 1 when in the fetch phase

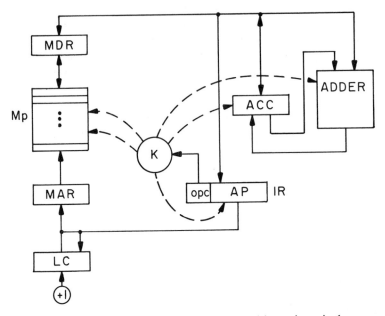

Figure 7.2   Main data paths, registers and buses in a single accumulator machine

and an execute flip-flop is set when in the execute phase. We assume a semi-conductor technology for Mp which implies a nondestructive read-out.

To simplify further, we present only examples of instruction timings which take either zero or one execute cycle. Although some of the timing is idealized, the concept can be easily extended by dividing the major cycle into several minor cycles and by allowing some operations such as Mp read to span several minor cycles.

In the following examples we utilize a CDL-like notation. We do not ex-

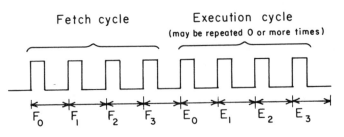

Figure 7.3   Major cycle and subcycles (synchronous variable)

plicitly include register and clock declarations, some of which are evident from our discussion (4-phase clock) and some from the figure. The first instruction is CLA or "clear the accumulator and add". The initial state has the MAR containing the address of the instruction to be fetched, the flip-flops F set to 1 and E set to 0.

$/F * F_0/$	MDR ← M(MAR),	\$Read from Mp
$/F * F_1/$	IR ← MDR, LC ← Countup LC,	
$/F * F_2/$	K ← opc, decode,	\$Next step depends on op-code
$/F * F_3/$	ACC ← 0, MAR ← LC	

Since F is still 1, the next action will be similar to the first one in CLA, i.e., a fetch of the next instruction.

For an "add" instruction, which adds the contents of the accumulator to that of the contents of an operand whose address is in the address part of the instruction, we have:

$/F * F_0/$	MDR ← M(MAR),	
$/F * F_1/$	IR ← MDR, LC, ← countup LC,	
$/F * F_2/$	K ← opc, decode,	
$/F * F_3/$	MAR ← AP, F ← 0, E ← 1,	\$Fetch operand; switch states
$/E * E_0/$	MDR ← M(MAR),	\$read operand
$/E * E_1/$	ADD1 ← MDR, ADD2 ← ACC,	\$Gate to inputs of adder
$/E * E_2/$	ACC ← ADDR,	\$Gate result to ACC
$/E * E_3/$	E ← 0, F ← 1, MAR ← LC	\$Prepare to fetch

In order to realize this control, we construct sequences which at each clock phase will activate gates according to the logic shown in the sequencing labels between bars at the left of each line. They can frequently be simplified. For example, an Mp read would occur if:

$$(F * F_0) + (E * E_0) \text{ is true.}$$

Furthermore, many operations such as "Add", "Subtract" on one hand, and "CLA", "load accumulator complemented" etc. . . . on the other, will have common subsequences. The control is constructed as a (clocked) finite state automaton with conjunctions of clock pulses and of decoder outputs providing the inputs to trigger transitions between states. A schematic view of the process is shown in Figure 7.4.

As can be seen the process is *ad hoc*. Modifications to completed designs are difficult; debugging and maintenance are overly complex. The remainder of this chapter deals with a more coherent approach to control, namely microprogramming.

7.2 MICROPROGRAMMING

The concept of microprogramming, a systematic and orderly approach to the design of the control portions of a Pc, was introduced in the early fifties by Wilkes. Since then, technology has allowed a cost-effective implementation and variations in the designs. The scope of applications of microprogramming has been extended from the interpretation of machine language instructions for a given instruction set to more general emulations and the direct execution of high-level languages. In this section, we restrict ourselves to the original goal, that is the design of the K portion of the Pc.

7.2.1 ROM Implementation

We have just seen that the execution of a machine language instruction can be broken out into a series of elementary steps that Wilkes called *micro-operations*. Sequences of these microoperations constitute *microprograms*. These microprograms are stored in a memory, the *control store* or Mcs. In

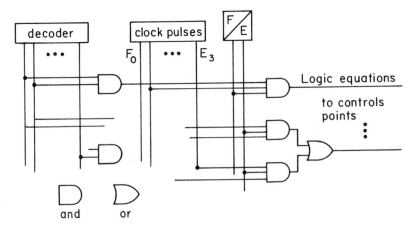

Figure 7.4 Control implemented via random logic

the same vein as we have (machine language) program instructions (also called macroinstructions) stored in Mp, with a program counter indicating the location from which the next instruction to be executed will be fetched, decoded and executed, we shall have microprograms stored in Mcs with logic indicating the location of the next microinstruction. The set of micro-operations (one or more) contained in a microinstruction will be decoded and will activate the control points in the Pc. Alternatives in the grouping of microoperations (or commands) and in the sequencing scheme will provide variations in the implementations. However, these variations are all based on Wilkes' scheme which we now describe.

The fundamental layout is shown in Figure 7.5. Matrices A and B store the microprogram with each column in matrix A reserved for a specific micro-operation. When a row, say row i, has been selected as the output of a 1-out-of-2^n decoder (the tree decoder in the figure with register $R2$ being n-bits wide), those commands indicated by dots in the matrix on row i are activated. The selection of the next microinstruction is left to matrix B where dots indicate the setting of bits for the next address. The bit pattern is then transmitted to $R1$. Selection of a row in matrix B can be modified as a result of testing flip-flops in the Pc such as an accumulator sign or an overflow bit. The two registers $R1$ and $R2$ (only one of which was present in the original design) allow one of them to hold the address of the microinstruction presently executed, while the other contains the address of the next microinstruc-

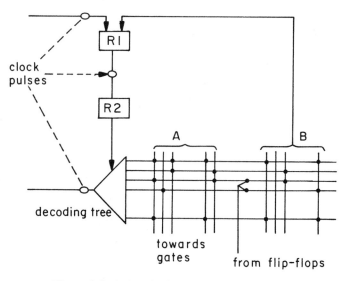

Figure 7.5 Wilkes' microprogramming scheme

tion. This latter register can be loaded from sources external to the K unit such as the opcode part of the instruction register holding the next machine language instruction to be executed. Transfers from $R1$ to $R2$ are performed at fixed times under orders from the microprogram.

This original idea has not received many conceptual modifications. Matrices A and B, which were diode matrices in the original design, were too costly to implement on a large scale basis. But with integrated-circuit technology, they can be easily built as ROM's (cf. Chapter 5) or even RAM's and PLA's. It is in fact the advent of fast and cheap semi-conductor memories which brought Wilkes' concept to reality, since the overhead of (control store) memory fetches is not as detrimental as it would have been if core or diode based memories were used. With the progress in memory technology, the control Mcs can be:

- part of Mp (e.g., IBM System/360 Model 25, some models of the Burroughs B1700);
- in a fast dedicated RAM thus allowing user written microprograms (e.g., IBM System/370 which is not user microprogrammable, HP21MX, Cal Data etc. ... which have writable Mcs);
- in a fast ROM (e.g., IBM System/360 Models 30, 40, 50, 65, 85, DEC PDP 11-45).

From the microprogramming viewpoint, the organization looks like that of Figure 7.6. The K unit as shown in this figure is often referred to as the microengine. The Mcs has an address register McsAR and a data register McsDR. Once the McsAR has been loaded with the address of the next microinstruction, a read (of Mcs) can be performed. Interestingly enough there is no command to read Mcs in the microprogram, i.e., it has to be performed synchronously, and all microinstructions must be designed so that in the worst case they take the same amount of time. We shall see implications of this constraint on various architectures. The McsDR holds the microinstruction to be executed; it plays the role of an instruction register (MIR for Microengine Instruction Register). In some machines, mostly those allowing writable control stores, we shall have distinct MIR and McsDR registers. Parts of the McsDR, or equivalently of the microinstruction, can contain a field giving the address of the next microinstruction or some modifier of the McsAR contents. The McsAR, or a microengine location counter MLC which, again, can be a separate register, can also be loaded or modified via the Pc instruction register, flip-flops in the D-units and/or a counter. Other parts of the McsDR will contain information leading to the activation of control points. Encoding of these commands will be discussed shortly.

In Figure 7.6 we have also included some registers which can only be ac-

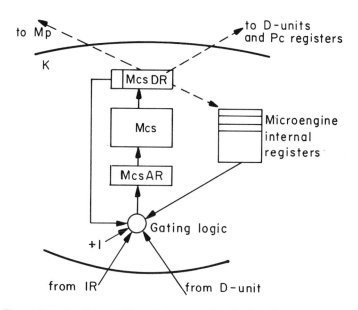

Figure 7.6   Implementation of the control unit via microprogramming

cessed by the microengine. Very often, we shall have a control stack linked to the McsAR for microprogram subroutine linkages and interrupt handling purposes, and some scratchpad registers. Typical examples will be seen later.

For the time being, we return to the machine of Figure 7.2. The microengine and the microinstruction formats are very simple. Microinstructions either contain a single command which directs a register to register transfer (or a similar action) or perform a (conditional) jump in the microprogram. When the microinstruction is of the command type, its successor is the one stored in the next Mcs word. Hence microprograms will look like ordinary (machine language) programs. Table 7.1 lists a subset of the possible microinstructions with the encoding being the ordinal number of the command. Microinstructions 16 to 19 are the only ones requiring some explanation. Microinstruction 16 will occur at the end of a "machine language instruction fetch" microprogrammed sequence to transfer control, in the microprogram, to the beginning of a routine selected by the macroinstruction's opcode. For example, assume the following opcodes (in decimal):

0   ADD
1   CLA
2   STO

3   SUB
4   TRA   (unconditional jump)
5   TRN   (jump on accumulator negative)
etc. ... ,

and let us also suppose that the opcode part is 6 bits wide, allowing 64 different opcodes. Then a possible layout for the microprogram interpreting this instruction set is shown in Figure 7.7. The first 64 locations in Mcs are used as a transfer vector. At location 64 is the beginning of the IFETCH routine which performs the macroinstruction fetch. At the end of this sequence (location 67), microinstruction 16 transfers control to the microinstruction whose address is equal to the macroinstruction's opcode. There, microinstruction 19 performs an unconditional jump to the appropriate routine. For example, if the macroopcode was 3, we would go from location 67 to location 3 and finally to location 83 corresponding to the beginning of the SUB routine.

From the microengine's viewpoint, command 16 implies a transfer from the IR's opcode part to McsAR. Command 19 cannot be by itself and another field of the McsDR will contain the label of the target location (we do not discuss the encoding problem in detail and utilize a simple but unrealistic scheme). Similarly, commands 17 and 18 imply testing of a flip-flop, or a whole register, and consequent setting of the McsAR. We do not elaborate on the remainder of Table 7.1 and of Figure 7.7. The reader is encouraged to study this example to comprehend the meaning of the various commands (cf. Exercise 1).

We can obviously improve on this purely sequential process. Parallel commands could be found in a microinstruction, e.g., 3 and 4, to gate inputs to the adder, 12 and 15 since an Mp read and clearing the adder have no data

Table 7.1   Microoperations for the machine of figure 7.2

1.	ACC ← MDR	11.	LC ← LC + 1
2.	Adder ← MDR	12.	Read (MDR ← Mp[MAR])
3.	Adder ← $\overline{\text{MDR}}$	13.	Write (Mp[MAR] ← MDR)
4.	Adder ← ACC	14.	ACC ← 0
5.	ACC ← Adder	15.	ADD ← 0
6.	ACC ← MDR	16.	McsAR ← OPC
7.	IR ← MDR	17.	If ACC = 0 GO TO LABEL
8.	MAR ← AP	18.	If ACC < 0 GO TO LABEL
9.	LC ← AP	19.	GO TO LABEL
10.	MAR ← LC		

Microinstruction label	Microcommand	Comment
0	19, 68	GO TO ADD
1	19, 75	GO TO CLA
2	19, 79	GO TO STO
3	19, 83	GO TO SUB
4	19, 90	GO TO TRA
5	19, 92	GO TO TRN
⋮	⋮	⋮
64 (IFETCH)	10	MAR ← LC
65	12	Read
65	7	IR ← MDR
66	11	LC ← LC + 1
67	16, OPC	MCSAR ← OPCODE
68 (ADD)	8	
⋮	⋮	
74	19, 64	GO TO IFETCH
75 (CLA)		
⋮		
78	19, 64	GO TO IFETCH
79 (STO)		
⋮		
82	19, 64	GO TO IFETCH
83 (SUB)	8	MAR ← AP
84	12	Read
85	15	ADD ← 0
86	3	ADD ← $\overline{\text{MDR}}$
87	4	ADD ← ACC
88	5	ACC ← ADD
89	19, 64	GO TO IFETCH
90 (TRA)	9	LC ← AP
91	19, 64	GO TO IFETCH
92 (TRN)	18, 90	IF ACCO GO TO TRA
93	19, 64	GO TO IFETCH

Figure 7.7   Microprogram layout for the machine of figure 7.2

path conflict, and 7 and 11 as an instance of the frequently encountered overlap of LC incrementing and some other operation. But naturally we shall have to pay a price for this speed-up. This will certainly occur at the encoding level, but there will also be some other repercussions. Our next task is therefore to examine encodings and means to determine the next microinstruction address.

7.2.2   Variations in the Microinstruction formats. Vertical vs. Horizontal Microprogramming

Even for the very simple microengine just described, there was a choice as to the power of a single microinstruction. We could limit ourselves to a single command/microinstruction or exploit the potential parallelism by having several control points simultaneously activated. The first approach which, as we have already noticed, is quite similar to conventional programming is called *vertical microprogramming* while the second has been named *horizontal microprogramming*. Evidently, there are advantages and disadvantages in each option and, as always, some middle-of-the-road designs have been implemented trying to combine the best of two worlds. Sometimes this combination has been dubbed "diagonal" microprogramming. The differences between these implementations reside in:

- the amount of hardware used;
- the speed of execution of the microprogram;
- the difficulty in coding the microprograms.

We first consider the required hardware resources. A simple way to encode commands would be to assign a bit per command in each microinstruction. The length of each microinstruction (or at least of that part directing the activation of control points) would be n if there were n commands, independently of the number of microoperations which could be processed in parallel. This appears very wasteful, especially for the vertical case, since only a few (one in the vertical approach) out of n bits would be of significance for a given microinstruction. However, it has the advantage that no further decoding is necessary. In fact Wilkes' scheme was following that idea. At the other extreme, in the vertical case each of the n possible commands could be encoded in $\lceil \log_2 n \rceil$ bits. This necessitates further decoding. This method must be modified for the horizontal case. One possibility is to partition the commands in groups, each group being related to a particular resource. For example, one group could control Mp, another the gating of registers to one internal buffer for a D-unit, another the actions taken by the D-unit etc. . . . . If there were k possible commands for a group, then $\lceil \log_2(k + 1) \rceil$ bits would be sufficient since a $(k + 1)$st command, a no-op, must be included.

This resource encoding can also be used efficiently in vertical microprogramming. A vertical microinstruction would have two fields: one, the "opcode", indicating the resource(s) to be controlled and the other determining the action for this resource. Naturally, this second field could be divided into subfields, as those naming the source and the sink in a register-register transfer. Both fields need not be of the same length for each microinstruction, although all microinstructions have equal length. This is illustrated in Table 7.2 showing the Burroughs B1726 microinstruction formats. The microinstruction is 16 bits wide but the opcode field can be either 4, 8 or 12 bits. We shall return to this coding method, called *expanding opcodes*, when we discuss minicomputers (cf. Chapter 9).

For the horizontal technique, we shall encode actions for every possible resource in every microinstruction. Figure 7.8 shows a simplified version of the data paths found in the IBM System/360 Model 30. Figure 7.9 shows those parts of the microinstruction format which control the data flow. The "next microinstruction address" field, some extraneous fields and parity bits are omitted. The Model 30 is not the most horizontal machine of the Sys-

Table 7.2   Microinstruction format for the B1726

Microinstruction format
$i \langle 0:15 \rangle$
$i1: = i \langle 0:3 \rangle$ Microinstruction
$i2: = i \langle 4:7 \rangle$ opcode 1
$i3: = i \langle 8:11 \rangle$ opcode 2
                       opcode 3
    ⋮

Microinstruction interpretation
$((i1 \neq 0) \rightarrow ((i1 = 1)/*$ Move instruction $*/ \rightarrow R[i \langle 10:15 \rangle] \leftarrow R[i \langle 4:9 \rangle]$;
              $(i1 = 2)/*$ Scratchpad move $*/ \rightarrow \cdots$

        ⋮

            $(i1 = 15)/*$ Call relative backward $*/ \rightarrow \cdots$);
$(i1 = 0 \wedge i2 \neq 0) \rightarrow ((i2 = 1)/*$ Swap memory with register $*/ \rightarrow \cdots$

        ⋮

            $(i2 = 8)/*$ Inc/Dec FA register $*/ \rightarrow \cdots$);
$(i1 \square i2 = 0 \wedge i3 \neq 0) \rightarrow ((i3 = 3)/*$ Bias $*/ \rightarrow \cdots$

        ⋮

            $(i3 = 6)/*$ Variant $*/ \rightarrow \cdots$);
$(i1 \square i2 \square i3 = 0) \rightarrow ((i = 0)/*$ No-op $*/ \rightarrow$;

        ⋮

            $(i = 3)/*$ Normalize $*/ \rightarrow \cdots$))

    ⋮

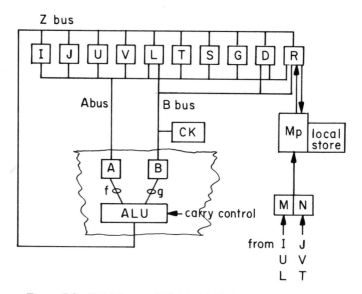

Figure 7.8   IBM System/360 Model 30 data paths (simplified)

Figure 7.9   IBM System/360 Model 30 microinstruction format

tem/360 series (cf. Table 7.3) but is simple enough for our explanatory purposes. The command fields can be classified into:

(i) ALU control fields (24 bits total) with:

- CA (4 bits) indicates one of 10 registers (all data paths and registers are 1 byte wide) as input to the internal A register;
- CB (2 bits) indicates one of 3 registers as input to the internal B register or indicates that the replicated CK field will yield a constant input;
- CK (4 bits) specifies half of the constant just alluded to;
- CF (3 bits) allows straight/cross, high/low gating between register A and the ALU (this is labelled f in Figure 7.8);
- CG (2 bits) as CF but for the B register; there are fewer options but see next field;

- CV (2 bits) controls true/complement input from the B register as well as special action for decimal arithmetic;
- CC (3 bits) specifies the arithmetic operation (ADD, AND, OR, XOR) as well as carry-in and out conditions;
- CD (4 bits) indicates the output register, or discarding of the output;

(ii) Mp Control fields (5 bits):

- CM (3 bits) indicates which pair of registers to use as source for the MAR (note that register R is always the MDR); this field also controls reading and writing;
- CU (2 bits) indicates whether Mp or a local store is to be controlled; the latter is not addressable by macroinstructions;

(iii) Status bit settings (4 bits):

- CS (4 bits) indicates how status bits, in register S, will be set according to conditions found in the ALU; for example if CS = 8 and the result of the ALU operation is 0, status bit $S2$ will be set to 0.

The status bits will be checked via two address fields, CH and CL, which in conjunction with a third field, CN, will determine the next microinstruction's address.

To get an idea of the "power" of such a format the following microinstruction (the values of the fields are expressed in decimal):

CA	CB	CF	CG	CV	CK	CC	CD	CM	CU	CS
7	3	3	2	0	13	0	0	0	0	3

would directly gate register R as the A input (CA, CF), take the constant $X'DD'$ (CB, CK) and gate only the high part (CV, CG), i.e., the constant $X'D'$, as the B input. Then it would add without carry (CC) and discard the output (CD). If the high order bits of the results are 0, then $S4$ would be set to 1, and if the low order bits are 0, then $S5$ would be set to 1 (CS). At the same time the contents of register R would be written back in Mp (CM, CU) presumably in the same location from where it was read (Mp is a core memory).

The microinstruction format appears powerful enough but a fair amount of subsequent decoding is necessary. However, the decoders are small (1-out-of-16 is the largest one). This power is quite relative though, since it takes almost 100 microinstructions to perform an integer multiply between 2 half-words resulting in a full word product. The data path width (one byte) and the absence of real shift instructions (only 4 bit crossing seems to be available) appear to be reasonable explanations for this particularly long

Table 7.3   Control store dimensions in IBM System/360 and /370

			Width (bits)	Length (words)	Amount of storage (bits)
System/360	Model	25	16	8192	131072
		30	60	4096	245760
		40	60	4096	245760
		50	90	2816	253440
		60	100	2816	281600
		85	108*	2560	276480
System/370	Model	145	32	16384	524288
		155	72	8192	589824
		165	108	2560	276480

* Hardwired fetch and decode.

microprogram (the Model 30 might be the only model to have this peculiar arrangement). A floating-point package takes 500 microinstructions.

If we compare this layout with that of a comparable vertical machine, such as the IBM System/370 Model 125 which has a 19-bit wide microinstruction format with an expanding opcode method, the same example as above would require approximately 6 microinstructions, namely:

- one to gate to the left input of the adder;
- one to gate to the right input;
- one to add;
- two to test specific conditions and set status bits;
- one to perform the Mp write.

Obviously then, horizontal microprogramming will execute faster but requires additional decoding hardware. In general, encoding will be less efficient in the horizontal case and more Mcs bits will be needed. Table 7.3 shows the amount of control store given to models of System/360 and System/370. These figures appear to confirm the tendency to have more Mcs for a horizontal machine. It is also apparent that between the System/360 (announced in the early sixties) and System/370 (announced in the late sixties) technology has advanced rapidly enough so that more functions can be embedded in the microprogram at a reasonable cost.

It is also quite clear that generating efficient, and correct, horizontal microprograms is more difficult than for vertical ones. Potential conflicts in bus transfers and in data dependent microoperations must be handled. Furthermore, the avenues open to optimization are so enormous that complete automated systems do not appear to have yet reached a satisfactory level of performance. We shall return to this problem in the last section of this chapter.

Before leaving the vertical vs. horizontal dilemma, we observe a further advantage to the "resource encoding" method, that is the ability of introducing new commands at no cost. Assume for example that we would like to encode the following commands for the gating to one of the inputs of a 56 bit adder (as in the IBM System/360 Model 40):

- no input, (clear the adder);
- register A to bit positions 32–63 of the adder (the adder has bit positions 8-63);
- Register B to bit positions 32–63 of the adder;
- Register B to bit positions 32–63 but shifted left 2 bits (useful when accumulating partial product in a multiplication);
- Bit positions 8–31 of register A to bit positions 8–31 of the adder (useful for shifting mantissas in floating-point additions).

Since we have 5 commands we shall need 3 bits leaving 3 possible new commands. Assuming that the data paths from registers A and B to the adder are distinct, one could (at no cost) implement a new command:

- Register B to bit positions 32–63 of the adder and bit position 8–31 of register A to bit positions 8–31 of the adder.

This is a combination of two of the original specifications and could be very useful in adding floating-point mantissas.

We now turn our attention to the "next address" or sequencing problem.

Sequencing

In Wilkes' scheme, each microinstruction carried the address of its successor. This method has been retained in some implementations, mostly in the horizontal case, while in others the usual sequentiality found in machine language programming is the rule. In this latter case, branching, conditionally or unconditionally, requires specific microinstructions. This second approach is most often found in vertical implementations. For example, the Burroughs B1700 has provisions for unconditional transfers forward and backward, for branch on conditions, for skipping the next microinstruction and for calling a subroutine, pushing the next address on the top of a hardware stack. Popping is done by transferring the top of the stack register to the McsAR.

The first option is well illustrated in the IBM System/360 Model 30.

However, it should not be concluded that a very long microinstruction is needed to have this form of sequencing. The Microdata 3200 has only a 32 bit microinstruction but each of them contains the address of its successor with many jump options. In the Model 30, the McsAR is 13 bits wide. Therefore, 8K of control store can be accessed, although the Mcs is limited to 4K. The next address is computed as follows. The 6 leftmost bits of the McsAR are not modified, except in some very special cases which involve a module switch, i.e., the addressing of a new block of 256 words of control store. This is done via a special instruction. The next 5 bits are stored directly in the microinstruction in the so-called CN field. The last 2 bits, X12 and X13, act as a four way switch. Two 4 bit fields, CH and CL, control the respective settings of X12 and X13. For example, if CH = 9, then X12 will take the value of status bit $S2$; if CH = 6 then X12 is set to 1 if the last ALU operation generated a carry out etc. . . . . Higher models in the System/360 hierarchy have even more complex branching arrangements.

It should be noted that the method just described prevents prefetching, or look-ahead, of microinstructions. In the next section, we shall describe how this prefetching is implemented on a particular machine. We have implied until now that all microinstructions required the same time and that there was no clocking involved in the timing of actions. This is what is called a *monophase* design. We can have *polyphase* (asynchronous or synchronous) implementations, where a microinstruction execution cycle is divided into minor cycles. Then the microinstruction cycle control has a hardwired component which resembles that of a hardwired Pc control unit but which is much simpler.

To close this discussion on microprogramming implementation options, we remark that coding microprograms is:

- simple in the vertical approach;
- difficult and requires much optimization in the horizontal case even with simple sequencing;
- even more difficult when the next microinstruction address is encoded in the current microinstruction. This requires a sophisticated (micro-assembler) software package to generate the microprogram addresses. This is especially true for machines which allow user microprogramming, i.e., those having writable control stores.

7.2.3 Two Example Architectures

To make more concrete the concepts just described, we present two examples of microprogrammed central processors. The first one, the Cal Data 100, is a microprogrammable machine whose main goal is to interpret the instruction

sets of minicomputers and, more specifically the PDP-11. The second, the
QM-1, is unique in the sense that it combines, at two different levels, the
horizontal and vertical approaches to microprogramming.

The Cal Data 100

A block diagram of the Pc and the connections with other components of the
Cal Data 100 is depicted in Figure 7.10. The top of the figure shows the
Mp − Pc switch called Macrobus (similar to the UNIBUS to be described in
Chapter 9) and the communication registers between the Pc and other
devices. We do not elaborate on these components of the architecture outside
of the Pc which have no relevance on the microprogramming aspect.

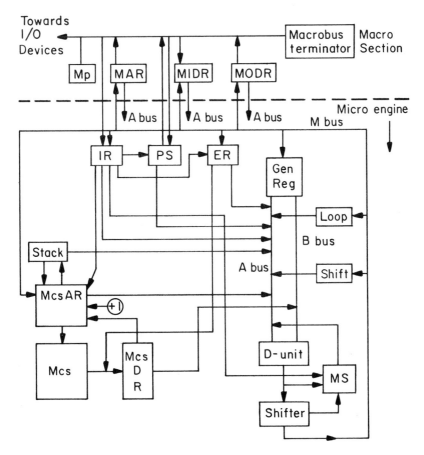

Figure 7.10 Cal Data block diagram

The registers providing the interface between the macro and microengines are:

MAR $\langle 0:15 \rangle$	Mp address register (Mp has a maximum of 128K words);
MIDR $\langle 0:15 \rangle$	Mp input data register (a word in Mp is 16-bit long);
MODR $\langle 0:15 \rangle$	Mp output data register;
IR $\langle 0:15 \rangle$	Macroinstruction register;
PS $\langle 0:7 \rangle$	Macro status register.

Most communications to the Macrobus are one way, from the microengine to Mp and other devices through MAR and MODR, and from the outside world to the microengine via IR and MIDR. Not surprisingly, the PS register has a two-way linkage. The distinction between MIDR and MODR is singular and can be explained by the fact that the Macrobus is a switch between several devices.

The microengine can be divided into 3 sections: the control section, the registers and the D-units.

(i) The control section consists of the following:

Mcs [0:4095] $\langle 0:47 \rangle$	Microprogram control store;
McsAR $\langle 0:11 \rangle$	Mcs address register;
McsDR $\langle 0:47 \rangle$	Mcs data register;
Stack [0:15] $\langle 0:11 \rangle$	Control store stack;
Loop $\langle 0:7 \rangle$	Replication counter.

The maximum capacity of the control store is 4K words of 48 bits each. Each microprogram can branch within 2K and a special instruction is needed to transfer control from one 2K block to the other. Up to 512 words can be writable control store, i.e., the machine is user microprogrammable. These 512 words can be loaded via the Macrobus like any I/O device. The microinstruction currently being executed is held in the McsDR. The system is monophase and while microinstruction i is executed, microinstruction ($i +$ 1) is prefetched. Thus, under normal sequencing execution takes place at the basic Mcs cycle rate of 165 ns. A microinstruction generating a branch or a skip will double the execution time. As seen in the figure, the microinstruction entering the McsDR can be modified by the contents of an emulate board of which we show only the emulate register ER. This modification is for sequencing purposes and is used to speed up the emulation of specific architectures.

Under normal sequencing, the McsAR is incremented by 1 after every fetch. However, it can also be loaded directly from the McsDR for programmed branches, as a sink from the microbus, called Mbus, connecting all registers with the output of the D-units, and from the IR and emulating circuitry. A 16 register stack is used for saving an Mcs address when calling microsubroutines or when processing interrupts. Pushes and pops are embedded in the branching conditions as will be seen later. The contents of the stack can be read, but not modified, except of course through pushes from McsAR. A stack pointer is provided but is not directly accessible by the microprogram. There is no provision for stack overflow and wrap arounds will occur if no precaution is taken.

The loop register allows the automatic replication of a set of microinstructions. It is loaded via the Mbus. It can be tested for zero or non-zero values and decremented or incremented in the same microinstruction.

Not shown in the figure is a block of 32 words of writable control store which can overlay any part of the Mcs. This can be a useful tool for inserting temporary microprograms for testing and debugging.

(ii) The registers

In addition to the registers already mentioned, the microengine has access to:

GR [0:15] ⟨0:15⟩	16 general registers;
XR ⟨0:15⟩	Shift register;
MS ⟨0:15⟩	Microstatus register;
ER ⟨0:15⟩	Emulate register.

The GR registers are sinks and sources for the D-units. The shift register is used as an extension of the shift unit for double length shifts. The MS register can receive inputs from IR and from the D-units to store condition codes regarding the presence of overflow and carry, as well as the status (zero, positive, negative, odd) of a resulting value. These conditions can be tested to force branches or skips, either dynamically at the end of the microinstruction in which they were generated, or statically after they have been stored in MS.

(iii) The D-units

The D-units consist of an ALU and a shift unit. The inputs are carried on two buses, A-bus and B-bus, and the output is transmitted through the Mbus.

All registers introduced until how can be gated to the A-bus except for PS and McsDR. The GR's and 16 bits of the McsDR (a literal value) can provide the second input through the B-bus. The Mbus is the main link through the microengine and can carry results to all registers except McsDR, PS and the control store stack.

The ALU can perform standard logical, integer add and subtract operations with provisions for carries as a third input. The shift unit and the ALU cannot be operated by the same microinstruction with a couple of exceptions for multiply and divide steps.

There are 3 classes of microinstructions: logical, arithmetic and special. Within each class, we distinguish between branch and skip formats (branch formats include no branch, i.e., normal sequencing). The formats are shown in Figure 7.11.

Some fields require further explanations. The *SB* field can be decomposed into:

branch Bit := *SB* ⟨0⟩ — Branch bit = 0 indicates a branch, otherwise a skip;

Test conditions := *SB* ⟨1:3⟩

T bit := *SB* ⟨4⟩ — If (test condition is present and *T* bit = 0) or (test condition is absent and *T* bit = 1) then skip or branch;

D bit := *SB* ⟨5⟩ — If *D* bit = 0 test on dynamic conditions else test on MS register.

For example we have:

branch bit	test cond	*T* bit	*D* bit	Actions
0	010	0	0	Branch on dynamic overflow
1	111	0	X	Unconditional skip (X = don't care)
0	010	0	1	Branch if overflow status reset

The *NX* field provides control to either allow or disallow the execution of microinstruction $(i + 1)$ after microinstruction i, if the latter is a branch. This permits saving a clock cycle. The 4 choices are:

- Execute the next microinstruction unconditionally;
- Inhibit the next microinstruction unconditionally;
- If a branch condition is met then execute the next microinstruction else inhibit it;
- If a branch condition is met then inhibit the next microinstruction else execute it.

The *OP*, *DN*, and *BO* fields have evident interpretations. The *AO* field is 6 bits long although only 27 registers can be an A source. The first bit indicates whether the source is also a sink. The *MC* field is used to indicate carry input for the ALU, links for double word shifts and microstatus modifications. The *MX* field defines modifications that can be applied to the operand fields of the next microinstruction and is used in conjunction with the emulate

mi/microinstruction ⟨0:47⟩	microinstruction
SB := mi ⟨0:5⟩	branch condition code
OP := mi ⟨6:10⟩	basic command
DN := mi ⟨11:15⟩	destination address
NX := mi ⟨16:17⟩	special control functions
AO := mi ⟨18:23⟩	operand 1 (A-bus)
MC := mi⟨24:27⟩	microstatus specifications
MX := mi⟨28:31⟩	modified functions
BO := mi ⟨32:35⟩	operand 2 (B-bus) for branch types in logical and arithmetic classes
SO := mi ⟨32:35⟩	specific control function for "special" class
LL := mi ⟨32:47⟩	literal value for skip types in logical and arithmetic classes
BF := mi ⟨36:47⟩	branch address or auxiliary functions in branch and "special" branch classes
FN := mi ⟨36:47⟩	auxiliary control in "special" skip class

Figure 7.11   Microinstruction formats for the Cal Data

register. The SO field is specific for each special microcommand. The LL field contains the B-source for logical and arithmetic commands of the skip type which have two operands. The BF field contains an 11 bit address for target addresses of branches plus a bit for push and save return addresses on the stack. When no branch condition is specified in the test condition field of SB, then the BF field and the FN field indicate control stack, interrupt or special purpose operations. In particular this provides the loading of McsAR from the stack (pop), various incrementations or decrementations of the stack pointer, and access to Mp.

As an example, assume that we wish to perform a floating-point addition. The exponents are in general registers $X11$ and $X14$ in excess notation (base 2) and the mantissas are right justified (24 bits) in registers $(X9, X10)$ and $(X12, X13)$ respectively. We first subtract the exponents and test for the larger of the two. This can be done by the following program where "•" indicates part of the same microinstruction:

```
    SUB X11, X14, LC    (Loop register ← X11–X14;
  • BNGDT SHIFTA        If the result is negative branch to SHIFTA;
  • SKIPB               Skip the next instruction if the branch is taken)
    MVA X12, XR         (Shift register ← X12, i.e., highest part of the
                        mantissa)
```

DRAS ∗ $X13$; RPT   (Do a double arithmetic right shift of XR, $X13$
 • BRU ADDSUB   the count being held in LC; transfer to
 • DONXT   ADDSUB after doing the next instruction)
   MVA XR, $X12$ ($X12 \leftarrow XR$; restore new high order bits of the
                     mantissa)
SHIFTA SUB $X14$, $X11$, LC ($LC \leftarrow X14-X11$)
   MVA $X9$, XR
   DRAS ∗ $X10$; RPT
   MVA XR, $X9$
   MVA $X14$, $X11$ (The exponent of the result is in $X11$)
ADDSUB etc. . . .

As can be seen the horizontality is not extreme. However microprogram optimization is already a challenge.

The Nanodata QM-1

The QM-1 is a unique and rather complex architecture. We shall not consider it in as much detail as the Cal Data. Our goal here is to introduce the concept of *nanoprogramming* (cf. Figure 7.12).

The QM-1 has two levels of writable control store. The macroinstruction program is stored in an Mp of 256K 18-bit words. The macroinstructions are interpreted by vertical microprograms stored in an Mcs of 16K 18-bit words. A microinstruction consists of one opcode and two or more operands fields, possibly in subsequent microwords. The vertical microprograms are interpreted by other microprograms, called nanoprograms, stored in a control memory Ncs of 1K words of 360 bits. A nanoinstruction consists of two vectors, a K vector and a T vector, each 72 bits long. The K vector fields indicate interrupt and branching conditions as well as the operations that may be initiated by a T vector. The latter indicates specific operations. A K vector can be shared by successive T vectors and a nanoword contains one K vector and 4 T vectors.

Before proceeding with a succinct explanation of how macro, micro, and nano programs execute, we examine the architecture of the Pc. Besides Mp, Mcs and Ncs, there are several other banks of registers.

(i) Local store: LS [0:31] $\langle 0:17 \rangle$, 32 local registers some of which have specific capabilities. In particular LS [31], an McsDR, is divided into 3 fields of 6 bits each which can be used in conjunction with other registers (the F store to be seen shortly) to control part of the Pc. The four registers LS [24:27] can be used as McsAR or microprogram location counters; one of the F register designates which of the 4 is currently in use. The contents of the current McsAR are modified under nanoprogramming control. The LS

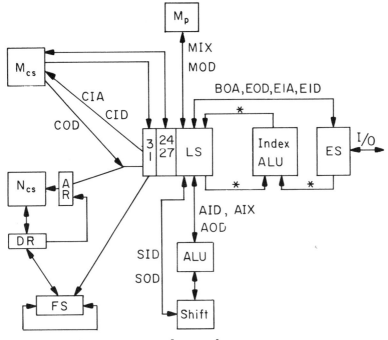

31 is for LS[31]; $\frac{24}{27}$ is for LS[24:27]

* indicates indirectly referenced buses

Legend for busses controlled by FS:

        Letter I M for Mp, C for Mcs, A for ALU,

                   S for Shift, E for ES

        Letter 2 I for input, O for output, L for left, R for right

        Letter 3 A for address, D for data, X for multiplex

Lines without legend are for direct connections

Figure 7.12   Nanodata QM-1 block diagram (simplified)

registers can serve as source or sinks of the D-units with some possible exceptions for *LS* [24:27].

    (ii) External store: *ES* [0:31] ⟨0:17⟩ is partitioned into several groups. *ES*
[0:7] provide the interface with Mp and the "outside world," *ES* [8:19] can
be an input to one of the D-units (the Index ALU) and *ES* [20:31], are reserved to service interrupts.

    (iii) The Fstore: *FS* [0:31] ⟨0:5⟩ provide indirect control over some hardware resources. Fourteen of these registers are used to provide control for the fourteen buses which connect all the stores and the D-units, six are special (e.g., one of these indicate the current McsAR), and twelve can be used as temporaries.

The processing power of the QM-1 is shared by 3 D-units:

(i) A conventional ALU, for logical operations and integer add and subtract with a wide range of carry possibilities controlled by a field in the K vector of a nanoinstruction;

(ii) A shifter, with extension for double shifts, also controlled within the K vector of a nanoinstruction. The output of the ALU can pass through the shifter before being sent on the output bus;

(iii) An index ALU, to help in fast indexing and masking operations on LS registers.

Since both Mcs and Ncs are writable, it is possible to emulate several macrolevel architectures as well as various microengines. It is even possible to consider Mcs as the main store and Mp as a back-up memory.

Let us examine how programs are executed. The opcode of a vertical microinstruction generates an entry point in Ncs. A nanoword consists of a K vector and 4 T vectors, $T1, T2, T3, T4$. Each T vector is executed in 75 ns although it can be stretched to 150 ns when ALU operations need this longer period. Furthermore, each 75 ns is subdivided into a leading edge and trailing edge and some commands will be obeyed on either one of these subperiods (hence a polyphase implementation).

When a nanoword is loaded in NcsDR, $T1$ is executed under the conditions specified by K. Then, at 75 ns intervals, $T2, T3, T4, T1, T2$, etc. . . . will be executed under the same K control until one of the following events occur:

- a program check condition: Mp parity or address error, attempt to execute in master mode, or time-out (i.e., the same nanoword being in NcsDR for over one second);
- a branch operation initiating a new nanoword load in NcsDR; this branching can be unconditional or conditional (this uses K vector specifications);
- A skip condition, making the next 75 ns a no-op and skipping over the next T vector.

When two or more of these conditions arise, a priority scheme resolves the conflicts.

The K and T vectors provide an effective 144 bit nanoinstruction, a very horizontal layout, with little encoding and much parallelism. The loading of NcsDR can be controlled so that prefetching is possible without delay.

Microprogrammability and especially nanoprogrammability require some expertise. The following simple example is a sketch of a nanoprogram to fetch a microinstruction. We do not show the K vector. The $T1$ through $T4$ vectors would do the following:

$T1$:   Read Mcs with McsAR being one of the LS [24:27] as indicated by a designated F register;

$T2$:   Load NcsAR with the opcode of the microinstruction just read, concatenated with the contents of some F register;

$T3$:   Read Ncs and increment McsAR by one;

$T4$:   Gate the result of the read to NcsDR and transfer the contents of McsDR (not shown in the figure) to LS [31].

Now, the next nanoword is in NcsDR and new K and $T1$ vectors are ready to be processed. Note that reading Ncs and gating the contents of the nanoword read to NcsDR are different commands which provide the prefetching capability.

7.3   APPLICATIONS OF MICROPROGRAMMING

In addition to the interpretation of a given instruction set, microprogramming can also be effectively applied to other tasks of an interpretative nature such as emulation, high-level language direct execution and enhancement of specific aspects of a given architecture.

7.3.1   Emulation

Microprogramming as we have described it can be considered as the interpretation of a native (macro) instruction set. *Emulation* can be defined as the interpretation of an instruction set different from the native one. Obviously, this definition is not precise for a machine such as the Cal Data 100 where no instruction set was imposed, although the microengine was geared to efficiently interpret a 16-bit macroarchitecture. In the case of the Nanodata QM-1, the definition is even less adequate. This is not the only blatant exception (cf. e.g., the Burroughs B1700 which does not have a native macroinstruction set). But, on the other hand, the definition fits well for interpretation of the IBM 7090 or IBM 1401 code on a System/360. In fact, it is emulation which provides the "compatibility" between these machines, or even between very closely related computers such as System/360 and System/370. As a final example, a new 32-bit entry in the computer market, DEC's VAX 11/780, has both a native instruction set and a PDP-11 emulated set, with the possibility of switching back and forth between the two modes.

Emulation does not necessitate microprogramming. The interpretation could be done entirely in software; we would then call it simulation. Thus, in the remainder of this section we imply that emulation is performed principally at the microprogramming level with some software support. Specialized hardware could also be present as in the emulate board and emulate register of the Cal Data.

A microprogrammed emulator is therefore a microprogram in a host machine executing the six steps of the instruction execution cycle of another machine. In order to be efficient, the emulated location counter, program status word and as much of the emulated Pc state as possible should be in the host microengine registers. The backbone of the emulator is what has been called the DIL (Do Interpretive Loop) which performs the fetching and decoding of a new emulated instruction. In addition, general utility routines are necessary for duties such as the alignment of the effective addresses in the proper format (i.e., the computation of the effective addresses according to the emulated machine and their modifications, if necessary, so that they will be sent in the proper form to the host's MAR), or such as the conversion of operands from the emulated to the host formats. For example, to emulate a 36 bit machine on the Cal Data, fetching of an operand would require 3 memory fetches ($3 \cdot 16 = 48$) and a masking operation of 12 bits. If these 36 bits were to represent a floating-point number in a given format, they would have to be transformed into a multiprecision format for the host, a task which is not complex in principle but not trivial in terms of number of required microinstructions. Each opcode of the emulated machine will correspond to a microroutine to perform the final operation. This can be followed again by some clean-up utility routines, such as those setting condition codes.

From the above paragraph, it is apparent that emulation speeds will vary greatly depending on the architectures of the host and of the emulated machines. If the instruction sets resemble each other and if the basic data types have the same length, then the emulation will be fast; it is conceivable that an emulated version of machine A and host B will be faster than the original version, if computer B has a faster Mp cycle that A, a fast Mcs and some horizontality which might not have been present in the original hardwired implementation. On the other hand, the example given previously (the interpretation of a 36-bit Pc on a 16-bit microengine) could yield nightmarish figures of performance.

The type of emulation that we have described is fairly simple. It requires the understanding of the emulated instruction set and of the host's microprogramming facilities. When I/O and/or privileged instructions are included in the emulation, then another level of complexity is added. Code conversions, buffering, interrupt and exception conditions must be handled. The reader is referred to Mallach's paper for a good introduction to this difficult topic.

The Burroughs B1700 can be called a pure emulating machine. The strengths of the B1700 as a host are primarily in the facts that it can directly access memory to the bit level and that all field lengths can be defined with the bit as a unit. The Mp accessing hardware, transparent to the (microprogrammer) user, allows fetching and storing of any number of bits from a given location with equal ease. Resources in the microengine can be used iteratively and/or fractionally under microprogramming control so that their physical structure is hidden from the user. As an example of this flexibility the fetching of a 36-bit instruction as mentioned above would be microprogrammed in a much simpler manner on the B1700 than on, say the Cal Data. Although the Burroughs B1700 has a 24-bit internal data path, a masking operation would not be required for the (36-24) bits of the second fetch but this field length would be indicated directly in the microoperation.

7.3.2   High-Level Language Direct Execution

The translation and subsequent execution of a program written in a high-level language (abbreviated HLL) can take one of two forms. In a compilation process, the whole source program is first translated into machine language (or some language very close to it). The machine language version, or object program, is then executed. In the interpreter process, source language statements are executed without going through the object program phase. This latter method can lead to very inefficient procedures since a source statement has to be analyzed everytime it is encountered. Therefore, the interpreter is usually split into two phases: a translation phase which transforms the source language into an intermediate language, and an execution phase which directly performs computations on this intermediate string.

Figure 7.13 summarizes these two concepts when the target machine is microprogrammed. In the interpreter case, the interpretive routine can be either written in machine language (itself interpreted by the target machine microprogram) or be microprogrammed (cf. Figure 7.13.c). It is in this latter case that we have what is called a *direct execution* of the HLL.

This application of microprogramming should not be confused with the design of HLL machines which are geared to the efficient execution of one (or more) HLL's. We shall briefly discuss this interesting approach to Computer Architecture in Chapter 11.

The intermediate language, or direct execution language (DEL), has to be a good output medium for the translation phase and a good input language

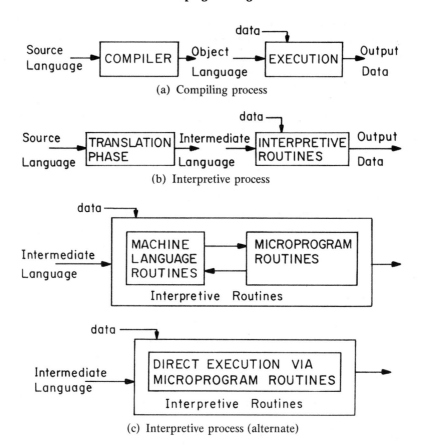

(a) Compiling process

(b) Interpretive process

(c) Interpretive process (alternate)

Figure 7.13 Execution and translation of high-level language source programs in a microprogrammed target machine

for the microprogram interpretation. This implies a series of constraints which we now summarize.

The translator's output, a DEL representation of the source language, should be compact. The translation should not be too time consuming (note that the translator itself could be microprogrammed directly), should take advantage of the idiosyncrasies of the HLL, e.g. for scanning, but should deliver a DEL code which is geared to the microengine. This latter requirement is of course void in machines such as the Burroughs B1700 which can tailor their microengines to various DEL's and hence have a different DEL and a different interpretation for each HLL (in Burroughs terminology a DEL is called an S-language). It is debatable whether the DEL should allocate critical resources such as registers since they might be used more efficiently by the interpretive routines.

This last point leads us to the expected characteristics of the DEL from the microengine's viewpoint. Since we have an interpretive process, a reverse polish notation, with associated data stacks, is quite appropriate. The operator representations in the polish stream should be encoded in such a way that they reflect the data types on which they operate. The decoding of these operators should be easy since it is performed often. For the same reason the decoding should be fast, that is take few microinstructions. Since there might be a rather large number of interpretive (micro)routines, the number of parameters to pass should be minimized. This parameter passing can become a lengthy process if Mp locations have to be used.

Some of the components of these two wish lists are contradictory. Moreover, in order to use a common DEL for several HLL's or a common DEL for various microengines, or both, the difficulties are compounded and executions become less efficient. Again, it appears that a flexible microengine is the best solution. The price to pay is a high level of expertise to be expected from the microprogrammers.

A well-known example of a DEL study is that of the direct execution of EULER, a subset of ALGOL 60 with semantics defined via an interpretive language, on an IBM System/360 model 30. (Recall the data paths and microinstruction format of Figures 7.8 and 7.9.) The EULER system consists of 3 segments:

(i) A translator (microprogrammed) which transforms EULER source code in reverse polish notation;
(ii) An interpreter (microprogrammed) which "executes" the polish string;
(iii) An I/O control program (written in System/360 machine language) linking the translator and the interpreter to the operating system.

The reverse polish string is contained in the program area. Each operator is represented by a single byte with some of them having "trailer" bytes. For example, a reference to a local variable in a given block is encoded by the operator followed by two bytes, the first one giving the block number and the second the ordinal number of the variable within the block. There also exist a stack area and a variable area. The run-time stack contains 32-bit words of which the first 4 bits indicate the type of variable stored in that location (undefined, integer, logical, stack label, variable area reference, procedure call and return masks, list head). The variable area has values of variables and elements of lists.

The translator is a one pass syntax-driven compiler which takes approximately 500 microwords. The interpreter is longer, about 2500 microinstructions. As an example of the interpretation, consider the execution of part of the polish string where the operator is 'and'. The semantics of the operation are as follows. The top of the run-time stack is accessed; if it does not contain a logical variable, an error routine will be entered; if the logical variable has value 'false', then control is transferred to the operator in the polish string whose address is contained in the two trailer bytes of the 'and' operator; if the value is 'true', then the next operator (found 3 bytes further) has to be interpreted and the stack is popped.

The 'and' operator has internal representation $X'52'$ (X means hexadecimal). Two operators which have closely related semantics, 'or' and 'then', have internal representations $X'50'$ and $X'53'$. The microprogram will take advantage of this to overlap decoding of the operator, access to the stack and testing if the top of the stack contains a logical value.

The current operator in the polish string is in a location (byte) whose address is in registers I and J. The top of the stack address is in the pair of registers UV. A Boolean variable has the following byte format:

byte 1: $X'31'$ if true, $X'30'$ if false;
byte 2-4: undefined.

The microroutine is then as follows (refer to Figure 7.8):

- Microword 1: Fetch the next operator, i.e., $IJ \rightarrow MN$, read Mp; result in R;
  Increment string pointer $J + 0 + 1 \rightarrow JC$ (meaning $J \leftarrow J + 1$);
- Microword 2: Transfer R to G (R will be needed for reading the top of the stack);
  Write back (recall Mp is core);
  Do a 4-way transfer depending on bits 0 and 1 of R;
- Microword 3: (Common to all operators with the first two bits being 10)
  Increment I if a carry out results from the incrementation of J, $I + 0 + C \rightarrow I$;
  Read the top of the stack from Mp, $UV \rightarrow MN$; Read Mp;
  Result in R;
  Do a 4-way transfer depending on bits 2 and 3 of G (bits 2 and 3 of the opcode);
- Microword 4: (Common to all operators with an opcode starting with $X'5'$)
  Test the top of the stack (now in R) by adding the con-

stant $X'D0'$ and setting $S4$ to 1 if the result is 0 (the carry is ignored) (Recall the example in Section 7.2.2); This can be written as: $R + KH \rightarrow Z$;
At the same time $S5$ is set to 1 if the low byte was 0 (value 'false');
Write back (recall Mp core);
Do a 4 way transfer depending on bits 5 and 6 of G;

- Microword 5: (Common to all operators with an opcode starting with $X'5'$ and 2 0's; common still to 'and', 'or' and 'then')
Increment string pointer saving the possible carry $J + 0 + 1 \rightarrow JC$; Read Mp;
Do a 4 way branch depending on bit 7 of G and $S5$;

- Microword 6: (Common to 'and' and 'then' and assuming a logical value of 'false')
Increment I; write back;
Test if the type was logical (by testing $S4$) and do a 2-way branch on $S4$;

- Microword 7: (Common to 'and' and 'then' and assuming a logical value of 'true')
Increment J again to skip the second trailer byte and save carry on $S3$; write back;
Do a 4-way branch based on $S4$ (wrong type) and $S3$ (carry-out of J);
(In fact we have a duplicate microword for $S4$ wrong type and both values of $S3$).

Let us now assume that the path went through microword 6 and that the type was indeed logical. Then:

- Microword 8: (Common to 'and' and 'then', assuming a logical type and a value 'false')
The two trailer bytes (one of them is already in R) become the next values of I and J;
$R \rightarrow I$;
$IJ \rightarrow MN$; Read;
Do a two way branch depending on bit 7 of $G7$;

- Microword 9: (Only for 'and', variable of type logical and value 'false')
$R \rightarrow J$; write back; go back to microword 1.

The reader is referred to Exercise 6 for another possible path. The compactness of the microcode should be noticed. In the above case, it takes 8 microinstructions to realize the execution of the two (macro)instructions:

Get top of stack and compare with logical and 'false' (compare immediate);
Branch if equal (Branch on condition);

But between 8 and 10 microinstructions would also be the longest path in the other cases which correspond to the full (macro) program (the difference depends on carry-outs during the incrementing of *IJ*). It could be as follows:

ANDROUTINE   Get top of stack and compare with logical and 'false' (compare immediate);
Branch if equal (branch on condition);
Compare with logical and 'true' (compare immediate);
Branch on not equal (type error) (branch on condition);
Pop stack (subtract immediate);

Furthermore the compiler has been assumed here to generate on-line code which is wasteful of space while the microprogram shared its code among many opcodes.

It is difficult to compare different implementations of a high-level language. In this particular example the microprogram can take advantage of stack accessing and similar features. But if floating-point operations were introduced, the microprogram would have no advantage over a machine language interpretation. In general, the DEL technique will be useful when the microengine is flexible and the HLL has features which can be easily interpreted.

7.3.3 Tuning of Architectures

Microprogramming gives the opportunity to computer designers to modify and expand classical (von Neumann) instructions sets. The trend is apparent in modern machines where powerful machine language instructions resembling HLL constructs are available. For example, the DEC VAX 11/780 has the following machine instructions:

- "POLY *X*, deg, Tab" which computes the polynomial of degree 'deg' and variable '*X*' with the coefficients found in the table of address 'Tab'. This instruction is used extensively in the run-time scientific library for the calculation of sine and cosine functions. The microcode carries the evaluation through Horner's method;
- "INDEX subscript, lowerbound, upperbound, dimension, index in, index out" which performs the operation:

  indexout ← (index in + subscript)·dimension, and checks if the subscript is within the lower and upper bounds. This instruction is useful for accessing unidimensional arrays, with each element of the same size, or by cascading it for multidimensional arrays. For example, if a FORTRAN declaration were:

Integer A (10, 5) then the compiler would generate:

INDEX J, 1, 5, 10, 0, RO;
INDEX I, 1, 10, 1, RO, RO;

to gain access to $A(I, J)$;

- "INSQUE" and "REMQUE" to respectively insert and delete an element at the front or the rear of a circular doubly linked list (queue). These operations frequently occur in operating system functions;

- "CASE Selector, base, limit, displace 1, . . . , displace n", which performs the equivalent of a Pascal case or FORTRAN computed GOTO;

- "CALL G" (Call procedure with general argument list);

- "CALL S" (Call procedure with actual arguments or addresses on the stack);

- "RET" (return from procedure) which provides standard procedure calls and returns with savings of all the registers that are used by the procedure and setting of entries in the stack for argument and address linkages (cf. Chapter 9 Section 3.7).

Obviously, there is a trade-off in introducing complex instructions: the gain incurred in execution speed vs. the amount of space taken in the Mcs. Tuning of an instruction set then consists of monitoring instruction usage, modifying the "native" instruction set, measuring the gain (or loss) in efficiency and cost, and iteratively repeating this procedure until a reasonable improvement has been achieved.

Ideally the process just described could be done dynamically for machines which have writable Mcs. Monitoring can be done in a few microinstructions (modern machines should have this capability in their microcode in the same sense as compilers should monitor the frequency of execution of each HLL statement). Analysis of the (macro)instruction trace would reveal instruction sequences which could be lumped together. A microprogram generator would then assemble the microcode for those sequences and insert these new microroutines in the microprogram. The last action would be to replace the original sequences by new instructions whose interpretation would be the new microroutines.

While the state of the art certainly does not allow this complete dynamic tuning, each subprocess can be done in turn. For example, to tune a line-oriented text-editor for a given machine we could start by monitoring which commands are often called and which service routines are most frequently activated. Then, for each of these subroutines (at the macroinstruction level), we would monitor where the bulk of the computing takes place. This could lead to the microprogramming of a sequence such as:

*LB, R*1	loc 1, index	(Load byte (or character) from loc 1 indexed);
*CB, R*1	loc 2	(compare with byte at loc 2);
BCS	add	(branch on nonequal to some address);

which could be part of the main loop of the command "Search for string *X*". Another example would be the microprogramming of a search through line numbers until a given line has been found (or discovered missing), assuming that a line is linked via a pointer to its successor.

Some precautions have to be taken. Assume that instead of microprogramming the above 3 instructions as a sequence, we microprogram the whole loop which does that search. If pending interrupts are tested only when a machine language instruction is fetched, then interrupts might not be serviced for the time it takes to read the text residing in Mp. Care is also required in saving and restoring the microengine registers used in the new microroutines so that no conflict arises.

Manual tunings of this kind have been reported in the literature with gains ranging from 4:1 to 8:1 in Pc execution speed and number of Mp references.

The future will bring more of this enhancement of computer architectures via a redefinition of the instruction sets tailored to specific applications.

7.4 MICROPROGRAMMING SYSTEM

In the same sense that we can define a computer system as more than the hardware and the operating system but less than the hardware, operating system, language translators and application programs, or a programming system as more than a programming language but less than an operating system, we can envision a microprogramming system as more than the microengine, the microstore and the permanent microprograms but less than the computer system as described above. A very ambitious microprogramming system could have the components shown in Figure 7.14.

7.4.1 Components of a Microprogramming System

The generation of a microprogram is the result of a process which receives as input descriptions of the algorithm to be executed and of the hardware resources needed to perform and sequence the operations. In conventional programming, these inputs are, generally, high-level language source pro-

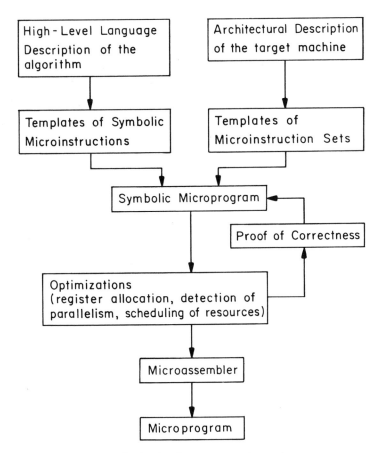

Figure 7.14 A microprogramming system

grams and machine language instruction sets. A single or multi-phase compiler, more or less optimized depending on available options, takes care of the translation. In a microprogramming system, the task is more difficult since:

- The microengine hardware is more detailed and the efficient allocation of some resources (e.g., microengine registers) is even more at a premium than in conventional compilers;
- The sequencing of microoperations in horizontal machines offers more variety than the two-way branches found in machine language instruction sets;

- The parallelism allowed in horizontal implementations imply that concurrent operations have to be detected and scheduled;
- Optimization of microcode is to be performed both in a space related manner since microprograms have to be short to cut down on the cost of Mcs (longer microprograms also imply a larger microinstruction width since the "next address" field will be larger) and shorter microprograms result in fewer microinstruction fetches, and in a time related fashion since microprograms are executed frequently.

Looking at Figure 7.14 we see two paths converging towards the final microprogram. On the left-hand side we start with a HLL description of the algorithm to be described. Although we could use any HLL, it appears more practical to use modifications of existing languages with new features emphasizing the microprogramming aspects. For example, we might have "shift" statements, tests on specific conditions such as carry or overflow, and declarations of fixed resources such as MAR and MDR. The language, like any high-level language, should be machine independent but efficiency constraints dictate that some machine dependency be included. Most current HLL's geared to microprogramming have facilities to "declare" hardware resources such as (microengine) registers, bit width of data paths, status control bits etc. . . . . Similarly, at the highest level on the right-hand side, we could have a description of the microengine and of its communication with the rest of the system. Languages such as ISP or CDL could be used with extensions to show potential concurrent use of resources.

Ideally, it would be desirable to automatically translate these descriptions into a symbolic microprogram analogous to the macroassemblers found in a conventional translating system. This intermediate step is mandatory here because of the need for optimization. While the translation of the HLL language into this symbolic microprogram, given the formats of the symbolic microinstructions, appears to be within the state of the art, the automated translation of the microengine description into templates of microinstructions is a problem which is far from being solved.

It is on the symbolic microprogram that optimization, resource allocation and scheduling should be performed. The next section will cover these topics in more detail. Concurrently, we would like to prove the correctness of the microprogram. Semi-automatic proofs might be realistic since we are dealing with small enough sequences of code so that almost exhaustive searches (in the worst case) would not be overly time-consuming.

The result of the optimization phase would be a microprogram in symbolic form analogous to a typical assembly language program in a conventional translating system. The final transformation to the absolute microprogram presents no conceptual difficulty.

As of the mid to late seventies, the paucity of user microprogrammable machines has hampered the development of microprogramming systems. There are some production microassemblers, and a number of HLL's specific to microprogramming have been proposed and translators do exist. Work is in progress to describe (horizontal) microengines in a fashion useful to the microprogrammer. As we shall see, several aspects of the optimization phases are being investigated and proofs of correctness for microprograms is a topic which is of interest to academia and industry. What is lacking is a unified system which will be mandatory in the future if the concept of user-microprogrammable machines is to be successful.

7.4.2 Microprogram Optimization

Our concern here is limited to the optimization of a microprogram once the algorithm and the microengine are fixed. Assume that the symbolic microprogram is a sequence of almost vertical microoperations. It consists of quadruplets of the form:

Command, source operands, sink operand, resources,

when the operation is not of the branch type. For branch operations, the quadruplets take the form:

Command, testing operand, destination, resources.

For example, we could have:

Shift left 1, $R6$, $R6$, {Shifter, bus A, bus M}

for a left shift of one of register $R6$, and

BOVON, MS, overflow, {Microstatus register, bus A, bus M}

for a branch on the overflow bit of the microstatus register.

Optimization steps common in compilers such as the removal of code from loops if the operands do not depend on the loop index can be readily performed on the microprogram in this format. We will not deal here with this so-called global optimization and once again refer interested readers to books on compiler construction.

The next steps of the optimization procedure before passing the resulting microprograms to the microassembler depend on the type of microengine. If it is of the vertical kind, then the only remaining task is to allocate resources such as registers and completely verticalize the microinstructions. But if a horizontal machine is the target, then we can detect parallelism and construct microinstructions from concurrently executable microoperations according to some scheduling algorithm. The resource allocation will generally take place prior to the detection and the scheduling, but could as well be embedded in either one.

Register Allocation

As mentioned at the end of Chapter 4, register allocation is one of these "hard" problems for which it is conjectured that (in the worst case) optimal solutions can be obtained only through an exhaustive search. However if we restrict ourselves to straight-line microcode sequences, with a single entry and a single exit, then we can have some heuristics which yield "good" microprograms where the quality of the microprogram measure is the number of Mp references needed to execute the sequence. We can even envision branch and bound techniques which would yield an optimal solution "rapidly" if the heuristics during the selection of partial solutions are well selected.

There are some differences which make the microprogramming register allocation process different from the one for machine language generation. First the set of microregisters is more heterogeneous: there exist special counters for loop execution, the MAR and MDR connections to Mp are highly specialized etc. .... Second, not all registers can be sources of all operations. For example, only some of them could be gated to a given operand source of the ALU (recall the IBM System/360 Model 30 CB field). Finally, not every microregister can be directly loaded from Mp. Secondary differences also exist if the function to be optimized is execution time rather than number of loads and fetches. This belongs more to the domain of scheduling which we consider shortly.

Detection of parallelism

We mentioned in Chapter 4 the conditions for concurrent execution of two sequential instructions. In Chapter 10 we shall see how this can be applied in a multiprocessing environment. Here, as was the case for look-ahead processors, we are concerned only with straight-line microprograms. The reason why we do not have to generalize is that, in addition to the data dependency constraints, we have resource dependencies. Hence finding that two segments of microcode can be executed concurrently from the data viewpoint will not help since in most instances these two segments would need common resources such as the ALU. Thus, the main objective here is to detect parallelism within straight-line sequences. Some authors are of the opinion that even in this restricted case, an automatic procedure will fail to discover most of the inherent parallelism and that this phase should receive the assistance of HLL features. In particular, "the single assignment rule" has been advocated. This rule dictates that a variable can be assigned only a single value during the execution of a program. Assignments can then be executed as soon as the input operands are ready (notice that here we have some contradiction with the register assignment problem which will result in assigning different values to the same register).

Independently of the HLL and of the place of the register allocation process, a possible strategy for the automatic detection of parallelism is to first disregard the resource conflicts and to consider only the data dependency precedence requirements. For each straight line sequence, a directed acyclic graph whose nodes are microoperations and whose arcs indicate the precedence relationships (recall Figure 4.11) is obtained. The method to obtain such graphs is a straightforward application of the conditions expressed in System (1) (Chapter 4 Section 3) except that some additional parallelism can be detected by considering subtle points such as typical in-gate/out-gate timings for register-register transfers and polyphase microinstruction cycles. For example the two microoperations:

$$\text{AND}, \{R3, R6\}, R6, \{\text{ALU, bus } A, \text{bus } B, \text{bus } M\}$$
$$\text{SHL}, \{R4\}, R3, \{\text{Shifter, bus } A, \text{bus } M\}$$

can be considered data independent (but not necessarily resource independent) if the control pulse to transfer out from a register is applied a significant amount of time before the in-gating control pulse (obviously both pulses are within a clock cycle). Or in a two-phase system the first operation could be during phase 1 and the second during phase 2.

The second part of the detection of parallelism is to resolve resource conflicts. At the same time microinstructions are generated and sequenced. Hence it is difficult to separate these two processes.

Resource conflict detection and scheduling

The output of the previous pass is a directed acyclic graph with nodes representing microoperations and arcs showing precedence constraints. As in Chapter 4 we could restrict ourselves to the transitive reduction of that graph. In order to make the explanation less abstract, we will refer to the example graph of Figure 7.15.a. The graph has been drawn in such a way that all nodes on the same horizontal level, say level i, can start at the earliest at time i (we assume the source to start at time 1 and all microoperations to take the same amount of time). In Figure 7.15.b we show the same graph but with the nodes arranged so that the latest starting times are readily apparent. Those microoperations which appear at the same levels in both graphs have fixed starting times and can be called critical microoperations (in the same way as we have critical paths in PERT-like networks). These critical microoperations are grouped into L microcritical sets C_i where L is the number of levels in the graph. In our example we would have:

$$C_1 = \{1\}, C_2 = \{2, 4\}, C_3 = \{5, 8\}, C_4 = \{9, 10, 11\},$$
$$C_5 = \{12, 13\}, C_6 = \{14\}.$$

The ideal situation would be to have a microprogram of L microinstructions. However if any 2 members of a given C_i have a resource conflict this will not be possible. The first step of the scheduling procedure is to test this criterion and create new critical sets in case of resource conflict. Because an optimal scheduling would require an exhaustive search of all possibilities, the choice of which critical operations to delay must be based on heuristics. For example, we could delay the microoperations with the smallest number of suc-

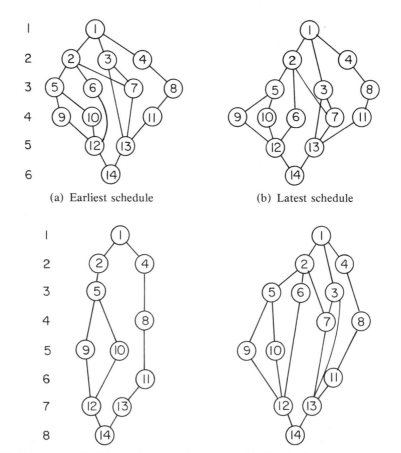

(a) Earliest schedule   (b) Latest schedule

(c) Scheduling of critical microoperations   (d) Final microprogram

Figure 7.15 Horizontal microprogram graph of microoperations and scheduling

cessors (if in the graph shown in Figure 7.15 microoperations 5 and 8 were using the same resource then we would delay 8). Once the critical microoperations have been scheduled, the non-critical ones are assigned in the same manner, with new microinstructions being created if the microoperations cannot be fitted within their earliest and latest times. Again adequate heuristics must be investigated. Finally, a last pass can "shrink" the microprogram which may be longer than necessary due to the above perturbations. This is better explained by continuing our example.

Assume that the resource conflicts between microoperations are:

(2, 3), (4, 5, 8, 13, 14), (6, 9, 12), (7, 10, 11), (4, 9), (6, 8, 10, 12), and (11, 13, 14).

The scheduling of critical microoperations would result in the graph of Figure 7.15.c. which now has 8 levels instead of the original 6. Notice that we chose 9 and 10 to be placed at the same level. We could have assigned 9 and 11 and this would not have changed the number of levels.

It remains to place the non-critical microoperations. We take them in lexicographical order and try to assign them as soon as possible. Microoperation 3 cannot be at level 2 since it conflicts with operation 2 but is possible at level 3. Microoperation 6 can also be placed at level 3. Continuing in this fashion, we obtain the graph of Figure 7.15.d. Since it also has 8 levels it cannot be reduced. Other heuristics might have resulted in a graph of more than 8 levels which could have been reduced by trying to move microoperations earlier (e.g., in our final graph 9 could be moved one level up).

Once the microoperations have been assigned a level, it becomes a simple matter to pass a reasonable output to the microassembler. The assumptions of equal timing could be relaxed for microoperations requiring resources such as Mp and the same techniques as those described for Hu's extended algorithm in Chapter 4 could be used.

From the preceding, it is apparent that the generation of microcode should be an interactive process with human input to direct and correct the automated procedures when necessary.

7.5   BIBLIOGRAPHICAL NOTES, REFERENCES AND EXERCISES

The machine represented in Figure 7.2 is essentially the same as the one used in [Rosin 69]. Wilkes' original scheme is from [Wilkes and Stringer 53] reprinted in [Bell and Newell 70]. Two monographs [Agrawala and Rauscher 76] and [Salisbury 76] give solid descriptions of several microprogrammed machines and in particular of the Nanodata QM-1. [Husson 70] is an encyclopedic view of the System/360 microprogramming implementation. The techniques used for the System/360 are also well exposed in [Tucker 67]. [Tanenbaum 76] has a good introduction to microprogramming and the subject is well treated in [Flynn 75].

More details on the Cal Data 100 and the Nanodata QM-1 can be obtained from specific manuals [California Data Processors 75, Nanodata 74]. [Wilner 72] is the standard paper on the Burroughs B1700 while additional references can be found in the two monographs cited above.

Emulation is discussed at length in [Mallach 75]. The DIL paramount importance for efficiency was first pointed out in [Tucker 65]. The presentation of the Burroughs Interpreter machine by [Reigel, Faber and Fischer 72] stresses the microengine requirements for interpretation as discussed in Section 3, The EULER implementation, as well as a description of the features of the IBM System/360 Model 30 microengine, are described in [Weber 67]. Table 7.3 is abstracted from [Case and Padegs 78]. Arguments for the tuning of computer architectures can be found in [Abd-Alla and Karlgaard 74] and [Rauscher and Agrawala 76].

Three special issues of IEEE Transactions on Computers have been devoted to microprogramming [IEEE TC 71, IEEE TC 74, IEEE TC 76]. Among many HLL's for microprogramming one can cite SIMPL, a single assignment ALGOL-like language, [Ramamoorthy and Tsuchiya 74], and STRUM a Pascal oriented language [Patterson 76]. Detection of parallelism is treated in the SIMPL article as well as in [Dasgupta and Tartar 76]. The general optimization procedure is well summarized in [Agerwala 76]. The scheduling aspect can again be found in the SIMPL reference as well as in [Tsuchiya and Gonzalez 76].

References

1. Abd-Alla, A. M. and D. C. Karlgaard, "Heuristic Synthesis of Microprogrammed Computer Architecture", *IEEE Trans. on Comp.*, *C-23*, (Aug. 1974), 802–807.

2. Agerwala, T., "Microprogram Optimization: A Survey", *IEEE Trans. on Comp.*, *C-25*, (Oct. 1976), 962–973.

3. Agrawala, A. K. and T. G. Rauscher, *Foundations of Microprogramming Architecture, Software and Applications*, Academic Press, New York, N.Y., 1976.

4. Bell, C. G. and A. Newell, *Computer Structures: Readings and Examples*, McGraw Hill, New York, N.Y., 1970.

5. California Data Processors *Cal Data 100 Engine*, Technical manual, 1975.

6. Case, R. P. and A. Padegs, "Architecture of the IBM System/370", *Comm. ACM*, *21*, (Jan. 1978), 73–96.

7. Dasgupta, S. and J. Tartar, "The Identification of Maximal Parallelism in Straight-Line Microprograms", *IEEE Trans. on Comp.*, *C-25*, (Oct. 1976), 986–991.

8. Flynn, M. J. "Interpretation, Microprogramming, and the Control of a Computer", in *Introduction to Computer Architecture*, H. Stone ed., SRA, Chicago, Ill., 1975, 432–472.

9. Husson, S., *Microprogramming*: *Principles and Practice*, Prentice-Hall, Englewood Cliffs, N.J., 1970.

10. *IEEE Trans. on Computers*, *C-20*, (Jul. 1971), 727–794.

11. *IEEE Trans. on Computers*, *C-23*, (Aug. 1974), 754–837.

12. *IEEE Trans. on Computers*, *C-25*, (Oct. 1976), 969–1009.

13. Mallach, E. G., "Emulator Architecture", *Computer*, *8*, (Aug. 1975), 24–32.

14. Nanodata Corp. *QM-1 Hardware Level User's Manual*, Nanodata Corp., 1974.

15. Patterson, D. A., "STRUM: Structured Microprogram Development System for Correct Firmware", *IEEE Trans. on Comp.*, *C-25*, (Oct. 1976), 974–985.

16. Ramamoorthy, C. V. and M. Tsuchiya, "A High-Level Language for Horizontal Microprogramming", *IEEE Trans. on Comp.*, *C-23*, (Aug. 1974), 791–801.

17. Rauscher, T. G. and A. K. Agrawala, "Developing Application Oriented Computer Architectures on General Purpose Microprogrammable Machines", *Proc. AFIPS 1976 Nat. Comp. Conf.*, *45*, AFIPS Press, Montvale, N. J., 715–722.

18. Reigel, E. W., Faber, U. and D. A. Fischer, "The Interpreter—A Microprogrammable Building Block System", *Proc. AFIPS 1972 Spring Joint Comp. Conf.*, *40*, AFIPS Press, Montvale, N. J., 705–723.

19. Rosin, R., "Contemporary Concepts of Microprogramming and Emulation", *Computing Surveys*, *1*, (Dec. 1969), 197–212.

20. Salisbury, A., *Microprogrammable Computer Architectures*, American Elsevier, New York, N.Y., 1976.

21. Tanenbaum, A. S., *Structured Computer Organization*, Prentice Hall, Englewood Cliffs, N. J., 1976.

22. Tsuchiya, M. and M. J. Gonzalez, "Towards Optimization of Horizontal Microprograms", *IEEE Trans. on Comp.*, *C-25*, (Oct. 1976), 992–999.

23. Tucker, S. G., "Emulation of Large Systems", *Comm. ACM*, *8*, (Dec. 1965), 753–761.

24. Tucker, S. G., "Microprogram Control for System/360", *IBM Systems Journal*, *6*, (1967), 222–241.

25. Weber, H., "A Microprogrammed Implementation of EULER on IBM System/360 Model 30", *Comm. ACM*, *10*, (Sep. 1967), 549–558.

26. Wilkes, M. V. and J. B. Stringer, "Microprogramming and the Design of the Control Circuits in an Electronic Digital Computer", *Proc. of the Cambridge Philosophical Society, 49,* 1953, 230–238.

27. Wilner, W. T., "Design of the Burroughs B1700", *Proc. AFIPS 1972 Fall Joint Comp. Conf., 41,* AFIPS Press, Montvale, N. J., 489–497.

Exercises

1. Complete the microprogram of Figure 7.7 for ADD, CLA and STO.

2. Label 6 of Figure 7.7 now reads

    6   19,93   GO TO MUL

    What additional hardware is needed to perform a multiplication (assume a 16 bit machine) without having a multiplier, i.e., the adder should be used. After having assessed the new resources needed, define additional microoperations (e.g. "Shift left one" etc. ...) and write the microprogram for the multiply routine.

3. You are given a microprogrammable computer with word length of 32 bits and standard binary arithmetic.

    (i)   Give a floating-point number representation (single and double precision).
    (ii) How would you microprogram a floating-point normalized addition instruction? You can consider only the case of single precision.

    You should define not only the algorithm but the microword format and indicate the "local" hardware set up (e.g., possible need for a subroutine register or stack). A horizontal approach to microprogramming is preferred but not mandatory. Indicate clearly which registers you will use and the bus structure. You can assume that the operands are already in internal registers and that the result will be placed in one of them.

4. Repeat Exercise 3 with a floating-point multiplication. Consider the case where you want to keep a double precision mantissa for the result. (You can assume normalized operands.)

5. Assume that you want to emulate the Sigma 5 presented in Chapter 2 on a Cal Data (you do not have an emulate board at your disposal). What parts of the Sigma 5's Pc state would you store in the Cal Data microengine registers? Sketch the DIL as microprogrammed on the Cal Data.

6. Continue the interpretation of the 'and' operator as in Section 7.3.2. in the case where we have the 'and' operator, a logical variable and a value 'true'. Recall that a branch occurs depending on $S3$ and that the stack must be popped.

Chapter 8

INPUT-OUTPUT

In previous chapters we have explained how the Pc manipulated information, under the supervision of a control unit, once this information was in Mp. We have indicated how the management of a memory hierarchy could be automated to direct transfers of information between Mp and Ms. We also introduced the devices (the DASD's) which could be used as Ms components.

In this chapter, we turn our attention to the process of transferring information in the memory hierarchy, extending this latter notion to all input-output devices. In a PMS sense, we consider the paths connecting the transducers T to Mp and vice-versa. These paths pass through a series of controllers K and possibly processors P that we call channels. Our goal is first to try and delineate the concepts leading to the control of the I/O function (Section 1). Then the hardware needed to assist in the different forms of control will be introduced (Section 2). In the third section, we shall briefly sketch the physical properties of I/O devices and of their local controllers. Section 4 will deal with I/O instructions seen from the Pc's viewpoint and with channel (i.e., Kio or Pio) programs. Finally, Section 5 will consider the performance gains attained with asynchronous I/O processing.

There are three principal considerations for the treatment of input-output: timing, speed and coding. By timing we mean that the clocks of the Pc and of the individual devices are not the same and that it will be necessary to synchronize messages and to control the access to the devices. The speed factor relates to the fact that the faster I/O devices, the DASD's, are at least three orders and can be as much as six orders of magnitude slower than Mp and Pc. Finally, the coding requirement reflects the fact that information stored inside Mp is machine rather than human oriented and consequently data will have to be encoded or decoded when it emanates from or reaches the world outside the machine.

Because of the immense variety of I/O systems, the concepts that we present are seldom found in their purest forms. For example, we classify interrupt systems in four categories but our examples do not fit neatly in any of them. The same will be true when we look at methods for transferring information between an I/O device and Mp. In a particular system we shall have a composite of the methods that we present. Our goal here is to show what are the main options and how I/O systems are organized conceptually.

8.1 CONTROLLING THE I/O FUNCTION

The final responsibility for the transfer of information between Mp and the "outside world" belongs to the Pc. However, the Pc can delegate some authority to controllers or other processors while performing other tasks. This method of control was not the original one and we start this section by looking at what has been called the *program directed* approach.

8.1.1 Program Directed Control

In the von Neumann model all information had to flow through the Pc. Before the advent of interrupts and channels, a typical I/O sequence (e.g., for an input or READ of a block of several words) was of the form:

1. Select the I/O device;
2. Loop until it is ready;
3. Transfer a word from the I/O device buffer to the Pc accumulator;
4. Transfer the contents of the accumulator to an Mp location;
5. Update the Mp location address and test if the whole block has been transmitted;
6. If the transfer is not completed then go back to step 2 else disconnect the device.

The selection of the I/O device and of the command (Read, Write, etc.) can be done in one instruction. Step 2, the test for readiness of a device, implies that each of these has a status bit indicating whether it is positioned at the correct place. For example, a tape controller will not be ready until it has located the exact section of tape which has to be read (or written). Thus Step 2 was usually implemented as a wait-loop such as:

*   Skip next instruction if device ready;
*   Jump to previous instruction.
    .
    .
    .

The advantage of using a conventional programming practice and a logical process for updating addresses and counts is more than counterbalanced by the disadvantages relative to the I/O requirements stated previously. The primordial inconvenience is that the Pc is slowed down to the speed of the I/O device it directs. In order to have the Pc maintain some freedom the I/O transfers should be made in parallel with the central processor's execution. But naturally we need to invest in some message passing capability.

8.1.2 Interrupts

If we assume that we have the capability of transferring information between Mp and the transducers while the Pc is kept busy by some other task, we must provide some mechanism to tell the Pc when the transfer is completed. This is evidently mandatory when the direction of transfer is from a T to Mp (a READ operation) but it is also necessary during a transfer from Mp to T (a WRITE) for the Pc must know when the contents of the Mp locations being transferred are free again. This is because this area of Mp is generally a buffer, used specifically for I/O transfers, and hence the Pc must neither overwrite what has not yet been transferred nor wait unduly when it could start refilling the buffer.

Testing of the status bits of the devices as introduced in the previous solution is sufficient for communication purposes. For example, the Pc, when becoming idle, could test which of the I/O devices which were busy are now free. This could also be done at periodic intervals. This *polling* mechanism has been used in a more sophisticated fashion in the communication between the peripheral processors Pio's and the Pc of the CDC 6600. It is one of the methods used for the interface between a large number of terminals and the Pio which controls them. This has been called *front-end processing*. As we shall see, it is also used in channels which control more than one I/O device.

Polling takes some valuable Pc time, especially in a multiprogramming environment where it can be safely assumed that the Pc will not be "idle". It is therefore more reasonable to open communication only when some message has to be passed. This leads to the concept of *interrupts*. Interrupts are not generated solely by I/O activities. The general philosophy is to have the Pc respond to stimuli other than those created by its current internal operations.

Different types, or classes, of interrupts can be recognized, such as:

- I/O interrupts: they are activated upon successful (or unsuccessful) completion of an I/O operation. For example, conditions such as a channel becoming free after the end of the transfer that it was controlling, the control unit of a device terminating its operation (tape rewind), special error conditions (unsuccessful read from a tape), generate I/O interrupts.

- Timer interrupts: hardware clocks might generate interrupts at different intervals of time. First a location (in Mp or a special register) is initialized to some "time" and at regular intervals this time is decreased and tested for 0. When a null value is encountered an interrupt occurs. This can be used for accounting, scheduling and protection from malfunction.
- Hardware failure interrupts: e.g., power failure, memory parity error, etc.
- Program interrupts (*traps*): e.g., arithmetic overflows, division by 0, memory reference outside of a user's field, illegal op-codes.
- Supervisory calls (SVC): these perform the switching of user mode to master mode. This is necessary when some instructions (e.g., I/O instructions) are not permitted to be executed in user mode (cf. Section 4).

Similar interrupts can be grouped into levels which have associated priorities. To simplify the presentation, we first describe the handling of a single level single priority system.

Interrupt Processing (simple case)

Assume that some program A is running and that an interrupt occurs. The questions to be answered are:

- When is an interrupt recognized?
- What is the source of the interrupt?
- What actions are to be taken to clear the interrupt?
- How is the execution of the interrupted program resumed?

Interrupts being exogenous events can arise at any time. Since the executing program A must be temporarily stopped and later resumed, this must be done when the program's state can be easily retrieved. This implies that the recognition points are to be clearly delineated. The most obvious time when this can be done is at the beginning of the instruction fetch cycle. Thus in general the instruction interpretation cycle will be of the following form, where IA is the program counter or instruction address register as in Figure 2.8:

$$\neg \text{ interrupt } \rightarrow (IR \leftarrow Mp[IA] \; ; \; IA \leftarrow IA + 1;$$
$$\text{next instruction execution});$$
$$\text{interrupt } \rightarrow \text{ call the interrupt routine.}$$

From the hardware viewpoint it is then sufficient (in this simple case) to set a flip-flop when an interrupt request occurs.

With this scheme, at instruction fetch time the Pc tests a flip-flop, F, indicating whether an interrupt is pending. This can be implemented as follows. Since interrupts are grouped into levels, each level can be the sink of several lines carrying the interrupt requests and an interrupt flip-flop F_i will be assigned to each level. Thus the recognition problem is to determine whether one of the interrupt request flip-flops F_i is set (this will become slightly more complex later). This can be done by ORing the outputs of the F_i into F which is tested by Pc.

There are two major exceptions to the procedure just outlined. The first one might arise when the Pc is microprogrammed. Then interrupt recognition can be done at the microinstruction fetch level. This might be necessary if the microcode has been optimized so that some rather lengthy looping construct in machine language was translated into a segment of microcode called by a single "super" machine instruction. In general though, interrupt occurrences imply a transfer of control at machine language instruction fetch times to a fixed location in Mcs (the control store) in a manner similar to what will be described for the transfer to fixed locations in Mp. In addition, since many microinstruction formats allow testing for pending interrupts, branching to the same fixed location in Mcs is possible.

The second exception is for time-consuming instructions such as those which move a source string to a destination string. If the source string is k words long, then at least k memory cycles will be needed for the transfer. Some interrupting sources might be unable to wait that long. However, in this case, the instruction can be interrupted after each word (or byte) transfer if care is taken in the hardware or microprogram which controls the instruction's execution. More specifically, let:

MOVE source address, destination address, count
be the format of the instruction. After each word (or byte) is transferred, the source and destination addresses are incremented and the count decremented appropriately in the instruction register. The location counter is not incremented until the count becomes zero. Thus, if an interrupt occurs, the instruction can be resumed from where it left off at the end of an information unit transfer.

Let us return now to the point where the Pc has sensed that one (or more) interrupt is pending. After recognition of an interrupt condition, several actions occur, some via software, some via hardware, the distinction depending on the particular machine. The first operation is to assess from which level the interrupt is coming. If there is only one level this is simple. If there are several, then let us assume that we remain in a simple case and that there is a built-in priority. For example, the vector of interrupt request flip-flops is scanned (hardware action) from left to right until the first set flip-flop is encountered. We shall soon return to this subject.

Once the Pc knows which level has triggered the interrupt it will (in a system without priority):

- reset the interrupt request and acknowledge the device for the interrupt;
- Disable the possibility of being interrupted (but the interrupt request flip-flops can still be set);
- Transfer control to a predetermined location, say IL, saving at least the location counter of the interrupted program A in another predetermined location, say IS.

Resetting of the interrupt request flip-flop and acknowledgment of the device follow a route parallel to that of the interrupt request itself. This acknowledgment is often called *handshaking*.

The third action is the reason why interrupt processing is often labelled a hardware subroutine call. One predetermined location can be reserved for each interrupt level. The location counter of the interrupted program, or most often its extension the program status word (PSW), will be saved in IS either automatically or this will be the action performed by the first instruction of the routine starting at IL. A new PSW is loaded, or exchanged, and the interrupt service routine can now proceed.

This service routine will first save the remainder of the Pc state; then it will clear the interrupt. Finally, it will restore the Pc state, reload the interrupted program's PSW and reenable the interrupt system. Assuming that there is no interrupt pending, program A will restart its normal instruction execution cycle by fetching the instruction which was suspended by the interrupt.

This simple interrupt processing is summarized in Figure 8.1. In part (a) an extended Petri Net shows when interrupt processing can start and in part (b) the actions taken to clear the interrupt (modelled by transition t_2) are expanded. The division between hardware and software operations in this second figure is quite arbitrary.

Up to now we have oversimplified the interrupt structure. Four types of interrupt systems can be defined.

Interrupt Systems

Type 1: Single-level, single-priority.

This is the simplest case from the hardware viewpoint. All interrupt lines are ORed into a single interrupt request flip-flop. When one interrupt is recognized, control is transferred to a specific location. After storing the Pc state, the interrupt clearing routine starting in this location must recognize the cause of the interrupt. This can be done by repeatedly testing the status bit of every device which can cause the interrupt. Since this polling is by necessity

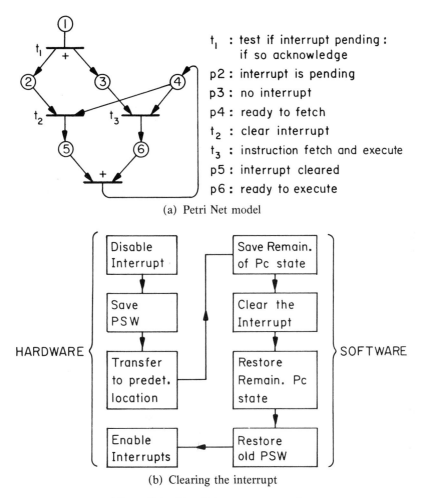

t_1 : test if interrupt pending :
     if so acknowledge
p2 : interrupt is pending
p3 : no interrupt
p4 : ready to fetch
t_2 : clear interrupt
t_3 : instruction fetch and execute
p5 : interrupt cleared
p6 : ready to execute

(a) Petri Net model

HARDWARE

| Disable Interrupt |
| Save PSW |
| Transfer to predet. location |
| Enable Interrupts |

| Save Remain. of Pc state |
| Clear the Interrupt |
| Restore Remain. Pc state |
| Restore old PSW |

SOFTWARE

(b) Clearing the interrupt

Figure 8.1   Simple interrupt processing

done in some order, we do have implied priorities set by the (system) programmer but they can be easily changed.

Type 2: Multiple-level, single-priority.

In addition to setting the flip-flop request as in the type 1 system, each device after sending an interrupt signal subsequently sends a code to indicate the interrupt's source. This code, called the *select code,* can be placed on the bus only when all previous interrupts have been acknowledged. Thus if device 1 has sent an interrupt and has not yet been acknowledged, device 2 can signal that it is requesting the Pc's attention but will not be allowed to send its select code until device 1 has been acknowledged.

Returning to Figure 8.1.b, we can modify the disable-enable interrupt sequence so that interrupts can be reenabled as soon as the Pc state has been stored, i.e., after the second box of the software flowchart. In type 2 systems the select code can indicate, either directly or through some indirect reference, the predetermined location of the interrupt clearing routine. If another interrupt occurs during processing of the clearing routine, the processor can decide if the new interrupt has higher priority. If so, the first interrupt can be interrupted and the second one cleared.

At this point there might be some confusion in the reader's mind about the meaning of "priority" since we have just defined type 2 systems as single priority but have allowed preemptions of some interrupts by others. By priority here, we refer only to the importance given directly by the hardware to an interrupt level. Thus deciding if a new interrupt has priority over another must be done by the Pc and therefore interrupts of lesser importance are momentarily disrupting the servicing of those which have higher "priorities" (in a system and not hardware sense). Note that this method of interrupting an interrupt processing routine could also be done in type 1 systems. The difference is that the multilevel select code technique provides a faster recognition of the source of the interrupt.

Type 3: Single-level, multiple-priority

As in type 1 there is only one interrupt request flip-flop but now the devices are positioned on the request line in priority order. When a device requests service, it prevents interrupts by devices of lower priority by opening a switch on the request line. The arrangement of the devices along a common line which can be broken for communication purposes is often referred to as a *daisy chain*.

After servicing the interrupt of the original device the switch is closed and devices of lower priority can send interrupt requests. Notice that while the processor services a given interrupt it can be interrupted by a device of higher priority. The handling of priority is different from type 2 since now only higher priority interrupts can arrive at the processor and it is unnecessary to check relative priorities. Hence the system is not degraded by the occurrence of low priority events.

Type 4: Multiple-level, multiple-priority

This general scheme is a combination of types 2 and 3. Devices are arranged in a daisy chain according to their priority as in type 3. In addition to sending interrupt requests, devices, upon acknowledgment, can also transmit a select code which identifies them as in type 2.

In multiple-level multiple-priority systems we might want to temporarily disable some particular interrupt sources. This is done with the use of a mask register. From the Pc viewpoint an interrupt is pending when an interrupt request is on and unmasked. From the hardware viewpoint each level can be given an interrupt request flip-flop and an interrupt mask flip-flop. Corresponding flip-flops are ANDed together and the AND network serves as input to an encoder which yields the next interrupt source to be serviced if any (cf. Figure 8.2). Notice that we can have a "priority" encoder where now levels can have priorities. This multiple-level encoding has been called a *vectored interrupt* scheme. From the software viewpoint, the mask register can be set by machine language instructions. The mask register encoding will often be part of the program status word (PSW). Since a new PSW is loaded at the beginning of an interrupt service routine, masking is readily available at the time it is most needed, when beginning to service another interrupt.

Referring to Figure 8.1, some of the places and transitions of the Petri Net can be extended to take into account the more complex schemes. For example, from the Pc's viewpoint a pending interrupt will have to be serviced if it

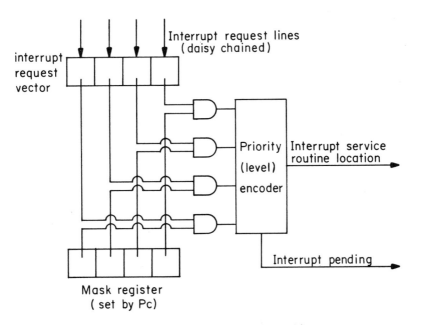

Figure 8.2 Multiple-level multiple-priority vectored interrupt system

has higher priority than the one being serviced (level-wise since on the same level the daisy chain arrangement would have prevented the request).

8.1.3 Two Examples of Interrupt Schemes

IBM Systems/360 and /370

The interrupt system of Systems/360 and /370 cannot be exactly mapped in any of the above schemes. However, it is quite close to a multiple-level multiple-priority vectored system. There are five levels of interrupts which are, in order of descending priority: machine check, program (traps), supervisory calls, external and I/O. (A sixth level, "restart", of highest priority is present in later models of System/370.) For each level, a pair old PSW—new PSW is assigned fixed locations in the Mp region dedicated to the operating system. Interrupts are grouped into sets called masked groups (cf. Figure 8.3). There are 32 such groups in System/360 and a few more in System/370. All external and I/O interrupt requests can be masked by setting specific bits in the PSW. This is also true of machine checks and of four traps. The remaining interrupt sources cannot be individually disabled via programmed operations. The I/O and external devices are daisy chained. Only one trap can be recognized at any time.

In case of an I/O interrupt the device address and the channel address of the interrupting device form the select code. When an I/O interrupt is ready to be serviced, either because it has the highest priority or because the other interrupt levels have been masked off, the select code is stored in bits 16–31 of the old PSW. This old PSW is stored in predetermined location 56 and a new PSW is fetched from location 120. The channel status word which encodes the status of the interrupting device is also stored in a predetermined location, location 64 to be precise (cf. Section 4).

The new PSW contains the new location counter and hence the address of the servicing routine. If several channels request service at the same time, priority is given to the one with smallest select code. In Section 4 we shall explain the types of I/O interrupts and how they are cleared.

The Xerox Sigma 5 Series

The Sigma 5 interrupt system is quite extensive. It is a direct outgrowth of the one implemented on the early SDS 9000 series which was geared towards time-sharing and real-time control of processes. Instead of having 32 sets grouped into 5 levels as in System/360, there are 237 individual "levels" (Xerox terminology) arranged into up to 17 priority groups. Each of the 237 levels has its own area of Mp for PSW exchange. Hence there is no need to

Source Identification	Interruption Code		PSW Mask Bits BC	Execution of Instruction Identified by Old PSW
Machine check (old PSW 48, new PSW 112)				
Exigent condition	machine dependent		13	terminated or nullified
Repressible cond.			13	unaffected
Supervisor call (old PSW 32, new PSW 96)				
Instruction bits	00000000	rrrrrrrr[1]		completed
Program (old PSW 40, new PSW 104)				
Operation	00000000	n0000001[2]		suppressed
Privileged oper.	00000000	n0000010		suppressed
Execute	00000000	n0000011		suppressed
Protection	00000000	n0000100		suppressed or terminated
Addressing	00000000	n0000101		suppressed or terminated
Specification	00000000	n0000110		suppressed or completed
Data	00000000	n0000111		suppressed or terminated
Fixed-pt. overflow	00000000	n0001000	36	completed
Fixed-point divide	00000000	n0001001		suppressed or completed
Decimal overflow	00000000	n0001010	37	completed
Decimal divide	00000000	n0001011		suppressed
Exponent overflow	00000000	n0001100		completed
Exponent underflow	00000000	n0001101	38	completed
Significance	00000000	n0001110	39	completed
Floating-pt. divide	00000000	n0001111		suppressed
Segment transl.	00000000	n0010000		nullified
Page translation	00000000	n0010001		nullified
Translation spec	00000000	n0010010		suppressed
Special operation	00000000	n0010011		suppressed
Monitor event	00000000	n1000000		completed
External (old PSW 24, new PSW 88)				
Interval timer	00000000	1nnnnnnn	7	unaffected
Interrupt key	00000000	n1nnnnnn	7	unaffected
External signal 2	00000000	nn1nnnnn	7	unaffected
External signal 3	00000000	nnn1nnnn	7	unaffected
External signal 4	00000000	nnnn1nnn	7	unaffected
External signal 5	00000000	nnnnn1nn	7	unaffected
External signal 6	00000000	nnnnnn1n	7	unaffected
External signal 7	00000000	nnnnnnn1	7	unaffected
Malfunction alert	00010010	00000000	7	unaffected
Emergency signal	00010010	00000001	7	unaffected
External call	00010010	00000010	7	unaffected
TOD clock sync chk	00010000	00000011	7	unaffected
Clock comparator	00010000	00000100	7	unaffected
CPU timer	00010000	00000101	7	unaffected
Input/Output (old PSW 56, new PSW 120)				
Channel 0	00000000	dddddddd[4]	0	unaffected
Channel 1	00000001	dddddddd[4]	1	unaffected
Channel 2	00000010	dddddddd[4]	2	unaffected
Channel 3	00000011	dddddddd[4]	3	unaffected
Channel 4	00000100	dddddddd[4]	4	unaffected
Channel 5	00000101	dddddddd[4]	5	unaffected
Channels 6 & on	cccccccc[3]	dddddddd[4]	6	unaffected

1. r = bits of register fields in SVC instruction.
2. n = possible bit significant indication of other concurrent interrupt conditions.
3. c = channel address bits.
4. d = device address bits.

Figure 8.3   Interrupt codes for IBM System/370 (slightly abridged)

test an interruption code in the PSW to determine which "level" has requested service. Within a group the priorities are fixed. Group priorities are assigned at installation time and can vary from one installation to another.

The only group which always has priority over all others is the override group. It has 7 interrupt levels: power on and power off which cannot be disabled, 4 count-pulse levels which are triggered by pulses from clock sources, and a memory parity level. The count-pulse interrupt locations contain a single instruction of the form:

"Modify and test word (or half-word or byte)"

which decrements by 1 (or by an integer between -8 and 7) the contents of the word (or half-word or byte) at the effective address. When these contents become 0, the appropriate interrupt is triggered in the "Counter-Equal-Zero" group.

This "Counter-Equal-Zero" group has 4 levels corresponding to the 4 count-pulse levels of the override group. They can be masked globally by setting a bit in the PSW (bit *CI* in Figure 2.8).

The other groups are an I/O group and external groups. The I/O group has two levels, one for the standard I/O system and one for the control panel. When an I/O interrupt occurs, control is transferred to the I/O predetermined location which in general will contain an XPSD, or exchange program status doubleword, instruction. The next instruction will be determined by the value of the location counter found in the new PSW. Control is then transferred to the I/O routine which contains an AIO (Acknowledge I/O) instruction that identifies the source and type of interrupt (i.e., finds a select code which will be loaded in a register designated by the AIO instruction). The (up to 14) external groups can contain 16 interrupt levels. The I/O interrupts can be masked within the PSW. The same is true for all external groups.

The masking of levels must be controlled in a more refined manner than just by masking complete groups. This is done by executing a privileged instruction which selects the group and levels within the group which are to be enabled or disabled.

A special feature of the Sigma 5 is that the Pc can trigger its own interrupts. This could be used for testing new software without having the I/O devices on hand (e.g., in a process-control environment). It allows more flexibility in the treatment of priority interrupts by letting the process of "clearing the interrupt" be performed by several subprocesses of various priorities. The urgent part can be performed immediately and then a lower priority level can be triggered allowing new high-priority interrupts to be acknowledged.

The Sigma 5 has also an extensive trap system very much like System/360's.

8.2 INPUT-OUTPUT PROCESSORS

8.2.1 Direct Memory Access

The program directed control of the last section can be somewhat improved when an interrupt system is present. Instead of looping in a busy wait mode, the Pc can be interrupted whenever the device is ready to transfer a word. Yet, the process is still very inefficient because the transferred word must pass through a Pc register and, since we have an interrupt, the Pc state must be saved. However, this type of facility is present in most systems from microprocessors, where sometimes this program directed control is the most sophisticated possibility, to medium and large computer systems (recall the switch S('DIO) in the PMS description of the Sigma 5 in Figure 2.8).

When the I/O device is fast and when the information block to transfer is several words long, a buffered approach can be used to make the program directed control method more efficient. A buffer area is reserved in Mp, one for each device, with two designated locations giving respectively its starting address and its length. To perform an input operation, the I/O device requests a transfer giving the block's length. The buffer control (some special hardware) initializes the length register. When the device is ready to send a word (or byte), it interrupts the Pc but the Pc state is not saved. Instead, under the special hardware control, the word is transferred in the buffer and the count incremented. If the whole block has not been transferred the sequence will be repeated later. After transfer of a word the Pc can continue its operations. An output operation would work in a similar fashion. The addition of a hardware buffer control saves an enormous amount of time since the Pc state does not have to be stored and restored. However, less disruptive (to the Pc) I/O operations can be done if separate paths for the Pc-Mp and I/O-Mp transactions are provided.

Conceptually, in terms of PMS, the program directed control follows the usual von Neumann model. With more than one Mp module and more than one I/O device, it can be represented as in Figure 8.4.a. At the left of Pc the switch is the Pc-Mp or Memory bus and at the right there is the I/O bus. A given device with buffer and its control is shown in Figure 8.4.b. Notice that Pc and Kbuffer cannot access Mp concurrently. This implies that Pc must be interrupted for a transfer between Mbuffer and Mp.

Figure 8.4.b can be expanded to allow concurrent access to Mp between Kbuffer and Pc, and at the same time Kbuffer and Mbuffer can be condensed into a single Kio. In order for Kio to directly access Mp the bus layouts must be changed, and several entry points, or *ports*, must be provided in each Mp module. A configuration with two such ports is shown in Figure

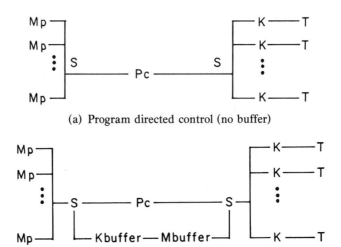

(a) Program directed control (no buffer)

(b) Program directed control with buffer

Figure 8.4   PMS structures for program directed control I/O

8.5.a. There can be several Kio's and additional programmable controllers, or equivalently I/O processors Pio, which can control several devices (recall Figure 2.4 and its abstraction here as Figure 8.5.b). Finally, there can be complete Cio's, i.e., dedicated computers to control part of the I/O as in front-end communication devices or back-end computers for controlling several disks in a large data base application. In Figure 8.5.c we show how this is done in the PDP-10 KL-10 system. Each Cio, from 1 to 4 PDP-11's, can directly access Mp via indirect address pointers. Similarly, several high-speed bus controllers (Kmassbus or Kio) are integrated within Pc. Up to 8 Pc or Pio as in Figure 8.5.b can access up to 16 Mp modules (there are 8 ports/memory module). The switch Mp-Pc is of the cross-bar type which allows maximum concurrency but other switch configurations exist (cf. Chapter 10). The Cio's are used for the control, formatting and checking of messages from slow peripherals such as terminals. The Kio's are used for high-speed transfers. The fact that the whole structure is integrated within Pc is more the result of technological advances than the implementation of a new architectural feature.

With the designs of Figure 8.5 we have a *Direct Memory Access (DMA)* between Mp and the I/O devices. After initialization from the Pc, transfers between Mp and I/O devices (or Ms) can occur in parallel with Pc activities. If a Pio is present, it will have its own program and will be able to execute it concurrently with that of Pc. The next section describes this organization.

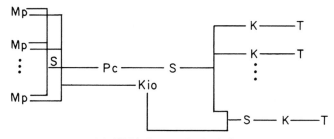

(a) DMA from a single device

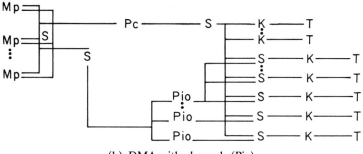

(b) DMA with channels (Pio)

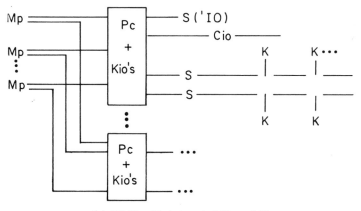

(c) DMA with integrated Pc and Pio

Figure 8.5   PMS structures for DMA for I/O devices

The Pio's are referred to as *channels*. If only a sophisticated controller directly connects Mp to the I/O bus, but still has a separate port to each Mp module, we have a *DMA interface* or *DMA channel*. The main difference with complete channels is that error checking is not provided within the DMA itself and that the operations allowed are not as sophisticated as the command or data chaining concepts which will be explained shortly. Finally, another method is to treat an I/O device like any Mp module attached to the unique bus of the system. This is typical of the architecture of minicomputers such as the PDP-11 (cf. Figure 1.4.a) and will be treated separately in the next chapter.

We have yet to address the problem of how to resolve conflicts when an Mp module is accessed at the same time by a Pc and a Pio or DMA channel. To do so, ports will be arranged in a priority fashion and the module will service the highest priority port. Because I/O transfer rates are much lower than the Pc accessing rate, channel ports will generally have priority. Thus when an I/O transfer must occur from/to an Mp module which at the same time was asked to service the Pc, a *"cycle stealing"* action will happen, i.e., the Pc will have to stay idle for the Mp cycle devoted to the other operation.

The cycle stealing priority scheme does not always favor the Pc. A particular exception is the implementation found in the CDC 6000 series where Pio's (in fact Cio's) are given the last chance at Mp access. The reader might look back at the stunt box organization (Chapter 5 Section 3) for a justification of this arrangement and for another way to implement the Mp-Pc and Pc-Pio connections. However in the remainder of this chapter we shall consider PMS structures as shown in Figure 8.5.b and interrupt driven I/O systems.

8.2.2 Channels

Channels can be treated as Pio's or Kio's depending on the levels of consideration. The more sophisticated channels are processors in the sense that they have their own instruction set and processor state, but they are only controllers if regarded as slaves to the Pc.

Channels must be able to:

• Select a particular device connected to the system for a given I/O transmission;
• Give commands for the type of operation requested by the Pc;
• Define the storage area in the external device from which information is stored or retrieved;
• Define the storage areas in Mp;
• Define the action at the end of transmission;

- Sense the state of the connected I/O device either in normal operations or when erroneous conditions occur;
- Convert data from the i-unit of the I/O device to the i-unit of Mp and vice versa. This is called the *assembly/disassembly process.*

Since Pio's execute commands, these commands must be ordered by means of programs. (We shall see later who has the responsibility of setting up these programs.) Thus the state of the channel must contain the equivalent of a PSW, that is, registers holding the opcode (or command), the external device address, the Mp address, the count of words to be transmitted and some buffer register for assembly/disassembly of data.

A channel command word (CCW or control word or instruction) specifies all of the parameters necessary for the transmission of a block of information between a device and Mp. Typical commands are: READ, WRITE, READ BACKWARD, SENSE (status), and TRANSFER of control. Commands can be chained to form a channel program, so that after the transmission of a block the Pio may automatically look for the transmission of another block.

As previously indicated, the Pio runs independently and in parallel with the Pc. However, it is the Pc which gives the "start" signal to the Pio and the Pio answers upon completion of its program, or of specific commands, by an I/O interrupt. The Pc is able to sense the state of a channel for decision making. The I/O programming from the Pc's viewpoint will be studied later.

The hardware requirements of a channel are in terms of:

- circuitry: for address modification, counting, assembly and disassembly of data, facilities to transmit data between Mp and I/O devices.
- storage facility: a counter, Mp address, address of current CCW, status information and flags (cf. Figure 8.6).

Because of widely different data rates in external devices, such as those of a disk and a teletype, channels may be divided into subchannels; that is, some of the hardware will be shared. Most often the circuitry is shared while the storage facilities are not. This leads us to consider two basic types of channels: *selector* and *multiplexor*, this latter type also divided into *block* and *byte multiplexors*.

Selector

Selector channels are dedicated to high-speed devices such as drums or disks; they can select only one I/O device at any given time and once the selection is done the operation runs up to completion. This is recognized as a "busy" condition on the channel.

The selector hardware will be very close to what is shown in Figure 8.6.

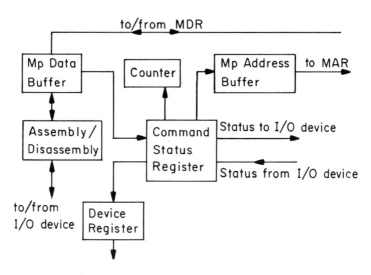

Figure 8.6   Hardware requirements for a channel processor (selector)

Some error detection circuitry may be added between the Assembly/Disassembly register and the Mp Data Buffer. Typically a selector channel will support maximum data rates of the order of 1 to 2 megabytes per second.

Byte Multiplexor

In multiplexors the circuitry is shared among several subchannels. Theoretically a multiplexor could be modelled as in Figure 8.7.a but a more typical configuration is illustrated in Figure 8.7.b where four I/O controllers (or devices) share a channel. The link and switch between the channel and the devices is called an *I/O interface* and contains address, data, and control lines. We shall discuss its design shortly.

When several subchannels carry I/O simultaneously, each I/O control unit is logically connected to the channel for the time required to transfer one byte of data. Thus, if device A were to send a string of bytes $A_0A_1A_2...$, device B a string $B_0B_1B_2...$, and device C a string $C_0C_1C_2...$, the resulting string in the channel-Mp interface would be $A_0B_0C_0A_1B_1C_1A_2B_2C_2$ etc. If only one I/O device is allowed to operate, then the multiplexor is in *burst mode* and it plays the same role as a medium speed selector.

In a byte multiplexor several subchannels contain their own storage for a byte buffer, device identification and some control flags. These subchannels share buffers for Mp addressing and transmission of data and circuitry for global channel control. While in the selector a single counter and Mp address

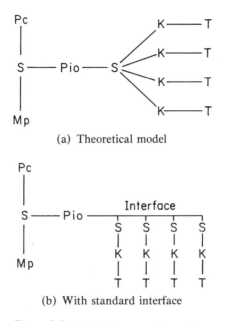

(a) Theoretical model

(b) With standard interface

Figure 8.7   Multiplexor configurations

buffer was sufficient, in the multiplexor one such pair per subchannel is required. Since it is prohibitive to keep them in the I/O channel (for example a byte multiplexor in the IBM System/370 can support up to 256 subchannels), these pairs of registers will be Mp memory locations. The loss in speed to access these registers is not critical since only slow-speed devices will be connected to the multiplexor.

The control of the multiplexor is such that it scans in a round-robin fashion the control flags of each subchannel. If a request is pending the subchannel will be serviced. The global control checks whether input or output is demanded and then takes appropriate actions, including the update of the Mp locations containing the count. A typical data rate for a byte multiplexor is 0.2 megabytes per second.

Block Multiplexor

A block multiplexor is a combination of the previous two channel configurations. Subchannels share the data path between the multiplexor and Mp, but each subchannel has its own hardware pair of registers indicating the Mp area of transfer and the size of the block to transfer.

A block multiplexor can operate in one of two modes. In the first one it performs like a selector (or a byte multiplexor in burst mode although faster since its hardware is more "local"). In the second mode, it operates like a multiplexor but interleaves blocks rather than bytes of data. We shall see how this can be of interest when we examine I/O devices with rotational position sensing.

On some models of the IBM System/370, like the Model 165, a block multiplexor channel servicing up to 8 I/O control units can be attached. Each control unit can have up to 8 devices, i.e., the channel can service 64 devices in the block multiplex mode. The maximum data rate is about the same as for a selector.

8.2.3   Interface to Devices

Looking at PMS descriptions such as the one depicted in Figure 8.7.b, we see that the information flow passing through a Pio goes through two different switches: the Mp-Pc switch, or memory bus, and an I/O bus. This situation is not mandatory and we have already encountered a system with a single bus (cf. Figure 1.4.a). This architecture will be discussed in detail in Chapter 9. Here, we consider the tree structured architectures of Figure 1.3, 1.4.b, and, more abstractly, of Figure 8.7.b. While we consider only the case of a single I/O bus connected to a given Pio, there exists another switching possibility, namely a cross-bar switch between Pio's and device controllers. However, since our interest at this time is in the protocols between Pio's and devices, we do not wish to confuse the issue with additional complexities. The cross-bar switch problem will be discussed in Chapter 10 in the context of multiprocessor structures.

When information has to be transferred between a given Pio and some device we have the following requirements:

(i) The data to be transferred must be present;
(ii) The source and sink of the transfer must be known;
(iii) The timing of the transfer must be set.

In the Mp-Pio interface these requirements are easily met. The data transferred is always present in Mp for an Mp-Pio transfer and for the other direction the Pio hardware can easily detect when the Mp data buffer is full (when the assembly process has been completed). The Mp source (or sink) destination is kept in the Pio or in an Mp register; there is no problem with the Pio sink (or source) destination. Finally, the protocol for information transfer is easily implemented via the cycle stealing procedure that we have already explained.

But with respect to the I/O bus, the situation is not as simple. First, the devices are not the same and their controllers will differ widely. Thus, there is a need for a standard interface between device controllers and the I/O bus. This interface can be embedded in the controller itself or it can be an independent circuit (for example, a simple microprocessor). Minimally there is a need for a data buffer and some status bits such as READY/NOT READY and BUSY/DONE. In the following, we shall assume that such a facility exists. Second, although a device might be free and ready to answer a given request this does not mean that the data is ready to be transferred; for example, the arm of a disk may have to be positioned at the right place. Third, if many devices share the I/O bus, the link between the Pio and the accessed device must be set. Finally, since several devices can request service at the same time, some priority mechanism must be included.

Let us look first at the physical structure of the I/O bus. It will consist of several parallel lines, some reserved for data transmission, some for address transmission, and some for control information. In practice, quite often some lines will play a dual role. Figure 8.8.a shows the IBM System/370 I/O

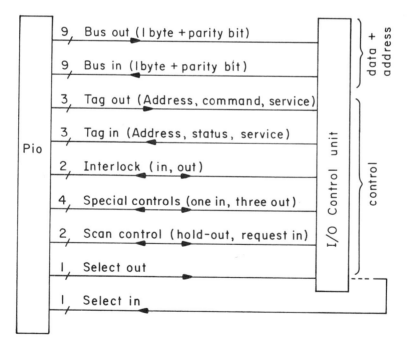

Figure 8.8 I/O bus in IBM System/370

bus lines (in Chapter 9 we will introduce the UNIBUS and its structure). As can be seen data and addresses share the same lines. The significance of the SELECT-IN and SELECT-OUT lines is related to the bus control protocol.

When several I/O devices share access to the same bus, protocols are implemented so that a given I/O unit can gain control of the bus and transmit data. There are 3 basic methods to do so, namely: *daisy chaining, polling* and *independent requests*.

In the daisy chain scheme all devices are connected serially along a common control line called the AVAILABLE line (cf. Figure 8.9.a where the control is centralized at the Pio and Figure 8.9.b where the control is decentralized among the Pio and the I/O units). In the centralized case, devices send requests along the REQUEST line and the BUSY line indicates whether the bus is busy or not. The bus controller, in our case the Pio, will answer a bus request only if the bus is not busy. Let us assume that this is the current situation and that a device wants to transmit data. The protocol is as follows (cf. also Figure 8.10 for a state diagram). The device activates the REQUEST line; the Pio receives the request and activates AVAILABLE; the available signal is daisy chained through all devices from the closest to the Pio to the farthest from it, and the first one (in that order) which has sent a request will acknowledge the signal by activating BUSY and deactivating REQUEST. Now data can be transmitted. Obviously, there is more to that protocol when commands to devices are included; this will be explained shortly using System/370's interface as an example. In the decentralized case, the first device which accepts the AVAILABLE signal keeps its

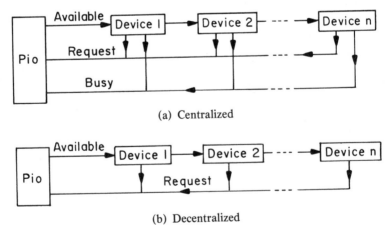

(a) Centralized

(b) Decentralized

Figure 8.9   Daisy chaining bus control

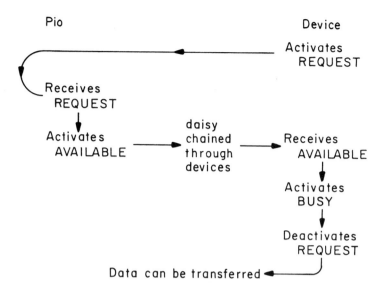

Figure 8.10 Daisy chain bus protocol

REQUEST line activated. When it has finished its transmission, if there is no REQUEST activated, then AVAILABLE is deactivated, otherwise the next in line will take over control. Thus instead of a priority scheme as in the centralized case, there is a round robin scheduling.

Daisy chaining has the enormous advantage of simplicity. However, if a device fails all subsequent ones (in the daisy chain ordering) are made unavailable. Redundant logic can be introduced in the control units to alleviate this reliability problem.

The second method, polling, is illustrated in Figure 8.11. (We show only the centralized version which is the only one relevant here; the same will be true for the independent request approach.) As in the daisy chain scheme each device can activate the REQUEST line. When the Pio receives the request, it interrogates (polls) each device in turn to ask whether it was a requestor. The polling is done by sending a count on the polling lines. When a requesting device recognizes this count as its own, it will activate the BUSY line. The Pio then stops the polling procedure until the end of the data transfer, at which point the BUSY line will be deactivated. Then the polling can resume, either from the start (priority-based polling) or from where it left off (round-robin scheduling).

The advantages of the polling method reside in its flexibility, since the polling procedure can be programmed, and reliability, since a failing device

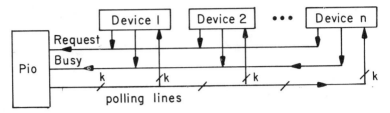

Figure 8.11   Bus protocol using polling lines

can be skipped during polling. On the other hand a minimum of $k = \lceil \log n \rceil$ polling lines are needed for n devices and therefore it is more costly than daisy chaining.

Finally in the independent request method (cf. Figure 8.12) each device has its own pair of REQUEST-GRANTED lines and there is a common BUSY line. Upon receiving one (or more) request(s), the Pio selects the one with highest priority and sends a GRANTED signal to it. The device then deactivates its REQUEST line and activates the BUSY line. At the end of the transmission the device deactivates BUSY and the Pio deactivates the GRANTED line and selects the next device (if any) which has a pending REQUEST activated.

This method is as flexible as polling. It leads to a fast assignment of the bus since the devices have their own communication lines to the Pio. But it is

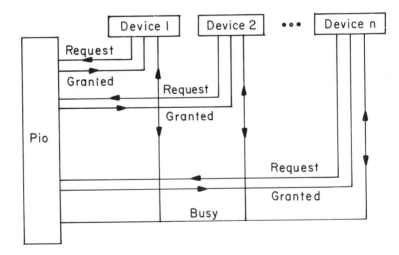

Figure 8.12   Bus protocol using independent requests

an expensive method since each device has its own line and the logic in the Pio is more complex.

Once the Pio and the I/O control unit are connected through one of the above schemes, the transmission of information, be it data, command or status, can begin. This can be done in either a synchronous or an asynchronous fashion, or in a mixture of both.

If synchronous communication is used, then each device must have its own time slot. This requires that a common clock be used by the Pio and all devices attached to it. This is not a good idea if the transmission is over long distances. Alternatively, distinct clocks with the same frequency could be used with periodic signals sent by the Pio to adjust potential drifts. The main disadvantage of the synchronous scheme is that all devices have to transmit at the speed of the slowest one.

On the other hand asynchronous communication lends itself well to the control of devices of different speeds. The basic "handshaking" procedure is provided by a pair of control lines READY-ACKNOWLEDGE for a source initiated transfer, or REQUEST-ACKNOWLEDGE for a destination initiated one. For example, for a source initiation from a device, the READY line will be activated and the data maintained on the bus until the device receives an ACKNOWLEDGE signal indicating that the data has been received without error. For the destination initiated case, the source unit will activate ACKNOWLEDGE to indicate that data is on the bus and will keep it in this state until the destination deactivates its REQUEST line, indicating that it has received the data.

We can now return to the System/370 I/O bus as shown in Figure 8.8. The protocol between the Pio and the I/O control units follows the centralized daisy chain scheme. The correspondence between lines is SELECT-OUT for AVAILABLE, OPERATIONAL-IN for BUSY, and REQUEST-IN for REQUEST. The asynchronous handshaking is performed via the (SERVICE-IN, SERVICE-OUT) pair.

Since the address lines can transmit one byte (8 bits), the number of I/O control units which can be addressed is 256. A typical transfer sequence between the Pio and one of these units will consist of an initial selection sequence followed by the data transmissions and terminated by an ending sequence. As an illustration, we show the synopsis for an initial selection where the Pio wishes to select a unit of given address (cf. Figure 8.13).

First, the Pio places on the address lines the address of the selected device and activates ADDRESS-OUT to tag the type of information placed on the bus. Then, it activates SELECT-OUT to start the daisy chain selection process. If a device recognizes itself in the address on the bus, it will activate OPERATIONAL-IN. If there is no device corresponding to the address, then

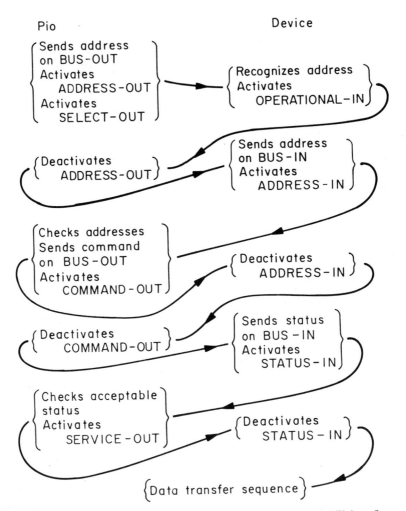

Figure 8.13 Initial selection sequence for the IBM System/370 interface

SELECT-IN will be activated and proper action will be taken by the Pio. When the Pio receives the OPERATIONAL-IN signal, it will deactivate ADDRESS-OUT. When the selected device sees this condition, it will send its address on BUS-IN tagging it with the activation of ADDRESS-IN. The Pio checks that both addresses are indeed the same (if not an error routine in the channel program will be entered) and sends a command (e.g., READ,

WRITE, etc.) on BUS-OUT tagged by COMMAND-OUT. The acknowledgment consists of the deactivation of ADDRESS-IN in the device followed by that of COMMAND-OUT in the Pio. Now the device sends its status, a byte indicating among other things whether it is ready or not, on BUS-IN tagged with STATUS-IN. The status is checked by Pio which, assuming that it finds it acceptable, then activates SERVICE-OUT. The device deactivates STATUS-IN and the data transfer can take place using SERVICE-IN and SERVICE-OUT for handshaking purposes. The ending sequence will deactivate OPERATIONAL-IN and SELECT-OUT with appropriate acknowledgments.

The other control lines have, either obvious meanings (e.g., OPERATIONAL-OUT), or correspond to situations too complex and not of sufficient generality to be of interest here.

8.3 I/O DEVICES

In the PMS notation the I/O devices are those transducers (T's) which permit the outside world to communicate with the Pc-Mp complex. This need is not limited to human communication but also includes analog devices monitoring real time processes or laboratory instruments. Moreover, as we have seen in Chapter 5, the division between devices used as secondary memories and those used for back-up storage is extremely fine. Therefore, the direct access storage devices already encountered will be considered here as I/O devices.

We shall not attempt to survey all possible kinds of I/O devices, nor do we plan to explain their electromechanical features. Our aim is to give an indication of the available media, of the functions that specific classes of devices will perform, and of the characteristics which are important from the architectural viewpoint. Details on specific devices can be found in the literature provided by manufacturers.

Broadly speaking, we can distinguish between devices used for interactive communication (on-line), those used for off-line communication, and those used for back-up storage. Some devices fit into more than one category (e.g., a paper tape reader and punch which can be used for off-line communication and back-up storage) and some are difficult to classify (for example, analog-digital and digital-analog converters). However, we shall use this classification in the following pages. A summary is presented in Table 8.1.

Table 8.1   Principal I/O devices

I/O device	Function	Medium	Transfer rate
Teletype	On-line communication	paper	10 to 60 cps
Display terminal	input-output on-line	visual image	10 to 240 cps
Paper tape			
reader	input off-line	paper	10 to 1000 cps
punch	output off-line	paper	10 to 150 cps
Card reader	input off-line	card	100 to 2000 cpm
Card punch	output off-line	card	100 to 250 cpm
Line printer	output off-line	paper	
impact			100 to 3000 lpm
electrostatic			100 to 40,000 lpm
Magnetic tape	backup storage	magnetic surface	15K to 300K cps
Cassette tape	backup storage	magnetic surface	10 to 400 cps
	input-output off-line		
Drum	backup storage	magnetic surface	30K to 2M cps
Disk	backup storage	magnetic surface	30K to 2M cps
Floppy disk	backup storage	magnetic surface	25K cps
	input-output off-line		

8.3.1 Types of I/O Devices

Interactive Terminals

Interactive terminals provide slow speed communication (input and output) between human operators and computing systems. The hard-copy terminals, or teletypes, consist of a keyboard and a printer. They can transmit and receive digital information to and from some local or remote computer on a character by character basis. In a display terminal, the printer is replaced by a cathode-ray-tube (CRT) screen.

The number of different terminals available is becoming astronomical. For example, a 1978 survey (Datamation, June 1978) listed 170 models of alphanumeric display terminals. The price range was approximately from $1,000 to $10,000 depending on the options available such as scrolling, brightness level, etc. Often microprocessors and some memory can be embedded in the terminal making it "intelligent", i.e., able to perform editing functions locally. Some external memory (an I/O device for the I/O device) can also be attached, so that whole files can be sent at once if need be (hence an off-line function). Cassette tapes, floppy disks and even bubble memories (as in a version of the Texas Instrument TI 700 teletype) can be used to that effect.

Keyboards are similar to typewriters with a few additional keys for special functions. Special characters can be sent by using a "control" key in conjunction with another key. Terminals transmit data serially, in general using an 8-bit character code, the ASCII (American Standards Committee on Information Interchange) code shown in Figure 8.14. (ASCII was originally a 7-bit code; in the figure the first bit, a one for all characters except the blank, has been omitted.)

Terminals can be connected directly to the computer or remotely via telephone lines. In this latter case, it is not possible to send digital information directly. A *modem* (abbreviation for modulator-demodulator) is used at each end of the transmission line. The sending modem modulates the carrier signals according to the data to be transmitted, and the receiving modem demodulates it and converts it back to digital form. Terminals and modems, and modems and computers are connected through "standard interfaces" of which the most common is the EIA RS232. Another interface circuit, named a UART (universal asynchronous receiver transmitter), performs serial-parallel and parallel-serial conversions.

Typical speed characteristics are 10 to 60 characters per second (cps) for a teletype and 10 to 240 cps for display terminals. Modems permit transmission at rates from 300 bits per second (bps), approximately 10 cps, to 9600 bps depending on their sophistication. Obviously, the fastest ones should be used only with displays.

Off-line Devices

These I/O devices are used to communicate indirectly with the computer. The information is encoded on some media such as punched cards or paper. The most common devices are listed below with a very short explanation of their main characteristics.

Paper Tape Reader and Punch

At one time paper tape readers were convenient as input devices to minicomputers. They have now become obsolete and been replaced by cassette tape units and/or floppy disks. The main disadvantages of paper tape devices are slow speed (10 to 100 cps for reading, 10 to 150 cps for punching), lack of flexibility and tendency to tear easily.

Card Reader and Punch

The 80 column punched card is still the main input medium used in off-line batch processing. Card reader speeds range from 100 to 2000 cards per minute. Card punch devices are almost abandoned since magnetic tapes and secondary memory devices can better perform the functions for which they were intended.

low/high	000	001	010	011	100	101	110	111
0000	NUL	DLE	SP	0	@	P	`	p
0001	SDH	DC1	!	1	A	Q	a	q
0010	STX	DC2	"	2	B	R	b	r
0011	ETX	DC3	#	3	C	S	c	s
0100	EOT	DC4	$	4	D	T	d	t
0101	ENQ	NAK	%	5	E	U	e	u
0110	ACK	SYN	&	6	F	V	f	v
0111	BEL	ETB	´	7	G	W	g	w
1000	BS	CAN	(	8	H	X	h	x
1001	HT	EM	)	9	I	Y	i	y
1010	LF	SUB	*	:	J	Z	j	z
1011	VT	ESC	+	;	K	[	k	{
1100	FF	FS	,	<	L	\	l	|
1101	CR	GS	–	=	M	]	m	}
1110	SO	RS	.	>	N	^	n	~
1111	SI	US	/	?	o	_	o	DEL

ASCII Control Characters
(From American Standards Institute Publication X3.4-1968)

ACK	acknowledge	ETX	end of text
BEL	bell	FF	form feed
BS	backspace	FS	file separator
CAN	cancel	GS	group separator
CR	carriage return	HT	horizontal tabulation
DC1	device control 1	LF	line feed
DC2	device control 2	NAK	negative acknowledge
DC3	device control 3	NUL	null
DC4	device control 4 (stop)	RS	record separator
DEL	delete	SI	shift in
DLE	data link escape	SO	shift out
EM	end of medium	SOH	start of heading
ENQ	enquiry	STX	start of text
EOT	end of transmission	SUB	substitute
ESC	escape	SYN	synchronous idle
ETB	end of transmission block	US	unit separator
		VT	vertical tabulation

Figure 8.14   ASCII code

Line Printer

This peripheral is generally mandatory for most installations except perhaps some microprocessor-based specific applications. Two types of line printers exist: impact and nonimpact (e.g., electrostatic). Impact printers print mechanically. The fastest ones can print lines (132 columns maximum) at a rate of 3000 lines per minute. The electrostatic nonimpact printers require special paper and hence are only useful for single copy output. They can be much faster than the impact printers. The characters are printed as dot matrices and are not as legible as those produced by the mechanical devices. There exist some nonimpact printers which use ink jets and do not require special paper. The reader is referred to specialized publications for more details.

There exist other off-line devices such as optical readers, plotters, etc. As mentioned earlier, this is only a summary of the most common I/O devices.

Back-up Storage

The back-up storage devices fall within two categories depending on the mode of access: sequential storage and direct access storage. The first category contains those devices using magnetic tape as the storage medium.

Magnetic Tape Drives

The most common magnetic tapes are long ribbons (typically 2400 feet), about half an inch wide, made of a plastic film (mylar) coated with magnetic oxide. Tapes are contained in reels about one foot in diameter. There are 7 or 9 tracks written across the width of the tape and hence there will be 7 or 9 read/write heads to store one character (6 bits + parity or 8 bits + parity depending on the internal representation) per frame. Several recording densities are possible with 200, 556, 800 or 1600 frames/inch being the usual ones. Thus a reel of tape at density 1600 can store: $2400 \cdot 12 \cdot 1600 = 46$ M bytes.

The most common recording technique is NRZI (recall Chapter 5.4.1) when the density is less than 1600 and PR when it is 1600 or greater. New data is read/written via a tape drive (cf. Figure 8.15). Transfer rates vary from 15K to 300K bytes per second. Rewind times are from 45 seconds to several minutes. Information is stored in (variable length) records separated by gaps of 1/2 to one inch. These gaps can limit considerably the amount of information which is stored on a tape (cf. Exercise 6).

Cassette Tapes

Cassette tapes have replaced the paper tape readers and punches as peripherals for micro and minicomputers. They are cheap and easy to load but

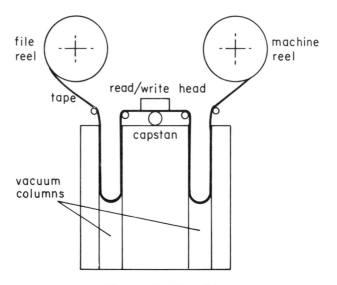

Figure 8.15   Tape drive

prone to error (about one erroneous bit/million recorded, or a few errors per cassette). A distinction is made between Phillips-type cassettes and others which are called cartridges. The Phillips cassette is 300 feet long, information is recorded serially with either interrecord gaps as in magnetic tape reels (continuous recording) or on a bit per bit (or character per character) basis. This second method alleviates the need for interrecord gaps but a lower density is necessary. Cassette tapes can store from 50K to 700K characters. Transfer rates range from 10 to 400 cps.

In Chapter 5, we have previously discussed the characteristics of the *drum, fixed-head disk,* and *movable-arm disk* which are the principal direct access storage devices (about which more will be said in the next section). To these we add the floppy disk.

Floppy Disk

Floppy disks are not different conceptually from magnetic disks. However, they are made of the same material as magnetic tapes. Floppy disks look like any 45 rpm record. They are in competition with cassette tapes for the same types of application.

A floppy disk stores approximately 250K bytes using a track-sector arrangement as in a regular disk. A movable-arm read/write apparatus is used. The disk rotates at 360 rpm and has about a 10 ms track-to-track access time. For typical floppy disks, average access times are of the order of 400 ms and transfer rates of the order of 25K bps.

There also exist a number of devices used for storing large amounts of data, e.g., IBM's and CDC's mass storage systems. Future mass memories might use optical (holographic) means of storing information. Read-only memories of that type are already present in very large installations.

Real Time Processes and Laboratory Monitoring Devices

In any particular installation, an unusual but useful peripheral device will be found. Very often in real time and process control environments as well as in the monitoring of laboratory conditions, analog-digital (A/D) and digital-analog (D/A) converters are required. Once more, we refer the reader to specialized publications on these important transducers. Suffice it to say here that digital-analog converters are simpler. They are used to transform a digital signal into a range of analog values; this can be achieved by a digital input grounding some resistors connected in a ladder network, thus allowing the output voltage to vary within a given range. Analog-digital converters must quantize the analog signal. For electronic analogs, a series of capacitors, either in parallel (of course at a cost in the number of capacitors), or serially in conjunction with a counter is used. Sophisticated A/D and D/A converters can handle, in a multiplexed fashion, up to 50,000 samples/second.

8.3.2   Direct Access Storage Devices (revisited)

In Chapter 5 (Section 4) we introduced drums and disks. We now cover, in greater detail, other aspects of the scheduling of these rotational devices.

Scheduling of Drums

There are two principal aspects which affect the performance of drums: organization and scheduling. As indicated earlier, the file drum (the "normal" drum) and the paging drum (where all records start on a sector boundary) are the two principal organizations. A paging drum in which all records are not of the same length (that is which might span over several sectors) is often called a *sectored drum*. Since the operation of the paging and sectored drums are similar from the scheduling viewpoint we shall not distinguish between them.

Many scheduling disciplines can be devised. From a practical viewpoint, the two important ones are first-in-first-out (FIFO) and shortest-access-time-first (SATF also called SLTF for shortest-latency-time-first). Before proceeding to give some results relative to these scheduling strategies, we introduce the drum models commonly used for their analysis.

We shall assume that we have a sequence of n records $R_1, R_2, \ldots, R_n$ to be processed. We shall not distinguish between read and write requests although, from a practical viewpoint, this might be debatable. Each record R_i is identified by a starting address s_i and a finishing address f_i. s_i and f_i can be given in terms of angular positions with the origin at a fixed position on the drum. In the case of a paging drum s_i and f_i may be assumed to be integers between 0 and S, where S is the total number of sectors, while for a file drum s_i and f_i can be real numbers between 0 and 1.

Let R_i and R_j be processed in succession. The (rotational) latency t_{ij} is defined as

$$t_{ij} = s_j - f_i \text{ if } s_j \geq f_i;$$
$$t_{ij} = (s_j - f_i) + 1 \text{ if } s_j < f_i \text{ in the file drum;}$$
$$t_{ij} = (s_j - f_i) + S \text{ if } s_j < f_i \text{ in the paging drum.}$$

At a given instant the read/write head will be at some position p.

The sequence of events leading to the servicing of a request is:
1. Request joins the queue for drum service;
2. Request R_i is selected to be the next one to be processed;
3. Wait until the head's position p is at position s_i (rotational latency);
4. Transfer of R_i; the length of this transfer is related to the rotation time of the drum, s_i, and f_i (cf. Exercise 7).

We initially assume that there are n records in the queue and we examine the effect of the scheduling policy. The following discussion and examples are explained in terms of a sectored disk but there is no loss in generality in doing so.

The FIFO policy is straightforward. Requests join the queue in a FIFO manner and the record R_i at the front of the queue is selected when the previous transfer is finished. For example, if the records shown in Figure 8.16.a (where the surface of the drum has been flattened) arrived in the order R_1, R_2, R_3 and a transfer has just been terminated, then the schedule of transfers is shown by the Gantt chart of Figure 8.16.b (the rotation time is 9 units, or sector transfer times).

The SATF discipline needs more data, namely the s_i and f_i of each R_i. If R_i is the last record transferred, the next one selected is the R_j such that t_{ij} is smallest (ties are broken randomly). In our example, if we assume an R_0 with $f_0 = 0$ then R_2 will be selected followed by R_3 and finally R_1. The schedule is shown in Figure 8.16.c.

It is obvious that the FIFO policy will not yield an optimal schedule in all cases and the above example shows that SATF will not either. However, the

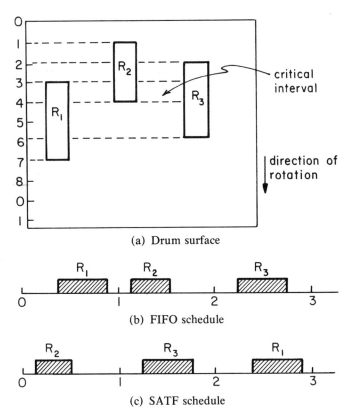

(a) Drum surface

(b) FIFO schedule

(c) SATF schedule

Figure 8.16   Drum scheduling policies

SATF has a very interesting property, namely that at the completion of all n transfers, the time spent will be at most one more complete revolution than the one given by an optimal schedule. The proof, left to the reader (cf. Exercise 8), is based on the concept of interval defined as a region of the drum bounded by neighboring end-points of the n records. A critical interval under the SATF schedule is any interval in which the schedule is never latent, i.e., an interval during which some portion of a record is transferred. In our example, the interval (3, 4) is critical. Then the proof is based on a lemma stating that every SATF schedule has at least one critical interval.

If neither FIFO nor SATF yield optimal schedules, how difficult is it to obtain one? Integer programming methods could be used but they are of exponential complexity. There exists an algorithm based on the matching of bipartite graphs, where one set of nodes corresponds to start points and one to final points, which runs in $O(n \log n)$. This is the same theoretical time complexity as SATF since SATF requires a sorting process. The optimal schedule has too many complex details to be included here; its practical significance appears limited when compared to the simpler near-optimal SATF.

In the above presentation we have assumed a static number of records. It is interesting to compare the behavior of file drums and paging drums scheduled under FIFO and SATF when the number of incoming requests vary dynamically. We have already shown (Chapter 5 Section 4) the superiority of paging drums over file drums when all requests are of equal size and the number of requests in the queue is kept constant. Studies relaxing these assumptions, that is, considering incoming requests arriving according to Poisson distributions and with records of unequal length, have shown that the resulting expected waiting times for the records to be serviced for the various drum organizations and scheduling policies could be ranked as (shortest waiting times first):

SATF paging, SATF file, FIFO paging, FIFO file.

The interested reader should consult the references given in Section 6 for more detail.

Scheduling of Disks

Disk scheduling deals mainly with reducing *seek time*, the time it takes for the moving arm to be positioned on the right cylinder. Since seek time is the major component in the access time characteristics (cf. Table 5.3), a great amount of research has been done in trying to find scheduling policies which minimize it. As a starting point, let us consider a single disk controlled by a channel, a uniform distribution of access to the cylinders, and a seek time linear with the number of cylinders traversed. We shall comment on each of these assumptions later.

The three most often used scheduling policies are FIFO, shortest-seek-time-first (SSTF) and SCAN. FIFO, as usual, schedules requests in their order of arrival. SSTF schedules first that request in the cylinder closest to the one currently under the read/write head. SCAN continually scans the disk surface from the inner to the outer cylinder, and then in the reverse direction, servicing the requests when encountering the correct cylinders.

At first glance it appears that the expected seek time will be shortest with SSTF. This has been confirmed by analysis and simulations (using a few more assumptions such as a Poisson distribution of arrivals and records of equal length to carry through an approximate queuing analysis). But SSTF can discriminate against individual requests; for example, this would happen if there were many requests for the center cylinders and only an exceptional one to the periphery. But even with our assumption of uniformity in the positions of the requests, the variance of the seek time is larger in SSTF than in SCAN and FIFO, while SCAN has an expected seek time close to SSTF's.

The results summarized in the above paragraph are true (under our simplifying assumptions) only under medium to heavy load. Under light load FIFO is competitive.

Let us now examine the three main assumptions. We start with the last one, the linearity of the seek time. The reader should look back at Figure 5.21 and the accompanying text to draw his/her own conclusions. Ours are that this is not unrealistic.

On the contrary, the uniformity of access to cylinders is not borne out by empirical evidence. Actual measurements of disk arm movements show that most of the time, the arms do not move! This can be explained by the same phenomenon of locality that we find in virtual memory systems. At some instant of time, there are a limited number of open files and the records of a given file are generally stored on the same, or adjacent, cylinders. Thus, instead of assuming a uniform access, some investigators have looked at a Markovian model of disk access such that, if i is the current cylinder for request j, then the cylinder for request ($j + 1$) will be either:

i (i.e., the source) with probability α, or
k ($k \neq i$) with probability $(1 - \alpha)/(c - 1)$

where c is the total number of cylinders. (The reader may want to compare assumptions in this model with those for the $\alpha - \beta$ model for interleaved memories in Chapter 5 Section 3). With these new assumptions, with $\alpha = 2/3$, and with records having exponentially distributed length with a mean of $1/2$ track, it has been shown that FIFO has a smaller expected seek time than SSTF under light and medium loads, and about the same seek time under heavy loads. For $\alpha = 0$, the same simulation showed the superiority of SSTF as soon as a non-trivial load was reached. Thus the scheduling strategy should be chosen carefully and it might well be that the simplest one, FIFO, is the most efficient.

The advantage of FIFO, namely "no scheduling", will be greater if we relax our third assumption by considering several spindles controlled by the same Pio. Then, the open files might be evenly distributed over the various disks, and individual arms will move even less.

The multi-spindle case provides another opportunity for speed-up of the overall operation (not of individual transfers). The arm positioning on one disk can be executed in parallel with other such seeks and with one data transfer. Channel programs, which we discuss in the next section, can be set up to command a seek, then to relinquish control, and finally to regain control when the arm has been correctly positioned. During the period where control has been relinquished, the Pio is free to execute another channel program, be it sending another seek command or monitoring a data transfer.

The final issue to be considered is that of data transfer and of minimizing latency time. Since there is only one head per disk, the situation is different from that of drums or fixed-head disks. There are two possible organizations. In the first one, each track has an arbitrary starting point and records are separated by gaps. Then a counting procedure can be used in order to locate the record to be read or the emplacement on which it should be written. A more sophisticated version of this organization is to have some contextual information, such as a key, stored in the gap. Then the channel programs can use this information while the next record is transmitted. This method, called *automatic key searching*, is better than the counter scheme but still requires a long searching time. This is why indexed files are used (their discussion is outside the scope of this book). The second organization is reminiscent of the paging drum. Tracks are divided into sectors and records can start only on record boundaries. Records can be directly addressed by track and sector numbers. Therefore a device can be ordered to search for that address, for example after the completion of the seek, thus allowing the Pio to relinquish control again. As soon as the desired sector will appear the device will attempt to regain the channel's attention. If it fails, a full rotation time will have to be spent until the same attempt is renewed. This method is known as *rotational position sensing* (RPS).

Seek operations and RPS are similar in the sense that they occur at the device level, thus freeing the channel for other activities. However, there is a major difference: once the seek is completed, the arm is in the correct position, while if the correct sector is missed a complete rotation is lost. While seek operations can be handled via some interrupt scheme, RPS must be more finely tuned since time is critical. Block multiplexor Pio's are an answer, as could be some switching apparatus between disk controllers and several Pio's.

8.4   GENERALITIES ON PIO PROGRAMMING

In Section 2 we described the architecture of channels (or Pio's). In this section, we give a general overview of the interactions between Pc and Pio's and

of the nature of the channel programs. Since channels are not part of all architectures it should be obvious that this is not the only means to perform
input-output operations. For example, direct transfers are used in microcomputers and simple DMA's with hardwired programs prevail in some
minicomputers.

Even within the context of architectures with channels, there exists a wide
variety of PMS and ISP structures. In general, the applications programmer
will not have to deal at a detailed level with I/O programming. His/her concern will be to define or work within some file (or data base) descriptions, to
be sure that files are open or closed at the right time, and to give commands
to read/write records on these files in a high-level language fashion. The code
produced by a compiler, or the one written by the user in assembly language,
will generate calls to specific I/O routines written by systems programmers.
These routines will use privileged instructions which will supervise the channel's activities while, in turn, channel programs will monitor the peripheral
devices.

There is more variation in these privileged instructions than in any other
part of the ISP descriptions of Pc's. The following is a sample of what is
available.

8.4.1 I/O Instructions at the Pc Level

As we just said, I/O instructions are privileged, that is, they cannot be initiated in "user" mode (the usual one) but only in "master" mode. Running
in "master" mode is restricted to some parts of the operating system but
there exist means to pass from one mode to another. Hopefully, modern
operating systems are well protected so that the passage from user to master
mode is allowed only under specific conditions.

An I/O instruction consists (either implicitly or explicitly) of an opcode
such as start, test, or halt, of the channel (and maybe device) address, and of
the address of the beginning of the channel program.

For example, in the UNIVAC 1108 the three basic I/O instructions have
the opcodes "Load input channel" (read), "Load output channel" (write)
and "Load function in channel" (send specific commands to a device). The
channel address is in a 4-bit field (the 1108 has a maximum of 16 channels)
and the effective address yields the location of a control word which will be
used by the channel programs.

As a second (more detailed) example, we consider the IBM System/370
I/O instructions. These instructions have the SI format (cf. Figure 2.9).
There are 8 of them, namely: START I/O (SIO), START I/O FAST RE-

LEASE (SIOF), TEST I/O (TIO), HALT I/O (HIO), HALT DEVICE (HDV), TESTCHANNEL (TCH), CLEAR I/O (CIO), and STORE CHANNEL ID (STIDC). The effective address yields an I/O address of 24 bits with the middle byte indicating the channel number and the rightmost byte the device number. Although there can be up to 256 channels, this number is usually less than 16 (lower models in the series are often limited to 7 channels). Up to 256 devices can be controlled by a channel. The only restriction in device addressing is that those sharing a control unit must have consecutive addresses.

The channel program's address is found in a prespecified location (address 72). This four-byte command address word (CAW) contains not only the 24-bit address but also a protection key for Mp accessing similar to the one found in the program status word (PSW).

We now give a brief summary of the functions of each of the 8 I/O instructions. Details on specific device commands and on the "states" of the I/O system are forthcoming.

SIO and SIOF initiate an I/O instruction on the channel and device selected by the effective address. The condition codes (CC) in the PSW will be set according to the state of the system. This allows the SIO to be followed by a "branch on condition" instruction to either continue normally if the SIO is accepted, or to transfer to some other routine otherwise. If the SIO is accepted, e.g., if the channel, the subchannel in the case of a multiplexor, and the device were all available, the CAW address part will be loaded in the Pio's location counter. In the case of an SIOF, used for block multiplexor channels, the Pc program can be continued sooner without testing the state of the device. An interrupt will be generated later if the operation could not be initiated.

TIO tests the state of the system and returns an appropriate condition code. Often the four possible conditions of the two bits of the CC in the PSW are not sufficient, mostly if some error has occurred. In these cases, the program must test the channel status word (64 bits), or CSW, which is stored, under certain conditions such as I/O interrupts or malfunction, in a prespecified Mp location (location 64). TCH performs the same function as TIO but only the channel's state is tested.

As their names indicate, HIO and HDV terminate I/O operations before all data has been transferred or before normal completion. In the case of a multiplexor, the HDV instruction does not interfere with the operations of the devices other than the one addressed by the instruction. CLRIO provides the same type of function. Finally, STIDC stores in a given Mp location additional information relative to the channel being addressed.

8.4.2 Channel Commands and Channel Programs

We continue our discussion using the System/370 as a model. As we said earlier, channels can be considered as Pio's; they have their own instruction sets and are directed by stored programs. These programs are stored in Mp and the address of the first word is found in the CAW. The channel programs are sequences of channel command words (CCW); as in any stored program processor, a location counter (initialized to the contents of the CAW) indicates the address of the next CCW. The current CCW will be loaded into the (channel) instruction register.

A CCW is composed (again implicitly or explicitly) of an order, an Mp address, a count and various flags. In the System/370, the Mp address and the count are in the CCW. In the UNIVAC 1108, they are in a different location which is passed to the channel as part of the "Load..." instruction (recall last section).

Orders (or commands in the IBM terminology) are actions that the channel wants the device to take. In general, a channel will order one of the following, after having been checked by the Pc to verify that everything is in the correct condition (via an accepted SIO):

- Write: Bytes are read from Mp and transferred to the device until either the device signals "channel end" or the byte count (see below) is 0 and there is no data chaining flag (again see below);
- Read: As above, but bytes are transferred from the device and written in Mp;
- Control: Special orders for specific devices (e.g., rewind for a magnetic tape) which do not involve the transfer of data;
- Sense: The device has to send back some information regarding its status. For example, the current sector address for a disk can be sought;
- Read backward: Same as read, but the device is started in reverse; this is used for magnetic tapes;
- Transfer in channel: This corresponds to a branch instruction in a conventional Pc and does not affect the device. This type of programming is called *command chaining*. This order loads a new CCW found at the address given in the Mp address field.

The Mp address field corresponds to the address in Mp where bytes are read or written. It is modified, in the channel, after transmission of each byte. The byte count stores the number of bytes to be transmitted. It is decreased by 1 at each transmission. When the count reaches 0, the current CCW is "terminated".

One of the flag bits is used for data chaining. If the flag is on, the next CCW is loaded and its order is ignored since it is implied that it is still the same as the previous one. But the Mp address and byte count for the previous order are now those found in this new CCW. If the flag is off, channel end is initiated and in general this indicates that a new SIO can be accepted. This SIO will not be accepted if other flags are on, such as those requesting an interrupt at the end of the transmission, command chaining (loading of the next CCW with decoding of the order), and error conditions.

8.4.3   A Simple I/O Programming Example

With the IBM System/370 in mind let us see how we would program Pc and Pio procedures to transfer a block of data of given length from some external device to a specified location in Mp. This corresponds to some form of READ statement from a high-level language. Before doing so, however, we explain what the states of the system can be. Each component of the chain between the Pc and the data to be transferred (channel, subchannel and device) can be in one of four states: available (A), interrupt pending (I), working (W), and not operational (N). A and N have obvious meanings; for the subchannel and the device, W means that they are executing some operation, while for the channel it means that it operates in burst mode; finally I means that the I/O interruption source is immediately available either in the channel, or from the CSW in the subchannel case, or is pending in the device for this last component. Not all of the 64 ($4 \cdot 4 \cdot 4$) possible states are relevant; less than a dozen are significant for the setting of the condition codes. As indicated earlier, the CSW will bring more information when needed.

We now return to our example. The first step is to set up a Pio program of one or more CCW's, and to generate a CAW with the desired protection key and the Pio program's address. The operating system will be cognizant of the location of the CAW. When it is time to activate the I/O routine, the following program is called in the Pc:

1. Load some prespecified address/register with the channel and device addresses; load the CAW in an assigned (reserved) location;
2. Disable the I/O interrupts;
3. Issue the SIO;
4. Test the condition codes to determine the outcome of the SIO; in particular if the CC's setting corresponds to states (XYZ means state X for the channel, Y for the subchannel, and Z for the device):

    AAA: the SIO was accepted; the Pc program continues normally;
    AAI or AAW: the SIO is not accepted; the CSW has been stored in Mp and should be examined;

AI-, *AW-*, *W--* (where - is any of the four possible states): the SIO is not accepted; the channel or subchannel was busy;

N--, *-N-*, *--N*: the SIO is not accepted; some part of the I/O system is not operational;

5. Enable I/O interrupts if the SIO was accepted (note that in the case IAA the SIO was accepted; the pending interrupt will be cleared at this point); if the SIO was not accepted other routines will be called (the branch on condition will direct the Pc to some error handling routine).

If the SIO was accepted, the Pc and Pio programs can run concurrently. The Pio program started as soon as the Pio received the SIO. At that point, the steps taken by the channel program were:

1. The CAW is fetched and checked for validity;
2. The CCW (of address given by CAW) is fetched and checked for validity;
3. The condition codes are set in the PSW. (This involves the interface protocol described previously to ascertain the state of the system.)

Assuming that the SIO was accepted, the channel program can now be executed, that is, in our case:

1. The first order (READ) is executed by the device;
2. The data transfer operation takes place and under normal conditions some end-status bits are set in the CSW;
3. An I/O interruption is initiated by the channel.

Obviously, there are other ways in which an I/O can terminate. Appropriate bits will be set in the CSW for specific malfunctions and I/O interrupts will be generated. Also the termination can be programmed via the HIO, HDV, and CLRIO instructions.

Asynchronous operations between Pio and Pc certainly enhance the performance of the whole system. How much can be gained is the subject of the next section.

8.5 SIMPLE MODELS FOR EVALUATING ASYNCHRONOUS I/O PROCESSING

After having discussed at length how I/O processing could be done while the Pc is executing some other program, we now attempt to evaluate the efficiency of such a scheme. The models that we present here are idealized and the characteristics of the systems and of jobs are certainly far from representing actual installations and workloads. However, this modeling will allow us to gain some insight as to how much can be gained by having Pio's and Pc's run in parallel.

The first type of models that we describe is a series of variations on the deterministic scheduling methods presented in Chapter 4. It is convenient here for the evaluation of batch processing. The second type of model is queueing theoretical in nature and is more appropriate for interactive systems. Since in this case the I/O processing part is perhaps not the most important subsystem to study, and since we have not laid the necessary mathematical foundations for this kind of problem, we shall not dwell too heavily on this aspect of the modeling. In particular, we shall deal only with models of batch processing.

In a batch processing environment, the important parameter is throughput which in the case of a single job can be equated to the reciprocal of the completion time. Thus, maximizing throughput and minimizing the completion time will be synonymous. In a time sharing or interactive environment, there are other variables that we would like to optimize such as the response time, the length of various queues, or the Pc utilization.

The factors which influence throughput and the other measures just mentioned are the speed and the size of the system's architectural components (hardware and software), the concurrency in the use of resources (this relates not only to the concurrency between Pc and Pio, but also to other facets of the system, such as the level of multiprogramming or the decomposition of a disk access into independent seek and read/write commands), and the workload (the number of jobs/terminals and their associated characteristics).

We start our evaluation with a simple model. Let us assume a batch processing environment and a unique job running through the system. This job can be decomposed into n steps, each step consisting of an input phase I_i, a compute phase C_i, and an output phase O_i, with $1 \leq i \leq n$. To simplify matters even more, let:

$$C_i = C, \ 1 \leq i \leq n,$$
$$I_i = O_i = IO, \ 1 \leq i \leq n.$$

We consider four possible system organizations, namely:

Organization 1: Sequential;
Organization 2: One Pio with either input or output running in parallel with the compute part (e.g., $I_i - C_{i-1}$, or $O_i - C_{i+1}$);
Organization 3: Two Pio's with an amount of concurrency of 2, i.e, any 2 out of the 3 phases can be performed in parallel (e.g., as above plus $I_i - O_{i-1}$);
Organization 4: Two Pio's but now with an amount of concurrency of 3 (e.g., $I_i - C_{i-1} - O_{i-2}$).

We must also include another parameter: the amount of Mp that each processor can consider as its own workspace. Otherwise it is obvious that the above organizations are ranked in increasing order of power, that is, the sequential one is the least powerful and Organization 4 is the most.

Instead of having a job of n steps, let us assume that N blocks, or records, must be processed and that the whole Mp can store m blocks. Mp is equipartitioned among Pio's and Pc according to the degree of concurrency allowed. We then have the following:

Organization 1: m blocks can be transferred/computed per phase;
Organization 2 and 3: $m/2$ blocks can be transferred/computed per phase;
Organization 4: $m/3$ blocks can be transferred/computed per phase.

Let us further define c and io to be the times to process one block. We compute the completion time for each organization (cf. also Exercises 9–10).
Organization 1:
   The number of (compute) phases is $n_1 = N/m$. Thus,

$$T_1 = \sum_{i=1}^{n_1} (I_i + C_i + O_i) = n_1(C_1 + 2IO_1) = N(c + 2io).$$

Organization 2:
   The number of steps is $n_2 = 2N/m$. We distinguish between compute bound and I/O bound jobs, namely whether:

$$C \geq 2IO \qquad \text{compute bound, or}$$
$$C < 2IO \qquad \text{I/O bound.}$$

It is simple to show (via a Gantt chart) that we have:

$$T_2^a = n_2 C_2 + 2IO_2 ; \qquad T_2^b = 2n_2 IO_2,$$

where superscript a indicates compute and b indicates I/O bound.
   With $C_2 = (m/2)c$, $IO_2 = (m/2)io$, we have:

$$T_2^a = Nc + mio ; \qquad T_2^b = 2Nio.$$

Organization 3:
   We have $n_3 = 2N/m$. The compute and I/O bound conditions are as above. Gantt chart analysis, on two consecutive cycles, show that:

$$T_3^a = n_3 C_3 + 2IO_3;$$
$$T_3^b = (n_3/3)(2IO_3 + C_3) + IO_3, \quad n_3 \text{ even,}$$
$$= \lceil n_3/2 \rceil (2IO_3 + C_3), \quad n_3 \text{ odd,}$$

and therefore:

$$T_3{}^a = Nc + mio \; ;$$
$$T_3{}^b = Nc/2 + (N + m/2)io, \qquad n_3 \text{ even}$$
$$= Nc/2 + mc/2 + (N + m)io, \qquad n_3 \text{ odd}.$$

Organization 4:

We have $n_4 = 3N/m$, $C_4 = (m/3)c$ and $IO_4 = (m/3)io$. Using the same technique we have:

$$T_4{}^a = n_4C_4 = 2IO_4;$$
$$T_4{}^b = (n_4 + 1)IO_4 + C_4;$$

and therefore:

$$T_4{}^a = Nc + (2m/3)io \; ;$$
$$T_4{}^b = (m/3)c + (N + m/3)io \; .$$

The above results are summarized in Table 8.2 (only the case of n_3 even is reported). As could be expected, organizations 2, 3 and 4 are equivalent, and better than sequential, in the compute bound case. In the I/O bound environment, organization 4 has a slight advantage over organization 3 which itself is better than organization 2.

One assumption in this model which could be easily removed is that the I/O time is proportional to the number of blocks transferred. Instead it could be assumed that:

$$IO = t_s + t_a + mt_r$$

where t_s would be the average seek time, t_a the average access time of a disk, and t_r the transfer time of one block. Then we would have:

$$IO_1 = t_s + t_a + mt_r \; ; \qquad IO_2 = IO_3 = t_s + t_a + (m/2)t_r \; ;$$

$$IO_4 = t_a + t_s + (m/3)t_r \, .$$

Table 8.2 can be revised in accordance with these new parameters. Since only the I/O bound computations are significantly changed, we limit ourselves to this case, yielding the results shown in Table 8.3 (cf. Exercise 11) with $t_{as} = (t_a + t_s)/m$.

The ranking of the various organizations depends on the respective values

Table 8.2   Simple model of asynchronous I/O (io proportional to m)

Organization	Completion time	
	Compute bound	I/O bound
Sequential	$N(c + 2io)$	$N(c + 2io)$
One channel	$Nc + m\,io$	$2N\,io$
Two channels (concurrency $= 2$)	$Nc + m\,io$	$\dfrac{Nc}{2} + \left(N + \dfrac{m}{2}\right)io$
Two channels (concurrency $= 3$)	$Nc + \dfrac{2m}{3}\,io$	$\dfrac{cm}{3} + \left(N + \dfrac{m}{3}\right)io$

Table 8.3   Simple model of asynchronous I/O
(io includes an access time)

Organization	Completion time I/O bound
Sequential	$N(c + 2t_{as} + 2t_r)$
One channel	$N(4t_{as} + 2t_r)$
Two channels (concurrency $= 2$)	$N\left(\dfrac{c}{2} + 2t_{as} + t_r\right) + m\left(t_{as} + \dfrac{1}{2}t_r\right)$
Two channels (concurrency $= 3$)	$N\left(3t_{as} + t_r\right) + m\left(\dfrac{c}{3} + t_{as} + \dfrac{1}{3}t_r\right)$

of c, t_{as} and t_r. For example, if the time for the Pc to process one record, c, is less than $2/m$ the average access plus seek times to find the $m/2$ blocks in organization 2, then a sequential organization will be better. This simply says that if the compute time is almost negligible and input and output cannot occur concurrently, then it is better to perform large blocks of I/O at a time. If c is less than t_{as}, then having two channels and complete overlap (organization 4) can be detrimental. Note though that organization 3 is always superior to the sequential structure (assuming $N \gg m$). The fact that organization 3 can be superior to organization 4 shows the importance of the partitioning of Mp. From a practical viewpoint, this can be translated into the fact that for an extremely I/O bound job it is important to have buffers as large as possible.

We now remove a second assumption, namely the equality of processing time for each phase. We still have an n-step job and each step consists of a compute phase C_i of expected time $E(C)$ and a single I/O phase of expected time $E(IO)$. We are therefore moving from a deterministic model to a stochastic one. We look first at the sequential and one channel organizations. As usual in this modeling aspect, we consider C_i and IO_i to be random variables following an exponential distribution, i.e., the random variables C and IO have the probability densities:

$$a(c) = \begin{cases} \mu_i e^{-\mu_i c} & \text{if } c \geq 0 \\ 0 & \text{otherwise} \end{cases}$$

$$b(io) = \begin{cases} \mu_2 e^{-\mu_2 io} & \text{if } io \geq 0 \\ 0 & \text{otherwise.} \end{cases}$$

Denoting by $E(t)$ the expected value of the random variable t we have in the sequential case

$$E(T_1) = n[E(c) + E(io)]$$
$$= n(1/\mu_1 + 1/\mu_2).$$

In the one channel case, when we can overlap one compute and one I/O phase, the expected time in a phase at steady-state is given by:

$$E(t) = E(\max(C, IO)).$$

With the common notation $(A \mid B)$ meaning "event A assuming event B," we have

$$E(t) = E(IO \mid C < IO) \Pr\{C < IO\} + E(C \mid C \geq IO) \Pr\{C \geq IO\}, \quad (1)$$

with the first term corresponding to an I/O bound phase and the second to a compute bound one. The probability that $C < IO$ can be easily computed if we assume that these two random variables are independent. Then we have:

$$\Pr\{C - IO < 0\} = \int_0^\infty \int_0^{io} b(io)\, a(c)\, dc\, dio = \mu_1/(\mu_1 + \mu_2) \quad (2)$$

and

$$\Pr\{C - IO \geq 0\} = 1 - \Pr\{C - IO < 0\} = \mu_2/(\mu_1 + \mu_2) \quad (3)$$

From the conditional probability definition, we have:

$$E(IO \mid C < IO) = 1/\Pr(C < IO) \int_0^\infty \int_0^{io} io\, b(io)\, a(c)\, dc\, dio$$

which yields (with the result from (2)):

$$E(IO \mid C < IO) = \frac{1/\mu_2 - \mu_2/(\mu_1 + \mu_2)^2}{\mu_1/(\mu_1 + \mu_2)}$$

$$= 1/\mu_2 + 1/(\mu_1 + \mu_2) \tag{4}$$

and similarly:

$$E(C \mid C \geq IO) = 1/\mu_1 + 1/(\mu_1 + \mu_2) \tag{5}$$

Substituting the results of (2)–(5) into (1) gives:

$$E(\max(C, IO)) = 1/\mu_1 + 1/\mu_2 - 1/(\mu_1 + \mu_2). \tag{6}$$

We have $(n - 1)$ "steady-state" phases plus one compute and one I/O phase of expected times $1/\mu_1$ and $1/\mu_2$ respectively. Therefore the expected completion time is:

$$E(T_2) = n(1/\mu_1 + 1/\mu_2) - (n - 1)(1/(\mu_1 + \mu_2)). \tag{7}$$

The relative expected speed gain over the sequential organization will be:

$$E(\text{gain}) = \frac{E(T_1) - E(T_2)}{E(T_1)} = \frac{(n - 1)(1/(\mu_1 + \mu_2))}{n(1/\mu_1 + 1/\mu_2)},$$

or

$$E(\text{gain}) = \frac{n - 1}{n} \frac{\mu_1 \mu_2}{(\mu_1 + \mu_2)^2}.$$

With $p = \mu_1/\mu_2$, this yields:

$$E(\text{gain}) = \frac{n - 1}{n} \frac{p}{(1 + p)^2}. \tag{8}$$

This is maximum for $p = 1$ and hence the maximum gain is 0.25 for large n. Figure 8.17 shows the gains for various values of p and n.

This analysis cannot be easily extended to several channels. Another possible model is to limit the concurrency to two (i.e., one channel) but allow an unlimited amount of buffering (that is up to n "output" buffers). It can be shown that under ideal conditions, with the appropriate value of the ratio between I/O and compute phases, an expected gain of up to 0.50 can be realized.

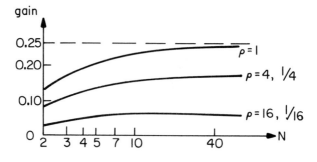

Figure 8.17   Expected gain of the single overlap organization over the sequential one

Rather than trying to expand the deterministic scheduling approach to a stochastic environment, it is more convenient to use analytical tools provided by queueing theory. For example, our batch processing model can take the form of Figure 8.18 with two servers, a Pc and a Pio of different speeds (figures (a) and (b)), or two classes of servers (figures (c) and (d)), the Pc with its input queue and 2 Pio's either having each their input queue, or sharing an input queue (this is certainly less realistic). There is a fixed number (N) of jobs in the system. After passing through a compute phase a job joins the I/O queue (or one of the two I/O queues randomly with probability 1/2). After being serviced by a Pio, the job joins the Pc queue. The process is repeated indefinitely. This latter assumption is justified since we can consider a job leaving the system as being immediately replaced by a new one. Organizations 2, 3 and 4 in a sense double the I/O capacity of the system and it would be interesting to see which one is best for a given ratio μ_2/μ_1. There exist computational methods to solve for this type of queueing networks with some assumptions on service times and the like. With the same probability distributions for the compute and I/O phases as before, the curves in Figure 8.19 show the percentage of time the Pc is busy versus the (fixed) number of jobs in the system for a ratio of service times $\mu_2/\mu_1 = 0.3$. As could be expected, the architectures of (b) and (d) are most efficient with a slight advantage to organization (b). For more practical models we have to consider simulations, or even empirical measurements.

8.6   BIBLIOGRAPHICAL NOTES, REFERENCES AND EXERCISES

A general overview of I/O architecture can be found in [Buzen 75]. Many books on computer organization deal with interrupt systems. A simple but lucid explanation is

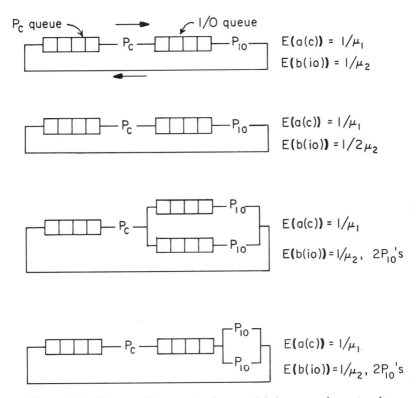

Figure 8.18   Four possible organizations modeled as queueing networks

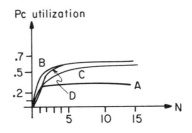

Figure 8.19   Pc utilization for the 4 organizations of figure 8.18 with $p = 0.3$

discussed in [Sloan 76]. Details on the System/360 and /370 and on the Sigma 5 interrupt schemes are available in the respective reference manuals [IBM 74, Xerox 71].

An example of the evolution of PMS structures for I/O processing is contained in [Bell, Kotok, Hastings and Hill 78]. [Thurber, Jensen, Jack, Kinney, Patton and Anderson 72] provides an encyclopedic view of bussing structures. A detailed explanation of the IBM Standard interface can be found in [IBM 76].

Stochastic aspects of drum and disk scheduling are covered in detail in [Coffman and Denning 73]. The SATF discipline has been known for a long time but first appeared in the technical literature in [Denning 67]. The fact that SATF is near-optimal is due to [Stone and Fuller 72]. The ranking between file and paging organizations under FIFO and SATF is extracted from [Fuller and Baskett 75]. [Teorey and Pinkerton 72] analyze various disk scheduling policies. [Wilhelm 76] uses [Lynch 72] measurements to show that FIFO can behave as well as SSTF.

The simple model of asynchronous I/O processing is analyzed in [Hellerman and Smith 70]. Its extension to a stochastic model and the derivations leading to Figure 8.17 are from [Cotten and Abd-Alla 74]. The queueing network model of Figure 8.8 is sketched in [Lipsky and Church 77] where many other references can be found on this topic.

References

1. Bell, C. G., Kotok, A., Hastings, T. N. and R. Hill, "The Evolution of the DEC System 10," *Comm. ACM, 21,* (Jan. 1978), 44-63.

2. Buzen, J. P., "I/O Subsystem Architecture," *Proc. IEEE, 63,* (Jun. 1975), 871-879.

3. Coffman, E. G. and P. Denning, *Operating Systems Theory,* Prentice Hall, Englewood Cliffs, N.J., 1973.

4. Cotten, L. W. and A. M. Abd-Alla, "Processing Times for Segmented Jobs with I/O Compute Overlaps," *J. ACM, 21,* (Jan. 1974), 18-30.

5. Denning, P. J., "Effects of Scheduling on File Memory Operations," *Proc. AFIPS 1967 Spring Joint Comp. Conf., 30,* AFIPS Press, Montvale, N.J., (1967), 9-21.

6. Fuller, S. H., "An Optimal Drum Scheduling Algorithm," *IEEE Trans. on Comp., C-21,* (Nov. 1972), 1153-1165.

7. Fuller, S. H. and F. Baskett, "An Analysis of Drum Storage Units," *J. ACM, 22,* (Jan. 1975), 83-105.

8. Hellerman, H. and H. J. Smith, Jr., "Throughput Analysis of Some Idealized Input, Output and Compute Overlap Configurations," *Computing Surveys, 2,* (Jun. 1970), 111-118.

9. IBM System/370 *Principles of Operation,* GA22-7000-4, 1974.

10. IBM Corp. *IBM System/360 and System/370 I/O Interface Channel to Control Unit,* Form GA22-6974-3, 1976.

11. Lipsky, L. and J. D. Church, "Applications of a Queueing Network Model for a Computer System," *Computing Surveys, 9,* (Mar. 1977), 205-222.

12. Lynch, W. L. "Do Disk Arms Move?" *Performance Evaluation Review, 1,* (Dec. 1972), 3-16.

13. Sloan, M., *Computer Hardware and Organization,* SRA, Chicago, Ill, 1976.

14. Stone, H. S. and S. H. Fuller. "On the Near-optimality of the Shortest-Latency-Time-First Drum Scheduling Discipline," *Comm. ACM, 16,* (Jun. 1973), 352-353.

15. Teorey, T. J. and T. B. Pinkerton, "A Comparative Analysis of Disk Scheduling Policies," *Comm. ACM, 15,* (Mar. 1972), 177-184.

16. Thurber, K. J., Jensen, E. D., Jack, L. A., Kinney, L. L., Patton, P. C., and L. C. Anderson, "A Systematic Approach to the Design of Digital Bussing Structures," *Proc. AFIPS 1972 Fall Joint Comp. Conf., 41 part II,* AFIPS Press, Montvale, N.J., (1972), 719-740.

17. Wilhelm, N. C., "An Anomaly in Disk Scheduling: a Comparison of FCFS and SSTF Seek Scheduling Using an Empirical Model for Disk Accesses," *Comm. ACM, 19,* (Jan. 1976), 13-17.

18. Xerox Data Systems. Xerox Sigma 5 Computer. *Reference Manual* 900959E, 1971.

Exercises

1. Show how one can implement servicing routines for I/O interrupts when all I/O devices share the same interrupt level. What data structure is needed in the servicing routine to allow devices with higher priority to interrupt devices of lower priority? Is there any critical instruction(s) for which the I/O interrupts considered as a group are to be disabled?

2. In machines which use base registers like System/370 the instruction to save registers might use a base register R to indicate where to save those registers, R included. How would you solve this problem in the context of interrupt handling?

3. Consider the computer(s) available to you. Describe its interrupt structure and attempt to classify it according to its number of levels and its priority scheme. Is masking available? How are multiple interrupts handled? Draw a flowchart (or Petri Net) of the handling of an interrupt. Distinguish between hardware and software actions.

4. Consider the computer(s) available to you. Does it have a channel? If so, compare the channel's architecture to the ones described in this chapter. If there is no channel, investigate the DMA mechanism.

5. Discuss advantages and disadvantages of the daisy chaining, polling, and independent request schemes. Which method is used for the I/O devices of the computer system available to you?

6. How many bytes can be stored on a 2400 foot long reel of tape recorded at 800 bits per inch with records of 1K bytes separated by gaps of 0.7 inch?

7. Give a formula for the transfer time of a record R_i with starting position s_i and final position f_i in the cases of
    (a) a file drum
    (b) a paging drum
    Assume an angular rotational speed of θ.

8. Prove that the SATF scheduling discipline for a drum yields a completion time at most one revolution time longer than an optimum schedule.

9. Prove the formulas given in the text for the simple model of asynchronous processing.

10. Consider the simple model of asynchronous processing but assume now that $I_i < O_i$, (e.g., $I_i = O_i/2$). Rework the formulas for each organization. Repeat this problem assuming that $I_i = O_{i+1} < I_{i+1} = O_i$.

11. Derive the formulas found in Table 8.3.

Part III

COMPLETE SYSTEMS: FROM MICROS TO SUPERCOMPUTERS

It is already becoming clear in the use of these new machines that they demand purely mathematical techniques of their own, quite different from those in use in manual computation or in the use of machines of smaller capacity.

N. Wiener

I am no prophet—and here's no great matter.

T. S. Eliot

Chapter 9

FROM MICROPROCESSORS TO SUPERMINICOMPUTERS

In the third part of this book we present architectures of complete systems, from the smallest end of the spectrum, microcomputers, to the largest represented by supercomputers and (local) networks of processors and memories. This chapter is devoted to the machines which are in the very small to medium range.

First, it should be clear to the reader that a fair representation of a medium-size machine can be obtained by piecing together material found in previous chapters. This will be done in Section 1 of this chapter. Then we will define mini and microcomputers and discuss their roles. In order to present a coherent description of these machines, we shall look first at single bus architectures and more specifically at the DEC PDP-11 and its successor the VAX 11/780. Then we shall descend one level in power and introduce microprocessors. As we shall see, the most powerful entries in that market will compete with some minis, in the same sense as superminis are as efficient as medium-size machines. Finally, we shall close this chapter by looking at a stack-oriented minicomputer, namely Hewlett-Packard's HP-3000.

9.1 MEDIUM-SIZE COMPUTERS. IBM SYSTEM/370 MODELS 155 TO 168 (A REVIEW)

The IBM System/360 and /370 have been used as examples in many instances in all previous chapters. Their architecture is typical of medium-size machines of the third generation. As stated previously, there exist many different models in the 360 and 370 series. We summarize here the characteristics of those in the medium-to-upper range. We leave the study of the most efficient models (or derivatives) for the next chapter. We do not treat the bottom of the line which is not as interesting, pedagogically speaking at least, as single bus or other mini and micro architectures presented in forthcoming sections of this chapter. In the following then, System/370 will be an abbreviation for System/370 Models 155 to 168. We shall also refer to specific entries in this book where the reader can find more details on the topics under discussion (e.g., see Chapter 1 Section 3 for a listing of the models in the 360 and 370 series).

From the PMS viewpoint, System/370 is representative of a tree-structured, multibus architecture, with Mp accessible from Pc (there could even be more than one Pc) and Pio's (channels as discussed in Chapter 8 Section 2.2). The Pio's control one or more Ms (drum, fixed-head and movable arm disks) and a large variety of peripheral devices. The block diagram of Figure 1.3, or better yet the PMS descriptions of Figures 2.4 and 2.5, are good schematic descriptions of representative models.

The System/370 ISP is based on a one-address + general register scheme. The instruction set has a full complement of register-register and register-memory operations, and a few memory-memory instructions for data transfers. There are five instruction formats of either 2, 4 or 6 bytes in length (cf. Chapter 2 Sections 2.3.2 and 2.3.3). Mp addressing is in terms of bytes (1 byte = 8 bits and 1 word = 4 bytes) although the information units transferred to and from Mp are words (Model 155) and double words (Model 165), and the transfers between Mp and Mcache are 4 or 8 words. The basic data types are integer (two's complement), floating-point (short, long and extended, cf. Chapter 3 Section 4) and decimal (packed, either BCD or zoned). Addressing can be immediate (restricted to 1 byte masks), direct (restricted to addresses at most 2^{12}), indexed, and based. The base register scheme, equivalent to double indexing, provides the means for easy relocation of segments of code and data less than 2^{12} bytes in length. Sixteen 32-bit general registers and four 64-bit floating-point accumulators are part of the Pc state. A double word program status register, PSW, contains the location counter, two condition codes (akin to the Sigma 5's CC's described in Chapter 2 Section 3.1), various interrupt masks (recall Chapter 8 Section 1.3), and protection keys. In addition, 16 control registers (not all of them are used in current versions) can be considered as extensions to the PSW. They are not program addressable in application mode but they can be modified by specific privileged instructions.

The Pc is controlled via horizontal microprograms. The microinstruction width is from 72 to 108 bits depending on the specific model. The system is not user microprogrammable but there exist operating systems enhancements via microprograms. The Pc contains at least 2 D-units: a general-purpose binary adder and a decimal (1-byte) adder. Some models might also have an extra D-unit for floating-point calculations. The basic data paths are

4 bytes for the Model 155 and 8 bytes for the 165. These widths correspond to the basic widths of the general-purpose adders and we can see why a floating-point extension is more needed in the 155 than in the 165. Although there are always at least two D-units, they cannot operate in parallel. In the case of the 165 some look-ahead, and look-behind, is provided with an instruction buffer and an auxiliary buffer for prefetching both paths of a branch instruction (cf. Figure 4.7).

The general-purpose adder is of the carry look-ahead type. Depending on the models, a number of techniques are utilized to speed up multiplication such as fixed length decoding, skipping over 0's and 1's, and even extensive table look-up as in the Model 158 floating-point extension. Division algorithms always consider a positive dividend, with a potential precomplementing, and generate the quotient either directly (Model 155) or by a post-complementation when the divisor is precomplemented to be positive (Model 165).

In terms of memory hierarchy, caches of 8K and 16K bytes are present in the models of this range. They are organized according to the set associative concept with an LRU replacement algorithm within each set (of 4 blocks) and a write through policy (cf. Chapter 6 Section 5). Models 158 and 168 have a memory hierarchy managed via a virtual memory scheme. Linear segmentation is used. The Memory management policy is a software adaptation of a global LRU replacement algorithm (cf. Chapter 6 Sections 3.2 and 4.1).

The Pio's of System/370, selector and multiplexor channels, have been described in Chapter 8. The Ms and peripheral devices attached to the channels include direct access storage devices described in Chapter 5 (Section 4) and Chapter 8 (Section 3) as well as a wide range of other devices such as terminals, card readers and punches, line printers, magnetic tapes, mass storage systems, etc. . . .

Multiprocessor (dual processor) System/370's are available. Networks of System/370's do exist. Their study is outside the scope of this chapter.

9.2 MINICOMPUTERS AND MICROCOMPUTERS: DEFINITIONS AND ROLES

9.2.1 Minicomputers

In the late sixties and early seventies, at the time when the minicomputer revolution, an explosion, was reaching its peak, it was fairly straightforward to define a minicomputer. It was simply a system where a minimal main frame containing a Pc and Mp of at least 4K words (1 word $\leq$ 16 bits) could be obtained for less than $20,000. The Pc was to have a general purpose instruction set and more often than not would be microprogrammed. The Mp should be expandable to at least 64K. The operating system and basic software (compilers, utilities, ect....) were rather primitive and many systems were intended for stand-alone applications or turn-key operations. The specific applications most often cited were process control, laboratory monitoring and communication handling. Thus, the number of peripherals to be interfaced for a given installation was in general limited but the variety of devices to be linked to a given main frame could be quite large.

Soon, though, a number of trends changed this simplistic description, making it inappropriate by the late 70's. Some of these trends are:

- Lower cost: The $20,000 figure mentioned above soon became $10,000 and even less. However, this decrease in cost was not matched by a comparable increase in the number of different available systems (of course more models were sold). For example, Datamation surveys of the period show that:
  * In 1969 there were 39 minicomputers available from 24 manufacturers.
  * In 1971 there were 49 minicomputers available from 28 manufacturers.
  * In 1974 there were 44 minicomputers available from 23 manufacturers.
  (These figures do not include various models in the same series.)
  Price is still the main parameter used for placing a machine into the minicomputer category, but it is the whole system which is appraised. A $200,000 to $250,000 figure is an upperbound for "superminicomputers".
- Higher performance: Most of the improvements seen in medium size machines of the third generation found their way to minicomputers: with cheaper semiconductor RAM's, larger Mp's became available (up to 128K words is usual); virtual memory and cache memory were implemented; stack computers or the use of a large number of accumulators (general-purpose registers) became the rule rather than the exception. The evolution of the DEC PDP-11 family presented in the next section will illustrate this point.
- More microprogramming: With the advent of cheaper ROM's, more functions were embedded in the microengine. Integer multiply and divide which were optional became part of the original instruction set; (microprogrammed) floating-point packages were offered (with possibly floating-point hardware extensions).

- More comprehensive software: Sophisticated multiprogrammed and time-shared operating systems appeared. The number of language processors and of utilities was also increasing rapidly. Similarly, the number of peripherals which could be linked, without saturation, to a given mainframe was large enough so that the system could be used as a general-purpose computer.

Thus, it becomes difficult to differentiate between minicomputers and medium-size machines. The main limitation in the minis is the addressing range given to a task (in general 2^{16} bytes). Although a lot of effort has been invested in finding schemes (patches?) to circumvent this defect, it was not until the late seventies that "superminis", machines with a 32 bit addressing space (e.g., Interdata/32, SEL-32, VAX 11/780) selling for less than $250,000, were introduced.

With this new addressing dimension, it seems that superminis are to replace medium-sized machines in the upper end of the spectrum; on the other hand at the lower end, microcomputers are taking the place of the smallest minis as will be discussed soon. So, defining minicomputers might be easier by stating what they cannot do rather than their capabilities. If we do not consider superminis, then they cannot be used in large Artificial Intelligence projects, they cannot run extensive simulation programs, they cannot support large databases, they cannot provide fast and extended floating-point arithmetic. This list is certainly not exhaustive. In addition, because of their physical dimension, they cannot be used in many specialized applications where microcomputers can fit (see below). But it is readily apparent that these limitations are not overly restrictive and that the field of applications of minicomputers remains large enough. Distributed processing and local networks (cf. Chapters 10 and 11) rely heavily on the uses and on advances in the design of minicomputers. It can be expected that they will continue to do so.

9.2.2 Microcomputers

The literature on microcomputers is growing as rapidly as the number of microprocessors being offered. Panegyrics on microcomputers, stating how they will revolutionize our daily habits and how they will transform computing facilities, can be found in every trade publication. At the risk of disappointing the reader, let us quote F. Brooks: "The 25-year computer man exposed suddenly to the architecture and software of today's microcomputer is swept with nostalgia and a deep feeling of deja vu". To this, we could add that microprocessors are not a universal panacea and that there exist limits to their use! But, of course, we shall have to agree that they have, and are going to have, an enormous impact on the automation of many functions and on the design of computing utilities.

In the above paragraph, we have used the terms microcomputer and microprocessor interchangeably. From now on, we shall be more precise and adopt the following definitions.

When the Pc of a stored program computer is implemented on a single, or a very small number, of integrated circuit chips we call it a *microprocessor*. Because of the programmable requirement, the arithmetic units of hand-held calculators do not qualify as microprocessors. A *microcomputer* is the combination of a microprocessor (and associated clock and control circuits), memories and circuits providing I/O capabilities. If all the Pc, Mp and I/O capability is on a single chip, we shall call this system a *one-chip microcomputer*.

We have to distinguish further between *"word size"* and *"bit-slice"* microprocessors. The former class, built around MOS technology, corresponds to classical architectures, i.e., we have monolithic registers of the given word size, currently 4, 8, 12 or 16 bits. Bit-slice microprocessors, 2 or 4 bits wide, are cascaded under microprogram control to form larger word lengths. Generally, they are based upon bipolar technology. In Section 4 we shall consider the advantages and disadvantages of the two architectures.

In complexity, microcomputers lie between the hand-held calculators and the small minicomputers. In cost, they can be as cheap as calculators. Performance-wise, we shall see that the most powerful micros can compete with medium-range minis, although the amount of software available is not as extensive. However, there exist many microcomputers having a BASIC interpreter and several having COBOL or Pascal translators. But, they are still restricted to function in a uniprogramming environment.

An 8-bit microcomputer system with 128K bytes of memory, 20 to 25KB of it reserved for the operating system and a BASIC interpreter, 4 floppy disks and a hard-copy printer can be available for $10,000, this price (circa 1978) including hardware and software. This is about half as much as a minicomputer with the same capabilities.

The above system would be convenient for a small business firm. But the applications of microcomputers cover a much wider range. For example, we can cite:

- Controllers for appliances, cars, calculators, games (4-bit systems);
- Intelligent terminals, hobby markets, small business systems, communication switches, disk controllers, word processing, office automation, laboratory data acquisition, etc., (8-bit systems);

- Intelligent terminals, process control and many applications where low-scale minis are used (16-bit systems).

At this point we may conjecture where the borderline between minis and micros should be drawn, in the same sense that we have attempted to draw one between minis and medium-size machines. Again, it is by looking at what micros cannot do that the question must be answered. In the late seventies, it is fair to say that most minis are 16-bit machines and most micros are 8-bits. Thus, if computations are to be performed primarily on 16-bit or larger entities micros should not be selected. This might be wrong by the time this book is published but then the same argument could be repeated by changing 16 to 32. The inherent limitation of the computer on a chip is, from a technological viewpoint, that the number of pins cannot increase unduly. Therefore the number of address/data lines is restricted.

In terms of instruction sets, or more broadly of the ISP, there is not much difference as will be seen in the remainder of this chapter. Both minis and micros can have extensive sets comparable to those of any third generation machine.

Mp is larger on minis than on micros, and more importantly miniinstallations will have larger Ms since the relative incremental cost is less. Therefore, more sophisticated software packages will be available on minis making them good candidates for environments with general-purpose applications. In terms of transfer rates and of the possibility of having DMA's, minis are currently slightly faster and may be more flexible but this is a marginal situation changing every day. Finally, we must remember that the small size and cost of some microcomputers make them available for many situations where it would be impossible to think of having a minicomputer.

From the above, it should be apparent that the distinctions between "supermicros" and minis on the one hand, and between "superminis" and medium machines on the other, are unclear at least from the user's viewpoint. The following sections where we present some mini and microcomputer families should reinforce this impression.

9.3 A MINICOMPUTER FAMILY: THE DEC PDP-11

In the same sense that the IBM System/360 and /370 series have had a profound impact on the design of third generation computer systems, the DEC PDP-11 family has been, and continues to be, a success story and has influenced many minicomputer manufacturers. With hindsight, it is possible to fault some of the design decisions. But the 50,000 PDP-11's sold in the years 1970–1977 and the attention given to its successor, the VAX 11/780, indicate the value of the PDP-11's architecture. In this section, we shall give a rather detailed view of the system following the approach taken in the previous chapters. We shall discuss the historical perspective of the PDP-11 development, the PMS and ISP structures, the Pc design and its microprogramming features, the cache and memory extensions, and the bussing and I/O structures. Finally, we shall present the architecture of the VAX 11/780.

9.3.1 Historical Perspective

The PDP-11 series was planned during the late sixties. The first model, the 11/20, was announced in 1970. Since then, about ten other models (this number depends on authors even within DEC) have been produced. Figure 9.1 shows the PDP-11 family tree, as a cost vs. time graph. Three directions in the evolution of the machine can be seen. The first one is simply an improvement caused by technology. The basic design of the 11/20 was kept in

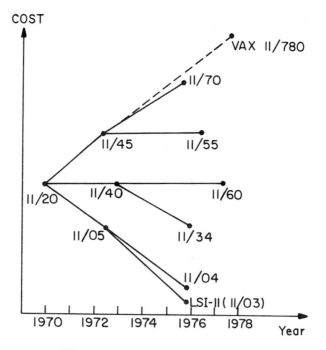

Figure 9.1   The PDP-11 family tree

the 11/40 but microprogramming was introduced and, henceforth, some new instructions (multiply/divide and floating-point) could be added. The 11/60 follows the same line with the addition of a cache as a principal difference.

The second line of PDP-11's is that of minimal-cost processors. The 11/05, contemporary of the 11/60, also took advantage of medium scale integration (MSI) technology but its microprogramming features are reduced to the bare essential (e.g., no microinstruction overlap). The 11/04, although even simpler than the 11/05, has a few features in its microengine, such as an extra scratch pad register and a swap byte facility, which make it as effective as its predecessor. Going down the cost coordinate, the LSI-11 (LSI = large scale integration), sometimes known as the 11/03, is a microcomputer system. A PDP-11/40 instruction set and 4K words of memory are available on a single board. The Pc consists of 4 LSI chips and associated packages for clock generation and interfacing circuits. Because the LSI-11 PMS is slightly different from all other members of the family, and because it is more a microcomputer than a minicomputer, we shall not discuss it here. Finally, the 11/34 can be considered as either an improved version of the 11/04 or a simplified 11/40.

The third line of evolution is towards high-performance minicomputers. The 11/45 has 6 additional registers for its floating-point instruction set (this is also true of other members of the family such as the 11/60 and 11/34 designed after the 11/45), a memory management unit for physical address management and virtual (segmented) memory (also added later to the 11/40, 11/34 and 11/60), a second set of general registers, and, most importantly, a very fast bipolar Mp (instead of core). The internal Pc organization is more complex than in the 11/40. The 11/55 has no conceptual difference with the 11/45. A cache has been added in the 11/70 with a high hit ratio, making it a very high-performance oriented minicomputer.

In Figure 9.1 we have drawn a broken line from the 11/45 to the VAX 11/780. As we shall see, there are some basic differences between these two machines, but it can be argued that the VAX 11/780 is part of the family.

Table 9.1 shows for several PDP-11 models the average instruction execution time given by the sum:

number of instructions in the instruction set

$$\sum_{i=1} (\text{Time for instruction } i) \cdot (\text{Frequency of instruction } i)$$

This table can be used to calibrate the coordinates of Figure 9.1.

Table 9.1 Average instruction execution time (in microseconds) for members of the PDP-11 family.

	Time	Speed Relative to 11/20
LSI-11	5.883	0.60
PDP-11/04	4.043	0.87
PDP-11/05	4.096	0.86
PDP-11/20	3.529	1.
PDP-11/34	3.029	1.16
PDP-11/40	2.087	1.69
PDP-11/45 (bipolar memory)	0.863	4.09
PDP-11/60 (87% cache hit ratio)	1.578	2.23

9.3.2 PMS Description

The PMS structure of the PDP-11 is shown in Figure 9.2. We have selected the PDP 11/40 as a "middle of the line" example and we shall continue to do so in the remainder of this section. We shall mention and elaborate on interesting features that appear in other models.

The salient feature of the PDP-11's PMS structure is its single switch, or bus, called the UNIBUS. All components, Pc, Mp modules, Kio's, communicate with each other through this bus. We shall soon describe how it functions in some detail. For the PMS level it is sufficient to note that any two components can communicate through the UNIBUS and that the bus protocol is of the master-slave type. That is, a requesting device will try to take control of the bus, thus becoming its master, and will transmit/receive data to/from the slave. The bus control is centralized at the Pc. Under this scheme Direct Memory Access (DMA) can be easily implemented. Program controlled transfers and interrupt I/O are also possible.

The UNIBUS has 16 data lines and 18 address lines. The principal information unit is a word of 16 bits although Mp is byte-addressable (one byte = 8 bits). Since the address field in an instruction is at most 16 bits, only 2^{16} bytes (64K bytes) can be accessed by a given user (in fact only 56K bytes as will be seen when we treat the handling of I/O programs). But the address lines being 2 bits wider, four times the amount of physical memory can be accessed in the UNIBUS if a mapping device is included. This memory management unit, introduced with the 11/45, will be discussed later.

An enormous advantage of the UNIBUS is that it can link Mp's and

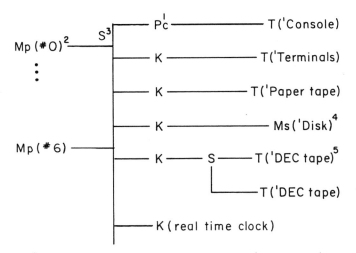

1. Pc('Model 40; microprogrammed; 16b/word; 8b/byte; (1|2|3) words/inst; 8 gen regs; Mps: 9 words; options: mult/div, floating-point, memory management, stack limit)
2. Mp(tech:core; t.cycle=850ns.; capacity: 4K words)
3. S('UNIBUS; data path: 16b; add. path: 18b; concurrency:1)
4. Ms ('Movable arm disk RK-11; t.access: 10~85ms.; capacity: 2.5 Mbytes)
5. T('DEC Tape; capacity: 300Kbytes/reel; i-rate: 200 μs/word)

Figure 9.2   PMS structure of a PDP-11/40

devices of various speeds since data transfers are handled in an asynchronous fashion. The same bus design can be kept for numerous performance ranges; as a matter of fact, many manufacturers have introduced "DEC-compatible" memories and transducers simply by providing a UNIBUS interface. On the other hand, the UNIBUS is too slow (a maximum transfer rate of 1 word per 0.75 μs, or 21.3 megabytes/second) when fast memories, like the 300 ns. bipolar memory for the 11/45, and caches are added. In that case a second bus can be introduced for the Pc—Mcache or Pc—Mp switch. Figure 9.3 shows generic PMS's for the 11/45, 11/70 and 11/60. Notice that in the case of the 11/60 the cache is between Pc and UNIBUS and that a second bus has

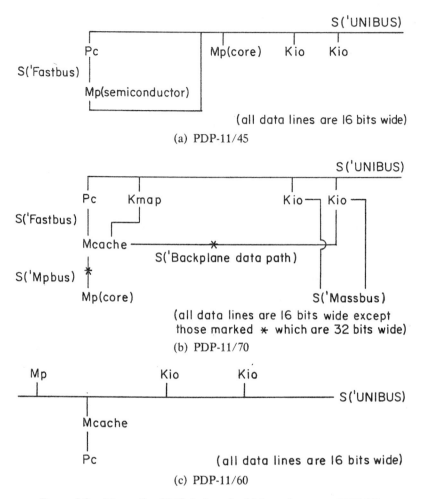

(a) PDP-11/45

(b) PDP-11/70

(c) PDP-11/60

Figure 9.3   Alternative PMS designs for high-performance PDP-11's

not been added. An alternative would have been to place Mcache between Mp and UNIBUS. But then, standard Mp's cannot be used. The disadvantage of the solution shown in Figure 9.3 is that the cache has to monitor DMA transfers (recall Chapter 6 Section 5.2).

The remainder of the PMS structure shows no surprising features. The Pc is microprogrammed (all models are except the 11/20). The processor state and instruction set will be covered in detail next. Mp is divided into 8K byte modules, up to a maximum of 8 modules when there is no memory extension unit. Technology is core, except for the 11/45, but even the 11/60 announced in 1977 has core memory. Naturally the Mcache, when present, uses semi-conductor technology. The Ms and T can be extremely varied. Interfacing to the UNIBUS is fairly straightforward.

9.3.3 ISP Description

The instruction set of the PDP-11 is an extensive set of operations on a limited number of data types. The PDP-11 can be considered as a 0-address, 1-address, or 2-address machine with or without general registers. The basic data type is the 16-bit integer with a 2's complement representation but there are also many byte-oriented instructions.

Because of the large variety in instruction formats and addressing modes, a complete formal description would be unwieldy. Even, C. G. Bell, one of the designers of the PDP-11 and co-inventor of the ISP description, seems to have balked at the magnitude of the task as an expository tool. Obviously, ISP could still be used in a reference manual which should cover all details. In the following, we shall mix ISP notation and descriptive language in an attempt to present as clear a view as possible of the ISP level of the PDP-11. In the ISP notation we shall adhere with DEC terminology and number bits from right to left. This will bring some discrepancy with figures in Chapter 2 but the reader should have no difficulty in making the conversion.

Pc State

The Pc state consists of 8 general registers and a processor status register.

$R[0:7]\langle 15:0 \rangle$	General Register
$SP: = R[6]$	Stack Pointer
$PC: = R[7]$	Program Counter
$PS\langle 15:0 \rangle$	Program Status Register
$P\langle 2:0 \rangle: = PS\langle 7:5 \rangle$	Priority level of current program
$CC\langle 3:0 \rangle: = PS\langle 3:0 \rangle$	Condition Codes
$C: = CC\langle 0 \rangle$	Arithmetic Carry
$V: = CC\langle 1 \rangle$	Overflow
$Z: = CC\langle 2 \rangle$	Zero Result
$N: = CC\langle 3 \rangle$	Negative Result
$T: = PS\langle 4 \rangle$	Trace bit

Some comments are in order here on the roles of $R[6]$ (SP) and $R[7]$ (PC). SP is used to access a "system" stack which stores the information needed to handle the linkage in procedure calls, interrupts and traps. PC is the program counter; its use as a general register will have a profound influence on the addressing modes.

The *PS* as shown above has since been expanded (note that there were 8 unused bits). These extensions, not present in the low performance line, are:

$$CM\langle 1:0\rangle: = PS\langle 15:14\rangle$$ Current mode (00 Kernel, 01 Supervisor, 11 user)

$$PM\langle 1:0\rangle: = PS\langle 13:12\rangle$$ Previous mode

$$GR: = PS\langle 11\rangle$$ General register set (for the 11/45 family only)

These extensions allow a protected environment for multiprogramming and a master-slave type of operating system with privileged instructions. In the case of the 11/45 a second set of general registers is available.

To this Pc state, six 64-bit floating-point registers must be added for models (11/45, 11/55, 11/70, 11/34, 11/60) that have the floating-point processor option. An additional 46 instructions are available for this data type. The floating-point format was discussed in Chapter 3 Section 4.1.

Mp State

Primary memory is byte-addressable but the *i*-unit for transfer is the word. Leaving aside for the moment the memory extension and the virtual segmented memory concepts, each user can address 64K bytes. However, 8K bytes are reserved for use by the I/O devices.

Addressing Modes

With its wide variety of addressing modes, a PDP-11 can be programmed as a stack machine, a single accumulator machine, a 2-address machine, or one of the above plus a general register scheme. Its use as a stack machine is a mixture of a stack and a one address scheme. For example, the sequence:

    A: = B + C*D

would be executed as:

    Load stack with C   (stack + 1-address)
    Multiply stack with D
    Add stack with B
    Store stack in A

instead of the "pure":

    Load stack with address of A
    Load stack with B

Load stack with *C*
Load stack with *D*
Multiply
Add
Store stack (in *A*)

In a PDP-11 instruction each memory address, source or destination, is specified by a 6 bit field. The first 3 bits indicate the mode of addressing, including one bit for deferred (or indirect) addressing, and the last 3 indicate the register involved in the address computation. The 8 possible modes are summarized in Table 9.2.

If both source and destination in a 2-address instruction, or the unique address in the 1-address instruction scheme, are addressed with one of the first six modes, then the instruction takes one word. If mode 6 or 7 is used for one address, then the instruction will be two words long and, finally, if both addresses use modes 6 or 7, then the instruction will be 3 words long.

To see the power of this scheme, where immediate, absolute, direct, and indexed addressing are easily implemented, with the option of post indirect

Table 9.2   Addressing modes in the PDP-11

Mode	Name	Interpretation
0	Register	The operand is in the register
1	Register deferred	The register contains the address of the operand
2	Autoincrement	As mode 1 but after the effective address calculation the register is incremented by 1 or 2 depending on the opcode
3	Autoincrement deferred	The register contains the address of a location which contains the address of the operand. The contents of the register are then incremented by 1 or 2
4	Autodecrement	The contents of the register are decremented, and then used to address the operand
5	Autodecrement deferred	The contents of the register are decremented and then used to address the location which contains the address of the operand
6	Indexed	The word following the instruction is fetched and added to the contents of the register to form the effective address
7	Index deferred	The word following the instruction is fetched, added to the contents of the register to form the address of the location which contains the address of the operand

addressing, consider the following versions of "ADD'" and associated PDP-11 encodings:

$R_i \leftarrow R_i + R_j$ — Destination, source mode 0;

$R_i \leftarrow R_i + \text{Mp}[EA]$ — Destination mode 0, source mode 1,6 or 7 (with the effective address possibly indexed or indexed and indirect);

$\text{Mp}[EA] \leftarrow R_i + \text{Mp}[EA]$ — Destination mode 1, 6 or 7, source mode 0;

$\text{Mp}[EA_1] \leftarrow \text{Mp}[EA_1] + \text{Mp}[EA_2]$ — Destination mode 1, 6 or 7, source mode 1, 6 or 7. But even $A[I] \leftarrow A[I] + B[I]$; $I \leftarrow I+1$ can be realized with both source and destination addressed in mode 2;

$R_i \leftarrow R_i + \text{Constant}$ — Destination mode 0, source mode 2 with Register 7;

$\text{Mp}[EA] \leftarrow \text{Mp}[EA] + \text{Constant}$ — Destination mode 1, 6 or 7, source mode 2 with register 7;

$R_i \leftarrow R_i + \text{Top}[\text{stack}];\text{pop}$ — Destination mode 0, source mode 2;

$\text{Mp}[EA] \leftarrow \text{Mp}[EA] + \text{Top}[\text{stack}];\text{pop}$ — Destination mode 1, 6 or 7, source mode 2;

Other modes are better illustrated by stack operations such as:

$\text{Mp}[\text{Top}[\text{stack-1}]] \leftarrow \text{Top}[\text{stack}]$ — Destination mode 3, source mode 2 (store top of stack in address found at top [stack-1]);

$\text{Top}[\text{stack}] \leftarrow \text{Constant}$ — Destination mode 4, source mode 2 with register 7 (Push);

Duplicate $\text{Top}[\text{stack}]$ — Destination mode 4, source mode 1;

This addressing scheme is quite extensive and has some interesting new features. For example, it is the use of the *PC* as a general register which allows full length immediate operands (mode 2 with register 7), relative addressing for branching purposes, and absolute addressing (mode 1 with register 7). The autoincrementing and decrementing features are mostly for stack-oriented instructions.

However, not all modes are used as often as others. Table 9.3 shows the frequency of addressing modes. These figures taken from Marathe's dissertation (cf. Section 6) and from data provided by Strecker, represent composites of respectively 12 million and 7.6 million instructions. We shall comment on them after looking at the instruction set.

Table 9.3 Frequency of mode addressing in the PDP-11

	One address Instruction (18.2%)	2 address Instruction (46.8%) Source	Dest
Mode 0	50	24.8	42.4
1	11.8	8.2	7.2
2	8.5	43.1	15.5
3	7.8	6.5	5
4	4.5	1.3	18.2
5	0	0	0.02
6	16.1	15.5	11
7	1.3	0.6	0.7
R7 used 13% of the time		23%	11.8%
R6 used 15.8% of the time		15.9%	22.2%

(a) Marathe's Data

	Source (40.6%)	Destination (63.7%)
Mode 0	34	50
1	8.2	9.4
2	39.3	13.3
3	2.8	4.6
4	8.5	13.0
5	0	0
6	6.5	8.5
7	0.5	1.2

(b) Strecker's Data

Instruction Formats

The PDP-11 has 8 instruction formats (some authors would say 13). To understand why there exist so many different formats, we must remember that the designers of the PDP-11 wanted a complete instruction set (more than 64 operations) and the wide range of addressing modes just introduced. This led to the concept of what has since been called the *expanding opcode* encoding of the instruction set.

If we return to the constraints of the addressing modes, we can see that for two address instructions only 4 bits are left for the opcodes ($16 - 2 \cdot 6 = 4$), under the constraint of a single word per instruction (assuming addressing modes 0 through 5). Thus, we can encode 15 two-address instructions plus a pattern (e.g., 0000) indicating that this is not a two-address instruction. Thereafter, one-address instructions opcodes can be encoded in 16 bits minus 6 for the address, minus 4 reserved for two-address instructions, i.e., 6 bits, yielding another 63 operations. This can be repeated again for 0-address instructions.

Of course, the encoding of the PDP-11 is not as simple (hence the 8 formats) but it follows this principle. The main formats are:

- Two-operand instructions: The opcode is in the 4 first bits except for 4 "opcodes" which are the respective first 4 bits of 3 other groups and of the floating-point operations. The remaining 12 bits are for the source and destination addresses as explained before.
- One-operand instructions: The opcode is 10 bits leaving 6 bits for the operand's address.
- Branch instructions: There are different groups including one with an 8 bit opcode and an 8 bit offset from the *PC*; a subroutine call which stacks (on the system stack whose pointer is $R[6]$ or *SP*) the contents of a linkage register, stores the *PC* in this linkage register, and then transfers to a new location by setting *PC* to the address determined by the destination field (hence an opcode of $16 - 6 - 3 = 7$ bits); a subroutine return (opcode 13 bits since only the linkage register's name is needed).
- Some miscellaneous instructions such as the setting or clearing of the condition codes (12 bit opcode plus 1 bit/condition code) and some 16 bit opcode operations such as WAIT or HALT.

Instruction Set

There is no outstanding feature in the approximately 80 instructions, the number depending on particular options. (The 46 floating-point instructions are not included in this count.) However, an instruction like MOVE has a deceptively simple ISP description, namely:

$$MOV(: = op = 0001) \rightarrow (D \leftarrow S, CC)$$

But, depending on the addressing modes of S and D we can have:

- 2-address MOVE

  $A \leftarrow B$
  $A \leftarrow$ constant
  $A[I] \leftarrow B[I]$
  $A[I] \leftarrow B[I]; I \leftarrow I + 1;$

- 1-address + general-register MOVE yielding a load or store direct, indexed, indirect, or indexed and post-indirect.
- Stack-oriented operations:

  Push constant; Push operand; Push operand whose address is on the top of the stack;
  Pop in a given Mp location; Pop in address specified by second topmost location on the stack; Duplicate top of stack.

The CC function is similar to the one described for the Sigma 5 in Figure 2.8.

The frequency of execution of individual instructions is summarized in Table 9.4. The sources for these figures are the same as for Table 9.3.

Evaluation of the PDP-11 ISP

Table 9.4 should be compared with Table 2.1 which shows statistics taken from programs running on a one-address + general-register machine. At first glance, there does not seem to be much difference. Branch instructions occur approximately every third instruction and the load-store group is used about as often in both machines. However, we should be aware that in the case of the PDP-11, this load-store is through the MOVE (move word or move byte) instruction and hence might be a memory-to-memory or a stack operation. (There seems to be some discrepancy between the two sets of measurements for the PDP-11 in the use of the MOVE instruction.) It would be interesting to see how frequently these last two addressing facilities were used but we can already gather from Table 9.3 that mode 0 (the operand is in a register) is used quite extensively for two address instructions.

Turning our attention to the addressing modes, we see that mode 5 is practically never used. Mode 4 corresponds to a "Push" instruction with an adequate decrement for the register used as stack pointer and mode 5 could be a "Push Indirect". In mode 5 the register would point to a stack pointer but it is then difficult to interpret the meaning of the decrementing part since the

Table 9.4   Instruction frequencies on the PDP-11

Move	31.2%	(2-address)
Branch on not equal	5.6%	
Branch on equal	4.1%	
Compare	4.0%	(2-address)
Jump	3.9%	
Decrement word	3.9%	(1-address)
Add	3.7%	(2-address)
Jump to subroutine	3.6%	
Test	3.5%	(1-address)
Arithmetic Shift Left	3.4%	(1-address)
Unconditional Branch	3.1%	
Return from Sub	3.0%	

(a) From Marathe's dissertation

Branch on True	17.4%
Branch on False	11.1%
Move	15.2%
Decrement word	8.1%
Compare	6.2%
Add	5.2%
Move byte	5.2%
Test	3.3%
Bit Clear (Mask)	3.1%
Arithmetic Shift Left	3.0%

(b) From Strecker's data

Load/Store	36/23	Floating-point	2/N.A.
Branch	34/34	Logical/Shift	9/9
Arithmetic	19/33		

(c) By groups (Marathe/Strecker)

contents of the register and not of the location are decremented. Similarly indexing plus post-indirection (mode 7) is rarely used. As a general rule, the indirect modes are used only about 10 to 20% of the time. It would be interesting to see whether suppressing the deferred (indirect) option and keeping only 4 modes would be detrimental. But how to use the two bits saved in the two address instructions is not readily apparent!

It should be useful to have more data on the use of the SP and PC registers. Marathe's measurements (not reproduced here) show that the PC is much more heavily used in Systems and Real-time programming while SP has more usage in Scientific computing. An educated guess could be that assembly language programs make use of the *PC* more often than compiled programs and that scientific programming has more expressions to compute and hence uses a stack and reverse polish notation, as well as possibly more calls to subroutines.

9.3.4 Pc Design

The central processor of the PDP-11 consists of an arithmetic unit (ALU), associated registers and data paths, and a microprogrammed control unit (the 11/20 is an exception). As before, we continue to take the 11/40 as a model.

The ALU is shared by the I-unit and the D-unit as defined in Chapter 4 Section 1. A diagram of the data paths and the ALU is shown in Figure 9.4. As can be seen all the ingredients necessary for a typical Pc are present (remember that the *PC* is register 7). The data paths in the ALU can operate on bytes or words. The interface to Mp is through the UNIBUS with 4 possi-

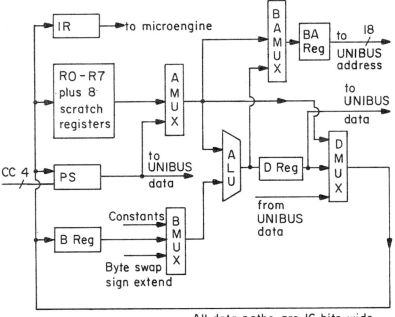

All data paths are 16 bits wide
unless noted otherwise

Figure 9.4   PDP-11/40 Pc data paths

ble operations: read word (DATI), write word (DATO), read-modify-write word (DATIP), write byte (DATOB). The read-modify-write is made possible by locking the access to the UNIBUS. This can be especially convenient when core memories are involved, since the write cycle following the read can be made useful.

The ALU can perform the usual Boolean operations, 2's complement addition and subtraction with various carry controls (a carry look-ahead adder is used), and rotate/shifts to the left. Rotate/shifts to the right are handled in the DMUX (D-multiplexor) which is slightly more complex than a switch selecting one of several inputs to pass through its single output. Inputs to the ALU come from two sources: on the A side is one of 16 registers, the 8 general registers plus 8 scratchpad registers which are not accessible from machine language programs, or the PS (program status register); on the B side, is an internal register (the B-reg) or a constant. Functions such as byte swap or sign extension are handled in the BMUX. The output of the ALU can be either an address when the arithmetic unit plays the role of a I-unit, or data when it is used in an execute cycle (D-unit). In the address case, the 16 bit output is converted to an 18-bit address in the BA register (note that this address can be directly out of the AMUX, e.g., if the addressing mode were mode 1). If data is generated, it can be sent to the UNIBUS or to the registers (RO-$R7$, 8 scratchpad, PS, B-Reg). The DMUX also receives data from the UNIBUS and therefore the instruction register is connected to its output. When extensions like a floating-point processor are present, they can be attached easily to the outputs of the DMUX and of the AMUX.

We noticed above that the inputs to the BA register could come either from the AMUX or the ALU. Similarly, a data "computation" can bypass the ALU (e.g., a register-register transfer) by going from the output of the AMUX to the DMUX.

Consequently, we shall have different microinstruction cycle lengths. Another interesting feature in Figure 9.4 is the presence of the D register. This allows reading and writing access to the general registers in one cycle by having the D register hold a "store" during a clock phase while a "read" is performed on a register. For example, this can be useful in autoincrement and autodecrement modes, where the value to be modified can be put in the BA register and stored back in one cycle.

The microprogrammed control unit is shown in Figure 9.5. It consists of a control store (Mcs) of 256 words of 56 bits. Thus, the microprogramming can be considered horizontal. The output of Mcs is stored in a 48-bit McsDR with the 8 extra bits containing the next microinstruction address sent back as the possible contents of the McsIR. This next address, therefore, is either contained in the current microinstruction, or, in case of branches, is ob-

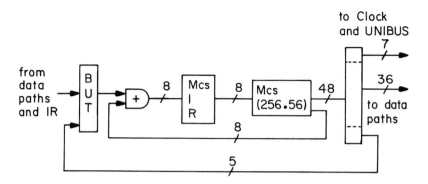

Figure 9.5   PDP-11/40 control unit

tained as the output of the branch-on-microtest multiplexor (BUT) which has inputs from the MDR and from the data paths. The presence of the McsDR allows prefetching but branch conditions have to be set up one microinstruction in advance (or otherwise no-op microinstructions must be inserted). The reader should refer to the CalData microengine organization (cf. Chapter 7 Section 2.3) to appraise this compromise in the PDP-11/40 implementation.

The microinstruction layouts can be divided into 3 groups:

• Group 1: Clock and UNIBUS control (7 bits).

These bits allow the microprogram to select a cycle length (3 possibilities depending, e.g., on whether the ALU is to be bypassed or if only micro-branching is accomplished), to turn the clock off so that the microprogram is temporarily stopped (to be used in conjunction with UNIBUS operations), and to gate the contents of the *BA* register to the UNIBUS address lines as well as to indicate to the UNIBUS the type of operation requested. The presence of a CLOCKOFF command allows the UNIBUS and the micro-program to operate concurrently (overlap operation) until, of course, the CLOCKOFF bit is set. In other PDP-11 implementations, a request to the UNIBUS automatically stops the microengine (interlock operation) until the UNIBUS operation is completed. The interlocking at some point is necessary because the UNIBUS and the Pc operate asynchronously. However, the CLOCKOFF option can take advantage of the fact that the UNIBUS opera-tion will take at least two microinstruction cycles to complete (and perhaps more depending on the particular microengine).

• Group 2: Data paths control (36 bits).

Subgroups are used to gate data into registers (8 bits), select registers (8 bits), select ALU functions (9 bits), and control the three multiplexors (11 bits).

- Group 3: Next microinstruction address (5 bits in the McsDR plus 8 bits directly out of the Mcs).

Five bits are used for inputs to the BUT and 8 bits are used as the next microinstruction address when there is no branching.

9.3.5   Memory Extensions and Caches

Memory Management Unit

The designers of the PDP-11 foresaw to some extent the inadequacy of 16-bit addresses. By having 18-bit address lines on the UNIBUS the addressing space could be quadrupled. However, a mapping device is needed to transform the 16-bit address into an 18-bit one.

First, it should be realized that from the individual program's viewpoint, the 16-bit address limitation remains. It is possible to double this addressing capacity if 64K bytes are reserved for the program and 64K bytes for data, that is implicitly we have a 17-bit address space (although from a practical viewpoint it is not always true that programs and data have the same order of magnitude for space requirements). But also in this case, a mapping device is necessary.

In the PDP-11/45 a memory management unit was designed to perform this address mapping. It is now available on other models including the 11/40. Basically, it is a segmentation map with a maximum of 8 segments per address space. Therefore, it combines some concepts from segmentation and some from paging.

The Memory Management (or segmentation) Unit consists of 2 sets (3 for the 11/45) of 16 32-bit segmentation registers, one for user mode and one for supervisor mode. Each set is divided into 8 registers for instruction references and 8 for data references. Each segment register contains the following fields:

Segment Starting (Real) Address (SSA): 12 bits
Segment Length: 7 bits
Activity Bit: 1 bit
Dirty Bit: 1 bit
Stack Bit: 1 bit
Protection: 3 bits

and 7 unused bits.

Since only the leftmost 12 bits are included in the (real) address map, segments can start only at multiples of $2^{18-12} = 2^6 = 64$ bytes. Or, in other words, segments are at least 64 bytes long. The length is thus between 64 bytes and 64 bytes $\cdot 2^{|\text{length}|} = 64 \cdot 2^7 = 2^{13} = 8K$ bytes. (Notice that with 8 segments of 8K bytes we have the maximum 64K bytes.) A virtual address has the form:

SRI: bits 15–13: Index of a segment register
BD: bits 12–6: Block displacement
DB: bits 5–0: Displacement within block.

The real address is then computed as shown in Figure 9.6. The segment register chosen by the SRI field will contain the segment starting address. (The instruction set or data set is selected with the knowledge that we are in either an instruction-fetch or operand effective address calculation cycle.) To this field of 12 bits we add the block displacement, and to this sum we concatenate the displacement within block field.

If the segment is not in Mp, the protection field will be 0. An interrupt will be generated and some replacement (or placement) algorithm will be called to find a "hole" for the missing segment. The length is also checked during address translation and an error routine will be called if the address exceeds the range of the segment. If the protection field is non-zero, it shows the type of access (read-only, read, write) allowed for the particular user for the segment in question. As usual, the dirty bit is set when a location in the segment is modified and the activity bit is set when the segment is referenced. Since the PDP-11 stacks grow in decreasing address order, this fact must be reflected for segments addressed as stacks. Therefore, a 1K byte segment, for

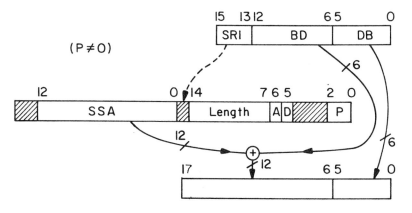

Figure 9.6   PDP-11/45 real address computation

example, used as a stack will be assigned addresses 8K to 7K instead of 0 to 1K. This is indicated by the stack bit.

As can be seen we have variable length blocks, the segments, but a fixed maximum number of blocks in the virtual space like in a paging system. This hybrid situation is reflected in the DEC literature where the memory management unit is sometimes referred to as a segmentation unit and sometimes as a paging unit!

Caches

Two models, the 11/70 and 11/60, have caches. As shown in Figure 9.3 their placement with respect to the UNIBUS is quite different (see also the previous section).

The 11/70 cache is 1K word, of the set associative type (recall Chapter 6 Section 5) with set size of two and block size of two words. The replacement algorithm for the two blocks is random and a write through policy is used. The hit ratio is of the order of 0.93.

In the 11/60 (cf. Figure 9.7), the cache has blocks of only one word. It has the same capacity as the 11/70 but has a direct mapping organization. The hit ratio is slightly decreased to 0.87. One of the reasons for this new organization is the availability of 1024.1 bit memory chips while only 256.1 were available for the 11/70. The component count is therefore decreased to one fifth, only one address comparator is needed instead of two, and there is no need to have a multiplexor to select the output from the halves of the cache as in the 11/70 (cf. Exercise 4).

9.3.6 UNIBUS and I/O Programming

I/O operations on the PDP-11 are relatively simple and flexible because the UNIBUS structure unifies the addressing of all components connected: all control status and data registers of the peripheral devices are given fixed Mp addresses in an 8K range (hence the restriction to 56K bytes/user space noted earlier when the memory management unit is not present).

Since the registers attached to the peripheral devices are addressable, it is trivial to perform some I/O in a program directed way. For example, the transfer of a word from the peripheral device X to an Mp location L can be done as:

LOOP: Test for ready X's status register   (Boolean operation)
           Branch if not ready to LOOP   (Branch operation)
           Move X's data register to L

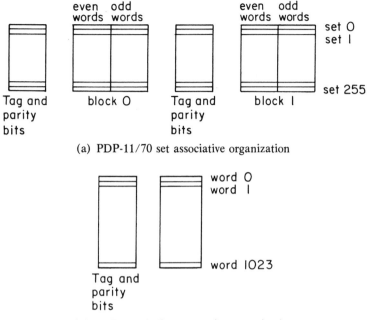

(a) PDP-11/70 set associative organization

(b) PDP-11/60 direct mapping organization

Figure 9.7   Cache organizations in the PDP-11 family

But, naturally, I/O on the PDP-11 is not restricted to the program direct approach. DMA transfers are possible with simple DMA "channels" attached to the UNIBUS. They will consist of a few registers indicating the I/O unit sink or source of the transfer, the count of words to be transferred, the Mp address of the source or sink, and the data. The DMA channel increments the Mp address, decrements the count and can send interrupts to the Pc.

The interrupt structure on the PDP-11 can be classified as a multiple-level multiple-priority vectored interrupt scheme (cf. Chapter 8 Section 1.2). The *PS* carries the priority of the running program encoded in 3 bits, hence we have 8 "priority levels". With each device are associated two Mp locations (in low-memory addresses) which contain the new *PC* (with the address of the interrupt handling routine) and the new *PS*. (These addresses are sent on the UNIBUS data lines by the device's controller requesting the interrupt). There are 4 hardware levels with devices daisy chained on these levels, plus a separate request line for the DMA channel (see below). When an interrupt request is received by the Pc, an arbitrator in the latter checks the relative priorities of the running program and of the request. If the request has higher priority, the *PC* and *PS* of the running program are stacked on the system stack (managed by *SP* or Register 6), and the new *PC* and *PS* are loaded from the preassigned locations. The new *PS* carries the priority of the interrupt handling routine. Furthermore, interrupts can be masked within a "level" by clearing the enable bit of a particular device in its status register. Returns from interrupt handling routines are performed by popping the stack and resetting the *PC* and *PS* to their original values.

Throughout our description of the PDP-11 we have stressed the importance of the UNIBUS as the single "*S*" in the PMS sense. Its organization is a mixture of independent requesting and daisy chaining. The arbitration between the requests is centralized at the Pc.

The UNIBUS consists of 56 lines (cf. Figure 9.8). The 16 data lines and 18 address lines require no further explanations. Fourteen of the other lines are used by the devices to try to gain control of the bus which is operated in a master-slave mode, and 6 are used for the interlocking procedure for the data transfers. Finally, the last 2 lines are for power failure conditions.

The bus mastership is determined by the current priority of the Pc (as indicated by the 3 bits in the *PS*), the priority of the line upon which a request is made (one of the 5 BRi lines), and the physical placement of the request on the line when a request on that line is granted (daisy chain). The handshaking procedure to obtain control of the UNIBUS is shown in Figure 9.9. When a device controller requests the bus mastership, it raises the BRi line to which it is attached. The arbitrator, in the Pc, waits until the Pc can be interrupted. Then the line BGi with highest priority and a BRi pending will be raised by the Pc (assuming that line *i* has priority over the running program). The first (in a daisy chain sense) device on line *i* which sent a request will acknowledge the grant signal by deactivating BRi and sending a selection acknowledge (SACK). Upon receiving SACK, the Pc deactivates BGi. Now, when there is no data transfer occurring on the UNIBUS, i.e., when SSYNC is not raised, the device controller obtains mastership by raising bus busy (BBSY) and deactivating SACK. This protocol is slightly simplified in the sense that one of the BR-BG pair is reserved for DMA channels and has highest priority for obtaining the bus mastership (but not from the interrupt viewpoint). In other words, the DMA line can steal a cycle at any time without causing a Pc interrupt.

Once a controller has received the bus mastership, it can "interrupt" the Pc by sending the addresses of the preassigned locations in Mp which give the necessary information for clearing the interrupt, or it can initiate some data transfers. The data transfers can be Read (DATI), Read Modify Write

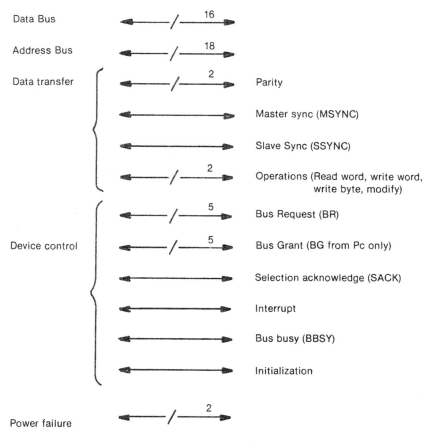

Figure 9.8   The 56 UNIBUS lines

(DATP, data in pause), Write Word (DATO) and Write Byte (DATB). The interlocked transfer procedure is shown for a DATI in Figure 9.10.

When the bus mastership has been secured, the slave's address is put on the address lines and the operation to be performed, in this case DATI, on the control lines. The slave will recognize its address (a delay of 150 ns. is allowed for this process). Then the MSYNC (Master synchronization) line is raised and upon receiving this signal the slave will fetch the data to be transferred. After this has been done, and the time to do so depends on the device, the data is put on the data bus and the slave signals that it is ready by raising SSYNC (slave synchronization). Upon receiving SSYNC, the master copies the contents of the data bus, deactivates MSYNC, and, after a 75 ns.

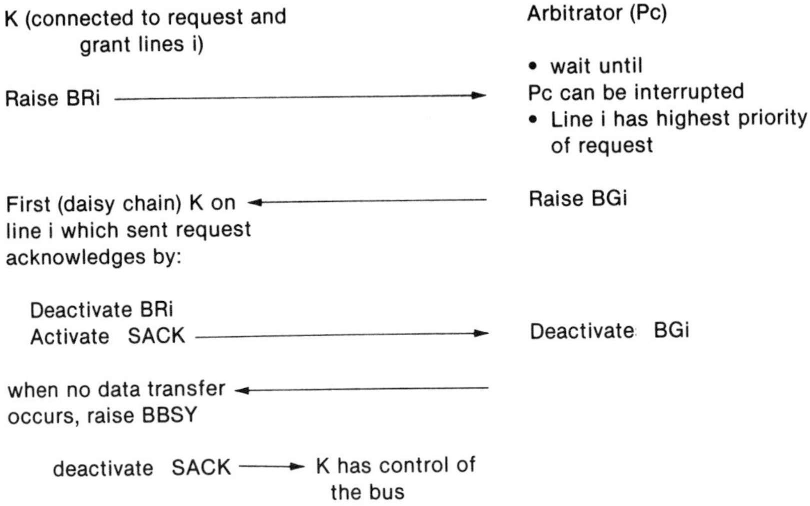

K (connected to request and
    grant lines i)

Arbitrator (Pc)

Raise BRi   ⟶

• wait until
Pc can be interrupted
• Line i has highest priority
    of request

First (daisy chain) K on   ⟵
line i which sent request
acknowledges by:

Raise BGi

Deactivate BRi
Activate SACK   ⟶

Deactivate BGi

when no data transfer ⟵
occurs, raise BBSY

deactivate SACK ⟶ K has control of
                                    the bus

Figure 9.9   Hand shaking procedure to obtain control of the bus

delay, clears the address and control lines and deactivates BBSY. Upon seeing MSYNC deactivated, the slave clears the data bus and deactivates SSYNC. The UNIBUS is now available to the request of highest priority.

There are a few problems with this design; the most important is that UNIBUS is a potential bottleneck since it is involved in all transfers. Secondly, with increasing Mp speeds, it can be considered as slow (1.7 megabyte/second or slightly less than a word transfer per microsecond). And finally, its addressing range is limited to 18 bits. But these disadvantages have not prevented the success of the UNIBUS, achieved mostly because of the ease of hooking devices or memory modules on the bus. This flexibility is due, in large part, to the asynchronous mode of operation and the clean interface for the data transfer protocols.

9.3.7   The VAX 11/780

The greatest weakness in the PDP-11 architecture is the limited addressing capability. Although the 16 bit addressing space can be expanded physically to 18 bits with the addition of a Memory Management Unit, it is still insufficient for many applications. The VAX (Virtual Address Extension) 11/780, which provides a 32-bit virtual address space and 30 address lines on its internal bus, is DEC's response to this problem. It can be argued that the VAX is not a minicomputer because it is based on a 32 bit information unit.

Master	Slave

Wait   for SSYNC to be deactivated

Raise   BBSY

Deactivate   SACK

Slave's address on Address Bus

Data-In Code on Control ————————————► Decode   content of address

        ⅼ wait 150 ns
           (decode time)

Raise   MSYNC ————————————► Fetch data to be transferred
                                                     ⅼ delay depending on device

                                            Data on data bus

Copy data from ◄———————————— Raise   SSYNC

Data bus

Deactivate   MSYNC ————————————► Clear Data Bus
      ⅼ Wait 75 ns   Deactivate SSYNC

Clear Address and
Control lines
Deactivate   BBSY

Figure 9.10   A Data-In (Read) operation on the UNIBUS (interlocked transfer)

However, if price is the metric behind the classification of minicomputers, and if one takes (1978) $250,000 as the figure which separates mini from medium-range systems (including secondary memory devices), then a minimal VAX 11/780 configuration falls within the mini category. A second argument for considering the VAX as a (super) minicomputer is that it is of the PDP-11 family and can execute PDP-11 programs using an emulated instruction set.

The two other main criticisms of the PDP-11 which have been corrected in the VAX design are: (1) a larger number of addresses assigned to the registers of I/O peripheral devices (although 8K bytes were reserved to that effect in the PDP-11, the number of different devices interfaced to the UNIBUS finally overflowed the original capacity and ad hoc measures had to be taken on an installation by installation basis), and (2) an increased number of opcodes and a simpler encoding for the native instruction set.

In the following, we give a brief overview of the machine. At the time of writing, there is not enough data to appraise the value of some of the architectural and implementation innovations, but the concept of 32 bit minicomputers, which is not limited to the VAX, deserves careful examination.

PMS Description

Figure 9.11 shows the PMS structure of the VAX 11/780. As in the PDP-11 we have a single bus connecting Pc, Mp and I/O devices. However, the I/O devices are not directly connected to the unique bus named SBI (Synchronous Backplane Interconnect). Instead, one UNIBUS and up to 4 Massbus adaptors are connected to the SBI; I/O devices, in turn, are connected to the UNIBUS or Massbus (a bus dedicated to fast controller-peripheral transactions). The SBI uses a synchronous transmission mechanism with a cycle time of 200 ns. Its maximum transfer rate is about one order of magnitude faster than UNIBUS's and greater than the sum of the maximum rates of one UNIBUS and 4 Massbus.

The horizontally microprogrammed Pc has a writable control store which can be loaded from the console subsystem for diagnostic purposes, an 8-byte

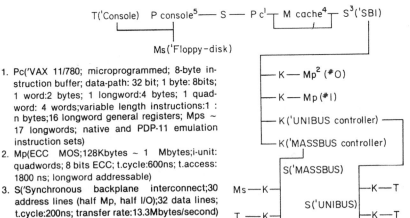

1. Pc('VAX 11/780; microprogrammed; 8-byte instruction buffer; data-path: 32 bit; 1 byte: 8bits; 1 word:2 bytes; 1 longword:4 bytes; 1 quadword: 4 words;variable length instructions:1 : n bytes;16 longword general registers; Mps ~ 17 longwords; native and PDP-11 emulation instruction sets)
2. Mp(ECC MOS;128Kbytes ~ 1 Mbytes;i-unit: quadwords; 8 bits ECC; t.cycle:600ns; t.access: 1800 ns; longword addressable)
3. S('Synchronous backplane interconnect;30 address lines (half Mp, half I/O);32 data lines; t.cycle:200ns; transfer rate:13.3Mbytes/second)
4. Mcache(8Kbytes;t.cycle: 200ns; set associative)
5. Pconsole ('LSI-11)

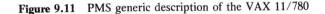

Figure 9.11 PMS generic description of the VAX 11/780

instruction look-ahead buffer, and separate D-units which can perform, in parallel, integer arithmetic, shifting, and floating-point arithmetic. The microprogram can interpret two instruction sets: the native mode and the PDP-11 compatibility mode, with the facility for switching easily from one to the other. The datapaths are 32-bit wide with instructions, in the native mode, taking from 1 to $(n + 1)$ bytes where n is the number of bytes necessary to encode the addresses of m operands ($m \geq 0$ and not limited). Addressing is in terms of bytes with a virtual address space of 2^{32} bytes (from a user's viewpoint only 2^{30} bytes are addressable). The processor state contains 16 32-bit general registers, a processor status word (see the ISP description below), and several non-user-addressable registers.

The memory hierarchy consists of Mcache, Mp, and a paging mechanism to translate virtual addresses into real addresses. Mp has one or two memory controllers, each one addressing from 128K to 1M bytes. The first memory modules were built with 4K RAM chips, but 16K chips are now available. Memory is organized in quadwords (64 bits) with 8 bits of error correcting code performing all single error correction and double error detection with 70% of the latter being corrected. The memory cycle time is 600 ns. but it takes 1800 ns. for a read access from Pc because of the SBI overhead as shown later. Note however, that 64 bits are "transmitted at a time" although the SBI's data width is only 32 bits. This long access time is compensated by the 8K byte cache which has a 200 ns. cycle time. It is organized along the set associative concept (2 long words of 32 bits/set) with a write-through policy. On a cache miss, 32 bits are sent to the Pc and 32 to the cache. A buffer is provided for the write back so that it can be done in parallel with a subsequent cache access. Measurements have shown a hit ratio of 0.95 yielding an effective read access time of 290 ns. Since the cache organization is the same as that of the 11/70 which has a hit ratio of 0.93, the slightly better performance can be presumed to derive from the 4-fold increase in capacity.

The virtual memory mechanism is page oriented with a small page size (512 bytes). The virtual address space is divided into two halves: system space and user space. The user space is further divided, again in half, into program and user data on one hand, and data space allocated by the system for stack and process-specific data on the other. Separate page tables exist for system and user space. Dedicated registers contain the start and end of page tables for the system space and user space. These two pairs of registers are part of the Pc state and will be saved and restored automatically by context switching instructions. A translation look-aside buffer (TLB) contains 128 entries for virtual to real address translation. DEC manuals report a 97% hit rate on the TLB. The first operating system delivered with the VAX for virtual memory systems uses fixed primary memory allocation and a local FIFO replacement algorithm backed up by a pool of frames shared by all tasks and managed as an approximation to global FIFO. The combination of the replacement algorithms seems to approximate LRU. Page sharing is possible but sharable pages must be declared in advance.

The Pc is also connected to a console subsystem consisting of an LSI-11, a console and a floppy disk. In addition to its usual role as an operating system terminal, it is also used for diagnostics since it can access the major control points of the system through a special internal diagnostic bus. The floppy disk peripheral is used for bootstrapping, storing diagnostics and for software updates.

ISP Description

We consider only the native instruction set. The VAX 11/780, even more so that the PDP-11, can be considered as having a very flexible addressing mechanism. The processor state consists of:

$R[0:15]$ $\langle 31:0 \rangle$	16 general registers (although 4 have reserved functions as shown below and $R[0]$ to $R[5]$ can also be reserved for specific tasks)
PC: = $R[15]$	Program counter
SP: = $R[14]$	Stack pointer; in fact we have 4 SP registers, one for each of the kernel, executive, supervisor and user access modes
FP: = $R[13]$	Frame pointer used for procedure calls
AP: = $R[12]$	Argument pointer used in procedure calls
PSL $\langle 31:0 \rangle$	Processor status longword
PSW $\langle 15:0 \rangle$: = PSL $\langle 15:0 \rangle$	Processor status word
CC $\langle 3:0 \rangle$: = PSW $\langle 3:0 \rangle$	Condition codes (cf. PDP-11)
T: = PSW $\langle 4 \rangle$	Trace bit (cf. PDP-11)
Trap bits: = PSW $\langle 7:5 \rangle$	Integer, floating and decimal overflows
Unused: = PSW $\langle 15:8 \rangle$	
IPL: = PSL $\langle 20:16 \rangle$	Interrupt priority level
Previous mode: = PSL $\langle 23:22 \rangle$	
Current mode: = PSL $\langle 25:24 \rangle$	Kernel, executive, supervisor, user
Compatibility bit: = PSL $\langle 31 \rangle$	Either PDP-11 or native mode

Other bits of the *PSL* have very specialized meanings. The *PSW* is modifiable by the user but the upper part of *PSL* can be accessed only by privileged instructions (i.e., not in user mode). There are five data-types, namely: integer with byte, word, long word or quadword carrier using the two's complement representation system, single and double precision floating-point with the same format as the PDP-11, variable bit field (that is, a bit vector of 0 to 32 bits), character string of 0 to 64K contiguous bytes, and decimal.

The instructions have variable lengths although their format follows the same template. The opcode is one or two bytes long but two-byte opcodes do not exist in the first implementation. The opcode is followed by $m(m \geq 0)$ operand specifiers. Each specifier has the same format: a one-byte addressing mode (the index mode, see below, is an exception since it has a 2-byte specifier) plus possibly some bytes carrying additional information in a manner similar to the encoding of the PDP-11. The opcode also provides some information on the type (byte, word, integer, floating-point, etc.) and access rights (read, write, etc.) of the operands.

The addressing modes are those of the PDP-11, except for the autodecrement deferred which was not implemented (recall that for all practical purposes it is never used), to which have been added:

- A *literal* mode in which small integer constants between 0 and 63 are stored directly in the operand specifier. This is somewhat similar to the immediate addressing of the IBM System/370. But, in addition, 64 common floating-point values, e.g., 1, 2, 4, 1/2, 3/4, etc., can also be encoded by 3 exponent bits and 3 mantissa bits. The distinction between fixed and floating-point is carried out by the opcode.
- A more powerful index mode, called here *displacement* mode, where either byte, word or long displacements can be added to the contents of a register. This saves space for small offsets. Deferred modes are possible for the 3 types of displacement. When the *PC* is used as the index register, these modes are called *relative*. As in the PDP-11, they are of interest for writing relocatable code and setting transfer vector tables.
- An *index* mode which uses two one-byte specifiers, the index specifier followed by the base specifier. The effective address is the sum of the address yielded by the base specifier in a normal way and the contents of the index register of the first specifier multiplied by either 2, 4 or 8 depending on the byte, word or long word specification of the opcode. We have then a combination of (extended) base indexing as in System/370 and generalized, size-wise, indexing as in the Sigma 5 (recall the effective address calculation of Figure 2.8). The advantages are that indexing takes space in the instruction format only when needed, that it

can be superimposed on any other mode (double indexing, post-indexing, etc.), and that it can be performed according to the type of the data. Thus byte, word, or long word arrays can be easily traversed.

As an example Figure 9.12 shows the format of the instruction which performs the operation:

$$X \leftarrow 3.75 + Y[11]$$

assuming that the address of Y is contained in register 8 and that the address of X is known relative to the beginning of the program segment. This is not necessarily the code that would be generated by a compiler which most certainly would take advantage of the INDEX instruction discussed previously (Chapter 7 Section 3.3).

The instruction set is quite extensive. We gave examples of powerful instructions in Chapter 7 Section 3.3. Here, we examine the extent to which opcode selection and addressing modes can optimize the use of instructions. For example, the conventional ADD can take the following forms (cf. Figure 9.13):

- Sum ← sum + addend (byte, word, long word, floating-point, double floating-point);
- sum ← addend1 + addend2 (same types as above);
- sum ← sum + addend + condition code C (long word); (i.e., add with carry-in)
- looping instructions on each of the 5 types:
  index ← index + addend;
  If ((add ≥ 0) ∧ (index ≤ limit)) ∨ ((add < 0) ∧ (index > limit))
  then $PC \leftarrow PC$ + displacement;
- optimized looping instructions when the addend is 1 (integer mode only); one instruction for <, and one for ≤ :
  index ← index + 1;
  if index < limit then $PC \leftarrow PC$ + displacement;
- decimal add (one per packing method);
- add as an indivisible operation for multiprocessing systems.

The procedure control instructions are also of interest. The reader should compare them with those of the HP3000 (cf. Section 5). There are two call instructions, the CALLG which has for operands the address of the procedure and the address of the argument list, and CALLS which has the same first operand but for which the second operand is the number of arguments. These are assumed to have been pushed on the stack whose stack pointer is

Byte 1:   41   Opcode specifying a floating-point add with 3 operands
Byte 2:   17   The first two bits of the operand specifier are 00. This im-
                 plies a literal mode. The exponent in the next 3 bits is 010
                 and the mantissa is .1111 (recall all numbers are normalized)
                 This yields $15/16 \cdot 2^2$, i.e., 3.75
Byte 3:   A8   "A" indicates a byte displacement mode. Register 8
                 will contain the address of Y
Byte 4:   0B   This is the displacement
Byte 5:   9F   9 is autoincrement mode and F is the PC register. Hence
                 we have a relative mode
Bytes 6 to 9 address of X

Figure 9.12   Example of a VAX 11/780 instruction to compute $X = 3.75 + Y(11)$

80 ADDB2 Add byte 2 Operand
81 ADDB3 Add byte 3 Operand
A0 ADDW2 Add word 2 Operand
A1 ADDW3 Add word 3 Operand
C0 ADDL2 Add long 2 Operand
C1 ADDL3 Add long 3 Operand
40 ADDF2 Add floating 2 Operand
41 ADDF3 Add floating 3 Operand
60 ADDD2 Add double 2 Operand
61 ADDD3 Add double 3 Operand

D8 ADWC Add with Carry

58 ADAWI Add aligned word Interlocked

9D ACBB   ⎡ byte
3D ACBW   ⎢ word
F1 ACBL Add Compare ⎨ long
4F ACBF and Branch   ⎢ floating
6F ACBD   ⎣ double

F2 AOBLSS Add One and Branch
                less than
F3 AOBLEQ Add One and Branch
                less than or equal

20 ADDP4 Add Packed 4 Operand
21 ADDP6 Add Packed 6 Operand

Figure 9.13   The ADD instructions on the VAX 11/780

SP. When CALLS is used, the argument count is pushed on the stack and *SP* is set to the new top. In the case of CALLG, the first byte at the address of the argument list must contain the argument count. When either CALLG or CALLS is expected (cf. Figure 9.14), all registers which are to be used by the procedure must be saved. The "names" of these registers are contained in a mask which is the first word of the called procedure. After these registers have been saved on the stack, *AP*, *FP*, *PC*, *PSW* and the entry mark are pushed on the stack and a long word is reserved for condition handling. This portion of the stack constitutes a frame and will be monitored by the two stack, *SP*, and frame, *FP*, pointers. The new *AP* is loaded with the argument list address. The next instruction, the first one in the procedure, can now be executed. To RETURN, the necessary information is located through *FP*. A special bit in the entry mask will be set to indicate if the frame belonged to a

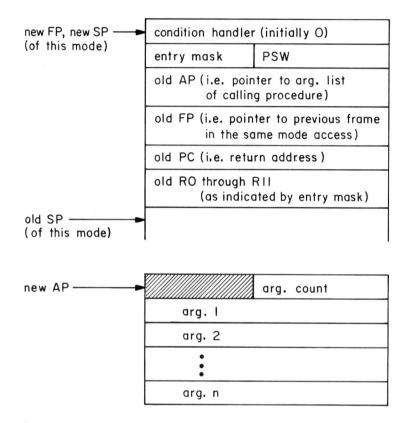

(the argument list is on the stack if bit 13 of the entry
mask is on, indicating a CALLS instruction)

Figure 9.14 Stack frame and argument list in the VAX 11/780

CALLG or CALLS instruction. In the latter case, the return protocol must
also pop the arguments from the stack, that is, change *SP* appropriately.

Instruction execution takes place in one of four modes: kernel (the mode
for the basic operating system functions such as interrupt handling, paging,
etc.), executive (the mode for logical I/O operations), supervisor (the command interpreter), and user. A "change mode" instruction permits transfers
from one mode to a more privileged one and a "return from exception or interrupt" does the converse. Each mode has its own stack and stack pointer
SP.

On context switching, the Pc state is saved, or restored, in a single instruction. The two instructions which perform these operations are LDPCTX "load process context" and SVPCTX "save process context". The Pc state, or Process Control Block in VAX terminology, consists of what was declared in our ISP description (recall that there are 4 different *SP's*, one per access mode) and of the two base and limit registers for the page tables of the user and system spaces.

The I/O and interrupt capabilities are comparable to those of the PDP-11. The multiple-level multiple-priority vectored interrupt scheme has 31 "levels", 16 for the hardware and 15 for the software. The protocols for access to the SBI are interesting since this is our first discussion of a synchronous bus.

The Synchronous Backplane Interconnect Bus

A master clock synchronizes the bus operations. Actions occur at given time intervals or *slots*. On the VAX, slots are 200 ns. long. The SBI has 32 "data" lines, used either for data or addresses, and a number of control lines. During a slot, either an address or data is transferred. Two data transfers, 64 bits, can follow an address transfer. There is no central arbitration for getting control of the bus. Each controller attached to the bus is given a fixed priority and can activate a REQUEST line. When a controller wishes to transfer data, it raises its request line, say R_i, at the beginning of a time slot. At the end of the time slot, it senses the status of all lines R_j which have a higher priority. If none of them is raised, then it has control of the bus, otherwise it repeats the same sequence on the next time slot. Thus, we have a distributed control with fixed priorities. Once a controller has control of the SBI, it can either send data or addresses. A FLAG control line indicates the interpretation to be given to the transfer. In addition, some lines carry the identity (ID) of the source/destination controller when necessary.

For example, let us see schematically how a 64-bit read request from the Pc might be performed on a slot by slot basis. (This is our own interpretation and might not be totally accurate.)

- Slot 1.   The Pc requests control of the SBI. We assume it is granted (although the Pc has lowest priority).
- Slot 2.   The Pc sends a memory address and a read command on the 32 "data" lines, as well as its own ID. This is acquired by the controllers connected to the SBI.
- Slot 3.   The controllers decode the contents of the message sent in slot 2; one of the two Mp controllers will have recognized that the address belongs to one of the memory modules it controls.

- Slot 4.   The controller acknowledges.
- Slots 5–7.   64 bits, a quadword, are read from Mp. (The Mp cycle is 3 slots.) During that time the SBI can be used by some other devices.
- Slot 7.   The Mp controller requests access to the SBI since it knows that at the end of that slot, data will be ready for transfer. Let us assume it takes control of the SBI. (Note that this action is overlapped with the Mp read.)
- Slots 8–9.   Two consecutive data transfers are done. The ID lines carry the destination's ID. The Pc recognizes its ID and accepts the data. In addition, error-checking is performed for each SBI transfer.

The VAX 11/780 clearly answers the main criticism addressed to the PDP-11 through its large virtual and physical memory ranges. But the appraisals of the uses of the instruction set, of the adequacy of the SBI, and of the efficiency of small pages among other features are yet to be determined.

9.4 MICROCOMPUTER AND MICROPROCESSOR ARCHITECTURES

9.4.1 One-Chip vs. Bit-Slice Microprocessors

According to manufacturers claims, we are periodically witnessing the birth of new "generations" of microprocessors. Within the space of a few years, we have seen 4-bit (INTEL 4004 in 1971), then 8-bit (INTEL 8008 in 1973) and finally 16-bit processors (NATIONAL PACE in 1975), where the number of bits corresponds to the internal data path width. It does not seem that we are to reach quickly 32-bit microprocessors, not so much because of technological limitations on the number of pins or on gate density, but because of lack of applications for such "giant" microprocessors (cf. Chapter 11 Section 3 for some contradictory predictions). Although a number of companies are introducing 16-bit microcomputers to upgrade their lines, e.g., INTEL 8086, ZILOG Z8000, Motorola 68000, their 8-bit counterparts, the INTEL 8080, ZILOG Z-80 and Motorola 6800, are still extremely popular since they are the right size and have adequate power for numerous applications as shown in Section 2.

The passage from one "generation" to another is linked naturally to the data path width in the chip as well as to the number of address and data lines which can connect the chip to other components. This is linked to the advances in the manufacturing technology of large-scale integrated circuits.

With those advances in MOS technology, gates can be more densely packed and hence more "real estate" can be put on a single chip. Therefore, not only will the data paths become wider, but there will also be more internal registers and control logic on the chip. As we shall see, the ISP of a 16-bit microprocessor such as the ZILOG Z8000 is of the same order of complexity and generality as those of a PDP-11 or of an IBM System/370. But MOS technology has speed limitations which are not as critical in bipolar circuitry. Transistor-transistor logic (TTL) and emitter-coupled logic (ECL) circuits, among others, are faster but they cannot be as densely packed and they require more power. Therefore, it is not possible to manufacture complete processing units of large enough size on a single bipolar chip; instead, an ALU "slice" and associated registers, called a RALU, will be built. These bit-slices, typically 2 or 4-bit RALU's, will be connected very much like groups of a carry look-ahead adder and controlled through a special microprogrammed sequencer. For most applications, bit-slice processors will be faster than single chip processors. On the other hand, they are more difficult to program and their use will be generally restricted to specific applications which require "one-shot" programming. Typical examples are the designs of mini or even medium-size computer central processing units and of special hardware attachments.

Before dwelling further on the differences at the register transfer level between one-chip, also called fixed-instruction, and bit-slice microprocessors, we examine the PMS structure of microcomputer systems. At this descriptive level, we need not differentiate between the two possible central processor implementations. The microprocessor, μPc, will be the arbitrator of a centralized single bus architecture (cf. Figure 9.15.a). Microcomputer manufacturers prefer to label this structure a "3-bus" architecture by separating the address, data and control lines into 3 different buses (cf. Figure 9.15.b). The data bus is bidirectional and the address bus unidirectional; although the control is mostly in the μPc, some control signals can be sent from controllers, such as priority interrupt or DMA devices, and therefore the control bus is bidirectional. The "3-bus" labelling might not be accurate in some cases. For example in the ZILOG Z8000, address and data share the same lines.

In Figure 9.15.b, we have split Mp into an Mcs ROM and an Mp RAM to underline that we have two types of microcomputer systems: those which can be considered as user-programmable and which derive from minicomputer systems, and those which could be labelled as user-packaged coming with a fixed program for a given application. In the former case, RAM's will dominate in Mp while in the latter there will be a majority of ROM modules.

We have not shown an Ms module since most systems will not have any. Of

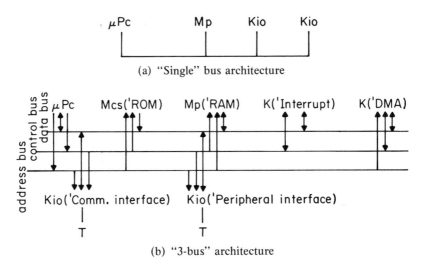

Figure 9.15　Generic PMS description of a microcomputer system

course, there will be some connection to T elements, such as terminals, instruments, or larger computers. Secondary storage, floppy disks or cassettes, is more of the archival type and hence is also represented as T elements although there are exceptions.

Let us now more closely examine the structure of the μPc, starting with the case of a fixed instruction microprocessor. The internal organization of the chip is built around an internal data bus and the means to communicate with the rest of the system, the "3" buses mentioned above. This is shown in Figure 9.16, with Figure 9.16.a giving the pin assignments for the external buses and Figure 9.16.b depicting the internal organization. As can be seen from the latter, it is a simple arrangement reminiscent of the basic requirements for a Pc with the I-unit and D-unit merged into a single entity, as outlined in Chapter 4 Section 1. (We have assumed that the program counter is one of the general registers.)

From the external viewpoint, a bit slice microprocessor looks like its fixed instruction counterpart; Figure 9.16.a remains accurate. From a less macroscopic viewpoint, there are several chips organized in two main sections. The first one (cf. Figure 9.17) constitutes the arithmetic and logic section, or central processing element, and consists of cascaded RALU's. The second is the microprogram control section with the sequencer and ROM, or programmable ROM (PROM). Each RALU will have connections to the data and address bus via "sliced" data and address buffers, an ALU for 2 or

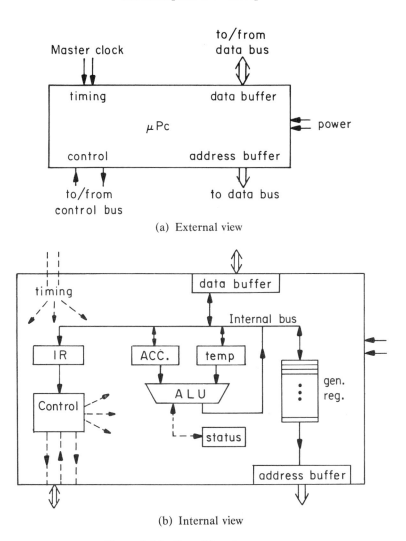

(a) External view

(b) Internal view

Figure 9.16 One-chip microprocessor

4 bits with carry-in, carry-out and look-ahead carry outputs, "slices" of general registers, and scratchpad registers. It will also have a minimal decoding facility to direct the operation of the ALU. The sequencer has the logic necessary to generate the address of the next microinstruction in the PROM; it is connected to the data and control buses and it receives signals from the central processing element and the PROM. Often the output of the

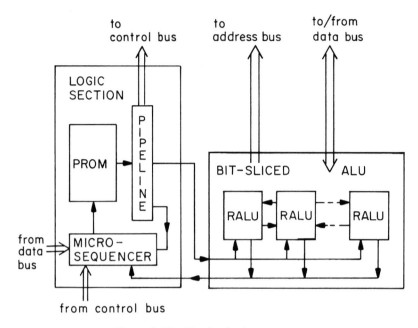

Figure 9.17   Bit-sliced microprocessor

PROM is stored in a so-called pipeline register which, in our terminology, is nothing else than an McsDR, or data register from the microstore. It allows prefetching of microinstructions and the overlap of fetch and execution (cf. Chapter 7).

Looking back at the single bus PMS structure, we see that Mp and I/O connections will have to be performed in a manner similar to other single bus systems or subsystems. An address recognition scheme and some transfer protocols will be required. The microcomputer literature often states that I/O facilities are organized by ports. These ports are simply groups of n parallel lines, where n is the width of the data bus, and associated logic to read/write. The ports are connected to interfaces which frequently are programmable microprocessors.

Most microcomputer systems have provisions for priority interrupts and DMA transfers. This is why the conceptual difference between micros and minis is so difficult to assess, if it exists at all. For example, a micro like the Motorola 6800 has an I/O scheme quite similar to the PDP-11's.

Although there are many varieties of microprocessors, they have more similarities than differences. Consequently, we limit ourselves to two representative μPc's, the INTEL 8080 which is currently the most popular 8-bit microprocessor, and the ZILOG Z8000, which has numerous features reminiscent of more powerful systems. Readers should consult specialized articles if they are interested in bit-sliced micros or in other fixed-instruction microprocessors which have distinctive characteristics (as e.g., the Texas Instruments TMS 9900 with its concept of "registers in memory" and the very advanced Motorola 68000).

9.4.2   The INTEL 8080

The INTEL 8080 is the paradigm of the 8-bit microcomputers. Its basic cycle time is an order of magnitude improvement over its predecessor the 8008. It has 78 instructions and its instruction format is of the form one address + general register, although some instructions use the (implied) single accumulator format.

A somewhat simplified block diagram of the 8080 is shown in Figure 9.18. In Figure 9.18.a, we have shown the "external" view of the chip with its 40 pin assignments: 16 for the unidirectional address bus, 8 for the bidirectional data bus, 4 for power, 2 for a master clock, and the remaining 10 for control purposes as explained later. Figure 9.18.b representing the internal organization requires some explanation.

The three main components of the chip are the ALU, the register array, and the control section. The ALU can perform 8-bit, or 1 byte, operations. It receives its input from an accumulator and a temporary register. A "decimal adjust" block allows decimal arithmetic to be performed. It is activated by the test of an auxiliary carry. Five flags (zero, carry, sign, parity, auxiliary carry) are set by the ALU.

In addition to the accumulator A, the 8080 has other registers which can be considered as 8-bit registers, or combined in pairs to form 16-bit registers. There are six 8-bit registers B, C, D, E, H, and L, which can be treated as three 16-bit register pairs $B\text{-}C$, $D\text{-}E$, and $H\text{-}L$, and two 16-bit registers, a program counter PC and a stack pointer SP. The 8-bit registers may contain data to be transferred to the ALU, or when treated as pairs, can contain addresses; hence, their connection to the address buffer. SP is used for subroutine calls and returns. Finally, there is an extra 16-bit pair $W\text{-}Z$ which is not accessible to the programmer.

The control section has an 8-bit instruction register which transfers information in the decoder. The decoder sends signals to the timing and control unit which can also receive inputs from the master clock and 4 control lines (ready, interrupt, reset and hold). The timing and control unit activates the internal control points and 6 external control lines (interrupt enable, hold acknowledge, data bus in, sync, write and wait).

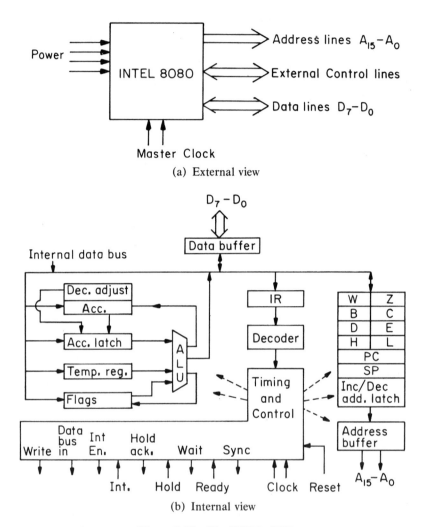

(a) External view

(b) Internal view

Figure 9.18   The INTEL 8080

The 3 sections are connected through an internal 8-bit data bus which can also transmit information to the data buffer or receives information from it.

·Each of the 78 instructions is from 1 to 3 bytes long. The opcode is 1 byte. Then, depending on the addressing mode, there is one of the following:

- a two-byte trailer for direct addressing (a 16-bit address);
- a one or two-byte trailer for immediate instruction (one or two bytes of data);

- no trailer for register addressing and memory addressing when the address is implied in the *H-L* pair (so-called register-indirect addressing).

The instruction set consists of an arithmetic group (14 instructions), a data transfer group (11 instructions), a logical group (15 instructions), a branch group (29 instructions), and a last group (9 instructions) for stack manipulation, interrupt handling and I/O. The two I/O instructions, IN and OUT, address 256 special registers not included in Mp. Instructions take from 4 to 18 clock cycles of 0.5 μs/cycle, that is their execution is between 2 and 9 μs.

The interrupt scheme on the 8080 is extremely simple since there is a single external interrupt line. However, more complex interrupt systems can be provided by adding on a special interface. This is required for a DMA capability.

We have seen before how instruction sets were exercised in medium scale machines and in minicomputers. It is interesting to note that the usage of a microprocessor like the 8080 follows the same lines. For example, Peuto and Shustek report that only half of the instruction set accounts for 99.2% of the instructions written and that, depending on the applications, from 7 to 10 instructions represent over 50% of the instructions executed. As in IBM System/370 and the PDP-11, load and conditional jumps are the most frequently executed instructions (about 15% each). The average instruction length varies from 1.4 to 1.8 bytes, the number of operand bytes read per instruction is 0.35, and the number of those written is 0.2 per instruction.

Because of the wide acceptance of the 8080, a sizable amount of basic software has been produced to help potential users. In particular, PL/M, a high level programming language resembling PL/1 but with fewer features and more responsive to structured programming practices and to the architecture of microprocessors, is popular.

The INTEL 8086

In 1978, INTEL announced a 16-bit microprocessor, the 8086, upward compatible with the 8080. Among the new features, in addition to the internal data path width of 16 bits, are more registers, an expanded addressing capability for both memory and I/O ports, a more extensive addressing mechanism, an instruction set with byte-string operations, and a more sophisticated interrupt system.

The switch from 8 to 16-bit data path width has no impact on the memory addressing range. To be able to go beyond the 64K bytes given by a 16-bit address, a relocation or segment register approach is taken. It is somewhat reminiscent of the PDP-11 memory extension unit described previously. Here, the memory space, which can be as large as 1M byte, is logically divided into four segments: the current code, data, stack, and extra segments. Each segment begins at an address evenly divisible by 16. A 16-bit segment register, one for each of the four segments, contains the 16 most significant bits of the 20-bit address. The final address, e.g., for a data reference, is computed as:

$$\text{(contents of data segment } \square \text{ 0000)} + \text{effective address.}$$

If the contents of all segment registers are the same, we have a 64K address range like in the 8080. But the programs have become relocatable. Note that code can be made re-entrant by imposing that the code segment does not overlap with any of the other three.

The register structure of the 8086 is a superset of the 8080's. The additions are the four segments registers just mentioned, a pair of stack pointers instead of a single one, and two index registers for the data segment (hence an index addressing capability). There is also a 16-bit accumulator instead of an 8-bit one and the number of flags set by the ALU is increased to 9.

The improvements in the instruction set are mostly in the area of byte-string manipulations. Unhappily, the new instructions are mostly limited to 1-byte operations.

The passage from 8 to 16 data lines is reflected in the I/O accessing capabilities: 64K ports are addressable instead of 256. There are two pins for external interrupts: one for maskable and one for non-maskable. Two hundred and fifty-six interrupt types can be triggered by software. Finally, provision for multiprocessor systems is apparent with the inclusion of a test-and-lock mechanism (cf. Chapter 10).

It is too early to conclusively assess the performance of the 8086. Initial benchmarks, advertised by INTEL, indicate a 10 to 25% decrease in program size and a 7 to 12 improvement in speed (with a basic clock cycle two to three times faster) over the 8080.

9.4.3   The ZILOG Z8000

In 1976, the ZILOG Corporation announced an 8-bit microcomputer, the Z-80, which looked very much like an improved INTEL 8080. Programs running on the 8080 could be executed on the Z-80. The main additions in the chip's architecture were in the duplication of the registers, the presence of two index registers, and multiple level interrupts. The instruction set consisted of 158 instructions but many of the new 80 opcodes were for the handling of the extra registers.

In 1978, ZILOG announced its new product, a 16-bit microprocessor named the Z8000 which is not completely upward compatible with the Z-80. A new chip architecture has been created, a much more powerful instruction set is implemented, a wide addressing range is available when a memory management unit is added, and performance has improved greatly. ZILOG claims that the Z8000 can compete successfully against minicomputers like the PDP-11/45, both in terms of performance and versatility. The Z8000 is easier to program in assembly language than previous 8-bit microcomputers and its instruction set includes operations for helping in the compilation of high-level languages and for operating system support. Furthermore, the Z8000 has been designed with an eye on the future; it has facilities for synchronizing asynchronous parallel computations.

From the external viewpoint, the Z8000 comes in two versions: a 40-pin chip without memory extension and a 48-pin "segmented" chip with a Memory Management Unit complement. In the following, we will describe the second organization for which the pin arrangement is shown in Figure 9.19.a, and the physical connections, from the address lines viewpoint, in Figure 9.19.b. Besides the addition of a Memory Management Unit, whose role will be described later, the other distinguishing features of the external view of the Z8000 are the sharing of data and address lines (at the PMS level we still have a single bus architecture), 3 external interrupt lines, and the 2 pins dedicated to multiprocessing functions.

The ISP level of the Z8000 is quite interesting. Regularity has been stressed: registers are general-purpose, most instructions can operate on the seven available data types, and addressing modes are quite general. The instruction set includes some instructions for compiler design, operating system support, and multiprocessing facilities.

The μPc state consists of 16 16-bit registers RO through $R15$. All 16 can be used as accumulators and all, except RO, as index registers. The 8 registers RO through $R7$ can serve as 16 8-bit registers RHO, RLO, $RH1$, ..., $RL7$. These 8-bit registers can be used as accumulators. The 16-bit registers can also be paired in 8 32-bit registers $RR0$, $RR2$, ..., $RR14$ and as 4 64-bit quadruples $RQ0$, ..., $RQ12$ for operations such as multiply and divide.

One of the registers, namely $RR14$ in segmented mode, contains the stack pointer implicitly used by the CALL and RET instructions. PUSH and POP instructions can use any other register as stack pointer. The reason for a 32-bit stack pointer will become clear when we describe the memory management. Since the Z8000 can run in either system or user mode, we have two stack pointers, one for each mode (recall the same feature in recent PDP-11 models). In the event of an interrupt or trap, the program status is pushed on

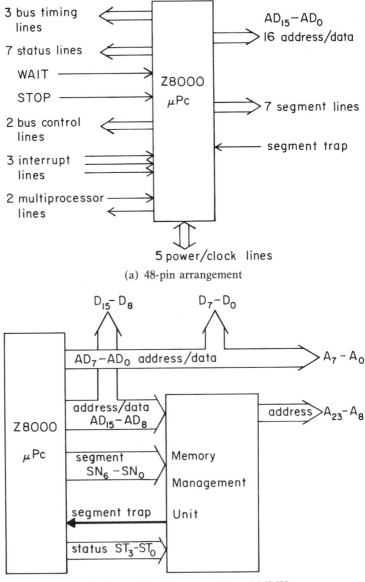

(a) 48-pin arrangement

(b) Connections between μPc and MMU

Figure 9.19   External view of the segmented version of the ZILOG Z8000

the system stack. This program status consists of a 32-bit *PC*, and of a 16-bit flag control word (*FCW*). Only 10 flags are used. An extra word has been reserved for future use.

The instructions are from 1 to 5 words long. The first word gives, for example, the opcode (up to 110 different opcodes), the addressing mode (8 modes described below), information as to whether the data is a byte or a word assuming that the opcode allows both, and two register designator fields. Following words, if necessary, yield addresses or immediate data. Up to 3 operands can be designated explicitly.

Instructions can operate on 7 data types: bits, BCD digits, bytes, words, double words, byte strings and word strings. Functionally, the instruction set can be divided into 9 groups: Move, Arithmetic, Logical, branches, bit manipulations, rotate and shift, block transfer and string manipulation, I/O, and Pc control. Some interesting characteristics are as follows: the first group includes compiler-oriented instructions such as POP and PUSH with autoincrement and decrement of the register used as a stack pointer and Operating System support instructions such as LOAD MULTIPLE (to register or to memory); the second has multiply and divide operations on 16 and 32-bit quantities (2's complement 16 and 32-bit arithmetic is a standard feature); the third has calls or jumps "relative" by adding small offsets to the *PC*, thus yielding shorter instructions; the I/O instructions can have autoincrements or decrements of the source or destination address and some can be repeated until a count, stored in a register, becomes null (hence block transfers can be initiated by a single instruction); the Pc control instructions are for trap and interrupt handling and multiprocessing facilities. The most novel features, at least for a microprocessor, are found in the block transfer and string groups with, among others, instructions which allow the comparison of byte or word strings until the comparison is unsuccessful or the strings have been exhausted, or the transfer of strings from a source to a destination as an IBM System/370 MOVE instruction. There are a number of instructions on the Translate, and Translate and Test theme as in System/370 (e.g., in the Translate instruction each byte in the first string operand is replaced by its translation found in a table whose address is the second operand. These instructions can be very useful in the lexical analysis phase of a compiler).

The 8 addressing modes of the Z8000 are: register, register indirect (modes 0 and 1 in the PDP-11), direct address (the address follows in subsequent words), indexed (mode 6 of the PDP-11), immediate (the data follows in subsequent words; this is similar to the PDP-11's mode 2 with the *PC* used as the index register), base address (equivalent to index for the non-segmented version; for the segmented version, see below), base indexed (as in

System/370 but without a displacement field, i.e., the address is computed as the sum of two registers), and relative (offset relative to the *PC* as explained above).

One of the most interesting innovations in the Z8000 architecture is the presence of a Memory Management Unit (MMU). With this addition, addressing spaces are 2^{23} bytes, or 8M bytes. The physical address range is twice as large, that is, 16M bytes (24 address lines). There are 6 addressing spaces, 3 for system mode and 3 for user mode, namely code, data and stack address spaces. The distinction between these spaces is communicated to the MMU by the status lines. When the MMU is not present, the non-segmented mode, the 16 address lines impose an addressing space of only 64K bytes, but the 6 spaces do exist as in the segmented case.

A (segmented) address consists of a 7-bit segment number and a 16-bit offset for a full address 3 bytes long. However, it is always represented as two words in a register or in memory. But in instructions, it can be represented either in a single word or in a double word. The distinction is made by the setting of the leftmost bit of the first word which is not significant for addressing purposes since segment numbers are only 7 bits. If this bit is 1, we have a long offset, or regular address, and if it is 0, we have a short offset which is contained in the second byte of the word, that is the most significant byte of the offset is implicitly 0.

The transformation of a 23-bit logical address into a 24-bit physical address is done in the MMU as shown in Figure 9.20. The segment number indicates a segment base address (SBA). The SBA contains the 16 high-order bits of the base address of the physical segment. The high-order byte of the offset is added to the SBA's contents and the low order byte is concatenated to the result to form the 24-bit physical address. This low order byte does not have to pass through the MMU as can be seen in Figure 9.19.b which shows the address lines $A_7 - A_0$ coming directly from the μPc. It is clear from this address translation mechanism that segments must be at least 2^8 (256) bytes and at most 2^{16} (64K) bytes long.

Each MMU can contain 64 SBA's. A pair of MMU's is needed to support the full number of segments possible for a given address space, and therefore 3 pairs for the 3 addressing spaces. MMU's are loaded and unloaded as any I/O peripheral.

In addition to the SBA, the MMU contains attributes for each translation entry which checks for the validity of the memory reference. For example, the size of the segment (in increments of 256 bytes) is stored in the MMU so that out of bounds checks can be done by comparing with the high-order byte of the offset. There are some protection bits for the code vs. data space, the read/write status of a segment, and the absence of a segment translation en-

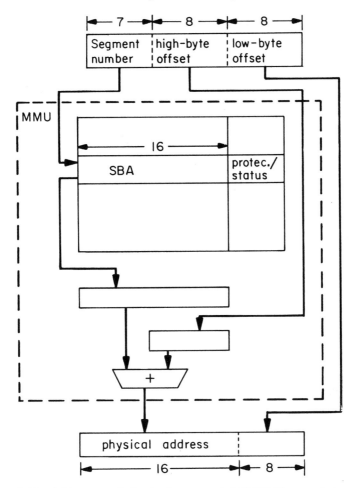

Figure 9.20   Address translation in the segmented Z8000 (the area between the
dotted lines is on the MMU chip)

try (so that 6 MMU's are not always needed). In case of an error, the segment
trap line is raised and a trap will occur in the μPc.

We now return to the consideration of the index and base address modes
for the segmented Z8000. In the non-segmented case, the two modes are
equivalent, that is the effective address is computed as:

$$EA \leftarrow C(\text{Index register}) + \text{Displacement},$$

where displacement is a 16-bit address.

In the segmented mode, the effective address is one of the following:

- Index mode: $EA \leftarrow$ Address $+ C$(Index register), where "Address" (following the first word of instruction) is either a long or short offset and the index register is a single 16-bit register, whose contents are therefore an offset.
- Base Address mode: $EA \leftarrow C$(32-bit index register) $+$ Displacement, where the index register contains a 23-bit address, i.e., it is a double length register, and the displacement is a 16-bit offset.

Therefore in the index mode, the "base address" is fixed at run time since the segment number is not modifiable, while in the base mode it is the opposite with a fixed displacement and a variable base (cf. Exercise 5). In the base indexed mode, the base register is a register pair while the index register is a single 16-bit register.

The remaining aspect of the Z8000 which makes it more sophisticated than previous μPc's is its more extensive interrupt and trap scheme. The 3 interrupt lines correspond to non-maskable, non-vectored, and vectored interrupts (up to 256 daisy chained levels). Upon a trap or interrupt, the *PC* (two words in the segmented mode), the *FCW*, and a word indicating the "reason" for the trap are pushed on the system stack. A new program status area pointer containing a segment number and a high-byte offset (the low byte offset is implicitly 0) indicates where the new *PC* and *FCW* can be obtained.

Although it is too early to judge the Z8000's performance, we can say that it is able to provide on a few chips, the μPc and MMU's, as much as a sophisticated minicomputer. The ZILOG literature indicates that the timing of individual instructions places the Z8000, which has a rather slow clock rate (250 ns.), between a PDP-11/45 and a PDP-11/70.

9.5 A MINICOMPUTER STACK ARCHITECTURE: THE HP-3000

In our descriptions of the PDP-11, INTEL 8080 and ZILOG Z8000 instruction sets, we noted the presence of PUSH and POP operations, either implicitly as a form of the MOVE instruction or explicitly. The PDP-11 and the Z8000 have general registers dedicated to the roles of stack pointers. In the VAX 11/780, the stack philosophy is even more a part of the architecture; for example, the procedure CALL and RETURN instructions use hardware maintained frames for storing and restoring the state of the Pc. However, none of these systems can qualify as "stack" computers. On the other hand, the Hewlett-Packard HP-3000 is a minicomputer which has the attributes of a stack computer. The environment of an executing process is based on the management of a data stack and the instruction set is biased towards stack rather than general register operations, with 4 hardware registers in the Pc used as top of the stack locations.

Besides its data stack organization, the HP-3000 has other interesting features such as a virtual memory mechanism for code segments which follows the principles of pure segmentation, a two-bus architecture with I/O channels (not common in minicomputers), and a microcoded implementation of the processor which favors the efficient interpretation of high-level languages.

We start by giving a generic PMS description of the HP-3000 (cf. Figure 9.21). The central processor and an I/O processor are integrated within a single computing unit. They have connections to the memory bus and to the I/O bus. Devices attached to the memory bus communicate through module control units (MCU). The control is distributed among the MCU's. The memory bus is synchronous with 175 ns. slot times. There is no handshaking. Instead, the MCU's determine that a given receiver module is ready and that no higher priority module is requesting the bus before it sends data on the next cycle. (This is to be compared with the VAX's SBI in Section 3.) Typically, memory modules have priority over the Pio which, in turn, has priority over Pc. Communication with I/O devices can be done in two ways. When direct I/O is performed, a word of data is transferred, or a command is sent, on the I/O bus under control of the Pc-Pio module. When programmed I/O is desired, an SIO instruction starts either a selector channel or a multiplexor channel program. The selector is connected directly to the memory bus, while transfers monitored by the multiplexor have to pass through the Pio. The Pc-Pio module also controls an extensive interrupt system: up to 125 external interrupt sources are possible, as well as 17 internal interrupts (e.g., power failure, memory error) and 7 traps. The interrupt system uses polling and daisy-chain priority rules.

At this point, an ISP description of the Pc would be nebulous. We must first explain the environment in which a task is executed. In the HP-3000, code and data have separated address spaces. Programs are organized into pure procedures which are contained in variable-length segments (a segment can contain several procedures). A virtual memory mechanism (pure segmentation) manages the primary memory allocation according to some variant of the working set policy. Each executing task has a code segment table which contains the base addresses of the segments currently in Mp. Every segment contains a segment transfer table to handle interprocedure references. Intra-segment references are displacements from the base while intersegment references are processed through the code segment table by giv-

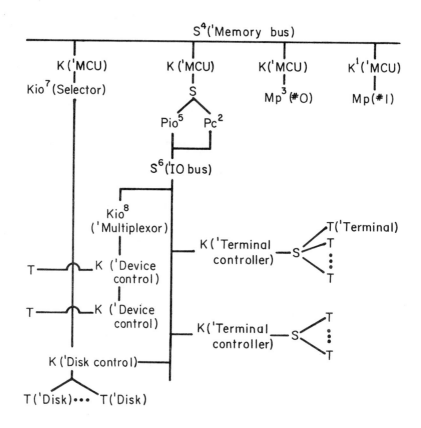

1. K('Module control unit; interfaces to the memory bus)
2. Pc('Hp 3000; microprogrammed; 16 b/word; (1|2)instr/word; stack oriented; 4 top of stack registers; 16 other programmable registers; multi-level priority interrupt system)
3. Mp(semiconductor;(128|192| 256)KBytes; 16 b + 5 ECC b/word)
4. S('Memory bus; synchronous; 175ns/slot time)
5. Pio (integrated with Pc; for direct I/O and control of multiplexor)
6. S('I/O bus; totally dedicated to I/O transfers)
7. Kio('Selector; provides direct access to memory bus)
8. Kio ('Multiplexor; can control up to 16 device controllers)

Figure 9.21   Generic PMS description of the Hewlett-Packard HP-3000

ing a segment number and displacement (the reader should compare this organization with that of MULTICS as described in Chapter 6 Section 3; here the binding is more static).

More interesting though, is the stack architecture for data. Each process has its own stack. The HP-3000 uses 5 registers to manage the stack (cf. Figure 9.22.a): *DL* (data limit) marking the lower limit of the process' data area; *DB* (data base) marking the bottom of the execution stack; *Q* (stack marker or frame register) which delimits the data belonging to the currently executing procedure; *S* or top of stack register; and *Z* (stack limit) marking the upper limit beyond which the stack cannot grow without requesting additional space. Actually, *S* has two components: *SR* which indicates how many valid elements are in the 4 "top of the stack" registers in the Pc, and *SM* which points to the stack extension in Mp (recall Chapter 4 Section 6).

All references to data lie between *DB* and *Z*. From the executing procedure viewpoint, the stack has the configuration shown in Figure 9.22.b. The bottom of the stack, the locations above *DB*, is used for storing global data

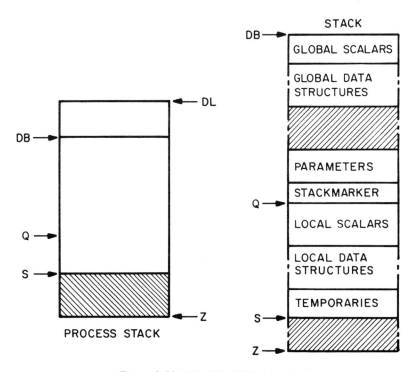

Figure 9.22   The HP-3000 data stack

(scalar and arrays). Similarly, locations between Q and S contain scalars and arrays local to the executing procedure, and temporaries. Locations just below Q contain the parameters passed by the procedure which called the one currently executing and the environment of the calling procedures (e.g., a code segment address, displacement with the code segment, location on the stack of its own stack marker, etc. ...). Therefore, it is possible to access parameters with a negative displacement from Q, local data with a positive displacement from Q, temporaries with a negative displacement from S, and global data with a positive displacement from DB. The stack markers can be used for static displays to access intermediate procedure levels (note that in the B6700 the display is implemented in high-speed registers; for the use of displays in the translation of block structured high-level languages, the reader is referred to texts on compiler construction). Finally, the area between DL and DB can be accessed through indirect addressing. Its usage is not obvious.

These 6 stack registers (recall that S is divided into two parts), the 4 "top of the stack" registers, and 3 registers for the code segment base, code segment limit and program displacement, are the main components of the Pc state which can be modified by the programmer. In addition, there are 7 other registers for base and index addressing and for status saving. The instruction set has over 200 instructions, with a number of 0-address operations and 1-address operations which use the top of the stack as an implicit operand. For example, the arithmetic expression:

$$A + B + C*(D + E + F*G),$$

would be compiled as:

LOAD A	Push A onto stack
ADDM B	$(A + B)$ on top of stack
LOAD D	Push D on top of stack
ADDM E	$(D + E)$ on top of stack
LOAD F	Push F on top of stack
MULM G	$F*G$ on top of stack
ADD	$D + E + F + G$ on top of stack
MULM C	$C*(D + E + F + G)$ on top of stack
ADD	$A + B + C + (D + E + F + G)$ on top of stack

This 9 instruction segment of code has to be compared with the corresponding 9 instructions for a one-address + general register scheme and the 13 instructions for a "pure" stack machine as described in Chapter 4 Section 6 when the same degree of optimization is performed (that is when the loading of C is delayed appropriately).

The HP-3000 Pc is microcoded with vertical microinstructions (32 bits). Prefetching is performed at the microinstruction and at the machine language levels. The microinstruction execution is pipelined in two stages, one for selecting data from Pc registers, and the second for activating the ALU and shifter. Some special microinstructions can be repeated a given number of times without having to be fetched anew from the Mcs.

This incomplete description of the HP-3000 is sufficient to ascertain that it can be truly labelled a stack computer. Certainly, it does not have the power of a Burroughs B6700. For example, it does not use a descriptor scheme but its replacement, the displacement from DB, is sufficient for most cases. In the same vein, it is difficult to access variables which are neither global nor local to the currently executing procedure. In other words, the HP-3000 data stack organization is fine for languages such as FORTRAN, BASIC, or SPL/3000 the native systems programming language, but not necessarily efficient for ALGOL-like block structures if block nesting is widely used. Finally, we already reported simulation studies which showed that it was sound to decide to limit the number of top of the stack registers in the Pc to 4 (cf. Chapter 4 Section 6).

9.6 BIBLIOGRAPHICAL NOTES, REFERENCES AND EXERCISES

There exist many texts and papers dealing with microcomputers and minicomputers. The state of the art for minis in the mid-seventies is adequately described in [Koudela 73]. Microprocessors of 4 and 8-bit are well covered in [Hilburn and Julich 76]. [Brooks 76] presents some personal views on microcomputer architecture with which this author often concurs.

The architecture of the PDP-11 was first presented in [Bell, Cady, McFarland, Delagi, O'Loughlin and Noonan 70]. The implementation of various PDP-11 models and comparison tradeoffs are reported in [Snow and Siewiorek 78]. Tables 1 and 3 are summaries of data gathered by Strecker (published in [Snow and Siewiorek 78]) and Marathe [Marathe 77]. Description of buses used in the PDP-11 family can be found in [Levy 78]. The microprogramming level of the PDP-11/40 is treated clearly in [Tanenbaum 76]. Cache designs for the PDP-11/70 and PDP-11/60 are contrasted in [Mudge 77]. The LSI-11 is described in [Sebern 76]. An introduction to the VAX 11/780 can be found in [Strecker 78]. These papers, and some additional ones dealing with the PDP-11, are reprinted in [Bell, Mudge and McNamara 78].

In addition to [Hilburn and Julich 76], the reader interested in specific microprocessors should consult user manuals (for example, see [Intel 75] for the Intel 8080). [Adams 78] is a complete survey of bit-slice microprocessors. The Intel 8086 is described in [Morse, Pohlman and Ravenel 78]. Performance considerations are discussed in [Peuto and Shustek 77]. Among the high-level languages for microcomputers, one should be aware of PL/M [Kildall 74]. The ZILOG Z8000 is presented in [Peuto 79].

[Bartlett 73] and [Sell 75] give a nice introduction to the HP-3000 and its stack architecture.

References

1. Adams, P. M., "Microprogrammable Microprocessor Survey," *SIGMICRO Newsletter, 9,* (Mar. 1978 and Jun. 1978), 23–49 and 7–38.
2. Bartlett, J. F., "The HP-3000 Computer System," *Proc. ACM-IEEE Symposium on High-Level Language Computer Architecture,* 1973, 61–69.
3. Bell, C. G., Cathy, R., McFarland, H., Delagi, B., O'Laughlin, J. and R. Noonan, "A New Architecture for Minicomputers—The DEC PDP-11," *Proc. AFIPS 1970 Spring Joint Comp.Conf., 36,* AFIPS Press, Montvale, N.J., 1970, 657–675.
4. Bell, C. G., Mudge, J. C., and J. McNamara, *Computer Engineering: A DEC View of Hardware Systems Design,* Digital Press, Bedford, Mass., 1978.
5. Brooks, F., "An Overview of Microcomputer Architecture and Software," *EUROMICRO 76,* 1976, 1–4.
6. Hilburn, J. L. and P. N. Julich, *Microcomputers/Microprocessors: Hardware, Software, and Applications,* Prentice-Hall, Englewood Cliff, N.J., 1976.
7. Intel Corp. *8080 Microcomputer System's User Manual,* Santa Clara, Calif., 1975.
8. Kildall, G. A., "High-Level Languages Simplifies Microcomputer Programming," *Electronics,* (Jun. 1974), 103–109.
9. Koudela, J., "The Past, Present and Future of Minicomputers: A Scenario," *Proc. of the IEEE, 61,* (Nov. 1973), 1526–1534.
10. Levy, J., "Buses, the Skeleton of Computer Structures," in *Computer Engineering,* Bell, et al., eds., Digital Press, Bedford, Mass., 1978, 269–299.
11. Marathe, M. *Performance Evaluation at the Hardware Architecture Level and the Operating Systems Kernel Design Level,* PhD. Dissertation, Carnegie-Mellon Univ., 1977.
12. Morse, S. P., Pohlman, W. B., and B. W. Ravenel, "The Intel 8086 Microprocessor: A 16-bit evolution of the 8080," *Computer, 11,* (Jan. 1978), 18–27.
13. Mudge, J. C., "Design Decisions Achieve Price/Performance Balance in Mid-Range Minicomputers," *Computer Design, 16,* (Aug. 1977), 87–95.
14. Peuto, B. L. and L. J. Shustek, "Current Issues in the Architecture of Microprocessors," *Computer, 10,* (Feb. 1977), 20–25.
15. Peuto, L., "Architecture of a New Microprocessor," *Computer, 12,* (Feb. 1979), 10–22.
16. Sebern, M. J., "A Minicomputer compatible microcomputer system: the DEC-LSI-11," *Proc. of the IEEE, 64,* (Jun. 1976), 881–888.

17. Sell, J. V., "Microprogramming in an Integrated Hardware/Software System," *Computer Design,* (Jan. 1975), 77–84.

18. Snow, E. and D. P. Siewiorek, *Impact of Implementation Design Tradeoffs on Performance: The PDP-11, A Case Study,* Tech. Report CMU-CS-78-104, Carnegie-Mellon Univ., (Feb. 1978).

19. Strecker, W. D., "VAX 11/780: A Virtual Address Extension to the DEC PDP-11 Family," *Proc. AFIPS 1978 Nat. Comp. Conf., 47,* AFIPS Press, Montvale, N.J., 1978, 967–980.

20. Tanenbaum, A. S., *Structured Computer Organization,* Prentice-Hall, Englewood Cliffs, N.J., 1976.

Exercises

1. Give an ISP description for the effective address calculation (e.g., of a destination operand) in the PDP-11.

2. Consider the Pc design of the PDP-11/40 as shown in Figure 9.3. For which addressing modes is the BA loaded from the output of the ALU?

3. Draw a diagram similar to that of Figure 9.10 for a data-out operation.

4. For each of the cache organizations shown in Figure 9.7, answer the following:
    a) How many comparisons are needed to check whether a given word at Mp address L is in the cache.
    b) Assuming that each byte has a parity bit associated with it in the tag and parity registers, how wide is this register (do not forget a validity bit and the parity bit for the address; recall that addresses are 18 bits).
        Assuming the availability of 256.1 bit chips for the 11/70 and 1024.1 bit chips for the 11/60 give the ratio of the component counts for each organization. Assuming that the larger chips are about 20% more expensive, discuss the relative merits of each organization in terms of cost and performance.

5. Consider the index mode and the base address mode of the Z8000 in the segmented version. Give examples of program constructs where one of these is preferable to the other.

Chapter 10

SUPERCOMPUTERS

The range of applications where micro and minicomputers can be used effectively is enormous. With the new "small" machines that have versatile instruction sets, addressing ranges as large as those encountered in the most powerful models of the third generation, and operating systems and basic software sufficient to satisfy sophisticated users, we may wonder if there is still a need for large computers. The answer is definitely positive. For example, "a supercomputer that is a hundred times faster than the Control Data 7600 is being sought at NASA for wind tunnels" (Datamation, 1977). Many applications such as weather prediction, the solution of large partial differential equations (as in nuclear physics problems), image processing, "real-time" speech recognition, medical applications (tomography, biomedical analysis), astronomy, etc . . . , require a processing power which cannot be delivered by small machines. Even in more mundane situations, as in large computing centers, there is a need for a central facility to perform chores such as the management of large data bases which, as of yet, cannot be accomplished by sophisticated "small" systems by themselves.

Processing power for most of the applications listed above has two main components: speed and precision. The units for gauging powerful Pc's will not be MIPS (millions of instructions per second) but rather Mflops (millions of floating-point operations per second). The floating-point results should have a high precision (if not the results, at least the intermediate data when manipulations such as Fourier transforms are performed). As a point of reference, a typical definition of a supercomputer (in the late 1970's) is a system which can perform 20 Mflops and has a physical primary memory of over 1M words. In order to achieve computational rates of the order of 100 Mflops with adequate precision, the architecture of supercomputers will have to depart from the strict von Neumann concept. One of the main reasons is that the point where communication delays between switching elements, or integrated circuits on chips, play a dominant role in the speed of the computation has been reached. Therefore, the decomposition of computations into tasks which can be executed concurrently will be mandatory.

This form of computation, or parallel processing, is not new (cf. Chapter 1). We have seen instances of it when studying powerful processors (the CDC 6600 and IBM 360/91 in Chapter 4) and, at a lower level, when looking at horizontal microprogramming. In this chapter, our goal is to consider the various organizations which have been proposed (and some of them realized) for achieving large computational power. In Section 1 we introduce a taxonomy for parallel processors based in great part on Flynn's original classification. Section 2 will be devoted to the study of pipeline and vector processors. In Section 3, we introduce the array processors. Section 4 looks at multiprocessors which, as we shall see, present more flexibility but also more synchronization and scheduling problems.

10.1 CLASSIFICATIONS OF COMPUTER SYSTEMS

10.1.1 Flynn's Classification

As early as 1966, Flynn classified computer organizations into 4 categories according to the uniqueness or multiplicity of instructions and data streams. By instruction stream is meant the sequence of instructions as performed by the machine. The sequence of data manipulated by the instruction stream forms the data stream. Then, looking at the cartesian product:

(*Single Instruction, Multiple Instruction*) × (*Single Data, Multiple Data*)

we obtain the 4 architectures:

Single Instruction Single Data abbreviated SISD;
Single Instruction Multiple Data abbreviated SIMD;
Multiple Instruction Single Data abbreviated MISD;
Multiple Instruction Multiple Data abbreviated MIMD.

This taxonomy is still currently in use although, as we shall see, the SIMD and MIMD categories need to be subdivided. We proceed by examining how current architectures of large computers fit in these categories.

SISD

The systems in this category are the usual uniprocessor computers. As always, we can argue with definite statements like this one. For instance, let us consider the Amdahl 470 V/6 (this specific example was chosen since G.

Amdahl has always been an advocate of the SISD organization, even for large computers). It consists of an I-unit, a D-unit (E-unit in Amdahl's terminology), a storage control unit for cache access, virtual address translation through a TLB, and Mp storage access, and a C-unit for executing Pio (channel) commands. If we concentrate only on the I-unit-D-unit complex, we see that the execution of an instruction is highly overlapped with that of its predecessors and successors. Thus, in our opinion, the Amdahl 470 V/6 can be considered as a pipeline computer. Since pipeline computers can be fit in any of the SIMD, MISD, and MIMD categories, we are left with trying to find another "usual" uniprocessor. In the area of large computers, this will be difficult because, as we mentioned in the introduction, parallelism is required at some level to obtain the desired execution rates. It is for this reason that in the remainder of this chapter, we shall deal only with systems which have an "*M*" component in Flynn's classification. They form the class of multiprocessing systems.

There are two definitions that have been used with respect to multiprocessing systems. The ANSI Vocabulary of Information Processing defines a multiprocessor, broadly, as a system composed of two or more processing units under integrated control. A more restrictive attitude is to define multiprocessing as the simultaneous processing of two or more portions of the same program by two or more processing units.

Every major manufacturer offers a multiprocessing system which can fit the broad definition given above. A comprehensive tabulation can be found in Enslow's book. On the other hand, the number of multiprocessors adhering strictly to the second definition is quite limited. Most of these multiprocessors are either intended for special-purpose applications (e.g., array processors) or their processing units are tightly-coupled and consist of functional units which perform dedicated tasks (e.g., CDC 6600, and IBM System/360 Model 91). With the advent of cheaper hardware and hence cheaper processing units, the trend to distribute tasks over several components of the system is a natural one. Flynn's classification will shed some light on the types of multiprocessing system organizations that are pursued.

MISD

To our knowledge, there exists no system which can be labeled uniquely this way. Pipeline, or vector, processors discussed below could be construed to be included in this category. However, we do not subscribe to this view.

SIMD

In SIMD architectures, a single control unit (CU) fetches and decodes instructions. Then the instruction is executed either in the CU itself (e.g., a jump instruction) or it is broadcast to some processing elements (PE's). These PE's operate synchronously but their local memories have different contents. Depending on the complexity of the CU, the processing power and addressing method of the PE's, and the interconnection facilities between the PE's, we can distinguish between pipeline, or vector, processors, array processors, processing ensembles and associative processors.

Pipeline processors are difficult to classify. They can be considered either SIMD, MISD or MIMD architectures. Pipelining, or overlap, has been discussed already at the instruction fetch (look-ahead) level in Chapter 4. In the same chapter, we studied the design of pipelined functional units such as those implemented in the floating-point unit of the IBM System 360/91 with its two-stage adder and a multiplier/divider where pipelining is enforced in the iterative hardware. In the next section, we look at systems whose designs are predicated on an extensive use of pipelining. The concept is quite powerful; it can be applied equally well to some small units such as floating-point adders or to large ones such as complete Pc's sharing a common memory or to networks of microcomputers. As already stated, pipeline processing is analogous to an assembly-line organization. The computational power is segmented into consecutive stations. Processes are decomposed into subprocesses which have to pass through each station or stage.

Let us return to our classification problem. If we consider that a single instruction, e.g., a two stage floating-point add, treats simultaneously (two) different items of data, then our processor is of the SIMD type; if we consider instructions in consecutive stages to be different but working on the same aggregate (vector) of data, then it will be MISD; if we combine the above two interpretations, we have an MIMD architecture. We favor the first interpretation.

In array processors the CU has limited capabilities. PE's communicate with their neighbors through a network switch. The array processors are therefore well suited for problems involving vector processing and, in some cases, for grid problems. But the range of applications is severely limited by the synchronous operations of the PE's. This drawback can be circumvented if a powerful CU is present. Examples, presented later in this chapter, will make this clear.

In processing ensembles the CU is a complete computer and in order to communicate the PE's have to pass their messages through the CU. In general, each PE will operate on an associative memory. This is mandatory in the case of associative processors for which the associative memories are larger and interconnections are more extensive. Because the concept of associative processing requires a large amount of hardware (recall Chapter 5

Section 5), it has not yet been proven cost-effective except for very specific functions. Thus, processing ensembles and associative processors are even more special purpose machines than array processors. We will give a very brief overview of two of these unconventional architectures, namely PEPE and STARAN, in the next chapter.

MIMD

In MIMD architectures, several Pc's operate in parallel in an asynchronous manner and share access to a common memory. Two features are of interest to differentiate among designs: the coupling or switching of processor units and memories, and the homogeneity of the processing units.

In tightly-coupled MIMD multiprocessors, the number of processing units is fixed and they operate under the supervision of a strict control scheme. Generally, the controller is a hardware unit. (Note that this tight-coupling is also present in array processors and pipeline computers.) Most of the hardware controlled tightly-coupled multiprocessors are heterogeneous in the sense that they consist of specialized functional units (e.g., adders, multipliers) supervised by an instruction unit which decodes instructions, fetches operands and dispatches orders to the functional units. Typical examples of these are the CDC 6600 and the IBM System/360 Model 91 (recall Chapter 4).

In more recent homogeneous multiprocessing systems, not dedicated uniquely to the fast computations of scientific problems, we see looser and more modular connections. Three main types of organizations are possible for the Pc — Mp switch: the cross-bar switch, time-shared buses, and multiport memory systems. They will be reviewed in more detail in Section 4.

Looking back at the evolution of multiprocessing systems, a general trend can be detected. When the goal of the system is raw computing power, the architecture will be tightly coupled, either SIMD for more specialized applications or MIMD with custom-designed functional units, or a mixture of both such as in pipeline processors. The coupling is still tight, but not as much, when a homogeneous multiprocessor is designed with a general application in mind but with many variations being possible. When the system consists of numerous small modules and when it is intended for general purpose applications, the connections are necessarily of the loose type. The MIMD classification can then be stretched to include distributed function architectures and local networks. We shall mention these in Chapter 11. Flynn's classification is not unique. Readers interested in another notation should look at Exercise 1 after having read this chapter.

10.1.2 Software Requirements

Multiprocessing systems add levels of complexity for both the operating system and the application software. In the following sections, we shall give examples of these problems and of some of their solutions. Here, we briefly introduce the major difficulties encountered in the design of the software for the SIMD and MIMD architectures.

When array processors and pipeline computers are considered, the SIMD structure imposes some constraints that make a direct transplantation of conventional (multiprogrammed) operating systems extremely inefficient. For this reason, either a satellite computer or virtual (peripheral) processors are almost mandatory. Programming languages should be modified both in their control and their data structures. It appears that the difficulties in producing efficient compiled code have slowed new language developments and one current trend is to let the applications programmer bear the burden of designing algorithms with the implied knowledge of the machine architecture, while providing efficient means of distributing the data in the elements' memories. In the case of pipeline processors, vector operations have been added to algorithmic languages such as ALGOL-60 or FORTRAN, but it is somewhat surprising that a vector language such as APL has not been more widely used.

In the MIMD architecture, control, synchronization and scheduling of the processors are sensitive areas. Two main types of control can be envisioned. In the fixed mode, one or more processors are dedicated to execute the operating system. When some other processor terminates its current task, or when all processors are busy and a higher priority task has to be initiated, it is the responsibility of the dedicated processor(s) to schedule, terminate and/or initiate processes. An advantage of such a scheme is that special-purpose hardware, e.g., associative memory, can be embedded in the design hence decreasing the executive's overhead. The main disadvantage is that failure in the dedicated processor brings the whole system to a halt, unless there are several identical controlling processors. In the floating control mode, each processor can have access to the operating system and schedule itself. For reliability, graceful degradation, and protection between users, this is certainly a better approach. The overhead in memory contention and synchronization could appear to be superior to that of the fixed control scheme but there is less centralized message passing.

The synchronization of concurrent processes has been a topic of intense investigation since Dijkstra's famous letter. Numerous solutions for the harmonious cooperation of sequential tasks addressing common variables have appeared. They can be classified according to:

- The use of special primitive operations such as Dijkstra's semaphores;
- The priority scheme given to the processes;
- The fairness of scheduling, that is the maximum amount of time that a process has to wait before entering its "critical section" (the portion of code where it should find a stable environment and be the only one to modify it);
- The graceful degradation of the system if one of its components (processors) fails.

This important problem will be considered in Section 4. In this same section, we shall review how we can take advantage of the multiprocessor structure within a single program or, in other words, how to realize the strict definition of multiprocessing. To do so, the conventional program structure has to be modified. Three nonmutually exclusive options are open: design algorithms such that they take into account the parallel architecture (this is mandatory for array processors); express potential parallelism in the high-level and assembly languages; and automatically detect the parallelism (cf. Chapter 4 Section 3.2 for a first look at this problem).

When designing new algorithms for parallel environments, an ideal situation would be to perform n times "better" than a uniprocessor if n (parallel) processors are available. This word "better" has to be qualified and we have to define measures of performance. Two metrics are possible: the completion time of a given program and the throughput of the whole system when the multiprocessor is also multiprogrammed. For these criteria, the ideal situation is not generally attainable because in particular:

- In a given program, the amount of parallelism is not uniform and it is seldom that the n processors can be kept consistently busy;
- The n processors share resources, e.g., main memory, and the contention will in most cases degrade performance;
- The transposition of serial algorithms to parallel ones does not yield necessarily a theoretical speed-up of n.

Specific examples of these limitations will be given in the remainder of this chapter. To give an idea of the efficiency losses that can occur when the amount of parallelism within an algorithm is not constant, we present a geometrical model which, albeit crude, is sufficient to prove the point. It is also more relevant for SIMD than for MIMD systems.

We assume a single job stream. During a period of time t_1 the program is purely sequential. During time t_2, it can be decomposed into W parallel tasks. An ideal computing situation, assuming as many processors available as necessary, can be represented graphically as in Figure 10.1.a. The area enclosed in the straight lines represents a (time·processor) product. If now,

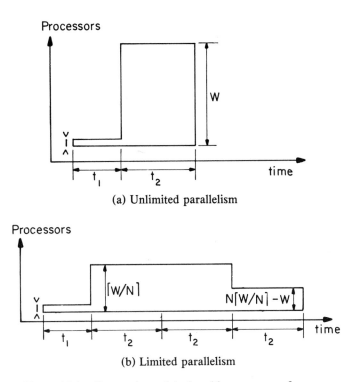

(a) Unlimited parallelism

(b) Limited parallelism

Figure 10.1   Geometric model of multiprocessor performance

we have only N processors ($N < W$), the (time·processor) product has the form of Figure 10.1.b. Processing time has increased by ($\lceil W/N \rceil - 1$) periods of length t_2.

If we had only one processor, the processing time would have been:

$$T_1 = t_1 + Wt_2;$$

with an "infinite" amount of processing power, we would have:

$$T_\infty = t_1 + t_2,$$

and, as shown in Figure 10.1.b, with N processors:

$$T_N = t_1 + \left\lceil \frac{W}{N} \right\rceil t_2.$$

The speed gain is (T_1/T_N), with (T_1/T_∞) an upper bound. We can define a parallelism ratio ρ as:

$$\rho = \frac{(\text{time} \cdot \text{processor}) \text{ showing parallelism}}{\text{total (time} \cdot \text{processor})} = \frac{Wt_2}{t_1 + Wt_2}, \qquad (1)$$

where ρ is independent of N (i.e., of the implementation) and is a measure of the parallelism within the algorithm. An efficiency measure E (discarding bookkeeping, scheduling, etc. ...) can be defined as:

$$E = \frac{\text{total (time} \cdot \text{processor})}{T_N \cdot N} = \frac{t_1 + Wt_2}{N\left(t_1 + \left\lceil \dfrac{W}{N} \right\rceil t_2\right)}. \qquad (2)$$

It shows the rates of useful processor occupancy over total processor occupancy.

We can write:

$$E = \frac{1}{N\left[\dfrac{t_1 + \left\lceil \dfrac{W}{N} \right\rceil t_2}{t_1 + Wt_2}\right]} = \frac{1}{N\left[1 - \left[\dfrac{W - \left\lceil \dfrac{W}{N} \right\rceil}{t_1 + Wt_2}\right] t_2\right]}$$

$$E = \frac{1}{N\left[1 - \left[1 - \dfrac{\left\lceil \dfrac{W}{N} \right\rceil}{W}\right] \rho\right]}$$

If we have no parallelism ($\rho = 0$), then, as expected, $E = (1/N)$. If t_1 is null (full parallelism, $\rho = 1$), then:

$$E = \frac{W}{N \cdot \left\lceil \dfrac{W}{N} \right\rceil}$$

If furthermore $W = kN$, then $E = 1$; if $W \neq kN$, then E is closer to 1 when (W/N) is large.

But, we are mostly interested in the influence of ρ over E. Let us assume $W = N$. Then E becomes:

$$E = \frac{1}{N \left[1 - \left[1 - \frac{1}{N}\right] \rho\right]}.$$

A plot of E vs. ρ with $N = 16$ is shown in Figure 10.2. For $\rho = 0.95$, E is only 0.57, and for $\rho = 0.8$, only a quarter of the attainable efficiency is reached. This leads us to compute ρ as a function of E, or from (3) (we still assume a "best" efficiency case of $W = N$):

$$\rho = \frac{1 - \frac{1}{NE}}{1 - \frac{1}{N}}$$

With $N = 16$, we see that E drops to 0.75 when $\rho = 0.978$ and to 0.5 when $\rho = 0.933$. This shows how the efficiency of parallel processing systems is sensitive to small amounts of imposed sequential code. However, it should be noted that for the same ρ of 0.978 and $E = 0.75$ and under the same assumptions, we have:

$$\frac{T_1}{T_N} = \frac{t_1 + N t_2}{t_1 + t_2} = NE = 12,$$

that is although E is quite degraded, the speed factor is still non-negligible (cf. Exercise 2).

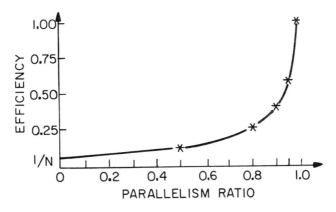

Figure 10.2   Efficiency vs. parallelism ratio ($W = N = 16$)

10.2 PIPELINED AND VECTOR PROCESSORS

10.2.1 Generalities

At the risk of becoming repetitive, let us reiterate the basic concepts of pipelining. Processes running on a pipelined processor are decomposed into a series of sequential subprocesses. Each subprocess is executed on a dedicated facility, called a stage or station. Stations are connected via buffers or latches. The time to execute a subprocess, say t, is the same in all stations; this constraint has to be enforced through a worst case analysis. If there are p stations, then a process (subdivided into at most p subprocesses) will be executed in $p \cdot t$. However, since each station is isolated from its neighbor, successive processes can be overlapped. Therefore k consecutive processes will be executed in $p \cdot t + (k - 1) \cdot t$, delivering a result at every interval t after a set-up time of $(p - 1) \cdot t$.

The pipelining concept can be implemented at several levels depending on the degree of subdivision of processes. In look-ahead processing, the subprocesses are steps of the instruction execution cycle. In the pipelining of an arithmetic function, a subprocess can be one (or more) step of the algorithm. We can distinguish between pipelined functional units dedicated to one algorithm and those that are multifunctional. In the first case, a new set of operands can be input at every interval t while in the latter the pipe may have to be "flushed" between two consecutive and different operations. The functional unit pipelining can be extended so that it caters to vector as well as to scalar operands. Finally, we can even consider the pipelining of software processes, thus extending the concept of coroutine to that of "parallel coroutines".

In the remainder of this section, we shall examine the architecture of computers such as the Amdahl 470 V/6, the CRAY-1, the CDC STAR-100, and the Texas Instruments Advanced Scientific Computer (TI ASC) on which one or more of the levels of pipelining mentioned above can be found. First, we show in general terms what hardware facilities are required to implement these various levels. At the same time, we indicate potential improvements which have been proposed but not yet included in commercial machines. (The reader should also consult Chapter 4 Sections 2 through 4 where look-ahead processing and the organization of the Pc's of the CDC 6600 and IBM System/360 Model 91 are discussed).

Our definition of pipelining imposes that every station performs its operation in the same amount of time. This is often unrealistic. For example, an instruction fetch requiring an Mp cycle will be more time consuming than an instruction decode. To smooth such variations in station time prevalent at the lower level of pipelining, buffering (or look-ahead) has to be used extensively. This was apparent in the design of the IBM System/360 Model 91 (recall Fig. 4. 25). A double buffering of instructions and operands exists in the TI ASC. The CRAY-1 uses an extensive set of back-up registers. An alternative is to provide a fast cache with a very good hit ratio; this is the method chosen by the designers of the Amdahl 470 V/6.

If several pipelines coexist, i.e., if we have systems with multifunctional units like the IBM System 360/91, TI ASC, CDC STAR-100, and CRAY-1, some means to control the concurrent execution of successive instructions are required. A scoreboard method, as in the CDC 6600, or a common databus scheme, as in the IBM 360/91, can be used. A simple interlock scheme allowing overlap between successive operation but no result obtained out of sequence is another possible option (cf. the TI ASC) with the advantage of simplicity at the expense of lower performance. We shall not dwell on the designs of the controllers for parallel execution since we have already looked at them in detail in Chapter 4.

Within a functional unit, the same station can be used several times during the execution of an instruction. An obvious example is the use of the stages of the CSA tree of the multiplier/divider in the IBM System/360 Model 91. But the scheduling of operation initiations is not a trivial matter when looping is allowed and when, in addition, we wish to overlap several instructions. In the method that we present next, we assume that the only control decision is when to initiate a new instruction and that the pipeline is restricted to a single function (this constraint is imposed here only for simplicity; it is known how to schedule multifunctional units). The goal of the scheduling algorithm is to keep a maximal rate of initiations while avoiding collisions (two or more subprocesses attempting to use the same station at the same time). We shall use latency (the interval of time between successive initiations) as a measure of performance instead of throughput rate.

A "looping" pipeline function can be modeled in the manner illustrated by the following example. Consider the pipeline of Fig. 10.3.a. A process running on this pipeline is completed in 6 time units assuming t (the station time) is 1 by passing through the stations:

$S1$ at times 1 and 5,
$S2$ at times 2 and 6,
$S3$ at time 3,
$S4$ at time 4.

This can be displayed in the "reservation table" of Figure 10.3.b where the rows correspond to stations, the columns to time units, and an X in row i, column j, indicates that station i is busy at time j. It is readily seen that a col-

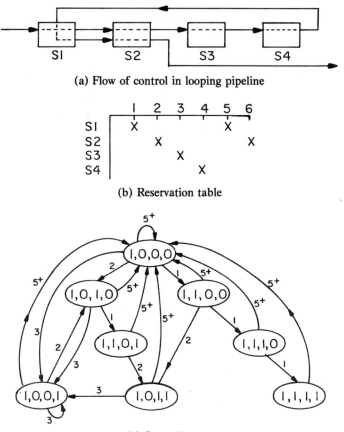

(a) Flow of control in looping pipeline

(b) Reservation table

(c) State diagram

Figure 10.3   Model of a pipeline with internal looping (single function)

lision will occur if two instructions are initiated with a latency equal to the distance between two X's in a given row. From an examination of the reservation table, we can obtain a list of these forbidden latencies (in our example, 4 is the only forbidden latency; it corresponds to collisions in stations $S1$ and $S2$). With these forbidden latencies, we build a collision vector:

$$(c_n, c_{n-1}, \ldots, c_1)$$

where

$$c_i = 1 \quad \text{if } i \text{ is a forbidden latency,}$$
$$c_i = 0 \quad \text{otherwise.}$$

In our example, the collision vector is $(1, 0, 0, 0)$.

The collision vector can be interpreted as meaning that an initiation is allowed at every time unit such that $c_i = 0$. Thus, we can start building a finite state diagram of possible initiations. A state will be a vector $(x_n, x_{n-1}, \ldots, x_1)$ such that x_i is 0 if an initiation is allowed after i time units. The initial state is the collision vector.

In our example, we can have a new initiation at time 1, or at time 2, or at time 3, or evidently at time 5 or more (corresponding to c_{n+1}, c_{n+2}, etc...). It remains to define the new state after an initiation. If this initiation occurred after i units of time, collisions which occurred at time j ($j > i$) will occur now at time ($j - i$). This can be represented by the current state vector shifted i places right with injections of 0 on the left hand side. The initial collisions are still possible and the new state is therefore the union of the previous state, initially the collision vector, shifted right i places where i is the time of the next initiation, with the collision vector. In our example, the state after an initiation at time 1 is:

$$(1, 0, 0, 0) \cup (0, 1, 0, 0) = (1, 1, 0, 0);$$

after an initiation at time 2, it is:

$$(1, 0, 0, 0) \cup (0, 0, 1, 0) = (1, 0, 1, 0);$$

and so on.

From this latter state, we can have a new initiation at either the next time unit, yielding the new state:

$$(1, 0, 0, 0) \cup (0, 1, 0, 1) = (1, 1, 0, 1),$$

or 3 time units later, yielding:

$$(1, 0, 0, 0) \cup (0, 0, 0, 1) = (1, 0, 0, 1).$$

A complete state diagram is shown in Figure 10.3.c where labels on arcs indicate the latency before the next initiation.

From this diagram, we can easily design a controller. The only hardware required is a shift register storing the results of the union operations defined above. Cycles in the diagram indicate all steady-state sequences possible (from these off-line controllers can be designed). Of special interest are those cycles which result in a minimal average latency. In our example, there are two such cycles, namely:

$$(1, 0, 0, 0), (1, 1, 0, 0), (1, 1, 1, 0), (1, 1, 1, 1), \text{ and}$$

$$(1, 0, 1, 0), (1, 1, 0, 1), (1, 0, 1, 1), (1, 0, 0, 1)$$

that each have an average latency of 2. The former corresponds to a "greedy" control, i.e., one in which a subprocess is executed as soon as one is available and allowed to by the control. These cycles are identified in the state diagram by following the smallest labels of outbound arcs. It can be shown, by counter example, that a greedy cycle might yield a non-optimal average latency. However, it is also possible to prove that an upper bound on the "greedy" average latency is one plus the number of non-zero entries in the collision vector (cf. Exercises 3 and 4). To our knowledge, such a controlling scheme has not yet been implemented but it seems worth studying since it can be extended to multifunctional units. In this latter case extraneous delays may have to be included. Practically speaking, all current multifunctional pipeline units are static in the sense that they have to be reconfigured when consecutive operations are of a different type. Dynamic pipes, controlled via microprogramming, have been envisioned.

Pipelining finds its most natural application with vector processing. However, vector processing has associated with it some definite overhead. In order for such processing to be worthwhile, the *set-up time*, or time taken to structure the pipeline and prepare the streams of vector operands, and the *flush time*, or time to empty the pipe at the conclusion of the operations and set the termination conditions, must be small in comparison to the amount of processing. Three of the pipeline processors to be described (STAR-100, TI ASC and CRAY-1) have vector processing capabilities. Although, as we shall see, their treatment of vector operations differ significantly, the basic vector instructions necessarily have to indicate:

- The type of operations to be performed (e.g., floating-point add);
- The beginning address of each vector and the amount by which this address has to be incremented to find the successive elements to be processed.

The alternatives appear when only some of the elements according to some control vector are to be selected, or when special long-registers containing the operand(s) are desired (that is we may wish to have memory-memory,

memory-register, or register-register operations), or when a resulting vector can be routed as an input operand for the next instruction. These options will be examined in more detail with each individual processor.

The presence of vector processing should influence the software to be made available. First, compilers should be able to generate "vector code" but not indiscriminately because of the influence of the set-up and flush times. High-level language constructs such as FOR-loops and DO-loops will provide a first hint for this "vectorization". Better yet, languages like APL which are fundamentally vector-oriented could be used. Second, algorithms have to be changed so that they take advantage of the pipelining. (This second type of optimization will be a recurring theme in this chapter.) For example, lexical analysis of source programs is better handled as a multipass process through the source object. One pass could remove blanks; another find operators; another find matching pairs of parentheses, etc.

To conclude this introductory section, we return to the performance evaluation aspect of pipelining. The geometric model of Figure 10.1, slightly modified, is still applicable. Let L be the number of tasks which can be presented to the pipe without incurring new set-up and flush times; let t_i be the time required by the ith station to process a task and t_j be the bottleneck, i.e., $t_j \geq t_i$, $1 \leq i \leq n$ where n is the number of stations in the pipe. Then the speed up gain is:

$$\frac{T_1}{T_{\text{pipe}}} = \frac{L \sum\limits_{i=1}^{n} t_i}{\sum\limits_{i=1}^{n} t_i + (L-1)t_j}$$

If t_i is the same for all stations, then the speed up becomes:

$$\frac{T_1}{T_{\text{pipe}}} = \frac{nL}{n + L - 1}.$$

This is an ideal condition and, as could be expected, at the limit ($L \to \infty$) we have an n-fold speed-up. We can define the efficiency of the pipeline as:

$$E = \frac{\text{time spent computing}}{\text{time stations are used}} = \frac{L \sum\limits_{i=1}^{n} t_i}{\sum\limits_{i=1}^{n} \left[\sum\limits_{i=1}^{n} t_i + (L-1)t_j \right]}$$

which reduces to $L/(n + L - 1)$ in the ideal situation. For L much larger than n, the efficiency approaches 1.

The latter case with large L corresponds to vector processing. However, the model does not take into account the set-up and flush times. With these two constraints, we can express a vector processing time as:

$$T^v = T^v_{\text{set-up}} + (L - 1)\, t_j^v + T^v_{\text{flush}}.$$

This has to be compared to the execution of L operations in scalar mode in the same pipe which can be expressed as:

$$T^s = T^s_{\text{set-up}} + (L - 1)\, t_j^s.$$

The differences between $T^v_{\text{set-up}}$ and $T^s_{\text{set-up}}$ are in the setting of additional registers for the vector instructions. But these registers will speed-up the operand fetches as well as the computations of their effective addresses so that t_j^v will be smaller than t_j^s. From the above two equations, we deduce that vector processing will be advantageous when:

$$T^v_{\text{set-up}} + (L - 1)\, t_j^v + T^v_{\text{flush}} \leq T^s_{\text{set-up}} + (L - 1)\, t_j^s,$$

or for vector size L such that:

$$L \geq 1 + \frac{T^v_{\text{set-up}} - T^s_{\text{set-up}} + T^v_{\text{flush}}}{t_j^s - t_j^v}.$$

This is shown in graphical form in Figure 10.4. A typical figure for L is 10.

10.2.2   The Amdahl 470 V/6

Pipelining at the lowest level, that is the overlapping of the steps of the instruction cycle execution, is quite extensive in the Amdahl 470 V/6. From the PMS and ISP viewpoints, there are no significant differences between this machine and the IBM System/370. For example, the operating systems for System/370 run without modification on the 470 which can then be considered as a top of the line model of the 370 (and 303X) series.

The 470 V/6 (delivered in 1975) has a basic (minor) cycle time of 32.5 ns. and the 470 V/7 (delivered in 1978) has a 29 ns. cycle time. The former is advertised as delivering 4.6 MOPS (million operations per second), and the latter can perform 7 MOPS. This second figure makes the V/7 1.2 to 1.4 times faster than IBM's 3033. The 10% improvement on the cycle time is not

Processing time

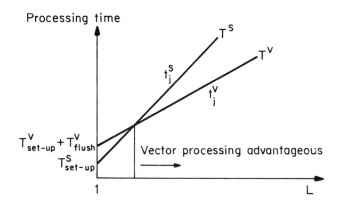

Figure 10.4   Determination of the vector size for scalar vs. vector processing in a pipelined processor

sufficient to explain the speed-up between the two models: a larger cache (32K bytes instead of 16) and a 16-way interleaving factor instead of 4-way might account for much of the improvement. In the following, we will describe succinctly the Pc of the V/6 expanding on the pipelining aspects.

The 470 V/6 central processor consists of 4 units: an I-unit where most of the pipelining is implemented, a D-unit (E-unit in Amdahl's terminology) for manipulating data, an S-unit for the control of the cache and Mp, and a C-unit which executes channel (Pio) commands. The instruction execution cycle is controlled in the I-unit.

The instruction execution cycle is divided into an I-fetch phase and six consecutive phases A to F. Some of these phases are subdivided into several minor cycles according to the following breakdown (we assume a one address + general register scheme and a System/370 RX format, i.e., $R_i \leftarrow R_i$ op. Mp [loc]).

- I—fetch: Cycle 1: Request the S-unit
             Cycle 2: Initiate a cache fetch
             Cycle 3: Instruction is available in the instruction register (assuming a cache hit).
- Phase A (Instruction decode plus reading of general purpose register if ready)
             Cycle 1: Decode
             Cycle 2: Read general-purpose register
- Phase B (Generates operand address using effective address generator; the latter, part of the I-unit, is connected to the

instruction register, the general registers for base and index addressing, and to the S-unit).

Cycle 1: Generate operand address

Cycle 2: Initiate a cache fetch

Cycle 3: Operand is available (assuming a cache hit)

- Phase C (First part of the execution)

  Cycle 1: Pass data to D-unit; start execution; early condition codes can be set in case of branches (note that the target of a branch instruction is prefetched).

- Phase D (Second part of the execution)

  Cycle 1: (and maybe more) Continuation of the D-unit execution.

- Phase E (Check results)

  Cycle 1: Results from the D-unit are checked by the I-unit.

- Phase F (Write results).

  Cycle 1: Final update and write back.

Because errors are checked in phase E and write back occurs in phase F all instructions can be retried. Similarly, interrupts can be handled at every minor cycle since all instructions in progress have not modified any information contained in the process state until phase F. Hence, we have precise interrupts unlike in the IBM System/360 Model 91.

The bottlenecks of this scheme are the slowdowns which appear when the D-unit takes more than one cycle in phase D and when there are cache misses in the I-fetch and phase B. The D-unit accepts new instructions every other minor cycle and can generate results every minor cycle thereafter. It is composed of 4 functional units (multiplier, adder, shifter, and byte mover for single byte arithmetic and logical operations). A logical unit and checker (LUCK) placed before these units can perform some preliminary operations such as operand comparison and condition code settings for most operations (recall phase C). Each functional unit performs its operation in a single cycle but several cycles are necessary for operations that have to be iterated through the functional units (e.g., those involving floating-point operations).

We have described previously (Chapter 6 Section 5) the operations of the S-unit for cache access. It should be noted that a cache address is identified by bits 19–26 of the effective address. Bits 21–26 will not be changed in the virtual-real address translation (pages are 2K bytes). Thus, when a cache fetch is initiated the following actions take place:

- The translation look-aside buffer (TLB) address is determined; this address depends on the segment and page number. At the same time, bits

21-26 of the virtual address are sent to the cache, yielding 4 possible blocks (lines in Amdahl's terminology) of 32-bytes.

- After the virtual address translation is performed, in one cycle if the TLB entry was valid, the "real" bits 19-20 permit the selection of one of the 4 blocks prefetched from the cache. It remains to align the byte(s) which have been demanded. Thus, in the case of a valid TLB entry, there is no overhead incurred in the virtual-real address translation.

It appears that improvements would be difficult to achieve in the S-unit control but that D-unit execution could be speeded up. At any rate, the extensive overlapping and the improved reliability due to the use of LSI chips make the Amdahl 470 V/6 a successful supercomputer if not a typical pipeline processor.

10.2.3 The CRAY-1

The CRAY-1 has been advertised as the most powerful computer of the late 1970's. Some benchmarks indicate that it can perform at rates of over 100 Mflops. When only the scalar functional-units are active, the CRAY-1 is still twice as fast as the CDC 7600. This tremendous speed is achieved by the symbiosis of several factors:

- the possible concurrent activation of 12 tightly-coupled functional units (D-units);
- the pipelining of these D-units;
- the presence of vector processing units among the D-units;
- the "chaining" of results from D-unit to D-unit avoiding references to Mp;
- an extremely fast minor cycle (12.5 ns., or approximately 2½ times faster than the Amdahl 470 V/6).

Although we are mainly interested in the systems architecture of the CRAY-1, we cannot fail to mention that the clock cycle of 12.5 ns. could only be achieved through some amazing technological advances in LSI (only 4 types of chips are used for the entire machine) and in the cooling system. These complimentary remarks are also addressed to the designers of the packaging of the Amdahl 470.

The PMS and ISP structures of the CRAY-1 resemble that of the CDC 6600 and 7600. This is not surprising since S. Cray is the main architect of these 3 machines. (The reader may wish to reread Chapter 4 Section 4 for a description of the CDC 6000 series.) Figure 10.5 shows the division of the system into 3 sections: the computation section, or Pc, the main memory section, or Mp, and the I/O section.

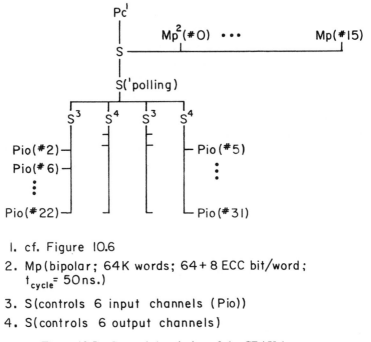

1. cf. Figure 10.6
2. Mp(bipolar; 64K words; 64 + 8 ECC bit/word; t_{cycle} = 50ns.)
3. S(controls 6 input channels (Pio))
4. S(controls 6 output channels)

Figure 10.5　General description of the CRAY-1 system

Most of the following will deal exclusively with the Pc. However, the Mp and I/O sections deserve some comments. The Mp is 16-way interleaved. Each of the 16 "banks" contain 72 modules, each contributing 1 bit to the 64-bit words and to an 8-bit ECC scheme (single error correction, double error detection). A bank can have 64K words yielding a total capacity of 1M words. The bank cycle time is 50 ns., and the access time from Mp to a Pc register is 11 minor cycles, or 137.5 ns. When there is no bank conflict, a word can be transferred to the scalar Pc registers at every other clock period, to the vector registers and the back-up scalar registers at every clock period, and 4 words/clock period can be sent to the instruction buffer.

The I/O section consists of 24 channels, 12 for input and 12 for output, divided into 4 groups. These groups share a common communication link to Mp. Therefore each group is polled every 4 cycles for pending memory requests. When two channels in the same group request Mp at the same polling time, priority is given to the channel with lowest number. This channel is then prevented from requesting Mp at the next polling time, 4 cycles later. In case of a memory bank conflict, scalar instruction requests will have priority over I/O requests. Vector transfers block the access to Mp for the length of the transfer plus 4 cycles.

The Pc structure is shown in Figure 10.6. The 12 pipelined D-units, which can all operate concurrently, are able to receive inputs at every minor cycle. The D-unit times to provide results, i.e., the lengths of the pipelines, are shown in Table 10.1. In this table, as well as in Figure 10.6, the D-units are divided into 4 groups according to the registers that serve as sources and sinks for the instructions. As in the CDC 6600, the D-units operate only on registers.

The CRAY-1 has five sets of operand registers. Three of these sets have direct links to the D-units and two sets are back-up registers. The registers have the following functions:

$A <0:7> <0:23>$ Address registers.

The A registers are used for addressing, indexing, holding shift counts, and for I/O operations.

$B <0:63> <0:23>$ Back-up to A registers.

Transfers between A and B registers take only one minor cycle. As stated earlier, block transfers between B registers and Mp can be pipelined every minor cycle.

$S <0:7> <0:63>$ Scalar registers.

The S registers are scalar accumulators. They are backed up by:

$T <0:63> <0:63>$ Back up to S registers.

Finally, we have:

$V <0:7> <0:63> <0:63>$ Vector registers.

The V registers are blocks of 64 words. Their accessing will be discussed shortly. They provide operands to the vector processing units and to the (scalar) floating-point units.

Instructions can be either short (16 bits) or long (32 bits). The latter are not constrained to be in the same 64-bit word. The 16-bit instruction is a 3-register instruction. The 32-bit instructions are for access to Mp and for immediate operand addressing. Thus, the instruction formats are very similar to those of the CDC 6600.

Instruction issuing and control is reminiscent of the CDC 6600 scoreboard. Four 16-word buffers hold 64 parcels of 16-bits each, that is a total of between 128 and 256 instructions. Loop mode execution is possible both intra and inter-buffer, with a slight time penalty for the latter. In case of a branch

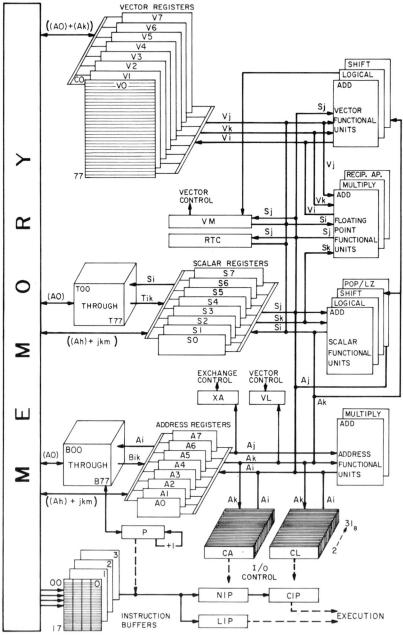

This figure appears courtesy of Cray Research.
Hardware Reference Manual, CRI publication 2240004.

Figure 10.6   CRAY-1's central processor

Table 10.1   Register usage and D-unit timing in the
CRAY-1

D-unit group	D-unit time	Operand registers
Vector		
add	3	V, S (source only)
shift	4	"
logical	2	"
Floating-point		
add	6	V, S
multiply	7	"
reciprocal	14	"
Scalar		
add	3	S
shift	2 or 3	"
logical	1	"
pop. count	3	"
Address		
add	2	A
multiply	6	"

out of the 4 buffers, one of the buffers is loaded from Mp (1 word/bank). The program counter is a 24-bit register (P in Figure 10.6) that indicates which parcel of 16 bits is to be executed next (the high-order 22 bits are the Mp address; the lower two bits indicate the parcel). Programs and data have to be in contiguous locations in Mp with the BA (base address) and LA (limit address) registers used for relocation and protection purposes. The CIP, NIP and LIP registers play the role of the instruction register with a one-parcel look-ahead. Context switching is facilitated by the XA, P and M registers (details can be found in the references). Issuing of an instruction depends on the availability of a D-unit and of registers. An unavailable D-unit is one involved in a vector operation that has not been completed. All others are available at every minor cycle.

The control for vector processing is further simplified by forbidding the concurrent use of input vector registers. Thus, the two vector operations:

$$V1 \leftarrow V2 + V3$$
$$V4 \leftarrow V2 * V5$$

cannot be executed in parallel. (This has to be contrasted with the CDC 6600 operations which would have allowed the parallel operation with X instead of V registers; the reader should be able to provide a simple explanation for this restriction after reading the next paragraphs; see also Exercise 5). The vector instruction above has the form:

$$V_i \leftarrow V_j \text{ op. } V_k$$

It is only one of four possible types. These register-register operations are controlled by the vector length (VL) register. Operands are transmitted from the V_j and V_k registers to the D-unit at every minor cycle and a result is obtained at every minor cycle thereafter, once the pipe has been filled. For example, the time to perform a vector addition on two n-long vectors ($3 \leq n \leq 64$) will be

$$t''_{\text{add}} = (t_{\text{add}} - 1) + n = n + 2 \text{ (cf. Table 10.1)}.$$

A second type of instruction involves a scalar register as source, as in:

$$V_i \leftarrow S_j \text{ op. } V_k$$

Instructions of this type allow the addition of the contents of S_j to all elements of V_k (integer arithmetic is performed in the vector add unit; floating-point arithmetic in the scalar floating-point adder; all floating-point arithmetic is performed in scalar units).

Since D-units accept operands from registers and store results in registers, two more types of instructions are needed for transfers to and from Mp: memory-(V) register and (V) register-memory. During the transfers all other requests to Mp are blocked.

Vector operations such as:

$$V1 \leftarrow V2 * V3$$
$$V4 \leftarrow V1 + V5$$

seem to be prevented from being executed in parallel because of the $V1$ register conflict. The concept of "*chaining*" will (in some cases) circumvent the problem. We can view the above two operations as the replication (n times, $2 \leq n \leq 64$, where n is the length of the vectors involved) of:

$$V1(i) \leftarrow V2(i) * V3(i)$$
$$V4(i) \leftarrow V1(i) + V5(i)$$

But the $(i + 1)$st multiplication and the ith addition can be pipelined, that is the two computations:

$$V1(i + 1) \leftarrow V2(i + 1) * V3(i + 1)$$
$$V4(i) \quad\quad \leftarrow V1(i) * V5(i)$$

can be carried on simultaneously (after the set up times) if the results of the multiplication can be gated directly as one of the inputs to the add unit.

Chaining is performed by having the second instruction attempt to issue as soon as the first D-unit yields a result. At that minor cycle, called "chain slot time" which happens only once for a potential chaining, the second D-unit can issue only if:

- It is free;
- The other one or two register(s) involved are free (or Mp is free if we have a register-memory operation).

If the second D-unit cannot issue, the first instruction will have to be completed before the second one can start. The reasons for having the "chain slot time" be the only possible time where the second D-unit can start are similar to those preventing the concurrent operation of seemingly independent vector instructions (cf. Exercise 5). If the chaining fails at "chain slot time", the common register is "reserved" by the first unit for its entire operation; on the other hand, if chaining succeeds, then the result register of the first operation is reserved for the time to perform the succession of the two operations, namely:

$$t = (t(\text{1st unit}) + t(\text{2nd unit}) - 1) + n$$

(cf. Exercise 6). Chaining can be cascaded to more than two operations.

Since vector registers are 64 elements long, processing of vectors with more than 64 elements will have to be decomposed into "short" loops, such as (for an addition):

> **While** all vectors are not processed **do**
>> **begin** Load (from Mp) the next (initially first) group of 64 elements of the first operand in V_j;
>> Load (from Mp) the next (initially first) group of 64 elements of the second operand in V_k;
>> Compute $V_i \leftarrow V_j + V_k$;
>> Store the next (initially first) group of 64 elements of the result
>> **end**;

Note that the second load and the compute can be chained. The store cannot be chained since Mp is busy reading the second operand.

The advantages of using vector operations instead of scalars are shown in Figure 10.7 for a number of arithmetic functions. We can observe almost immediately that vector operations are advantageous. In Figure 10.8, we show the timings of (square) matrix multiplications for various dimensions. The execution rate is almost constant (above 100 Mflops) for matrices that are larger than 64 × 64.

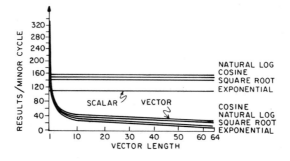

Figure 10.7   Scalar vs. vector processing in the CRAY-1

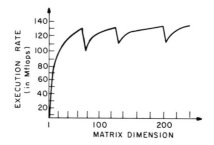

Figure 10.8   Matrix multiplication rates in the CRAY-1

We have not explained yet the role of the Vector Merge (*VM*) register. This 64-bit register is set on a bit by bit basis as the result of an element by element comparison to 0 (equal, unequal, greater than, less than). As its name indicates it can control merging operations. For example, a typical instruction using *VM* is:

If $VM(m) = 0$ transmit $V_j(m)$ to $V_i(m)$
     else   transmit $V_k(m)$ to $V_i(m)$

Although this might help in interchanging values in the inner loop of sorting algorithms, there are no vector operations truly geared to internal sorting. This is one of the weaknesses of the machine.

The unique features of the CRAY-1, parallelism between scalar and vector D-units, chaining, vector and back-up registers, present interesting challenges to compiler writers. The registers can be seen as a programmable cache with advantages such as controlled prefetching and disadvantages such as storing of these registers during context-switching. Several schemes have been proposed to utilize these fast registers as efficiently as possible. One proposed method is:

- Keep local scalars for a given procedure in the B and T registers;
- Keep local arrays, records and long strings in Mp since the B and T registers cannot be indexed;
- Perform all arithmetic expression calculations by loading the A and S registers with source operands and temporaries, and storing the results back in the B and T registers;
- Upon a procedure call, save the local "stack frame" from the B and T registers back into Mp using a "block store"; do a "block load" upon a procedure return;
- Because one cannot "block store" from the A and S registers, these should not contain any part of the procedure's environment.

This scheme can be improved by allowing several procedures to share the B and T registers. This is possible in languages like Pascal where compilation of procedures do not have to be separated.

For a system like CRAY-1, the need for special software is limited to the expression of vector operations and detection of parallelism at the arithmetic expression level. We delay the first topic until we discuss ILLIAC IV (the problems are similar) and the second one has been treated in Chapter 4 Section 3.2.

10.2.4 Two Vector Processors: CDC STAR-100 and TI ASC

While CRAY-1 can be considered as a multifunctional unit look-ahead processor with vector capabilities, both the CDC String-Array-100 (STAR-100) and Texas Instruments' Advanced Scientific Computer (ASC) were designed with mostly vector processing in mind. Estimates of the relative speeds of these 3 systems indicate that in vector mode CRAY-1 has a slight edge and that in scalar mode it outperforms the other two processors by a factor of 2 to 4. This can be due to the architectural design as well as to the advances in technology found in CRAY-1; its minor cycle is from 3 to 5 times faster than its competitors'.

An undetailed PMS description of the STAR-100 is given in Figure 10.9. One feature is worth noticing. A special I/O processor, the maintenance station, is used for error monitoring and performance evaluation. A second feature, not shown at the PMS level, is that the STAR-100 has a paged virtual memory. The virtual address space is 2^{48} bits or 2^{42} 64-bit words. Pages are either 512 words (4Kbytes) the normal size, or 128 times this normal size (the large size). A global true LRU replacement algorithm is used. Its im-

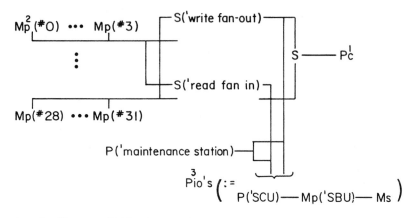

1. cf. Figure 10.10; in the CDC literature, the Pc−Mp complex
   is called central processor

2. Mp(core; 2K superwords; 1 superword = 512 bits; tcycle:
   1.28 ms; transfer rate 1.28/32 = 40 ns.)

3. Pio('some have SBU's, some don't)

Figure 10.9   Simplified PMS description of the CDC STAR-100

plementation is helped by a 16-entry associative memory of 40 ns. search
time; the remainder of the page table, which resides in Mp, is also built
according to the associative mapping concept. Therefore, a single page table
is shared by all users with appropriate mechanisms to ensure the mapping of
virtual pages of same number for different users. Searching in the Mp table
can proceed at the rate of 50 searches/microsecond; the LRU stack is
modified at the same time. The secondary memories are controlled by paging
stations consisting of minicomputers and associated fast core memories.
Prepaging in the form of predictive loading of vectors is available.

A global view of the central processor is shown in Figure 10.10. It consists
of the arithmetic components, the stream unit, and the storage access control
unit which provides the interface with Mp and Pio's. The 3 read and 2 write
buses between the storage access control and the stream units are 128 bit
wide; the connections between the floating-point pipes and the stream unit
are 1 word, or 64-bit, wide while the string unit processes 16-bit entities.

The string unit works on decimal or binary scalar data. The two floating-
point pipes are shown in more detail in Figure 10.11. Each pipe is multifunctional and static, that is, it has to be flushed between instructions of different
types. Pipe 1 can perform pipelined floating-point operations (addition and
multiplication) and address operations (on integers); Pipe 2 has capabilities

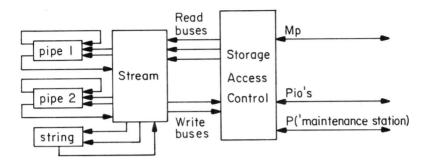

Figure 10.10   CDC STAR-100 central processor

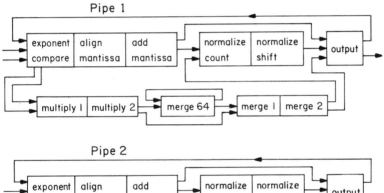

Figure 10.11   Pipelines in the CDC STAR-100

for pipelined floating-point addition, non-pipelined floating-point division, and has a multipurpose unit which can perform floating-point multiplication, division or square root. These units can yield 64-bit results every minor cycle (or 40 ns.). When used in pipe mode the floating-point add pipeline can be split into two 32-bit add pipes, thus doubling the execution rate. The pipes are reconfigured under the control of a microprogrammed control unit. The output of a pipe can be used as one of its own inputs, but not as an input to the other pipe.

The stream unit is the controlling agent for the pipes and the string unit (cf. Figure 10.12). It contains a set of 256 64-bit high-speed registers (40 ns. access time). The instruction buffer can hold 32 64-bit words. Branching is allowed in this look-behind buffer so that the processor can function in loop-mode. Note that the buffer can be filled by a single request to the interleaved Mp. In addition to controlling the arithmetic components, the stream unit initiates all Mp references and provides buffers for operands and results.

The vector operations are not in a register-register format; vector addresses, offsets and increments must be explicitly indicated within a vector instruction. A 64-bit vector instruction, VOP R, M, N $(R \leftarrow M$ op. $N)$, has the form:

$i \langle 0:7 \rangle$ main opcode
$i \langle 8:15 \rangle$ subopcode
$X := i \langle 16:23 \rangle$ register holding the offset for operand M
$A := i \langle 24:31 \rangle$ register holding the base address and field length of M
$Y := i \langle 32:39 \rangle$ register holding the offset for operand N
$B := i \langle 40:47 \rangle$ register holding the base address and field length of N
$Z := i \langle 48:55 \rangle$ register holding the address of the control vector
$C := i \langle 56:63 \rangle$ register holding the address and field length of the result vector; $C + 1$ will hold the offset for control and result vectors

For example, let us assume that A contains 10000 (base address) and 24 (field length), and that X contains 4 (offset). Assume all elements are 64-bit entities. Then, the start address of the first operand M will be its fifth element at address 10004 (decimal) and there will be only 20 elements to be processed. The contents of registers B, C, and Y are encoded similarly. The contents of register Z is a mark indicating which elements of the source operands are to be processed. For example, assuming that in conjunction with the contents of $C + 1$, we find the start bit of the control vector and its 7 successor bits to be:

$$1\ 0\ 0\ 1\ 0\ 0\ 1\ 1$$

only the 5th, 8th, 11th and 12th elements of M will be operated upon since only bits 1, 4, 7 and 8 of the control vector are on (recall the offset of 4 for the M operand).

It should be apparent that the set up time which includes the reading of addresses from the register, the computation of the offsets, start addresses, and field lengths, and the setting of the read/write buses depending on the subopcode is not trivial. Therefore, vectorization will not pay off for small

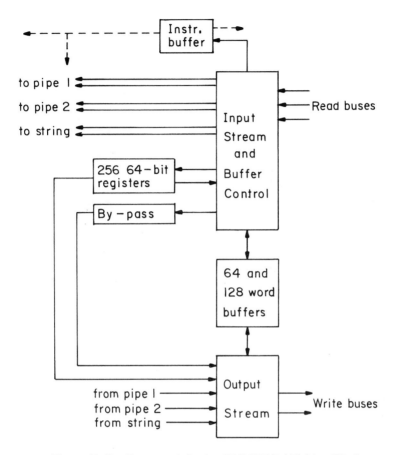

Figure 10.12   Stream unit in the CDC STAR-100 (simplified)

vectors. If we assume that the vector flush time and the scalar set-up time are equal, and this is a fair assumption since it corresponds roughly to a complete operation within all but one stage of the pipe, then the advantageous vector size L can be computed as:

$$L \geq 1 + \frac{t^v_{\text{set-up}}}{t_j^s - t_j^v}.$$

For example, with all times expressed in minor cycle units, we have:

floating-point add: $t^v_{\text{set-up}} = 96$, $t^s = 13$; $t^v = .5$ (splitting pipe) yielding $L \geq 8$;

floating-point multiply: $t^v{}_{\text{set-up}} = 156$, $t^s = 17$; $t^v = 1$, yielding $L \geq 10$; square root: $t^v{}_{\text{set-up}} = 152$, $t^s = 73$, $t^v = 2$, yielding $L \geq 3$.

It is easy to see that under the above assumption, the speed-up due to vectorization is linear with the size of the vector for a given operation. In reality this speed-up is even more important for long vectors, when memory loads and stores are included, since the scalar operations might not know how to take advantage of the interleaving features as well as the vector operations.

The STAR-100 has a large vector instruction set. In addition, to the 3 operand instructions whose format has just been outlined, there exist vector macro instructions and sparse vector instructions. The macro instructions allow the coding of APL-like statements such as the count of non-zero elements in a vector or finding the index i for which $A_i > B_i$ and all $A_j \leq B_j$, $0 \leq j < i$. This latter condition can be used in conjunction with marking from the control vector so that, in another pass, the second such element can be found and so on. As another example, a control vector with 1 bits for each occurrence of $A_i > B_i$ and 0 otherwise can be created with the macro instruction set. The sparse vector instruction set is useful for compressing vectors with a large number of zero values. The sparse vector and a control vector used as a bit map give all the information necessary with a potential great amount of saving in storage space.

As an application, consider how the core of a QUICKSORT procedure could be coded in vector form. This procedure has the following specifications.

Input: An unsorted vector of M elements, $X[1]$ to $X[M]$;
Output: An unsorted vector of M elements such that the value of $X[1]$ has been moved to $X[I]$ and

$$X[J] < X[I] \qquad 1 \leq J < I$$
$$X[K] \geq X[I] \qquad I \leq K \leq M.$$

The algorithm to perform this transformation is immediate if we use scalar mode. Using vector mode efficiently requires that we scan the vector, maybe more than once, in a uniform manner, that is with indices monotonically modified. This can be realized (following Stone) as follows:

1. Compare all elements of X with $X[1]$ and set a Boolean vector Z with $Z[i] = 0$ if $X[1] < X[I]$ and $Z[i] = 1$ otherwise;
2. Using Z as a control vector, copy all elements $X[i]$ such that $Z[i] = 1$ in a temporary vector $Y[i]$ (i.e., compress X into Y with mask Z; note that $X[1]$ becomes $Z[1]$);

3. Using the complement of Z as a control vector, compress X in place;

4. Count the number of one's in Z; this will give the number of elements in Y and the index I ($I = M -$ count $+ 1$);

5. Move (copy) the elements of Y in $X[I]$ to $X[M]$.

The serial and vector mode realization of QUICKSORT have an average time complexity of $O(M \log M)$. Hand-coded versions of the algorithms have been analyzed and show that for M of the order of 1000, the vector solution runs 10 times faster.

The macro and sparse instruction sets are certainly a factor in favor of the STAR-100. Their implementation is helped by the control vector scheme which is absent from the CRAY-1 architecture. However, there is no chaining and no register-register operation in STAR-100. The third pipeline processor that we present, the TI ASC, is closer to the STAR-100 than to CRAY-1.

As for the other two vector processors, our emphasis in describing the ASC will be on the central processor. The PMS description of Figure 10.13.a points out some other interesting features, namely the cross-bar arrangement between the 8-way interleaved Mp and the eight processor ports. Four of these ports are for the Pc, three for the specialized channels, and the last one for the processor handling the operating system. This special processor, depicted in more detail in Figure 10.13.b, has an architecture reminiscent of the peripheral processors of the CDC 6600. It consists principally of eight "virtual processors" (VP). Each VP has its own program counter and internal registers. The VP's share a ROM, for often executed portions of code, an ALU, an I-unit and buffers to communicate with Mp. They can address a set of 64 communication registers which are mostly holding static information relative to the whole system. A VP accesses the shared resources on a time-multiplexed basis. Every 85 ns., a new VP has control. The sequence of control has a period of 16 85 ns. cycles. The eight VP's can be distributed equally, giving them two accesses per period, or one or more of the VP's can be favored by letting them have more than two accesses per period. The distribution of accesses can be varied dynamically. A typical VP instruction requires two accesses.

The central processor is shown in Figure 10.14. It consists of an I-unit preparing instructions for from one to four homogeneous pipes. Each of these pipes is connected to a buffer which communicates through a dedicated port with Mp. In the case of a four-pipe Pc, we need five of the eight available ports to communicate with Mp. This situation imposes the use of memory port expanders; for example, one of them could be shared by the tape channel and the data concentrator. The I-unit is itself pipelined in four stages: in-

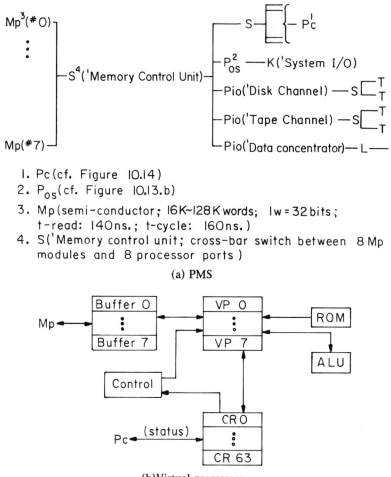

1. Pc (cf. Figure 10.14)
2. P_{os} (cf. Figure 10.13.b)
3. Mp (semi-conductor; 16K~128K words; lw = 32 bits; t-read: 140ns.; t-cycle: 160ns.)
4. S ('Memory control unit; cross-bar switch between 8 Mp modules and 8 processor ports)

(a) PMS

(b) Virtual processors

Figure 10.13 The TI ASC

struction fetch, decode, effective address calculation, and register operand fetch (this is slightly simplified). The I-unit has a dedicated port to the memory control unit. Two 8-word (1 word = 32 bits) buffers are used for instruction look-ahead.

The memory buffer unit (MBU) has three double buffers of eight words: two for input (X and Y) and one for output (Z). Double buffering permits a high rate of communication with Mp (all requests are for eight words). The Z buffer can be transferred directly to the X or Y buffer of the same MBU.

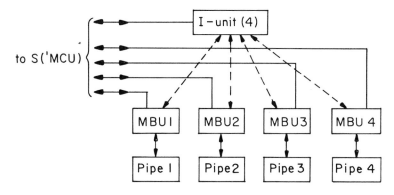

Figure 10.14   A four-pipe TI ASC central processor

A homogeneous pipe is shown in Figure 10.15. It consists of 8 stages. Thus, with the 4-stage I-unit, a single pipe ASC can have 12 instructions in execution at one time. With four pipes, this number becomes $4 + 4 \cdot 8 = 36$. The minor cycle time is 60 ns. (The ASC was started in 1966 and became operational in 1972, hence this rather slow minor cycle.) In Figure 10.15.a we show the paths that would be taken by a floating-point add (on the left) and a fixed-point multiply (on the right). We have assumed 32-bit quantities. The reader can observe that in the case of the multiplication, the path is: input-multiply-add-output. The reason for the add stage is that, in reality, the multiply is performed by a Wallace tree of carry save adders (recall Chapter 3 Section 3) and that the output of that stage is a pseudo-carry and a pseudo-sum (the accumulator stage performs the same function). Although the accumulate stage is not used in these two operations, its presence is mandatory for an implementation of a "Vector dot product" in an efficient manner. This latter condition was one of the primary design specifications. The pipeline path for the vector dot operation is shown in Figure 10.15.b for the case of floating-point elements. The output of the normalizer has to be fed back to the exponent subtract for the alignment and addition of partial products. Thus in steady-state, four products are accumulated in an overlap fashion. The reconfiguration of the pipe is controlled with a microprogrammed control unit with a $512 \cdot 256$ ROM (i.e., highly horizontal).

The Pc's instruction set includes both scalar and vector instructions. The instruction size is one word and operands are either 16, 32 or 64 bits. The I-unit has 48 32-bit internal registers: 16 for base-addressing, 16 accumulators, 8 for index addressing and 8 for vector parameter registers. These last 8, forming the vector parameter file (VPF), are extremely useful. They allow the compilation of a doubly nested loop such as:

> **for** $I := 1$ **step** 1 **until** 3 **do**
> **for** $J := 1$ **step** 1 **until** 5 **do**
> $X[I, J] := Y[I, J] +$
> $K;$

into a single vector add with appropriate settings of the VPF.

To see how this is done, we consider first the instruction format. Its ISP description is:

$i \langle 0:31 \rangle$ instruction

opcode$:= i \langle 0:7 \rangle$

Register$:= i \langle 8:11 \rangle$ Accumulator or C-D registers

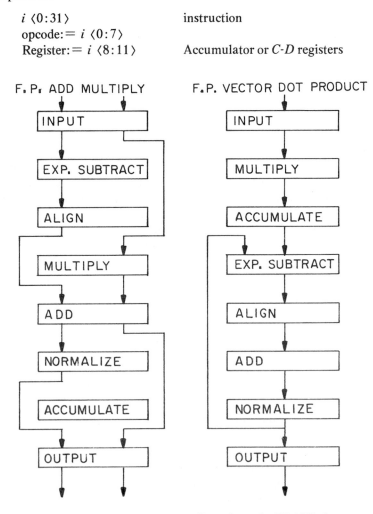

F.P. ADD MULTIPLY

INPUT
EXP. SUBTRACT
ALIGN
MULTIPLY
ADD
NORMALIZE
ACCUMULATE
OUTPUT

F.P. VECTOR DOT PRODUCT

INPUT
MULTIPLY
ACCUMULATE
EXP. SUBTRACT
ALIGN
ADD
NORMALIZE
OUTPUT

Figure 10.15   Three sample configurations of a TI ASC pipe

Index:$= i \langle 12:15 \rangle$ Index or I registers
Base:$= i \langle 16:19 \rangle$ Base of A-B registers
Displacement:$= i \langle 20:31 \rangle$

The effective address is then:

$$EA := \text{Displacement} + I[\text{Index}] + A - B[\text{Base}].$$

In the case of a vector-vector instruction, this effective address does not indicate an operand but the address of where to find the contents of the VPF (the loading of the VPF can be avoided if the previous contents are those needed). The 8 registers of the VPF contain respectively:

Register 1:   The opcode, type (single or double dimension), and length of the vectors considered (all vectors must have the same length).

Register 2-4:   For each operand, the base address and the index register containing the offset.

Register 5-6:   The increment for each operand and the number of iterations for the inner loop (the increment can be 0, i.e., we can have a scalar as one of the operands).

Register 7-8:   As Registers 5-6 for the outer loop.

The loading of the VPF is part of the set-up time for a vector instruction. The VPF scheme allows the processing of two dimensional vectors and variable vector increments, two features not found in the other two pipeline processors presented previously.

The reader interested in further studies of pipeline processors should consult the bibliography as well as the manufacturers machine reference manuals.

10.3   ARRAY PROCESSORS (SIMD)

10.3.1   ILLIAC IV

We defined the Single Instruction Multiple Data (SIMD) organization at the beginning of this chapter. Rather than dealing in generalities, we illustrate this type of architecture with ILLIAC IV, its most renown representative.

The ILLIAC IV project was started in 1966, under the direction of D. Slotnick, as a joint venture between the University of Illinois and Burroughs under a contract to the Department of Defense's ARPA. The system is currently in operation at NASA Ames Research Center. Its size is one-fourth of what had been planned originally. Because ILLIAC IV is not meant to be used in scalar mode, the basic software (operating system, compilers, assembler) resides in a satellite computer. Communications with the outside world, e.g., ARPANET, are handled by a "central system" (cf. Figure 10.16). With this terminology, ILLIAC IV can be considered as a very expensive and powerful special attachment. The readers who find this view to be too restrictive should nonetheless acknowledge the special-purpose function of the ILLIAC IV.

In terms of raw performance, ILLIAC IV can be from 2 to 4 times faster than the CDC 7600, that is significantly slower than the vector processors discussed previously (only vector mode comparisons are relevant). But we should remember that ILLIAC IV does not use as advanced a technology as the pipeline processors (e.g., its Mp cycle is 5 times slower although ILLIAC IV was the first computer to use uniquely semi-conductor memories).

A block diagram of the ILLIAC IV is shown in Figure 10.17 (a PMS description is not interesting for this architecture). A brief outline of the system is as follows. The 64 processing elements (PE) have the capabilities of a standard multipurpose D-unit. They operate synchronously under the control of the control unit (CU) which itself can be considered as an I-unit with look-ahead features. Each PE has an associated 2K-word (1 word = 64 bits) memory. Not shown on the figure are the memory control units which interface the memory modules (ME) to the control unit and to the I/O system. There are three main paths of communication in the internal structure of ILLIAC IV (we shall not deal with the disk and the "central" systems): the unidirectional link between the CU and the PE's broadcasts operands, sends parts of the effective address and enables/disables some of the PE's; the

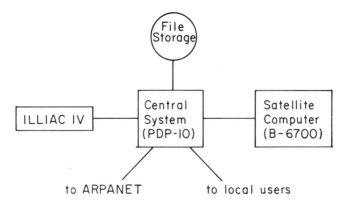

Figure 10.16   The ILLIAC IV system at NASA Ames

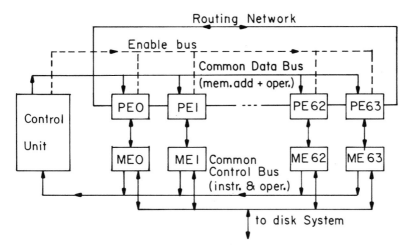

Figure 10.17 ILLIAC IV system

unidirectional link between the ME's and the CU sends instructions and operands; and finally the routing network permits transfers of information between PE's.

We return to each component of the ILLIAC IV in more detail, starting with the control unit. In addition to its conventional role as an I-unit, that is the fetching and decoding of the instructions, and the generation of commands to the D-units (here the PE's), it generates and broadcasts memory addresses and constants to the PE's, and communicates with the central system for traps and I/O interrupts. All flow of control decisions are taken in the CU. Therefore, the instruction set of the ILLIAC IV consists of a CU set and a PE set.

The CU has three components: local storage, processing unit (called Advanced Instruction Station, ADVAST), and PE communication. The local storage contains an instruction look-ahead buffer of 64 words (128 32-bit instructions), a 64-word data buffer, the program counter and the instruction register. The instruction register and four local accumulators are connected to an address adder; these four 64-bit accumulators can also be operands of an ALU whose other inputs may be taken from the data buffer or from a 64-bit vector made of one of the 8 mode bits from each of the PE's (this will be explained later). The ALU is limited to operations such as addition, subtraction and Boolean operations. The outputs of the ADVAST (i.e., the address adder, the four accumulators and the ALU) are memory addresses and data operands which are stored in a final queue register (FINQ) for broadcast to the PE's. A final instruction station holds the PE instruction to be executed and controls the broadcast from FINQ.

The loading of the instruction look-ahead buffer is interesting. Since the CU has no Mp, the programs are stored in the ME's (in an interleaved fashion). When the program counter is halfway through a block of 8 words of instruction, the next block is prefetched from eight consecutive ME's (unless it is already in the buffer). When the block arrives, it replaces the oldest one as in a circular queue. An associative memory connected to the instruction buffer takes care of the sequencing of instructions within the buffer. With respect to the data buffer, either one word or eight words can be fetched from one or eight ME's.

The PE's have a structure similar to conventional Pc's with a microprogrammed control unit receiving orders from the CU. The main registers of an individual PE are:

$A \langle 0:63 \rangle$ Accumulator (input and output of adder)
$B \langle 0:63 \rangle$ Second operand; communicates most directly with external data
$C \langle 0:63 \rangle$ Carry register
$R \langle 0:63 \rangle$ Routing register for communication with other PE's
$S \langle 0:63 \rangle$ Temporary storage
$M \langle 0:7 \rangle$ Mode register (see below)
$X \langle 0:15 \rangle$ Index register

The 8-bit mode register contains flip-flops to enable/disable the operation of the PE for the next instruction, to store faults (overflow, underflow), and to hold test conditions temporarily.

The index register is used for the computation of the effective address:

$$EA = A + \mathrm{CAR}(j) + X,$$

which is the sum of a 24-bit base address found in the instruction (A), the contents of one of the four 64-bit accumulators ($\mathrm{CAR}(j)$) and of the local index register X. $A + \mathrm{CAR}(j)$ is broadcast to all enabled PE's and in each PE a 16-bit address adder is used to form EA. One of the outputs of this adder is the associated ME's Memory Address Register.

The PE's can function in either 64-bit or 32-bit floating-point format, or in 64-bit or 8-bit unsigned word format. Addition is performed in a 3-stage CLA, multiplication in a CSA Wallace tree of four levels with the multiplier decoded 8-bits at a time. A synchronous shifting unit is present. Floating-point addition takes 350 ns. and multiplication 450 ns. A CU instruction can be performed during a PE operation. This overlap can provide substantial time savings.

In an array processor like ILLIAC IV, where each PE has its own memory and where there is no shared primary memory, a means of communication between processors is required. Although it could be argued that processes could exchange messages through the CU, this is unrealistic since it would destroy all attempts at parallelism (only one processor at a time could send a message!). Therefore, a switching, or routing, network between PE's is mandatory. In the ILLIAC IV, each PE can communicate directly with four "neighbors", i.e., processing element i is wired to processors $i - 1$, $i + 1$, $i - 8$, $i + 8$ where the PE's are numbered modulo 64. The routing network can therefore be visualized as a torus (cf. Figure 10.18; there exist other interconnection schemes which will be reviewed in the next section). To transfer a word from processor i to processor j ($j \neq i$), a sequence of one to seven one-step routings is taken; the number of steps depend on the respective values of i and j (cf. Exercise 7). However, simulation and actual programs have shown that routings of one step are most common and routings of over two steps are very rare. This is because many algorithms use either cyclic interconnections (processor i requires values computed by processors ($i + 1$) or ($i - 1$), or both) or four-point iterations (e.g., solution of 2-dimensional field problems via finite differences approximations of partial differential equations) where each point on the grid needs the values computed at adjacent points. Note that in some sense ILLIAC IV is restrictive since 3-dimensional problems require at least six-point iterations.

It should be apparent to the reader that programming ILLIAC IV to obtain efficient code is not a simple matter. Algorithms must be developed to keep the 64 PE's busy as often as possible, with the enormous constraint that the PE's must perform the same instructions at the same time. To achieve such a goal, algorithms tailored to the architecture must be designed, data structures which can be accessed with a minimal amount of routing between processors must be specified, and, maybe as a less important feature, programmers and analysts should be provided with high-level language procedural and declarative statements which reflect the ILLIAC IV environment.

We consider two examples which will give a good idea of the problems facing ILLIAC IV users. The first one is to sum the elements of a vector as in the final phase of a dot product computation. To simplify, we assume that the vector X has 64 elements and that x_i is in the A register of PE i. A log-sum process can be programmed by routing half of the elements to neighbors and add (with only 32 processors being busy), then route half of these results

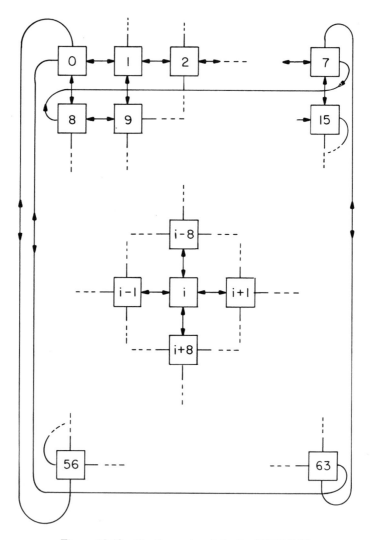

Figure 10.18   Routing network in the ILLIAC IV

again (only 16 processors busy) and add etc., until a unique result is obtained. It is easy to verify that the efficiency of this process, in the sense of the first section of this chapter, is going to be dismal. However, in the same amount of time the same computation can be performed and the final result be present in all 64 PE's. This will save some time if the result has to be used subsequently by all processors and, at any rate, does not cost anymore. The computation of the sum with the final result available to all processors is shown in Figure 10.19 along with the necessary number of adds ($\log_2 64$) and one-step routings.

As a second example, we consider the accessing of arrays. Consider first a 64×64 matrix multiplication:

$$C \leftarrow A \times B$$

where the main body of the procedure after the initialization of C to 0 is:

for $i := 1$ **step** 1 **until** 64 **do**
for $j := 1$ **step** 1 **until** 64 **do**
for $k := 1$ **step** 1 **until** 64 **do**
$C[i, j] := C[i, j] + A[i, k] * B[k, j];$

Let us assume first that we have what has been called straight storage, that is

	Number of add	Number of one-step routings
Initialization: $A_i = x_i$		
Route one left and add ($A_i = x_i + x_{i+1}$)	1	1
Route two left and add ($A_i = \sum_{i}^{(i+3)\bmod 64} x_i$)	1	2
Route four left and add ($A_i = \sum_{i}^{(i+7)\bmod 64} x_i$)	1	4
Route eight left and add ($A_i = \sum_{i}^{(i+15)\bmod 64} x_i$)	1	1
Route 16 left and add ($A_i = \sum_{i}^{(i+31)\bmod 64} x_i$)	1	2
Route 32 left and add ($A_i = \sum_{i}^{(i+63)\bmod 64} x_i$)	1	4
	6 ($\log_2 64$)	14

Figure 10.19   Accumulation in ILLIAC IV

each matrix has the elements of its rows interleaved on each ME (cf. Figure 10.20.a). Then the above procedure would require the instructions shown in Figure 10.20.b.

We can see that this process has to be repeated 64^2 times. The bottleneck resides in the first two instructions where only one PE at a time is active. This can be speeded up by loading eight PE's at a time and using an 8-word broadcast to the CU. Even more optimization can be performed by overlapping broadcast to the CU with PE operations which can proceed in parallel (a better than two-to-one speed-up has been obtained on some programs by a judicious use of this overlap).

However, another representation of the matrix, called skewed storage, can

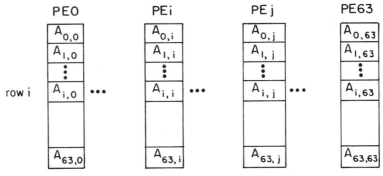

(a) Straight storage of a 64 × 64 matrix

```
Repeat i = 0,63
Repeat k = 0,63
   Load A_{i,k} from PEk
   Transfer in CU
   Broadcast to all PE's (e.g., in Accumulator A)
   Load PEn with B_{k,n}(in parallel for n=0,···,63; e.g., in acc. B)
   A ← A.B (e.g., in PEn we have A ← A_{i,k} · B_{k,n} )
   Load PEn with (accumulated) C_{i,n} (in parallel for n=0,···,63)
   A ← A+B (i.e., accumulate C_{i,n})
   Store in C_{i,n}(in parallel n=0,···, 63)
```

(b) Matrix multiplication with straight storage

Figure 10.20   Example of the use of straight storage in ILLIAC IV

be used (cf. Figure 10.21.a). Now, column elements are also interleaved in the ME's. As can be seen from the figure, all elements of row i can be accessed by indexing the base address with i, while elements of column j require the index $(i - j)$ mod 64 in PE i. In a 64×64 matrix multiplication, the skewed storage does not seem to present any advantage. The broadcasting is replaced by a log-sum process as shown in Figure 10.21.b. But if the dimensions are larger, only one log-sum process is necessary since we can first accumulate the partial products:

$$A[i, k] \cdot B[k, j] \text{ for } k, k + 64 \ldots, k + m \cdot 64$$

in ME i and perform a unique log-sum process per resulting element at the end. Therefore, the process is speeded up by some factor proportional to the logarithm of the number of processors and not to the dimension of the matrix (the 64×64 example is unfortunate in this respect). The reader is encouraged to work out Exercise 8 in order to obtain more insight into the tradeoff between straight and skewed storage.

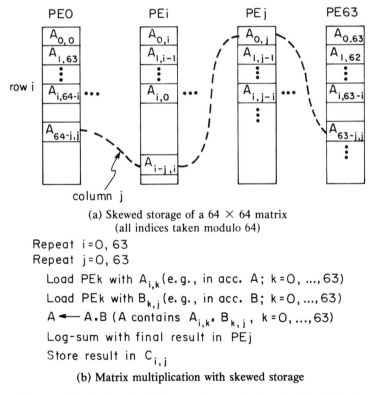

(a) Skewed storage of a 64×64 matrix
(all indices taken modulo 64)

Repeat i=0, 63
Repeat j=0, 63

    Load PEk with $A_{i,k}$ (e. g., in acc. A; k=0, ...,63)

    Load PEk with $B_{k,j}$ (e. g., in acc. B; k=0, ...,63)

    A ⟵ A.B (A contains $A_{i,k} \cdot B_{k,j}$, k=0, ...,63)

    Log-sum with final result in PEj

    Store result in $C_{i,j}$

(b) Matrix multiplication with skewed storage

Figure 10.21   Example of the use of skewed storage in ILLIAC IV

order to obtain more insight into the tradeoff between straight and skewed storage.

The last question we raised was relative to the availability of high-level languages tailored to ILLIAC IV. A number of such languages have been proposed and the two that are most used are GLYPNIR (an ALGOL-based language) and CFD (FORTRAN-based). In GLYPNIR, there exist statements which facilitate the control of parallel executions. Variables can be declared to be CU variables (one word, or a vector of given dimension), or PE variables (one sword or 64 words one in each ME, or a vector of swords). For example:

> PE $A[100]$,

is actually a two-dimensional 64 $\times$ 100 array.

In CFD, we can have array statements such as:

$$A(*) = B(*) + C(*, j)$$

which sums the vector B and the jth column of C and stores the result in the vector A. In both languages Boolean vectors can represent the enable/disable flip-flops of the PE's. An interesting peculiarity is the implementation of "**go to**" (either implicit or explicit). Consider the following statement:

"**If** Boolean expression **then go to** here **else go to** there" which is executed by all PE's simultaneously. Some of the PE's will return a "true" value for the Boolean expression while the others will return a "false" value. But, because of the synchronous control, some PE's cannot start executing at "here" while the remainder start at "there". To circumvent this problem, the semantics of the statement are:

> **If** any PE returns a true value for the Boolean expression
> **then all** PE's **go to** here
> **else all go to** there;

The same philosophy is applied to other control statements.

Finally, we should mention that there exist automated methods to transform FORTRAN DO-loops into a form amenable to efficient ILLIAC IV processing. We shall discuss some of these methods in Section 4.3.

10.3.2   Interconnection Networks (SIMD)

As previously indicated, each ILLIAC IV processing element can communicate with four neighbors. The connection pattern allows processor i to route data to processors $i \pm 1$ and $i \pm \sqrt{N}$, where N is the number of processors. Many other connection schemes have been proposed, and some implemented, which are less restrictive than ILLIAC IV's. In this section, we give only a brief summary of this highly technical issue which continues to attract a sizeable degree of research. The interested reader should consult the bibliography at the end of the chapter.

We restrict ourselves to interprocessor connections. (The discussion of the Pc − Mp switch in an MIMD environment is delayed until next section). We assume that each processor has its own private primary memory. The role of the network is to allow the transfer of data, in a single operation, from processor i ($i = 0, 1, \ldots, n − 1$) to processor j ($j = 0, 1, \ldots, n − 1$) according to some mapping $j = f(i)$ with all processors being active. If this function is such that it can perform all possible one-to-one mappings from inputs to outputs, we have a *permutation* network. If we have one-to-many mappings of inputs to outputs, we have a *broadcast* network (if only a subset of the outputs can be reached then we have a *selective broadcast* network). As we shall see, permutation networks are expensive. Often only a subset of the connections will be wired in. In this case, there are two metrics of importance:

- the number of switches needed in the connection network;
- the time it takes to perform a given mapping (i.e., we might need several iterations through the network before realizing the intended transfers).

For example, in ILLIAC IV the number of switches is $O(n)$ (four per processor). The time to perform a mapping is more difficult to assess because some mappings are "impossible" according to our present conventions. To understand this last point, consider this very simple transfer: we want the even $(2k)$ and odd $(2k + 1)$ processors to exchange their contents. The permutation is:

$$(0, 1, 2, \ldots, 2k, 2k + 1, \ldots) \rightarrow (1, 0, 3, \ldots, 2k + 1, 2k, \ldots).$$

Masking and temporary storage are required so that a program like the following can be executed.

1. Mask (disable) even processors;
2. Store contents of accumulator in temporary storage T_i (for processors i, i odd);
3. Mask odd processors for the next two steps;
4. Transfer accumulator to routing register (only in even processors);
5. Transfer routing register to accumulator of processor $(i + 1)$;
6. Mask even processors for the next two steps;
7. Load routing register from T_i (recall i is odd);
8. Transfer the routing register to the accumulator of processor $(i − 1)$.

In the examples of connection networks to follow, we shall first consider that there is no masking and no possibility of temporary storage.

In order to build a permutation network, an immediate solution is to have a cross-bar switch from any processor to all other processors. It is well known that this complete connectivity requires $n \cdot (n - 1)/2$ or $O(n^2)$ links, or n^2 switches if we allow processor i to connect to itself. It is therefore very expensive and impractical for large n. It is not only impractical but also wasteful since the number of links needed to realize a permutation network is smaller than $O(n^2)$. This can be shown as follows. A cross-bar switch can map all permutations of inputs to outputs. There are $n!$ such permutations. The Stirling approximation to $n!$ is:

$$n! \simeq \sqrt{2\Pi n}\left(\frac{n}{e}\right)^n.$$

On the other hand, with n^2 switches, we can encode 2^{n^2} states. Since:

$2^{n^2} >> n!$ (easily verified from the above approximation)

a cross-bar switch is unnecessarily powerful. What is needed is a device with $O(\log n!)$ devices, or approximately $O(\log (\sqrt{2\Pi n}\ (n/e)^n)) = O(n \log n)$.

At first glance, it looks like the transfer of data with a cross-bar switch needs a single unit of "time" since we have direct connections between each processor. However, if the decoding time necessary to set up the connection is counted, we have an $O(\log n)$ process. This can be considered as a set-up time which can be discarded if transfers are lengthy but which is of great importance if connections are to be changed often. In the following, we succinctly describe networks with less than $O(n^2)$ switches. (We shall assume that n is a power of 2.)

Interconnection networks of the SIMD type derive from telephone switching networks. In this latter application, it is mandatory to have a permutation network, that is each customer must be able to talk to any other customer. However, since the communications are long, a short set-up time is not required. The network can be "rearranged" for every mapping. A rearrangeable network can be built by connecting together 2×2 cross-bar switches. Then, the following property can be proved:

- A permutation network for n processors requires at most $2 \log n - 1$ (2×2) cross-bar switches stages, where each stage has $n/2$ components.

Therefore, we have $(n/2)$ $(2 \log n - 1)$ components $(O(n \log n))$ for a mapping time of O(log n). But we have to set the 2×2 cross-bar switches; the best known algorithm requires O(n log n) time to do so. An 8×8 re-arrangeable network before set-up is shown in Figure 10.22.a; Figure 10.22.b shows the setting of the cross-bar switches to perform the permutation:

$$(0, 1, 2, 3, 4, 5, 6, 7) \rightarrow (0, 2, 4, 6, 7, 5, 3, 1)$$

(Note the $(8/2) \cdot (2 \cdot 3 - 1) = 20$ cross-bar switches and the $(2 \cdot 3 - 1) = 5$ stages for the mapping).

In computer applications the O(n log n) set-up time is unbearable. But often a complete permutation network is not necessary. A good compromise is to have an extensive subset of all possible connections which require little set-up time and perform transfers in a reasonable amount of time. Many such networks are based on the perfect shuffle which, itself, derives from merge and sort networks proposed by Batcher.

Let us look first at merging networks. We wish to merge two sorted lists $(a_1, a_2, \ldots, a_n)$ and $(b_1, b_2, \ldots, b_n)$. If $n = 1$, we have a single comparator. For $n = 2$ the reader can convince himself that the network of Figure 10.23.a will give the right answer. For larger n, we decompose our problem into series of 2×2 merges. The odd-indexed of each list are paired as input to an odd-merge network and the even-indexed to a similar even-merge. The ith output of the even merge e_i is compared with the $(i + 1)$st output of the odd merge d_{i+1} to form the $(2i)$th c_{2i} and $(2i + 1)$th c_{2i+1} final outputs. Figure 10.23.b illustrates the concept and Figure 10.23.c shows a 4×4 odd-even merge network applied to an example. (The proof that this yields a sorted output list is not as trivial as it appears and can be found in Batcher's original paper.) It can be shown that the network needs O(n log n) comparators for a merging time of O(log n), and naturally there is no set-up time.

Given the possibility of merging sorted lists, a sorting network can be built by taking an n-element unordered list and building sequences of 2, then 4, 8, $\ldots, n/2$ ordered lists which are finally merged. A 4 element sorting network is shown in block diagram form in Figure 10.24. An n-element sorting network built along these lines will require O(n log^2 n) comparators for an O(log^2 n) sorting time.

Batcher sorting networks can be considered as a collection of 2×2 switches interconnected by a series of stages built according to a (perfect) shuffle pattern and its inverse, since links can be bidirectional. The *perfect shuffle* interconnection, which takes its name from the shuffling of a card deck, connects processor i to processor j whose address is derived from that of i by a circular shift of one position to the left in the binary representation

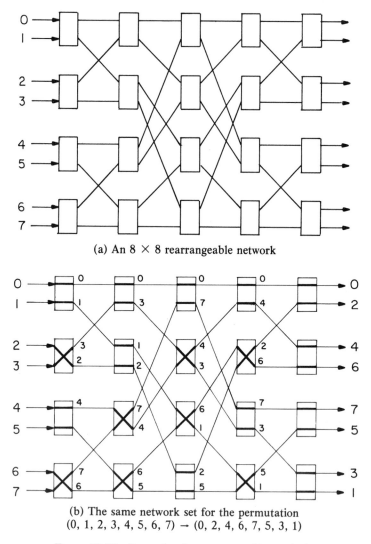

(a) An 8 × 8 rearrangeable network

(b) The same network set for the permutation
(0, 1, 2, 3, 4, 5, 6, 7) → (0, 2, 4, 6, 7, 5, 3, 1)

Figure 10.22   Example of a rearrangeable network

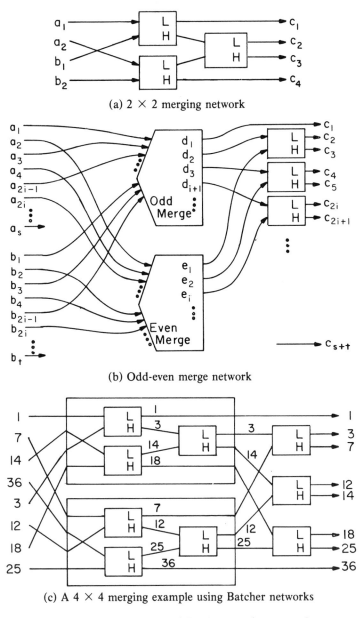

(a) 2 × 2 merging network

(b) Odd-even merge network

(c) A 4 × 4 merging example using Batcher networks

Figure 10.23   Examples of Batcher merging networks

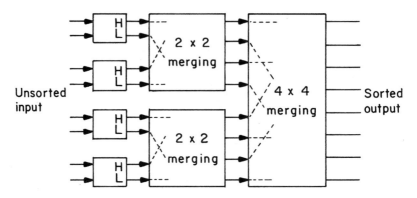

Figure 10.24   Schematic view of a Batcher sorting network

of i (we assume that processors are numbered 0 through ($n - 1$)). An 8 processor shuffle is shown in Figure 10.25. Figure 10.26 depicts the permutation:

$$(0, 1, 2, 3, 4, 5, 6, 7) \rightarrow (0, 2, 4, 6, 7, 5, 3, 1)$$

as in Figure 10.22.b, with a sequence of appropriate shuffles and unshuffles.

The perfect shuffle can be used effectively for sorting, fast Fourier transform, polynomial evaluation, etc. It serves as the basis for other $O(n \log n)$ networks. The interested reader should consult the bibliography.

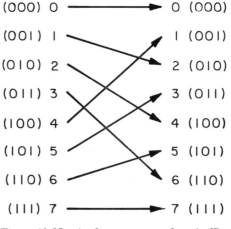

Figure 10.25   An 8 processor perfect shuffle

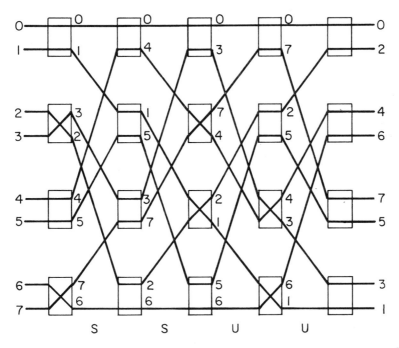

Figure 10.26   A sequence of shuffle and unshuffle permutations to realize the mapping (0, 1, 2, 3, 4, 5, 6, 7)→(0, 2, 4, 6, 7, 5, 3, 1)

10.3.3   Future Array Processors

The history of ILLIAC IV and of pipeline processors provides us with enough data to assess the critical points in the design of an SIMD array processor, namely:

- In all scientific computations amenable to vector processing there is a non-negligible amount of scalar computations; hence, a fast scalar unit should be available with the facility of overlapping its processing with that of the synchronous parallel processing elements;
- The system should have efficient means to provide memory access to all processing elements via some "alignment" network;
- The processors should be interconnected through a network allowing as many permutations (mappings) as possible;
- The application software (compilers for, possibly tailored, high-level languages) should take advantage of vector operations as much as possible, independently of the lengths of the vectors.

We have seen that some of these criteria are not answered satisfactorily by ILLIAC IV. The Burroughs Scientific Processor (BSP), announced in 1977 but not delivered by 1979, is another approach to SIMD computation worth some discussion.

The BSP is not meant to be an independent computer. It is an attachment to a powerful general purpose machine, a Burroughs B7800, which plays the role of a system manager. In line with the Burroughs tradition, the BSP is a "high-level" language machine, more precisely a FORTRAN machine. It is capable of performing 50 Mflops. This speed is achieved by a conjunction of array processing (16 arithmetic elements (AE's) working synchronously in parallel) and of pipelining memory access and computations.

A PMS description of the BSP system is shown in Figure 10.27. The BSP communicates with its system manager through a memory file which can be considered as a secondary memory for both the system manager and the BSP. This memory file uses CCD technology with 64K-bit chips of average access time of less than one ms. and transfer rates of the order of 12.5 Mw/sec. Under control of the file controller, the memory file can transfer data to or receive data from:

- The system's manager Mp at transfer rates of 250 Kw/sec;

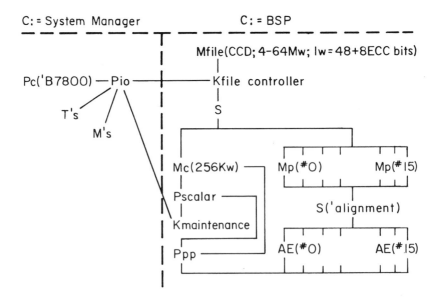

Figure 10.27   PMS description of the Burroughs Scientific Processor BSP

- The parallel memory (in 16 word blocks) and the control task memory (in 4 word blocks) at rates of 12.5 Mw/sec.

The remaining major components of the BSP can be divided into those belonging to the control processor (Mc, Pscalar, Kmaintenance, Ppp) and those which are part of the parallel processor (Mp's, S('alignment), AE's).

The control processor supervises many tasks: it runs the BSP's operating system and in particular provides the interface with the system manager; it executes the non I/O and the scalar portions of code (I/O is sent to the file controller); and it prepares vector operations to be executed by the arithmetic elements of the parallel processor. The scalar processing unit (Pscalar in the figure) is a fast central processor with an 80 ns. cycle time, a 16 word look-behind instruction buffer, 16 48-bit registers, a stack for subroutine linkage, and 16 120-bit vector data buffers for preparing instuctions for the AE's (120 bits is the maximum width of a vector instruction). The control processor memory (Mc) is a 256Kw semi-conductor memory of 160 ns. cycle time (4 words are accessed in a single cycle). It is used to store parts of the BSP operating system (with overlap in Mfile) and user programs in execution. The parallel processor control unit (Ppp) has two functions, each one implemented in a separate unit: one unit receives and stores temporarily the vector operations sent by Pscalar and transforms them into a sequence of steps to be followed by the parallel processor unit (at a 160 ns. rate); the other unit queues these control steps and presents them to the parallel processor (at an 80 ns. rate). In addition, there is a control and maintenance unit (Kmaintenance) which provides the interface between the Pio's of the system manager and Pscalar.

The importance of the preparation of the control steps is apparent when we look at the organization of the parallel processor. It consists of 17 memory modules (Mp's) each of which can contain from 32 to 512K words (the basic chip is 4K bit, bipolar, of 160 ns. cycle time); an alignment network which is a cross-bar switch connecting the 17 Mp's and the 16 AE's; and finally these 16 AE's, each with a 160 ns. cycle time, 8 scratchpad and 2 temporary registers, and an instruction set of over 100 vector operations. Floating-point add, subtract and multiply take two cycles, divide takes eight.

The reader might have noticed that there are 17 memory modules. With a straight storage scheme, rows, columns and diagonals of a matrix can be accessed without conflict by the 16 AE's as long as the distance between consecutive elements is not a multiple of (the prime number) 17. This is a clever way to implement a "simple" alignment network with few conflicts. The fetching and storing of array elements is controlled by descriptors prepared by Pscalar and sent to Ppp. The literature on the BSP gives many examples where FORTRAN DO-loops with two levels of nesting can be executed in a single vector operation. This optimization is realized through the use of precompiled "templates" which can have up to 5 operands for a given vector instruction. There exist capabilities for interprocessor communication but the BSP literature does not provide any detail.

An additional speed increase is achieved by pipelining in the parallel processor complex. A typical (vector) operation consists of the sequence of 5 steps:

> Fetch (from Mp's)
> (Input)   Align (in S('alignment))
> Compute (in AE's; at least 2 cycles)
> (Output) Align (in S('alignment))
> Store (in Mp's)

Functionally, the alignment network is divided into input and output switches so that the input and output align operations of consecutive instructions can be overlapped. The conflicts which can arise are between stores and fetches which cannot occur simultaneously.

In order to prepare templates which will result in as few conflicts as possible, the BSP system relies both on hardware and software optimizations. In the former case, instructions can be executed out of sequence if there are no procedural conflicts; loop orderings can be changed, for example during the initialization of arrays, if the results are not affected. On the software side, a FORTRAN optimizing compiler is helped by language extensions as in ILLIAC IV's CFD. There also exists some automatic recognition of parallelism within loops and for recurrence relations. In this latter case, the interprocessor communications and "special instructions" are used.

The BSP design meets some of the criteria presented at the beginning of this section. We shall have to wait until the BSP is in operation to judge the efficiency and feasibility of the hardware and software optimizations, and of the "template" strategy.

While the BSP presents an architecture quite distinct from that of ILLIAC IV, there is a proposal to build a system more powerful than ILLIAC IV but based on some of the same premises. The Phoenix array processor is the result of investigations performed at the NASA Ames Research Center, where ILLIAC IV is housed, pertaining to the interplay between the architectures of SIMD machines and the computing power needed in some specific applications (recall that the existing ILLIAC IV is only one-fourth of the system as originally planned). Phoenix would consist of a number of sextants of 64 processors where sextants could collaborate if need be. Each sextant would have a scalar processor and control unit. A super control unit would direct the topology and coordination of the sextants. Within a sextant, the 64 processors could operate either synchronously in lock-step fashion or asynchronously. The interconnection network, with some memory elements at each switch to store a small number of useful permutations, would permit more mappings than the four point connections of ILLIAC IV. According to the Phoenix proponents, the goal is to achieve computational rates of a few thousand Mflops that is several orders of magnitude over those of present day computers.

10.4   MULTIPROCESSING SYSTEMS (MIMD)

In this section our emphasis is on multiprocessing systems where each processor has the power of a complete Pc. The reader interested in more tightly coupled systems is referred to the description of look-ahead processors (CDC 6600, IBM System 360/91) in Chapter 4 and to the study of the pipelined processors (CRAY-1, CDC STAR-100, TI ASC) in Section 2 of this chapter.

10.4.1   Topologies of the Processor-Memory Switch

The interconnection network between processors and memories, or the Pc-Mp switch in PMS terminology, can have various topologies depending on the desired transfer concurrency and the investment in hardware. In the following, we emphasize the Pc-Mp switch but we shall also indicate how Pc's communicate. Thus, some of the features of the interconnection networks of SIMD systems are relevant.

Cross-bar switch and C.mmp

The cross-bar switch is the most extensive, and expensive, scheme providing direct paths from processors to memories (cf. Figure 10.28). With m processors and n memory modules, a concurrency of min (m, n) can be achieved. The cross-bar requires $m \cdot n$ switches; with m and n of the same order of magnitude, the number of cross-points grows as n^2. Since each cross-point must have hardware capable of switching parallel transmissions and of resolving conflicting requests for a given memory module, the switching device can rapidly become the dominant factor in the cost of the overall system. This trend will accelerate in the future since, with the advances in LSI technology, memory and processor costs will decrease more rapidly than that of the switch structure.

Cross-bar switches have been used in Burroughs multiprocessors. The

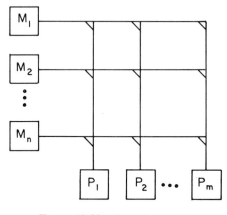

Figure 10.28   Cross-bar switch

most representative system today is C.mmp (multiminiprocessor), a research system at Carnegie-Mellon University. C.mmp (cf. Figure 10.29) is a multiprocessor consisting of 16 slightly modified PDP-11's (5 PDP 11-20 and 11 PDP 11-40) connected to 16 memory modules. Five of the Mp modules use semi-conductor and 11 use core technology; they all have the same average cycle time (650 ns.). When the delay due to the switching is taken into account, the average access time is of the order of 1 ms. in the absence of conflict; in the next section we present some experimental data on the impact of the memory interference problem. Each processor has its own 4K words of private memory (Mlocal).

Fixed-head disks (Mpaging) and movable-arm disks (Mdisk) can be attached to the UNIBUS's of the Pc's. Each Pc has its own memory mapping device Dmap. The initial mapping consists of adding two bits of the program status (PS) register to the 16-bit user address to form an 18-bit address. If the two PS bits are 11, 8K words of the possible address space corresponding to this combination are used to reference Mlocal and the I/O devices (as in any PDP-11). For the three other combinations of the PS bits and the remainder of the (11) combination, the 18-bit address is mapped into a 21-bit address by having the 5 high-order bits select one of 30 relocation registers (and not 32 because of Mlocal and the I/O page). Each relocation register contains an 8-bit "page" number referring to a global Mp page frame to which is concatenated the low order 13 bits of the user's address.

Communication between Pc's is through a time-shared multiplexed bus (interbus) with controllers (Kibi) on each individual Pc UNIBUS and a common centralized controller (interbus).

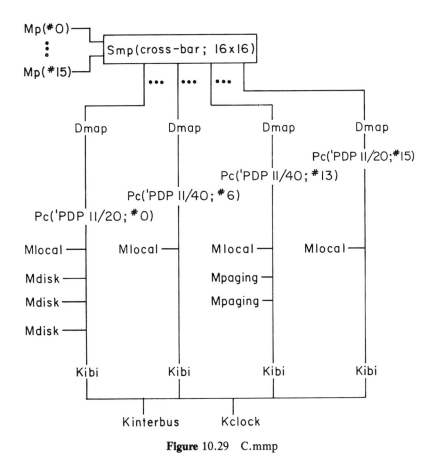

Figure 10.29 C.mmp

Time-shared bus

We have just mentioned this organization for inter-Pc communication in
C.mmp. This is the simplest organization although there are several degrees
of complexity depending on the number of buses. The simplest one is to have
all processors, memories and I/O units connected to a single bus which can
be totally passive. We have seen examples of this scheme in Chapter 9 with
the asynchronous UNIBUS and the synchronous SBI. Obviously, the concurrency is minimal (one transaction at a time) but so is the investment in hardware. The single bus structure can be applied to (virtual) processors sharing
a common memory, and even some circuitry, in a synchronous multiplexed
fashion. This is the architecture chosen for the peripheral processors of the
CDC 6600 and the virtual processors of the TI ASC (recall Section 2.4).

The time-shared bus concept can be used in distributed function architectures and local networks for interconnection between processors. In Chapter 11 we shall briefly discuss ring structures and contention schemes in these environments. They fall outside the area of MIMD organizations since the processors cannot be considered as having a shared primary memory. In the MIMD architectures, more parallelism can be attained, at the price of more complexity, by having several buses, either uni or multi-directional. Priorities can be given to specific units if a bus arbiter is added to resolve them. We can even envision different topologies for the transfer buses and control buses.

Multiport Memory Buses

In this organization, reminiscent of the cross-bar switch, the switching is concentrated in the memory module. Each processor has access through its own bus to all memory modules (cf. Figure 10.30). Conflicts are resolved by assigning a fixed priority to the memory ports. This organization is used quite often in uniprocessors for allowing concurrent memory access by the Pc and Pio's (recall Chapter 8). An interesting feature of the multiport architecture is that Pc's can have private memories, or equivalently be denied the use of some memory modules, in a very easy fashion.

In this scheme the concurrency is again min (n, m). The amount of hardware needed is of the same order of magnitude as in the cross-bar (m connections per memory module) but it is more localized. It appears easier to increment the number of memory modules but, on the other hand, the number of ports in a memory module limits the number of processors to which it can be linked.

Some trade-offs are apparent for the choice of one of the above three topologies. Costwise the time-shared bus is cheaper and the cross-bar is the most expensive. The memory modules of the multiport organization must

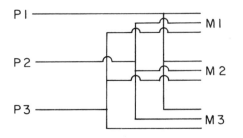

Figure 10.30   Multiport memory buses

have additional logic in their controllers and this might drive their cost fairly high. The time-shared bus allows easy expansions but the performance of the system might degrade rapidly if the bus is overloaded. We have discussed previously the modularity difficulties for the multiport system. In terms of reliability, the time-shared bus and cross-bar switches appear equally poor. However, redundancy can be built in the cross-bar (at more cost). Finally, both the cross-bar and multiport schemes allow maximal concurrency. Table 10.2 summarizes this discussion.

Table 10.2 Summary of the attributes of Pc-Mp switches

	Concurrency	Cost	Modularity	Reliability
cross-bar	maximum	high	easy	poor
time-shared bus	1	low	very easy	very poor
multiport memory	maximum	medium	hard	medium

Some of these topologies may be mixed. For example, Figure 10.31 shows an abstraction of a multiprocessor (PLURIBUS) used as a modular switching node for ARPANET (the I/O buses are not shown). In essence there are 7 pairs of dual processors (Lockheed SUE minicomputers) with each pair sharing 2 modules of 4K word of local memories on a single bus structure. Through a bus arbiter and extender, these dual processors can access 8K

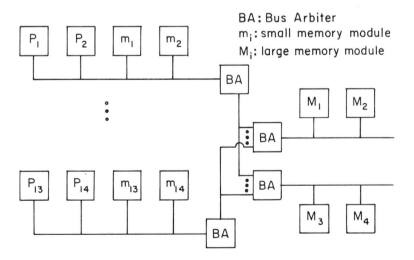

Figure 10.31   Multiminiprocessor connection scheme

word modules of shared memory. These larger modules are again grouped in pairs and it is not necessary for every dual processor to be connected directly to every bus arbiter of the large memory module pairs.

In the PLURIBUS architecture, the premise of a memory hierarchy can be distinguished. It should take less time for a processor to access a local memory than to access a large module. This clustering of processors and memories is at the heart of the design of another Carnegie-Mellon University research project, called Cm*.

Clusters of Microcomputers: Cm*

The basic "building block" of the Cm* architecture is the computer module Cm (cf. Figure 10.32.a). It consists of a processor (LSI-11) and 4 to 124K words of primary memory. Peripherals such as teletypes or disks can be present in the Cm. In addition, an address mapping device (Slocal) is attached to the LSI-bus and provides the interface between a Cm and other Cm's in the same cluster. A cluster is composed of several modules connected through a map bus. Cm* consists of several clusters connected via intercluster buses. The traffic control and memory address translations inter and intra clusters are provided by powerful controllers (Kmap). Each Kmap can communicate with two intercluster buses. A three-cluster Cm* system is shown in Figure 10.32.b. In 1979, the Cm* configuration had 5 clusters of 10 modules for a total of 50 modules. The architecture is extendable in terms of number of modules per cluster (up to 14) and in the number of clusters.

It is interesting to follow the paths that can be taken when a memory reference is generated by a processor. This memory reference can be either local, i.e., in the module itself, or non-local. The resolution of this first level of mapping is performed in the Slocal of the module. The Slocal contains a relocation table for 32 pages of 4K bytes (although the LSI-11 is limited to an addressing range of 64K bytes, i.e., 16 pages, two address spaces are provided for each Pc for the protection of the operating system and of interrupt handlers; the address space selection is performed by concatenating a bit of the processor status word to the high-order 4 bits of the virtual address). The result of the mapping process is either a local 18-bit real address or a "fault" indicating that the virtual address corresponds to a non-local reference. A bit is included to that effect in the Slocal relocation table.

When the reference is non-local, the Kmap will provide the next level in the translation process. The Kmap (cf. Figure 10.33) contains three major components, Kbus, Pmap and Linc. The Kbus, a microprogrammed processor, provides the interface between the map bus (and therefore the Slocal's) and Pmap. One of its major tasks is to arbitrate the Slocal requests. This is

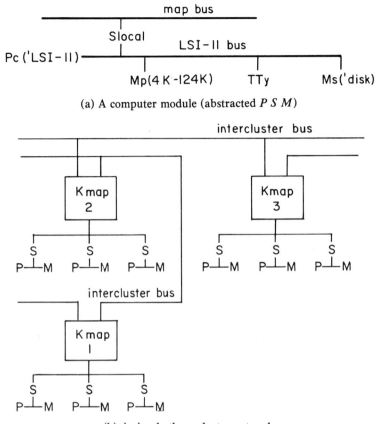

(a) A computer module (abstracted *P S M*)

(b) A simple three cluster network

Figure 10.32   C.m∗: a clustering approach

done via a round-robin discipline. Pmap is a special-purpose processor with sufficient hardware to be multiprogrammed (e.g., it has 8 sets of 32 16-bit registers). It holds the mapping tables for intra and inter-cluster references. Finally, the Linc is the interface to the two intercluster buses. Messages between Kmap's are transferred in a package-switching mode (a message is at most 8 words) as in a store-and-forward computer network. Each Linc has a buffer for 128 8-word messages.

Let us return to our memory referencing problem (the following discussion is necessarily schematic; more details can be found in the references). Assume that the Slocal relocation map has shown that the reference is non-

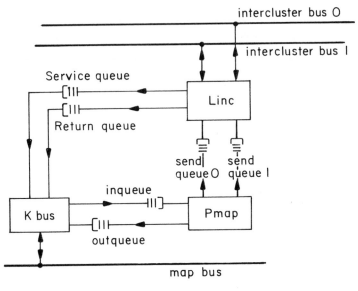

Figure 10.33   C.m*'s Kmap

local. The Slocal requests the attention of the Kbus. The source module number and a 16-bit address is sent to Kmap and queued for processing by Pmap. If Pmap discovers, through its mapping tables, that the reference is to a location within the cluster, then it generates the 18-bit address and 4-bit module number and places them in the Kbus output queue. Then the Kbus, which gives priority to Pmap requests, transfers the address to the Slocal of the destination module; in case of a write operation the Kbus initiates the transfer of data from the source Slocal to the destination Slocal. The destination Slocal performs a DMA to its Mp module and, at completion, signals the Kbus. In case of a read, the data is transferred between Slocal's and in case of a write, an acknowledgment is sent.

If the Pmap determines that the reference is to another cluster, it prepares a message containing its own identification, including one of eight "contexts", i.e., an identification of the process handling this reference in its multiprogrammed environment, the destination, the operation, the system wide internal address which is a segment number (2^{16} possible segments) of variable size (between 2 bytes and 4K bytes) and an offset within the segment. The message is sent to one of the two input queues of the Linc. The Linc is responsible for acquiring control of the designated intercluster bus and sending the message to the destination Linc which acknowledges on a word per word basis. At the destination Kmap, the Linc sends requests to the Kbus as if it were a local Cm. The only difference is that the Pmap translates a full virtual address instead of a 16-bit address. Assuming that the destination cluster contains the referenced address (if not a forwarding call will be performed exactly as the original one), a return message is prepared with either the data (read) or an acknowledgement (write). Upon receipt of the return message, the original source Linc places it in the return queue. This will be treated as a return from an intra-cluster reference.

It is obvious that the access times to memory depend on their position with respect to the processor generating the request. Preliminary investigations show that intra-cluster and inter-cluster references are respectively 2.7 and 7 times slower than local ones. This imposes structural properties for the operating system and application programs such as assignment of code to local memories, duplication of code and algorithm modifications to improve locality of referencing (e.g., stack environments should be on local memories). Moreover, the local referencing cannot always pass straight through Slocal and may need the assistance of Kmap. This is due to the segmentation of the address space and the inability of Slocal to check whether a reference is within the limits of a segment size if the size is less than 4K bytes. The description of the complete virtual to physical address mapping is outside the scope of this book; we can only mention that it is based on a hierarchy of capability lists where a capability consists of a segment name and access rights. A special page, addressed through a specific relocation register in Slocal, contains "window registers" defining the binding between the processor's local space and the virtual (segmented) address. Modifications to the mapping have to be performed through Kmap.

With Cm* we have an MIMD architecture quite close to that of a network. Other examples of distributed processing environments will be discussed in the next chapter.

10.4.2   Memory Interference

The Processor-Memory interconnection networks allowing concurrency would present no advantage if all processors were requesting information from the same memory module. When several processors simultaneously address the same memory module, we have a *memory interference*. We have already seen this problem arise in two situations: the conjunction of look-ahead processing with memory interleaving (Chapter 5 Section 3) and the competition between Pc and Pio's resolved by cycle stealing (Chapter 8 Section 2.1). In this section, we examine memory interference in the context of p processors of equal priority addressing m memory modules.

Let us start with an example which shows the importance of the degradation caused by memory interference. We consider a C.mmp organization ($p = 16$, $m = 16$) where all processors can be busy doing useful work at the same time provided that they either access their local memories or different modules of the shared memory. Let us assume further that all Pc's work on the same problem and that they must share information (infrequently).

The specifics of the algorithm are not relevant here; the reader is referred to Oleinick's dissertation cited in the references for an example involving the root finding problem. The program implementing the algorithm is the same for all Pc's; only the data is different. Furthermore, the amount of data needed is very small compared to the length of the program (e.g., one value is needed to perform a lengthy iterative process). There are two options for the placement of code. It is possible to save space by allowing all Pc's to share a common code "page" (placed in one of the memory module) or the code in each memory module can be replicated. Alternatively, one copy of the code could be interleaved among the m modules. We dismiss this last strategy since the interleaving in C.mmp is done on the high-order bits of the address (for graceful degradation and enhancement purposes) and we do not have any data to evaluate this latter model. Figure 10.34 shows the degradation due to memory conflicts. With private code pages, an increase in the number of processors results in a decrease in total processing time (the decrease is not linear but this is not unexpected). On the other hand, if one copy of the code is present we see that when only a few processors (2 or 3) are competing, then we do have a satisfying speed-up. As soon as too many processors are requesting code from the same memory module, each processor is slowed down and, because they need to communicate, the whole process is even slower than if a single processor were working alone. Naturally this example is somewhat extreme.

In order to study memory interference in more general terms, let us consider the following model. At a given instant of time, the p processors generate p requests. These p requests are distributed among the m modules. It is useful to view this process as each processor depositing a ball (with its name) into an urn corresponding to a memory module. For example with $p = 4$ and $m = 4$, the request:

p 0 1 2 3
m 2 2 2 3

would deposit three balls (marked 0, 1 and 2) in urn 2 and one ball (marked 3) in urn 3. Once these requests have been made, we can consider two different modes of operation. In the first one, all requests have to be satisfied

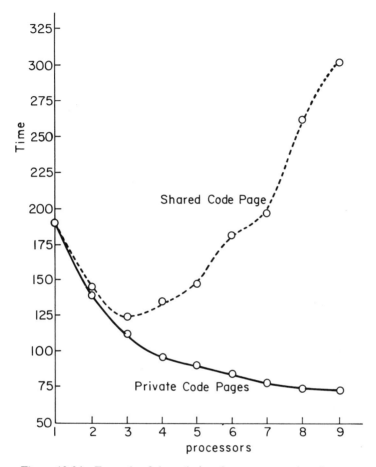

Figure 10.34   Example of degradation due to memory interference

before (p) new requests are generated. In the second mode, as many requests as possible are satisfied during one memory cycle and the processors which have been serviced (or maybe even all processors) can generate new memory requests at the next memory cycle time. As we shall see, this second model can have several interesting variations.

The first mode of operation is quite close to what is needed in SIMD architectures, that is, all processors must have their operands in order to proceed synchronously. The bandwidth of the memory can be defined as the number of requests serviced per cycle. In the above example it would be:

$$\frac{\text{processors}}{\text{number of cycles}} = \frac{4}{3} = 1.33,$$

where the number of cycles is the maximum number of balls in any one urn. The average bandwidth B is then:

$$B = \frac{p}{\sum\limits_{h=1}^{p} hg(h)}, \tag{1}$$

where $g(h)$ is the probability that the maximum number of balls in any one urn is h. There exists no closed form for equation (1). However, it has been observed that for a fixed ratio p/m, B increases almost linearly with p.

The second mode of operation resembles more that of MIMD organizations. In order to analyze the impact of the interference problem, a step of the computation can be abstracted as follows:

- The p processors generate a request; each processor requests service from any of the m memory modules with uniform probability $(1/m)$;
- B ($B \leq \min(m, p)$) requests are serviced by the memory and returned to the processors.

In the next computation step, all p processors will generate p new requests even if some of the previous ones have not been serviced. We shall deal with this assumption soon. At the present time, we give an average value for B. In terms of our urn and ball model, B is the average number of non-empty urns.

The probability that processor i has a request for memory module j is $1/m$. The probability that processor i has a request for a memory module other than j is therefore $1 - (1/m)$. Now, the probability that r requests are queued for memory module j is:

$$P(r) = \binom{p}{r} \left(\frac{1}{m}\right)^r (1 - 1/m)^{p-r}$$

(This is a straightforward application of the binomial theorem). The average memory bandwidth corresponds to the average number of modules with at least one request. If we define the random variables b_j as having the value 1 if memory module j is busy and 0 otherwise, then:

$$B = \sum_{j=1}^{m} b_j.$$

But $b_j = 1 - P(0)$ (1 minus the probability of no request). Hence

$$B = \sum_{j=1}^{m} b_j = m (1 - P(0))$$

or,

$$B = m (1 - (1 - 1/m)^p).\qquad(2)$$

The function B has the important property that it is non-decreasing with increasing m and p. It is an asymptotically linear function of either p or m given a constant p/m ratio.

The average bandwidth as computed in (2) is optimistic for two reasons: first, it assumes that at each step all p processors generate random requests independently of the previous step and, second, it assumes that the processing time is null. This second assumption can be rephrased as stating that the processing time is equal to the time it takes for the memories and switching network to stabilize (e.g., this can be a "rewrite time").

In order to be more realistic, we must modify our model. The price that we shall pay is the absence of a closed form solution as in (2) and thus additional computational complexity. Furthermore, when we want to include the processing time (assumption #2), we shall have to make new assumptions. For example, we can consider processing times to be distributed geometrically or we can have a binomial distribution of processors generating requests at a given step. The reader is referred to the references for specific analyses. In the remainder of this section, we assume a "null" processing time but we force a processor to have its ith request be serviced before generating its $(i + 1)$ st. In other words, we provide some queueing control in the Pc $-$ Mp switch.

The computation can be viewed as a Markovian process. The state of the computation is the disposition of the processors queued at the memory modules (or the number of balls in each urn). Since we are interested in the average number of busy memory modules and not in the behavior of each individual module, the state is an m-tuple $(p_1, p_2, \ldots p_m)$, $p_i \geq p_{i+1}$, with $\sum_{i=1}^{m} p_i = p$. (In our example the state is (3, 1, 0, 0)). In the simplified analysis leading to equation (2), any state is reachable from any other state. When we introduce queueing, the number of new states are restricted as follows:

- Set $p_i' = \max(0, p_i - 1)$

- Generate $p'' = p - \sum_{i=1}^{m} p_i'$ new requests, say $(p_1'', p_2'', \ldots, p_m'')$
- The new state is $(p_1' + p_1'', p_2' + p_2'', \cdots, p_m' + p_m'')$

In our example, after servicing two requests from $(3, 1, 0, 0)$ we have the "prime" state $(2, 0, 0, 0)$ and generate one of the 4 new states $(4, 0, 0, 0)$, $(3, 1, 0, 0)$, $(2, 2, 0, 0)$, $(2, 1, 1, 0)$ instead of the 5 possible states (i.e., $(1, 1, 1, 1)$ is not reachable). Transition probabilities can also be computed. For example, from $(2, 0, 0, 0)$ we can reach the (partial) state $(3, 0, 0, 0)$ with probability $1/4$ and the final state $(4, 0, 0, 0)$ with probability $1/16$ (cf. Exercise 10). More generally, the transition probability from state $(p_1, \ldots, p_m)$ to $(p_1' + p_1'', \ldots, p_m' + p_m'')$ is:

$$\frac{p''!}{p_1''! \, p_2''! \cdots p_m''!} \cdot \left(\frac{1}{m}\right)^{p''}$$

Unfortunately, there is no "good" method to generate the state transitions and their probabilities. With $p = m = 16$, over an hour of computer time (on a medium-size machine) is needed to generate the average number of busy modules! The encouraging result, though, is that Equation (2) is a good, optimistic, approximation (within 8%) of the Markov model. Simulation, which in this case can be less time consuming than the state transition method, has confirmed the accuracy of equation (2).

Instead of using this Markovian approach, we could assume that each processor is a look-ahead processor and can generate a new request after every memory cycle. Of course its previous request, if not serviced, remains queued at the memory module. With this model, reminiscent of the improved α-β model of Chapter 5, we can surmise intuitively that we should improve on the results of Equation (2) since we are distributing more requests per memory cycle. Simulations have shown that 5 to 10% improvements can be expected for queue lengths of 1 or 2 allowed at the memory modules.

Table 10.3 summarizes some of the points raised in this discussion: it shows the number of busy modules in a $p \times p$ ($p = 2, 4, 8$) MIMD machine computed by equation (2), by the Markov chain approach, and as derived by simulation (average of results obtained by Baskett and Smith).

Before closing this section, we have to return to an assumption that we have not examined, namely the uniform access probabiltiy of every memory module. This assumption is not realistic in the case of a uniprocessor accessing an interleaved memory. In the case of a multiprocessor system, this is not important since if processors were to generate sequential references over the m modules, they would have a tendency to synchronize themselves and, actually, decrease the memory interference. But if a memory module is favored

Table 10.3 Influence of the memory interference problem

Expected number of busy memory modules

$p = m =$	Equation (2)	Markov chain approach	Simulation
2	1.5	1.5	1.56
4	2.73	2.62	2.68
8	5.25	4.95	5.04

consistently by more than one processor, then we have a sizeable degradation. This was the point of the example presented at the beginning of this section and shows the danger of interleaving with the high order bits of the address when there is a large amount of sharable code or data. Naturally, the presence of private memories can circumvent the problem for read-only code but not for writable data since then all private memories or caches must have consistent contents (cf. Section 4.3).

10.4.3 Software Requirements

MIMD architectures add levels of complexity to the operating system, assemblers, compilers and application software. The more sensitive areas are: the design of algorithms to take advantage of potential concurrency, the introduction of language features to explicitly express parallelism, the automatic detection of parallelism at the compiler level, the synchronization problems betwen cooperating or competing processors, and scheduling and load balancing. We do not treat the first area (design of algorithms) in this section. The reader should consult the literature on this advanced research topic. We shall introduce some of its aspects in Chapter 11 when we discuss alterable architectures.

Concurrent Programming

The ISP level of a multiprocessor should reflect the new dimension in the power of the MIMD PMS structure. The new capabilities must also be available to high-level language programmers. New instructions, or language constructs, are required to express the desires of the programmer to initiate concurrent paths and to have these paths merge when necessary. Since concurrent tasks can access shared data or use common resources, means to synchronize these accesses must also be provided.

Let us look first at the initiation and merging of concurrent paths. At the

ISP level, the instructions which control these actions have received various names. As an example, we introduce the pair FORK-JOIN whose semantics are as follows:

FORK A Initiate process at address A; the current process continues with the next sequential instruction;

FORK A, J As FORK A; in addition a counter at address J is incremented by one;

FORK A, J, N As FORK A; in addition the counter at address J is set to N;

JOIN J The counter at address J is decremented by one; if the counter becomes null, initiate processing at address $(J + 1)$ else release the processor executing the JOIN;

JOIN J, B As JOIN J except that instead of executing instruction $J + 1$ when the counter becomes null, a branch to address B is performed.

The example of Figure 10.35 illustrates the use of these instructions for the

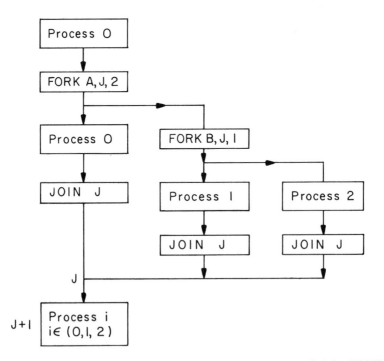

Figure 10.35   Concurrent execution of three processes controlled by FORK and JOIN

control of three concurrent processes. It should be noted that these instructions do not allow a task to terminate by itself without coming to a merging point. Additional instructions, e.g., a QUIT, and variations on the semantics of JOIN would allow this extension.

Within high-level languages, FORK-JOIN pairs can be indicated in two fashions. On a statement per statement basis the brackets BEGIN ... END can be replaced by PARBEGIN ... PAREND where it is understood that the individual statements within the brackets can be performed in parallel. Another possibility is to add a "parallel" separator to the sequential separator. For example in ALGOL-68, statements separated by a "," can be processed in parallel while sequential execution is imposed for statements separated by a ";". At the procedure level, the concept of "tasking" (i.e., a FORK-JOIN-QUIT scheme) was introduced in PL/I with the TASK, EVENT, RETURN, or EXIT options in the procedure call-return mechanism. A similar feature is present in ALGOL-68. More recent languages, or their extensions, permit the concurrent execution of processes (i.e., instantation of procedures) and provide mechanisms for their synchronization.

The synchronization between concurrent tasks is mandatory. To illustrate this point, consider the instruction JOIN J, B with the semantics defined above. A "statement per statement" execution of this instruction becomes:

$$\text{counter} \leftarrow \text{counter} - 1;$$
$$\text{If counter} = 0 \text{ then go to } B;$$

Assume now that two processes, process 1 and process 2, want to merge with a third process, say process 0 at address J. Process 1 and process 2 execute JOIN J, B and JOIN J, C respectively. Assume that process 0 has already executed its JOIN J and therefore the counter at address J is equal to 2. Depending on the interleaving of the two steps of JOIN J, B with the two steps of JOIN J, C, either process 1 will transfer control to B, or process 2 will transfer control to C, or both processes will execute their respective "go to" parts. This last alternative was certainly not intended, otherwise the two JOIN's would have been coded as "JOIN J, D" where at address D we would have found the instantation of processes at addresses B and C. In order to avoid the last alternative, the JOIN J, B instructions must be made *indivisible*.

This indivisibility can be achieved by instructions of the form "Test and Set" as implemented in many systems (e.g., IBM System/370, but also in microcomputers such as the Motorola 68000), or the pair Lock-Unlock. The semantics of the Lock-Unlock are as follows:

- Lock *w*   If *w* = 1 (locked state), the instruction is repeated until *w* = 0; in this case the process can proceed after setting *w* to 1;
- Unlock *w* Set *w* to 0;

In the IBM System/370, the Test and Set instruction fetches the byte at the effective address, temporarily setting the whole byte to a string of 1's. If the fetched byte has a leftmost bit of 0, the condition code 0 is set and the process can proceed. Otherwise the condition code 1 is set. At the same time, all other Pc's are prevented from accessing the byte at the effective address between its fetching and its setting to all one's. Thus, in essence, this is a Lock instruction. Unlock can be executed with a store instruction.

The conflict between the two JOIN instructions can be generalized. We can have several portions of code wishing to access some shared data or a common resource. These portions of code are called *critical sections.*

In order to simplify the programming of critical sections, Dijkstra has introduced new variables called *semaphores.* Semaphores are variables which can only take non-negative integer values. Two primitive, indivisible, operations are defined on semaphores, namely (with S being a semaphore):

$V(S): S \leftarrow S + 1;$

$P(S): L:$ **If** $S = 0$ **then go to** L **else** $S \leftarrow S - 1.$

To enter a critical section, we perform a P operation on a common semaphore, say **mutex** (for mutually exclusive; **mutex** is initialized to 1). The first process performing **P(mutex)** will be able to enter its critical section. All other processes are blocked since **mutex** has become null. After leaving its critical section, the process performs a **V(mutex)** and allows another process to execute successfully **P(mutex)**. The critical section problem is summarized in the Petri Net of Figure 10.36 where the place p_{mutex} represents the semaphore and transitions P(mutex) and V(mutex) control the entry and exit to the critical sections.

As we said in the introduction of this chapter, there is still some extensive research on the synchronization of concurrent processes related to scheduling and reliability problems (e.g., what would happen in Figure 10.36 if the processor on which process 1 is running would fail while process 1 is in its critical section?). Similarly, high-level language constructs which can be implemented in terms of semaphores have been proposed and incorporated in some new languages. For example, *monitors*, a collection of associated data and procedures with mutual exclusion on the code of the monitor, have been incorporated in Concurrent Pascal. We do not dwell on these aspects of the synchronization problem; they are treated in texts on operating systems and are still subject to intense investigation.

The sharing of resources by several processors may lead to a dangerous

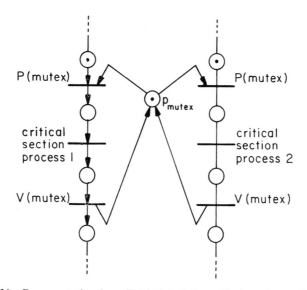

Figure 10.36   Representation by a Petri Net of the critical section problem solved with a semaphore

situation called *deadlock*. Consider the following example where two processes, process 1 and process 2, require the use of two resources, say A and B (cf. the Petri Net of Figure 10.37). Process 1 acquires resource A first and then needs resource B to continue. After having used resources A and B, it releases them. Process 2 proceeds in a similar fashion but requires B first and then both A and B. If the scheduler, or the operating system's resource allocator, services requests dynamically, the following situation may occur. Process 1 acquires resource A (transition $t_{1,A}$ in the net) and process 2 acquires resource B (transition $t_{2,B}$). From there on neither process can continue (the places p_A and p_B are empty and neither $t_{1,AB}$ nor $t_{2,AB}$ can fire). Many solutions to the deadlock problem have been proposed (see the references). For example, we may impose all processes to declare in advance which resources they are planning to use, and at which steps of the computations, so that resources can be granted, maybe too early, in a fashion avoiding a deadlock. In the previous example processes 1 and 2 would be granted both resources A and B at once, so that they would have to proceed sequentially. It is interesting to note that avoiding deadlock is possible as a global strategy, i.e., when all requests are known in advance. However, if these requests are dynamic, or if the number of resources is so large as for ex-

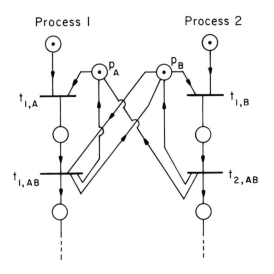

Figure 10.37   Illustration of the deadlock problem

ample the records of a large data base that it precludes a computationally feasible analysis, then we must be able to detect and recover from deadlock. Here again, we are stepping outside the scope of this book but the reader should be aware of the difficulties of computing in a parallel processing environment.

Our final example showing the implications of parallel computations on the correct behavior of tasks is related to the use of personal memories, or caches. Assume two processors P_1 and P_2, each with their own cache, C_1 and C_2, and accessing a common memory Mp. An inherent problem with this organization is the updating of both caches and Mp when we have shared modifiable data. For example, let A be a common scalar shared by the programs running on P_1 and P_2. Let P_1 access A first with a "Load" instruction; A is brought into C_1. Let P_2 perform the same operation. Now the initial value of A is in Mp and there are copies in C_1 and C_2. The next operation of P_1 is to store a new value in A. A's value in C_2 must be modified before P_2 can access it, and similarly it should be modified in Mp and other caches if instead of two processors we had several more which can access A.

Several solutions have been proposed for this problem. The first one is reminiscent of the cache's scheme described in Chapter 6 Section 5.2 for keeping a consistent cache during I/O transfers. Each cache "listens" to the activities of all processors and a write-through policy is implemented. For example when P_1 stores a new value in A, C_2 "listens" to this storage requirement, sees that A's address is a valid entry, and either modifies A or in-validates the corresponding entry. The difficulties in this method are that the control logic in each cache can become extremely cumbersome when there are many processors (and many cache cycles might be devoted to the check-ing of external requests) and that the Pc $-$ Mp switch is liable to be ex-tremely congested if all store requests must be broadcast to all Pc's. The first drawback can be alleviated by having the control logic of a cache duplicated; one half "listens" to the activities of the other Pc's and interrupts the second half only when there is a conflict. It is likely that it will not happen often.

A second method would be to have some additional control embedded in the Mp. Bits indicating whether data is private or sharable, and in this latter case if it can be present in several caches at once, can be appended to each word (or it could be part of the protection bits in a paging or segmented system). Similar control bits would exist in each cache. Protocols between Mp and caches are necessary for keeping consistent copies of those sharable items. The reader is referred to the references for more detail.

Automatic Detection of Parallelism

We have seen previously (Chapter 4 Section 3.2) how to detect parallelism at the arithmetic expression level. We have also stated the conditions re-quired for two instructions to be allowed to operate concurrently. These con-ditions, that we repeat here, are still valid when we extend the range and do-main O_i and I_i to be that of statements or groups of statements. To derive these conditions, we classify the variables which are referenced by a segment of program P_i into 4 categories:

- W_i representing read-only variables,
- X_i representing write-only variables,
- Y_i representing variables first read and then modified,
- Z_i representing variables first modified and then read-only.

In order for two segments of program P_i and P_j to be allowed to proceed con-currently before joining into P_k, the following three conditions must be realized:

- Variables read by P_i should not be modified by P_j, i.e.,

$$(W_i \cup Y_i \cup Z_i) \cap (X_j \cup Y_j \cup Z_j) = \emptyset;$$

- Variables read by P_j should not be modified by P_i, i.e.,

$$(W_j \cup Y_j \cup Z_j) \cap (X_i \cup Y_i \cup Z_i) = \emptyset;$$

- The state of the computation when entering P_k must be independent of the order of computations between P_i and P_j, i.e., the variables first read in P_k should be independent of the order of the store operations in P_i and P_j; this yields

$$(W_k \cup Y_k) \cap (X_i \cup Y_i \cup Z_i) \cap (X_j \cup Y_j \cup Z_u) = \emptyset,$$

which simplifies to:

$$X_i \cap X_j \cap (W_k \cup Y_k) = \emptyset.$$

If P_i's are high-level language statements, then the 3 conditions above are reduced to:

$$I_i \cap O_j = \emptyset,$$
$$I_j \cap O_i = \emptyset,$$
$$O_i \cap O_j = \emptyset,$$

which is system (1) of Chapter 4 Section 3.1.

Analyzers which automatically detect the interstatement parallelism in FORTRAN or ALGOL-60 source programs have been written based on this system of 3 conditions and the decomposition of programs into straight-line code segments. These segments are such that the flow of control allows one entry and one exit to the segment. Many analysis programs proceed similarly. They consist of several phases summarized here:

Phase 1.   Build a directed graph of the program where each node is a statement and arcs represent the flow of control;

Phase 2.   Detect loops and cycles; suppress the feedback arcs yielding an acyclic graph;

Phase 3.   Record the procedural dependencies (loops, IF statements etc.);

Phase 4.   Build the input-output sets I_i and O_i for each statement;

Phase 5.   Detect parallelism (on the acyclic graph) and modify the graph accordingly;

Phase 6.   Build a new "parallel" graph by combining the acyclic graph from phase 5 and the procedural dependencies of Phase 3. This new graph is an AND/OR graph with AND's showing FORK's and JOIN's, and OR's showing tests and loops.

For example, assume that phase 1 yields the graph of Figure 10.38.a. Node 2 represents an IF statement; this segment of program is a DO-loop with the feedback arc (8, 1). Phase 2 will detect the loop and phase 3 will record it as well as the fact that arcs (2, 3) and (2, 5) are to be kept in the final graph. After phase 4, phase 5 will detect (for example) that statements 3 and 4 on the one hand, and 5 and 6 on the other can be done in parallel. (Note that the results of phase 3 can be used here to indicate that segments (3, 4) and (5, 6)

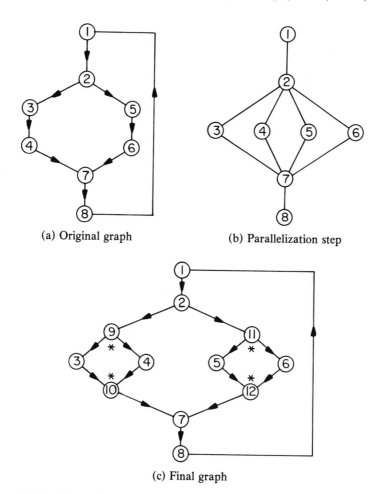

(a) Original graph   (b) Parallelization step

(c) Final graph

Figure 10.38   Illustration of the phases in an analyzer for automatic detection of parallelism

are mutually exclusive and hence there is no need to try and find any parallelism between them; each of these two segments is a straight-line segment as is (1, 8).) The parallel graph of phase 5 is then shown in Figure 10.38.b (in a more general case, a transitive reduction of the graph should be performed first to suppress unnecessary control structures). It remains to inject the procedural dependencies as shown in Figure 10.38.c, where 9 and 11 represent FORK's, and 10 and 12 are JOIN's.

This automatic detection of parallelism can be useful only if it is accompanied by a further analysis of the loop structures. We have not indicated how to interpret a subscripted variable in the I_i and O_i sets. If we consider whole arrays to be a single element of the set, then a loop such as:

> **for** I: = 1 **step** 1 **until** N **do**
> **begin** $A[I]:= B[I] + 1$;
> $B[I + 1]:= C[I]$
> **end;**

would have to proceed sequentially. But if our program could analyze subscripts, it would find out that the two statements within the loop can proceed in parallel. Furthermore, it would then notice that the N assignments to B can be done in parallel. However, the "pipelining" between a B assignment and an A assignment would be difficult to express even in common high-level languages (or extensions), so that the best that an automatic analyzer could produce would be the two parallel loops:

> **for** I: = 1 **step** 1 **until** N **do together**
> $B[I + 1]:= C[I]$;
> **for** I: = 1 **step** 1 **until** N **do together**
> $A[I]:= B[I] + 1$;

General conditions for such loop distributions can be defined. Other techniques, such as the wave-front method can be used. For example, the loop

> **for** I: = 1 **step** 1 **until** N **do**
>   **for** J: = 1 **step** 1 **until** N **do**
> $A[I, J]:= A[I - 1, J] + A[I, J - 1]$;

can be decomposed into:

- Compute $A[1, 1]$ from the initial values $A[0, 1]$ and $A[1, 0]$;
- Compute in parallel $A[2, 1]$ and $A[1, 2]$;
- Compute in parallel $A[3, 1]$, $A[2, 2]$ and $A[1, 3]$ etc. . . . .

In this case the "wave front" proceeds at a $45°$ angle in the array.

The combination of these techniques as well as improvements in the handling of conditional and unconditional transfer of control statements have given viable results. Kuck and his coworkers have shown that 16 processors could be kept busy when processing ordinary programs. However, system programs are not amenable to such improvements. Other techniques, such as pipelining, can be used but they require human analysis.

Processor Scheduling

Operating Systems for MIMD architectures must contain a scheduler which assigns tasks to Pc's. We have noted in Section 1 that this scheduling could be done by a specialized Pc (fixed-control) or that each Pc could schedule itself (floating-control). Case studies have shown the superiority of the latter scheme when there is no special hardware for the scheduler (this extra hardware could be in the form of an associative memory and/or tailored microprograms; recall the TI ASC virtual processors). In this section, we review some performance aspects of the scheduling of processors.

Multiprocessors consisting of n identical Pc's can be evaluated by queueing theory models. Poisson arrival (rate λ) and exponential service time (average execution time $1/\mu$) are assumed yielding a utilization factor of $\rho = \lambda/n\mu$. The n processors are to execute jobs whose only known characteristics from the distribution of their execution times are the mean m_k and standard deviation σ_k of the k independent subjobs comprising a job. Then, we can compare three policies:

- Multiprogramming: The k subjobs of a job are assigned to the same processor (i.e., $k = 1$);
- Multiprocessing: The k subjobs are distributed among the n processors and two jobs cannot be present in the system at the same time;
- Parallel processing: The first free processor executes the first (in a FIFO sense) subjob available.

For the parallel processing case, the throughput rate is $n\mu/m_k$; in the multiprocessing case, it is $1/m_0$ where m_0 is the mean execution time of an entire job. If m_k is large, the multiprocessing approach will tend asymptotically to be as efficient as parallel processing but when m_k is small, pure multiprocessing can become very disadvantageous. Another interesting conclusion which can be obtained from the analysis is that the number of subjobs in the system in a parallel processing mode is larger for n processors with a service time $1/\mu$ than with $n/2$ processors which are twice as fast (i.e., of service time $1/2\mu$) for the same utilization factor. This should not be surprising in light of the analysis of I/O systems as seen in Chapter 8 Section 5.

These general conclusions reached from the queueing analysis are consistent with our intuition. At the other end of the spectrum, we can look at specific cases and apply deterministic scheduling techniques. We do not repeat here the definition and goals of deterministic scheduling. The reader is referred to Chapter 4 Section 3.3 where some scheduling algorithms in the case of procedural dependencies of the tasks forming a tree were presented. A more general case where the precedence relationship of the tasks form a directed acyclic graph (dag) is considered here.

The model is as follows. The tasks system is represented by a dag $G(T, U)$

where $T_i \in T$ is a task and the arcs U show the precedence relationships, that is, if $(T_i, T_j) \in U$ then T_j cannot be scheduled before T_i's execution is completed. Each task takes $\mu(T_i)$ time units (we restrict ourselves to integer $\mu(T_i)$'s). The MIMD system consists of n identical Pc's. As in the case of trees, we consider only list scheduling algorithms.

The practical importance of this type of study should not be overemphasized since no real system, hardware and software, can realistically be represented by the abstraction of deterministic scheduling. However, some interesting insights can be obtained. For example, the following anomalies can occur while scheduling tasks on a multiprocessor system. If we vary singly one of the four parameters:

- Using a new labelling algorithm;
- Relaxing the precedence constraints, i.e., having more parallelism by erasing some arcs in U;
- Decreasing the execution times;
- Increasing the number of processors;

then the total completion time can increase! The latter case is illustrated in Figure 10.39 with a task system of 7 tasks $(T_1, T_2, \ldots, T_7)$. The precedence relationships and execution times are shown in Figure 10.39.a. With a priority list $(T_1, T_2, T_3, T_4, T_5, T_6, T_7)$ the completion time is 6 time units on 2 processors and 7 on 3 processors (cf. Figure 10.39.b and c).

A bound for the ratio of completion time for two task systems $G(T, U)$ and $G'(T, U')$ with $U' \subseteq U$, $\mu'(T_i) \le \mu(T_i)$ for all $T_i \in T$, with two different

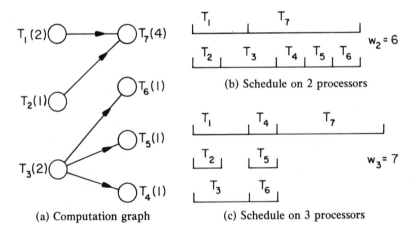

(a) Computation graph   (b) Schedule on 2 processors   (c) Schedule on 3 processors

Figure 10.39   Anomaly in deterministic scheduling

labelling algorithms L and L', and running on n and n' processors respectively is:

$$w'/w \leq 1 + (n - 1)/n'$$

where w and w' are the respective completion times of G and G'. If we let $n = n'$, then the bound becomes $(2 - 1/n)$. This means that for a given set of tasks and a given multiprocessor system, no schedule will turn out to be worse than twice the optimal one. This result is important since the number of polynomial time algorithms yielding optimal algorithms is severely limited. For example, the two apparently simple problems:

- Find an optimal schedule for m independent tasks T_i of various integer execution times $\mu(T_i)$ on 2 processors;
- Find optimal schedules on any k processors for a task system with all tasks taking unit time;

are in the class of NP-complete problems (those "hard" problems mentioned several times in preceding chapters).

We have seen before that Hu's algorithm yielded an optimal schedule for a tree and all $\mu(T_i)$ equal. Hu's algorithm could not be extended to the case of unequal $\mu(T_i)$. We show here that it cannot be extended to the case of dags with equal task times. The counter-example of Figure 10.40.a and Figure 10.40.b is sufficient to prove this point. However, a polynomial time optimal algorithm exists for the case $n = 2$.

This algorithm, due to Coffman and Graham, labels nodes level by level as in Hu's algorithm but with an extra constraint. The algorithm involves the comparison of decreasing sequences of integers. We say that $N = \{n_1, n_2, \ldots, n_s\}$ is smaller than $N' = \{n_1', n_2', \ldots, n_t'\}$ if either:

(1) $n_j = n_j'$, $1 \leq j \leq i - 1$ and $n_i < n_i'$ for some $i \geq 1$, or
(2) $s < t$ and $n_i = n_i'$, $1 \leq i \leq s$.

Now, for a given task T_i, let $N(T_i)$ be the decreasing sequence of the labels of its successors. The labelling algorithm is:

(1) Label the nodes without successors as $1, 2, \ldots, m$.
(2) Assume that $(k - 1)$ nodes have been labelled. Consider all unlabelled tasks $T_{i_1}, \ldots, T_{i_n}$ which have all their successors in these $(k - 1)$ nodes. Let $N(T_{i_1}), \ldots, N(T_{i_n})$ be the decreasing sequences corresponding to the respective labels of their successors. Label as k that T_{i_1} for which $N(T_{i_j})$ is minimal. Repeat step 2 until all tasks have been labelled.
(3) The priority list is by decreasing label order.

This algorithm applied to the task system of Figure 10.40.a yields the label-

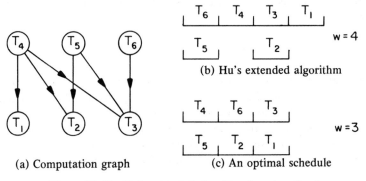

(a) Computation graph

(b) Hu's extended algorithm

$w = 4$

(c) An optimal schedule

$w = 3$

Figure 10.40   Hu's extended algorithm is not optimal

ling (T_4, T_5, T_6, T_3, T_2, T_1) and the (optimal) scheduling on 2 processors of Figure 10.40.c.

This algorithm is not directly extendable to either the case of three processors, or two processors of different speeds, or of tasks with unequal execution time even if these times are only 1 or 2 units. This latter problem is NP-complete; there is a strong conjecture that the second one could be solved in polynomial time and the first problem still remains as an open question.

In the deterministic scheduling algorithms presented in Chapter 4 and in this section, we have assumed that once a task was assigned to a processor, it would be executed without interruption. Another policy is to allow preemptions. A task T_i can be interrupted and resumed later, possibly on another processor. Keeping the assumption that all $\mu(T_i)$ are integers, scheduling m independent tasks becomes a trivial problem and the optimal schedule has a completion time (for an n-processor system) of:

$$w = \max\left(\max\left(\mu(T_i)\right), \frac{1}{n} \sum_{i=1}^{m} \mu(T_i)\right).$$

The duals of Hu's algorithm (optimal scheduling on any number of processors in the case of a tree) and that of Coffman and Graham (optimal scheduling on two processors in the case of a dag) exist in the case of preemptive scheduling. The algorithm (due to Muntz and Coffman) can be explained as follows.

When a task T_i has a weight $\mu(T_i)$ larger than one, we expand it into $\mu(T_i)$ tasks, T_{i_1}, T_{i_2}, ..., $T_{i_{\mu(T_i)}}$ such that T_{i_1} precedes T_{i_2} which precedes T_{i_3} etc .... This is repeated for all T_i of execution time greater than one. We continue by building a priority list on this new task system according to Hu's extended labelling algorithm (longest path or level labelling). To build the schedule, we consider the tasks at the highest level. Say that there are k of them and n processors. We assign them as a set of independent tasks. If $k >$ n and $k \bmod n \neq 0$, then we must preempt some tasks and reschedule them during the (k/n)th time period so that no processor is idle. We continue in this fashion level by level until all tasks are assigned.

For example, consider the dag of Figure 10.41.a and its expansion in Figure 10.41.b. The optimal schedule on two processors without preemption is shown in Figure 10.41.c (it was not obtained by a known scheduling algorithm), and the preemptive optimal algorithm is in Figure 10.41.d. Note that tasks $T_{1.2}$, $T_{2.2}$ and $T_{4.1}$ "share" one and a half time units.

This algorithm is not extendable to the case of a dag and more than two processors. Because of all the limitations on optimal algorithms, it is necessary to use heuristics and it is useful to have bounds on their performance.

We have already given a general bound. Tighter ones can be obtained for either a given dag or for a given algorithm. We shall not dwell further on this topic since it is more in the realm of Operating Systems Theory or of Opera-

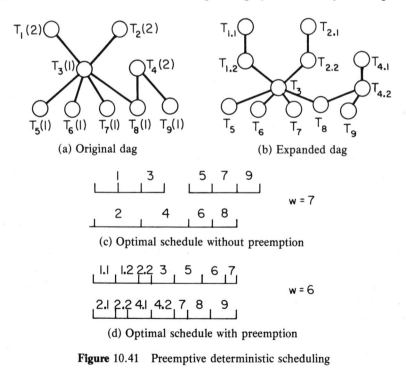

(a) Original dag

(b) Expanded dag

(c) Optimal schedule without preemption

(d) Optimal schedule with preemption

Figure 10.41 Preemptive deterministic scheduling

tions Research than of Systems Architecture. It is important to know however that heuristics based on the longest path labelling perform extremely well and are close to optimality except in pathological cases.

Multiprocessing Overhead

In the queueing and in the deterministic scheduling analyses, we have not taken into account the overhead accrued by the use of several processors. This overhead takes the form of synchronization or locking steps and can be extremely important. The analysis of real systems, or simulation, are currently the only tools that can be used to assess the impact of this overhead. We give the results of two studies to shed some light on this problem which has not yet received as much attention as it deserves.

The first study is Oleinick's work already cited when memory interference was evaluated. Several processors in the C.mmp system cooperate to find the root of an equation. Each processor, after having terminated its computation for a given subinterval, waits until all others are finished in order to know whether the root has been found or what its next subinterval will be. This synchronization has been implemented by several mechanisms in order to evaluate their performance. We present only two for comparison purposes. The most rudimentary is a "Spin-lock", in which a processor continually tests a semaphore until it can perform a P operation successfully. The two drawbacks are that the processor is busy waiting, that is, it cannot do any other useful work, and that the processor continually references the memory module where the semaphore is stored thus increasing memory interference. A second mechanism is to have the synchronization be performed by the Operating System. When a process blocks on a P operation, it is put in a queue attached to the semaphore and swapped out. It will be awakened when the blocking condition is not true anymore and when the process is the first (in some scheduling sense) in the semaphore's queue. Because of the swapping overhead this second solution is two orders of magnitude slower than the spin-lock but it frees the processor. When the compute time for each iteration is of the same order of magnitude as the synchronization time of the second primitive, the maximum speed-up for 8 processors is 2.8 under a spin-lock synchronization and 2.4 for the other primitive. When the computation time is significantly larger, the differences between the two synchronization modes is insignificant. Oleinick's data shows that 50% of the optimal speed-up can be obtained with a spin-lock synchronization if the compute time is 2ms. while this figure must be almost 10 times as large for the other primitive. When the compute times are sufficiently large (half a second), there is no distinction between all the primitives which were tested.

Concurrent search and insertion in balanced trees is the topic of the second study. An MIMD architecture is assumed without memory interference (i.e., the results will be optimistic). The measured overhead due to parallelism is limited to the locking and unlocking of nodes in the tree mainly by the processes performing insertions, and by the presence of extra fields in the nodes which have to be updated in the case of multiple processors and which need not be present if there were a single processor. Figure 10.42 (taken from C. Ellis' work) shows the number of inserting processors kept busy for two different algorithms as the tree size increases. As can be seen the choice of a judicious algorithm is quite important. Figure 10.43 shows the speed-up vs. the number of processors. It indicates that for the best algorithm almost 50% of the time is spent in overhead (and recall that memory interference is not taken into account). It is a figure which is far from negligible and which has to be kept in mind when assessing the performance of MIMD systems.

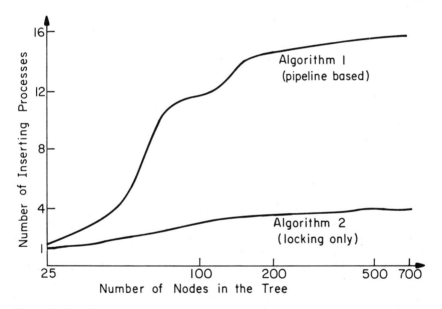

Figure 10.42   Number of processors kept busy in concurrent insertions in 2-3 trees

10.5 BIBLIOGRAPHICAL NOTES, REFERENCES AND EXERCISES

There have been many surveys on various aspects of supercomputers. We mention them first in alphabetical order and will refer to them in specific instances later in this

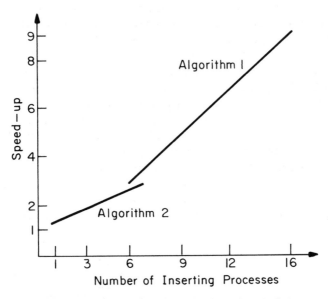

Figure 10.43   Speed-up in concurrent insertions in 2-3 trees

section [Baer 73, Baer 76, Chen 75, Enslow 74, Enslow 77, Higbie 73, Kuck 77, Ramamoorthy and Li 77, Stone 75].

Flynn's classification of computer systems appeared in the classical paper [Flynn 66]. Other classifications have been attempted [Baer 73, Händler 77] with the goal of making more precise some of Flynn's broad classes. The geometric performance model presented in Section 1 is due to Chen [Chen 71]. More elaborate derivations can be found in [Chen 75].

Pipeline and vector processors are extensively surveyed in [Chen 75, Ramamoorthy and Li 77]. The reservation table and looping pipeline analysis are derived from [Davidson, Shar, Thomas and Patel 75]. Some examples of software pipelining can be found in [Baer and Ellis 77 and Ellis 80]. The Amdahl 470 V/6 is described in [Amdahl 75]. [Russell 78] is a general introduction to the CRAY-1. More details can be found in [Cray 77]. The concept of chaining is explained in [Johnson 78]. [Baskett and Keller 77 and Sites 78] present some interesting analyses and suggest improvements for the performance of the CRAY-1. Various aspects of the CDC STAR-100 are described in [Hintz and Tate 72, Hohn and Jones 73 and Requa 78]. The reference manual for this machine is [Control Data 72]. The Quicksort example of Section 2.4 is abstracted from [Stone 78]. A general presentation of the TI ASC can be found in [Watson 72] with more details in [Texas Instruments 72]. The ALU design is treated in [Stephenson 75].

The ILLIAC IV system is described in [Barnes et al. 68]. The implementation of the processing element is presented in [Davis 69]. The concepts of skewed and straight storage were first outlined in [Kuck 68]. An introduction to Glypnir can be found in [Lawrie, Layman, Baer and Randall 75] and CFD is mentioned in [Waldken, McIntyre and Laws 77].

Interconnection networks have their origins in telephone rearrangeable switching networks [Benes 65, Opferman and Tsao-Wu 71]. Batcher networks were first described in [Batcher 68]. The perfect shuffle has been thoroughly investigated by Stone [Stone 71, Stone 75]. Other alignment networks are described in [Lawrie 75] and surveyed by Kuck [Kuck 77]. An assessment of the research on switching networks up to 1974 can be found in [Thurber 74]. [Siegel 77] discusses the impact of masking on several interconnection schemes.

The Burroughs BSP is introduced in [Jensen 78]. [Feinbach and Stevenson 79] are the proponents of the Phoenix array processor.

Multiprocessing systems and their topologies are extensively surveyed in [Baer 76, Enslow 74 and Enslow 77]. [Wulf and Bell 72] is the first presentation of C.mmp. A later configuration and performance analyses on memory interference and synchronization overhead can be found in [Oleinick 78]. The PLURIBUS multiprocessor is described in [Heart et al. 73]. Cm*'s architecture and implementation are presented in [Swan et al. 77 and Swan, Fuller and Siewiorek 77]. The implementation of a subset of ALGOL-68 on Cm* is outlined in [Hibbard, Hisgen and Rodeheffer 78].

The memory interference problem is surveyed in [Chang, Kuck and Lawrie 77]. For alternate derivations the reader is referred to [Strecker 70, Bhandarkar 75 and Baskett and Smith 76]. This latter reference reports the results of simulations used for Table 10.3. Figure 10.33 showing memory interference in C.mmp is from [Oleinick 78].

The FORK-JOIN concept is due to [Conway 63]. Many variants can be found (e.g., see [Baer 73]). The study of the synchronization of concurrent processes was started by Dijkstra [Dijkstra 65] who also introduced the concept of semaphores [Dijkstra 68]. Since then numerous extensions and improvements have been published. The more well-known are monitors [Hoare 74, Brinch Hansen 77]. Alternate synchronization methods not using semaphores are examplified by Lamport's bakery algorithm [Lamport 74]. Deadlock properties in computer systems, and methods to avoid deadlocks are surveyed in [Coffman, Elphick and Shoshani 71 and Holt 72]. The cache synchronization problem is studied in [Tang 76 and Censier and Feautrier 78].

Automatic detection of parallelism in FORTRAN programs is the subject of Russell's thesis [Russell 69]. A similar approach is found in [Ramamoorthy and Gonzales 69]. Loop analysis has been studied in [Lamport 74, Muraoka 71] and is summarized in [Kuck 77]. Experiments on the number of paths which can be executed concurrently in ordinary programs can be found in [Kuck, Muraoka and Chen 72].

[Gonzalez and Ramamoorthy 72] presents a convincing case study for the use of decentralized control. Queueing theory approaches to scheduling can be found in [Coffman 67] while deterministic scheduling is the subject of [Coffman 76]. General bounds on multiprocessor deterministic scheduling are found in [Graham 72]. The optimal scheduling algorithm on two processors without preemption is due to [Coffman and Graham 72] while the preemptive counterpart is from [Muntz and Coffman 69]. The two studies on multiprocessor overhead are [Oleinick 78 and Ellis 80].

References

1.   Amdahl Corp. Amdahl 470 V/6 Machine Reference, Sunnyvale, Cal. 1975.

2.   Baer, J.-L., "A Survey of Some Theoretical Aspects of Multiprocessing", *Computing Surveys, 5,* (Mar. 1973), 31-80.

3.   Baer, J.-L., "Multiprocessing Systems", *IEEE Trans. on Comp., C-25,* (Dec. 1976), 1271-1277.

4.   Baer, J.-L. and C. Ellis, "Model, Design, and Evaluation of a Compiler for a Parallel Processing Environment", *IEEE Trans. on Soft. Eng., SE-3,* (Nov. 1977), 394-405.

5.   Barnes, G. H., Brown, R. M., Kato, M., Kuck, D. J., Slotnick, D. L. and R. A. Stokes, "The ILLIAC IV Computer", *IEEE Trans. on Comp., C-17,* (Aug. 1968), 746-757.

6.   Baskett, F. and T. W. Keller, "An Evaluation of the CRAY-1 Computer", in *High Speed Computer and Algorithm Organization.* D. Kuck et al., eds., Academic Press, New York, NY, 1977, 71-84.

7.   Baskett, F. and A. J. Smith, "Interference in Multiprocessor Computer Systems with Interleaved Memory", *Comm. ACM, 19,* (Jun. 1976), 327-334.

8.   Batcher, K. C., "Sorting Networks and their Applications", *Proc. AFIPS 1968 Spring Joint Comp. Conf., 32,* AFIPS Press, Montvale, NJ, 1968, 307-314.

9.   Benes, V. E., *Mathematical Theory of Connecting Networks and Telephone Traffic,* Academic Press, New York, NY, 1965.

10. Bhandarkar, D. P., "Analysis of Memory Interference in Multiprocessors", *IEEE Trans. on Comp., C-24,* (Sep. 1975), 897-908.

11. Brinch Hansen, P. *The Architecture of Concurrent Programs,* Prentice-Hall, Englewood Cliffs, N.J. 1977.

12. Censier, L. M., and P. Feautrier, "A New Solution to Coherence Problems in Multicache Systems", *IEEE Trans. on Comp., C-27,* (Dec. 1978), 1112-1118.

13. Chang, D. Y., Kuck, D. J. and D. H. Lawrie, "On the Effective Bandwidth of Parallel Memories", *IEEE Trans. on Comp., C-26,* (May 1977), 480-490.

14. Chen, T. C., "Parallelism, Pipelining, and Computer Efficiency", *Computer Design,* (Jan. 1971), 69-74.

15. Chen, T. C., "Overlap and Pipeline Processing", in *Introduction to Computer Architecture,* H. Stone ed., SRA, Chicago, Ill., 1975, 375-431.

16. Coffman, E. G., "Bounds on Parallel Processing of Queues with Multiple Jobs", *Naval Research Logical Quaterly, 14,* (Sep. 1967), 345-366.

17. Coffman, E. G. ed. *Computer and Job-Shop Scheduling Theory,* John Wiley, New York, N.Y. 1976.

18. Coffman, E. G., Elphick, M., and A. Shoshani, "System Deadlocks", *Computing Surveys, 3,* (Jun. 1971), 67–78.

19. Coffman, E. G., and R. L. Graham, "Optimal Scheduling for Two Processor Systems", *Acta Informatica, 1,* (1972), 200–213.

20. Control Data Corporation. Control Data STAR-100 Computer Hardware Reference Manual, Minneapolis, Minn, 1972.

21. Conway, M., "A Multiprocessor System Design", *Proc. AFIPS 1963 Fall Joint Comp. Conf., 24,* Spartan Books, Baltimore, Md, 1963, 139–146.

22. Cray Research Inc. CRAY-1 Computer System. Hardware Reference Manual, Minneapolis, Minn, 1977.

23. Davidson, E. S., Shar, L. E., Thomas, A. T., and J. H. Patel, "Effective Control for Pipelined Computers", *COMPCON Digest,* 1975, 181–184.

24. Davis, R. L., "The ILLIAC IV Processing Element", *IEEE Trans. on Comp., C-18,* (Sep. 1969), 800–816.

25. Dijkstra, E. W., "Solution of a Problem in Concurrent Programming", *Comm. ACM, 8,* (Sep. 1965), 569–570.

26. Dijkstra, E. W., "Cooperating Sequential Processes", in *Programming Languages,* F. Genuys ed., Academic Press, New York, NY, 1968, 43–112.

27. Ellis, C., "Concurrent Search and Insertion in 2–3 Trees", to appear in *Acta Informatica,* (1980).

28. Enslow, P. H., Jr., ed., *Multiprocessors and Parallel Processing,* Wiley-Interscience, New York, NY, 1974.

29. Enslow, P. H., Jr., "Multiprocessor Organization", *Computing Surveys, 9,* (Mar. 1977), 103–129.

30. Feierbach, G. F. and D. K. Stevenson, "The Phoenix Array Processor', *IAC Newsletter, 3,* (Jun. 1979), 0–9.

31. Flynn, M. J., "Very High Speed Computing Systems", *Proc. IEEE, 54,* (Dec. 1966), 1901–1909.

32. Gonzalez, M. J. and C. V. Ramamoorthy, "Parallel Task Execution in a Decentralized System", *IEEE Trans. on Comp., C-21,* (Dec. 1972), 1310–1322.

33. Graham, R. L., "Bounds on Multiprocessing Anomalies and Packing Algorithms", *Proc. AFIPS 1972 Spring Joint Comp. Conf., 40,* AFIPS Press, Montvale, N.J., 1972, 205–217.

34. Händler, W., "The Impact of Classification Schemes on Computer Architecture", *Proc. 1977 Int. Conf. on Parallel Processing,* 1977, 7–15.

35. Heart, F. E., Ornstein, S. M., Crowther, W. R., and W. B. Barker, "A New Minicomputer/Multiprocessor for the ARPA Network", *Proc. AFIPS 1973 Nat. Comp. Conf., 42,* AFIPS Press, Montvale, N.J. 1973, 529–537.

36. Hibbard, P., Hisgen, A., and T. Rodeheffer, "A Language Implementation Design for a Multiprocessor Computer System", *Proc. 5th Symp. on Comp. Arch.*, 1978, 66-72.

37. Higbie, L. C., "Supercomputer Architecture", *Computer, 6,* (Dec. 1973), 48-58.

38. Hintz, R. G. and D. P. Tate, "Control Data STAR-100 Processor Design", *COMPCON Digest,* 1972, 1-4.

39. Hoare, C. A. R., "Monitors: An Operating System Structuring Concept", *Comm. ACM, 17,* (Oct. 1974), 549-557.

40. Hohn, W. C. and P. D. Jones, "The Control Data STAR-100 Paging Station", *Proc. AFIPS 1973 Nat. Comp. Conf., 42,* AFIPS Press, Montvale, N.J. 1973, 421-426.

41. Holt, R. C., "Some Deadlock Properties of Computer Systems", *Computing Surveys, 4,* (Sep. 1972), 179-195.

42. Jensen, C., "Taking Another Approach to Supercomputing", *Datamation,* (Feb. 1978), 159-172.

43. Johnson, P., "An Introduction to Vector Processing", *Computer Design,* (Feb. 1978), 89-97.

44. Kuck, D. J., "ILLIAC IV Software and Application Programming", *IEEE Trans. on Comp., C-17,* (Aug. 1968), 746-757.

45. Kuck, D. J., "A Survey of Parallel Machine Organization and Programming", *Computing Surveys, 9,* (Mar. 1977), 29-59.

46. Kuck, D. J., Muraoka, Y., and S. C. Chen, "On the Number of Operations Simultaneously Executable in FORTRAN-like Programs and their Resulting Speed-up". *IEEE Trans. on Comp., C-21,* (Dec. 1972), 1293-1309.

47. Lamport, L., "The Parallel Execution of DO-loops", *Comm. ACM, 17,* (Feb. 1974), 83-89.

48. Lamport, L., "A New Solution of Dijkstra's Concurrent Programming Problem", *Comm. ACM, 17,* (Aug. 1974), 453-454.

49. Lawrie, D. H., "Access and Alignment of Data in an Array Processor", *IEEE Trans. on Comp., C-24,* (Dec. 1975), 1145-1155.

50. Lawrie, D. H., Layman, T., Baer, D., and J. M. Randal, "Glypnir—A Programming Language for ILLIAC IV", *Comm. ACM, 18,* (Mar. 1975), 157-164.

51. Muntz, R. R., and E. G. Coffman, "Optimal Preemptive Scheduling on Two Processor Systems", *IEEE Trans. on Comp., C-18,* (Nov. 1969), 1014-1020.

52. Muraoka, Y., *Parallelism Exposure and Exploitation in Programs,* Ph.D. Dissertation, University of Illinois, 1971.

53. Oleinick, P. N., *The Implementation and Evaluation of Parallel Algorithms on C.mmp*, Ph.D. Dissertation, Carnegie-Mellon University, 1978.

54. Opferman, D. C. and N. T. Tsao-Wu, "On a Class of Rearrangeable Switching Networks", *Bell System Technical Journal, 50*, (May 1971), 1579-1618.

55. Ramamoorthy, C. V., and M. J. Gonzalez, "Recognition and Representation of Parallel Processable Streams in Computer Programs, II (Task/Process Parallelism)", *Proc. ACM 24th Nat. Conf.*, ACM, New York N.Y. 1969, 387-397.

56. Ramamoorthy, C. V. and H. F. Li, "Pipeline Architectures", *Computing Surveys, 9*, (Mar. 1977), 61-102.

57. Requa, J. E., "Virtual Memory Design Reduces Program Complexity", *Computer Design*, (Jan. 1978), 97-106.

58. Russell, E. C., *Automatic Program Analysis*, Ph.D. Dissertation, UCLA, 1969.

59. Russell, R. M., "The CRAY-1 Computer System", *Comm. ACM, 21*, (Jan. 1978), 63-72.

60. Siegel, H. J., "Analysis Techniques for SIMD Machine Interconnection Networks and the Effect of Processor Address Masks", *IEEE Trans. on Comp., C-26*, (Feb. 1977), 153-162.

61. Sites, R. L., "Analysis of the CRAY-1 Computer", *Proc. 5th Annual Symp. on Comp. Architecture*, 1978, 101-106.

62. Stephenson, C., "Case Study of the Pipeline Arithmetic Unit for the TI Advanced Scientific Computer", *Proc. 3rd Symposium on Comp. Arithmetic*, 1975, 168-173.

63. Stone, H. S., "Parallel Processing with the Perfect Shuffle", *IEEE Trans. on Comp., C-20*, (Feb. 1971), 153-161.

64. Stone, H. S., "Parallel Computers", in *Introduction to Computer Architecture*, H. S. Stone, ed., SRA, Chicago, Ill., 1975, 318-374.

65. Stone, H. S., "Sorting on STAR", *IEEE Trans. on Soft. Eng., SE-4*, (Mar. 1978), 138-146.

66. Strecker, W. D., *An Analysis of the Instruction Execution Rate in Certain Computer Structures*, Ph.D. Dissertation, Carnegie-Mellon University, 1970.

67. Swan, R. J., Bechtholsheim, A., Lai, K. W. and J. K. Ousterhout, "The Implementation of the Cm* Multimicroprocessor", *Proc. AFIPS 1977 Nat. Comp. Conf., 46*, AFIPS Press, Montvale, N. J., 1977, 645-655.

68. Swan, R. J., Fuller, S. H. and D. P. Siewiorek, "Cm*—A Modular Multimicroprocessor", *Proc. AFIPS 1977 Nat. Comp. Conf., 46*, AFIPS Press, Montvale, N. J., 1977, 637-644.

69. Tang, C. K., "Cache System Design in the Tightly Coupled Multiprocessor System", *Proc. AFIPS 1976 Nat. Comp. Conf., 45,* AFIPS Press, Montvale, N.J., 1976, 749-753.

70. Texas Instruments Inc. A Description of the Advanced Scientific Computer System, Austin, Texas, 1972.

71. Thurber, K. J., "Interconnection Networks- A Survey and Assessment", *Proc. AFIPS 1974 Nat. Comp. Conf., 43,* AFIPS Press, Montvale, N. J., 1974, 909-919.

72. Waldken, F., McIntyre, H. A. J. and G. T. Laws, "A Users View of Parallel Processors", *IAC Newsletter, 1,* (Aug. 1977), 1-14.

73. Watson, W. J., "The TI ASC- A Highly Modular and Flexible Supercomputer Architecture", *Proc. AFIPS 1972 Fall Joint Comp. Conf., 41 vol. 1,* AFIPS Press, Montvale, N. J., 1972, 221-228.

74. Wulf, W. A. and C. G. Bell, "C-mmp- A Multimini Processor", *Proc. AFIPS 1972 Fall Joint Comp. Conf., 41,* AFIPS Press, Montvale, N. J., 1972, 765-777.

Exercises

1. Händler has proposed a classification of computer systems as follows. Each system is represented by a triple:

$C = (K, D, W)$ where,

K is the number of control units,

D is the number of ALU's controlled by each unit,

W is the i-unit length of the entities managed by the D's.

For example, we have:

IBM System/370 $= (1, 1, 32)$,

CDC 6400 $= (1, 1, 60)$,

IBM System/360 dual processor $= (2, 1, 32)$,

ILLIAC IV $= (1, 64, 64)$,

C.mmp $= (16, 1, 16)$.

In addition, each element of the triple can be written in the form $i \times i'$, where i' indicates the parallelism or the number of pipeline stages in the ith component. Then, in $K \times K'$, we have K' independent computers of the same type processing programs, in $D \times D'$, we have D' functional units or ALU's per processor, and in $W \times W'$, W' expresses the number of stages in a pipelined ALU. We can thus represent:

TI ASC $= (1, 4, 64 \times 8)$,

CDC 6600 $= (1, 1 \times 10, 60)$.

What advantages does this representation have over Flynn's classification? What are its limitations? Give examples of systems which are not easily classified under this scheme. What operators would you add in order to make the notation more amenable to represent your latter examples?

2. Consider the geometric model of Section 1. Express the speed-up T_1/T_N as a function of ρ assuming $N = W$. Draw a curve similar to the one in Figure 10.2 replacing E by T_1/T_N.

3. Find the minimum average latency and the greedy cycles for the single function pipeline described by the reservation table

	1	2	3	4	5	6	7	8	9
$S1$	X								X
$S2$		X	X					X	
$S3$				X					
$S4$					X	X			
$S5$							X	X	

4. Prove that an upper bound for the average latency of a greedy cycle in a single function pipeline is one plus the number of non-zero entries in the collision vector.

5. In the CDC 6600, the following two operations can be executed concurrently:
$$X1 \leftarrow X2 + X3$$
$$X4 \leftarrow X5 * X2$$
In the CRAY-1, the vector operations
$$V1 \leftarrow V2 + V3$$
$$V4 \leftarrow V5 * V2$$
cannot be executed in parallel. Can you give some reasons for this (apparent) restriction? What kind of constraint could be imposed on D-unit times and issuing to make the concurrency possible? It is worthwhile? (Hint: Can you deliver two different elements of the same vector simultaneously?).

6. What is the time to perform the following operations on the CRAY-1 (refer to Table 10.1)
   a) $V1 \leftarrow V0 * S1$
      $V2 \leftarrow V1 + V3$
   b) $V2 \leftarrow V0 + V1$
      $V3 \leftarrow$ Left shift $(V2)$ by (contents of $A3$) places
      $V5 \leftarrow V3 \wedge V4$
   c) $V1 \leftarrow V0 * S1$
      $V2 \leftarrow V0 + V3$

7. Consider the ILLIAC IV routing network. Which PE's can be accessed from PE i
   a) in two one-step routings?
   b) in seven one-step routings?

8. With an ILLIAC IV architecture of 64 PE's, which of the straight and skewed storage is more efficient with respect to:
   a) Adding the elements of row i of a 64×64 matrix
   b) Adding the elements of column j of a 64×64 matrix
   c) Same as (a) but for all rows and save the result in a 64-element vector
   d) Same as (b) but for all columns and save the results in a 64-element vector
   What happens if the dimension of the matrix exceeds the number of processors?

9. Draw an 8 × 8 Batcher merging network; draw a sorting network to sort 12 elements.

10. Starting with an initial state of (3, 1, 0, 0) with 4 processors and 4 memory modules, what are the reachable next states and the probabilities to reach them in an MIMD cross-bar switch organization according to (cf. Section 4.2):
    a) a model without queueing?
    b) a model with queueing?

Chapter 11

FUTURE TRENDS IN COMPUTER SYSTEMS ARCHITECTURE

In this last chapter, we first briefly outline some architectures which have been proposed in the last two decades and which have not achieved a complete success because of their lack of generality. We shall be extremely specific and present examples rather than general concepts. We shall then consider some designs which have generated interest among the academic and industrial communities. Finally, the impact that very large scale integration (VLSI) may have on the architecture of future systems will be discussed.

11.1 OUTLINE OF SOME SPECIALIZED ARCHITECTURES

11.1.1 Associative Processors and Ensembles

Associative processors belong to the SIMD architectures. As such, they consist of several processing elements capable of performing synchronously the same operation under the supervision of a common control unit. In addition, data can be retrieved using the associative concept, i.e., by contents rather than by address (recall Chapter 5 Section 5). The SIMD and associative properties are useful for tasks encountered in many information retrieval projects, large data-base searches, radar signal tracking and processing, and, generally, for operations which can be performed in parallel on large sets of data. Associative processors can be classified according to the type of associative memory used. The two most important classes are *fully parallel* and *bit serial*.

The fully parallel associative processors can be word oriented or can use distributed logic. In the first case, comparison logic is present at each bit cell of the associative memory and decision logic (match or no-match) at the output of each word. In the second case, comparison logic is present only at each byte or group of bytes. In the bit serial organization, the bits in the same position in all words are processed simultaneously and only one such column at a time can be operated upon. This second organization is therefore slower but also cheaper. In the remainder of this section, we present an example of a distributed logic associative ensemble (PEPE) and of a bit-serial associative processor (STARAN). The term ensemble has the connotation of a powerful control unit by contrast with a simpler one in an associative processor.

PEPE (Parallel Element Processing Ensemble)

PEPE is a special-purpose "attachment" to a general-purpose computer called the host. It is housed in the Ballistic Missile Defense Agency quarters in Huntsville (Alabama). PEPE's main application is radar processing. A block diagram of the system is shown in Figure 11.1. The host is a CDC 7600 and the test and maintenance station is controlled by a Burroughs B1700. PEPE itself consists of a control system and up to 288 processing elements (PE's). PE's can be added or disconnected without impeding the normal operation of the system. One reason for this flexibility is that, unlike other SIMD systems, there is no direct connection between PE's. If data has to be transferred between PE's it will have to be routed through the host.

A PE consists of 3 units: the arithmetic unit (AU), correlation unit (CU), and associative output unit (AOU) sharing an element memory (EM). The three types of unit are under the global control of three control units: arithmetic control unit (ACU), correlation control unit (CCU) and associative output control unit (AOCU) which are part of the control system. Not shown in the figure are units in the control system for output data control and element memory control to resolve conflicts in data access, the interconnection logic between ACU, CCU and AOCU, and an I/O unit to connect to the host.

The PE's perform most of the computational work. For example, in a radar processing application each PE would have the responsibility of an object in the sky, maintaining a data base for this object in its EM. Arithmetic computations such as track updating and prediction can be performed, in parallel, in each AU. As in ILLIAC IV each PE can be enabled/disabled by setting a control flip-flop. The AU's execute under control of the ACU which sends microprogrammed sequences to them. Individual AU's do not have a stored program of their own.

Inputs to the PE's are controlled by the CU's under the supervision of the CCU. For example, information on a new object can be broadcast to all CU's at the same time. Each CU will correlate the new coordinates with predictions performed by the AU in the same element. The new information can

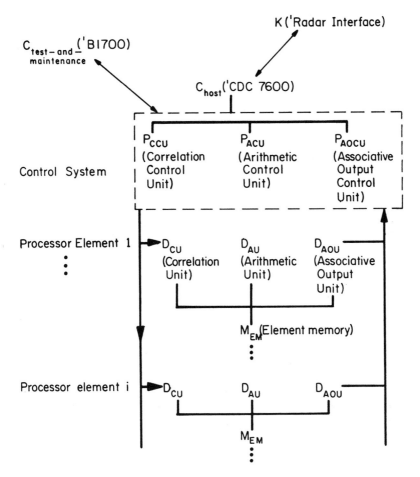

Figure 11.1.   PEPE PMS description

then be input to the CU whose data correlates, or to the first empty element if there were no correlation. It is this type of processing which gives to PEPE its associative label since the broadcast data can be viewed as an argument to be matched by the CU's acting as memory cells.

The AOU's, under control of the AOCU in an enable/disable fashion similar to the ACU's, provide data for the radar connected to the host. The data has to be ordered on an object by object basis and this ordering is performed through an associative maximum-minimum search.

The three units in a PE can operate concurrently. Since PEPE can have

288 elements, up to 864 operations can be in execution at the same time. In order to alleviate the loads on the input and output buses connecting the global control units and the PE's, most programs for the latter are loaded at initialization time with very few parameter modifications during execution.

The three global control units have the responsibility of the control flow. Each control unit has its own program and data memories. They can communicate with each other. A program is a mix of instructions executed either in the global control unit or broadcast to all PE's as in ILLIAC IV. Further details on the implementation can be found in the references.

This architecture is well suited for parallel tasks with low intertask communications requirements. The associative processing and the fact that the system can be in operation with a variable number of PE's are interesting and original features.

STARAN

Since the early seventies, Goodyear Aerospace Corporation has produced an associative processor called STARAN. The latest model, Series E, has the same general architecture as its predecessors. The main improvement is an expanded memory capacity. The salient features of STARAN are that it can simultaneously perform search, arithmetic and logical operations on either all or selected words of its memory. The memory can be accessed on a word by word basis or in a bit-slice manner. A processing element is associated with each memory word of 256 bits. The words are grouped into arrays of 256 words. STARAN can have from 1 to 32 array elements.

Because STARAN's designers felt that each system should be custom built for its users, the overall configuration has the form of Figure 11.2.a with STARAN interconnected through a custom interface unit to peripherals and other computers. The parallel I/O channel, PIO, can transfer in parallel up to $32.256 = 8192$ words, i.e., it has a direct connection to all memory words. An example installation, the RADCAP facility at the Rome Air Development Center, is shown in Figure 11.2.b. STARAN's internal organization is depicted in PMS form in Figure 11.3. The key elements are the associative control processor P_{AP}, the associative control memory M_{AP}, and the associative arrays. The function of P_{AP} is to perform data manipulations within the associative arrays as indicated by the program stored in M_{AP}. M_{AP} also contains data buffers.

An array element is shown in Figure 11.4.a. It consists of a 256×256 multidimensional access memory (in STARAN E, this has been expanded to several plans of 256×256 bits), 256 processing elements (one per memory word) and a flip (also called scramble/unscramble) interconnection network

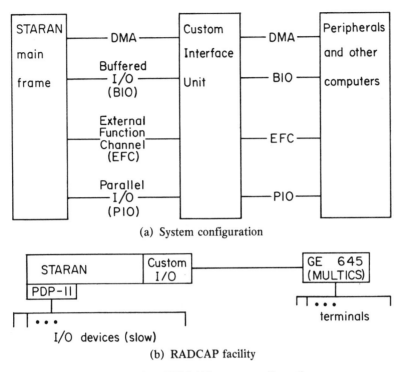

(a) System configuration

(b) RADCAP facility

Figure 11.2. STARAN system configuration

between the memory and the processing elements. From an operational viewpoint, the array has the form of Figure 11.4.b. The flip network is designed in such a way that words and bit-slices, as well as other templates, can be accessed easily while the multidimensional access memory (MDA) is implemented using conventional RAM chips.

For the purposes of illustrating how the MDA and flip networks are designed, we assume an 8×8 MDA. The 2^3 words of 2^3 bits are stored in 2^3 chips of 2^3 bits. The method can be generalized to any power of 2 ($2^8 = 256$ for STARAN). Memory words, bits within a word, chips, and bits within a chip have 3-bit addresses that will be denoted by 3-element vectors (capital letters will denote these vectors). The storage pattern is as follows. Bit B of word W will be stored on chip $B \oplus W$. Conversely, bit B on chip C stores bit B of word $B \oplus C$. Figure 11.5 shows the 8×8 MDA with a_{ij} being the ith bit of word j. We can observe that each bit-slice and each word are spread over the 8 chips. However, accessing is not restricted to these two modes; there

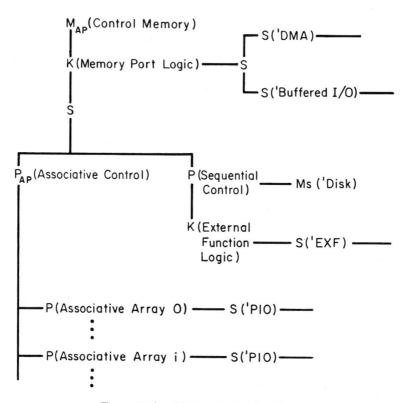

Figure 11.3.   STARAN PMS description

can be as many as 2^3 templates and this is important when only subsets of 256-bit words or bit-slices are required. An accessing mode can be represented by a 3-element vector M. In particular, bit-slice accessing will be $(0, 0, 0)$ and word accessing will be $(1, 1, 1)$. Let us denote by G the address of a template. Restricting ourselves to words and bit-slices, G will be the n-bit address of one of the 2^n words or bit-slices. The MDA is wired in such a way that to retrieve the bit corresponding to access mode M and address G on chip C, the local address on the chip is $G \oplus (M \cdot C)$. For example, if we want to access word 4 $(G = (1, 0, 0))$ under word access $(M = (1, 1, 1))$ then the local addresses are:

Chip 0: $(1, 0, 0) \oplus ((1, 1, 1) \wedge (0, 0, 0)) = (1, 0, 0)$
Chip 1: $(1, 0, 0) \oplus ((1, 1, 1) \wedge (0, 0, 1)) = (1, 0, 1)$
$\vdots$
Chip 7: $(1, 0, 0) \oplus ((1, 1, 1) \wedge (1, 1, 1)) = (0, 1, 1)$

This corresponds to $(a_{44}, a_{54}, \ldots, a_{34})$ as can be verified in Figure 11.5. Similarly, the 4th bit-slice can be retrieved by applying the local address $(1, 0, 0)$ to all chips since $M = (0, 0, 0)$. One more transformation is necessary to process the ith bit by the ith processing element. This can be achieved by sending the data on the output pin of chip C to processor $G \oplus C$. In the above example, the output of chip 0 will be sent to processor $(1, 0, 0) \oplus (0, 0, 0) = (1, 0, 0)$ independently of the accessing mode. Conversely, the data computed at processor P will be stored on chip $G \oplus P$.

This example shows how a multidimensional access memory can be built with ordinary RAM chips. The additional hardware required is a second set of address lines (the M lines) and a flip network. It has been shown that n levels of 2^n two-input selectors are sufficient to construct a flip network for a $2^n \times 2^n$ MDA and 2^n processing elements. Alternatively, a single level of selection and a perfect shuffle interconnection network could be used.

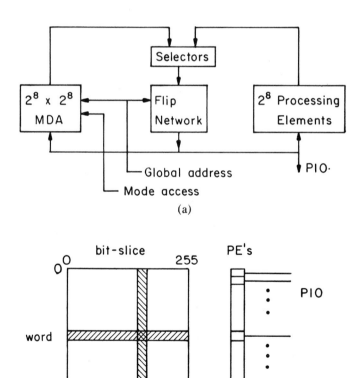

(a)

(b)

Figure 11.4. STARAN's array element

$$^{a}00 \quad ^{a}11 \quad ^{a}22 \quad ^{a}33 \quad ^{a}44 \quad ^{a}55 \quad ^{a}66 \quad ^{a}77$$

$$^{a}01 \quad ^{a}10 \quad ^{a}23 \quad ^{a}32 \quad ^{a}45 \quad ^{a}54 \quad ^{a}67 \quad ^{a}76$$

$$^{a}02 \quad ^{a}13 \quad ^{a}20 \quad ^{a}31 \quad ^{a}46 \quad ^{a}57 \quad ^{a}64 \quad ^{a}75$$

$$\vdots$$

$$^{a}07 \; \cdots \qquad\qquad \cdots\, ^{a}61 \quad ^{a}70$$

Figure 11.5. An 8 × 8 MDA memory

STARAN is well suited for applications which require parallel processing at the bit level (e.g., data base management, air traffic control) and word (or bit-group) level (e.g., arithmetic operations). Furthermore, the inclusion of the permutation network facilitates the efficient programming of functions such as the Fast Fourier Transform. Nonetheless, STARAN cannot be used as a stand-alone facility but must be part of a complex where it only performs parallel tasks.

11.1.2. High-level Language Architectures

Since the days when high-level languages were first accepted as the main tools for programming, computer architects have strived to include features which can help the translation and execution of source programs. Depending on the amount of hardware invested in that effort and on the mode of execution of the source program, we can distinguish between architectures with the following features:

- Instruction sets and stack organizations helping the execution of block-structured languages;
- Microprogram implementations geared to the interpretation of a given high-level language;
- Hardware specifically designed for the translation and subsequent execution of a high-level language.

The first category includes the stack computers presented previously such as the Burroughs B5500 and B6700 series and the HP-3000. To a lesser degree, more recent machines, such as the VAX 11/780, with an extensive instruction set can be considered as part of this class. We have discussed in Chapter

7 Section 3.2 high-level language direct execution by microprogram interpretation which forms the basis for architectures of the second category. In
addition to the EULER machine described in that chapter, there exist FOR-
TRAN, APL and ALGOL machines. The Burroughs B1700, which can interpret various high-level languages by changing microprograms, is also included in this class. Our interest in this section is in the third category whose
paradigm is SYMBOL.

The SYMBOL Computer

SYMBOL was developed in the late sixties by a team at Fairchild Camera
and Instrument Corporation under the direction of Rice and Smith. The sole
system ever built was delivered at Iowa State University in 1971. More than
20 research papers have been published on various aspects of SYMBOL. Our
presentation is succinct with emphasis on the system's architecture (for additional information see the references).

SYMBOL is a multiprocessor with several functional units dedicated to
specific tasks. The hardware (hardwired and not microprogrammed, and
hence with some lack of flexibility) translates and directly executes a high-
level language named the SYMBOL Programming Language (SPL). In addition, several other functional units execute operating system functions such
as scheduling, virtual memory management and command interpretation. A
block diagram of the system is shown in Figure 11.6 (in a PMS description we
would replace all units by processors except for the main memory Mp and the
disk). Before giving some details on the function of each processor, we emphasize the fact that there is no ISP for this machine. The programming
language is SPL, a mixture of ALGOL, APL and list-processing constructs,
geared towards non-numeric rather than scientific processing as is the whole
SYMBOL system.

Although SYMBOL can be characterized as a multiprocessor, no two
parts of the same program can be active at any given time. A task passes
from processor to processor during the editing, computing and executing
phases. However multiprogramming is possible. Four of the processors, the
channel controller (CC), the interface processor (IP), the translator (TR) and
the central processor (CP) can each execute a different task. The memory
controller (MC), memory reclaimer (MR) and system supervisor (SS) are
used as service processors for the other four. Up to 32 terminals can be linked
to CC and queues are provided for each processor. They are managed by SS.

Assuming a single task to be edited, compiled and executed, the control
flow would be as follows. The source code is entered through CC directly into
Mp bypassing MC. The SS receives control input from CC and passes control
to IP when a buffer has been filled in Mp. Text editing is handled in IP. Vir-

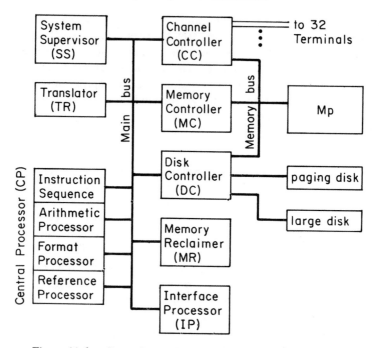

Figure 11.6.   General organization of the SYMBOL processor

tual memory allocation of the source program is performed by *MC* (the virtual memory scheme of SYMBOL is quite complex and would require another section to be adequately treated; since it is not the major point we wish to emphasize, we omit such a description). When the editing is completed to the user's satisfaction, he/she sends a RUN command. The *SS* then transfers control to the *TR* which "compiles" the source program into a reverse polish string and associated name tables as described later in the next paragraph. At the completion of the translation, control is transferred (through *SS*) to *CP* which executes the program. I/O transfers are handled by *SS*, *IP* and *CC* in a manner similar to the source program entry above. This oversimplified view is complicated by memory access conflicts which are resolved by a priority scheme on the main bus, by a paging mechanism which is handled by *SS* and the disk controller, and by multiprogramming context switching which is supervised by *SS*.

The high-level language architecture features are highlighted in the translator and in the central processor. The translator receives as input the edited source program which it transforms into a reverse polish string where each 32-bit instruction consists of an opcode followed by either an address, a literal, or nothing (e.g., for "add"). The address is an index in a name table with a distinct name table created for each block in the source program. The contents of the location pointed to by the index contain the virtual address of the operand, or its value if the latter is six or less characters. This latter case stems from the structure of the virtual memory and the fact that SYMBOL is a decimal machine. With some slight simplification, we can view the translated program as a string of operators and associated addresses ordered according to a reverse polish notation, with the addresses being references to descriptors pointing to operand values. The *TR* processor also performs the linking to library procedures which are stored in source form since the translation process is rapid enough to allow this representation.

The central processor is divided into 4 units: instruction sequencer, arithmetic, format and reference subprocessors. Only one of these units can be active at a time. They are internally connected by a local bus and they have access to the main bus. The instruction sequencer plays the role of an I-unit. It fetches and decodes the next instruction. This instruction is executed if it is a transfer flow of control, otherwise the instruction sequencer invokes one of the three other subprocessors. The arithmetic subprocessor performs arithmetic and numerical comparisons. The format subprocessor performs conversions between the external representation of data as strings of characters and the internal numeric form. It also executes scalar and Boolean instructions. The last subprocessor handles references to name tables, assignments of new values and the manipulation of complex data structures (these structures are complex because of the aforementioned virtual memory scheme which is partially based on "list of strings").

The other processors manage the virtual storage facility (*MC*, *MR*, parts of *SS*), the scheduler and multiprogram context switching (*SS*), text editing (*IP*) and I/O control (*CC*). Each of these processors has features of interest but they are not particularly germane to a discussion of high-level language architecture.

SYMBOL is one of the precursors to the distributed function architectures of the future (see next sections). Among its advantages is a very high "edit, load and go" speed. It is tailored to direct processing of source text thus bypassing several steps with respect to a normal job flow. On the negative side, SYMBOL only accepts source code from a single language. Modifications to the processors are practically impossible since they are hardwired. It would be interesting to see how such a design could be modified, with little loss in efficiency, if it were user microprogrammable so that it could accept several (related in structure) high-level languages.

11.2 DISTRIBUTED-FUNCTION ARCHITECTURES

In Chapter 10 we have presented several architectures which enhance multi-programming and multiprocessing facilities. In this section, we introduce some designs which also are intended to allow the concurrent use of many resources. These architectures depart from the von Neumann model even more than the SIMD and MIMD models.

11.2.1. Data-Flow Architectures

In the SIMD and MIMD schemes, the parallelism is controlled by procedural statements embedded (implicitly or explicitly) in the control flow of the programs. The basic idea behind the data flow architectures is that the computation is data driven. The data flow concept is based on the following two premises:

- An instruction executes when and only when all the operands required are available;
- Instructions are purely functional and produce no side-effects.

In this second condition the term instruction is quite general. It can be interpreted as the equivalent of a machine language instruction or as a complete procedure. It implies that iterative constructs should be abandoned in favor of recursive ones and of data streams.

Research in the data-flow area has concentrated more on the programming language aspects than on the implementation of data flow machines. This can be explained by the need (for data-flow proponents) to convince potential users that programming is feasible within the data-flow philosophy. This is not to say that there has been no attempt at building data-flow machines. A data-flow computer is operational at the University of Utah, another one near completion (1979) in Toulouse, France, and projects at MIT and UC Irvine have shown (via simulation) that such an approach is viable.

Since an instruction can be executed as soon as its operands are available, asynchronous concurrency must be easily represented in the data-flow language. Several graph models of computations, and their translation into textual programming languages, are appropriate for that purpose. The simple example of the computation of the roots of a quadratic equation will show the main concepts. The graphical representation is given in Figure 11.7. Operators are nodes of the graph and arcs represent the paths followed by the data. Data is queued on these arcs in a FIFO fashion and can be represented by tokens. An operator (instruction) can process its operands as

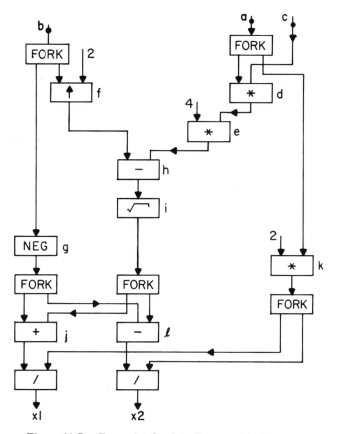

Figure 11.7.   Example of a data-flow graphical program

soon as all its input arc(s) carry a token (recall the Petri Net firing rules). An execution consists of removing tokens from the input arcs and of placing tokens on the output arc(s). (We assume that constants have an irremovable token.) In contrast with Petri Nets, each operator is fully specified, i.e., the net is completely interpreted. In Figure 11.7, the first two operations ready to be executed are the FORK's for duplicating a and b. After these two operations, $-b$, b^2, $a \cdot c$ and $2 \cdot a$ can be computed in any order. A textual description of the same program is shown in Figure 11.8. We have expanded the number of "let" statements at its extreme so that the maximum parallelism can be achieved. Note also that the "let" statements, which loosely speaking correspond to assignment statements, assign a single value to any given

```
procedure roots (input:a,b,c:real; output: x1,x2:real);
   var d,e,f,g,h,i,j,k,l:real;
      begin let d = a.c;
            let e = 4.d;
            let f = b↑2;
            let g = -b;
            let k = 2.a;
            let h = f - e;
            let i = SQRT(h);
            let j = g + i:
            let l = g - i;
            let x1 = j/k;
            let x2 = l/k
   end;
```

Figure 11.8.   Example of a data-flow textual program

variable. This *single assignment rule*, already encountered in the optimization of horizontal microprograms (Chapter 7 Section 4.2), is mandatory since the "let" statements can be executed in any order, as long as their operands are ready, and they should be void of side-effects.

This simple example does not shed any light on some important features required of all programming languages: expression of predicates, repetitive constructs, procedure calls and returns, and allocation of aggregate data structures. The first of these is treated in the graphical form in a manner reminiscent of the EOR extension of Petri Nets (cf. Chapter 2 Section 5.2). A loop can be seen as the replication of the body of the loop with new values computed from the initial and old values. In the graphical form, special operators are required to show the instantation of new values. In textual form, an operator, for example called **new**, plays the same role. Summing the first n integers could be written as:

> **let** $i = 1$; **let** sum $= 0$; ($*$ Initialization $*$)
> **while** $i \leq n$ **do**
>   **let new** $i = i + 1$;
>   **let new** sum $=$ sum $+ i$;
> **end;**

An important aspect of this segment of program is that the new sum is computed from the old sum and the old i so that the effect of the loop is to compute in parallel the recurrence equations:

$$i_{j+1} = i_j + 1,$$
$$\text{sum}_{j+1} = \text{sum}_j + i_j.$$

In the same spirit, if one of the recurrence relations took longer to compute than the other, computation of the second one need not be slowed down since we can individualize each newly created instance of a variable by attaching to it an activity number. In this case, the number could be the index of the recurrence (note that **let** $i = i + 1$ is illegal since it violates the single assignment rule). In essence, this fills the FIFO queues on the data arcs in the graphical representation. Similarly, the "application" of a procedure consists of providing the procedure definition and the list of its actual parameters to an "apply" operator. Several instances of the same procedure can be applied concurrently. This can be viewed as either replication of the procedural graph or as providing the arguments of the consecutive applications on the input arcs, again in a FIFO sense, and with activity numbers so that only arguments corresponding to the same activation are parts of the same operation. Finally, structured variables are handled in a manner reminiscent of record variables in Pascal.

We now give a schematic view of a data-flow architecture which can interpret languages of the type just described. The basic processor shown in Figure 11.9 consists of a memory which is an array of cells, an arbitration, a

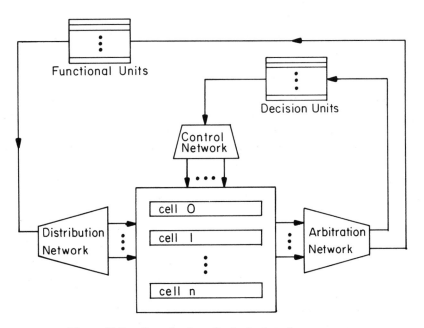

Figure 11.9. Organization of a basic data-flow processor

distribution and a control network, and some functional and decision units. Each cell contains an opcode and two registers with operand values. It corresponds to an operator in the data-flow graph. When both registers (assuming a binary operation) are holding values, a packet containing these values and the opcode is sent to the arbitration network which forwards it to the appropriate functional unit, or decision unit in case of a predicate. The outputs are sent to the distribution network in the form of (address + data) messages and are stored in the memory under the direction of either the distribution or the control network. This basic architecture can be expanded to contain a multi-level memory with the array shown in Figure 11.9 acting as a cache and with several modules similar to the basic one for the replication of procedures under the control of a scheduler. It is to be noted that the interconnection networks or modes of communication between the functional units and the memory are especially sensitive points in the design.

11.2.2   Distributed Processing and Local Networks

Distributed Processing and Distributed Function Architecture are terms which have taken so many different meanings that it has become difficult to pinpoint clear definitions. In this section we present some system designs which undoubtedly belong in these categories. They consist of several processor-memory pairs, or even several bona fide computers, connected to form cooperating systems under a decentralized control scheme. Cm*, presented in Chapter 10 Section 4, could be considered part of this class of systems although in the examples to follow the processors will not be able to communicate directly through shared memory. Rather, protocols similar in spirit to those implemented in geographically distant computer networks will be used. This will lead us to consider alternative communication designs for local networks. Because this field is in constant development, we renew our caution to the reader: we are only presenting a few specific examples with emphasis on the interprocessor communication aspects and do not strive for generality. We start by giving some rationale for the existence of such systems.

Multiprocessors of the MIMD type are limited in extensibility by the inflexibility of the $Pc - Mp$ switch. Adding or deleting elements is difficult because of features which have been incorporated for efficiency considerations (e.g., memory interleaving). Failure in one component might bring the whole system to a halt if a centralized control scheme is implemented. Distributed processing will try to alleviate these defects by allowing extensibility and graceful degradation (or enhancement) and by operating in a decentralized mode such that the failure of a component shuts down only a portion of the system. At the same time, processes, implemented on different processors, will cooperate towards a common goal of performance improvement. Some of the problems already cited for multiprocessors such as the contention for shared resources, here the communication links instead of memory, and the overhead for message passing or locking will still be present. The three systems whose descriptions follow are representative of a large class of distributed systems.

The Honeywell Experimental Distributed Processor (HXDP)

The HXDP consists of up to 64 processor-memory pairs (PE) connected through a bus interface unit to a synchronous bus. As of 1978, the experimental system had 5 PE's. The decentralized operating system was under implementation. The limitation to 5 PE's is not due to design difficulties but to the cost of building the interface units which are one order of magnitude more complex than the minicomputers they support. Figure 11.10 shows a schematic view of the HXDP which is meant to supervise real-time control tasks.

All communications between processes are in the form of messages (up to 255 words) transmitted over the global bit-serial bus even if the communicating processes are in the same PE. Each message is addressed by software defined names and each bus interface unit can recognize 8 names. In a PE, messages are transmitted from one circular FIFO output queue and received in eight circular FIFO input queues. When the output queue of a PE is not empty, the bus interface unit waits for its "turn" to take possession of

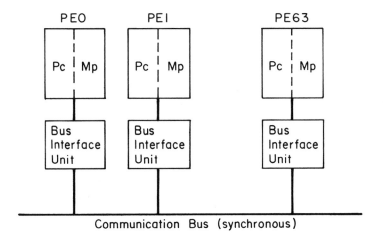

Figure 11.10. Honeywell Experimental Distributed Processor

the bus (see below for the detailed protocol) and sends the first message in the output queue. All bus interface units listen to the bus all the time and the one recognizing its (destination) name receives the message and places it in one of its input queues. A number of error checking and recovery procedures are included in the receiving of a message, hence the complexity of the bus interface unit.

Claiming of the bus by a bus interface unit proceeds as follows. Each interface unit contains a Boolean vector of 256 bits whose value, in each unit, is set at configuration time according to planned priorities, expected load etc.. An index to the vector is shifted simultaneously in all units at the end of a message transmission through a command sent on the bus. The Boolean vectors are such that of all indices (up to 64, one per unit), at most one points to a value "1". The unit which has such an index is the one allowed to transmit the next message. If the output queue is not empty the message is transmitted, otherwise a command signalling the end of a message is sent to increment the indices. This method is one of the most "synchronous" approaches. A dangerous error which could arise because of the requirement for all indices to be pointing to the same element is that some of them would become "out of synch". This is prevented by having the end of message command, a message broadcast to all units, carry the value of the index in the unit sending the command. Then all other units can synchronize themselves to the source's value.

Ethernet

Ethernet is one of several local networks which have been recently introduced. A local network in contrast with remote, or geographically dispersed, networks is one which connects computers and terminals within a 100 meter to 10 kilometer range at a speed of .1 to 10 megabits per second. Ethernet is housed at the Xerox Palo Alto Research Center and consists of over a hundred ALTO minicomputers, some larger computers, back-up storage devices, printing and duplicating facilities etc., connected via a shared passive communication facility called the Ether. In Figure 11.11, we show an Ethernet segment which can be expanded to several segments by including signal regenerators. Special nodes on the network, the gateways, provide the interfaces to other (local or remote) networks.

Ethernet's topology is that of an unrooted tree. There is a single path between any two nodes of the network, thus avoiding the possibility of a transmission interfering with itself. The "unrooted" property allows easy extension in any direction which is important since a new node, or station in Ethernet's terminology, can be inserted at the nearest convenient point. This

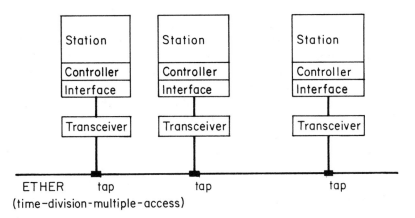

Figure 11.11. An Ethernet segment

topology implies a central connection scheme, implemented as the Ether, and distributed control since there is no active central facility.

Stations communicate by sending messages on the Ether. Since there is no central control, it is likely that two (or more) stations wish to transmit at the same time or, if not exactly at the same time, a second station might wish to transmit before the completion of the first station's message transmission. Therefore, we shall have collisions which must be detected and mechanisms to reschedule the aborted transmissions must be included. Messages are sent in packet form with source and destination physical addresses. All stations "listen" to the Ether and the one matching the destination address accepts the message. A destination address of 0 is interpreted as a broadcast to be accepted by all stations. Ethernet's philosophy is based on the high probability that a message placed on the Ether, and which has not been part of a collision, will be accepted. Thus at the lowest level, called packet transport level, there is no acknowledgment of the reception of a message. Naturally, higher level protocols (e.g., file transport) will embed acknowledgments and ask for transmission retries when necessary.

The high probability of having a packet reaching its destination is made possible by mechanisms implemented in the elements connecting the Ether and the stations (cf. Figure 11.11). The Ether, low-loss coaxial cable, is tapped with off-the-shelf CATV taps and connectors. The transceivers which connect directly to the Ether are designed to work and/or tolerate failures or disruptions so that a station can be removed without harm to the rest of the network. The transceivers contain hardware to sense that information is carried by the Ether and to defer transmitting until the Ether is silent. The sending receivers detect interference by comparing the values of the bit they receive with the one they sent. When they are different, the transceiver knows that a collision has occurred and transmission is aborted. Since a transceiver would not transmit if the Ether were busy, collisions occur only when two stations wish to transmit simultaneously during an interval equal to the time taken by a bit to perform a round trip through the network (this is called a slot, typically 10 μs for a network limited to 1 Km). When a station determines that a collision has occurred, it "jams" the Ether to ensure that all stations, or rather their transceivers, are aware of the problem. It then reschedules itself within a random interval, determined in the controller, of mean equal to a slot. If the new transmission again collides, the mean of this random interval is doubled and so on repeatedly until success is achieved. It has been shown that this Binary Exponential Backoff procedure is stable, i.e., the throughput of the network (transmission intervals/(transmission + contention) intervals) is a non-decreasing function of the load (number of stations desiring to transmit). The interface of a given station is responsible for accepting only those packets whose destination address corresponds to its station, for checking errors in the packet through cyclic redundancy checking, and for discarding packets which have been truncated because of interference detection or collision.

Ethernet which has been in operation for over five years has been highly successful. It has spawned a number of networks following the same "time-division-multiple-access", also called "carry-sense-multiple-access", to a broadcast channel policy.

The Distributed Computing System (DCS)

DCS, developed at the University of California at Irvine under Farber in the early seventies, is a network of minicomputers arranged in a ring topology (cf. Figure 11.12). Communication is between (software) processes by means of messages placed on the 2.3 megabits per second ring. Each minicomputer C is linked to the ring by an interface which contains buffers, a shift register and an associative memory loaded with the names of the processes currently active in C. To communicate, a process, via the minicomputer via the ring interface, places a message on the ring when it discovers an empty slot, that is when the ring does not carry any message for a sufficient time interval. This message contains a destination address, a process name, as well as the source address. It passes from ring interface to ring interface, with each interface checking the destination address against the names of its currently active processes. If a match is found, the interface copies the message and transmits it to its associated computer. Independently of the result of the

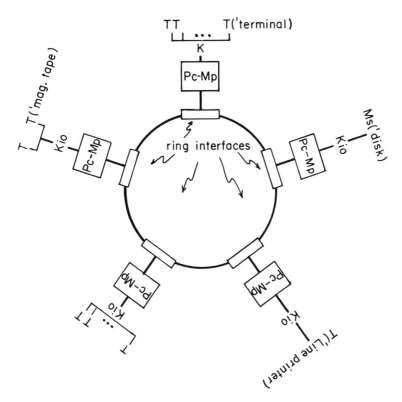

Figure 11.12. A schematic view of a ring network

comparison, the message is forwarded (on the ring) to the next interface. When the originator of the message recognizes the message it has sent, it retires the message from the ring. Broadcasting within this scheme is possible; it simply requires destination processes with the same name on all computers. An advantage of this method is that there is no need for tying physical addresses. As the other local networks or distributed architectures, the ring network is modular, its control is decentralized, and it can degrade gracefully.

11.2.3 Alterable and Fault-Tolerant Architectures

Multiprocessors of the MIMD and SIMD organizations have a rigid structure. Distributed function architectures and local networks most often will require building blocks larger than the memory and ALU chips currently available. With these latter building blocks, it is tempting to design systems meeting one or more of the following criteria:

- speed: as in conventional multiprocessing structures;
- modularity: the possibility of graceful degradation and enhancement without having to modify the architecture and operating system philosophies;
- flexibility: the possibility of having the system be configured or partitioned according to the problem(s) to be solved.

This last criterion leads to what has been called various names such as variable structure, restructurable, configurable, reconfigurable, and varistructured architectures. Distributed and federated systems can be added to this list. All the above systems are essentially multi- Pc or multi-functional units. Because single Pc systems whose microprograms can be modified at run time should be included, we will discuss "*alterable*" architectures. By adding the adverb "dynamically" we imply that this alteration be possible under program control.

A first classification of alterable architectures could be done according to the components (in a PMS sense) which can be altered. In ascending order of "looseness" in the coupling of the units we might have the classification summarized in Table 11.1.

Any microprogrammed processor with writable control store can be considered as alterable. Not only can we change the instruction set but also we can tune the architecture according to the problem to be run (recall Chapter 7 Section 3.3). This becomes important in the larger context of a local network of microprogrammable machines where some units have a specific role, this specificity being embedded in the microprogram. If a particular special-purpose unit fails it can be replaced "on the spot" by a general-purpose one by loading a new microprogram in the latter. We can stretch the definition of alterable architectures by including processors with microprogrammed multifunctional pipeline units. The control of the pipeline could change according to the application rather than according to the sequence of instructions, mostly if stages of the pipeline are microprocessors.

The next component which might be altered is the data word width. Again microprogrammed machines do it implicitly (cf. IBM System/370). However, a hardwired solution similar to ILLIAC IV might be preferred (cf. Chapter 10 Section 3.1). The processing elements can function either in a 64-bit mode, or as 2.32, or as 8.8 bit subprocessors. But these subprocessors are not independent since they share a common index register, that of the PE, and a routing register for communication with neighboring PE's. A more

Table 11.1   Classification of alterable architectures according to the modified components

Components	Examples
• K (Control Unit)	• Uniprocessors with writable control store
	• Multipurpose pipeline unit
• Data word size within the processors	• ILLIAC IV processing element
• Data word size by combining ALU's or Pc's	• Dynamic Computer Group
	• Varistructured arrays
• Addition of functional units	• Variable structure computer
	• Federated systems
• Topology (static)	• Variable topology multicomputers
	• SIMD networks
• Topology (dynamic)	
• Mp-Pc switch	• "Home memory" multiprocessors
• Coalescing Pc's	• Dynamic computer group
	• Varistructured arrays
• Hierarchy of Pc's	• Master/slave organizations
	• X-tree
• Structured Pc's	• Restructurable computer
• Cluster of Pc's and Mp's	• C.m*
• Task oriented Pc's	• Configurable systems
	• Distributed systems
• Algorithm oriented units	• Data-flow machines

appealing approach is to combine "small" ALU's and/or microprocessors to form a larger ALU. In a sense, we have a dynamically extensible sliced ALU.

We have already mentioned the possibility of having some special-purpose units within a local network of processors. Following the same idea, but in a tighter coupling environment, we might want functional units which provide fast executions of various algorithms. A typical example would be an array or FFT attachment. Extension of this concept leads to a variable structure computer (the variable structure idea antedates most of the special-purpose attachments) and what has more recently been called federated systems. Typical federated units could be garbage collectors, lexical analyzers, string processors and page monitors. The difficulties are the same as in MIMD structures: memory interference and synchronization between federated units and main processor. The utility of such a design is based on a flexible way to attach new units without disrupting the already configured machine.

The next component that we have listed is the topology of the system which by necessity must be a multiprocessing structure. This topology, or interconnection network, can be modified statically for a given application or various schemes for SIMD machines can be investigated as in the Phoenix proposal (cf. Chapter 10 Section 3.3). In MIMD architectures, it is advantageous to think in terms of processors showing a preference for some particular memory modules as in Cm* clusters. More interesting, because of a more dynamic nature, are those architectures which connect processors and memories under software control and which allow modular extensions in both the processor and memory domains. Table 11.1 lists some of the proposed designs. The reader is referred to the bibliography for further details.

The list of Table 11.1 is far from exhaustive. In particular, we have not included *fault-tolerant* architectures. In these systems, failures of components can either be detected and masked by using replication of elements or be corrected by a dynamic reconfiguration of the system. The static masking can be performed by methods such as triple modular redundancy and voting. The dynamic reconfiguration is controlled by hardware or software or a combination of the two. Although the term fault-tolerant computer is most often associated with space-borne systems, it should be remembered that current memories include error correcting and detecting schemes (cf., Chapter 5 Section 2.4) and that local networks have provisions, in the hardware interfaces and in the software protocols, to continue operating in the presence of errors.

11.3 THE IMPACT OF VLSI ON FUTURE ARCHITECTURES

Large scale integration (LSI) has modified the economics of the computer market without bringing major conceptual changes in the architecture of computer systems. With LSI it has been possible to expand the capacity of memory chips and to place a complete 16-bit microprocessor on a chip. The number of active elements that can be placed on a chip is doubling every year although the predictions are that the slope of the growth curve should decrease by half (cf. Figure 11.13 based on the views of Intel Corporation's President G. Moore). Speculations on the impact that very large scale integration (VLSI) will have on the future of computer architectures appear more and more frequently. We summarize here some of the principal ideas which have been publicly defended.

The most pessimistic view is that the computer industry is not ready for VLSI. Chip design which necessarily will require some computer-aided design assistance because of the enormous number of components, packaging, and manufacturing are often cited as problems which are far from solved. This leads to the prediction that VLSI, for some extensive period of time, will only be used in memories which are easier to design since the patterns are ex-

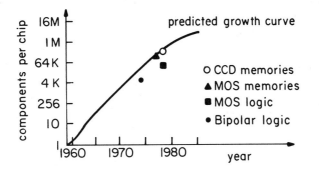

Figure 11.13.   Expected and realized growth in IC complexity

tremely regular. This is partially confirmed by the LSI experience which shows that the number of components on memory chips can be as much as five times that of a processor chip.

A slightly more optimistic forecast is to predict the expansion of 16-bit microprocessors to 32-bit (by 1981) and 64-bit (by 1985) with in addition the integration on a single chip of memory and input/output circuitry. The architecture of these wider paths microprocessors will not depart significantly from that of current systems because of compatibility reasons. In the same sense as the Zilog Z8000 and the Motorola 68000 have incorporated some of the best features of the IBM System/370 and DEC PDP-11 series, the future microprocessors will have the enhancements found today in superminis such as the VAX 11/780.

The more adventurous, and longer term, predictions foresee radical changes in our way of thinking about chip design and computer system architectures. Parallel processing on a single chip, in either an MIMD, SIMD or pipelining fashion, is advocated. Distributed function architectures with special-purpose functional chips such as file servers, text editors, language interpreters, etc., will be the common environment according to some authors (and we agree with them). The design of these chips will rely heavily on the regularity of patterns for communication between active elements. To quote Sutherland and Mead, "the relative costs of wiring and logic must change the nature of the computers built in the future . . . regular patterns of wiring will play an increasing role in future designs". Many of the techniques alluded to in Chapter 10 for the design of algorithms for parallel processors will have to be adapted for "parallel computing on a chip". The amount of parallelism exhibited by an algorithm will not be sufficient to characterize its potential: communication between processing elements will become part of the cost function. Redundancy and/or superfluous elements might be included to allow ease in communication paths.

VLSI design as perceived in the above paragraph is not uniquely of the domain of circuit designers in the semiconductor industry. It becomes a systems enterprise requiring design methodologies and the development of tools such as computer-aided design with large data bases of already produced subsystems. Conversely, the main frame manufacturers of today will have to learn of the opportunities offered to them and of the technological advances they should expect. The challenge is not limited to hardware specialists. Software tools will become more and more important in the design and testing stage; production of a new chip will require software as well as hardware engineering. Finally, computer scientists with a more theoretical background will have an important role to play in developing new algorithms and new communication techniques to make use of VLSI.

11.4   BIBLIOGRAPHICAL NOTES AND REFERENCES

A survey of associative processors is given in [Yau and Fung 77]. [Enslow 74] provides additional information on PEPE and STARAN. More complete details can be found in [Evensen and Troy 73] for PEPE and [Rudolf 72 and Batcher 77b] for STARAN. The RADCAP facility is described in [Feldman and Fulmer 74] while the multidimensional access memory design is due to [Batcher 77a].

High-level language architecture is the subject of two books [Chu 75] and [Myers 78]. The original description of the SYMBOL computer can be found in several papers presented at the 1971 Spring Joint Computer Conference (in particular see [Rice and Smith 71] for a general description). The two books mentioned above include detailed presentations of SYMBOL [Laliotis 75 and Myers 78] as well as complete bibliographies.

The data-flow languages presented in Figures 7 and 8 have features taken from [Dennis 74 and Arvind, Gostelow and Plouffe 77]. The basic data-flow processor of Figure 9 is adapted from the research conducted at MIT under the direction of Dennis [Dennis and Misunas 75]. Arvind and Gostelow at Irvine head another group involved in data-flow architectures [Arvind and Gostelow 77]. Davis is the designer of the existing data-flow computer [Davis 78] while Syre and his coworkers are reportedly near completion of their implementation of a single assignment machine [Syre, Comte, and Hidfi 77]. The concept of the single assignment rule is originally due to [Tesler and Enea 68]. Additional references on data-flow languages and architectures can be found in the recent survey [Treleaven 79].

The motivations, goals and importance of distributed systems are clearly exposed in [Jensen 78]. This reference also presents the Honeywell Experimental Distributed Processor. Ethernet, at the system level, is described in [Metcalfe and Boggs 76]. Analysis of Ethernet-like networks can be found in [Almes and Lazowska 79]. The DCS ring network is presented in [Farber and Larson 72].

Alterable architectures are surveyed in [Baer 78]. The concept of a variable structure computer can be traced to [Estrin 60]. For the architectures listed in Table 1 which have not been treated in previous chapters, further details on the Dynamic Computer Group can be found in [Kartashev and Kartashev 77], on varistructured arrays in [Lipovski and Tripathi 77], and on hierarchical architectures in [Despain and Patterson 78 and Harris and Smith 77]. An extensive discussion of fault-tolerant systems is presented in [Avizienis 77] which also includes an abundant bibliography.

Predictions on the impact that VLSI will have on future computer architectures are given in [Moore 79] from which Figure 13 is abstracted, in [Faggin 78], and in [Sutherland and Mead 77]. This last reference makes a convincing case for a new approach to chip design, computer systems architecture, and more generally Computer Science. [Kung and Leiserson 78] is an example of what future special-purpose systems may look like.

References

1. Almes, G. T. and E. D. Lazowska, "The Behavior of Ethernet-Like Computer Communications Networks", *Proc. 7th Symp. on Oper. Systems Principles,* 1979.

2. Arvind and K. P. Gostelow, "A Computer Capable of Exchanging Processors for Time", *Proc. 1977 IFIP Congress,* North-Holland, Amsterdam, 1977, 849-853.

3. Arvind, Gostelow, K. P. and W. Plouffe, "Indeterminacy, Monitors and Dataflow", *Proc. 6th Symp. on Oper. Systems Principles,* 1977, 159-169.

4. Avizienis, A., "Fault-tolerant Computing-Progress, Problems, and Prospects", *Proc. 1977 IFIP Congress,* North-Holland, Amsterdam, 1977, 405-420.

5. Baer, J.-L., "Software Control and Program Design Issues for Alterable Architectures", *Proc. COMPSAC 1978,* 1978, 769-774.

6. Batcher, K. E., "The Multidimensional Access Memory in STARAN", *IEEE Trans. on Comp., C-26,* (Feb. 1977), 174-178.

7. Batcher, K. E., "STARAN Series E", *Proc. 1977 Int. Conf. on Parallel Processing,* 1977, 140-143.

8. Chu, Y. ed., *High-Level Language Computer Architecture,* Academic Press, New York, N.Y., 1975.

9. Davis, A. L., "The Architecture and System Methodology of DDM1: A Recursively Structured Data Driven Machine," *Proc. 5th Symp. on Comp. Arch.,* 1978, 210-215.

10. Dennis, J. B., "First Version of a Data Flow Procedure Language" in *Lecture Notes in Computer Science, 19,* Springer-Verlag, Berlin, 1974, 362-376.

11. Dennis, J. B. and D. P. Misunas, "A Preliminary Data Flow Architecture for a Basic Data Flow Processor", *Proc. 2nd Symp. on Comp. Arch.,* 1975, 126-132.

12. Despain, A. M. and D. A. Patterson, "*X*-tree—A Tree Structured Multiprocessor Computer Architecture", *Proc. 5th Symp. on Comp. Arch.,* 1978, 144-151.

13. Enslow, P. H. Jr., ed., *Multiprocessors and Parallel Processing,* Wiley-Interscience, New York, N.Y., 1974.

14. Estrin, G., "Organization of Computer Systems: the Fixed-plus-Variable Structure Computer", *Proc. Western Joint Comp. Conf.,* 1960, 33-40.

15. Evensen, A. J. and J. L. Troy, "Introduction to the Architecture of a 288-element PEPE", *Proc. of the 1973 Sagamore Comp. Conf. on Parallel Processing,* 1973, 162-169.

16. Faggin, F., "How VLSI Impacts Computer Architecute", *IEEE Spectrum, 15,* (May 1978), 28-31.

17. Farber, D. J. and K. C. Larson, "The Structure of a Distributed Computer System—The Communications System", *Proc. Symp. on Communications Networks and Teletraffic,* 1972, 21-27.

18. Feldman, J. D. and L. C. Fulmer, "RADCAP—An Operational Parallel Processing Facility", *Proc. AFIPS 1974 Nat. Comp. Conf., 43,* AFIPS Press, Montvale, N.J., 1974, 7-15.

19. Harris, J. A. and D. R. Smith, "Hierarchical Multiprocessor Organizations", *Proc. 4th Symp. on Comp. Arch.,* 1977, 41-48.

20. Jensen, E. D., "The Honeywell Experimental Distributed Processor", *Computer, 11,* (Jan. 1978), 28-38.

21. Kartashev, S. and S. Kartashev, "A Multicomputer System with Software Reconfiguration of the Architecture", *Proc. of the 1977 Sigmetric/CMG VII,* 1977, 47-62.

22. Kung, H. T. and C. E. Leiserson, "Systolic Arrays (for VLSI)", *Computer Science Research Review,* Carnegie Mellon Univ., 1978, 37-58.

23. Laliotis, T. A., "Architecture of the SYMBOL Computer System", in *High-Level Computer Architecture,* Y. Chu, ed., Academic Press, New York, N.Y., 1975, 109-185.

24. Lipovski, G. J. and A. Tripathi, "A Reconfigurable Varistructured Array Processor", *Proc. 1977 Int. Conf. on Parallel Processing,* 1977, 165-174.

25. Metcalfe, R. M. and D. R. Boggs, "Ethernet: Distributed Packet Switching for Local Computer Networks" *Comm. ACM, 19,* (Jul. 1976), 395-404.

26. Moore, G., "VLSI: Some Fundamental Challenges", *IEEE Spectrum, 16*, (Apr. 1979), 30-37.

27. Myers, G. J., *Advances in Computer Architecture*, John Wiley, New York, N.Y., 1978.

28. Rice, R. and W. R. Smith, "SYMBOL—A Major Departure from Classic Software Dominated von Neumann Computing Systems", *Proc. AFIPS 1971 Spring Joint Comp. Conf., 38*, AFIPS Press, Montvale, N.J., 1971, 575-587.

29. Rudolf, J. A., "A Production Implementation of an Associative Array Processor STARAN", *Proc. AFIPS 1972 Fall Joint Comp. Conf., 41*, AFIPS Press, Montvale, N.J., 1972, 229-241.

30. Sutherland, I. E. and C. A. Mead, "Microelectronics and Computer Science", *Scientific American, 237*, (1977), 210-229.

31. Syre, J.-C., Comte, D. and N. Hifdi, "Pipelining, Parallelism and Asynchronism in the LAU System", *Proc. 1977 Int. Conf. on Parallel Processing",* 1977, 87-92.

32. Tesler, L. G. and H. J. Enea, "A Language Design for Concurrent Processes", *Proc. AFIPS 1968 Spring Joint Comp. Conf., 32*, AFIPS Press, Montvale, N.J., 1968, 402-408.

33. Treleaven, P. C., "Exploiting Program Concurrency in Computing Systems", *Computer, 12*, (Jan. 1979), 42-50.

34. Yau, S. S. and H. S. Fung, "Associative Processor Architecture—A Survey", *Computing Surveys, 9*, (Mar. 1977), 3-28.

INDEX